SIPRI Yearbook 2012
Armaments, Disarmament and International Security

STOCKHOLM INTERNATIONAL PEACE RESEARCH INSTITUTE
Signalistgatan 9
SE-169 70 Solna, Sweden
Telephone: +46 8 655 97 00
Fax: +46 8 655 97 33
Email: sipri@sipri.org
Internet: www.sipri.org

SIPRI Yearbook 2012

Armaments, Disarmament and International Security

**STOCKHOLM INTERNATIONAL
PEACE RESEARCH INSTITUTE**

OXFORD UNIVERSITY PRESS
2012

OXFORD
UNIVERSITY PRESS

Great Clarendon Street, Oxford OX2 6DP,
United Kingdom

Oxford University Press is a department of the University of Oxford.
It furthers the University's objective of excellence in research, scholarship,
and education by publishing worldwide. Oxford is a registered trade mark of
Oxford University Press in the UK and in certain other countries

British Library Cataloguing in Publication Data
Data available

Library of Congress Cataloging in Publication Data
Data available

ISSN 0953–0282
ISBN 978–0–19–965058–3

Typeset and originated by SIPRI
Printed in Great Britain on acid-free paper by
CPI Group (UK) Ltd, Croydon, CR0 4YY

*Before 1987 the Yearbook was published under the title
'World Armaments and Disarmament:
SIPRI Yearbook [year of publication]'*

Contents

Preface   xv
Abbreviations and conventions   xvii

Introduction

Introduction. International security, armaments and disarmament   3
BATES GILL

   I. *Assessing the past year*   3
  II. SIPRI Yearbook 2012: *overview, themes and key findings*   5
     Overview—Key trends and findings
 III. *Looking ahead*   11

1. Responding to atrocities: the new geopolitics of intervention   15
GARETH EVANS

   I. *The challenge of civilian protection*   15
  II. *New paradigms for a new century: protection of civilians and the*   18
     responsibility to protect
     Protection of civilians in armed conflict—The responsibility to
     protect—The relationship between protection of civilians and the
     responsibility to protect
 III. *Libya and its aftermath: the limits of intervention?*   25
     Implementing Resolution 1973: a case of overreach?—The
     geopolitical environment after Libya: potential for a new
     consensus?
 IV. *The future for civilian protection*   33
     Criteria for the authorization of military force—Measures falling
     short of coercive military intervention—Long-term preventive
     strategies—Developing appropriate institutional response
     capacities—Rethinking the concept of 'national interest'

Part I. Security and conflicts, 2011

2. Armed conflict   43
     Overview   43
     NEIL MELVIN

   I. *The first year of the Arab Spring*   45
     MARIE ALLANSSON, JONAS BAUMANN, SAMUEL TAUB, LOTTA THEMNÉR
     AND PETER WALLENSTEEN

     Domestic developments—External involvement—Conclusions

     Table 2.1. The Arab Spring, 2011   46

II. *Organized violence in the Horn of Africa*   57
JONAS BAUMANN, MARCUS NILSSON, LOTTA THEMNÉR AND
PETER WALLENSTEEN

Armed conflict: the regional effects of Somalia's instability—
One-sided violence: abuses in Ethiopia's Somali Region—Non-state
conflicts: unrest in border areas

Figure 2.1. Map of the Horn of Africa   58

III. *Patterns of organized violence, 2001–10*   65
LOTTA THEMNÉR AND PETER WALLENSTEEN

Armed conflicts—Non-state conflicts—One-sided violence—
Organized violence: a comparison

Figure 2.2. Numbers of armed conflicts, non-state conflicts and 66
one-sided violence, 2001–10
Figure 2.3. Average number of fatalities in non-state conflicts, 75
2001–10
Figure 2.4. Subcategories of non-state conflict, by region, 2001–10   75
Figure 2.5. Fatalities in one-sided violence, by type of actor, 78
2001–10
Figure 2.6. Fatalities, by category of organized violence, 2001–10   80
Table 2.2. Armed conflicts in 2010   68
Table 2.3. Armed conflict, by intensity, type and region, 2001–10   71
Table 2.4. Non-state conflicts in 2010   72
Table 2.5. Non-state conflict, by subcategory and region, 2001–10   74
Table 2.6. One sided-violence in 2010   76
Table 2.7. One-sided violence, by actor and region, 2001–10   77
Sources and methods   81

IV. *The Global Peace Index 2012*   84
CAMILLA SCHIPPA AND THOMAS MORGAN

Table 2.8. Countries with the greatest change in Global Peace   85
Index scores, 2011–12
Table 2.9. The Global Peace Index 2012   86
Sources and methods   87

3. Peace operations and conflict management   89
Overview   89
SHARON WIHARTA

I. *Global trends in peace operations*   91
CLAIRE FANCHINI

Figure 3.1. Number of multilateral peace operations, by type of 92
conducting organization, 2002–11
Figure 3.2. Number of personnel deployed to multilateral peace   92
operations, 2002–11

Figure 3.3. The top 10 contributors of troops to multilateral peace   93
operations, including and excluding the International Security
Assistance Force (ISAF) in Afghanistan, 2011
Figure 3.4. The top 10 contributors of civilian police to multilateral   93
peace operations, 2011

II. *New peace operations in 2011*   95
CLAIRE FANCHINI

Sudan and South Sudan: the UN Mission in the Republic of South
Sudan and the UN Interim Security Force for Abyei—Libya:
NATO's Operation Unified Protector and the UN Support Mission
in Libya—Syria: the Arab League Observer Mission to Syria—
Conclusions

Figure 3.5. Map of South Sudan and Sudan   96

III. *Regional developments in peace operations*   106
CLAIRE FANCHINI

Africa—The Americas—Asia and Oceania—Europe—The Middle
East

Table 3.1. Number of peace operations and personnel deployed, by   108
region and type of organization, 2011

IV. *Table of multilateral peace operations, 2011*   112
CLAIRE FANCHINI

Table 3.2. Multilateral peace operations, 2011   113
Sources and methods   143

Part II. Military spending and armaments, 2011

4. Military expenditure   147
Overview   147
SAM PERLO-FREEMAN

I. *Global developments in military expenditure*   149
SAM PERLO-FREEMAN AND CARINA SOLMIRANO

Table 4.1. Military expenditure by region, by international   150
organization and by income group, 2002–11
Table 4.2. The 15 countries with the highest military expenditure   152
in 2011
Table 4.3. Key military expenditure statistics by region, 2011   153

II. *The economic cost of the Afghanistan and Iraq wars*   156
SAM PERLO-FREEMAN AND CARINA SOLMIRANO

Table 4.4. Estimates of the costs of the Afghanistan and Iraq wars   160
to selected participating states

III. *The United States' military spending and the 2011 budget crisis* 162
ELISABETH SKÖNS AND SAM PERLO-FREEMAN

Table 4.5. US outlays for the Department of Defense and total 164
national defence, financial years 2001, 2005, 2007, 2009 and
2011–13

IV. *Military expenditure in Africa* 167
OLAWALE ISMAIL AND SAM PERLO-FREEMAN

Oil and counterterrorism in Algeria—Oil and counterterrorism in
Nigeria—Developments in other countries

V. *Europe and the impact of austerity on military expenditure* 173
SAM PERLO-FREEMAN

The crisis countries of Southern Europe—The implications of
reduced spending

Figure 4.1. Changes in military spending versus gross domestic 174
product, Western Europe and Central Europe, 2008–11

VI. *The reporting of military expenditure data to the United Nations,* 181
2002–11
NOEL KELLY

The United Nations reporting system—Trends in reporting,
2002–11—The report of the Group of Governmental Experts

Table 4.6. Number of countries reporting their military 182
expenditure to the United Nations, 2002 and 2006–11
Table 4.7. Reporting of military expenditure data to the United 184
Nations, by region and subregion, 2011

VII. *Military expenditure data, 2002–11* 187
SAM PERLO-FREEMAN, OLAWALE ISMAIL, NOEL KELLY,
ELISABETH SKÖNS, CARINA SOLMIRANO AND HELEN WILANDH

Table 4.8. Military expenditure by country, in local currency, 188
2002–11
Table 4.9. Military expenditure by country, in constant US dollars 195
for 2002–11 and current US dollars for 2011
Table 4.10. Military expenditure by country as percentage of gross 202
domestic product, 2002–2010
Sources and methods 214

5. Arms production and military services 217
Overview 217
SUSAN T. JACKSON

I. *Key developments in the main arms-producing countries*   219
SUSAN T. JACKSON

The US National Defense Authorization Act for 2012—
Acquisitions, spin-offs and sell-offs in the United States—The
debate on arms industry cooperation in the European Union—
Diversification into cybersecurity

Table 5.1. Arms sales of companies in the SIPRI Top 100   220
arms-producing and military services companies, 2002–10
Table 5.2. Selected cybersecurity acquisitions by OECD   228
arms-producing and military services companies, 2011

II. *The military services industry*   230
SUSAN T. JACKSON

Military services companies in the SIPRI Top 100—Developments
in selected military services sub-sectors—Conclusions

Table 5.3. Military services companies in the SIPRI Top 100 for   232
2010

III. *The Indian arms-production and military services industry*   239
SUSAN T. JACKSON AND MIKAEL GRINBAUM

India's arms industry structure—India's arms production
framework—India's military services industry—Conclusions

IV. *The SIPRI Top 100 arms-producing and military services*   247
companies, 2010
SUSAN T. JACKSON

Table 5.4. Regional and national shares of arms sales for the SIPRI   248
Top 100 arms-producing and military services companies, 2010
compared to 2009
Table 5.5. The SIPRI Top 100 arms-producing and military   251
services companies in the world excluding China, 2010
Sources and methods   257

6. International arms transfers   259
Overview   259
PAUL HOLTOM

I. *Developments in arms transfers in 2011*   261
PAUL HOLTOM, MARK BROMLEY, PIETER D. WEZEMAN AND
SIEMON T. WEZEMAN

Major supplier developments—Recipient developments

Figure 6.1. The trend in international transfers of major   262
conventional weapons, 2002–11
Table 6.1. The 10 largest suppliers of major conventional weapons   264
and their destinations, by region, 2007–11

Table 6.2. The 50 largest suppliers of major conventional weapons,   266
2007–11

Table 6.3. The 10 largest recipients of major conventional weapons   270
and their suppliers, 2007–11

Table 6.4. The 50 largest recipients of major conventional   272
weapons, 2007–11

Sources and methods   273

II. *Policies on exports of arms to states affected by the Arab Spring*   275
MARK BROMLEY AND PIETER D. WEZEMAN

Table 6.5. Suppliers of major conventional weapons to states   276
affected by the Arab Spring, 2007–11

III. *The maritime dimension of arms transfers to South East Asia,*   280
2007–11
SIEMON T. WEZEMAN

Maritime security in South East Asia—Arms transfers related to
maritime security

Figure 6.2. Map of South East Asia   282
Table 6.6. Suppliers of major conventional weapons to Brunei   281
Darussalam, Indonesia, Malaysia, the Philippines, Singapore and
Viet Nam, 2007–11

IV. *Arms transfers to Armenia and Azerbaijan, 2007–11*   286
PAUL HOLTOM

Armenia—Azerbaijan

Figure 6.3. Map of Armenia and Azerbaijan   287
Table 6.7. Suppliers of major conventional weapons to Armenia   287
and Azerbaijan, 2007–11

V. *Transparency in arms transfers*   293
PAUL HOLTOM AND MARK BROMLEY

The United Nations Register of Conventional Arms—National and
regional reports on arms exports

Figure 6.4. Reports submitted to the United Nations Register of   294
Conventional Arms, 2001–10

Table 6.8. Reports submitted to the United Nations Register of   294
Conventional Arms, by region, 2006–10

Table 6.9. States participating in international, regional and   299
national reporting mechanisms on arms transfers, 2009–11

VI. *The financial value of states' arms exports, 2001–10*   303
MARK BROMLEY

Table 6.10. The financial value of states' arms exports according to   304
national government and industry sources, 2001–10

7. World nuclear forces 307

    Overview 307
    SHANNON N. KILE

    Table 7.1. World nuclear forces, January 2012 308

  I. *US nuclear forces* 309
    SHANNON N. KILE, PHILLIP SCHELL AND HANS M. KRISTENSEN

    Nuclear modernization—Nuclear strategy and planning—
    Land-based ballistic missiles—Ballistic missile submarines—
    Non-strategic nuclear weapons

    Table 7.2. US nuclear forces, January 2012 310

  II. *Russian nuclear forces* 315
    SHANNON N. KILE, VITALY FEDCHENKO, PHILLIP SCHELL AND
    HANS M. KRISTENSEN

    Strategic bombers—Land-based ballistic missiles—Ballistic missile
    submarines and sea-launched ballistic missiles—Non-strategic
    nuclear weapons

    Table 7.3. Russian nuclear forces, January 2012 316

  III. *British nuclear forces* 322
    SHANNON N. KILE, PHILLIP SCHELL AND HANS M. KRISTENSEN

    The British–French nuclear cooperation agreement

    Table 7.4. British nuclear forces, January 2012 324

  IV. *French nuclear forces* 325
    SHANNON N. KILE, PHILLIP SCHELL AND HANS M. KRISTENSEN

    Table 7.5. French nuclear forces, January 2012 326

  V. *Chinese nuclear forces* 327
    SHANNON N. KILE, PHILLIP SCHELL AND HANS M. KRISTENSEN

    Land-based ballistic missiles—Ballistic missile submarines—
    Aircraft and cruise missiles

    Table 7.6. Chinese nuclear forces, January 2012 328

  VI. *Indian nuclear forces* 332
    SHANNON N. KILE, PHILLIP SCHELL AND HANS M. KRISTENSEN

    Strike aircraft—Land-based missiles—Sea-based missiles

    Table 7.7. Indian nuclear forces, January 2012 334

  VII. *Pakistani nuclear forces* 337
    SHANNON N. KILE, PHILLIP SCHELL AND HANS M. KRISTENSEN

    Strike aircraft—Land-based missiles

    Table 7.8. Pakistani nuclear forces, January 2012 338

VIII. *Israeli nuclear forces*   341
SHANNON N. KILE, PHILLIP SCHELL AND HANS M. KRISTENSEN

    Table 7.9. Israeli nuclear forces, January 2012   342

IX. *North Korea's military nuclear capabilities*   343
SHANNON N. KILE, PHILLIP SCHELL AND HANS M. KRISTENSEN

X. *Global stocks and production of fissile materials, 2011*   345
ALEXANDER GLASER AND ZIA MIAN

    Table 7.10. Global stocks of highly enriched uranium (HEU), 2011   346
    Table 7.11. Global stocks of separated plutonium, 2011   347
    Table 7.12. Significant uranium enrichment facilities and capacity worldwide, as of December 2011   349
    Table 7.13. Significant reprocessing facilities worldwide, as of December 2011   350

Part III. Non-proliferation, arms control and disarmament, 2011

8. Nuclear arms control and non-proliferation   353
Overview   353
SHANNON N. KILE

I. *Russian–US nuclear arms control*   355
SHANNON N. KILE

Implementation of data exchanges, notifications and inspections—New START and missile defence—Next steps after New START

    Table 8.1. Russian–US nuclear arms reduction treaties' force limits   356
    Table 8.2. Russian and US aggregate numbers of strategic offensive arms under New START, as of 5 February 2011 and 1 September 2011   357

II. *Syria and nuclear proliferation concerns*   363
SHANNON N. KILE

III. *Iran and nuclear proliferation concerns*   366
SHANNON N. KILE

The IAEA's assessment of alleged Iranian military nuclear activities—New US National Intelligence Estimate on Iran—IAEA Board of Governors resolution on Iran—Status of Fordow enrichment plant

IV. *North Korea's nuclear programme*   374
SHANNON N. KILE

V. *Developments in the Nuclear Suppliers Group* 376
SIBYLLE BAUER

Revision of the guidelines for export of sensitive technology—
Other Nuclear Supplier Group discussions during 2011—The future
of nuclear export controls

VI. *International cooperation on non-proliferation, arms control and* 387
nuclear security
SHANNON N. KILE

UN Security Council Resolution 1977—Extension of the Group of
Eight's Global Partnership programme—The P5 states' discussion
of multilateral arms control

9. Reducing security threats from chemical and biological materials 391
Overview 391
JOHN HART

I. *Biological weapon arms control and disarmament* 393
JOHN HART

II. *Chemical weapon arms control and disarmament* 397
JOHN HART

Destruction of chemical weapons—Political tension

III. *Allegations of chemical and biological weapon programmes* 406
JOHN HART

North Korea—Iran and Libya—Syria

IV. *Chemical and biological warfare prevention and response* 409
JOHN HART

Scientific research—Future implications of science and technology

10. Conventional arms control 415
Overview 415
IAN ANTHONY

I. *Limiting conventional arms for humanitarian reasons: the case of* 417
cluster munitions
LINA GRIP

The Fourth Review Conference of the Certain Conventional
Weapons Convention—The Convention on Cluster Munitions—
Prospects and challenges

II. *Limiting the military capabilities of others: developments in arms* 425
export control
MARK BROMLEY AND GLENN MCDONALD

Export control regimes—The European Union—Regional efforts to
control small arms and light weapons in the Americas and

Europe—The United Nations Programme of Action on small arms and light weapons

III. *Multilateral arms embargoes*   431
PIETER D. WEZEMAN AND NOEL KELLY

Libya—Syria—Other multilateral arms embargoes—Embargo violations

Table 10.1. Multilateral arms embargoes in force during 2011   439

IV. *Limiting conventional arms to promote military security: the case of*   442
conventional arms control in Europe
HANS-JOACHIM SCHMIDT AND WOLFGANG ZELLNER

The Treaty on Conventional Armed Forces in Europe—Subregional arms control in South Eastern Europe—Prospects and challenges

V. *Confidence- and security-building measures*   447
HANS-JOACHIM SCHMIDT AND WOLFGANG ZELLNER

Confidence building in South America—Revision of the Vienna Document—Blockade of the Open Skies Consultative Commission

Annexes

Annex A. Arms control and disarmament agreements   455
NENNE BODELL

  I. *Universal treaties*   456
 II. *Regional treaties*   472
III. *Bilateral treaties*   482

Annex B. International security cooperation bodies   487
NENNE BODELL

  I. *Bodies with a global focus or membership*   487
 II. *Bodies with a regional focus or membership*   494
III. *Strategic trade control regimes*   505

Annex C. Chronology 2011   509
NENNE BODELL

About the authors   525
Errata   533
Index   534

Preface

Welcome to the 43rd edition of the SIPRI Yearbook, our flagship publication. This volume—published initially in English in hard copy and online, and soon to be translated into Arabic, Chinese, Russian and Ukrainian—will be read by political leaders, policymakers, security experts, business strategists, diplomats, journalists, researchers and other keen observers of the global scene around the world. Since 1969, readers have sought and found in the SIPRI Yearbook the single most comprehensive annual compendium on developments in international security, armaments and disarmament.

The global and regional security situation has become ever more complex and uncertain in recent years, with many new and often unforeseen threats, risks and opportunities. In this environment, the findings and insights of the SIPRI Yearbook (as well as SIPRI's other published work) are all the more anticipated and in demand. We are especially pleased this year to have our opening chapter—on the evolution and future of the protection of civilians (POC) and responsibility to protect (R2P) norms—penned by Gareth Evans, a former Australian foreign minister and a person integrally involved in developing the R2P concept.

This year's edition also reviews the evolution of conflict and armed violence over the past decade, the geopolitics of peace operations, trends in military spending, arms production, the conventional arms trade and nuclear arsenals, and the most recent developments in the control and disarmament of weapons of mass destruction, conventional weapons, and their related delivery systems and technologies.

Readers will find some changes in how we present the work of the SIPRI Yearbook. Our partnership with the Uppsala Conflict Data Program now presents data on three types of organized violence: armed conflicts involving states, non-state conflicts and one-sided violence against civilians. This new approach means that the SIPRI Yearbook offers a more comprehensive accounting and analysis of armed violence.

To make the volume easier to navigate and use, readers will find a two-page overview at the start of each chapter, while the individual sections have been given greater prominence. We hope you will find these changes helpful. Unchanged is the core mission of the SIPRI Yearbook: to be a global public good in support of sound research, public awareness and well-crafted policy choices for a more secure, stable and peaceful world.

The past year has seen some important changes at the institute as well. Most important among these was the establishment of SIPRI North America, whose offices in Washington, DC, join our headquarters in Stockholm and outpost in Beijing. Led by Dr Chantal de Jonge Oudraat, it will bring new global perspectives to security and foreign policy debates across North

America and strengthen cooperation between SIPRI and its transatlantic partners.

On a sad note, all of SIPRI regrets the passing of former colleague Professor Thomas Ohlson in early 2012. He worked at SIPRI from 1979 to 1987 and led SIPRI's groundbreaking work on the arms trade and arms production. He remained a close professional colleague and personal friend to many of us at SIPRI. We send our condolences to his family and friends.

In overseeing the publication of the SIPRI Yearbook, I remain, as ever, deeply impressed by the enormous energy and intellectual firepower which goes into preparing and publishing this indispensible annual reference work. I would like to extend a special thanks to all the authors and researchers, from SIPRI and around the world, for their expert contributions to *SIPRI Yearbook 2012*. I am also grateful to the many external referees who reviewed the chapters. A special thanks goes to the tireless SIPRI editorial team—Dr David Cruickshank, Jetta Gilligan Borg, Dr David Prater and Annika Salisbury—for their unstinting professionalism and dedication in shepherding the Yearbook to publication.

Numerous others at SIPRI make exceptional contributions to the completion of the Yearbook and to SIPRI's many other achievements. These include Daniel Nord, Deputy Director, Dr Ian Anthony, Research Coordinator, Elisabet Rendert, SIPRI Financial Officer, Nenne Bodell, Library and Documentation Director, Gerd Hagmeyer-Gaverus, Information Technology Director, Stephanie Blenckner, Communications Director, Cynthia Loo, Senior Management Assistant and Special Assistant to the Director and Chairman, and all of the great administrative and research staff at SIPRI. I am also grateful to the SIPRI Governing Board, its Chairman, Göran Lennmarker, and to SIPRI supporters and partners worldwide for their service and commitment.

This is the fifth edition of the SIPRI Yearbook for which I have been responsible as Editor and Publisher. This is also the last edition I will have the privilege to oversee. In late 2012, after a five-year term as SIPRI Director, I will step down to undertake new pursuits as the CEO of the United States Studies Centre in Sydney, Australia.

It has been an extraordinary honour to serve as Director of SIPRI. Working with SIPRI's outstanding Governing Board, our world-class researchers and staff from around the globe, and our numerous supporters and stakeholders worldwide, I have been privileged to help further build the institution's distinctive reputation as a global public good. I thank all of these colleagues and friends for their confidence and support that allowed me this singular and remarkable opportunity.

Dr Bates Gill
SIPRI Director
May 2012

Abbreviations and conventions

ABM	Anti-ballistic missile	CDS	Consejo de Defensa Suramericano (South American Defence Council)
ACV	Armoured combat vehicle		
AG	Australia Group		
ALCM	Air-launched cruise missile	CEEAC	Communauté Economique des Etats de l'Afrique Centrale (Economic Community of Central African States, ECCAS)
APC	Armoured personnel carrier		
APEC	Asia–Pacific Economic Cooperation		
APM	Anti-personnel mine	CFE	Conventional Armed Forces in Europe (Treaty)
APT	ASEAN Plus Three		
ARF	ASEAN Regional Forum	CFSP	Common Foreign and Security Policy
ASAT	Anti-satellite		
ASEAN	Association of Southeast Asian Nations	CICA	Conference on Interaction and Confidence-building Measures in Asia
ATT	Arms trade treaty		
ATTU	Atlantic-to-the Urals (zone)	CIS	Commonwealth of Independent States
AU	African Union		
BCC	Bilateral Consultative Commission (of the Russian–US New START treaty)	COPAX	Conseil de Paix et de Sécurité de l'Afrique Centrale (Central Africa Peace and Security Council)
BMD	Ballistic missile defence	CSBM	Confidence- and security-building measure
BSEC	Organization of the Black Sea Economic Cooperation		
		CSDP	Common Security and Defence Policy
BTWC	Biological and Toxin Weapons Convention	CSTO	Collective Security Treaty Organization
BW	Biological weapon/warfare		
CADSP	Common African Defence and Security Policy	CTBT	Comprehensive Nuclear-Test-Ban Treaty
CAR	Central African Republic	CTBTO	Comprehensive Nuclear-Test-Ban Treaty Organization
CBM	Confidence-building measure		
		CTR	Cooperative Threat Reduction
CBRN	Chemical, biological, radiological and nuclear	CW	Chemical weapon/warfare
CBSS	Council of the Baltic Sea States	CWC	Chemical Weapons Convention
CBW	Chemical and biological weapon/warfare	DDR	Disarmament, demobilization and reintegration
CCM	Convention on Cluster Munitions		
		DPKO	UN Department of Peacekeeping Operations
CCW	Certain Conventional Weapons (Convention)	DPRK	Democratic People's Republic of Korea (North Korea)
CD	Conference on Disarmament		

DRC	Democratic Republic of the Congo		ICTY	International Criminal Tribunal for the former Yugoslavia
EAEC	European Atomic Energy Community (Euratom)		IED	Improvised explosive device
EAPC	Euro-Atlantic Partnership Council		IFS	Instrument for Stability
ECOWAS	Economic Community of West African States		IGAD	Intergovernmental Authority on Development
EDA	European Defence Agency		IGC	Intergovernmental conference
ENP	European Neighbourhood Policy		INDA	International non-proliferation and disarmament assistance
ERW	Explosive remnants of war			
EU	European Union		INF	Intermediate-range Nuclear Forces (Treaty)
FATF	Financial Action Task Force			
FMCT	Fissile material cut-off treaty		IRBM	Intermediate-range ballistic missile
FSC	Forum for Security Co-operation (of the OSCE)		ISAF	International Security Assistance Force
FY	Financial year		JCG	Joint Consultative Group (of the CFE Treaty)
FYROM	Former Yugoslav Republic of Macedonia		LEU	Low-enriched uranium
G8	Group of Eight (industrialized states)		MANPADS	Man-portable air defence system
GCC	Gulf Cooperation Council		MDGs	Millennium Development Goals
GDP	Gross domestic product			
GGE	Group of government experts		MIRV	Multiple independently targetable re-entry vehicle
GLCM	Ground-launched cruise missile		MOTAPM	Mines other than anti-personnel mines
GNEP	Global Nuclear Energy Partnership		MTCR	Missile Technology Control Regime
GTRI	Global Threat Reduction Initiative		NAM	Non-Aligned Movement
			NATO	North Atlantic Treaty Organization
GUAM	Georgia, Ukraine, Azerbaijan and Moldova		NBC	Nuclear, biological and chemical (weapons)
HCOC	Hague Code of Conduct			
HEU	Highly enriched uranium		NGO	Non-governmental organization
IAEA	International Atomic Energy Agency		NNWS	Non-nuclear weapon state
ICBM	Intercontinental ballistic missile		NPT	Non-Proliferation Treaty
			NRF	NATO Response Force
ICC	International Criminal Court		NSG	Nuclear Suppliers Group
			NWFZ	Nuclear weapon-free zone
ICJ	International Court of Justice		NWS	Nuclear weapon state
			OAS	Organization of American States
ICTR	International Criminal Tribunal for Rwanda			

OCCAR	Organisation Conjointe de Coopération en matière d'Armement (Organisation for Joint Armament Cooperation)	SALW	Small arms and light weapons
		SAM	Surface-to-air missile
		SCO	Shanghai Cooperation Organisation
ODA	Official development assistance	SCSL	Special Court for Sierra Leone
OECD	Organisation for Economic Co-operation and Development	SECI	Southeast European Cooperative Initiative
OHCHR	Office of the UN High Commissioner for Human Rights	SLBM	Submarine-launched ballistic missile
		SLCM	Sea-launched cruise missile
OIC	Organization of the Islamic Conference	SORT	Strategic Offensive Reductions Treaty
OPANAL	Organismo para la Proscripción de las Armas Nucleares en la América Latina y el Caribe (Agency for the Prohibition of Nuclear Weapons in Latin America and the Caribbean)	SRBM	Short-range ballistic missile
		SRCC	Sub-Regional Consultative Commission
		SSM	Surface-to-surface missile
		SSR	Security sector reform
		START	Strategic Arms Reduction Treaty
OPCW	Organisation for the Prohibition of Chemical Weapons	TLE	Treaty-limited equipment
		UAE	United Arab Emirates
OPEC	Organization of the Petroleum Exporting Countries	UNASUR	Unión de Naciones Suramericanas (Union of South American Nations)
OSCC	Open Skies Consultative Commission	UAS	Unmanned aerial system
		UAV	Unmanned aerial vehicle
OSCE	Organization for Security and Co-operation in Europe	UCAV	Unmanned combat air vehicle
P5	Five permanent members of the UN Security Council	UN	United Nations
		UNDP	UN Development Programme
PFP	Partnership for Peace	UNHCR	UN High Commissioner for Refugees
PRT	Provincial reconstruction team	
PSC	Peace and Security Council (of the African Union)	UNODA	UN Office for Disarmament Affairs
PSC	Private security company	UNROCA	UN Register of Conventional Arms
PSI	Proliferation Security Initiative	WA	Wassenaar Arrangement
R&D	Research and development	WEU	Western European Union
SAARC	South Asian Association for Regional Co-operation	WMD	Weapon(s) of mass destruction
SADC	Southern African Development Community	WMDFZ	WMD-free zone

Conventions

. .	Data not available or not applicable
–	Nil or a negligible figure
( )	Uncertain data
b.	Billion (thousand million)
kg	Kilogram
km	Kilometre (1000 metres)
m.	Million
th.	Thousand
tr.	Trillion (million million)
$	US dollars, unless otherwise indicated
€	Euros

Geographical regions and subregions

Africa	Consisting of North Africa (Algeria, Libya, Morocco and Tunisia, but excluding Egypt) and sub-Saharan Africa
Americas	Consisting of North America (Canada and the USA), Central America and the Caribbean (including Mexico), and South America
Asia and Oceania	Consisting of Central Asia, East Asia, Oceania, South Asia (including Afghanistan) and South East Asia
Europe	Consisting of Eastern Europe (Armenia, Azerbaijan, Belarus, Georgia, Moldova, Russia and Ukraine) and Western and Central Europe (with South Eastern Europe); in discussions of military expenditure, Turkey is included in Western and Central Europe
Middle East	Consisting of Egypt, Iran, Iraq, Israel, Jordan, Kuwait, Lebanon, Syria, Turkey and the states of the Arabian peninsula

Introduction

International security, armaments and disarmament

Chapter 1. Responding to atrocities: the new geopolitics of intervention

Introduction
International security, armaments and disarmament

BATES GILL

I. Assessing the past year

The past year saw new and old uncertainties and instabilities around the globe, even as pressures built for further cutbacks, especially in the United States and among its closest allies, to already-dwindling military budgets. Economic austerity measures took hold in many states, including significant economic and military powers in the developed world, further constraining their financial wherewithal, political willingness and military capacity to respond to complex challenges. The balancing of security needs with economic realities received further serious debate in many countries, including a growing realization that narrowly constructed military solutions are likely to be less and less relevant to addressing the actual security challenges of the future. Indeed, in 2011 the argument gained ground in Western capitals that it is not traditionally defined security threats but financial irresponsibility and profligacy—including the long-term costs of the ongoing wars in Iraq and Afghanistan—that pose some of the greatest long-term challenges to the prosperity and security of the developed world, and to the current international security institutions more broadly.

The 2011 uprisings and regime changes in the Arab world drew international attention. Hundreds of civilians and soldiers were killed in Bahrain, Egypt, Libya, Tunisia and Yemen. International responses included the United Nations-mandated and NATO-led intervention in Libya, Operation Unified Protector, which facilitated the downfall of the Libyan regime. In Syria, despite escalating sanctions and other punitive measures throughout the year on the part of the UN, the Arab League, Turkey, the USA, the European Union (EU) and others, violence continued unabated with well over 5000 people, mostly civilians, reportedly killed in 2011. Thousands more lives were lost to armed violence in other parts of the world in 2011 as well. In Côte d'Ivoire more than 1000 people were killed as a result of heavy fighting between rival political groups and inter-ethnic conflict. High-profile and deadly extremist attacks occurred in Afghanistan, Iraq, Nigeria, Pakistan and Somalia, as well as in Norway, Russia's North Caucasus, western China and elsewhere around the world. While the overall incidence of organized armed violence appears to have been in decline over the decade 2001–10, in 2010 there were 30 armed conflicts (involving at least one state), 26 non-state conflicts, and at least 18 armed actors carrying out one-sided violence against unorganized civilians. To help bring peace to unstable parts of the world, more than 262 000 peacekeepers in 52 operations were deployed around the world in 2011.

In June 2011 US President Barack Obama announced that, having largely met its aims in Afghanistan, the USA would withdraw 10 000 troops from the country by the end of the year, with a further withdrawal of 20 000 troops anticipated by mid-2012. In December 2011, after nine years of war in Iraq, the US military presence there came to a formal end, with the last US combat soldiers leaving the country on 18 December. But prospects in Afghanistan and Iraq are clouded at best. Both countries will continue to grapple with the internal challenges of factional conflict, and foreign powers will for the indefinite future intervene in various ways to influence developments. Controversial leaders Osama bin Laden, Muammar Gaddafi and Kim Jong-il all died in 2011, but left legacies that will continue to have an impact on regional and global security for years to come.

World military expenditure was $1738 billion in 2011, making it the first year since 1998 that spending did not increase. This results from the fact that 10 of the world's top 15 military spenders—among them the USA and some of its major allies in Europe and the Asia–Pacific region—saw flat or reduced military budgets in 2011. However, while global military spending may have peaked for now, there was continued growth in the volume of conventional arms transfers and in the arms sales of the 100 largest arms-producing and military services companies. In addition, while total world military spending did not increase between 2010 and 2011, 5 of the world's top 15 military spenders—China, Russia, Saudi Arabia, South Korea and Turkey—increased their defence budgets. Of the top 15 military spenders, the greatest increases in military budgets in the period 2002–11 occurred in China (whose spending increased by 170 per cent), Saudi Arabia (90 per cent), Russia (79 per cent) and India (66 per cent). Meanwhile, the world's nuclear-armed states continued to modernize and in some cases expand their arsenals; as of the end of 2011, eight states had a total of approximately 19 000 nuclear weapons, with nearly 2000 kept on high operational alert. Concerns about the Iranian and North Korean nuclear programmes continued, while a three-year investigation by the International Atomic Energy Agency (IAEA) concluded that a facility in Syria destroyed by an Israeli air strike in 2007 was 'very likely' a nuclear reactor which the Syrian Government had failed to report, in contravention of its international obligations.

A number of encouraging developments in 2011 arose in certain parts of the world, although many uncertainties linger in all of these cases. Expectations in early 2011 that the January referendum vote in favour of South Sudan's independence would lead to an all-out bloodbath did not come to pass, and the country entered the United Nations as its 193rd member in July. However, by early 2012, violence across the new South Sudan–Sudan border had begun to escalate toward war. The Basque separatist movement in Spain, Euzkadi ta Azkatasuna (ETA, Basque Homeland and Liberty), declared a permanent ceasefire in January 2011 that still holds. In May a ceasefire was also agreed between Cambodia and Thailand over their border dispute, and the International Court of Justice ruled that a provisional demilitarized zone be established in the contested area. Despite this, a proposed agreement between the two countries to have Indonesian observers deployed to the disputed area had not been put in place by the end of the year.

With respect to arms control, in a February 2011 ceremony in Munich, Russia and the USA exchanged instruments of ratification for the 2010 Treaty on Measures for the Further Reduction and Limitation of Strategic Offensive Arms (New START). In addition, in June the five permanent members of the UN Security Council—China, France, Russia, the UK and the USA—came together to establish a regular exchange on nuclear transparency, verification and confidence-building measures, a potential first step toward multilateral disarmament discussions at some point in the future. In November, in a step forward for regional confidence-building, the South American Defence Council, made up of the region's defence ministers, reached agreement on the transparent exchange of military spending information.

II. *SIPRI Yearbook 2012*: overview, themes and key findings

Overview

In examining the above-noted developments and more, this 43rd edition of the SIPRI Yearbook includes contributions from 39 experts from 17 countries. These experts chronicle and analyse important trends and developments in international security, armaments and disarmament in 2011, including those in armed conflict and violence, multilateral peace operations, military expenditure, arms production, international transfers of conventional arms, non-proliferation, arms control, and confidence- and security-building measures.

This year the featured opening chapter is by former Australian Foreign Minister Gareth Evans. Drawing from his extensive international experience, his chapter explores the new geopolitics of intervention and in particular the advances seen over the past decade in relation to the protection of civilians (POC) in conflict and the responsibility to protect (R2P) concept. Evans was himself deeply involved in the development and global acceptance of POC and R2P norms and practice, and his chapter highlights the strength of the international community's emerging commitment to these two principles. The chapter is also particularly timely, as it speaks directly to the intervention in Libya in 2011 and the mounting concern in 2011 and early 2012 over the violence and bloodshed in Syria, and provides readers with a structured analysis of practical steps for further strengthening an effective consensus for protecting civilians in armed conflict.

The remainder of *SIPRI Yearbook 2012* is built around three principal parts: part I examines developments in relation to armed conflict and conflict management; part II documents and analyses important global, regional and national trends in armaments, including military expenditure, arms production, arms transfers and nuclear arsenals; and part III elaborates important recent developments in disarmament, including assessments of nuclear non-proliferation and arms control, chemical- and biological-related threats, and efforts to control conventional arms. The chapters are supported by extensive tabular data and by annexes giving details of international arms control and non-proliferation agreements, multilateral security institutions, and a chronology of major events in 2011. In addition, *SIPRI Yearbook 2012* provides a platform for publishing the work of three important partner organizations: the Uppsala Conflict Data Program's extensive data on organized violence; the Institute for Economics and Peace's Global Peace Index, produced in collaboration with the Economist Intelligence Unit; and the International Panel on Fissile Materials' tables of global stocks and production capabilities of enriched uranium and plutonium.

Key trends and findings

Taken together, the contributions to *SIPRI Yearbook 2012* offer the single-most comprehensive and in-depth annual assessment of developments in international security, armaments and disarmament. The current and recent editions of the SIPRI Yearbook point to persistent contemporary trends that define and shape developments in global and regional security, armaments and disarmament. These trends underpin a more dynamic and complex global security order where established powers will face constraints, new power centres will emerge, and traditional norms and institutions will struggle to cope with current and future security challenges.

Constraints on established powers

Established powers in the world system—especially the USA and its major transatlantic allies—will face continued constraints on their economic, political and military capacities to address global and regional security challenges. This seems to be particularly true in relation to military-centred responses but also applies across the spectrum of developmental and diplomatic responses. These constraints are primarily imposed by budget austerity measures in the wake of the crisis in public finances experienced throughout most of the developed world.

Some of the findings and data in this volume underscore this trend towards austerity. Perhaps it is most evident in relation to military spending. As detailed in chapter 4, for example, over the period 2002–11, with the exception of the UK, the military spending of most of the USA's major allies in Europe fell. Taken as a whole, in real terms the military budgets of European members of the North Atlantic Treaty Organization (NATO) have now fallen back to 2002 levels and are expected to decline further for the next several years. Japan's military spending also shrank over this period, by 2.5 per cent. Chapter 4 discusses in detail some of the implications of austerity for US and European military budgets. These figures do not take into account the effects of the 'war fatigue' that is found in the USA—whose continued involvement in the conflict in Afghanistan makes this its longest war—and among its allies, which will place intangible but nonetheless politically real constraints on their military action for the years ahead.

It is true that the USA and its allies still dominate indicative tables of military power. As described throughout part II of this volume, the USA is far and away the world's largest military spender—indeed, it spends more on its military than the next 14 countries combined—and is likely to remain so for many years to come, despite the budgetary cutbacks. A number of the USA's allies—including the UK, France, Japan, Germany, South Korea, Australia and Turkey—are also likely to retain some of the world's highest military budgets. Investments by these countries, and particularly the USA, in new weapons and technologies will also help them to retain military advantages for the foreseeable future. Further, as some of the world's principal exporters of major conventional weapons, countries such as the USA, the UK, France, and Germany will continue to exercise diplomatic and military influence through that trade. Nevertheless, the relative strengths of established powers will be constrained in comparison with the recent past as they struggle through a period of financial austerity and aim to 'do more with less' or, more likely, 'less with less'. The initial political and operational difficulties encountered in mobilizing and deploying the coalition for the NATO-led intervention in Libya are likely portents of the future. In the event, the coalition was made up of barely half of NATO's 28 members—with Germany taking a clear decision not to participate—plus Sweden, Jordan, Qatar and the United Arab Emirates.

Continuing emergence of new powers and non-state actors

As noted in recent editions of the SIPRI Yearbook and discussed in the current volume, numerous states around the world outside the traditional US alliance system continue to build greater economic, diplomatic and military capacity to affect regional and, in some cases, global security developments. The remarkable growth in China's, Russia's, India's and Saudi Arabia's military spending noted above is only part of the story. Other countries that are not among the top military spenders are nevertheless rapidly expanding their military investments as a result of rapid economic growth or resource wealth. Algeria increased its military spending by 44 per cent between 2010 and 2011. Indonesia and Viet Nam have both increased their military budgets by over 80 per cent since the early 2000s and, as outlined in chapter 6, the top five importers of major conventional weapons in the period 2006–11—India, South Korea, Pakistan, China and Singapore—accounted for 30 per cent of arms imports over that period and were all located in Asia. Giving some focus to the Indian case, chapter 5 on arms production and military services notes that India expects to spend approximately $150 billion on equipment to modernize its military in the coming years.

As chapter 3 details, 32 of the 52 peace operations active in 2011 were conducted by regional organizations, alliances or ad hoc coalitions. While most of these were led by North Atlantic institutions—including the EU, NATO and the Organization for Security and Co-operation in Europe (OSCE)—regional organizations outside the transatlantic space have also become more politically and even militarily active. As discussed in chapters 1, 2, 3 and 10, such organizations as the African Union, the Arab League and the Gulf Cooperation Council took a higher profile in calling on the UN and the international community to take measures to quell the violence erupting in such places as Côte d'Ivoire, Libya and Syria. Significantly, the Arab League formed and deployed its first peace operation, an observer mission, at the close of 2011, in an effort to resolve the Syrian uprising and bring the escalating violence against civilians to an end. These and other regional organizations still lack sufficient political and military capacity to act entirely independently, but it is a sign of the times that the international community, and in particular established powers, will look to such regional groupings to take on more responsibilities in defining and addressing security challenges which affect them.

States and state-based regional organizations are not alone in gaining in relative influence and impact. The research in the current and recent editions of the SIPRI Yearbook clearly underscores the continuing role played by non-state actors in defining regional and even global security developments. The impact of non-state actors is most clearly seen in the findings of chapters 2 and 3, which follow trends in armed conflict and conflict management, respectively. In-depth tracking of armed violence around the world reveals the destabilizing role of non-state actors in prosecuting conflicts and engaging in violence against civilians. The research presented in chapter 2 examines violence by state and non-state actors alike, whether directed against other states, non-state groups or civilian populations. The work in chapter 3 also details the critically important impact of non-state actors across all forms of organized violence, and the often central role they play in conflict areas including Afghanistan, the Democratic Republic of the Congo, Côte d'Ivoire, Libya, Mexico, Nigeria, Somalia, South Sudan, Syria and Thailand. The research and findings in this and previous editions of the SIPRI Yearbook on both conventional arms transfers and conventional arms control point out that non-state groups continue to access a range of military equipment and weapons—mainly small arms and light weapons but also, occasionally, major weapon systems such as anti-ship missiles.

Other types of non-state actor also raise new and potentially more troubling concerns. Technologically sophisticated security threats in the form of cyberattacks and cybertheft, often emanating from non-state and quasi-state actors, pose a continuing concern in many circles. This in part explains the increase in major arms-producing companies' strategically significant and financially noteworthy acquisitions of cybersecurity firms, as discussed in chapter 5. Meanwhile, chapter 9, which focuses on biological and chemical threats, points out that we are effectively already living in a 'post-proliferation' world: the concern is less with the spread of weapon systems and more with the increased access to and capacity for work with materials and technologies that can be employed for malign purposes. A 2011 case involving a decision as to whether and how to publish research results on the transmissibility of avian influenza led a US Government-mandated advisory body on biosecurity to request that Dutch and US research groups withhold parts of their research methodology from publication. This underscores the potential security challenges posed by the increasing ability of scientists to create and manipulate pathogens with novel or predetermined (including more lethal) characteristics. Finally, SIPRI research increasingly draws attention to the role of non-state and quasi-state middlemen in the supply chain—brokers, shippers, banks and other financial institutions, scientists, and others—who may knowingly or otherwise play a part in the proliferation of materials, technology and know-how related to chemical, biological, radiological and nuclear weapons, particularly with respect to so-called intangible transfers of technology.

Struggling norms and institutions

The established powers' diminished capacity to shape the terms of discussion and implement preferred responses, combined with the diffusion of power to other players in the international system, contributes to a third important trend that is identified and illuminated in this and recent editions of the SIPRI Yearbook: struggling norms and institutions. Multilateral organizations tasked with promoting and enforcing norms for stability and security continue to face difficulties in generating the political will and financial resources needed to meet their mandates, and gaps remain which require new or more effective mechanisms.

The opening chapter by Gareth Evans argues that the norms that bolster policy and action for protecting civilians from the ravages of war and mass atrocities have steadily strengthened over the past decade, with the Libyan and Côte d'Ivoire interventions in 2011 being cases in point. However, Evans acknowledges that the lack of effective international responsiveness to the even more horrendous plight of civilians in Syria throughout most of 2011 and into 2012 may signal that the consensus around these norms is not as strong as it could be and may well have reached a 'high-water mark from which the tide will now retreat'. He lays out the difficult consensus-building steps that must be taken by the world's powers. Even if the process is ultimately successful, such a consensus will not be easy to achieve, especially in the wake of the Libyan intervention, and is likely to remain a work in progress for a long time to come.

The widespread support for and expansion of traditional peace operations over the past decade is also facing difficult obstacles in the years ahead. As described in chapter 3, these include expanded mandates and 'mission creep'; overstretched yet understaffed missions; and a lack of necessary equipment. Moreover, the world's major donors to global peace operations—predominantly the advanced economies most badly affected by the global financial crisis and economic recession—are largely looking to cut back support to multilateral institutions and to focus instead on smaller and quicker missions. A case in point is the forthcoming major cut of around $1 billion to UN peacekeeping support, which will force blue helmet missions to do more with less, a reality which has already begun to affect the scale and timing of current operations.

The chapters in this volume examining armaments and disarmament also confirm the difficulties that norms and institutions are facing regarding arms control, non-proliferation, and confidence- and security-building measures. The capacities of major international non-proliferation and arms control regimes such as the 1968 Non-Proliferation Treaty (NPT, see chapter 8), the 1972 Biological and Toxin Weapons Convention (BTWC, see chapter 9), and the 1993 Chemical Weapons Convention (CWC, also discussed in chapter 9) did not see significant improvements in 2011. At the same time, new concerns surfaced about the existence of military nuclear programmes in Iran, North Korea and Syria; possible chemical and biological weapons in Syria; and the existence of previously undeclared chemical weapon sites in Libya. The UN Working Group on Preventing and Responding to Weapons of Mass Destruction Attacks reported in 2011 that institutions with a mandate for dealing with chemical and biological threats were too diffuse in their organization and hampered by separate and partial mandates when it came to addressing such remedial measures as prevention, preparedness and response.

Similar normative and institutional difficulties are evident in the conventional weapons realm. As discussed in chapter 4, for example, the past decade has seen an overall decline in the number of UN member states publicly reporting their military spending via the UN Standardized Instrument for Reporting Military Expenditures. In 2011 the number of reporting countries dropped to 51—that is, fewer than one-third of UN member states—from a high of 81 in 2002. The UN Security Council was able to agree to an arms embargo on Libya in 2011 but was unable to agree to one on Syria (although the EU and the Arab League did so unilaterally). As in previous years, in 2011 there were significant violations of various arms embargoes imposed by the UN against countries such as Côte d'Ivoire, Iran, North Korea and the Darfur region of Sudan (see chapter 10). The most elaborate conventional arms control and confidence-building regime—the 1990 Treaty on Conventional Armed Forces in Europe (CFE Treaty)—held in September 2011 what was probably its last review conference. Russia unilaterally suspended its participation in the regime in 2007, and all NATO member states that are party to the CFE Treaty, as well as Georgia and Moldova, decided at the end of 2011 to stop exchanging treaty-relevant data with Russia. It is not clear what new mechanism, if any, will replace the CFE regime in the future. Regarding the banning of cluster munitions, developments in 2011 underscored the division within the international community between the states that negotiated the 2008 Convention on Cluster Munitions and are obligated to ban such weapons and those states that would prefer less categorical restrictions to be negotiated in the framework of the 1981 Certain Conventional Weapons (CCW) Convention but in the meantime face few restraints on their use of cluster munitions.

III. Looking ahead

The convergence of increased constraints on established powers, the emergence of influential states and non-states with diffuse objectives and capabilities, and the continuing struggle to stabilize norms and institutions leaves the world in a more precarious position in the short-to-medium term. The old constellation of power balances and institutional capacities, rooted in the second half of the 20th century, looks increasingly incapable of effective policy and action to address and manage the challenges of the current era. Major global or regional interstate wars appear unlikely in the near term, but the international system is nevertheless vulnerable to disruptive shocks arising from localized and intensive warfare and interruptions to the flows of people, capital, commodities, technologies and information that help sustain modernizing and stable societies. Many of these disruptions—such as cyberattacks and cybercrime, well-organized criminal networks, resource scarcity, violent displacement of peoples, pandemics, piracy and extremism, as well as destabilizing trafficking in weapons, sensitive technologies, narcotics, money and persons—will not necessarily arise from the deliberate strategic choices of states but will often come from non-state or sub-state sources. Unfortunately, the global community has yet to fully grapple with the ongoing structural changes that define today's dynamic, complex and transnationalized security landscape—changes that often outpace the ability of established institutions and mechanisms to cope with them.

It will certainly take time for established and newly emergent powers to reach an effective consensus on the most important requirements for international order, stability and peace, and on how to realize and defend them. It will also take time for states, still the dominant actors in the international system, to come to grips with and effectively respond to the increasingly critical role of non-state players. This needs to include more effective and genuine partnerships with those non-state actors that can make positive contributions—including businesses, philanthropists, religious and ethnic leaders and groups, and other civil society representatives. It also means working with other states and with constructive non-state actors to defuse and counter the threats to global, regional, and societal stability and security that malign non-state actors will increasingly pose.

At the level of high politics, institutions must continue bold reforms that more fully take into account the emerging power relationships among states at the global and regional levels. The reinvigoration of the Group of 20 (G20) in recent years has helped to ensure that more of the world's emerging powers can have an influence commensurate with their growing interests and capacities. However, given the indivisibility of economics and security in today's world, the G20 will also need to include security questions on its agenda. Expansion and reform of the UN Security Council would be a welcome move towards better reflecting the emergent realities of hard and soft power in the world today, but such measures seem unlikely given the understandable reluctance on the part of the current five permanent members to dilute their influence. Instead, it appears that members of the Security Council will look to regional organizations for political buy-in and, increasingly, material support for action. However, such 'outsourcing' would be more effective if regional organizations—such as the African Union, the Arab League, the Association of Southeast Asian Nations and others—significantly reformed their decision-making structures and improved their capacities for cooperative action in such areas as preventive diplomacy, peacekeeping, countering crime, border surveillance, disaster relief, disease surveillance and developmental assistance.

In much of this work, established and newly emergent states and their multilateral institutions will need to devote far more resources than in the past to engaging with non-state actors, particularly at the intersection of security and development. Such partnerships are needed both in immediate post-crisis responses and, more importantly, in long-term recovery phases that, to be successful, must engage and empower local society actors to build up sustained capacity in such areas as health care, education and technical training, and judicial and police systems. The increased focus across the international community on developing the peacebuilding capacities of civilian actors should facilitate the development of effective partnerships between states, state-based institutions and non-state civil society actors.

It is also clear that a far greater focus will need to be placed on less militarized solutions to the security challenges ahead. This is both a political and a practical necessity. The general public in the developed world, especially in North America and Europe, will be wary about new military interventions, and national governments are under growing pressure to cut costs and produce more credible strategies for managing and reducing their long-term debts. Moreover, the diffusing constellations of state and institutional power today can constrain the will and capacity for effective military action, whether under a UN mandate or by an ad hoc coalition. Perhaps most crucially, many of the most important security challenges in the years ahead will not readily lend themselves to traditional military solutions. Instead, what will be needed is an innovative integration of preventive diplomacy, pre-emptive and early-warning technologies, and cooperative transnational partnerships. This is not to say that military capacities are not needed—they will be. In some cases, they can be put to work as part of domestic law enforcement and counterterrorism efforts, for example through the use of overhead imagery, robots and information system protection. But, to put it simply, the balance between military and less- or non-militarized solutions should continue to tip in favour of the latter.

As important as these steps are to take, it will certainly not be easy to create a new framework for relations among the world's powers, reform institutions, respond to the influence of non-state players, and rebalance military and non-military resources. Nevertheless, the rapidly transforming global and regional scene will not wait. As a result, the world is likely to continue to face a lengthy period of uncertainty and a diffuse range of unmet and potentially destabilizing risks and challenges for security, armaments and disarmament. As an authoritative and respected resource for the international community for more than four decades, the SIPRI Yearbook will continue to monitor these complex developments and put forward well-informed perspectives on how to address them.

1. Responding to atrocities: the new geopolitics of intervention

GARETH EVANS

I. The challenge of civilian protection

Our age has confronted no greater ethical, political and institutional challenge than ensuring the protection of civilians, as victims of both war and of mass atrocity crimes. In wartime, civilians have for long now been killed and maimed in numbers far exceeding armed combatants. Whether in peacetime or war, the murder, torture, rape, starvation or forced expulsion of groups of men, women and children, for no other reason than their race, ethnicity, religion, nationality, class or ideology, has been a recurring stain on the world's collective conscience.

Many fewer wars are fought today than just two decades ago, and there are many fewer battle casualties, certainly across borders but within them as well.[1] Fewer instances, and fewer victims, of what is now called genocide and other major crimes against humanity occur today but the civilian tolls are still alarmingly high, and new threats continually arise.[2] In Iraq between 2003 and 2011, of the 162 000 deaths as a result of the US-led war, 128 000 were civilians.[3] At the end of 2011 the civilian death toll from the war in Afghanistan stood at 17 000 and still counting.[4] The war in the Democratic Republic of the Congo (DRC) formally ended in 2003 but the number of deaths from ongoing violence and war-generated malnutrition and disease continues to rise, and sexual violence continues on a horrendous scale.[5] In Sudan, the plight of 1.8 million displaced Darfuris is as acute

---

[1] Human Security Report Project, *Human Security Report 2009/2010: The Causes of Peace and the Shrinking Costs of War* (Oxford University Press: New York, 2011). This report draws on data from the Peace Research Institute Oslo (PRIO) and the Uppsala Conflict Data Program (UCDP). The original *Human Security Report 2005: War and Peace in the 21st Century* (Oxford University Press: New York, 2005) also contains much material that is still relevant. See also Pinker, S., *The Better Angels of Our Nature: The Decline of Violence in History and Its Causes* (Allen Lane: London, 2011), chapter 7, especially pp. 297–305.

[2] Human Security Report Project (note 1); and Pinker (note 1), pp. 336–43.

[3] 'Iraqi deaths from violence 2003–2011', Iraq Body Count, 2 Jan. 2012, <http://www.iraqbodycount.org/analysis/numbers/2011/>.

[4] United Nations Assistance Mission in Afghanistan (UNAMA), 'Civilian casualties rise for fifth consecutive year in Afghan conflict', Press release, 4 Feb. 2012, <http://unama.unmissions.org/Default.aspx?tabid=1762&ctl=Details&mid=1920&Itemid=16267>.

[5] See e.g. International Coalition for the Responsibility to Protect, 'Crisis in the Democratic Republic of Congo', <http://www.responsibilitytoprotect.org/index.php/crises/crisis-in-drc>; and Global Centre for the Responsibility to Protect (GCR2P), 'Imminent risk: Democratic Republic of the Congo', *R2P Monitor*, no. 1 (10 Jan. 2012), pp. 7–8. *R2P Monitor* documents situations of 'current crisis', 'imminent risk' and 'serious concern'.

as ever, and in late 2011 the new border with South Sudan witnessed the aerial bombardment of civilian areas, extrajudicial killings and the forced displacement of local populations opposed to Sudanese rule.[6] During the course of 2011, the international community had to respond to a merciless assault by the regime of Muammar Gaddafi in Libya on its initially unarmed civilian opponents, with the overall civilian death toll at the end of the year amounting to many thousands.[7] In the even more alarming situation in Syria, by early 2012 the death toll from 9 months of regime crackdown on initially unarmed protesters stood at well over 5000 and was increasing rapidly.[8]

Not all the news is bad. Awareness of the problem of civilian protection is as great as it has ever been, not least as a result of the emergence and consolidation in the post-cold war years of an array of actors, including effective media organizations (e.g. most recently and to spectacular effect during the Arab Spring, Al Jazeera); highly professional non-governmental organizations such as the International Crisis Group and Human Rights Watch; and more official institutions like the Office of the High Commissioner for Human Rights (OHCHR) and the United Nations Joint Office of the Special Advisers on the Prevention of Genocide and Responsibility to Protect. All this made it impossible for policymakers to pretend, as they could as recently as the Rwandan genocide in 1994, to be unaware of horrors that may be unfolding.

Consciousness of the problem has been accompanied by a much greater evident willingness—at least in principle—to do something about it. This chapter charts two big normative advances in this area: first, the dramatically upgraded attention given since 1999 to the law and practice relating to the protection of civilians (POC) in armed conflict; and, second, the emergence in 2001, and far-reaching global embrace since 2005, of the new concept of the responsibility to protect (R2P). There is now more or less universal acceptance of the principles that state sovereignty is not a licence to kill, but entails a responsibility not to do or allow grievous harm to one's own people (Pillar 1); a responsibility on the part of the wider international community to assist those states that need and want help in

---

[6] Global Centre for the Responsibility to Protect (note 5), pp. 4–6.

[7] No properly verified Libyan death toll figures exist. The best available evidence, according to an International Criminal Court (ICC) estimate, suggests that 500–700 civilians were killed in Feb. 2011, before the international intervention and outbreak of civil war. 'Hague court seeks warrants for Libyan officials', New York Times, 4 May 2011. However, estimates of the overall death toll from the fighting between Mar. and Oct. 2011 vary wildly, from 10 000 to 30 000 or more. Milne, S., 'If the Libyan war was about saving lives, it was a catastrophic failure', The Guardian, 26 Oct. 2011. The number of civilian deaths directly attributable to the NATO-led military action seems likely to have been fewer than 100. Chivers, C. J. and Schmitt, E., 'In strikes on Libya by NATO, an unspoken civilian toll', New York Times, 17 Dec. 2011.

[8] 'Syria should be referred to ICC, UN's Navi Pillay says', BBC News, 13 Dec. 2011, <http://www.bbc.co.uk/news/world-middle-east-16151424>.

meeting that obligation (Pillar 2); and—although this element has been harder to translate into consistent practice—a responsibility to take timely and decisive collective action in accordance with the UN Charter, including under the enforcement provisions of Chapter VII, if a state is manifestly failing to protect its populations from genocide and other mass atrocity crimes (Pillar 3).[9]

UN Security Council Resolution 1973, authorizing military intervention in Libya to halt what was seen as an imminent massacre, was a resounding demonstration of these principles at work, and seemed to set a new benchmark against which all future arguments for such intervention might be measured.[10] However, the subsequent implementation of that mandate led to the reappearance of significant geopolitical divisions. The Security Council's paralysis over Syria during the course of 2011, culminating in the veto by Russia and China on 4 February 2012 of a very cautiously drafted condemnatory resolution, has raised the question, in relation to the sharp-end implementation of R2P, of whether Resolution 1973 would prove to be the high-water mark from which the tide will now retreat.

China and Russia have always been susceptible to the suggestion that if Western powers are given an inch they will take a mile, and their position had real resonance through the course of 2011 with the major new emerging power bloc of India, Brazil and South Africa (the IBSA countries), which also had seats on the Security Council at the time. This was a fascinating foretaste of what might be expected if the Security Council's permanent membership can ever be configured to reflect contemporary power realities rather than those of the mid-20th century.

The crucial question to be explored is whether the new geopolitics of intervention that appeared to have emerged with Resolution 1973—with previously reluctant powers prepared not only to acknowledge in principle the imperative of civilian protection but also to accept strong practical action, and to do so squarely within the framework of the UN Charter—is in fact sustainable, or whether, as suggested by the subsequent response to the situation in Syria, a more familiar, and more cynical, geopolitics will in fact reassert itself. A no less important related question is whether powers such as France, the United Kingdom and the United States, which have been the strongest supporters of robust intervention in the past, will retain their appetite for strong action in an environment of acute financial constraint

---

[9] Charter of the United Nations, signed 26 June 1945, entered into force 24 Oct. 1945, <http://www.un.org/en/documents/charter>. The UN General Assembly unanimously endorsed the concept of the responsibility to protect in UN General Assembly Resolution 60/1, 24 Oct. 2005, paras 138–39. The 'Pillars' language was introduced in 2009 and is now generally accepted as usefully refining and clarifying the 2005 language. United Nations, General Assembly, 'Implementing the responsibility to protect', Report of the Secretary-General, A/63/677, 12 Jan. 2009.

[10] UN Security Council Resolution 1973, 17 Mar. 2011. The resolution was passed with several abstentions—Brazil, China, Germany, India and Russia—but no opposition.

and uncertain domestic support for any foreign adventures that are not seen to be squarely related to identifiable national interests.

This chapter takes the optimistic view that the new normative commitment to civilian protection is alive and well, and that, in the aftermath of the intervention in Libya, the world has been witnessing not so much a major setback for a new cooperative approach as the inevitable teething troubles associated with the evolution of any major new international norm. Section II summarizes the related concepts of protection of civilians and the responsibility to protect, and outlines some of the challenges that may affect their future applicability and effectiveness. Section III focuses on the 2011 intervention in Libya and the implementation of Resolution 1973, and seeks to answer two specific questions. First, was the intervention a case of overreach? Second, given the shifts in the geopolitical environment since the intervention, is there potential for a new consensus? Section IV, finally, argues for a set of policy approaches that could make the path back to effective consensus significantly easier to tread, both in principle and in practice.

II. New paradigms for a new century: protection of civilians and the responsibility to protect

Protection of civilians in armed conflict

International action to protect civilians in time of war has a long history, with legal foundations in the body of international humanitarian law that has been developed since the 19th century in successive Hague and Geneva conventions, especially as now enshrined in the 1949 Geneva Conventions and Additional Protocols of 1977 (the latter extending the relevant protections to non-international armed conflicts).[11] International human rights law and refugee law, most of which originated in the years following World War II, also create obligations on states to protect civilians in multiple ways in both war and peacetime. Many international organizations have also long exercised significant civilian protection mandates, including the International Committee of the Red Cross (ICRC), the OHCHR, the Office of the UN High Commissioner for Refugees (UNHCR) and the United Nations Children's Fund (UNICEF).

It is only since 1999, with the presentation of the first report by the Secretary-General to the UN Security Council on the protection of civilians in armed conflict, that there has been systematic policy focus on this issue

---

[11] For brief summaries of the 1949 Geneva Conventions and their 1977 protocols—which are the basis for international humanitarian law—see annex A in this volume.

at the highest international level.[12] The report was a comprehensive over-view, addressing the threats posed by attacks on and forced displacement of civilians; the mixing of combatants and civilians in camps for refugees and internally displaced persons; the denial of humanitarian assistance and access; the targeting of humanitarian and peacekeeping personnel; the specific problems faced by children and women; the destructive role played by small arms and anti-personnel mines; and the humanitarian impact of sanctions. It recommended a series of measures to strengthen both legal protection (including ratification and implementation of international instruments, and increasing accountability for war crimes) and physical protection (including more effective peace operations, stronger guarantees of humanitarian access and targeted sanctions).

Most of these recommendations were embraced, albeit in general terms, in a subsequent Security Council thematic resolution on POC and, in various permutations, have been the subject of regular annual debates and resolutions since.[13] Ban Ki-moon's reports and briefings since 2009, and the debates following them, have focused on the 'five core challenges' of enhancing compliance with international humanitarian and human rights law, including Security Council measures to initiate commissions of inquiry and refer relevant matters to the International Criminal Court (ICC); engaging more effectively with non-state armed groups to enhance compliance; properly training and resourcing peace operations to enhance the protection of civilians; enhancing humanitarian access to affected populations; and generally enhancing accountability for violations of international law.[14]

Building on these foundations, over the past decade the Security Council has frequently taken POC action in specific cases, including calling on parties to conflict to observe international humanitarian law; imposing sanctions on violators; creating special tribunals (notably for Rwanda and the former Yugoslavia) and making references to the ICC to hold individuals accountable; and using Chapter VII of the UN Charter to impose arms embargoes. Very importantly, the Security Council has also used Chapter VII to authorize peace operations to use force when providing physical protection to civilians under imminent threat of violence, with

---

[12] United Nations, Security Council, Report of the Secretary-General to the Security Council on the protection of civilians in armed conflict, S/1999/957, 8 Sep. 1999.

[13] UN Security Council Resolution 1265, 17 Sep. 1999.

[14] United Nations, Security Council, Report of the Secretary-General on the protection of civilians in armed conflict, S/2009/277, 29 May 2009; United Nations, Security Council, Report of the Secretary-General on the protection of civilians in armed conflict, S/2010/579, 11 Nov. 2010; United Nations, Security Council, 6650th meeting, 'Protection of civilians in armed conflict', S/PV.6650, 9 Nov 2011; and Security Council Report, *Protection of Civilians*, Cross-cutting Report no. 2 (Security Council Report: New York, 20 July 2011).

14 missions being so mandated since 1999.[15] An important further under-pinning of these expanded peacekeeping mandates came with the 2000 Report of the Panel on United Nations Peace Operations, chaired by Lakhdar Brahimi, which made absolutely clear that the principle of UN impartiality could not mean—as it had during the 1990s, much to the organization's discredit—a reluctance to distinguish victim from aggressor.[16]

Beyond the issue of peacekeeping mandates, the POC reports and debates have tended until recently to avoid the larger issue of coercive military intervention, although Kofi Annan opened up the issue in his initial 1999 report.[17] In Resolution 1296 in 2000 the Security Council noted

that the deliberate targeting of civilian populations or other protected persons and the committing of systematic, flagrant and widespread violations of international humanitarian and human rights law in situations of armed conflict may constitute a threat to international peace and security, and, in this regard, reaffirms its readiness to consider such situations and, where necessary, to adopt appropriate steps.[18]

The responsibility to protect

Important as this new emphasis on civilian protection was after 1999, some crucial ingredients were missing in the way the issue was being conceptualized. Nothing in the POC reports and resolutions addressed mass atrocity crimes occurring as one-sided violence—as had been the case for some of the worst atrocities of all, notably those in Cambodia in the 1970s and Rwanda in 1994—or other than in the context of full-blown war. Perhaps even more importantly, there was nothing directly politically responsive to the major debate on 'humanitarian intervention' that had been raging throughout the 1990s and deeply dividing the international community.

A fundamental conceptual gulf was evident throughout this decade between those, largely in the Global North, who rallied to the banner of humanitarian intervention or 'the right to intervene' (*droit d'ingérence* in Bernard Kouchner's influential formulation) and those, largely in the Global South, who defended the traditional prerogatives of state sovereignty, invoking the primacy of Article 2(7) of the UN Charter, and arguing

---

[15] See Security Council Report (note 14); Security Council Report, 'Publications on protection of civilians in armed conflict', 20 Dec. 2011, <http://www.securitycouncilreport.org/site/c.glKWLeMT IsG/b.2400839/>; and Global Centre for the Responsibility to Protect, 'The relationship between the responsibility to protect and the protection of civilians in armed conflict', Policy brief, Jan. 2009, <http://globalr2p.org/advocacy/>.

[16] United Nations, General Assembly and Security Council, Report of the Panel on Peace Operations, A/55/305-S/2000/809, Executive Summary, pp. ix–x; and Evans, G., *The Responsibility to Protect: Ending Mass Atrocity Crimes Once and For All* (Brookings Institution Press: Washington, DC, 2008), pp. 120–25.

[17] United Nations (note 12), para. 67.

[18] UN Security Council Resolution 1296, 19 Apr. 2000, para. 5.

that internal events were none of the rest of the world's business.[19] The outcome was that the international community reacted incompletely or not at all—as with the catastrophe of Rwandan genocide and the almost unbelievable default in Srebrenica in Bosnia and Herzegovina in 1995—or unlawfully, as in Kosovo in 1999 when the North Atlantic Treaty Organization (NATO), anticipating a Russian veto, intervened without the Security Council's authorization.

It was to find a way out of this political impasse that the 'Responsibility to Protect' concept was born, in the 2001 report of that name by the International Commission on Intervention and State Sovereignty (ICISS).[20] The Commission was established by the Canadian Government as an explicit response to the challenge issued by Kofi Annan in the UN General Assembly in 2000: 'If humanitarian intervention is indeed an unacceptable assault on sovereignty, how should we respond to a Rwanda, to a Srebrenica—to gross and systematic violations of human rights that offend every precept of our common humanity?'[21]

The ICISS report sought to meet this challenge in three main ways. First, in terms of presentation, it turned abrasive 'right to intervene' language into the potentially much more acceptable 'responsibility to protect'. Second, it broadened the range of actors in the frame: whereas humanitarian intervention focused just on the international response, the new formulation spread the responsibility, starting with the spotlight on the sovereign state itself and its responsibilities (the idea of 'sovereignty as responsibility' that had been earlier given prominence by Francis Deng and Roberta Cohen), and only then shifting to the responsibility of the wider international community.[22] Third, it dramatically broadened the range of possible responses: whereas humanitarian intervention focused one-dimensionally on military reaction, R2P involves multiple elements in the response continuum, including both long-term and short-term preventive action, reaction when prevention fails, with coercive military action only contemplated as an absolute last resort after multiple criteria are satisfied, and post-crisis rebuilding aimed at preventing recurrence.

---

[19] Article 2(7) of the UN Charter (note 9) requires the UN not to 'intervene in matters which are essentially within the domestic jurisdiction of any state'. *Droit d'ingérence* came to prominence at the time of the US-led intervention in Somalia in 1992 and was first articulated in Bettati, M. and Kouchner, B. (eds), *Le devoir d'ingérence: peut-on les laisser mourir?* [The duty to interfere: can one let them die?] (Denoël: Paris, 1987), p. 300. See also Evans (note 16), pp. 32–33.

[20] International Commission on Intervention and State Sovereignty (ICISS), *The Responsibility to Protect* (International Development Research Centre: Ottawa, 2001). For a fuller account of the birth and evolution of the concept see Evans (note 16), pp. 31–54.

[21] United Nations, General Assembly, 'We the peoples: the role of the United Nations in the 21st century', Millennium Report of the Secretary-General, A/54/2000, 3 Apr. 2000, p. 48.

[22] See Deng, F. and Cohen, R., 'Mass displacement caused by conflicts and one-sided violence: national and international responses', *SIPRI Yearbook 2009*, pp. 15–38.

Articulated this way, the new concept gained remarkable international traction within a very short time, winning unanimous endorsement by the more than 150 heads of state and government meeting as the UN General Assembly at the 2005 World Summit; and within another year it had been embraced in Security Council Resolution 1674.[23] Since 2005 the task has been to ensure that this new normative development—spectacular as it might look on paper, with the historian Martin Gilbert, for example, describing it as 'the most significant adjustment to sovereignty in 360 years'— actually translates into effective action in real-world situations that cry out for it.[24] That has meant surmounting conceptual, institutional and political challenges.

As to the conceptual challenge, it is evident—writing in early 2012—that this has largely been met. Assisted by a series of well-received reports to the General Assembly by the Secretary-General in 2009, 2010 and 2011 (written by his Special Adviser on R2P, Edward Luck), the debate about what constitutes an R2P situation is much less confused now than it was in the period shortly after 2005.[25] As successive situations have arisen and been debated, it has come to be widely understood and accepted that R2P is not about human security, human rights violations or conflict situations in general; nor is it concerned with natural disasters or other humanitarian catastrophes. Rather, R2P is about responding to the 'four crimes' specified in the 2005 Outcome Document—namely, genocide, war crimes, ethnic cleansing and crimes against humanity—and even here there has to be some scale and contemporaneity to the types of atrocity crime committed or feared if any kind of serious coercive response is to be justified.[26]

The institutional challenge, similarly, is being met, although much more remains to be done to fully develop the necessary preparedness—diplomatic, civilian and military—to deal with future situations of mass atrocity crime. Within key national governments and international organizations, 'focal points' are being established with officials whose job it is to worry

[23] For the key primary documents in the process of international take-up of the ICISS report see United Nations, *A More Secure World: Our Shared Responsibility*, Report of the Secretary-General's High-level Panel on Threats, Challenges and Change (United Nations: New York, 2004); United Nations, General Assembly, 'In larger freedom: towards development, security and human rights for all', Report of the Secretary-General, A/59/2005, 21 Mar. 2005; UN General Assembly Resolution 60/1 (note 9), paras 138–39; and UN Security Council Resolution 1674, 28 Apr. 2006.

[24] Gilbert, M., 'The terrible 20th century', *Globe and Mail* (Toronto), 31 Jan. 2007.

[25] United Nations, A/63/677 (note 9); United Nations, General Assembly, 'Early warning, assessment and the responsibility to protect', Report of the Secretary-General, A/64/684, 14 July 2010; and United Nations, General Assembly and Security Council, 'The role of regional and subregional arrangements in implementing the responsibility to protect', Report of the Secretary-General, A/65/877-S/2011/393, 28 June 2011.

[26] On the emerging consensus about particular cases see Evans, G., 'The raison d'etre, scope and limits of the responsibility to protect', Address, Centre de Droit International, Université Paris Ouest, 14 Nov. 2011, <http://www.gevans.org/speeches/speech456.html>; and Global Centre for the Responsibility to Protect (note 5).

about early warning and response to new situations as they arise, and to energize the appropriate action throughout their respective systems. One of the strongest examples is the USA, with a special unit in the National Security Council, and an inter-agency Atrocities Prevention Board being created with the object of taking whole-of-government responses to these situations to a new level of effectiveness.

The ICC and a number of other ad hoc tribunals have been established, enabling not only trial and punishment for some of the worst mass atrocity crimes of the past, but also potentially providing an important new deterrent for the future. Although the establishment of effective military rapid reaction forces on even a standby basis remains more an aspiration than a reality, key militaries are now devoting serious time and attention to debating and putting in place new force configuration arrangements, doctrines, rules of engagement and training to run what are being increasingly described as mass atrocity response operations (MARO).[27]

The most troubling challenge, as always, is the political one: finding the will to translate clear understanding of need, and available institutional capacity, into effective action. While the paralysed Security Council response to the situation in Syria since mid-2011 has brought this problem once again to the fore, the available evidence points to unequivocal in-principle acceptance of all the core elements of the R2P norm by the overwhelming majority of states. The clearest proof lies in the outcomes of the series of debates in the UN General Assembly since 2005, especially those in response to the Secretary-General's R2P reports in 2009, 2010 and 2011. For those who had never accepted the 2005 consensus, the 2009 debate was seen as a real opportunity to overturn it but it became apparent that, out of the whole UN membership, only four states—Cuba, Nicaragua, Sudan and Venezuela—wanted to go that far.[28] Since then, while lively debate continues about the pros and cons of particular responses to particular situations, general opposition to the R2P norm itself has been even more muted. That was so even in 2011 in the midst of concerns being widely voiced about the 'overstretching' of the Libya mandate.[29] Moreover,

---

[27] Sewall, S. et al., *Mass Atrocity Response Operations: A Military Planning Handbook* (Harvard University, Carr Center for Human Rights Policy: Cambridge, MA, 2010).

[28] Global Centre for the Responsibility to Protect (GCR2P), *Implementing the Responsibility to Protect—The 2009 General Assembly Debate: An Assessment*, GCR2P report (GCR2P: New York, Aug. 2009), p. 4.

[29] On the July R2P debate see International Coalition for the Responsibility to Protect, 'General Assembly holds third interactive dialogue on the role of regional and sub-regional arrangements in implementing the Responsibility to Protect', 13 July 2011, <http://www.wfm-igp.org/site/general-assembly-holds-third-dialogue-rtop-focuses-role-regional-organizations>. On the Sep. general debate see Global Centre for the Responsibility to Protect, 'The responsibility to protect and the 66th opening of the General Assembly, September 2011', 7 Oct. 2011, <http://globalr2p.org/advocacy/>. On the Nov. POC debate see International Coalition for the Responsibility to Protect, '12th Security Council Open Debate on the Protection of Civilians in Armed Conflict', 9 Nov. 2011, <http://www.responsibilitytoprotect.org/index.php/component/content/article/136-latest-news/3733>.   In   the

by the end of 2011 the Security Council itself had referred to R2P on three occasions since the Libya resolutions: in its resolutions on Sudan and Yemen, and in a presidential statement on prevention.[30] As Ban Ki-moon put it in September 2011: 'It is a sign of progress that our debates are now about how, not whether, to implement the Responsibility to Protect. No government questions the principle'.[31]

The relationship between protection of civilians and the responsibility to protect

The two new paradigms that have dominated international policy debate on civilian protection in the new century march comfortably alongside each other and there is no particular point, except as an intellectual exercise, in trying to disentangle them in the many real-world situations where they overlap.[32] The preamble to UN Security Council Resolution 1973 on Libya, for example, makes clear its reliance on both R2P and POC norms, in '*Reiterating* the responsibility of the Libyan authorities to protect the Libyan population and *reaffirming* that parties to armed conflicts bear the primary responsibility to take all feasible steps to ensure the protection of civilians'.[33]

The UN Under Secretary-General for Humanitarian Affairs, Jan Egeland, briefing the Security Council in its open debate on the protection of civilians in 2006, made clear the common normative foundations of the two bodies of doctrine, stressing that the responsibility to protect was a 'core principle of humanity' which must 'become a truly shared interest and translate into joint action by all members of this Council and our global Organisation'.[34] The first endorsement of R2P by the Security Council came in its POC resolution of 2006.[35] Both POC and R2P have the same legal

general debate opening the General Assembly, 2 of the most fascinating acknowledgements that R2P is here to stay came from ministerial contributions from 2 manifestly unlikely sources: Syria and Zimbabwe.

[30] UN Security Council Resolution 1996, 8 July 2011; UN Security Council Resolution 2014, 21 Oct. 2011; and United Nations, Security Council, Statement by the President of the Security Council, S/PRST/2011/18, 22 Sep. 2011.

[31] United Nations, 'Effective prevention requires early, active, sustained engagement, stresses Secretary-General at ministerial round table on "responsibility to protect"', Press Release SG/SM/13838, 23 Sep. 2011.

[32] For detailed analyses of the 2 concepts and their interrelationship ('sisters but not twins' in Popovski's account) see Popovski, V. et al., 'Responsibility to Protect and Protection of Civilians', *Security Challenges*, vol. 7, no. 4 (summer 2011). A succinct but very useful account is Global Centre for the Responsibility to Protect (note 15). See also Breakey, H. et al., *Enhancing Protection Capacity: A Guide to the Responsibility to Protect and the Protection of Civilians in Armed Conflicts* (Asia-Pacific Civil Military Centre of Excellence/Institute for Ethics, Governance and Law: Canberra/Brisbane, 2012).

[33] UN Security Council Resolution 1973 (note 10) (emphasis in original).

[34] United Nations Security Council, 5577th meeting, S/PV.5577, 4 Dec. 2006.

[35] UN Security Council Resolution 1674 (note 23).

underpinnings in international humanitarian law, human rights law and refugee law as far as the responsibility of individual states is concerned. In addition, neither body of doctrine is synonymous with military intervention: R2P is about a very wide range of preventive and reactive responses, and while POC is heavily focused, operationally, on peace operations mandates, its agenda is much broader than that.

The two norms differ in just two respects, neither of which is significant for present purposes. POC is broader than R2P to the extent that the rights and needs of populations caught up in armed conflict go well beyond protection from mass atrocities. However, in one major respect the scope of R2P goes well beyond POC, in that it is concerned with preventing and halting mass atrocity crimes regardless of whether they occur in times of armed conflict. Cambodia in the mid-1970s, Rwanda in 1994, Kenya in 2008 and Libya, at least at the time of Resolution 1973 in February 2011, are major examples of such non-war situations.

III. Libya and its aftermath: the limits of intervention?

Implementing Resolution 1973: a case of overreach?

Libya in 2011 was, at least initially, a textbook example of how R2P is supposed to work in the face of a rapidly unfolding mass atrocity situation during which early-stage prevention measures no longer have any relevance. In February, Gaddafi's forces responded to the initial peaceful protests against the excesses of his regime, inspired by the Arab Spring revolutions in Tunisia and Egypt, by massacring at least several hundred of his own people.[36] That led to UN Security Council Resolution 1970, which specifically invoked 'the Libyan authorities' responsibility to protect its population', condemned its violence against civilians, demanded that this stop and sought to concentrate Gaddafi's mind by applying targeted sanctions, an arms embargo and the threat of ICC prosecution for crimes against humanity.[37]

Then, as it became apparent that Gaddafi was not only ignoring that resolution but planning a major assault on Benghazi in which 'no mercy or pity' would be shown to perceived opponents, armed or otherwise—his reference to 'cockroaches' having a special resonance for those who remembered how Tutsis were being described before the 1994 genocide in Rwanda—the Security Council followed up with Resolution 1973.[38] This also invoked the R2P principle (and POC as well); reasserted a determination to ensure the protection of civilians; deplored the failure to

---

[36] See note 7.
[37] UN Security Council Resolution 1970, 26 Feb. 2011.
[38] UN Security Council Resolution 1973 (note 10).

comply with the first resolution; called for an immediate ceasefire and a complete end to violent attacks against and abuses of civilians; and explicitly authorized military intervention by member states to achieve these objectives.

That coercive military action was allowed to take two forms: 'all necessary measures' to enforce a no-fly zone, and—in an important and far-reaching addition proposed by the USA at the last minute—'all necessary measures . . . to protect civilians and civilian populated areas under threat of attack'. Only 'a foreign occupation force' was expressly excluded: ground troops were just a bridge too far for the Arab League to contemplate, and the political support of this regional organization was absolutely crucial in ensuring both a majority on the Security Council and no exercise of the veto by China or Russia. (That regional support was also, politically, an absolute precondition for the UK and the USA to act without leaving themselves open to the allegation throughout the Arab-Islamic world of being up to their old Iraq-invading, crusading tricks.)

NATO action commenced immediately, and can certainly be credited with stopping a major catastrophe in Benghazi that would have cost a great many civilian lives. To this extent R2P again worked exactly as it was intended, and justified the exultation at the time of those who, like the present author, believed that a major page had been turned and that maybe, just maybe, after centuries of indifference or worse to mass atrocity crimes, the world could look forward to a future in which there would be no more Rwandas or horrors like it. But not everyone shared even that initial exultation. Right from the outset there were critics who argued that the likely Benghazi death toll, with no international intervention, would have been much less than claimed, and that negotiations could have succeeded given more time.[39] It is impossible after the event to test such arguments, but these particular ones are unpersuasive. Whatever the distaste unquestionably felt for Gaddafi in both the West and the Arab League, it is inconceivable that the 'all necessary measures' resolution in the Security Council would have been pursued, let alone accepted, if there had not been at the time a widespread and quite genuine belief (shared by China, Russia and the others who did not oppose Resolution 1973) that Gaddafi's regime had killed many civilian protesters and was on the verge of killing a great many more in Benghazi. Gaddafi's behaviour over the three weeks since the preceding Security Council resolution had shown him to be determinedly resistant to any negotiated political settlement, certainly one that involved him relinquishing any significant power.

[39] See e.g. Roberts, H., 'Who said Gaddafi had to go?', *London Review of Books*, 17 Nov. 2011, pp. 8–18, and the subsequent exchange in 'Letters', *London Review of Books*, 15 Dec. 2011, pp. 4–5.

The criticisms of the intervention that have more traction, and continuing resonance, are those mounted not against the initial military response—destroying Libyan Air Force infrastructure, and attacking the ground forces advancing on Benghazi—but what came after, when it became rapidly apparent that the NATO-led forces would settle for nothing less than regime change and do whatever it took to achieve that. Such action included not only rejecting outright early ceasefire offers that may or may not have been serious, but also attacking from the air fleeing personnel who posed no immediate risk to civilians (including, in the October endgame, Gaddafi himself); striking locations that were not obviously militarily significant (such as the Tripoli compound in which Gaddafi's son Khamis and three grandchildren were reportedly killed in April); and, more generally, comprehensively supporting the rebel side (even to the extent of breaching the Security Council arms embargo in the case of France and Qatar) in what rapidly became a full-scale civil war.[40]

All these actions were characterized, inevitably, by a number of critics as exceeding the mandate conferred by Resolution 1973, or at the very least stretching its letter to the limits and breaching its spirit. They generated negative reactions as a result from the Arab League, which originally strongly supported that resolution, and from many of the countries that initially did not oppose the resolution including Brazil, Russia, India, China and South Africa (the BRICS countries). They were also used as justification, again by these states, for opposing any substantive Security Council resolution on Syria throughout 2011.[41] On the other side, the argument was made that, while the intervention was always about civilian protection, the only way civilians could reliably be protected in areas, such as Tripoli, that were under Gaddafi's control was by removing him from power. Some critics have been quick to ascribe darker commercial or other motives, or simply a congenital trigger-happiness on the part of the 'war party' of France, the UK and the USA but it seems fairer to describe the Western powers' response as primarily a genuinely motivated reaction to a genuinely perceived humanitarian need.[42]

The question remains, nonetheless, whether that reaction was an overreaction. Could it in fact have been possible to respond militarily to the situation as it presented itself in Libya without taking sides and fighting an all-out war? The original 2001 ICISS report certainly approached the issue of R2P military interventions from a limited perspective of this kind:

---

[40] On implementation of the arms embargo see chapter 10, section III, in this volume.

[41] See e.g. the statements, of varying degrees of explicitness but with a clear common message, by the permanent representatives of Brazil (pp. 15–17), India (pp. 17–18), South Africa (pp. 21–23), Russia (pp. 23–24) and China (pp. 24–25) in United Nations, S/PV.6650 (note 14).

[42] See e.g. Roberts (note 39); and, among many other critics of the relevance and utility of R2P in these situations, O'Connor, M., 'How to lose a revolution' and Hehir, A., 'The illusion of progress: Libya and the future of R2P', *The Responsibility to Protect* (e-International Relations: Nov. 2011).

Because the objective of military intervention is to protect populations and not to defeat or destroy an enemy militarily, it differs from traditional warfighting. While military intervention operations require the use of as much force as is necessary, which may on occasion be a great deal, to protect the population at risk, their basic objective is always to achieve quick success with as little cost as possible in civilian lives and inflicting as little damage as possible so as to enhance recovery prospects in the post-conflict phase.[43]

The present author, concerned about the backlash that the Libyan intervention was generating, went on record suggesting that it would have been preferable for the NATO-led coalition to conduct the operation on a more restrained basis: maintaining a no-fly zone, and attacking any concentration of forces clearly about to put civilians at risk, and beyond that leaving the rebels to fight their own war.[44]

This is, it must be acknowledged, a hard position to sustain. Conducting the operation in this way would certainly have led to a more protracted, messier war with the likelihood of larger civilian casualties as a result, and it may have given freer rein to Gaddafi to do his worst, without attackable concentrations of troops, in Tripoli and elsewhere.[45] The domestic politics of an open-ended but limited brief would have been much more difficult to manage in Europe and the USA than a short, reasonably sharp war with the avowed aim of removing a universally abhorred dictator, successfully accomplished. Additionally, militaries are always going to be hard to dissuade from conducting the kind of operations with which they feel most comfortable: using all available resources to defeat a clearly defined enemy. It may be that the Libyan intervention could not practicably have been conducted any other way.

And yet. The trouble is that there is no broad-based international constituency for an approach to mass atrocity crimes that does not set very carefully defined limits on the most extreme response option, military coercion. If the necessity, in a rule-based international order, for Security Council endorsement for any coercive use of military force other than self-defence is accepted, then operations must be conducted within a framework that is capable of generating, and sustaining, consensus in that body. If some key states act in ways that are seen by others to be pushing that consensus beyond endurable limits, then not only will it be almost impossible in the future to win Security Council consensus on any further use of

---

[43] International Commission on Intervention and State Sovereignty (note 20), para. 7.1, p. 57. See also Evans (note 16), p. 214.

[44] Evans, G., 'Letters' (note 39), p. 4.

[45] The argument that the international intervention as conducted resulted in more civilian casualties than would otherwise have been the case cannot be proven. It seems reasonable to assume that without it there would still have been a bloody civil war, with atrocity crimes ending only with either Gaddafi's overthrow or his crushing all dissent, and body counts either way impossible to guess. On this type of methodology see Seybolt, T. B., SIPRI, *Humanitarian Military Intervention: The Conditions for Success and Failure* (Oxford University Press: Oxford, 2007).

military force in atrocity crime situations, but it will be hugely difficult to get agreement on even lesser measures. This seems to be the lesson of Syria, at least while nerves remain raw about the Libyan experience.

The geopolitical environment after Libya: potential for a new consensus?

There are two basic directions in which the debate could now go. One is that mapped by David Rieff, who concludes that rather than trying to fashion a new, constrained concept of R2P military intervention—and indeed, rather than staying with the whole R2P project, with its multi-layered approach and focus on international consensus building across the whole spectrum of preventive and reactive atrocity crime responses—'we could have simply stayed with the concept of just war'.[46] Presumably, although he does not spell it out, this means relying on ad hoc inter-ventions—outside the framework of the Security Council and depending on moral legitimacy rather than legal authority—of the kind that have occasionally occurred in the past (e.g. in the humanitarian interventions periodically mounted in the 19th century to protect Christians at risk in various parts of the Ottoman Empire, and most recently with NATO in Kosovo in 1999).[47]

The other approach is not to throw the R2P baby out with the bathwater in this way, but to go back to basics, build on the very substantial foun-dations that have already been laid, and work at refining and further developing the R2P norm in a way that is capable of generating consensus around even the hardest cases. Achieving this will involve the key states on both sides of the post-Libya intervention debate stepping back a little from the positions they have staked out. In the present geopolitical environment that may not be as hard as it first seems: if the positions of each of the major current players are reviewed, it is evident that in every case there are contradictory dynamics at work, which are far from pushing them into inexorably opposed camps.

While the three Western permanent members of the Security Council have been by far the most overtly committed to R2P in all its dimensions (and the most willing to argue for coercive military force to be applied in appropriate cases), the UK and France are incapable of going it alone, except in relatively small-scale operations like the UK's Operation Palliser in Sierra Leone in 2000 or the France-led (although notionally an EU mis-

[46] Rieff, D., 'Saints go marching in', *National Interest*, July/Aug. 2011, pp. 6–15.
[47] Rodogno, D., *Against Massacre: Humanitarian Interventions in the Ottoman Empire 1815–1914* (Princeton University Press: Princeton, NJ, 2012); and Evans (note 16), pp. 19, 29–30.

sion) Operation Artemis in the DRC in 2003.[48] As for the USA—the 'indispensable nation' as Madeleine Albright famously described it in the context of its unique capacity to project power just about anywhere in the world—it can be expected to be deeply cautious in the future about plunging into new military commitments except when national interests, narrowly defined, are very obviously threatened.[49] The isolationist current always evident in US public and congressional sentiment is, if anything, strengthening. Some hard lessons have been learned in Afghanistan and Iraq over the past decade about the limits of military power; and the budgetary pressures imposed by the global financial crisis and its aftermath will bite hard on US military expenditure in the years ahead. Overall, there is much less cause for anxiety now than there may have been at the time of the Iraq war in 2003 about the major Western powers' willingness to engage in cynical neo-imperialist adventurism.

The other two permanent members of the Security Council, China and Russia, have been much more traditionally inclined to champion—cynically or otherwise, and some scepticism is permissible, particularly in the case of Russia—the principles of 'non-interference in countries' internal affairs and of respect for the sovereignty, unity and territorial integrity of states'.[50] Notwithstanding this, China, contrary to many expectations, did not play any kind of spoiling role in the discussion leading up to the World Summit debate which embraced R2P in 2005 and has not been the strongest obstructive voice since. It did not oppose the initial Resolution 1973 on Libya, and has framed its subsequent objections not absolutely but in terms of the need to use 'extreme caution' in authorizing the use of force to protect civilians, and to 'fully and strictly' implement Security Council resolutions and not 'wilfully misinterpret' them.[51] It is increasingly apparent that China is self-conscious about its need to be seen to be playing a constructive, responsible role in international affairs and should not be assumed to be instinctively unresponsive to the need for sometimes quite robust cooperative responses to mass atrocity crimes.[52] Its veto early in 2012, against the wishes of the Arab League, of the condemnatory but not

---

[48] The EU, not least as a result of Germany's continuing deep reluctance to contribute to any such missions (as evident in its abstention from UN Security Council Resolution 1973), remains unlikely for the foreseeable future to become a serious collective player in these enterprises.

[49] NBC Television, 'An interview with Secretary of State Madeleine K. Albright on "The Today Show" with Matt Lauer', 19 Feb. 1998, <http://usembassy-israel.org.il/publish/press/state/archive/1998/february/sd4220.htm>.

[50] E.g. Li Baodong, Chinese Permanent Representative, United Nations, S/PV.6650 (note 14), p. 24.

[51] E.g., again, Li Baodong, United Nations, S/PV.6650 (note 14), p. 25.

[52] China's potentially constructive multilateral role has started to generate some attention from commentators: 'It starts out still relatively poor, is geographically insecure and is short of almost any natural resource you can think of. Its economy relies on western markets. It needs a stable, open international system. It's an intriguing thought: how long before China emerges as the new champion of the multilateral order?' Stephens, P., 'How a self-sufficient America could go it alone', *Financial Times*, 12 Jan. 2012.

otherwise interventionist proposed Security Council resolution on Syria was unexpected and may have reflected other factors—in particular anxiety about the USA putting increasing pressure on its Middle East energy sources—more than a determination to reassert a hard line on R2P as such.[53]

Both in the lead up to 2005 and since, Russia has been a more obdurate opponent of robust action but in the event it did not oppose the World Summit Outcome Document, the 2011 Libya resolutions or other Security Council resolutions referring to R2P. In fact, Russia explicitly relied on R2P to justify its own military invasion of Georgia in 2008, not that the wider international community found this remotely persuasive.[54] Its subsequent objections have been more directed to the way in which R2P was applied in Libya ('double standards dictated by short term circumstances or the preferences of particular states') than to its inherent normative content.[55] Russia has been particularly supportive of the role of regional organizations in the prevention and settlement of conflicts and was clearly influenced, as were others, by the strong support of the Arab League for intervention in Libya. All that said, strong support by the Arab League—and 13 members of the Security Council—for the proposed resolution on Syria put to it on 4 February 2012, condemning the violence and backing an action plan for political transition but not threatening any coercive measures, was not enough to prevent Russia vetoing the resolution: the realpolitik of its close and long-standing economic and strategic relationship with Syria and the regime of President Bashar al-Assad prevailed.[56] But it is not to be assumed that its intransigence will be as complete in other contexts in the future.

Of the remaining BRICS countries, India was the last significant state to be persuaded to join the 2005 consensus, and has remained a generally unenthusiastic supporter of R2P since (save in the context of the Sri Lankan conflict in 2009, when the Foreign Minister, Pranab Mukherjee, called on the Sri Lankan Government to exercise its responsibility to protect its own citizens). Certainly it has been among the strongest critics, both in the Security Council and the Human Rights Council, of the way the Libyan intervention mandate was implemented. It did support the initial interventionist measures against Libya in Resolution 1970, while not

[53] 'Russia and China veto resolution on Syria at UN', BBC News, 4 Feb. 2012, <http://www.bbc.co.uk/news/world-16890107>. See also Sayigh, Y., 'China's position on Syria', Carnegie Endowment for International Peace, 8 Feb. 2012, <http://www.carnegieendowment.org/2012/02/08/china-s-position-on-syria/>.

[54] Global Centre for the Responsibility to Protect, 'The Georgia–Russia crisis and the responsibility to protect', Background note, 19 Aug. 2008, <http://globalr2p.org/advocay/>.

[55] The Russian Permanent Representative, Vitaly Churkin, refrained from mentioning Russia's invasion of Georgia in this context. United Nations, S/PV.6650 (note 14), p. 23.

[56] See Trenin, D., 'Russia's line in the sand on Syria', Carnegie Endowment for International Peace, 5 Feb. 2012, <http://carnegieendowment.org/2012/02/05/russia-s-line-in-sand-on-syria/9g77>.

opposing Resolution 1973; issued a condemnatory statement on Syria as president of the Security Council; and supported the proposed Syria resolution in February 2012.[57] Further, India supported the use of UN forces to protect civilians in Côte d'Ivoire, has itself been a willing provider of peacekeeping forces with strong POC mandates and has generally focused not on opposing military force so much as on setting conditions for its exercise, including that it 'be the measure of last resort and be used only when all diplomatic and political efforts fail' and that Security Council mandates be closely monitored.[58] India has wanted to be seen internationally as a champion of human rights and democracy, but at the same time to maintain its non-interventionist credentials with the Non-Aligned Movement (NAM), a difficult balance to maintain (as is its position as simultaneously a global champion and national resister of nuclear disarmament).[59] It seems reasonable to assume that as India looks more and more to assume a global leadership role, it will contribute to bridge building on these issues in a more active and systematically constructive way.

South Africa, in contrast, was an enthusiastic proponent of R2P at the 2005 World Summit, was a crucial player in mobilizing and articulating sub-Saharan African support for it, and has since been generally supportive and keen to maintain its post-apartheid human rights and democracy credentials. However, it has been pulled in a different direction by its other international personalities as an outspoken advocate for pan-African and South–South solidarity, and as a strong supporter of mediation and conflict resolution through dialogue. Above all, in the context of Libya, as a long-standing friend of the Gaddafi regime and the leader of the African Union mediation effort, South Africa has been an outspoken critic of the military intervention there, describing it as going 'far beyond the letter and spirit of Resolution 1973'.[60] If its explicit concerns about less than even-handed mandate implementation can be addressed, it seems reasonable to hope that it will again become a strong supporter of R2P in all its dimensions.

Brazil is another state visibly torn between its overall desire to maintain support from the Global South, and its increasing self-consciousness as a rapidly growing global player of real stature and willingness in that context to employ more human rights rhetoric in its foreign policy.[61] Again, more like South Africa than India, it was one of the key Latin American countries

---

[57] For the condemnatory statement on Syria see United Nations, Security Council, Statement by the President of the Security Council, S/PRST/2011/16, 3 Aug. 2011.

[58] Puri, H. S., Permanent Representative of India, United Nations, S/PV.6650 (note 14), p. 18. See also Tardy, T., 'Peace operations: the fragile consensus', *SIPRI Yearbook 2011*.

[59] See e.g. Piccone, T. and Alinikoff, E., *Rising Democracies and the Arab Awakening: Implications for Global Democracy and Human Rights* (Brookings Institute: Washington, DC, Jan. 2012), pp. 11–17.

[60] Sangqu, B., Permanent Representative of South Africa, United Nations, S/PV.6650 (note 14), p. 22. See also Piccone and Alinikoff (note 59), pp. 23–30.

[61] Piccone and Alinikoff (note 59), pp. 4–10.

embracing, in a historically significant way, limited-sovereignty principles in the lead-up to 2005 and has generally given quite strong support to the R2P norm. But as with all the BRICS countries, the bridge too far for Brazil was the perceived overreach by the NATO-led operation in Libya in implementing Security Council Resolution 1973. What has distinguished Brazil's role, however, is its evident willingness now to search actively for a way to regenerate consensus around the issue of forcible intervention in hard cases, with its proposal to develop, in parallel to the present concept of R2P, an 'agreed set of fundamental principles, parameters and procedures' on the theme of 'responsibility while protecting'.[62] As discussed in section IV, this does seem to have the potential to put back on track a multilateral, cooperative approach to civilian protection, including in the most difficult cases.

None of these three major emerging powers have taken as hard a negative line as China and Russia on the question of international engagement in Syria, and they seem more likely between them to play a more substantial and influential role than China or Russia in rebuilding international consensus about how to respond to mass atrocity crimes. Another extremely influential emerging power whose role will be important in the years ahead on this as on many other issues is Turkey, which has been a consistently strong supporter of the R2P principle, an increasingly active, forthright and respected player in its own region and beyond, and a particularly strong critic of the Syrian regime's murderous response to its civilian opponents.

IV. The future for civilian protection

It will not be easy to rebuild the consensus on the implementation of the R2P, and more general POC, norms that were fleetingly achieved at the time of the Security Council resolutions on Libya and Côte d'Ivoire in March 2011, but the best chance of doing so will be for civilian protection policymakers and advocates—building on the general political support for R2P that clearly exists among UN member states (as described in section II)—to focus in the period ahead on making progress in the following five specific areas.

Criteria for the authorization of military force

First, and most importantly, some understanding will need to be reached on the kinds of condition, or criterion, which should have to be satisfied before coercive military force is authorized, and on a process to ensure that the

---

[62] See statement of de Auguiar Patriota, A., Brazilian Foreign Minister, presented by Ribeiro Viotti, M. L., Permanent Representative of Brazil, United Nations, S/PV.6650 (note 14), pp. 15–17.

limits inherent in any mandate granted by the Security Council continue to be observed. These are the issues at the heart of the backlash that has accompanied the implementation of Resolution 1973, and the concerns of the BRICS countries in particular should be taken seriously by France, the UK and the USA. They are too serious to be simply dismissed as indicative of the kind of complaints, rationalizations or evasions of responsibility that are bound to arise whenever states have to make hard decisions that have the potential to offend international friends or domestic constituencies.

One way of approaching the criteria issue would be to return directly to the recommendations of the ICISS, the High-level Panel on Threats, Challenges and Change and Kofi Annan that the Security Council formally adopt the five following prudential guidelines for authorizing the use of force.[63]

1. *Seriousness of risk*. Is the threatened harm of such a kind and scale as to justify prima facie the use of force?

2. *The primary purpose of the proposed military action*. Is it to halt or avert the threat in question, whatever other secondary motives might be in play for different states?

3. *Last resort*. Has every non-military option been fully explored and the judgement reasonably made that nothing less than military force could halt or avert the harm in question?

4. *Proportionality*. Are the scale, duration and intensity of the proposed military action the minimum necessary to meet the threat?

5. *Balance of consequences*. Will those at risk ultimately be better or worse off, and the scale of suffering greater or less? This is usually the toughest legitimacy test.

Such criteria could clearly not guarantee consensus in any particular case, but requiring systematic attention to all the relevant issues—which simply does not happen at the moment—would hopefully make its achievement much more likely. One of the further virtues of this approach is that it would make it abundantly clear from the outset just how different coercive military action is to other response mechanisms, and how many hurdles should have to be jumped before ever authorizing it: that it is something that should not be contemplated as a routine escalation, but only in the most extreme and exceptional circumstances. If such criteria were able to be agreed, and applied with some rigour and consistency to new situations as they arise, it should be a lot easier to avoid the 'slippery slide' argument

[63] International Commission on Intervention and State Sovereignty (note 20), pp. 32–37, 74–75; United Nations, *A More Secure World* (note 23), p. 67; and United Nations, 'In larger freedom', A/59/2005 (note 23), p. 43. These recommendations differ slightly in their language and presentation but the core concepts are exactly the same.

which has contributed to the Security Council paralysis on Syria, making some countries unwilling to even foreshadow non-military measures like targeted sanctions or ICC investigation because of their concern that military coercion would be the inevitable next step if lesser measures failed.

Until now, however, all such arguments have foundered in the face of strong arguments by most of the relevant states and UN insiders—even those who agree on the utility of having such criteria in place—that getting there would be a procedural nightmare, generating endless wrangling about abstractions and unproductively diverting attention away from real issues. What has given fascinating new life to the question is Brazil's initiative in November 2011 in introducing the idea of 'responsibility while protecting' (RWP) to be pursued not as an alternative but a complement to R2P, evolving together with it.[64] The concept paper distributed to generate discussion recommends that there be an 'agreed set of fundamental principles, parameters and procedures' that include at least three of the five criteria described above (last resort, proportionality and balance of consequences).[65] Indications at the time of writing in early 2012 are that the Brazilian proposal has been well received, certainly by its fellow BRICS countries, and—with further development—is likely to feature centrally in the next General Assembly Interactive Dialogue on R2P in mid-2012, which will focus squarely on Pillar 3 enforcement issues.

It is clear that the Brazilian RWP proposal, in its initial formulation, is generating a positive response from other BRICS countries, not least because it also focuses specifically on the need for military action to 'abide by the letter and the spirit of the mandate conferred by the Security Council or the General Assembly', arguing that 'Enhanced Security Council procedures are needed to monitor and assess the manner in which resolutions are interpreted and implemented to ensure responsibility while protecting'.[66] While this part of the initiative will no doubt be particularly sensitive for the three Western permanent members of the Security Council, if it proves—as now seems very possible—to be the vehicle through which a new cooperative commitment to sharp-end implementation of R2P is capable of emerging, it would be irresponsible for France, the UK and the USA, and others who share their basic outlook, not to participate seriously in crafting workable procedures of the kind sought.

[64] de Auguiar Patriota (note 62).

[65] United Nations, General Assembly and Security Council, 'Responsibility while protecting: elements for the development and promotion of a concept', annex to Letter dated 9 November 2011 from the Permanent Representative of Brazil to the United Nations addressed to the Secretary-General, A/66/551–S/2011/701, 11 Nov. 2011.

[66] United Nations (note 65), para. 11(d), (h).

Measures falling short of coercive military intervention

The second major area to which more attention needs to be devoted by policymakers is the scope and limits of Pillar 3 measures that fall short of coercive military intervention, with Security Council members focusing on how they can better join up diplomatic initiatives, targeted sanctions, threats of reference to the ICC and other tools. A good example of the Security Council linking some of these tools reasonably effectively is Côte d'Ivoire, which became a threat to the UN's credibility in early 2011, with both Russia and South Africa blocking more decisive action. UN sanctions primarily implemented by the EU helped contain the crisis while African diplomats tried to negotiate a peace deal. When that proved impossible, with other options manifestly exhausted, a unanimous Security Council resolution approving the use of force by French and UN troops was readily achievable by the end of March.[67] That said, it is important that 'exhaustion of other options' not be seen as requiring non-military options to be physically worked through in circumstances where they are obviously likely to prove totally unproductive: where killing is occurring or imminent, the requirement is to be able to make a reasonable judgment, quickly, that no non-military action is likely to be productive.

Long-term preventive strategies

It will also be important to give, and for the key states to be seen to be giving, more systematic attention to longer-term preventive strategies. These should be relevant both to conflict generally and mass atrocity crimes in particular, not only before such events have ever occurred but—in many ways even more pertinently—after they have occurred, in the peace-building stage where the effort is to prevent recurrence. While the toolbox of relevant structural measures—across the whole spectrum of political and diplomatic, economic and social, constitutional and legal, and security strategies—is well known and regular lip service is paid to this need in the Security Council, including in regular thematic debates on conflict prevention, the record of effective action is not stellar.[68] One theme strongly emphasized in commentary from the Global South, and in lessons-learned analyses from Afghanistan and Iraq, is the critical need for more sensitive attention to be paid by external interveners and assisters to local social dynamics and cultural realities, and to perceptions of their own require-

---

[67] See Gowan, R., 'The Security Council's credibility problem', UN Security Council in Focus, Friedrich-Ebert-Stiftung, Dec. 2011, <http://www.fes.de/gpol/inhalt/publikationen_unsc.php>, p. 4. See also chapter 3, section III, in this volume.

[68] On structural measures see e.g. Evans (note 16), chapter 4. On Security Council debates see United Nations, Security Council, 6621st meeting, S/PV.6621, 22 Sep. 2011.

ments by local populations at all levels.[69] The more that states in the Global North, in particular, are seen to be taking seriously and sensitively their Pillar 2 assistance responsibilities, the less prospect there is of them being criticized as intolerably preoccupied with punitive measures.

Developing appropriate institutional response capacities

A fourth major need is for rapid further development of appropriate institutional response capacity, both preventive and reactive, and both civilian and military, of the kind referred to in section II. The main challenges here are the establishment, in many more governments and intergovernmental organizations, of early warning and response 'focal points'; and the organization and resourcing of civilian capability able to be used, as occasion arises, for diplomatic mediation, civilian policing and other critical administrative support for countries at risk of atrocity crimes occurring or recurring. Further, it will be important to create a culture of effective support—crucial at the national level in the absence of any international marshals service—for the ICC and the developing machinery of international criminal justice; and to have in place properly trained and capable military resources available both for rapid 'fire-brigade' deployment in Rwanda-type cases and for long-haul stabilization operations like those in the DRC and Sudan, not only in no-consent situations, but also where vulnerable governments request this kind of assistance. Again, a major, visible commitment by countries of the Global North to building this kind of capacity is not only very important in its own terms, but can also help to reduce scepticism about their good intentions when more sensitive policy responses have to be considered.

Here as elsewhere on global security issues in the future, regional organizations can be expected to play an ever more important role, exercising the full range of the responsibilities envisaged for them in Chapter VIII of the UN Charter. So far, although both the African Union and the EU have shown occasional willingness to act collectively, and the Arab League demonstrated in 2011 a hitherto-lacking capacity for concerted political action in the contexts of both Libya and Syria, only the Economic Community of West African States (ECOWAS) has so far shown a consistent willingness to respond with a full range of diplomatic, political, economic and ultimately military strategies in response to civilian protection crises. Still there will, and should be, ever more pressure on regional and subregional organizations elsewhere in Africa, and in Asia and Latin America, to be front-line responders in these situations. It may be going too far to

---

[69] See e.g. Mani, R. and Weiss, T. G. (eds), *Responsibility to Protect: Cultural Perspectives in the Global South* (Routledge: London, 2011); and Stewart, R. and Knaus, G., *Can Intervention Work?* (Norton: New York, 2011).

say that the engagement of regional organizations will over the next few years be either a necessary or a sufficient condition for any military intervention in mass atrocity cases—each situation will have its own dynamic—but their role will be ever more important.

Rethinking the concept of 'national interest'

A fifth need worth mentioning relates to those many states that are sensitive to potential domestic resistance to morally worthy foreign entanglements (or which are perhaps oversensitive in perceiving such resistance: it is not unknown for publics to be more generously and internationally minded than their own governments). There is much to be said for rethinking the concept of 'national interest' as involving not just the two traditional dimensions of economic and security interests, but a third as well: every state's interest in being, and being seen to be, a good international citizen. The argument is that, even when there may be no direct economic or strategic pay-off, actively helping to solve global public goods 'values' challenges—for example, climate change, drug trafficking, cross-border population flows, weapons of mass destruction and mass atrocity crimes—is not just the foreign policy equivalent of boy-scout good deeds. Selfless cooperation on these issues does actually work to a country's advantage, in terms of both reputation and the generation of reciprocal support: my help in solving your drug trafficking issue today will increase the chances of you supporting my asylum-seeker problem tomorrow. A story couched in these realist terms is likely to be an easier sell to domestic constituencies than one pitched as disinterested altruism.

Nobody suggests that the geopolitics of ensuring effective civilian protection is ever going to be easy, especially in cases where early-stage prevention, if any, has manifestly failed. What has to be accepted, and treated as a challenge rather than cause for despair, is that there is always going to be tough debate about the really hard cases, where violations that are occurring are so extreme that the question of coercive military force comes into play as something which, prima facie at least, might have to be seriously contemplated as the only way to halt or avert the harm that is occurring or feared. The higher the stakes, the higher the emotion and the more that realpolitik will come into play.

When it comes to generating consensus on military action, some cases will always be easier than others, for example, where small, relatively friendless countries with weak military forces are involved, and where a military intervention is not particularly likely to have wider regional ramifications, as compared to cases where it almost certainly will, perhaps because of cross-over ethnic or sectarian loyalties. What is most important in all of this is not to let the idea take hold that because—for any one of a number of reasons, good or bad or both—it will not be possible to intervene militarily everywhere that a mass atrocity crime situation arguably justifies this, then intervention should not take place anywhere. The bottom line is that, while the responsibility to protect and the protection of civilians generally face some real challenges after Libya, these challenges are not insuperable. The R2P principle is firmly and globally established and has demonstrably delivered major practical results but its completely effective implementation is going to be a work in progress for a long time yet.

Part I. Security and conflicts, 2011

Chapter 2. Armed conflict

Chapter 3. Peace operations and conflict management

2. Armed conflict

Overview

During 2011 the sudden and dramatic popular uprisings in parts of the Middle East and North Africa, which together constituted the Arab Spring, produced diverse patterns of conflict. From the street protests that led to the flight into exile of Tunisia's president, to the serious armed confrontations that developed in Libya and Syria, the emergence of mass opposition to the region's ruling regimes was the precursor to dynamic and complex forms of violence (see section I in this chapter).

The events of the Arab Spring in 2011 were not, however, isolated in terms of contemporary conflict trends. Rather, developments across the region served to underline some of the long-term changes that have occurred in armed conflict over recent decades. This has involved important shifts in the scale, intensity and duration of armed conflict around the world, and in the principal actors involved in violence. Together these changes point to the emergence of a significantly different conflict environment than that which prevailed for much of the 20th century.

Since 1988 the SIPRI Yearbook has, in cooperation with the Uppsala Conflict Data Program, published data on armed conflict that has reflected a focus on 'major armed conflict' as the predominant type of conflict around the globe. This form of conflict, like all types of state-to-state conflict, has been in long-term decline, even while other forms of violent conflict have emerged as a key issue shaping international security. The data suggests that new approaches are needed to capture empirically and convey effectively the nature of modern conflict, which is increasingly moving beyond established definitions.

In order to gain a fuller picture of the nature of contemporary conflict, the 2012 Yearbook presents for the first time data on three broader types of organized violence: armed conflict (involving one or more states), non-state conflict and one-sided violence (against civilians). While all three types of violence decreased over the decade 2001–10, the sharpest fall was in the number of the most intense armed conflicts—those with at least 1000 battle-related deaths in a year (see section III).

The shift to non-state conflicts and a decline in the scale of conflicts has been matched by a substantial long-term decline in the deadliness of warfare, with the number of battle-related deaths in the average conflict continuing to fall. At the same time, there have been falling rates of successful conflict termination, resulting in more recurring or protracted conflicts. Such situations of 'hybrid peace' involve low levels of near continuous or recurring violence.

The dynamic, multidimensional and fluid nature of contemporary violence was particularly highlighted in 2011 by the active conflicts in Afghanistan, Côte d'Ivoire, the North Caucasus and Turkey. In Afghanistan, the confrontation involving the armed forces of the United States and its allies, the Government of Afghanistan, and violent non-state actors—notably the Taliban and the Haqqani network—with support from Afghanistan's neighbours, principally Pakistan, continued into its 10th year.

In Côte d'Ivoire, armed violence erupted in March 2011 between forces loyal to President Laurent Gbagbo and supporters of the internationally recognized president-elect, Alassane Ouattara. Following months of unsuccessful negotiations and sporadic violence, United Nations and French forces intervened, resulting in the arrest of Gbagbo and his eventual extradition to face trial at the International Criminal Court.

In the North Caucasus, a broad insurgency continued despite the official end of the decade-long Russian counterterrorism operation in Chechnya in 2009. While violence was largely confined to the republics of Chechnya, Dagestan, Ingushetia and Kabardino-Balkaria, Russian authorities were unable to make substantial progress in bringing to an end the set of conflicts underpinning the insurgency. Similarly, in southern districts of Thailand an insurgency that has resulted in over 5000 deaths entered its eighth year.

The long-running conflict involving Turkey and various Kurdish insurgent groups resumed in 2011 following a partially observed ceasefire from the summer of 2010. A series of clashes and mass protests took place across the country and, in October, 26 Turkish soldiers were killed in fighting with armed rebels of the Partiya Karkerên Kurdistan (PKK, Kurdistan Workers' Party).

Finally, the many ongoing and long-running conflicts in the Horn of Africa point to the interaction of different forms of violence and state and non-state actors, as well as regional factors in shaping the form of conflict in the area (see section II).

The emergence of new patterns and dominant forms of armed violence, as the conflict incidents during 2011 highlight, constitutes a major challenge to the international community. Effective policy responses require clear understandings of both the nature of and trends in contemporary violence. The steady decline in the number of state-based conflicts, even while conflict has continued in different forms, has opened a growing debate about the scope and significance of armed violence in society. Boundaries between political, criminal and gender-based violence have become blurred, as has the distinction between war and peace, with significant violence occurring in conditions defined conventionally as peace or at least an absence of war.

NEIL MELVIN

I. The first year of the Arab Spring

MARIE ALLANSSON, JONAS BAUMANN, SAMUEL TAUB, LOTTA THEMNÉR
AND PETER WALLENSTEEN

UPPSALA CONFLICT DATA PROGRAM

The 2011 uprisings in the Arab world came as a surprise to most observers. While successive Arab Human Development Reports had identified lingering problems affecting the Arab regimes—including inequality, lack of economic development, low levels of participation in policy formation and the marginalization of women—few experts expected either the series of mass revolts that were carried out with such persistence and with such a global impact or the increasing use of violence to suppress them.[1]

The uprisings, which quickly became known as the Arab Spring, spread rapidly from country to country and soon affected large parts of North Africa and the Middle East (see table 2.1). While they shared a number of traits—including large-scale demonstrations, non-violent actions, the absence of single leaders and the use of central squares in major cities—they also differed in certain respects. The extent of the demands made by the protesters varied, ranging from improved economic situations to regime change, as did the level of violence. While there were comparatively few fatalities in Algeria and Morocco, other countries (including Bahrain, Egypt, Tunisia and Yemen) were much more severely affected. The highest levels of violence were reported in Libya and Syria.

This section first outlines domestic developments in the six countries—Bahrain, Egypt, Libya, Syria, Tunisia and Yemen—that experienced at least 25 fatalities related to the Arab Spring in 2011.[2] It then examines international involvement in the different cases, including external support given to aid one of the parties, and third-party involvement and neutral interventions carried out to attempt to solve the crises. It concludes with some general reflections on the first year of the Arab Spring.

Domestic developments

Bahrain

The 2011 protests in the Bahraini capital Manama and several nearby towns and villages were preceded by months of political repression and years of unfulfilled promises of democratic reforms. In mid-February, thousands of protesters assembled at the Pearl Roundabout in Manama, which became

---

[1] United Nations Development Programme (UNDP), Regional Bureau for Arab States, *Arab Human Development Report*, 2002–2005, 2009 (UNDP: New York, 2002–2005, 2009).

[2] Other conflicts occurred simultaneously in some countries in North Africa and the Middle East, notably those inspired by al-Qaeda. These had different dynamics and are not discussed here.

Table 2.1. The Arab Spring, 2011

The countries are the member states of the Arab League.

Country	Level of violence[a]	First fatality[b]	Regime type[c]	External support[d]	Third-party involvement[e]	Demand[f]
Algeria	Low	6 Jan.	Monocracy	No	No	Economic reform
Bahrain	Intermediate	14 Feb.	Monarchy	Yes	No	Regime change
Comoros	–	–	Other	–	–	–
Djibouti	Low	18 Feb.	Monocracy	No	No	Political reform
Egypt	Intermediate	25 Jan.	Monocracy	No	No	Regime change
Iraq	Low	16 Feb.	Other	No	No	Economic reform
Jordan	Low	25 Mar.	Monarchy	No	No	Political reform
Kuwait	None	–	Monarchy	No	No	Political reform
Lebanon	None	–	Other	No	No	Political reform
Libya	High	16 Feb.	Monocracy	Yes	Yes	Regime change
Mauritania	None	–	Monocracy	–	–	Political reform
Morocco	Low	20 Feb.	Monarchy	No	No	Political reform
Oman	Low	27 Feb.	Monarchy	No	No	Economic reform
Palestinian Authority	None	–	Other	–	–	Political reform
Qatar	–	–	Monarchy	–	–	–
Saudi Arabia	Low	21 Nov.	Monarchy	No	No	Political reform
Somalia	–	–	Other	–	–	–
Sudan	Low	30 Jan.	Monocracy	No	No	Political reform
Syria	High	18 Mar.	Monocracy	Yes	Yes	Regime change
Tunisia	Intermediate	8 Jan.	Monocracy	No	No	Regime change
United Arab Emirates	–	–	Monarchy	–	–	–
Yemen	Intermediate	16 Feb.	Monocracy	No	Yes	Regime change

[a] 'Level of violence' refers to the number of people killed in Arab Spring-related violence, with 'Low' indicating a death toll of 1–24, 'Intermediate' of 25–999 and 'High' of 1000 or more. 'None' indicates protests without fatalities and '–' indicates that there was no Arab Spring-related protests. Much of the violence connected to the Arab Spring was of a character that makes it difficult to record in UCDP's 3 categories of organized violence (armed conflict, non-state conflict and one-sided violence—see section III). Other fatalities are therefore included in these totals, such as from violence involving protesters throwing rocks or Molotov cocktails or attacking government institutions (e.g. the interior ministry or police or army barracks).

[b] 'First fatality' is the date of the first death connected to Arab Spring-related violence. All dates are in 2011.

[c] Regime type is as at 1 Jan. 2011. 'Monarchy' refers to both absolute and constitutional monarchies. 'Monocracy' is a term used to capture one-party or one-family states; it includes both electoral regimes and autocratic regimes where power is vested in an individual.

[d] 'External support' can range from the provision of sanctuary or financial assistance to aid a party, via provision of arms, logistics and military support, up to sending combat troops.

[e] 'Third-party involvement' is an intervention aiming to regulate or solve a conflict or crisis with diplomatic means. Typical third-party activities are mediating between the parties in a conflict, hosting negotiations or attending a peace conference, or monitoring a ceasefire or a peace agreement.

[f] 'Demand' is based on a hierarchy: economic reform is the least threatening to the regime, followed by calls for political reform and then by calls for a complete regime change. The demand noted here is the highest level voiced during 2011 by protesters or the opposition regarding domestic issues.

the centre of the protests. Initially, the protesters' demands focused on political reforms but as security force actions against them intensified, more and more protesters began calling for a complete regime change. Nevertheless, the demands of Wifaq, the largest opposition party, continued to focus on political reforms.[3]

While the state of emergency imposed in mid-March was lifted on 1 June, protesters as well as health workers who treated the wounded continued to be attacked and hundreds of people were detained and prosecuted in military courts.[4]

Egypt

By the time of the January 2011 protests in Egypt, the National Democratic Party (NDP) had led a de facto one-party state for 33 years, with Hosni Mubarak as president since 1982. In addition to the local context of rigged elections, corruption and mismanagement, Egypt's relatively organized opposition was inspired by earlier developments in Tunisia.[5]

Demonstrations against Mubarak had occurred before. But an announcement, made via Twitter and Facebook, of a protest on 25 January led to tens of thousands taking part in what was named a 'day of rage'.[6] Police harshly repressed the demonstrations but the protestors remained in Tahrir Square in central Cairo and other cities and the situation escalated as they clashed repeatedly with riot police.[7] To calm the situation, Mubarak offered several concessions. These were seen as 'too little, too late', and the protesters' repeated demands for regime change were finally met when Mubarak resigned on 11 February.[8]

The Supreme Council of the Armed Forces (SCAF), led by Field Marshall Mohamed Hussein Tantawi, stepped in to fill the political vacuum.[9] While SCAF initially received praise, the political situation soon appeared to be little more democratic than earlier.[10] Elections to the lower house of parliament were held between November 2011 and January 2012. Simultaneously with the first round of elections Egyptians once again took to the streets, this time to show their discontent with SCAF and the lack of progress since

[3] Katzman, K., *Bahrain: Reform, Security, and U.S. Policy*, Congressional Research Service (CRS) Report for Congress 95-1013 (US Congress, CRS: Washington, DC, 21 Feb. 2012), p. 8; and 'Mass march in Bahrain as Mullen wraps up visit', Agence France-Presse, 25 Feb. 2011.

[4] Human Rights Watch (HRW), *Targets of Retribution: Attacks against Medics, Injured Protesters, and Health Facilities* (HRW: New York, 2011), pp. 10–12.

[5] 'The view from Liberation Square', *New York Times*, 28 Jan. 2011.

[6] 'Egypt's day of rage goes on: is the world watching?', *The Guardian*, 27 Jan. 2011.

[7] 'Two die in Egypt protests as US urges concessions', Agence France-Presse, 26 Jan. 2011.

[8] 'Mubarak concessions "insufficient"', Al Jazeera, 2 Feb. 2011.

[9] Tantawi had been Minister of Defence since 1991, and was seen by many as Mubarak's right-hand man. Knell, Y., 'Egypt after Mubarak: Mohamad Hussain Tantawi profile', BBC News, 22 Nov. 2011, <http://www.bbc.co.uk/news/world-middle-east-12441512>.

[10] Amnesty International (AI), *Year of Rebellion: The State of Human Rights in the Middle East and North Africa*, Index no. MDE 01/001/2012 (AI: London, 9 Jan. 2012), p. 12.

February.[11] This resulted in demonstrations that were met with violence, resulting in further criticism, both domestically and internationally.

Libya[12]

The February 2011 demonstrations in Libya were related to a history of brutality by the regime of Muammar Gaddafi.[13] The massacre in June 1996 of over 1000 inmates in Abu Salim Prison—many of them political prisoners—had created a sense of resentment against Gaddafi.[14] In February 2006 security forces killed 12 people involved in a non-violent demonstration in Benghazi, while the arrest in early 2011 of Fathi Terbil, a human rights lawyer who represented the families of the victims of the 1996 massacre, led to new protests.[15] The unrest soon spread and, as more people took to the streets, repression increased. The opposition was particularly active in the east of the country, and Benghazi quickly became its centre. Gaddafi ordered his military to curb the demonstrations with harsh methods and this led the international community to condemn the atrocities.[16]

As the campaign of repression continued, the rebel organization operating from Benghazi began referring to itself as a National Transitional Council (NTC) with the explicit intention of removing Gaddafi from power.[17]

While the Gaddafi regime launched an offensive against the rebellious towns, the international community debated courses of action to prevent civilian casualties. This led to the passing of United Nations Security Council Resolution 1973 on 17 March, which authorized the establishment of a no-fly zone over Libya and authorized UN member states 'to take all necessary measures ... to protect civilians and civilian populated areas under threat of attack'.[18] The introduction of de facto air support for the rebel cause—led by the North Atlantic Treaty Organization (NATO) in Operation Unified Protector—changed the dynamics of the conflict; after inconclusive battles in the Libyan desert, during which towns changed hands on several

---

[11] Amnesty International, 'Egypt: military rulers have "crushed" hopes of 25 January protesters', 22 Nov. 2011, <http://www.amnesty.org/en/news/egypt-military-rulers-have-crushed-hopes-25-january-protesters-2011-11-22>.

[12] On developments in Libya in 2011 see also chapter 1 and chapter 3, section II, in this volume.

[13] Amnesty International, 'The battle for Libya: killings, disappearances and torture', Sep. 2011, <http://www.amnesty.org/en/library/info/MDE19/025/2011/en>, p. 7.

[14] Human Rights Watch, 'Libya: June 1996 killings at Abu Salim prison', 27 June 2006, <http://www.hrw.org/en/news/2006/06/27/libya-june-1996-killings-abu-salim-prison>; and Franklin, S., 'Abu Salim: walls that talk', The Guardian, 30 Sep. 2011.

[15] 'Libya protests: second city Benghazi hit by violence', BBC News, 16 Feb. 2011, <http://www.bbc.co.uk/news/world-africa-12477275>.

[16] 'Libya protests: pressure mounts on isolated Gaddafi', BBC News, 23 Feb. 2011 <http://www.bbc.co.uk/news/world-middle-east-12550719>.

[17] 'UPDATE 1-Rebel Libyan council chief vows "victory or death"', Reuters, 4 Mar. 2011.

[18] UN Security Council Resolution 1973, 17 Mar. 2011, paras 4–12.

occasions, the rebels, supported by NATO, slowly advanced towards the capital, Tripoli.

In late August the rebels gained the upper hand and by the end of the month Tripoli was under rebel control. Gaddafi, who had managed to escape, was not located until rebels took control of his hometown, Sirte, on 20 October. In the tumultuous situation following his apprehension, Gaddafi was killed, bringing a definite end to a regime that had been in place for over 40 years.

The situation following Gaddafi's death was turbulent. The NTC moved its base from Benghazi to Tripoli and attempted to steer Libya towards democratization. However, an abundance of weapons remained in circulation and unemployment was rampant. Combined with a traditionally divided society, this led to clashes between NTC soldiers representing different tribes.[19] While these clashes did not develop beyond skirmishes, the threat of tribal conflict remained. Another unresolved issue was the apparent abuses carried out by the rebel forces during the final phases of the conflict.[20] Shortly after the death of Gaddafi, Luis Moreno-Ocampo, the prosecutor of the International Crime Court (ICC), stated that NATO forces and rebel soldiers—as well as members of the Gaddafi regime— would be investigated for war crimes.[21]

Syria[22]

It initially seemed that the Arab Spring would not affect Syria, whose stability during past decades had been remarkable, particularly given its religious and ethnic heterogeneity. Prior to 2011, the only significant challenge to the 40-year rule of President Hafez al-Assad and his son and successor, President Bashar al-Assad, had been an uprising launched by the Muslim Brotherhood in the late 1970s which, while brought under control by 1982, led to 10 000–25 000 deaths, mostly civilians.[23]

Initial protests broke out in February 2011, but they were limited and quickly subdued by the regime. The situation changed on 18 March in Dará, in the south of the country, with a protest triggered by the arrest and torture of a group of young boys. The security services unsuccessfully attempted to end the protests with tear gas, water cannons and ultimately live ammunition, killing four people. From this point the protests quickly spread, resulting in further civilian deaths in Dará and other cities.

---

[19] 'Fighters clash again near Tripoli, several dead', Reuters, 12 Nov. 2011.

[20] Human Rights Watch, 'Libya: apparent execution of 53 Gaddafi supporters', 24 Oct. 2011, <http://www.hrw.org/news/2011/10/24/libya-apparent-execution-53-gaddafi-supporters>.

[21] United Nations, Security Council, 6647th meeting, S/PV.6647, 2 Nov. 2011.

[22] On developments in Syria in 2011 see also chapter 3, section II, in this volume.

[23] United Nations, Human Rights Council, Report of the independent international commission of inquiry on the Syrian Arab Republic, A/HRC/S-17/2/Add.1, 23 Nov. 2011.

For the rest of the year protests, often involving tens of thousands of people, occurred all over Syria. While Dará governorate remained a focal point, Homs governorate soon became the main hot spot, experiencing roughly one-third of all fatalities. Throughout the year, protests were coordinated via Facebook, usually taking place after Friday prayers or funerals of killed protesters. While they initially focused on economic and political reforms, protesters soon demanded the ousting of President Assad and free and fair elections. Apart from isolated incidents of looting and stone throwing, the demonstrations remained largely peaceful. In contrast, government responses included mass arrests, torture of detainees, deprival of medical treatment to the wounded and the use of snipers to kill protesters.[24] About one month into the protests, the government also began to besiege and shell whole cities that it considered hostile.[25]

In addition to the use of force, the regime also reacted politically, blaming the violence on 'foreign elements' and 'terrorists', and repeatedly promising reforms. Indeed, Assad lifted the state of emergency that had been in effect since 1963 and reshuffled the government, but such reforms remained cosmetic and were usually followed by even more brutal violence.[26]

The Syrian Army's violent actions led to a number of defections, mainly by lower-ranked Sunni conscript soldiers. To fight this trend, security agents positioned behind army lines reportedly threatened any soldiers who attempted to defect.[27] Some deserters organized themselves into small groups to protect demonstrators and occasionally even clash with the army. A group of defecting officers led by Colonel Riyad al-Asaad announced the creation of the Free Syrian Army (FSA) via YouTube on 29 July.[28] In late September, the FSA began fighting government forces, mainly in Aleppo, Hamah and Homs governorates, resulting in several hundred fatalities by the end of 2011, in addition to the several thousand fatalities resulting from the violent crackdown on the protesters.

Tunisia[29]

On 17 December 2010, Mohamed Bouazizi set himself on fire following a dispute with the police concerning his small vegetable business.[30] This act triggered increasing protests across Tunisia against police brutality and

---

[24] United Nations (note 23); and Human Rights Watch, 'We live as in war', Nov. 2011, <http://www.hrw.org/reports/2011/11/11/we-live-war>.

[25] Human Rights Watch (HRW), *We've Never Seen Such Horror* (HRW: New York, June 2011).

[26] International Crisis Group (ICG), *Uncharted Waters: Thinking Through Syria's Dynamics* Middle East Briefing no. 31 (ICG: Damascus, 24 Nov. 2011); and Human Rights Watch (note 25).

[27] Human Rights Watch (HRW), *'By All Means Necessary!'* (HRW: New York, Dec. 2011).

[28] 'Defected officers declare the formation of "Syrian Free Army", 29-7-2011', YouTube, 29 July 2011, <http://www.youtube.com/watch?v=Rk7Ze5jVCj4>.

[29] International Crisis Group (ICG), *Popular Protests in North Africa and the Middle East (IV): Tunisia's Way*, Middle East/North Africa Report no. 106 (ICG: Tunis, 28 Apr. 2011).

[30] 'How a man setting fire to himself sparked an uprising in Tunisia', *The Guardian*, 28 Dec. 2010.

corruption and, ultimately, in support of regime change. The escalation of the protests forced President Zine-Al Abidine Ben Ali into exile in Saudi Arabia on 14 January. The Prime Minster, Mohamed Ghannouchi, was also forced to resign in late February, making room for a new interim government without ties to Ben Ali. Elections to a Constituent Assembly were held on 23 October and on 12 December, Moncef Marzouki, a former human rights activist, was elected interim president. Meanwhile, Ben Ali was sentenced in absentia to 35 years in prison.

Yemen

By 2011, after more than three decades of rule by President Ali Abdullah Saleh, Yemen faced significant economic and social challenges including widespread corruption, an unemployment rate of about 40 per cent, falling oil production, a looming water shortage and widespread poverty. Furthermore, over recent years Yemen had experienced high levels of violence, including from al-Qaeda in the Arabian Peninsula (AQAP).[31]

In January, the ruling party—the General People's Congress—announced that it would seek to remove the limit on the number of presidential terms. This triggered widespread resistance, as many Yemenis feared that Saleh would retain office for life.[32] Calls for Saleh's resignation gained momentum with the resignation of Mubarak as president in Egypt. Thousands of protesters held largely peaceful demonstrations in Sana'a, Aden and Ta'iz, but they were met with lethal violence from government forces and supporters of the regime.[33]

In response to the growing number of people killed in the demonstrations, powerful tribes and high-ranking soldiers withdrew their support for Saleh. Towards the end of May, violent clashes erupted between loyalist forces and members of the powerful al-Ahmar tribe.[34] On 3 June Saleh was wounded in a rocket attack on the presidential residence allegedly launched by members of the al-Ahmar tribe.[35] Saleh was flown to Saudi Arabia for medical treatment but returned to Yemen in September. He retained full presidential powers until 23 November, when he agreed to relinquish them by February 2012 in return for amnesty in a plan negotiated by the Gulf Cooperation Council (GCC). He stood down following the

---

[31] International Crisis Group (ICG), *Breaking Point? Yemen's Southern Question*, Middle East Report no. 114 (ICG: Sana'a, 20 Oct. 2011), pp. 10–11; and Gardner, F., 'What next in Yemen', BBC News, 29 Jan. 2011, <http://www.bbc.co.uk/news/world-middle-east-12309909>.

[32] International Crisis Group (ICG), *Popular Protest in North Africa and the Middle East (II): Yemen between Reform and Revolution*, Middle East/North Africa Report no. 102 (ICG: Sana'a, 10 Mar. 2011), pp. 1–2.

[33] International Crisis Group (note 32), pp. 1–4.

[34] International Crisis Group (note 31).

[35] 'Yemen tribe leader denies link to palace attack', Reuters, 3 June 2011.

election on 21 February of Abdo Rabu Mansour al-Hadi, formerly vice-president, as interim president for a two-year period.[36]

Throughout the year, government forces pursued widespread violence against peaceful protesters, resulting in hundreds of fatalities. Hundreds more were killed in clashes between government forces, dissident troops and tribal fighters.

External involvement

External support[37]

International community reactions to developments in North Africa and the Middle East varied greatly. External support was provided to one or both sides in the two countries with high numbers of fatalities—Libya and Syria (see table 2.1). In three of the four countries with intermediate numbers of fatalities—Egypt, Tunisia and Yemen—the international community restricted itself to political statements expressing either support for or opposition to the current leader, although this often occurred only at a late stage of the protests, as in the case of Egypt.[38] Only the fourth country with an intermediate level of violence—Bahrain—received external support. This came in the form of military and police reinforcements from Saudi Arabia and the United Arab Emirates in response to a request to the GCC by the Bahraini Government.[39] In contrast to the condemnation of regimes elsewhere, the Bahraini Government received only muted regional and international criticism for its crackdown on peaceful protesters.[40]

The international community was directly involved in Libya, as demonstrated by the UN's rapid action, with France and the United Kingdom in the lead.[41] The approach built on the idea of protecting the civilian population from the government's indiscriminate actions.[42] Nineteen states took part in enforcement of the UN-imposed no-fly zone, which, after the first

---

[36] Amnesty International (note 10), pp. 22–23; Ghobari, M., 'Election preparations start in conflict-torn Yemen', Reuters, 6 Feb. 2012; and 'New Yemen President Abdrabbuh Mansour Hadi takes oath', BBC News, 25 Feb. 2012, <http://www.bbc.co.uk/news/world-middle-east-17163321>.

[37] On the term 'external support' see table 2.1, note d.

[38] 'Egypt power transfer not enough: Obama', Agence France-Presse, 11 Feb. 2011.

[39] 'Gulf Cooperation Council states pledge "full" support for Bahrain', BBC Monitoring, 19 Feb. 2011; and Katzman (note 3).

[40] 'Gulf Cooperation Council states pledge "full" support for Bahrain' (note 39); and Amnesty International (AI), *Arms transfers to the Middle East and North Africa: Lessons for an Effective Arms Trade Treaty*, Index no. ACT 30/117/2011 (AI: London, 19 Oct. 2011), p. 22.

[41] Five Security Council members—Brazil, China, Germany, India and Russia—chose to abstain from the vote on Resolution 1973. As permanent members of the Security Council, China and Russia in effect allowed the resolution to pass. UN Security Council Resolution 1973 (note 18); 'West mobilizes for Libya air strikes', Agence France-Presse, 18 Mar. 2011; and 'France, UK draft sanctions text on Libya violence', Reuters, 25 Feb. 2011, <http://in.reuters.com/article/2011/02/25/idINIndia-55147 320110225>.

[42] On protection of civilians see chapter 1 in this volume.

few days, was officially implemented by NATO.[43] NATO aircraft bombed Libyan Air Force and artillery targets, with the aim of preventing them from attacking civilians and rebel forces. The Libyan Army's headquarters were also bombed, significantly reducing the effectiveness of the army's command structure. The Arab League, initially supportive of UN Security Council Resolution 1973, criticized NATO for its interpretation of the mandate.[44] The rebels also received direct military or financial support from France, Italy, Qatar, Turkey, the UK and, to a lesser degree, Sudan.[45] Overall, international involvement greatly facilitated the rebels' armed struggle.

In Syria, Russia and, allegedly, Iran supported the government with arms, ammunition and technical assistance.[46] Iran is also alleged to have provided troops and military advisers to the government.[47] Russia occasionally deployed naval vessels to the region and to its naval base at Tartous, Syria, as a deterrent against possible NATO military action.[48] Politically, China and Russia repeatedly opposed proposals by France and the United States for a substantial UN Security Council resolution on Syria.[49] When these proposals were blocked, the European Union (EU) and the USA each imposed unilateral sanctions on Syria and increased political pressure on Assad, while continuing to stress that they had no intention of intervening militarily.[50] Turkey, despite having built an increasingly close relationship with Syria over recent years, was strongly critical of the Assad regime. It welcomed tens of thousands of refugees and hosted the first conference of

---

[43] The 19 participating states included 15 NATO members (Albania, Belgium, Bulgaria, Canada, Denmark, France, Greece, Italy, the Netherlands, Norway, Romania, Spain, Turkey, the UK and the USA) and 4 non-member states (Jordan, Qatar, Sweden and the United Arab Emirates). 'NATO to enforce no-fly zone in Libya—Rasmussen', Reuters, 24 Mar. 2011. See also chapter 3, section II, in this volume.

[44] 'Arab League condemns broad Western bombing campaign in Libya', *Washington Post*, 20 Mar. 2011.

[45] 'France says it gave arms to the rebels in Libya', *New York Times*, 29 June 2011; 'Qatar admits sending hundreds of troops to support Libya rebels', *The Guardian*, 26 Oct. 2011; 'Turkey reveals quiet rebel payments', *Wall Street Journal*, 24 Aug. 2011; 'Libya conflict: British and French soldiers help rebels prepare Sirte attack', *The Guardian*, 25 Aug. 2011; 'Sudan armed Libyan rebels, says President Bashir', BBC News, 26 Oct. 2011, <http://www.bbc.co.uk/news/world-africa-15471734>; and United Nations, Security Council, Final report of the Panel of Experts established pursuant to Security Council resolution 1973 (2011) concerning Libya, 17 Feb. 2012, annex to S/2012/163, 20 Mar. 2012.

[46] International Crisis Group (ICG), *Popular Protests in North Africa and the Middle East (VII): The Syrian Regime's Slow-motion Suicide*, Middle East/North Africa Report no. 109 (ICG: Brussels, 13 July 2011). On the policies of arms-exporting countries on supplying states affected by the Arab Spring see chapter 6, section II, in this volume.

[47] Abdo, G., 'How Iran keeps Assad in power in Syria', *Foreign Affairs*, 25 Aug. 2011; British Foreign and Commonwealth Office, 'Britain's relations with Iran', [n.d.], <http://www.fco.gov.uk/en/global-issues/mena/017-iran/>; 'Iran helping Syrian regime crack down on protesters, say diplomats', *The Guardian*, 9 May 2011; and Dagres, H., 'Viewpoint: Iran looms large in Syria conflict', Middle East Voices, 22 Mar. 2011, <http://www.middleeastvoices.com/2012/03/viewpoint-iran-looms-large-in-syria-conflict-25664/>.

[48] 'Russia sending warships to its base in Syria', Reuters, 28 Nov. 2011, <http://af.reuters.com/article/egyptNews/idAFL5E7MS1XT20111128>.

[49] On proposals for a UN arms embargo on Syria see chapter 10, section III, in this volume.

[50] International Crisis Group (note 46).

all Syrian exile opposition parties in June. Turkey was also the FSA's foremost supporter, as it hosted and protected FSA leader al-Asaad and tolerated the use of its territory as an area of retreat for the FSA.[51]

Third-party involvement[52]

In addition to directly supporting parties to the various conflicts in the Arab Spring, the international community was also active in searching for solutions to these conflicts. As with external support, third-party involvement was directed to both high-casualty countries. It also occurred in one intermediate-violence country: Yemen.

In Libya, Russia attempted to mediate between the government and the NTC. Kirsan Ilyumzhínov, a former Russian regional governor and president of the World Chess Federation, was sent on several official missions to Libya in June.[53] His meetings with Gaddafi, as well as with the rebels—which came weeks after bombing had commenced, and appeared not to have been coordinated with NATO—did not result in any substantial outcome. Regional organizations were initially hesitant and internally divided concerning the no-fly zone. The African Union (AU) tried to mediate in Libya, but since none of its proposals included Gaddafi's departure they were flatly rejected by the NTC.[54]

In Syria, the Arab League initially supported Assad's proposed reforms. However, as the violence against civilians increased, the League gradually adapted its position, first urging Assad to end the violence and then attempting to establish a dialogue between the parties involved. Faced with ongoing violence, the League suspended Syria's membership in November. Threatened with economic sanctions and further political isolation, Assad agreed to a peace plan on 19 December.[55] Under the terms of the plan, the League sent an observer mission to monitor and report on the situation in Syria. However, the opposition considered this mission to be biased. In early 2012 it was suspended.[56]

In Yemen, the GCC, supported by the UN, repeatedly negotiated with President Saleh in order to secure his resignation. These efforts proved fruitful and led to a handover of power in February 2012. Yemen's involvement in the fight against AQAP in close cooperation with the USA makes it a special case. However, as both the protests and the violence escalated, the

---

[51] 'Assad has less than week to heed reforms call—Turkey', Reuters, 20 June 2011; and 'In slap at Syria, Turkey shelters anti-Assad fighters', *New York Times*, 27 Oct. 2011.

[52] On the term 'third-party involvement' see table 2.1, note e.

[53] 'Russia meets with NATO in new push for Libyan peace', *New York Times*, 4 July 2011.

[54] 'Libyan rebels reject African Union proposal as fighting rages', CNN, 11 Apr. 2011, <http://articles.cnn.com/2011-04-11/world/libya.war_1_leader-moammar-gadhafi-libyan-people-african-union>.

[55] '3 killed as Syria urged to implement peace plan', Agence France-Presse, 20 Dec. 2011.

[56] On the Arab League Observer Mission to Syria see chapter 3, section II, in this volume.

USA eventually supported the GGC plan and urged Saleh to resign.[57] At the same time, the USA continued to cooperate with the Yemeni Government and conducted a number of air strikes against AQAP in Yemen.

Conclusions

The outcomes of the first year of the Arab Spring were mixed. There were examples of regime change but also cases where popular resistance was repressed. Nevertheless, Arab politics has been changed by this historically unique series of events.

There was a clear connection between the types of demand and the number of deaths: where the protesters demanded regime change, fatalities reached intermediate or high levels (see table 2.1). In addition, mono-cracies—regimes based on a single leader or family—were more susceptible to successful challenge than traditional monarchies or other regime types, at least in 2011. Egypt, Syria, Tunisia and Yemen are all in the first category, while Jordan, Morocco, Saudi Arabia and the Gulf states belong to the second. Notable exceptions include Bahrain, where a traditional monarchy was shaken but maintained power with external support, and Algeria, where a military authoritarian regime faced mostly modest demands. The most open Arab countries, including Lebanon, the Palestinian territories and Iraq, encountered fewer popular uprisings on domestic issues. In the Palestinian territories, demonstrators sought greater unity within the Palestinian community, rather than regime change.

International reactions varied, with external support limited to a few cases. Western powers, notably France and the USA, initially supported governments in Egypt and Tunisia but then began to push for change. In the case of Libya, they immediately took an active stand against the regime, with the UN's approval and NATO as the instrument. In Syria, the Western powers were positioned against China and Russia, both of which became increasingly critical of the international use of force. The scope for third-party involvement in solving the crises was remarkably limited, and serious negotiations only occurred in Yemen.

The role of neighbouring countries and regional organizations was important. In particular, the Arab League helped promote international involvement in Libya, and gave regional legitimacy to the first forceful UN application of the principle of the international responsibility to protect civilians. The Arab League attempted to hammer out an agreement on Syria, but its efforts were obstructed by both the Syrian Government and opposition groups. In Yemen, the GCC also pursued a mediating role.

---

[57] Carmichael, L., 'US watches Yemen chaos with growing concern', Agence France-Presse, 26 May 2011; and Amnesty International (note 10), p. 25.

The events of 2011 took place against a background of profound divisions in the Arab world. The prevalence of unrepresentative regimes, with no record of solving the problems faced by their populations, fuelled revolts. Monocracies had little space in which to make political concessions and quickly found themselves isolated domestically, regionally and internationally. The use of modern as well as traditional forms of communication exposed these regimes' fragility and stimulated further action.[58] The message of the Arab Spring is thus not just one for the Arab world but has implications for regimes globally.

[58] See also e.g. Melvin, N. and Umaraliev, T., 'New social media and conflict in Kyrgyzstan', SIPRI Insights on Peace and Security no. 2011/1, Aug. 2011, <http://books.sipri.org/product_info?c_product _id=429>.

II. Organized violence in the Horn of Africa

JONAS BAUMANN, MARCUS NILSSON, LOTTA THEMNÉR AND
PETER WALLENSTEEN

UPPSALA CONFLICT DATA PROGRAM

For decades, the countries in the Horn of Africa—Djibouti, Eritrea, Ethiopia, Kenya and Somalia (see figure 2.1)—have been plagued by organized violence. However, despite the vast scale of human suffering, the region tends to make the international headlines only when the focus is on piracy or droughts. To provide a coherent overview of the violence that affects the Horn of Africa, this section therefore analyses the region through the lens of UCDP's three categories of organized violence: armed conflict between and within states, one-sided violence against civilians, and violence between non-state actors.[1]

While all countries in the region experienced one or more of these categories of violence during the decade 2001–10, non-state conflicts were by far the most common. A total of 77 non-state conflicts, or 35 per cent of the global total, were recorded in the Horn of Africa. The annual number of active non-state conflicts was fairly stable during the first six years of the period, ranging between 11 and 13. However, the figure then oscillated wildly, first dropping to 2 in 2007, then increasing to 14 in 2008, after which it decreased to 5 in 2009 and 2010.

State-based armed conflict was less common in the Horn of Africa: only five were recorded in 2001–10, of which only one was at the level of war.[2] Nonetheless, states in the region have demonstrated a growing tendency to become militarily engaged in neighbouring countries. For instance, both Ethiopia and Kenya have at times sent troops in support of the Somali Transitional Federal Government (TFG) in its conflict with Harakat al-Shabab al-Mujahideen (Mujahedin Youth Movement, or al-Shabab), which has in turn received both arms and training from Eritrea.[3]

Six actors were responsible for acts of one-sided violence in the region: the Ethiopian Government; the Kenyan Government; Mungiki, a Kenyan religious sect; the Ogaden National Liberation Front (ONLF), an Ethiopian rebel group; the Sabaot Land Defence Force (SLDF), a militia active in the Mount Elgon district of Kenya; and al-Shabab. In the years 2001–2006, only

---

[1] For definitions of the UCDP's 3 categories of organized violence and a discussion of global trends see section III below.

[2] The 5 armed conflicts recorded for the region were Djibouti–Eritrea (common border), Eritrea, Ethiopia (Ogaden), Ethiopia (Oromiya) and Somalia. Throughout this section, when only the name of a country is given this indicates a conflict over government. When a conflict is over territory the name of the contested territory appears after the country name(s) in parenthesis.

[3] United Nations, Security Council, Report of the Monitoring Group on Somalia and Eritrea pursuant to Security Council Resolution 1916 (2010), 20 June 2011, annex to S/2011/433, 18 July 2011.

Figure 2.1. Map of the Horn of Africa

one actor was recorded as crossing the threshold of 25 deaths in a year in attacks targeting civilians (the Ethiopian Government; see below). In 2007 and 2008 there were five such actors, but the number then decreased to one again in 2009 and 2010.

This section continues with an examination of the armed conflict in Somalia, particularly its international aspects. It then describes one of the worst cases of one-sided violence in the Horn of Africa, taking place in Ethiopia's Somali Region. Finally, it discusses the prevalence of non-state conflicts in the region, focusing on two examples in the Ethiopia–Kenya border area.

Armed conflict: the regional effects of Somalia's instability

Of all the conflicts that are active in the world today, the struggle for government power in Somalia is clearly one of the most protracted. The most recent effort to find a solution led to the establishment of the internationally sanctioned TFG in 2004. However, it was only after Ethiopia's invasion of Somalia in December 2006 and later with the support of the United Nations-authorized African Union Mission in Somalia (AMISOM) that the TFG was able to move to the capital, Mogadishu.[4]

Prior to December 2010, Hizbul-Islam and al-Shabab, the two main armed Islamist groups in opposition to the government, were in armed conflict with both the TFG and each other. When the leader of Hizbul-Islam, Hassan Dahir Aweys, announced that month that his group had become part of al-Shabab, this made the latter the only explicit armed opposition to the TFG.[5] At the time, al-Shabab controlled all of southern and central Somalia, including large parts of Mogadishu.[6]

Even though the TFG is internationally recognized, its forces are weak and its control does not extend far.[7] AMISOM, rather than the TFG, has carried out much of the fighting against al-Shabab in Mogadishu.[8] A number of non-state groups and regional clan-based administrations have aligned themselves with the TFG and fought against al-Shabab.[9] These groups include Ahlu Sunna Waljamaca, which is supported and sometimes directly assisted by Ethiopia and, more recently, the Ras Kamboni movement, which is often seen as a proxy for Kenyan interests.[10]

When al-Shabab announced a 'tactical' departure from Mogadishu in August 2011, many hoped that the capital would, for the first time in many

---

[4] For details of AMISOM see chapter 3, sections III and IV, in this volume.

[5] 'Somalia: Aweys surrenders to Al Shabaab, 6 killed in bombing', Garowe Online, 20 Dec. 2010, <http://www.garoweonline.com/artman2/publish/Somalia_27/Somalia_Aweys_surrenders_to_Al_Shabaab_6_killed_in_bombing.shtml>.

[6] International Crisis Group (ICG), *Somalia: The Transitional Government on Life Support*, Africa Report no. 170 (ICG: Nairobi, 2011), p. 27.

[7] United Nations (note 3), p. 11.

[8] International Crisis Group (note 6), p. 17.

[9] On the rest of Somalia (e.g. the self-declared autonomous regions) see the UCDP Conflict Encyclopedia, <http://www.ucdp.uu.se/database/>; Pugh, A., 'Block party—breaking Somalia's political paralysis', *Jane's Intelligence Review*, 19 May 2011; and United Nations (note 3).

[10] United Nations (note 3); and '48 people killed in Somalia', Garowe Online, 25 Feb. 2011, <http://www.garoweonline.com/artman2/publish/Somalia_27/48_people_killed_in_Somalia.shtml>.

years, return to relative calm.[11] However, a series of suicide bombs and sporadic clashes in late 2011 demonstrated that Mogadishu remained far from secure.[12] The insecurity at that time was exacerbated by the presence of thousands of internally displaced persons (IDPs) who had streamed into the city as a result of widespread famine. In addition, a lack of funds had led to unpaid TFG troops looting international food distribution centres, setting up illegal checkpoints and at times clashing with other government forces.[13]

Al-Shabab itself has also encountered financial problems. Following the TFG–AMISOM offensives of February and July–August 2011, it lost control of Bakara Market, formerly an important source of taxation income. In addition, one goal of Kenya's intervention in southern Somalia in October 2011—Operation Linda Nchi, which followed a spate of kidnappings on Kenyan soil—was to enforce a blockade of Kismayo port, another former source of income for al-Shabab.[14]

While there seems to be a growing rift between the global jihadists and the Somali nationalists within al-Shabab's leadership, some analysts claim that increased internationalization of the conflict may transform the movement into a global actor and possibly provide it with new resources.[15] Al-Shabab's deliberate attempts to internationalize the conflict, including kidnappings and the 2010 bombings in Kampala, Uganda, have led to further international engagement against the group.[16] By the end of 2011, five African countries had troops in Somalia and in February 2012 the UN Security Council approved the expansion of AMISOM from a maximum of 12 000 to more than 17 000 troops, supported by international funding.[17] In turn, al-Shabab is extending its reach outside Somalia and in January 2012

---

[11] Khalif, A., 'Al Shabaab militants pull out of key positions in Mogadishu rout', *Daily Nation* (Nairobi), 6 Aug. 2011.

[12] E.g. on 4 Oct. a suicide bombing killed up to 120 people, according to local hospital sources. 'Hospitals overwhelmed as bombing death toll rises', IRIN, 5 Oct. 2011, <http://www.irinnews.org/Report/93896/SOMALIA-Hospitals-overwhelmed-as-bombing-death-toll-rises>.

[13] 'Somali government soldiers warned over killings', BBC Monitoring Africa, 7 Nov. 2011; and Guled, A., 'African Union troops reach outskirts of Mogadishu', Associated Press, 20 Jan. 2012, <http://news.yahoo.com/african-union-troops-reach-outskirts-mogadishu-083503256.html>.

[14] United Nations (note 3), p. 28; and 'Kenya–Somalia–West: Operation *Protect the Nation* follows wave of abductions', *Africa Research Bulletin*, 9 Nov. 2011, p. 19 032.

[15] Weinstein, M. A., 'Harakat al-Shabaab "gobbles up" Hizbul Islam', Garowe Online, 23 Dec. 2010, <http://www.garoweonline.com/artman2/publish/Somalia_27/Somalia_Harakat_al-Shabaab_Gobbles_Up_Hizbul_Isam.shtml>; and International Crisis Group (note 6), p. i.

[16] International Crisis Group (note 6), p. i.

[17] UN Security Council Resolution 2036, 22 Feb. 2012. The countries with troops in Somalia were Ethiopia and Kenya and, as contributors of troops to AMISOM, Burundi, Djibouti and Uganda. In addition, France and Israel are among the countries openly supporting Operation Linda Nchi with logistics and there are continuous reports of US drone attacks inside Somalia. 'France to support Kenya's incursion into Somalia', BBC Monitoring Africa, 25 Oct. 2011; and 'Some 19 civilians killed in "US drone attack" in southern Somalia', BBC Monitoring Africa, 17 Sep. 2011. See also chapter 3, sections III and IV, in this volume.

named a leader in Kenya, suggesting the organization's interest in increasing its regional influence.[18]

This regionalization of al-Shabab's actions has led to calls for a tougher response, particularly since the bombings in Kampala. Politicians and military commanders from Uganda—which contributes a large proportion of AMISOM's troops—have signalled that AMISOM should move towards peace enforcement.[19] While international engagement in Somalia has so far largely been driven by a desire to stabilize the situation, a likely consequence of internationalization could be an expansion of the conflict beyond Somalia's borders. Domestically, external intervention may also result in increased support for al-Shabab.

One-sided violence: abuses in Ethiopia's Somali Region[20]

As the global patterns predict, more non-state actors than governments carried out one-sided violence in the Horn of Africa in 2001–10.[21] However, the Ethiopian Government was the worst actor both in terms of the number of active years and the number of people killed. The years 2003 and 2004 were the bloodiest (with around 500 and 250 fatalities, respectively), while a more recent peak was recorded in 2007, when over 160 civilians were killed. In that year, almost all of the Ethiopian Government's one-sided violence was carried out in Somali Region, in the country's south-east, which has been the scene of an intermittent intrastate conflict between the government and secessionist rebel groups since the mid-1970s.

The crackdown on civilians in 2007 was preceded by the ONLF's escalation of its military struggle for an independent Ogaden, the southeastern part of Somali Region. Aided by arms entering the region from neighbouring Somalia, the ONLF became more active and in late April stormed a Chinese-run oilfield, killing 74 people. This led to an increase in counterinsurgency operations by the Ethiopian National Defence Force (ENDF) and in July a major military campaign was initiated, with large

[18] Sheikh Iman Ali was named al-Shabab representative in Kenya in 2012. 'Al-Shabaab names Kenyan leader', Somalia Report, 10 Jan. 2012, <http://somaliareport.com/index.php/post/2489/Al-Shabaab_Names_Kenyan_Leader_>. Other al-Shabab leaders with international experience include Swedish–Somali Fuad Shongole and Omar Hammami (also known as Abu Mansur al-Amriki), who was born and raised in the USA. McGregor, A., *Who's Who in the Somali Insurgency: A Reference Guide* (Jamestown Foundation: Washington, DC, 2009), pp. 10–13.

[19] The interpretation of AMISOM's mandate has already changed. 'Mandate of AU troops in Somali capital said changed to enforcement of peace', BBC Monitoring Africa, 30 June 2011.

[20] This section is based on Human Rights Watch, 'Ethiopia: crackdown in east punishes civilians', 4 July 2007, <http://www.hrw.org/news/2007/07/03/ethiopia-crackdown-east-punishes-civilians>; Human Rights Watch (HRW), *Collective Punishment: War Crimes and Crimes against Humanity in the Ogaden Area of Ethiopia's Somali Region* (HRW: New York, 2008); and Ethiopian Human Rights Council (EHRCO), 'EHRCO Condemns Massacre Committed on Innocent Oilfield Workers', Press release, 26 April 2007, <http://www.ehrco.org/index.php?option=com_content&id=14>.

[21] On the global pattern see section III below.

parts of Somali Region being cut off from the outside world. In late July 2007 the Ethiopian Government banned the International Committee of the Red Cross (ICRC) from the region, claiming that it had sided with the opposition forces. A few weeks later the security situation also forced Médecins sans Frontières (MSF, Doctors without Borders) to leave.

While independent coverage of events in the region was thus largely lacking, reports that did emerge indicated that the government's counter-insurgency campaign was marred by gross human rights abuses. The ENDF deliberately and repeatedly attacked civilian populations in an effort to root out the insurgency. Relatives of suspected ONLF members were particularly targeted but simply being an ethnic Somali, and more specifically a member of the Somali Ogaden sub-clan (which has a special link with the rebels), was enough for a person to be considered a suspect.

Non-state conflicts: unrest in border areas

Non-state conflicts form a heterogeneous category, but they can be crudely classified by organization type.[22] Non-state conflicts in the Horn of Africa follow the pattern seen in the rest of Africa, in that a majority (80 per cent) are fought between informally organized ethnic or religious communities. Further important distinctions can be made within this subgroup of actors on the basis of different geographical and topical clusters. The case studies below concern two distinct conflict clusters on the border between Ethiopia and Kenya.

The western Ethiopia–Kenya border cluster[23]

The remote area straddling the border between north-west Kenya and south-west Ethiopia is home to a large number of agro-pastoralist groups, between which relations are very fluid. While some groups are seen as 'eternal enemies', seemingly in a constant state of conflict, others serve as allies of convenience from time to time. This border area, on which neither state exerts much influence, is inhabited by the Turkana, Dassanech, Nyangatom, Suri and Dizi peoples, among others. Over the past decade the UCDP has recorded non-state conflicts between a number of these groups.[24]

[22] On the classification by organization level of the parties see section III below.

[23] This subsection is based on Schlee, G. and Watson, E. E. (eds), *Changing Identifications and Alliances in North-East Africa*, vol. 1, *Ethiopia and Kenya* (Berghan books: New York, 2009); Abbink, J., 'Ritual and political forms of violent practice among the Suri of southern Ethiopia', *Cahiers d'Études Africaines*, vol. 38 (1998), pp. 271–95; Abbink, J., 'Ethnic conflict in the "tribal zone": the Dizi and Suri in southern Ethiopia', *Journal of Modern African Studies*, vol. 31, no. 4 (Dec. 1993), pp. 675–82; and Abbink, J., 'Violence and the crisis of conciliation: Suri, Dizi and the state in south-west Ethiopia', *Africa*, vol. 70, no. 4 (2000), pp. 527–50.

[24] Specific conflicts recorded include those between the Turkana and Dassanech; the Nyangatom and Turkana; and the Dizi and Suri peoples.

While fighting can be triggered by a wide variety of events—for example, the killing of a person by an opposing group—several underlying reasons appear to explain many of the conflicts in the area. One of the most common causes is access to natural resources, particularly water and grazing land. As pressure on these resources has increased, underlying tensions based on a conflictual past have been exacerbated, resulting in intermittent fighting. The level of violence in the region tends to increase in the wake of droughts.[25] Cattle raiding, which has been practised in the area for centuries, is another major cause of deadly conflict between the groups. Raiding of neighbouring groups continues to be a way to replenish herds in the wake of disease or drought. One raid can create a vicious cycle of counter-raids that often leads to substantial violence. Yet another reason for fighting is that young men traditionally constitute their respective villages' fighting force. Once initiated, they are responsible for protecting both the tribe and its cattle. This has led to many instances of violence, with young men wishing to demonstrate their bravery.

The eastern Ethiopia–Kenya border cluster[26]

Between 2001 and 2010, four of the main tribes inhabiting the eastern part of the Ethiopia–Kenya border were involved in five different conflicts that shared a number of characteristics.[27] Typically, the conflicts occurred sporadically, resulted in comparatively low levels of violence and involved frequently shifting alliances.

There are several interrelated reasons for the high number of non-state conflicts in this cluster. One is shifts in affiliation to the two overarching clan families in the region, the Oromo and the Somali, which view each other as traditional enemies.[28] Some groups shift affiliation strategically as they can be viewed as Oromo according to one set of criteria (e.g. language) and Somali according to another (e.g. religion).

Another important reason is the historic westward expansion of the Garre from their traditional homelands in Somalia into present-day Kenya and Ethiopia. This led to conflicts with groups already present in the area, forcing some to move further westwards and encroach on other groups' traditional homelands, thus creating new conflicts. In addition to this his-

[25] On the links between natural resources and conflicts see Melvin, N. and De Koning, R., 'Resources and armed conflict', *SIPRI Yearbook 2011*.

[26] This subsection is based on eds Schlee and Watson (note 23); and Kefale, A., 'Federal restructuring in Ethiopia: renegotiating identity and borders along the Oromo–Somali ethnic frontiers', eds T. Hagman and D. Péclard, *Negotiating Statehood: Dynamics of Power and Domination in Africa* (John Wiley and Sons: Chichester, 2011).

[27] The areas that experienced conflict were Mandera, Marsabit, Moyale and Wajir districts of Kenya and the southern part of the Oromia and Somali regions of Ethiopia. The 4 tribes were the Borana, Gabra, Garre and Guji, which were involved in 5 dyads: Borana–Gabra, Borana–Garre, Borana–Guji, Gabra–Guji and Garre–Borana/Guji.

[28] Note that Somali here refers to ethnicity rather than nationality.

toric movement, groups also migrate as a reaction to environmental factors. Due to difficult living conditions in this arid region, droughts have a particularly destructive impact, provoking violent conflicts over scarce resources. As in the cluster further west, albeit to a lesser extent, livestock raids play into the conflicting relations between these tribes.

Political motives also add to the complexity. Domestically, this mainly concerns control over local administrations. In Ethiopia, for instance, the complexity stems from the country's reorganization as an ethnic federation in the early 1990s, which established a clear link between land and ethnicity. This resulted in increased interest in the possession of 'pure' ethnic territory, resistance to which led to non-state conflicts. Internationally, the dynamics of the relationship between Ethiopia and Kenya—which is dominated by the fear that Somalia's instability might spread beyond its borders—influences events in the cluster. Ethiopia and Kenya also fear each other's potential hegemonic aspirations. Thus, a number of non-state conflicts are drawn into the general entanglements of the Horn of Africa.

III. Patterns of organized violence, 2001–10

LOTTA THEMNÉR AND PETER WALLENSTEEN

UPPSALA CONFLICT DATA PROGRAM

In previous editions of the SIPRI Yearbook, the Uppsala Conflict Data Program (UCDP) presented information on patterns of 'major armed conflicts', defined as those conflicts where the use of armed force between two parties—at least one of which is the government of a state—has resulted in 1000 or more battle-related deaths in at least one calendar year.[1] The focus has now changed and broadened to include three types of organized violence: 'armed conflicts', 'non-state conflicts' and 'one-sided violence'. By including violence carried out by state and non-state actors alike, whether directed against other states, non-state groups or civilian populations, the data provides a broader look at organized violence.

Of the three types of organized violence, the definition of armed conflict most closely resembles that of major armed conflict; the difference is that, instead of applying a threshold of 1000 battle-related deaths in at least one calendar year, the cut-off point is set at 25 deaths in a calendar year. While at least one side in an armed conflict must be a government, non-state conflicts involve only non-state armed groups, which can be formally or informally organized. The third category, one-sided violence, is the intentional targeting of civilians by a state or an organized group.

This section provides an overview of armed conflict, non-state conflict and one-sided violence in the first decade of the 21st century. Over the period 2001–10 there were 69 armed conflicts and 221 non-state conflicts and 127 actors were involved in one-sided violence: thus, in total, there were more than 400 violent actions that each resulted in the deaths of more than 25 people in a particular year. The extent of organized violence at the end of the decade was lower than at its beginning, although the decline was not dramatic (see figure 2.2). Moreover, while in the 1990s there were wide fluctuations in the number of conflicts, this pattern was not repeated in the 2000s, indicating that the downward trend may be a promising indication of future developments. Within the overall trend, each of the three types of violence has its own internal dynamics, while also being affected by the dynamics of the other types. The full picture is, of course, more complex, but there is no clear indication that the three types of violence offset each other, with a decline in one type leading to an increase in the other two.

---

[1] For a more detailed definition of the concept of major armed conflict see e.g. Themnér, L. and Wallensteen, P., 'Patterns of major armed conflicts, 2001–10', *SIPRI Yearbook 2011*, pp. 69–70.

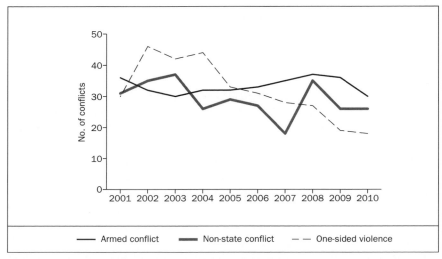

Figure 2.2. Numbers of armed conflicts, non-state conflicts and one-sided violence, 2001–10

Armed conflicts

Armed conflict is defined as a contested incompatibility between two parties—at least one of which is the government of a state—that concerns government or territory or both, where the use of armed force by the parties results in at least 25 battle-related deaths in a calendar year. An armed conflict that results in 1000 battle-related deaths in a year is classified as a 'war' in that year; other armed conflicts are classified as 'minor armed conflicts'.[2] This definition extends from low-intensity conflicts that are active for just one or a few years—such as the territorial conflict between the politico-religious movement Bundu-dia-Kongo and the Congolese government (active in 2007–2008)—right through to high-intensity conflicts that are active over a long period of time—such as the conflict over governmental power in Afghanistan that has pitted successive governments against a range of rebel groups since 1978.

In 2001–10 there were 69 active armed conflicts, including 30 that were active in 2010 (see table 2.2). Overall, the annual number declined somewhat during the period, but the decline was uneven, with the highest number of conflicts being recorded in 2008 (see table 2.3). Interestingly, wars have declined the most. While in 2001 there were 10 wars (28 per cent of the total), in 2010 there were just 4 (13 per cent of the total). The longest-

---

[2] Thus, a major armed conflict is an armed conflict that has been classified as a war in at least 1 year.

running wars were fought between the Afghan Government and the Taliban, and between the Iraqi Government and a plethora of rebel groups: both of these conflicts were on a war level in 7 of the 10 years (Afghanistan in 2001 and 2005–10, and Iraq in 2004–10).

There was also an overall reduction in battle-related deaths over the decade, but there were still close to 20 000 people killed in battles in 2010 (see figure 2.6 below).[3] Again, the decline was uneven, with the lowest number (c. 11 500) recorded in 2005 while the highest number (almost 31 000) was recorded in 2009. This peak was largely due to the dramatic escalation of the conflict in Sri Lanka, which ended in 2009 with the defeat of the Liberation Tigers of Tamil Eelam (LTTE). Developments in Afghanistan and Pakistan also played their part: the conflict between the Afghan Government and the Taliban escalated and a new, violent conflict erupted between the Pakistani Government and Tehrik-i-Taliban Pakistan (TTP, Taliban Movement of Pakistan).

UDCP data distinguishes between three types of armed conflict: interstate, intrastate and internationalized intrastate.[4] Intrastate conflicts are by far the most common; in most years they account for more than 80 per cent of all conflicts, and never less than 70 per cent (see table 2.3). Interstate conflicts are the least common. In 2001–10 there were only three: those between India and Pakistan (2001–2003), Iraq and the USA with its allies (2003), and Djibouti and Eritrea (2008). However, even though interstate conflicts are rare, they should not be neglected. Given the vast resources that can be mobilized by governments compared to rebel groups, conflicts between states may rapidly escalate to a deadly level.[5]

Internationalized intrastate conflicts have become increasingly common. Those since 2001 can be divided into two broad groups: (a) conflicts linked to the USA's 'global war on terrorism' such as the wars in Afghanistan and Iraq and the USA's conflict with al-Qaeda; and (b) cases of government intervention in internal conflicts in their neighbours, such as the conflict between India and the National Socialist Council of Nagaland–Khaplang faction (NSCN–K), during which the Indian Government received support from neighbouring Myanmar. Another example of this type of armed conflict was the conflict between the Angolan Government and União Nacional para a Independência Total de Angola (UNITA, National Union for the Total Independence of Angola), during which the government side was aided by troops from Namibia.

---

[3] For the full definition of battle-related deaths, see below.

[4] Interstate conflicts are fought between 2 or more governments of states. Intrastate conflicts are fought between a government of a state and 1 or more rebel groups. Internationalized intrastate conflicts are intrastate conflicts in which 1 or both sides receive troop support from an external state.

[5] See e.g. Lacina, B. and Gleditch, N. P., 'Monitoring trends in global combat: a new dataset of battle deaths', *European Journal of Population*, vol. 21 (2005), pp. 145–66.

Table 2.2. Armed conflicts in 2010

For more detailed definitions of the terms used see 'Sources and methods' below.

Location[a]	Parties	Incompatibility	Start year[b]	Fatalities, 2010	Change from 2009[c]
Africa					
Algeria	Government of Algeria, Niger				
	vs al-Qaeda in the Islamic Maghreb (AQIM)	Government	1998/ 1999	240	– –
CAR	Government of the CAR				
	vs Convention des patriotes pour la justice et la paix (CPJP, Convention of Patriots for Justice and Peace)	Government	2009/ 2009	26	0
Chad	Government of Chad				
	vs Front populaire pour la renaissance nationale (FPRN, Popular Front for National Renaissance)	Government	2010/ 2010	42	..
Ethiopia	Government of Ethiopia				
	vs Ogaden National Liberation Front (ONLF)	Territory (Ogaden)	1994/ 1994	25	0
Mauritania[d]	Government of Mauritania, France, Niger				
	vs al-Qaeda in the Islamic Maghreb (AQIM)	Government	2008/ 2010	33	..
Rwanda[e]	Government of Rwanda, DRC				
	vs Forces Démocratiques de Libération du Rwanda (FDLR, Democratic Liberation Forces of Rwanda)	Government	1996/ 1996	199	– –
Somalia	Government of Somalia, Ethiopia				
	vs Al-Shabab	Government	2008/ 2008	2 076	+
	vs Hizbul-Islam (Islamic Party)	Government	2009/ 2009	82	+
Sudan	Government of Sudan				
	vs Justice and Equality Movement (JEM)	Government	2003/ 2003	638	+ +
	vs Sudan Liberation Movement/Army (SLM/A)	Government	2003/ 2003	203	+ +
	vs Forces of George Athor	Government	2010/ 2010	90	..
Uganda[f]	Government of Uganda, CAR, DRC, Sudan				
	vs Lord's Resistance Army (LRA)	Government	1988/ 1988	51	– –
Americas					
Colombia	Government of Colombia				
	vs Fuerzas Armadas Revolucionarias de Colombia (FARC, Revolutionary Armed Forces of Colombia)	Government	1964/ 1964	376	0
	vs Ejército de Liberación Nacional (ELN, National Liberation Army)	Government	1965/ 1966	52	..
Peru	Government of Peru				
	vs Sendero Luminoso (Shining Path)	Government	1981/ 1982	28	–

Location[a]	Parties	Incompatibility	Start year[b]	Fatalities, 2010	Change from 2009[c]
USA[g]	Government of the USA, Canada, France, the Netherlands, Romania				
	vs al-Qaeda	Government	2001/ 2001	269	–
Asia					
Afghanistan	Government of Afghanistan, Multilateral coalition[h]				
	vs Hizb-i Islami-yi Afghanistan (Islamic Party of Afghanistan)	Government	1980/ 1980	96	+ +
	vs Taliban	Government	1995/ 1995	6 278	+
India	Government of India				
	vs Communist Party of India–Maoist (CPI–Maoist/Naxalites)	Government	2004/ 2005	531	0
	vs United Liberation Front of Assam (ULFA)	Territory (Assam)	1983/ 1990	30	– –
	vs National Democratic Front for Bodoland (NDFB)	Territory (Bodoland)	1992/ 1993	25	. .
	vs National Democratic Front for Bodoland–Ranjan Daimary faction (NDFB–RD)	Territory (Bodoland)	2009/ 2009	32	– –
	vs Kashmir insurgents	Territory (Kashmir)	1984/ 1989	362	0
Myanmar	Government of Myanmar				
	vs Karen National Union (KNU)	Territory (Karen)	1966/ 1966	63	+ +
	vs Democratic Karen Buddhist Army Brigade 5 (DKBA 5)	Territory (Karen)	2010/ 2010	58	. .
	vs Shan State Army–South command (SSA–S)	Territory (Shan)	1986/ 1996	36	–
Pakistan[i]	Government of Pakistan				
	vs Tehrik-i-Taliban Pakistan (TTP, Taliban Movement of Pakistan)	Government	2007/ 2008	4 787	–
Philippines	Government of Philippines				
	vs Communist Party of the Philippines (CPP)	Government	1969/ 1969	202	+
	vs Abu Sayyaf Group (ASG)	Territory (Mindanao)	1993/ 1993	85	– –
Tajikistan	Government of Tajikistan				
	vs Islamic Movement of Uzbekistan (IMU)	Government	2005/ 2010	98	. .
Thailand	Government of Thailand				
	vs Patani insurgents	Territory (Patani)	1965/ 2003	68	– –
Europe					
Russia	Government of Russia				
	vs Forces of the Caucasus Emirate	Territory ('Caucasus Emirate')	2007/ 2007	418	–
Middle East					
Israel	Government of Israel				
	vs Harakat al-Jihad al-Islami fi Filastin (Palestinian Islamic Jihad, PIJ)	Territory (Palestinian territories)	1987/ 1995	27	– –

Location[a]	Parties	Incompatibility	Start year[b]	Fatalities, 2010	Change from 2009[c]
Iran	Government of Iran				
	vs Jondullah (God's Army)	Government	2003/ 2006	74	–
Iraq	Government of Iraq, USA				
	vs Dawlat al-'Iraq al-Islamiyya (Islamic State of Iraq, ISI)	Government	2004/ 2004	1 015	0
Turkey[j]	Government of Turkey				
	vs Partiya Karkerên Kurdistan (PKK, Kurdistan Workers' Party)	Territory ('Kurdistan')	1983/ 1984	328	+ +
Yemen	Government of Yemen, USA				
	vs al-Qaeda in the Arabian Peninsula (AQAP)	Government	2009/ 2009	175	+ +

CAR = Central African Republic; DRC = Democratic Republic of the Congo.

[a] Location refers to the state whose government is being challenged by an opposition organization. If fighting took place in another geographical location, this is indicated in a note.

[b] Start year refers to the onset of a given dyad (i.e. the fighting between a government and a rebel group). The first year given is the year when the first recorded battle-related death in the dyad occurred and the second year is the year when fighting caused at least 25 battle-related deaths for the first time.

[c] 'Change from 2009' is measured as the increase or decrease in the number of battle-related deaths in 2010 compared to the number of battle-related deaths in 2009. The symbols represent the following changes: + + = increase in battle-related deaths of >50%; + = increase in battle-related deaths of >10 to 50%; 0 = stable rate of battle-related deaths (–10 to +10%); – = decrease in battle-related deaths of >10 to 50%; – – = decrease in battle-related deaths of >50%; . . = the conflict was not active in 2009.

[d] As well as Mauritania, fighting took place in Mali and Niger.

[e] Fighting took place in the DRC.

[f] Fighting took place in the CAR, the DRC and Sudan.

[g] Fighting took place in Afghanistan and Pakistan.

[h] The following countries contributed troops to the coalition in 2010: Albania, Armenia, Australia, Austria, Azerbaijan, Belgium, Bosnia and Herzegovina, Bulgaria, Canada, Croatia, Czech Republic, Denmark, Estonia, Finland, France, Georgia, Germany, Greece, Hungary, Iceland, Ireland, Italy, Jordan, Korea (South), Latvia, Lithuania, Luxembourg, Macedonia (Former Yugoslav Republic of), Malaysia, Mongolia, Montenegro, the Netherlands, New Zealand, Norway, Poland, Portugal, Romania, Singapore, Slovakia, Slovenia, Spain, Sweden, Turkey, Ukraine, the UAE, the UK, the USA.

[i] As well as Pakistan, fighting took place in Afghanistan.

[j] As well as Turkey, fighting took place in Iraq.

Source: UCDP/PRIO Armed Conflict Dataset, <http://www.pcr.uu.se/research/ucdp/datasets/>.

Of the 69 armed conflicts active in 2001–10, 27 (or 39 per cent) were fought in Africa, 25 (36 per cent) were in Asia, 8 were in the Middle East (12 per cent), 5 were in Europe (7 per cent) and 4 were in the Americas (6 per cent). This pattern was roughly constant over the decade (see table 2.3), although since 2003 Asia has been the region hardest hit by armed conflict, reflecting a dramatic fall in the number in Africa. Over the decade, the number of wars in Africa fell from five to one, accompanied by a drop in the annual number of battle-related deaths from well above 10 000 in 2001 to below 4000 in 2010. Driving this trend was the termin-

Table 2.3. Armed conflict, by intensity, type and region, 2001–10

	2001	2002	2003	2004	2005	2006	2007	2008	2009	2010
Total	**36**	**32**	**30**	**32**	**32**	**33**	**35**	**37**	**36**	**30**
Intensity										
Minor armed conflict	26	26	25	25	27	28	31	32	30	26
War	10	6	5	7	5	5	4	5	6	4
Type										
Interstate	1	1	2	–	–	–	–	1	–	–
Intrastate	30	28	26	28	26	27	30	30	28	21
Internationalized intrastate	5	3	2	4	6	6	5	6	8	9
Region										
Africa	15	15	10	10	7	10	12	13	12	9
The Americas	2	2	1	3	2	2	3	3	3	3
Asia and Oceania	14	12	15	14	16	15	14	15	15	12
Europe	2	1	1	2	2	1	2	2	1	1
Middle East	3	2	3	3	5	5	4	4	5	5

ation of the wars in Angola, Burundi and Liberia and the de-escalation of the conflicts in Algeria, Chad, Sudan and Uganda.

While Asia and Europe also saw a decline in the number of conflicts, it was not of the magnitude seen in Africa. In Europe, the reduction in conflicts was accompanied by a drop in battle-related deaths, but the reverse was true in Asia. After a decrease in the number of battle-related deaths in Asia in the first years of the decade, the total began to increase in 2006 and by 2010 it was more than 12 700. This reflected the escalation of the conflicts in Afghanistan and Pakistan.

In contrast, the number of armed conflicts increased in the Americas and the Middle East. In the Middle East, the number of battle-related deaths also increased: it almost quadrupled from about 400 to more than 1600. In the Americas, in contrast, the fatality figure decreased from around 2700 to a little over 700. Notwithstanding the 2001 attack on the USA by al-Qaeda, this decrease was largely due to a de-escalation of the conflict in Colombia.

Non-state conflicts

Non-state conflict is defined as the use of armed force between two organized groups—neither of which is the government of a state—that results in at least 25 battle-related deaths in a year. According to the groups' level of organization, non-state conflicts are divided into three sub-types: (*a*) conflicts between formally organized actors such as rebel groups; (*b*) conflicts between informally organized supporters and affiliates of political parties

Table 2.4. Non-state conflicts in 2010

For more detailed definitions of the terms used see 'Sources and methods' below.

Location[a]	Side A	Side B	Organization level[b]	Start year[c]	Fatalities, 2010	Change from 2009[d]
Africa						
Nigeria	Anagutas, Afisare, Birom	Fulani, Hausa	3	2001	555	..
Nigeria	Birom	Fulani	3	2010	150	..
Nigeria	Boje	Nsadop	3	2010	30	..
Somalia	Al-Shabab	Hizbul-Islam	1	2009	88	–
Somalia	Ahlu Sunna Waljamaca	Al-Shabab	1	2008	202	– –
Somalia	Ahlu Sunna Waljamaca	Hizbul-Islam	1	2010	45	..
Somalia	Forces of Shayk Muhammad Said Atom	Puntland state of Somalia	1	2010	109	..
Somalia	Suleiman subclan of Habar Gidir clan (Hawiye)	Qubeys subclan (Dir)	3	2010	88	..
Sudan	Atuot Dinka	Ciek Dinka	3	2010	27	..
Sudan	Dinka	Nuer	3	1997	228	..
Sudan	Gok Dinka	Rek Dinka	3	2010	28	..
Sudan	Misseria	Rizeigat Baggara	3	2008	342	+
Americas						
Honduras	Mara 18 (Honduras)	Mara Salvatrucha (Honduras)	1	2010	49	..
Honduras, Mexico	Gulf Cartel	Sinaloa Cartel	1	2004	40	– –
Mexico	Beltrán Leyva Cartel	Beltrán Leyva Cartel–Valdez Villareal faction	1	2010	182	..
Mexico	Gulf Cartel	Los Zetas	1	2010	412	..
Mexico	Juarez Cartel	Sinaloa Cartel	1	2008	2 515	+ +
Mexico	Los Zetas	Sinaloa Cartel	1	2010	29	..
Mexico	Tijuana Cartel	Tijuana Cartel–El Teo faction	1	2008	54	+
Asia						
Afghanistan	Hizb-i Islami-yi Afghanistan	Taliban	1	1994	99	..
Kyrgyzstan	Kyrgyz (Kyrgyzstan)	Uzbeks (Kyrgyzstan)	3	1990	45	..
Pakistan	Lashkar-e-Islam (Army of Islam)	TTP	1	2010	63	..
Pakistan	TTP–Momin Afridi faction	TTP–Tariq Afridi faction	1	2010	74	..
Pakistan	TTP–Mulla Rafique faction	TTP–Mullah Toofan faction	1	2010	80	..
Pakistan	Bangesh tribe	Mangal tribe	3	2010	200	..
Middle East						
Yemen	al-Shabab al-Mumin (Believing Youth)	al-Qaeda in the Arabian Peninsula (AQAP)	1	2010	26	..

TTP = Tehrik-i-Taliban Pakistan (Taliban Movement of Pakistan)

[a] Location refers to the geographical location of the fighting.

[b] Organization level: 1 = formally organized groups; 2 = informal 'supporters' groups; and 3 = informally organized ethnic or religious groups. See 'Sources and methods' for full details.

[c] Start year is the first year (since 1988) when conflict caused 25 fatalities.

[d] 'Change from 2009' is measured as the increase or decrease in the number of battle-related deaths in 2010 compared to the number of battle-related deaths in 2009. The symbols represent the following changes: + + = increase in battle-related deaths of >50%; + = increase in battle-related deaths of >10 to 50%; 0 = stable rate of battle-related deaths (−10 to +10%); − = decrease in battle-related deaths of >10 to 50%; − − = decrease in battle-related deaths of >50%; . . = the conflict was not active in 2009.

Source: UCDP Non-state Conflict Dataset, <http://www.pcr.uu.se/research/ucdp/datasets/>.

and candidates; and (c) conflicts between informally organized groups that share a common identification along ethnic, clan, religious, national or tribal lines. Thus, non-state conflict relates to a broad spectrum of violence that tends to greatly affect ordinary people but often has fewer implications for international relations than armed conflict. For example, the category includes conflicts between highly organized groups—such as the Colombian paramilitary group Autodefensas Unidas de Colombia (AUC, United Self-defence Forces of Colombia) fighting the rebel group Fuerzas Armadas Revolucionarias de Colombia (FARC, Revolutionary Armed Forces of Colombia)—as well as conflicts between ethnic communities in the Horn of Africa such as that between the Ari and the Mursi peoples in south-east Ethiopia.

There was a total of 221 non-state conflicts worldwide during the decade 2001–10, including 26 that were active in 2010 (see table 2.4). There was a decrease in the number of active non-state conflicts over the decade, but as with armed conflicts the decline was far from smooth (see table 2.5).

At the same time the average number of people killed in non-state conflicts increased markedly (see figure 2.3). While the 31 conflicts fought in 2001 caused just over 2800 fatalities (or an average of 91 people killed per conflict), the 26 conflicts in 2010 caused more than 5700 fatalities (an average of 222 fatalities per conflict). In fact, trends in conflict numbers and conflict fatalities rarely corresponded in this period. This is illustrated most clearly by the increase of 135 in the average number of fatalities per conflict between 2008 and 2010—which is substantial in the context of non-state conflicts—while the number of conflicts decreased by 9. This considerable increase was mainly driven by the violent escalation of the conflict between the Juarez and Sinaloa cartels in Mexico.[6]

The most common type of non-state conflict in 2001–10 was conflict between ethnic or religious communities. Of the 221 non-state conflicts, 133 (60 per cent) were fought between such groups. Eighty of the conflicts

---

[6] On the difficulties in coding non-state conflicts in Mexico see the entry for Mexico in the UCDP Conflict Encyclopedia, <http://www.ucdp.uu.se/database/>.

Table 2.5. Non-state conflict, by subcategory and region, 2001–10

	2001	2002	2003	2004	2005	2006	2007	2008	2009	2010
Total	31	35	37	26	29	27	18	35	26	26
Subcategory										
Formally organized groups	7	13	16	13	11	7	10	13	9	16
Informal 'supporters' groups	2	1	3	1	–	1	–	2	1	–
Informally organized ethnic or religious groups	22	21	18	12	18	19	8	20	16	10
Region										
Africa	23	30	32	20	22	21	10	23	18	12
Asia and Oceania	4	2	2	2	4	5	5	8	5	6
The Americas	4	2	2	3	3	–	–	3	3	7
Europe	–	–	–	–	–	–	–	–	–	–
Middle East	–	1	1	1	–	1	3	1	–	1

(36 per cent) were between formally organized groups, such as rebel groups or militias. Conflicts between supporters and affiliates of political parties and candidates were uncommon: only 8 (3 per cent) were recorded in the entire period.[7] Non-state conflict involving informal 'supporters' groups was the least common of the three subcategories in all years of the period 2001–10.

The vast majority of non-state conflicts in 2001–10 were located in Africa (see table 2.5). Most of the non-state conflicts in Africa are clustered in a few countries. Of the 169 non-state conflicts in Africa over the decade, 130 (or 77 per cent) were fought in Ethiopia, Kenya, Nigeria, Somalia or Sudan.

There are clear differences in the types of non-state conflict fought in each region. Africa was the only region where a majority of the non-state conflicts involved ethnic or religious communities (see figure 2.4). In all other regions, a majority of the conflicts were fought between formally organized groups; in the Middle East this category made up 100 per cent of all non-state conflicts.

While a majority of the deaths in non-state conflicts occurred in Africa, at 141 deaths per conflict the average number of fatalities in Africa was

---

[7] It should be noted, however, that there is a potential overlap between the various types of non-state conflict. E.g. in many countries supporters of different political parties are almost by definition members of a specific ethnic group. During election years these groups are mobilized under a political banner, whereas they are mobilized as an ethnic group in conflicts occurring in other years. To be able to get a good overview and to follow a conflict even though it is reported in different ways in different years, UCDP has a coding rule that if there is a conflict between 2 ethnic groups in 1 year, and these ethnic groups are then involved in fighting mobilized along political lines (i.e. as supporters of a party) in another year, all conflict years are coded as part of the same ethnic conflict.

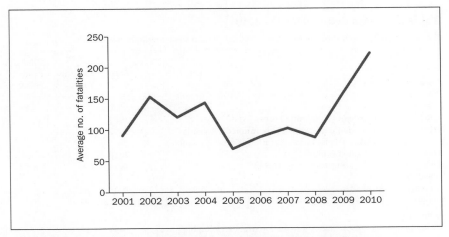

Figure 2.3. Average number of fatalities in non-state conflicts, 2001–10

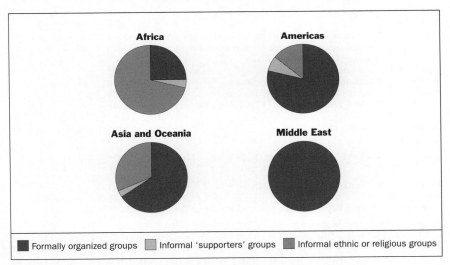

Figure 2.4. Subcategories of non-state conflict, by region, 2001–10

among the lowest globally. This is to be expected, since most non-state conflicts in Africa involve informally organized groups, such as ethnic or
religious communities, which cannot mobilize resources as effectively as
formally organized rebel groups or militias. Indeed, the average number of
fatalities is higher in conflicts between formally organized groups than
between informal ones.

The Americas is one of the regions with the highest proportion of non-
state conflicts between formally organized groups (see figure 2.4). As the
above logic would predict, it is also the region with the highest average

Table 2.6. One sided-violence in 2010

For more detailed definitions of the terms used see 'Sources and methods' below.

Location[a]	Actor	Start year[b]	Fatalities, 2010	Change from 2009[c]
Africa				
DRC	Alliance of Democratic Forces (ADF)	1997	38	..
DRC	Forces democratiques de liberation du Rwanda (FDLR, Democratic Liberation Forces of Rwanda)	1996	68	– –
DRC	Mayi Mayi Complet	2010	27	..
DRC, CAR, Sudan	Lord's Resistance Army (LRA)	1989	430	– –
Somalia	Al-Shabab	2008	88	..
Sudan	Janjaweed	2001	41	..
Americas				
Colombia	Fuerzas Armadas Revolucionarias de Colombia (FARC, Revolutionary Armed Forces of Colombia)	1994	29	0
Mexico	Los Zetas	2010	86	..
Asia				
Afghanistan	Taliban	2004	190	+
India	Communist Party of India–Maoist (CPI–Maoist/Naxalites)	2005	337	+ +
India	National Democratic Front for Bodoland–Ranjan Daimary faction (NDFB–RD)	2010	25	..
Myanmar	Government of Myanmar	1992	27	..
Pakistan	Baluchistan Liberation Army (BLA)	2010	33	..
Pakistan	Lashkar-e-Jhangvi (Army of Jhangvi)	1998	167	..
Pakistan	Tehrik-i-Taliban Pakistan (TTP, Taliban Movement of Pakistan)	2007	549	+ +
Thailand	Patani insurgents	2004	135	+
Middle East				
Iraq	Dawlat al-'Iraq al-Islamiyya (Islamic State of Iraq, ISI)	2004	707	+
Europe				
Russia	Forces of the Caucasus Emirate	2010	57	..

CAR = Central African Republic; DRC = Democratic Republic of the Congo.

[a] Location refers to the geographical location of the one-sided violence.

[b] Start year is the first year (since 1988) when one-sided violence caused 25 fatalities.

[c] 'Change from 2009' is measured as the increase or decrease in the number of battle-related deaths in 2010 compared to the number of battle-related deaths in 2009. The symbols represent the following changes: + + = increase in battle-related deaths of >50%; + = increase in battle-related deaths of >10 to 50%; 0 = stable rate of battle-related deaths (–10 to +10%); – = decrease in battle-related deaths of >10 to 50%; – – = decrease in battle-related deaths of >50%; .. = the conflict was not active in 2009.

Source: UCDP One-sided Violence Dataset, <http://www.pcr.uu.se/research/ucdp/datasets/>.

number of people killed in non-state conflicts (at 472 fatalities per conflict). Most conflicts in the Americas are fought between rebel groups and pro-government militias (e.g. the Colombian rebel group FARC and the pro-government AUC), rival criminal gangs (e.g. Comando Vermelho and Terceiro Comando in Brazil) or drug cartels (e.g. the Juarez and Sinaloa cartels in Mexico).

Table 2.7. One-sided violence, by actor and region, 2001–10

	2001	2002	2003	2004	2005	2006	2007	2008	2009	2010
Total	30	46	42	44	33	31	28	27	19	18
Actor										
Non-state actor	21	33	30	33	22	19	18	20	15	17
State actor	9	13	12	11	11	12	10	7	4	1
Region										
Africa	12	25	23	18	12	10	15	14	8	6
Asia and Oceania	10	14	13	13	9	15	10	10	7	8
The Americas	4	2	1	3	4	1	–	2	1	2
Europe	1	1	1	3	–	–	–	–	–	1
Middle East	3	4	4	7	8	5	3	1	3	1

One-sided violence

One-sided violence is defined as the use of armed force by the government of a state or by a formally organized group against unorganized civilians that results in at least 25 deaths. A state or group that kill 25 or more unarmed civilians during a year is registered as a 'one-sided actor' in the UCDP data. This includes a wide variety of situations, ranging from small-scale, day-to-day attacks, such as those by the Senegalese rebel group Mouvement des forces démocratiques de Casamance (MFDC, Movement of the Democratic Forces of Casamance) on inhabitants of the Casamance region, to large-scale cases such as the Rwandan genocide in 1994.

A total of 127 one-sided actors were recorded in 2001–10, including 18 that were active in 2010 (see table 2.6). The total number of actors targeting civilians has declined markedly, from 30 in 2001 to 18 in 2010, after peaking at 46 in 2002 (see table 2.7).

The decline in the number of actors targeting civilians over the decade was matched by a drop in the number of fatalities (see figure 2.5). The increase in fatalities between 2001 and 2002 (from about 6000 to more than 10 000) was largely due to a dramatic increase in the number of one-sided actors (from 30 to 46). The number of deaths decreased continuously from 2002 to 2008. Between 2004 and 2005, deaths fell by 45 per cent, due in part to a decline in one-sided violence by the Sudanese Government and the Janjaweed militia in Darfur. The number of fatalities increased again in 2009, as both the Forces démocratiques de libération du Rwanda (FDLR, Democratic Liberation Forces of Rwanda) and the Lord's Resistance Army (LRA) stepped up their campaigns against civilians in Central Africa.

As described for non-state conflicts above, the trend in fatality numbers can differ from the trend in actor numbers. For example, as the number of actors carrying out one-sided violence decreased from 27 to 19 between

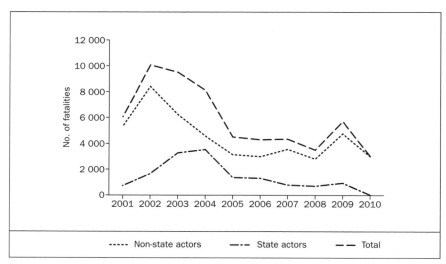

Figure 2.5. Fatalities in one-sided violence, by type of actor, 2001–10

2008 and 2009, the number of fatalities increased from approximately 3500 to almost 5700. Such dramatic increases are often caused by a single actor.

Non-state groups are the most common perpetrators of one-sided violence. In all years of the period 2001–10 more non-state actors were recorded than state actors (see table 2.7), and over the period as a whole 95 of the 127 one-sided actors (almost 75 per cent) were rebel groups or militias. Although individual government actors can be particularly lethal, as illustrated by the Sudanese Government in 2003 and 2004, non-state actors also killed more civilians than government actors did in every year of the period (see figure 2.5). The one-sided actors that killed the most civilians during any given year in 2001–10 were al-Qaeda, whose 2001 attack on New York resulted in over 2700 civilian deaths; the Sudanese Government, whose attacks in Darfur in 2004 led to the deaths of more than 2500 civilians; and the Iraqi rebel group Dawlat al-'Iraq al-Islamiyya (Islamic State of Iraq, ISI), which caused almost 2000 civilian deaths in 2007.[8]

Nearly half of the actors targeting civilians in 2001–10 were in Africa (60 of the 127 actors), followed by Asia (39), the Middle East (14), the Americas (9) and Europe (5). Over the decade, Africa saw the highest number of one-sided actors in all but two years, when Asia had more (see table 2.7). Africa was the region with the highest number of fatalities in all but four years of the decade: 2001, 2006, 2007 and 2010. The highest level of one-sided violence in 2001 was in the Americas as a result of al-Qaeda's attacks on the

[8] While the series of attacks on the USA on 11 Sep. 2001 also led to deaths in Pennsylvania and Washington, DC, only the attacks on New York were directed against civilian targets and subsequently counted as one-sided violence.

USA. In 2006 and 2010 most one-sided violence was in Asia, but this was due more to a decrease in Africa than to any increase in Asia, where violence remained more or less at the level of previous years. Finally, the 2007 peak in one-sided violence in the Middle East was a result of increased activity by ISI, which stepped up its use of booby-trapped fuel tankers in suicide car attacks, causing numerous deaths.

Organized violence: a comparison

Although the three types of organized violence described in this section have their own particular dynamics, there are some notable connections.

First, there is a close relationship between armed conflicts and one-sided violence: 125 of the 127 one-sided actors in the period 2001–10 were operating in countries that had experienced an armed conflict at some time since 1946.[9] The remaining 2 one-sided actors were active in just two countries: Brazil and Guyana. Two-thirds of one-sided actors were also recorded as parties in armed conflict. For instance, the LRA simultaneously pursued an armed conflict against the Ugandan Government and used violence against the civilian population. On the whole, the data suggests that one-sided violence is a phenomenon that to a large extent takes place in armed conflict settings. The practice of targeting civilians may even be used as a tactic in the conflict or the armed conflict may provide an opportunity for genocide.[10] Much reporting on conflicts makes no distinction between battle-related deaths and deaths as a result of one-sided violence; instead only aggregate fatalities numbers are recorded. The UCDP's differentiation between the two makes it possible to understand the different processes at work and, from the perspective of conflict management and resolution, makes it clear that there is a need to consider different strategies.

Second, non-state conflict is connected to armed conflict and one-sided conflict in at least two ways: they frequently occur in the same countries and sometimes include the same actors. The geographical overlap is almost perfect: during the decade 2001–10, 189 of the 221 non-state conflicts took place in countries that were also the scene of armed conflict or one-sided violence during the decade. Indeed, only two non-state conflicts in 2001–10 were fought in countries that have not been the scene of an armed conflict since 1946 or one-sided violence since 1989—the conflict in Jamaica between rival supporters of the Jamaica Labour Party and the People's

[9] The corresponding figure for countries that had experienced armed conflict in the period 2001–10 was 116 one-sided actors.

[10] Again, the LRA is a good example of this. On the LRA's use of one-sided violence as a tactic in its conflict with the Ugandan Government see UCDP Conflict Encyclopedia (note 6). On the general finding see Wallensteen, P., Melander, E. and Möller, F., 'The international community response', eds. I. W. Zartman, M. Anstey and P. Meerts, *The Slippery Slope of Genocide: Reducing Identity Conflicts and Preventing Mass Murder* (Oxford University Press: Oxford, 2012), pp. 280–305.

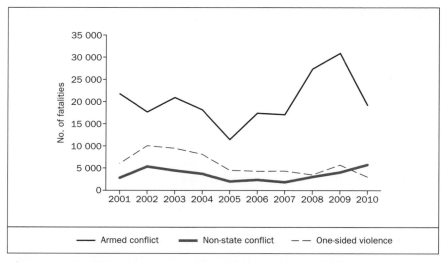

Figure 2.6. Fatalities, by category of organized violence, 2001–10

National Party; and the conflict in Kyrgyzstan between Kyrgyz and Uzbeks.[11] Moreover, 47 (21 per cent) of the 221 non-state conflicts included at least one party that had at some point also been active in an armed conflict or one-sided violence.

Third, all three types of organized violence are most prevalent in Africa. In 2001–10, Africa was the scene of 76 per cent of non-state conflicts, 47 per cent of one-sided violence and 39 per cent of armed conflicts. Asia was the second most affected region for all three categories. While it might have been reasonable to expect that the Middle East would be the most conflict-torn region, according to UCDP statistics only 11 per cent of armed conflicts, 3 per cent of non-state conflicts and 11 per cent of one-sided violence in 2001–10 occurred in the region.

Finally, a notable difference between the three categories of organized violence can be seen in the numbers of deaths caused. Armed conflict—in which at least one side is the government of a state—led to the highest number of fatalities, both on an annual basis and for the period as a whole (see figure 2.6). The average total number of people killed in each of the 69 armed conflicts was almost 3000, compared to 160 for non-state conflicts and 466 for one-sided violence. Clearly, the more organized the actors involved in violence, the more deadly that violence becomes. As the most deadly violence is so strongly driven by state actors or formally organized non-state actors, they are also the actors to which efforts at conflict containment, prevention and resolution should be directed.

---

[11] Note that the UCDP's data on armed conflicts involving a state stretches back to 1946 while that on one-sided violence begins in 1989.

Sources and methods

Definition of armed conflict

The UCDP defines armed conflict as a contested incompatibility concerning government or territory over which the use of armed force between the military forces of two parties, of which at least one is the government of a state, results in at least 25 battle-related deaths in a calendar year. The separate elements are defined as follows.

1. *Incompatibility that concerns government or territory*. This refers to the stated generally incompatible positions of the parties to the conflict. An *incompatibility that concerns government* refers to incompatible positions regarding the state's type of political system or the composition of the government. It may also involve an aim to replace the current government. An *incompatibility that concerns territory* refers to incompatible positions regarding the status of a territory and may involve demands for secession or autonomy (intrastate conflict) or aims to change the state in control of a certain territory (interstate conflict).

2. *Use of armed force*. This refers to the use of armed force by the military forces of the parties to the conflict in order to promote the parties' general position in the conflict. Arms are defined as any material means of combat, including anything from manufactured weapons to sticks, stones, fire or water.

3. *Party*. This refers to the government of a state, any of its allies, an opposition organization or an alliance of opposition organizations. The *government of a state* is the party that is generally regarded as being in central control, even by those organizations seeking to seize power. If this criterion is not applicable, the party controlling the capital of the state is regarded as the government. An *opposition organization* is any non-governmental group that has announced a name for itself as well as its political goals and that has used armed force to achieve them. A state or a multinational organization that supports one of the primary parties with regular troops may also be included in the table. In order to be listed in the table, this secondary party must share the position of one of the warring parties. A traditional peacekeeping operation is not considered to be a party to the conflict but is rather seen as an impartial part of a consensual peace process.

4. *State*. A state is an internationally recognized sovereign government controlling a specific territory or an internationally non-recognized government controlling a specific territory whose sovereignty is not disputed by an internationally recognized sovereign state that previously controlled the territory in question.

5. *Battle-related deaths*. This refers to deaths directly related to combat between the warring parties and can include both deaths on the battlefield and civilians caught in cross-fire. UCDP defines a conflict that has incurred at least 25 battle-related deaths during a calendar year as a minor armed conflict and any with at least 1000 battle-related deaths during a calendar year as a war in that year.

Definition of non-state conflict

The UCDP defines non-state conflict as the use of armed force between two organized armed groups, neither of which is the government of a state, which results in at least 25 battle-related deaths in a year. The separate elements are defined as follows.

1. *Organized groups*. There are three levels of organization. *Formally organized groups (organizational level 1)* are rebel and other organized groups whose level of organization is high enough to include them in the state-based armed conflict category. These include rebel groups with an announced name, as well as military factions. *Informally organized supporter groups (organizational level 2)* are groups composed of supporters and affiliates of political parties and candidates. These are commonly not groups that are permanently organized for combat, but which at times use their organizational structures for such purposes. *Informally organized ethnic or religious groups (organizational level 3)* are groups that share a common

identification along ethnic, clan, religious, national or tribal lines. These are not groups that are permanently organized for combat, but which at times organize themselves to engage in fighting

2. *Battle-related deaths.* The definition of battle-related death varies according to the level of organization of the fighting groups. For formally organized groups (organizational level 1) the recording of battle-related deaths follows the same criteria as for state-based armed conflict, that is, the warring groups must target representatives of the other formally organized group. Targeting of civilians, even if those civilians are of, for example, the same ethnicity as a group's rivals, is coded as one-sided violence. For informally organized groups (organizational levels 2 and 3), the definition of battle-related death is extended to include both civilian and armed victims as long as there is a pattern of violent (lethal) interaction between the groups, with both parties carrying out attacks.

Definition of one-sided violence

The UCDP defines one-sided violence as the use of armed force by the government of a state or by a formally organized group against civilians, which results in at least 25 deaths in a calendar year. Extrajudicial killings in custody are excluded. The separate elements are defined as follows.

1. *Use of armed force.* This is the use of arms in order to exert violent force, resulting in death. Arms are defined as any material means of combat, including anything from manufactured weapons to sticks, stones, fire or water.

2. *Government.* See above.

3. *State.* See above.

4. *Formally organized group.* This can be any non-governmental group of people that has announced a name for their group and that uses armed force. This corresponds to 'opposition organization' as defined for the armed conflict category and to 'formally organized group' as defined for the non-state category.

5. *Extrajudicial killings in custody.* This is the killing by the government of a state of a person in its custody. In custody is defined as when a person is located in a prison or another type of government facility.

Sources

The data presented here is based on information taken from a wide selection of publicly available sources, both printed and electronic. The sources include news agencies, newspapers, academic journals, research reports, and documents from international and multinational organizations and non-governmental organizations (NGOs). In order to collect information on the aims and goals of the parties to the conflict, documents of the warring parties (governments, allies and opposition organizations) and, for example, the Internet sites of rebel groups are often consulted.

Independent news sources, carefully selected over a number of years, constitute the basis of the data collection. The Factiva news database is indispensable for the collection of general news reports. It contains more than 25 000 sources in 22 languages from 159 countries and provides sources from all three crucial levels of the news media: international (e.g. Agence France-Presse and Reuters), regional and local.

The UCDP regularly scrutinizes and revises the selection and combination of sources in order to maintain a high level of reliability and comparability between regions and countries. One important priority is to arrive at a balanced combination of sources of different origin with a view to avoiding bias. The reliability of the sources is judged using the expertise of the UCDP together with advice from a global network of experts (academics and policymakers). Both the independence of the source and the transparency of its origins are crucial. The latter is important because most sources are secondary, which means that the primary source also needs to be analysed in order to establish the reliability of a report. Each source is judged in relation to the context in which it is published. The potential interest of either the primary or secondary source in misrepresenting an event is taken into account, as are the general climate and extent of media censorship. Reports from NGOs and international organizations are particularly useful in this context, complementing media reporting and facilitating cross-checking. The criterion that a source should be independent does not, of course, apply to sources that are consulted precisely because they *are* biased, such as government documents or rebel groups' Internet sites. The UCDP is aware of the high level of scrutiny required and makes great efforts to ensure the authenticity of the material used.

Methods

The data on organized violence are compiled by calendar year. It includes data on conflict locations, type of incompatibility, onset of the armed conflict, warring parties, total number of battle-related deaths, number of battle-related deaths in a given year and change in battle-related deaths from the previous year. See also the notes for tables 2.2, 2.4 and 2.6.

The data on fatalities are given the most attention in coding for the UCDP database. Information on, for example, the date, news source, primary source, location and death toll is recorded for every event. Ideally, these individual events and figures are corroborated by two or more independent sources. The figures are then aggregated for the entire year of each conflict. The aggregated figures are compared to total figures given in official documents, in special reports and in the news media. Regional experts such as researchers, diplomats and journalists are often consulted during the data collection. Their role is mainly to clarify the contexts in which the events occur, thus facilitating proper interpretation of the published sources.

UCDP codes three different fatality estimates—low, best and high—based on the reliability of reports and the conflicting number of deaths that can be reported for any violent event. All of the data presented here are based on the best estimate, which consists of the aggregated most reliable numbers for all incidents of each category of violence during a year. If different sources provide different estimates, an examination is made as to what source is the most reliable. If no such distinction can be made, UCDP as a rule includes the lower figure in the best estimate. UCDP is generally conservative when estimating the number of fatalities. As more in-depth information on a case of organized violence becomes available, the conservative, event-based estimates often prove more correct than others widely cited in the news media. If no figures are available or if the numbers given are unreliable, the UCDP does not provide a figure. Figures are revised retroactively each year as new information becomes available.

IV. The Global Peace Index 2012

CAMILLA SCHIPPA AND THOMAS MORGAN

INSTITUTE FOR ECONOMICS AND PEACE

Now in its sixth year, the Global Peace Index (GPI) measures the peacefulness of countries based on a scoring model that uses 23 indicators to rank 158 countries by their relative states of peace. The selected indicators are the best available data sets that reflect the incidence or absence of peace. They contain both quantitative data and qualitative scores from a range of trusted sources. The GPI is produced by the Institute for Economics and Peace (IEP), guided by an international expert panel of independent experts and supported by the Economist Intelligence Unit (EIU), which collates the data and calculates the rankings in conjunction with the IEP.[1]

The GPI's principal aim is to investigate positive peace. It does this by identifying correlations between GPI scores and a range of other indexes and databases that measure key social, economic, education, health, governance and political factors. Investigating the statistical relevance of these factors allows the identification of a range of potential determinants that may influence the creation and nurturing of a peaceful society.

The Global Peace Index 2012 records improvements in the average scores of all regions apart from the Middle East and North Africa (see table 2.9 below).[2] The uprisings, protests and revolutions of the Arab Spring (see section I above) made the Middle East and North Africa the least peaceful region; GPI scores deteriorated most sharply in Syria, Egypt, Tunisia and Oman (see table 2.8). For the first time since the GPI was launched, in 2007, sub-Saharan Africa was not the least peaceful region; there were notable improvements in Madagascar, Gabon and Botswana.

Iceland was the country most at peace for the second successive year. Small, stable democracies dominate the top 10 once more. Qatar, ranked 12th, is the highest-placed Middle Eastern country (and non-democracy). Bhutan moved into the top 20 for the first time, mainly as a result of easing tensions surrounding ethnic Nepali refugees. Norway fell out of the top 10, dropping from 9th to 18th position as a result of the July 2011 attacks in which 77 people were killed and deteriorations in several measures of militarization. Sri Lanka experienced the greatest improvement in its overall peacefulness, following the ending of decades of civil war.

---

[1] More information on the IEP is available at <http://www.economicsandpeace.org/>. The panel included the following experts in 2011–12: Kevin Clements, Chairman (University of Otago), Ian Anthony (SIPRI), Sultan Barakat (University of York), Nick Grono (International Crisis Group), Toshiya Hoshino (Osaka University), Manuela Mesa (Centro de Educación e Investigación para la Paz, Madrid) and Ekaterina Stepanova (IMEMO).

[2] For full details see IEP, *2012 Global Peace Index* (IEP: Sydney, 2012).

Table 2.8. Countries with the greatest change in Global Peace Index scores, 2011–12

Country	Score, 2012	Change in score, 2011–12	Rank, 2012	Change in rank, 2011–12[a]
Top 5 risers				
Sri Lanka	2.145	−0.292	103	+27
Zimbabwe	2.538	−0.186	140	−
Bhutan	1.481	−0.182	19	+11
Guyana	1.937	−0.178	69	+21
Philippines	2.415	−0.157	133	+2
Top 5 fallers				
Syria	2.830	+0.523	147	−31
Egypt	2.220	+0.215	111	−40
Tunisia	1.955	+0.193	72	−29
Oman	1.887	+0.150	59	−20
Malawi	1.894	+0.146	60	−19

[a] The Global Peace Index (GPI) 2011 included only 153 countries while the 2012 GPI includes 158 countries, which affects changes in ranking between 2011 and 2012.

War-ravaged Somalia remained the country least at peace in 2012 for the second successive year, with ongoing conflict in several regions (with the notable exception of Somaliland; see section II above). Afghanistan's score deteriorated and it dropped to second-lowest position. Iraq became slightly more peaceful as a result of a reduction in the likelihood of violent demonstrations and a fall in the number of displaced people, albeit from high levels. Syria's descent into civil war caused its score to deteriorate by the largest margin and it dropped by 31 places to 147th position.

The world has become slightly more peaceful in the past year. The average score for the 158 countries ranked in the 2012 GPI was 2.02 (based on a 1–5 scale), a slight decline—indicating an increase in peacefulness—compared with 2011, when the average was 2.05. This follows two consecutive years in which overall peacefulness fell, with many countries experiencing growing instability and heightened disharmony linked to rises in fuel, food and commodity prices and the global economic downturn. There is little variance between the scores of the top 25 countries in 2012: 0.435, from 1.113 for Iceland to 1.548 for Spain. The spread in scores of the 25 lowest-ranked countries was more than double this: 0.973, from 2.419 for Côte d'Ivoire to 3.392 for Somalia, a slight increase on the spread in 2011 (0.956).

Among the GPI indicators, the largest change from the 2011 GPI was the deterioration in perceptions of criminality in society. Other significant changes were all in measures of societal safety and the security situation, reflecting the turmoil in the Arab world and beyond. The greatest improvement was in the political terror scale, and there were gains in several indicators of militarization as defence budgets were squeezed.

Table 2.9. The Global Peace Index 2012

Rank	Country	Score	Change	Rank	Country	Score	Change
1	Iceland	1.113	−0.037	50	Ghana	1.807	+0.066
2	Denmark	1.239	−0.041	51	Zambia	1.830	−0.013
2	New Zealand	1.239	−0.034	52	Sierra Leone	1.855	−0.027
4	Canada	1.317	−0.033	53	Lesotho	1.864	..
5	Japan	1.326	+0.032	54	Morocco	1.867	+0.007
6	Austria	1.328	−0.001	55	Tanzania	1.873	+0.020
6	Ireland	1.328	−0.054	56	Burkina Faso	1.881	+0.054
8	Slovenia	1.330	−0.040	56	Djibouti	1.881	..
9	Finland	1.348	−0.015	58	Mongolia	1.884	+0.006
10	Switzerland	1.349	−0.077	59	Oman	1.887	+0.150
11	Belgium	1.376	−0.033	60	Malawi	1.894	+0.146
12	Qatar	1.395	−0.005	61	Panama	1.899	+0.080
13	Czech Republic	1.396	+0.064	62	Jordan	1.905	−0.009
14	Sweden	1.419	+0.010	63	Indonesia	1.913	−0.045
15	Germany	1.424	+0.011	64	Serbia	1.920	−0.136
16	Portugal	1.470	+0.018	65	Bosnia–Herzegovina	1.923	+0.026
17	Hungary	1.476	−0.028	66	Albania	1.927	+0.024
18	Norway	1.480	+0.113	66	Moldova	1.927	+0.026
19	Bhutan	1.481	−0.182	68	Macedonia, FYR	1.935	−0.095
20	Malaysia	1.485	+0.031	69	Guyana	1.937	−0.178
21	Mauritius	1.487	..	70	Cuba	1.951	−0.014
22	Australia	1.494	+0.034	71	Ukraine	1.953	−0.043
23	Singapore	1.521	−0.052	72	Tunisia	1.955	+0.193
24	Poland	1.524	−0.032	73	Cyprus	1.957	−0.059
25	Spain	1.548	−0.101	74	Gambia	1.961	+0.046
26	Slovakia	1.590	+0.002	75	Gabon	1.972	−0.095
27	Taiwan	1.602	−0.040	76	Paraguay	1.973	+0.007
28	Netherlands	1.606	−0.027	77	Greece	1.976	+0.035
29	United Kingdom	1.609	−0.016	78	Senegal	1.994	−0.041
30	Chile	1.616	−0.107	79	Peru	1.995	−0.076
31	Botswana	1.621	−0.080	80	Nepal	2.001	−0.153
32	Romania	1.627	−0.126	81	Montenegro	2.006	−0.098
33	Uruguay	1.628	+0.101	81	Nicaragua	2.006	−0.007
34	Viet Nam	1.641	−0.032	83	Brazil	2.017	−0.033
35	Croatia	1.648	−0.051	84	Bolivia	2.021	−0.008
36	Costa Rica	1.659	−0.027	85	Ecuador	2.028	−0.075
37	Laos	1.662	−0.013	85	Swaziland	2.028	+0.031
38	Italy	1.690	−0.089	87	Equatorial Guinea	2.039	+0.011
39	Bulgaria	1.699	−0.147	88	United States	2.058	−0.007
40	France	1.710	+0.016	89	China	2.061	−0.015
41	Estonia	1.715	−0.084	90	Dominican Republic	2.068	−0.061
42	South Korea	1.734	−0.100	91	Bangladesh	2.071	−
43	Lithuania	1.741	−0.027	92	Guinea	2.073	−0.040
44	Argentina	1.763	−0.100	93	Papua New Guinea	2.076	−0.053
45	Latvia	1.774	−0.029	94	Trinidad and Tobago	2.082	+0.042
46	United Arab Emirates	1.785	+0.099	95	Angola	2.105	−0.014
47	Kuwait	1.792	+0.141	95	Guinea-Bissau	2.105	..
48	Mozambique	1.796	−0.020	97	Cameroon	2.113	+0.012
49	Namibia	1.804	−0.039	98	Uganda	2.121	−0.032

Rank	Country	Score	Change		Rank	Country	Score	Change
99	Madagascar	2.124	−0.123		129	Honduras	2.339	+0.013
99	Tajikistan	2.124	−0.094		130	Turkey	2.344	−0.071
101	Liberia	2.131	−0.014		131	Kyrgyzstan	2.359	+0.069
102	Mali	2.132	−0.039		132	Azerbaijan	2.360	−0.009
103	Sri Lanka	2.145	−0.292		133	Philippines	2.415	−0.157
104	Republic of the Congo	2.148	−0.009		134	Côte d'Ivoire	2.419	−0.009
105	Kazakhstan	2.151	+0.007		135	Mexico	2.445	+0.092
106	Saudi Arabia	2.178	−0.003		136	Lebanon	2.459	−0.121
107	Haiti	2.179	−0.097		137	Ethiopia	2.504	+0.031
108	Cambodia	2.207	−0.085		138	Burundi	2.524	−0.005
109	Belarus	2.208	−0.080		139	Myanmar	2.525	−0.014
110	Uzbekistan	2.219	−0.017		140	Zimbabwe	2.538	−0.186
111	Egypt	2.220	+0.215		141	Georgia	2.541	−0.019
111	El Salvador	2.220	−		142	India	2.549	−0.026
113	Jamaica	2.222	−0.012		143	Yemen	2.601	−0.057
114	Benin	2.231	..		144	Colombia	2.625	−0.062
115	Armenia	2.238	−0.016		145	Chad	2.671	−0.074
116	Niger	2.241	−0.082		146	Nigeria	2.801	+0.074
117	Turkmenistan	2.242	−0.004		147	Libya	2.830	+0.037
118	Bahrain	2.247	−0.106		147	Syria	2.830	+0.523
119	Rwanda	2.250	+0.061		149	Pakistan	2.833	−0.070
120	Kenya	2.252	−0.031		150	Israel	2.842	−0.062
121	Algeria	2.255	−0.156		151	Central African Rep.	2.872	+0.022
122	Eritrea	2.264	+0.044		152	North Korea	2.932	−0.153
123	Venezuela	2.278	−0.110		153	Russia	2.938	−0.029
124	Guatemala	2.287	−0.107		154	Congo, Dem. Rep.	3.073	+0.057
125	Mauritania	2.301	−0.078		155	Iraq	3.192	−0.107
126	Thailand	2.303	+0.052		156	Sudan	3.193	−0.038
127	South Africa	2.321	−0.041		157	Afghanistan	3.252	+0.043
128	Iran	2.324	−0.036		158	Somalia	3.392	+0.021

.. = not ranked in 2011; − = no change.

Sources and methods

The GPI's 23 indicators are divided into three thematic categories: ongoing domestic and international conflict; societal safety and security; and militarization. All of the indicators are assigned a score ('banded') on a 1–5 scale. EIU country analysts score the qualitative indicators, and gaps in the quantitative data are filled by estimates. The GPI is intended to review the state of peace in countries over the period 16 March 2011–15 March 2012, but many indicators are based on available data from 2010 and 2011.

Weights are assigned to each indicator, based on their relative importance, on a 1–5 scale. Two sub-component weighted indices are then calculated from the 23 indicators: one that measures a country's level of internal peace and one that measures a country's level of external peace (its state of peace beyond its borders). The overall composite score and index are then calculated by applying a weight of 60 per cent to the measure of internal peace and 40 per cent for external peace. A heavier weight is applied to internal peace on the assumption that a greater level of internal peace is likely to correlate with a lower level of external conflict.

1. *Measures of ongoing domestic and international conflict.* The five indicators in this category are: (*a*) number of external and internal conflicts fought (from the UCDP Armed Conflict

Dataset), with weight 5; (*b*) estimated number of deaths from organized external conflict (UCDP), with weight 5; (*c*) number of deaths from organized internal conflict (International Institute for Strategic Studies, IISS, Armed Conflict Database), with weight 5; (*d*) level of organized internal conflict (EIU), with weight 5; and (*e*) relations with neighbouring countries (EIU), with weight 5.

Data reflecting a country's historical experience of domestic and international conflict is not included since the GPI uses data on ongoing intra- and interstate conflicts.

2. *Measures of societal safety and security.* The 10 indicators in this category are: (*a*) perceptions of criminality in society (EIU), with weight 3; (*b*) number of displaced people as a percentage of the population (UN High Commissioner for Refugees Statistical Yearbook and the Internal Displacement Monitoring Centre), with weight 4; (*c*) political instability (EIU), with weight 4; (*d*) political terror scale (Mark Gibney and Matthew Dalton, University of North Carolina/Amnesty International), with weight 4; (*e*) terrorist acts (IEP and Global Terrorism Database, University of Maryland)), with weight 2; (*f*) number of homicides per 100 000 people (UN Surveys on Crime Trends and the Operations of Criminal Justice Systems, CTS), with weight 4; (*g*) level of violent crime (EIU), with weight 4; (*h*) likelihood of violent demonstrations (EIU), with weight 3; (*i*) number of prisoners per 100 000 people (International Centre for Prison Studies, King's College London, World Prison Population List) with weight 3; and (*j*) number of internal security officers and police per 100 000 people (CTS), with weight 3.

3. *Measures of militarization.* The eight indicators in this category are: (*a*) military expenditure as a percentage of GDP (IISS, *The Military Balance*), with weight 2; (*b*) number of armed services personnel per 100 000 people (IISS, *The Military Balance*), with weight 2; (*c*) volume of transfers of major conventional weapons (imports) per 100 000 people (SIPRI Arms Transfers Database), with weight 2; (*d*) volume of transfers of major conventional weapons (exports) per 100 000 people (SIPRI Arms Transfers Database), with weight 3; (*e*) funding for UN peace operations (IEP), with weight 2; (*f*) aggregate weighted number of heavy weapons per 100 000 people (IEP), with weight 3; (*g*) ease of access to small arms and light weapons (EIU), with weight 3; and (*h*) military capability/sophistication (EIU), with weight 2.

This category reflects the assertion that the level of militarization and access to weapons is directly linked to how at peace a country feels internationally. Financial support to UN peace operations is considered a contribution to increasing peace.

For the precise definition of each indicator see Institute for Economics and Peace (IEP), *2012 Global Peace Index* (IEP: Sydney, 2012), annex A.

Changes to the methodology for 2012

The panel of experts that oversees the compilation of the Global Peace Index chose to include five additional countries in the 2012 edition: Benin, Djibouti, Guinea-Bissau, Lesotho and Mauritius. This brings the total coverage in the 2012 GPI to 158 states, encompassing more than 99 per cent of the world's population.

Subsequent editions of the GPI will include other states, but not microstates; the panel decided that countries in the GPI must either have a population of more than 1 million or a land area greater than 20 000 square kilometres.

The panel recommended that the Global Terrorism Database, an authoritative and up-to-date quantitative measure of terrorist acts compiled by the University of Maryland, would be a useful addition to the GPI. This year it replaces the qualitative indicator 'Likelihood of terrorist acts', which was scored by EIU analysts.

3. Peace operations and conflict management

Overview

The year 2011 was in many respects a year of contradiction for peacekeeping. On the one hand, after nearly a decade of record expansion in the numbers of operations and personnel deployed and the costs of financing these operations, peacekeeping showed initial signs of slowing down in 2010 and there were further indications in 2011 that peace operations—and in particular military-heavy, multidimensional operations—have reached a plateau. Fifty-two peace operations were active in 2011, with 262 129 personnel deployed, largely unchanged since 2010 (see section I in this chapter). New operations in Libya, South Sudan and Syria and expanded operations in the Democratic Republic of the Congo, Côte d'Ivoire, Haiti and Somalia were balanced by the closure or drawdown of missions elsewhere (see section III). On the other hand, 2011 saw the possible beginnings of a firm actionable commitment by the international community to the concepts of the responsibility to protect (R2P) and protection of civilians (POC) in relation to the conflicts in Côte d'Ivoire, Libya and Syria (see also chapter 1). Significantly, at the end of 2011 the Arab League deployed the first mission in its history, to Syria (see section II).

Several factors explain the consolidation trend of recent years. First and foremost is the global military overstretch: during the years of expansion the United Nations and other organizations had difficulty in persuading countries to contribute sufficient troops and force enablers such as helicopters. The emergence of new contributors such as Brazil, China and Indonesia, while a positive development, did not significantly fill the demand gap (as discussed in SIPRI Yearbook 2011). Certainly, the massive operations in Afghanistan and Iraq (each deploying over 100 000 personnel at its peak) amplified the demand for military personnel and diverted resources (particularly those belonging to Western states) that could have been applied to mainstream peacekeeping. However, the impending withdrawal of the International Security Assistance Force (ISAF) from Afghanistan in 2014 will not necessarily free up resources for other operations. A second factor is the ongoing global financial downturn, which had a more discernable impact on peacekeeping in 2011 as governments outlined budget cuts for their militaries and advocated leaner operations and quicker exits in multilateral frameworks such as the UN. Third, over the past decade contemporary peace operations have faced 'mission creep' in terms of the explosion of mandated tasks, which often require civilian expertise and open-ended time frames. This has led to a questioning of whether a heavy (and long-term) military footprint in peace operations is necessary.

As a result of the growing complexity of political objectives in contemporary operation mandates and the lack of civilian experts, the focus of policy discussions and development in 2010 and 2011 provided a strong impetus to develop global civilian capacities for peace operations. Additionally, the UN buttressed its mediation and conflict-prevention capacities and, when determining whether a UN peace operation was necessary or appropriate, sought alternative models to the multidimensional operations, such as the political mission in Libya (see section II).

The quest for alternate, more cost-effective models to a heavy on-the-ground military footprint may lead to future operations becoming more technology-oriented. For example, the use of drones to gather tactical information could improve force protection capabilities as well as the ability of operations to, for instance, implement POC mandates. However, access to and the transfer of technology among states remain highly political issues.

The North Atlantic Treaty Organization (NATO) operation in Libya falls outside the SIPRI definition of a peace operation (and so does not appear in the table of peace operations in section IV) but is nonetheless significant as it encapsulates the current global debate on how to demarcate the boundaries of peacekeeping. It was the first military intervention to be launched in the R2P framework and was mandated by the UN Security Council with no permanent member objecting. However, towards the end of the operation, whatever tentative consensus there had been disintegrated over the extent of the responsibility (see section II). More broadly, the NATO operation in Libya highlighted the complicated relationships and boundaries between protection of civilians in peace operations and actions undertaken to enforce peace.

SHARON WIHARTA

I. Global trends in peace operations

CLAIRE FANCHINI

A total of 52 peace operations were conducted in 2011, the same number as in 2010 and the second lowest in the period 2002–11, confirming a downward trend that started in 2009 (see figure 3.1).[1] However, the number of personnel deployed on peace operations in 2011 was the second highest of the period, at 262 129, just 700 fewer than in 2010 (see figure 3.2).[2]

The slight increases in the personnel numbers of some operations were due in part to temporary reinforcements to allow them to assist their host countries—the Democratic Republic of the Congo (DRC) and Haiti—to hold elections. These increases were balanced by decreases due to personnel withdrawals related to the actual or upcoming closure of United Nations missions in Nepal and Timor-Leste.[3] Similarly, deployments related to the launch of four new operations in 2011—the UN Interim Security Force for Abyei (UNISFA), the UN Mission in the Republic of South Sudan (UNMISS), the UN Support Mission in Libya (UNSMIL) and the Arab League Observer Mission to Syria—did not result in a net increase in personnel numbers. UNSMIL and the Arab League mission were small political or civilian operations, while most of the personnel for UNISFA and UNMISS were drawn from the UN Mission in the Sudan (UNMIS), which closed in July 2011.

The United Nations, which was responsible for 20 of the 52 peace operations in 2011 (38 per cent), remained the main conducting organization. However, just over half of the personnel deployed to peace operations worldwide—137 463 personnel (52 per cent)—were deployed to operations conducted by the North Atlantic Treaty Organization (NATO), mainly the International Security Assistance Force (ISAF) in Afghanistan, making NATO the largest conducting organization in terms of personnel deployed for the third consecutive year.[4]

---

[1] The quantitative analysis presented here draws on data collected in the SIPRI Multilateral Peace Operations Database, <http://www.sipri.org/databases/pko/>, to examine trends in peace operations in the 10-year period 2002–11. It is limited to operations that meet the SIPRI definition of peace operation. The data presented provides a snapshot of ongoing peace operations in 2011 and is meant to serve as a reference point to enable comparative analysis between 2011 and previous years.

[2] The figures for personnel deployments given in this chapter are generally estimates as of 31 Dec. 2011 or the date on which an operation terminated. They do not represent maximum numbers deployed or the total number of personnel deployed during the year.

[3] The UN Mission in Nepal (UNMIN) closed in Jan. 2011 and the UN Integrated Mission in Timor-Leste (UNMIT) is expected to close in Dec. 2012.

[4] UN figures include peace operations led by the UN Department of Peacekeeping Operations, the UN Department of Political Affairs and the African Union/UN Hybrid Operation in Darfur (UNAMID).

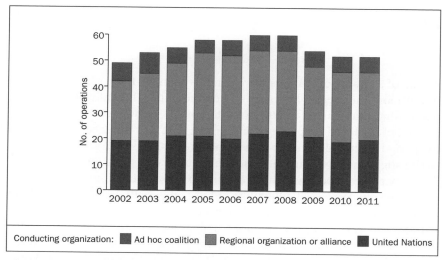

Figure 3.1. Number of multilateral peace operations, by type of conducting organization, 2002–11

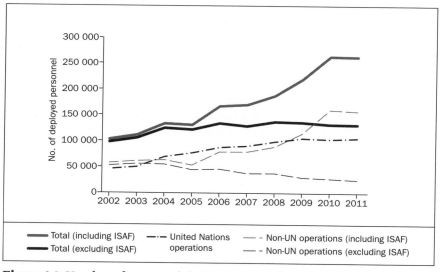

Figure 3.2. Number of personnel deployed to multilateral peace operations, 2002–11

ISAF = International Security Assistance Force

ISAF itself was the largest operation in 2011, for the third year running, with 131 386 troops deployed. The second and third largest were the African Union/UN Hybrid Operation in Darfur (UNAMID) and the UN Organization Stabilization Mission in the Democratic Republic of the Congo

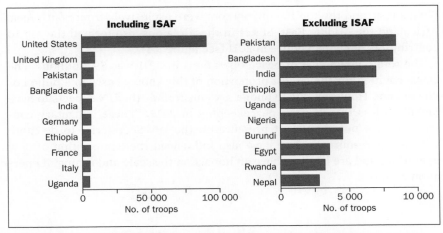

Figure 3.3. The top 10 contributors of troops to multilateral peace operations, including and excluding the International Security Assistance Force (ISAF) in Afghanistan, 2011

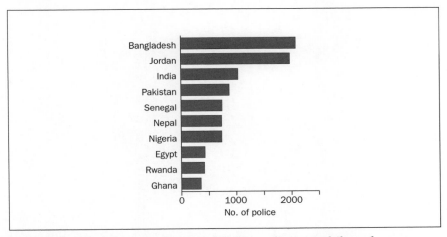

Figure 3.4. The top 10 contributors of civilian police to multilateral peace operations, 2011

(MONUSCO). Ten operations had more than 5000 personnel: seven under UN command, two under NATO command and one under African Union command.

Including ISAF, the largest contributor of troops to multilateral peace operations in 2011 was the United States, and the top 10 contributors included other, European contributors to ISAF such as the United Kingdom, Germany, France and Italy (see figure 3.3). Excluding ISAF, the picture changes: Pakistan was the largest contributor, followed closely by

Bangladesh, and the top 10 contributors were exclusively from South Asia, Africa and the Middle East. States in these regions also formed the top 10 contributors of civilian police in 2011 (see figure 3.4).

The total known cost of peace operations in 2011 was $9.8 billion.[5] The UN accounted for the largest proportion of this known cost—$7.8 billion or 80 per cent. However, due to budgetary constraints, the UN expects to have $1 billion less to spend on peacekeeping in 2012.[6] These budgetary constraints have put significant pressure on the UN Secretariat to do more with fewer resources. They have also influenced the composition of new operations and are likely to have an impact on the scale and timing of operation closures.

---

[5] The cost of most non-UN (e.g. European Union or NATO) operations does not include the cost of personnel contribution; therefore, the total known cost is a conservative estimate of the global cost of peace operations.

[6] Ladsous, H., UN Under-Secretary-General for Peacekeeping Operations, Press conference, Transcript, 8 Feb. 2012, <http://www.un.org/en/peacekeeping/articles/USG Ladsous.Transcript.PC. 08022012>.

II. New peace operations in 2011

CLAIRE FANCHINI

Sudan and South Sudan: the UN Mission in the Republic of South Sudan and the UN Interim Security Force for Abyei

South Sudan's proclamation of independence on 9 July 2011 was the culmination of a six-and-a-half-year peace process. The process began on 9 January 2005 with the signing of the Comprehensive Peace Agreement (CPA) between the Sudanese Government and the Sudan People's Liberation Movement (SPLM), ending the 28-year intrastate conflict.[1] Although almost 99 per cent of the participants in the January 2011 referendum supported independence, South Sudan was born into a complex and fragile environment. Between January and mid-May 2011, insecurity had resulted in more than 116 000 internally displaced persons in southern Sudan.[2] At the same time, humanitarian access to areas affected by conflict had been hampered. Conflict and deadly violence against large numbers of civilians persisted until early July.

South Sudan's independence also led to a significant reconfiguration of the UN presence in the former territory of Sudan. There were numerous discussions on whether the UN Mission in the Sudan (UNMIS) should essentially split into two operations, and how unresolved issues surrounding the states of Blue Nile and South Kordufan (in particular, the Abyei Area) would be treated (see figure 3.5).[3] However, immediately following the results of the referendum, the Sudanese Government signalled to the UN that it had no intention of consenting to an extension of UNMIS's mandate when it expired in July 2011.[4] It argued that, since the focus of the mandate was the implementation of the CPA and the mission's geographical focus was in what was to become South Sudan, it was no longer necessary for the UN to maintain a mission in Sudan. Sudan's opposition led to the closure of UNMIS, which represented the nominal withdrawal of over 10 000 military and police personnel and 965 international civilian personnel. In practice, the majority of the personnel were redeployed to the new UN Mission in the Republic of South Sudan (UNMISS) and to the

---

[1] Comprehensive Peace Agreement between the Government of the Republic of the Sudan and the Sudan People's Liberation Movement/Sudan People's Liberation Army, signed 9 Jan. 2009, annex to UN document S/2005/78, 10 Feb. 2005.

[2] United Nations, Security Council, Special report of the Secretary-General on the Sudan, S/2011/314, 17 May 2011.

[3] Lederer, E. M., 'UN votes to wrap up peacekeeping force monitoring 2005 Sudan peace deal', Associated Press, 11 July 2011, <http://www.680news.com/news/world/article/252442--un-votes-to-wrap-up-peacekeeping-force-monitoring-2005-sudan-peace-deal>.

[4] 'UNMIS's mandate will not be extended beyond July, Sudan says', Sudan Tribune, 15 Feb. 2011.

Figure 3.5. Map of South Sudan and Sudan

new border-monitoring mission, the UN Interim Security Force for Abyei (UNISFA).[5]

---

[5] UN Security Council Resolution 1997, 11 July 2011.

The UN Mission in the Republic of South Sudan

Planning for UNMISS was fraught with political uncertainties in the run-up to South Sudan's independence on 9 July 2011. Following several rounds of deliberation, the UN Security Council mandated UNMISS to support the South Sudanese Government in political transition and governance, and assist in security sector reform; the rule of law; disarmament, demobilization and reintegration (DDR) strategies; the protection of civilians; and conflict prevention.[6] The latter two areas of the mandate rely on the establishment and implementation of a mission-wide early-warning capacity, which in turn will rely on information sharing (gathering, monitoring, verification and dissemination) and follow-up mechanisms. The explicit inclusion of conflict prevention, in particular its early-warning component, is relatively novel.[7] UNMISS's other core responsibilities were essentially the same as UNMIS's. There were high expectations that UNMISS would be more successful in implementing its mandate than UNMIS, since the South Sudanese Government is more receptive to UNMISS's presence than the Sudanese Government was to UNMIS. However, concerns remain about the feasibility and appropriateness of the mission's DDR strategies, given that the security situation remains tense.

The new mission is only slightly smaller than its predecessor. The UN Security Council authorized a maximum of 7000 military personnel and 900 civilian police personnel and an appropriate civilian component. The appropriate size of UNMISS was apparently a point of contention among Security Council members: some thought it was relatively small given that protection of civilians was a central mandate coupled with the worsening situation in Abyei; others viewed it as disproportionately large for a country the size of South Sudan.[8] One of the key determinants of the authorized troop levels was the presence of UNISFA and its subsequent relationship with UNMISS.

The UN Interim Security Force for Abyei

The impending independence of South Sudan also led to the deterioration of the security situation along the border with Sudan and especially in the resource-rich territories on and near the border in South Kordufan (including the Abyei Area) and Blue Nile. Abyei is probably the most intractable of these heavily disputed territories, and the dispute over its future status was one of the greatest obstacles to the implementation of the CPA and a major cause of instability in the region. Competition over land

[6] UN Security Council Resolution 1996, 8 July 2011.
[7] Saferworld, 'UNMISS: A second chance for UN peacekeeping in South Sudan', *South Sudan Monitor*, Aug. 2011.
[8] 'South Sudan', *Security Council Report: Monthly Forecast*, July 2011.

ownership and use between local communities, which was intensified by the presence of high-quality oil reserves, meant that Abyei remained on the brink of conflict and resulted in serious clashes between the Sudan People's Liberation Army (SPLA) of South Sudan and the Sudanese Armed Forces.

In response to the escalation of deadly violence and population displacement in the area as South Sudan was preparing for independence, on 20 June 2011 the two parties to the CPA—facilitated by the African Union (AU) High-level Implementation Panel on Sudan, Ethiopia, UNMIS and other stakeholders—signed an agreement on the administration and security of the Abyei Area.[9] The agreement provides for the establishment of an Abyei Area Administration and for the total withdrawal and full demilitarization of all armed elements in the area. In order to support these arrangements and provide security in the Abyei Area, the parties requested that the UN deploy a peace operation.

The UN Security Council duly authorized the deployment of UNISFA on 27 June.[10] Notable elements of the mission's mandate include monitoring and verifying the redeployment of any troops of the Sudan Armed Forces or the SPLA (or its successor) from the Abyei Area; facilitating the delivery of humanitarian aid and the free movement of humanitarian personnel; and, when necessary, providing security for the region's oil infrastructure. The operation is also authorized to use force in protecting civilians and humanitarian workers in Abyei. It is comprised of a maximum of 4200 military personnel and 50 civilian police personnel and an appropriate civilian component.[11] Unlike other UN operations, only six countries have contributed to UNISFA (see table 3.2 in section IV below). It is led by Ethiopia, which provided an armoured brigade.

South Sudan's independence on 9 July 2011 transformed the nature of the dispute over the final status of Abyei and other South Sudan–Sudan border areas from an internal Sudanese matter into a bilateral concern between two sovereign states. The achievement of stable and peaceful relations between South Sudan and Sudan, as well as wider regional stability, will depend on the resolution of the Abyei issue and the broader problem of the growing militarization of the 2100 kilometre-long border.

On 30 July the South Sudanese and Sudanese governments signed an agreement on the establishment of a Joint Border Verification and Monitoring Mechanism (JBVMM), as well as a Joint Political and Security Mechanism (JPSM), to oversee the demilitarization and security of the 10-km-wide Safe Demilitarized Border Zone (SDBZ) that had been created

---

[9] Agreement between the Government of the Republic of the Sudan and the Sudan People's Liberation Movement on temporary arrangements for the administration and security of the Abyei Area, signed 20 June 2011, annex to UN document S/2011/384, 24 June 2011.

[10] UN Security Council Resolution 1990, 27 June 2011.

[11] UN Security Council Resolution 2032, 22 Dec. 2011.

on 29 June.[12] The agreement called for UNISFA's support for and protection of the monitoring teams. UN Security Council Resolution 2024 of 14 December 2011 extended UNISFA's mandate, requiring it to support the operational activities of the JBVMM in undertaking verification, investigations, monitoring, reporting and patrols, and to provide security as appropriate.[13]

Despite the successful deployment of UNMISS and UNISFA, the security situation in the border area at the end of 2011 remained of serious concern. Both the South Sudanese and Sudanese governments had yet to live up to their commitments under the 20 June agreement on Abyei, with the continued presence of security forces increasing the already considerable tension between the two countries. In December 2011 the border town of Jau was the scene of violent clashes between the Sudanese Armed Forces and the SPLA. In addition, Jungoli state in South Sudan was subjected to deadly violence for weeks on end.[14]

At the same time, the stability of the wider region was threatened, particularly in South Kordufan and Blue Nile, where a security vacuum had been created by the withdrawal of UNMIS and the Sudanese Government's ban on international aid agencies and media.[15] Many groups remain vulnerable to humanitarian crises and are victims of the escalating violence.

Libya: NATO's Operation Unified Protector and the UN Support Mission in Libya

After the successful and relatively peaceful protests in Tunisia and Egypt, the Arab Spring spread to Libya in February 2011.[16] The protests escalated rapidly, despite the violent attempts of the Libyan authorities to crush the uprising. The international community widely condemned the serious violations of human rights and international humanitarian law committed in Libya. On 20 February the European Union (EU) 'condemned the repression against peaceful demonstrators' and urged the Libyan authorities to immediately refrain from further use of violence against protesters.[17] Three

---

[12] Agreement on the Border Monitoring Support Mission between the Government of Sudan and the Government of South Sudan, signed 30 July 2011, <http://www.scribd.com/doc/61383096/Agreement-on-the-Border-Monitoring-Support-Mission>; and Agreement between the Government of the Sudan and the Government of Southern Sudan on Border Security and the Joint Political and Security Mechanism, signed 29 June 2011, <http://www.smallarmssurveysudan.org/pdfs/facts-figures/abyei/Agreement-Border-Security-JPSM-29-June-2011.pdf>.

[13] UN Security Council Resolution 2024, 14 Dec. 2011.

[14] 'South Sudan', *Security Council Report: Monthly Forecast*, Jan. 2012.

[15] Pantuliano, S., 'South Sudan: referendum—one year on', AllAfrica, 13 Jan. 2012, <http://allafrica.com/stories/201201131008.html>.

[16] On the conflict in Libya see also chapter 2, section I, in this volume.

[17] European Union, 'Declaration by the High Representative, Catherine Ashton, on behalf of the European Union on events in Libya', 6795/1/11, 20 Feb. 2011, <http://www.consilium.europa.eu/uedocs/cms_data/docs/pressdata/en/cfsp/119397.pdf>.

days later, the AU also condemned the crackdown, despite the extensive influence of the Libyan leader, Muammar Gaddafi, over the organization.[18] On 26 February the UN Security Council, through Resolution 1970, imposed an arms embargo.[19] However, despite repeated condemnations and sanctions, the situation deteriorated, resulting in heavy civilian casualties. On 8 March the Gulf Cooperation Council (GCC) called on the UN Security Council to impose a no-fly zone over Libya and the Arab League followed suit on 12 March.[20]

On 17 March, after Gaddafi indicated in a radio address to Benghazi residents that his armed forces would search every house in the opposition stronghold that night and show 'no mercy' to fighters who resisted them, and in response to the calls from the Arab League and the GCC, the UN Security Council adopted Resolution 1973. The resolution established the legal basis for military intervention in the Libyan conflict, authorizing the international community to use all means necessary to protect Libyan civilians and to implement a no-fly zone.[21] Resolution 1973 was unusual in several respects. First, its calling for a military intervention 'to protect civilians and civilian populated areas under threat of attack' led some observers to assert that it was the first time that the UN had referred to the 'responsibility to protect' (R2P) framework since its adoption of Resolution 1706 on the situation in Darfur, Sudan, on 31 August 2006.[22] Second, the resolution was adopted by a vote of 10 in favour to none against, with China and Russia, which could have vetoed it, among the five abstentions.

NATO and Libya: Operation Unified Protector

NATO responded to the UN resolution by launching Operation Unified Protector (OUP) on 22 March 2011.[23] On 31 March, NATO took control of

---

[18] African Union, Peace and Security Council, 261st Meeting, Communiqué on the situation in Libya, 23 Feb. 2011.

[19] UN Security Council Resolution 1970, 26 Feb. 2011. See also chapter 10, section III, in this volume.

[20] Joint Statement of the Joint Ministerial Meeting on the Strategic Dialogue between the countries of the Cooperation Council for the Arab Gulf States and Australia, Gulf Cooperation Council, 8 Mar. 2011, <http://www.gcc-sg.org/indexc23e.html?action=News&Sub=ShowOne&ID=1919> (in Arabic), para. 3; Australian Minister for Foreign Affairs, 'First Joint Ministerial Meeting on GCC–Australia Strategic Dialogue', Communiqué, 8 Mar. 2011, <http://www.foreignminister.gov.au/releases/2011/kr_mr_110308c.html>; and Leiby, R. and Mansour M., 'Arab League asks U.N. for no-fly zone over Libya', *Washington Post*, 12 Mar. 2011.

[21] UN Security Council Resolution 1973, 17 Mar. 2011; and Reuters, 'Gaddafi tells rebel city, Benghazi, "We will show no mercy"', Huffington Post, 17 Mar. 2011, <http://www.huffingtonpost.com/2011/03/17/gaddafi-benghazi-libya-news_n_837245.html>.

[22] International Coalition for the Responsibility to Protect, 'The crisis in Libya', <http://www.responsibilitytoprotect.org/index.php/crises/crisis-in-libya>. On the R2P principle see chapter 1 in this volume.

[23] Note that NATO's Operation Unified Protector does not meet SIPRI's definition of a peace operation (see section IV below) since it did not serve as an instrument to facilitate the implementation of a peace agreement (as there was no peace agreement in place); it was not mandated to support a peace operation; and it did not assist with conflict-prevention or peacebuilding efforts in the

all military operations in Libya under UN Security Council resolutions and was therefore charged with the enforcement of the arms embargo, the enforcement of the no-fly zone and the protection of civilians from attack or the threat of attack. The operation was carried out by air and sea, while, in accordance with the terms of Resolution 1973, forces on the ground only played a support role. OUP, far from being a purely defensive operation, consisted of daily air strikes across the country targeting Libyan Government ground forces, air defences, artillery, rocket launchers, command-and-control centres, radar systems, military bases, bunkers, ammunition storage sites, logistical targets and missile storage sites. NATO also used aircraft and warships to enforce a naval blockade of Libya. The approaches to Libyan territorial waters were patrolled and NATO forces worked to interdict ships and aircraft carrying weapons or mercenaries. At its peak, OUP used over 260 air assets—which flew over 26 500 sorties, including over 9700 strike sorties—and 21 naval assets, with the support of approximately 8000 troops.[24]

Members of the international community and civil society organizations actively challenged the way in which OUP was conducted, with some accusing NATO of not only interpreting Resolution 1973 in the broadest sense but also acting above and beyond its mandate.[25] In June 2011 leaders of several African states, along with China and Russia, demanded an immediate end to NATO's bombing campaign in Libya.[26] However, the case could also be made that the UN had deliberately granted wide powers to the operation as it was relying on NATO to make up for its own lack of military forces. Indeed, in late August as the UN was envisaging deploying a mission in Libya, the Special Adviser to the Secretary-General on Post-conflict Planning for Libya, Ian Martin, asserted in a leaked report that the military support required in order to stabilize Tripoli would remain

country. It is thus not included in the table of peace operations for 2011 in section IV and is excluded from the statistics presented in sections I and III.

[24] 'Air assets' refers to fighter aircraft, surveillance and reconnaissance aircraft, air-to-air refuellers, unmanned aerial vehicles and attack helicopters. 'Naval assets' refers to supply ships, frigates, destroyers, submarines, amphibious assault ships and aircraft carriers. North Atlantic Treaty Organization (NATO), 'Operation Unified Protector: final mission stats', Fact sheet, 2 Nov. 2011, <http://www.nato.int/cps/en/natolive/71679.htm>.

[25] 'More countries slam NATO action in Libya', ABC Radio Australia, 29 Mar. 2011, <http://www.radioaustralia.net.au/asiapac/stories/201103/s3177136.htm>; and Agence France-Presse, 'L'Otan outrepasse le mandat de l'ONU en Libya, affirme Moscou' [NATO goes beyond the mandate of the UN in Libya, says Moscow], France 24, 15 Apr. 2011, <http://www.france24.com/fr/20110415-russie-libye-crise-actions-otan-outrepassent-mandat-onu-nations-unies-resolution-diplomatie>.

[26] E.g. South African President Jacob Zuma stated on 14 June 2011 that the UN resolution authorizing military action was being abused for regime change, political assassinations and foreign military occupation. 'African leaders demand halt to NATO bombing campaign in Libya', Bloomberg, 15 June 2011, <http://www.bloomberg.com/news/2011-06-15/african-leaders-demand-halt-to-nato-bombing-campaign-in-libya.html>.

NATO's responsibility.[27] Martin also stated that if UN military observers needed military protection, this protection would have to come from a source other than a UN contingent, given the lengthy time needed for the UN to generate and deploy troops.

Despite the mixed reaction to the way the operation was conducted, NATO's intervention was a turning point in the conflict as it managed to galvanize rebel forces struggling against the Gaddafi regime's superior resources.

Following the opposition's capture of most strategic towns and locations, the widespread international recognition of the National Transitional Council (NTC) as the legitimate new representative of the Libyan people, the killing, defection or capture of a large part of the Gaddafi regime and family, and finally Gaddafi's death on 20 October 2011, NATO declared that it had, with the support of its partners, successfully implemented the UN mandate to protect the people of Libya and that it would terminate its operation in coordination with the UN and the NTC.[28] At a meeting of NATO defence ministers on 6 October the guidelines for determining when to terminate the operation were agreed as follows: the operation would end when Gaddafi and his regime no longer threatened the security of the Libyan people and the NTC would be able to provide for their security.[29]

On 27 October the UN Security Council, taking note of the NTC's 'Declaration of Liberation' of Libya on 23 October, decided to end the authorization for a no-fly zone, as well as the action to protect civilians, as of 31 October.[30] Operation Unified Protector thus ended after seven months of its sea and air operation.

The UN and Libya: the UN Support Mission in Libya

Concurrent to the NATO deployment, the UN Secretary-General, Ban Ki-moon, had appointed Ian Martin as Special Adviser on Post-conflict Planning for Libya, charging him with determining whether the UN could and would have a role in post-conflict Libya. As part of his mandate, in April 2011 Martin led a UN integrated pre-assessment process for post-conflict planning for Libya. He met with several UN agencies, funds and programmes as well as the World Bank and the International Organization for Migration and, later in the process, consulted with the new Libyan

---

[27] Martin, I., 'United Nations post-conflict deployment to Libya', Introductory note to the Consolidated report of the integrated pre-assessment process for Libya post-conflict planning, 22 Aug. 2011, <http://www.innercitypress.com/martin1unlibya1icp.pdf>.

[28] North Atlantic Treaty Organization (NATO), 'Statement by the NATO Secretary General on Libya', Press Release 128, 20 Oct. 2011, <http://www.nato.int/cps/en/SID-27364A7E-5456866F/nato live/news_79742.htm?mode=pressrelease>.

[29] North Atlantic Treat Organization (NATO), 'NATO and Libya—Operation Unified Protector: Ending the mission', [n.d.], <http://www.nato.int/cps/en/natolive/topics_71652.htm>.

[30] UN Security Council Resolution 2016, 27 Oct. 2011.

transitional authorities on areas in which they would like to receive UN support. On 16 September 2011, responding to the NTC's formal request for assistance from the UN, the UN Security Council established the United Nations Support Mission in Libya (UNSMIL).[31]

UNSMIL is essentially tasked with assisting the new Libyan authorities in restoring public security and the rule of law; promoting inclusive political dialogue and national reconciliation; and supporting the NTC as it embarks on the drafting of a new constitution and preparing for elections. Following Gaddafi's death, the NTC announced that it intended to organize elections within eight months.[32] Ban considered this to be a 'challenging timeline in a country where there has been limited or no electoral experience in over 45 years'.[33]

Regardless of the timeline, UNSMIL was initially established for a period of three months in order to give the UN the opportunity to continue its discussions with the Libyan transitional authorities on longer-term UN support, while delivering urgent initial advice and assistance.[34] The Libyan transitional authorities were expected to engage in defining the needs and wishes of Libya for the scope and nature of UN support beyond this initial phase. The Security Council subsequently extended UNSMIL's mandate for an additional three months, 'as the prolongation of the conflict had delayed the formation of the interim Government and other developments essential for the dialogue and assessment of needs required for mission planning'.[35] The resolution also broadened the mandate of UNSMIL to include assisting and supporting Libyan national efforts to prevent the proliferation of arms, especially from Libya. In doing so, it sought to address the risks of destabilization that Libya posed in the Sahel region; its potential fuelling of terrorist activities in the broader North Africa region; and its potential impact on regional and international peace and security. In mid-December 2011 well over a hundred Libyan militias had a total of 125 000 armed members.[36] Considering UNSMIL's broad and exacting mandate, its further extension is highly likely.

---

[31] 'Libya', *Security Council Report: Monthly Forecast*, Oct. 2011; and UN Security Council Resolution 2009, 16 Sep. 2011.

[32] 'Libya's Jibril sees elections within eight months', Reuters, 22 Oct. 2011, <http://www.reuters.com/article/2011/10/22/us-libya-elections-idUSTRE79LOLD20111022>.

[33] United Nations, Security Council, Report of the Secretary-General on the United Nations Support Mission in Libya, S/2011/727, 22 Nov. 2011.

[34] 'Security Council mulls resolution on potential UN mission for Libya', UN News Centre, 9 Sep. 2011, <http://www.un.org/apps/news/story.asp?NewsID=39497&Cr=libya&Cr1>.

[35] UN Security Council Resolution 2022, 2 Dec. 2011; and United Nations (note 33).

[36] International Crisis Group, 'Holding Libya together: security challenges after Qadhafi', Press release, 14 Dec. 2011, <http://www.crisisgroup.org/en/publication-type/media-releases/2011/mena/holding-libya-together-security-challenges-after-qadhafi.aspx>.

Syria: the Arab League Observer Mission to Syria[37]

The Arab League played a central role in attempts to address the conflicts related to the Arab Spring in 2011. Its adamant support for external military intervention in Libya came as a surprise to many observers. As the Libyan conflict worsened and the UN remained paralysed, the Arab League became a critical actor.

The Arab League expressed its first forceful condemnation of the violent repression of protests in Syria in August 2011.[38] Following a series of diplomatic démarches, it finally adopted an Arab Plan of Action on 2 November 2011, with the agreement of the Syrian Government.[39] The Arab League's peace plan attempted to facilitate a resolution to the Syrian uprising and protect civilians. It called on the Syrian Government to halt the violence directed at civilians, to withdraw all its security forces from civilian areas and to release tens of thousands of political prisoners.[40] A key aspect of the plan was the Arab League's demand for its immediate implementation.[41] However, the Syrian Government's failure to comply with this demand resulted in the Arab League suspending Syria's membership and imposing economic sanctions on 12 November.[42]

On 19 December 2011 the Syrian Government finally acquiesced and signed a protocol on the plan with the Arab League, including the deployment of the Arab League Observer Mission to Syria. By signing the protocol the Syrian Government agreed to fully cooperate with the mission; provide free movement in Syria to both observers and approved media; and assist the observers by providing necessary support. Approximately 150 observers (down from the initial 500 proposed by the Arab League) were to be deployed within a week of the signing of the protocol, with a limited mandate of one month.[43] Syria reportedly made the deployment conditional on a reduced number of observers and coordination of their activities with the

---

[37] Xenia Avezov, SIPRI Intern, assisted in the writing of this subsection.

[38] International Freedom of Expression Exchange, 'Arab League breaks its silence and condemns Assad's massacre of protesters; journalists disappear', 17 Aug. 2011, <http://www.ifex.org/syria/2011/08/17/arab_league_speaks_out/>.

[39] The plan of action is annexed to Arab League Council Resolution 7436, 2 Nov. 2011 (in Arabic). See also 'Syria accepts Arab League peace plan after Cairo talks', BBC News, 2 Nov. 2011, <http://www.bbc.co.uk/news/world-middle-east-15560322>.

[40] MacFarquhar, N., 'Arab League votes to suspend Syria over crackdown', New York Times, 12 Nov. 2011.

[41] Black, I., 'Syrian acceptance of Arab League ceasefire plan met with scepticism', The Guardian, 2 Nov. 2011.

[42] 'Syria calls Arab League decision to suspend its membership "violation of charter"', Al Arabiya News, 12 Nov. 2011, <http://english.alarabiya.net/articles/2011/11/12/176668.html>; and Mac-Farquhar, N. and Bakri, N., 'Isolating Syria, Arab League imposes broad sanctions', New York Times, 27 Nov. 2011.

[43] 'Syria unrest: Arab League monitors' advance team arrives', BBC News, 22 Dec. 2011, <http://www.bbc.co.uk/news/world-middle-east-16296255>.

government.[44] The observers were posted in 20 cities—with a concentration in high-conflict areas including Damascus, Homs, Rif Homs, Idlib, Dará and Hamah—in order to monitor and observe any cessation of violence. The mission was also mandated to ensure that the Syrian security services 'and so-called shabiha gangs do not obstruct peaceful demonstrations', and to verify the withdrawal of the military from residential areas and the release of detainees.[45]

However, from the start of its deployment, the mission was unable to effectively carry out its mandate and quickly became mired in controversy and criticism.[46] On 28 January 2012 the Arab League Observer Mission to Syria suspended its operations due to an escalation of violence against civilians and observers. On 12 February 2012 the Arab League proposed a joint peacekeeping mission with the UN to supervise the ceasefire process in Syria. The proposal drew support from the United States, European powers and Turkey but was opposed by Russia and China. Finally, on 14 April 2012, the UN Security Council voted unanimously to authorize a UN observer mission to monitor the ceasefire.[47]

Conclusions

The criticism of the way in which OUP was conducted and the international community's hesitation over the Syria crisis highlight the differences that exist between countries and regions on how R2P principles should be implemented. Despite these differences, both the international community's call for military intervention to protect the Libyan people and the UN's use of R2P principles in Resolution 1973 in order to provide a legal basis for this military intervention suggest that a consensus is forming around these principles.

While it is unlikely that future operations will adopt the OUP model wholesale, elements of it may be used for similar operations. For example, future operations may become increasingly dependent on air support for the protection of civilians. Peacekeeping is in a state of flux and the boundaries between humanitarian and military intervention and peace operations have been eroded and blurred.

[44] 'Negotiations on Syria Draft Resolution', What's in Blue blog, Security Council Report, 22 Dec. 2011, <http://whatsinblue.org/2011/12/negotiations-on-syria-draft-resolution.php>.

[45] Arab League, Report of the Head of the League of Arab States Observer Mission to Syria for the period from 24 December 2011 to 18 January 2012, English translation available at e.g. <http://un-report.blogspot.se/2012/02/al-dabis-report-on-arab-league-observer.html>.

[46] Fahim, K., 'Chief of Arab League's mission in Syria is lightning rod for criticism', New York Times, 2 Jan. 2012.

[47] UN Security Council Resolution 2042, 14 Apr. 2012; and United Nations, Security Council, 'Security Council unanimously adopts Resolution 2042 (2012), authorizing advance team to monitor ceasefire in Syria', Press Release SC/10609, 14 Apr. 2012, <http://www.un.org/News/Press/docs/2012/sc10609.doc.htm>.

III. Regional developments in peace operations

CLAIRE FANCHINI

Africa

As in preceding years, the largest concentration of peace operations in 2011 was in Africa: there were 16 operations in the region, most under the command of the United Nations, with a total of approximately 87 000 personnel, of which 83 000 were troops and civilian police and the remaining 4000 were civilian staff (see table 3.1). The number of operations deployed in Africa was unchanged from 2010. While three operations closed in 2011, three of the four new operations—the UN Interim Security Force for Abyei (UNISFA), the UN Mission in the Republic of South Sudan (UNMISS) and the UN Support Mission in Libya (UNSMIL)—are located in Africa. The deployment of UNISFA and UNMISS, which have significant military components, did not lead to a significant increase in personnel numbers as the two new operations in Sudan and South Sudan were mostly composed of personnel transferred from the UN Mission in the Sudan (UNMIS) after its closure in July 2011.

The rise in personnel numbers in the region was linked to the expansion of the African Union (AU) Mission in Somalia (AMISOM)—which had been authorized in 2010 but did not take effect until 2011—and the temporary reinforcement of the UN Operation in Côte d'Ivoire (UNOCI). Developments related to these two operations in 2011 are outlined below.

The AU Mission in Somalia

In December 2010, as the civil war in Somalia led to further deterioration of the security and humanitarian situation, the UN Security Council endorsed the AU's proposal to increase AMISOM's force strength from 8000 to 12 000 troops.[1] However, by December 2011 the AU had only generated an additional 2000 troops, to reach a force strength of 9800 troops. The gap between the authorized strength and the actual number of troops deployed is partly due to the technical and financial incapacities of AU member states but also points to contributing countries' reluctance to expose their soldiers to the constant attacks of Harakat al-Shabab al-Mujahideen (Mujahedin Youth Movement, or al-Shabab).[2] In 2011 AMISOM suffered 94 fatalities, making it the operation with the

---

[1] UN Security Council Resolution 1964, 22 Dec. 2010. On the conflicts in Somalia and their links to conflicts across the Horn of Africa see chapter 2, section II, in this volume.

[2] United Nations, Security Council, Letter dated 18 July 2011 from the Chairman of the Security Council Committee pursuant to resolutions 751 (1992) and 1907 (2009) concerning Somalia and Eritrea addressed to the President of the Security Council, S/2011/433, 18 July 2011.

second highest number of fatalities, for the third consecutive year, after the International Security Assistance Force (ISAF) in Afghanistan.

Despite the fact that AMISOM had not reached its authorized strength in 2011, the AU proposed raising the authorized level to 17 000 troops as it considered the mission too small in size to fulfil its mandate.[3] It also requested that the UN increase its financial support from UN assessed contributions. One reason for the AU's proposal to increase the authorized strength may have been the presence of Kenyan troops in southern Somalia. In October, with the agreement of the Transitional Federal Government (TFG) of Somalia, Kenya launched a unilateral operation against al-Shabab. There are indications that the Kenyan troops may be incorporated into AMISOM in 2012.[4]

The first tangible results of the EU Training Mission in Somalia (EUTM), which was launched in 2010, were seen in 2011 with the deployment of the first batch of Somali troops under AMISOM command. However, despite this short-term achievement at the operational level, questions were raised as to the appropriateness and strategic value of the mission given the fragility of the TFG's legitimacy and the lack of a functioning government in Somalia.[5] Notwithstanding these concerns, in July 2011 the Council of the European Union approved a 12-month extension of EUTM's mandate, to December 2012.[6]

The UN Operation in Côte d'Ivoire

The political stand-off between the incumbent Ivorian president, Laurent Gbagbo, and Alassane Ouattara, a former prime minister and the declared winner of the November 2010 presidential election, erupted into violent clashes between their supporters and continued into 2011. Deeply concerned over the ongoing violence and human rights violations in the country, including against UN peacekeeping personnel, the UN Security Council agreed on 19 January 2011 to deploy an additional 2000 military personnel to UNOCI until 30 June 2011.[7]

However, the security situation continued to deteriorate, with clashes taking place in both Abidjan and the rest of the country, especially in the west. This intense fighting escalated the use, by both sides, of heavy weapons—including mortars, rocket-propelled grenades and heavy

[3] African Union, Peace and Security Council, 306th meeting, Communiqué on the situation in Somalia, 6 Jan. 2012.

[4] International Crisis Group (ICG), *The Kenyan Military Intervention in Somalia*, Crisis Group Africa Report no. 184 (ICG: Nairobi, 15 Feb. 2012).

[5] Oksamytna, K., *The European Union Training Mission in Somalia: Lessons Learnt for EU Security Sector Reform*, Istituto Affari Internazionali (IAI) Working Papers 1116 (IAI: Rome, June 2011).

[6] Council Decision 2011/483/CFSP of 28 July 2011 amending and extending Decision 2010/96/CFSP on a European Union military mission to contribute to the training of Somali security forces (EUTM Somalia), *Official Journal of the European Union*, L198, 30 July 2011.

[7] UN Security Council Resolution 1967, 19 Jan. 2011.

Table 3.1. Number of peace operations and personnel deployed, by region and type of organization, 2011

Conducting organization	Africa	Americas	Asia and Oceania	Europe	Middle East	World
United Nations[a]	10	1	3	2	4	20
Regional organization or alliance	5	1	2	13	5	26
Ad hoc coalition	1	–	3	–	2	6
Total operations	**16**	**2**	**8**	**15**	**11**	**52**
Total personnel	**86 642**	**12 201**	**134 727**[b]	**11 932**	**16 627**	**262 129**[b]

[a] United Nations figures include peace operations led by the UN Department of Peacekeeping Operations, the UN Department of Political Affairs and the African Union/UN Hybrid Operation in Darfur (UNAMID).

[b] These figures include the International Security Assistance Force (ISAF) in Afghanistan, which had 131 386 troops in 2011.

Source: SIPRI Multilateral Peace Operations Database, <http://www.sipri.org/databases/pko/>.

machine guns—against the civilian population, and also resulted in intensified attacks on UNOCI. On 30 March 2011 the UN Security Council called for UNOCI to 'use all necessary means to carry out its mandate to protect civilians under imminent threat of physical violence'.[8] Thus, in early April, with the support of French troops from Operation Licorne, UNOCI attacked military camps of pro-Gbagbo forces and the presidential palace.

Following the arrest of Gbagbo on 11 April 2011 and the installation of Ouattara as president, UNOCI was tasked with assisting the new Ivorian Government in disarming and demobilizing illegal armed groups.[9] Although the security situation had improved, the UN Security Council decided to prolong the deployment of UNOCI and Operation Licorne until 30 July 2012 and to maintain UNOCI at the authorized strength of 9800 troops and observers and 1350 civilian police, while reducing Operation Licorne's size by half, to 450 troops.[10]

The Americas

The UN Stabilization Mission in Haiti (MINUSTAH)—the biggest of the two operations deployed in the Americas—operated at a reinforced authorized strength of 12 500 personnel (including an additional 1900 troops and 1600 police) for most of 2011, in part to complete post-earthquake recon-

[8] UN Security Council Resolution 1975, 30 Mar. 2011.
[9] UN Security Council Resolution 1980, 28 Apr. 2011.
[10] UN Security Council Resolution 2000, 27 July 2011.

struction activities but also to support the electoral process.[11] However, given the relatively calm security situation, the UN Security Council, during its annual discussion on MINUSTAH's mandate extension, decided to reduce the total number of military and police personnel to 10 600.[12] MINUSTAH's mandate renewal became a subject of serious debate and protest within the Haitian community as allegations (and video clips) of Uruguayan soldiers involved in the sexual abuse of a young Haitian surfaced on the Internet and as Nepalese peacekeepers were accused of being the cause of a cholera outbreak in the country.[13] The legitimacy of the operation, dependent partly on its moral authority, had been undermined to an extent by the conduct of its personnel.[14]

Asia and Oceania

Eight peace operations were active in Asia and Oceania in 2011, with a total of 135 000 personnel deployed (see table 3.1). This represented one fewer operation than in 2010 and a slight decrease in the total number of personnel. The International Security Assistance Force (ISAF) in Afghanistan continued to account for the overwhelming majority of personnel deployed in the region and made Asia the region with the most peacekeeping personnel. In line with the overall global trend of consolidation, 2011 was marked by crucial transition-related developments and planned withdrawals for two operations in Asia: the UN Integrated Mission in Timor-Leste (UNMIT) and ISAF.

In the case of Timor-Leste, a first step towards the long-planned withdrawal of peacekeepers was the transfer of executive responsibility for the conduct, command and control of all police operations from UNMIT to the East Timorese National Police in March 2011. In September 2011 the East Timorese Government and UNMIT signed the Joint Transition Plan for UNMIT's closure in December 2012. The plan envisages the early transfer of some UNMIT equipment to national authorities, allowing them to familiarize themselves with its use and maintenance while the mission is still in place and able to provide assistance. UNMIT will continue to provide a high level of support in the first half of 2012, around and during the presidential and parliamentary elections, after which the UNMIT police component and military liaison officers will begin to gradually

---

[11] These figures are as of 31 Oct. 2011.

[12] UN Security Council Resolution 2012, 14 Oct. 2011. Accordingly, and as recommended by the UN Secretary-General, military troops will be reduced from 8940 to 7340 and police from 4391 to 3241. United Nations, Security Council, Report of the Secretary-General on the United Nations Stabilization Mission in Haiti, S/2011/540, 25 Aug. 2011.

[13] 'Haiti: UN troops must go, say Haitians after rape scandal', GlobalVoices, 9 Sep. 2011, <http://globalvoicesonline.org/2011/09/09/haiti-un-troops-must-go-say-haitians-after-rape-scandal/>.

[14] See also Wiharta, S., 'The legitimacy of peace operations', SIPRI Yearbook 2009.

downsize.[15] The plan also sets out different models for a post-UNMIT UN presence and engagement in Timor-Leste.[16]

Europe

There were 15 peace operations in Europe in 2011, the same as in 2010, while the total number of personnel deployed to the region fell from 15 000 in 2010 to 12 000 in 2011 (see table 3.1) owing to the phased drawdown strategy of the NATO-led Kosovo Force (KFOR).

KFOR's strategy envisaged that the operation would reach the third phase of troop reduction to a level of 5000 personnel by its 12th year, 2011, with the eventual goal of a minimal 'deterrent' presence if the political and security conditions allowed. However, some countries found the downsizing plan to be overly cautious and drawn-out, and there were indications of mission fatigue as early as 2009 as these countries declared end dates for their withdrawals.[17] Nevertheless, although the third phase was achieved in March 2011, clashes between Serbs and Kosovan police forces at the end of 2011 resulted in KFOR having to raise its troop level to 6700, perhaps reaffirming NATO's argument for a cautious transition strategy for KFOR.[18]

The Middle East

The Arab League's deployment of an observer mission to Syria, albeit briefly, was perhaps one of the most significant developments for peacekeeping in 2011 (see section II). This was the first time in the Arab League's history that it had conducted a peace operation.

Another significant development was that, after nine years of operation, the Multinational Force–Iraq (MNF-I) ended its mission on 18 December 2011.[19] MNF-I had a total budget of $6.8 billion dollars and, at its peak, comprised over 183 000 military personnel from approximately 30 countries.[20] MNF-I is a prime example of how peace operations evolve over the course of their mandate and how the lines between a robust peace operation and a combat operation have been blurred as a result of the USA's

[15] United Nations, Security Council, Report of the Secretary-General on the United Nations Integrated Mission in Timor-Leste (for the period from 20 September 2011 to 6 January 2012), S/2012/43, 18 Jan. 2012.

[16] United Nations (note 15).

[17] US Mission to NATO, 'NAC stresses that KFOR drawdown must remain conditions-based', Cable to US State Department, no. 09USNATO409, 25 Sep. 2009, <http://wikileaks.ch/cable/2009/09/09USNATO409.html>.

[18] Nativi, A., 'NATO updates plans for Kosovo draw down', Aviation Week, 10 Feb. 2012.

[19] The Multinational Force in Iraq (MNF-I) was established by UN Security Council Resolution 1511 in 2003. On 1 Jan. 2010, MNF-I transformed into USF-I on the basis of a bilateral security framework agreement between the USA and Iraq. See also note 21 below.

[20] On the total cost of the war in Iraq see chapter 4, section II, in this volume.

'global war on terrorism'.[21] MNF-I, ISAF and, more recently, Operation Unified Protector in Libya have undoubtedly affected host populations' perceptions of peacekeeping. More importantly, they have influenced the way in which peacekeeping is carried out; for example, while there is now arguably a greater disposition to use force, strategies for 'winning the hearts and minds' are being introduced to gain local acceptance and legitimacy through the use of quick impact projects or provincial reconstruction teams.[22] The deployment of MNF-I and ISAF has also taken a toll on peacekeeping resources, as Western countries have diverted both military and financial resources to these missions. The full impact of MNF-I will probably not be known for several years.

---

[21] In some previous editions of the SIPRI Yearbook, MNF-I was classified as a peace operation (although its activities included counterinsurgency) and it appeared in the tables of multilateral peace operations for 2003–2006. MNF-I was excluded from the table from 2006 onwards, after a review, because its focus had largely shifted from peacekeeping to counterinsurgency and it thus no longer met SIPRI's definition of a peace operation.

[22] Wiharta, S., 'Peacekeeping: keeping pace with changes in conflict', *SIPRI Yearbook 2006*, pp. 107–28.

IV. Table of multilateral peace operations, 2011

CLAIRE FANCHINI[1]

Table 3.2 provides data on the 52 multilateral peace operations that were conducted during 2011, including operations that were launched or terminated during the year. By definition, a peace operation must have the stated intention of (a) serving as an instrument to facilitate the implementation of peace agreements already in place, (b) supporting a peace process or (c) assisting conflict-prevention or peacebuilding efforts.

SIPRI follows the United Nations Department of Peacekeeping Operations (DPKO) description of peacekeeping as a mechanism to assist conflict-afflicted countries to create conditions for sustainable peace. Peacekeeping tasks may include monitoring and observing ceasefire agreements; serving as confidence-building measures; protecting the delivery of humanitarian assistance; assisting with the demobilization and reintegration processes; strengthening institutional capacities in the areas of the judiciary and the rule of law (including penal institutions), policing, and human rights; electoral support; and economic and social development. Table 3.2 thus covers a broad range of peace operations, reflecting the growing complexity of operation mandates and the potential for operations to change over time. The table does not include good offices, fact-finding or electoral assistance missions, nor does it include peace operations comprising non-resident individuals or teams of negotiators, or operations not sanctioned by the UN.

The table lists operations that were conducted under the authority of the UN, operations conducted by regional organizations and alliances, and operations conducted by ad hoc (non-standing) coalitions of states that were sanctioned by the UN or authorized by a UN Security Council resolution. UN operations are divided into three subgroups: (a) observer and multidimensional peace operations run by the DPKO, (b) special political and peacebuilding missions, and (c) the joint African Union/UN Hybrid Operation in Darfur (UNAMID).

The table draws on the SIPRI Multilateral Peace Operations Database, <http://www.sipri.org/databases/pko>, which provides information on all UN and non-UN peace operations conducted since 2000, including location, dates of deployment and operation, mandate, participating countries, number of personnel, costs and fatalities.

---

[1] Xenia Avezov, SIPRI Intern, assisted in the compilation of table 3.2.

Table 3.2. Multilateral peace operations, 2011

New states joining an existing operation in 2011 are shown in bold type. Individual state participation that ended in 2011 is shown in italic type. Where operations were launched in 2011 the legal instrument is shown in bold type. Where operations closed in 2011 the legal instrument is shown in italic type. Designated lead states (i.e. those that either have operational control or contribute the most personnel) are underlined for operations that have a police or military component.

Legal instrument/ Deployment date/ Location	Countries contributing troops, observers (Obs.), civilian police (Civ. pol.) and civilian staff (Civ. staff) in 2011	Troops/Obs./ Civ. pol./Civ. staff		Deaths: to date/ 2011/ (by cause^a)	Cost ($ m.): 2011/ unpaid
		Approved	Actual		
United Nations (UN) **Total: 15 operations**	115 contributing countries*	73 091** 1 528** 10 045** 4 119**	64 599** 1 700** 9 350** 4 339**	1 350 88	5 528.9 1 071.1

* Due to the unavailability of data on the nationalities of civilian staff for special political and peacebuilding missions, this figure only includes countries deploying uniformed personnel to UN Department of Peacekeeping Operations (DPKO) operations during 2011.

** To avoid double counting, since most of the personnel of the UN Interim Security Force for Abyei (UNISFA) and of the UN Mission in the Republic of South Sudan (UNMISS) were drawn from the UN Mission in the Sudan (UNMIS) that closed in July 2011, these totals do not include UNMIS personnel.

UN Truce Supervision Organization (UNTSO)

UNTSO was established by SCR 50 (29 May 1948) and mandated to assist the Mediator and the Truce Commission in supervising the truce in Palestine after the 1948 Arab–Israeli War. In subsequent years it also assisted in observing the General Armistice Agreement of 1949 and the ceasefires in the aftermath of the 1967 Six-Day War. UNTSO cooperates with UNDOF and UNIFIL. A positive decision by the UN Security Council is required to terminate the operation.

SCR 50	Obs.: Argentina, <u>Australia</u>, Austria, Belgium, Canada, Chile, China, Denmark,	–	–	50	30.3
June 1948	Estonia, <u>Finland</u>, France, Ireland, Italy, *Malawi*, Nepal, Netherlands, New	150	150	–	–
Egypt, Israel,	Zealand, Norway, Russia, Slovakia, Slovenia, Sweden, Switzerland, USA	–	–		
Lebanon, Syria		120	101*		

* The operation is supported by 132 locally recruited staff.

Legal instrument/ Deployment date/ Location	Countries contributing troops, observers (Obs.), civilian police (Civ. pol.) and civilian staff (Civ. staff) in 2011	Troops/Obs./ Civ. pol./Civ. staff		Deaths: to date/ 2011/ (by cause^a)	Cost ($ m.)/ 2011/ unpaid
		Approved	Actual		

UN Military Observer Group in India and Pakistan (UNMOGIP)

UNMOGIP was established by SCR 91 (30 Mar. 1951) and mandated to supervise the ceasefire in Kashmir under the Karachi Agreement (July 1949). A positive decision by the UN Security Council is required to terminate the operation.

SCR 91	Obs.: Chile, Croatia, Finland, Italy, Korea (South), Philippines, Sweden,	–	–	11	8.1
Mar. 1951	Uruguay	48	39	–	–
India, Pakistan (Jammu, Kashmir)		–	–		
		26	25*	25*	

* The operation is supported by 51 locally recruited staff.

UN Peacekeeping Force in Cyprus (UNFICYP)

UNFICYP was established by SCR 186 (4 Mar. 1964) and mandated to prevent fighting between the Greek Cypriot and Turkish Cypriot communities and to contribute to the maintenance and restoration of law and order. Since the end of hostilities in 1974, the mandate has included monitoring the de facto ceasefire (Aug. 1974) and maintaining a buffer zone between the two sides. SCR 2026 (14 Dec. 2011) extended the mandate until 19 July 2012.

SCR 186	Troops: Argentina, Austria, Brazil, Canada, Chile, **China**, Croatia, Hungary,	860	872	181	58.2
Mar. 1964	Paraguay, Serbia, Slovakia, UK	–	–	1	::
Cyprus	Civ. pol.: Australia, Bosnia and Herzegovina, Croatia, El Salvador, India,	69	69	(–,–,–,1)	
	Ireland, Italy, Montenegro, *Netherlands*, **Serbia**, Ukraine	39	38*		

* The operation is supported by 112 locally recruited staff.

UN Disengagement Observer Force (UNDOF)

UNDOF was established by SCR 350 (31 May 1974) and mandated to observe the ceasefire and the disengagement of Israeli and Syrian forces as well as to maintain an area of limitation and separation in accordance with the 1973 Agreement on Disengagement. SCR 2028 (21 Dec. 2011) extended the mandate until 30 June 2012.

SCR 350	Troops: Austria, Canada, Croatia, India, Japan, **Philippines**	1 047	1 043	43	49.2
June 1974		–	–	–	18.3
Syria		47	41*		

* The operation is supported by 103 locally recruited staff.

___

UN Interim Force in Lebanon (UNIFIL)

UNIFIL was established by SCRs 425 and 426 (19 Mar. 1978) and mandated to confirm the withdrawal of Israeli forces from southern Lebanon and to assist the Lebanese Government in re-establishing authority in the area. In 2006, following the conflict between Israel and Hezbollah, the operation's mandate was altered by SCR 1701 (11 Aug. 2006) to encompass tasks related to establishing and monitoring a permanent ceasefire. SCR 2004 (30 Aug. 2011) extended the mandate until 31 Aug. 2012.

SCRs 425 and 426	Troops: **Austria**, Bangladesh, **Belarus**, Belgium, Brazil, Brunei Darussalam,	15 000	12 017	293	532.1
Mar. 1978	Cambodia, China, Croatia, Cyprus, *Denmark*, El Salvador, France, Germany,	–	–	3	..
Lebanon	Ghana, Greece, Guatemala, Hungary, India, Indonesia, Ireland, Italy, Korea	–	–	(-,1,1)	
	(South), Macedonia (FYR), Malaysia, Nepal, **Nigeria**, Portugal, Qatar, Serbia,	407	353*		
	Sierra Leone, Slovenia, Spain, Sri Lanka, Tanzania, Turkey				

* The operation is supported by 666 locally recruited staff.

___

UN Mission for the Referendum in Western Sahara (MINURSO)

MINURSO was established by SCR 690 (29 Apr. 1991) and mandated to monitor the ceasefire between the Polisario Front and the Moroccan Government; to observe the reduction of troops; and to prepare for an eventual referendum on the integration of Western Sahara into Morocco. SCR 1979 (27 Apr. 2011) extended the mandate until 30 Apr. 2012.

SCR 690	Troops: Bangladesh, Ghana	27	27	15	61.6
Sep. 1991	Obs.: Argentina, Austria, Bangladesh, Brazil, China, Croatia, Djibouti, Egypt,	203	195	–	44.7
Western Sahara	El Salvador, France, Ghana, Greece, Guinea, Honduras, Hungary, Ireland, Italy,	6	6		
	Jordan, Korea (South), Malaysia, Mongolia, Nepal, Nigeria, Pakistan,	108	102*		
	Paraguay, Poland, Russia, Sri Lanka, Uruguay, Yemen				
	Civ. pol.: Chad, Egypt, El Salvador, Jordan, Yemen				

* The operation is supported by 165 locally recruited staff and 19 UN volunteers.

Legal instrument/ Deployment date/ Location	Countries contributing troops, observers (Obs.), civilian police (Civ. pol.) and civilian staff (Civ. staff) in 2011	Troops/Obs./ Civ. pol./Civ. staff		Deaths: to date/ 2011/ (by cause[g])	Cost ($ m.): 2011/ unpaid
		Approved	Actual		

UN Interim Administration Mission in Kosovo (UNMIK)

UNMIK was established by SCR 1244 (10 June 1999) and mandated to promote the establishment of substantial autonomy and self-government in Kosovo; to perform civilian administrative functions; to maintain law and order; promote human rights; and to ensure the safe return of refugees and displaced persons. Following Kosovo's declaration of independence and the deployment of EULEX Kosovo, UNMIK's mandate altered to monitoring and supporting local institutions. A positive decision by the UN Security Council is required to terminate the operation.

Legal instrument/ Deployment date/ Location	Countries contributing	Approved	Actual	Deaths	Cost
SCR 1244	Obs.: Czech Republic, *Denmark*, Norway, Poland, **Portugal**, Romania, Spain,	–	–	54	46.4
June 1999	**Turkey**, Ukraine	8	9	–	..
Kosovo	Civ. pol.: Germany, Ghana, Italy, Pakistan, Romania, *Russia*, Turkey, Ukraine	8	7		
		173	150*		

* The operation is supported by 215 locally recruited staff and 26 UN volunteers.

UN Organization Stabilization Mission in the Democratic Republic of the Congo (MONUSCO)

The UN Organization Mission in the DRC (MONUC) was established by SCR 1279 (30 Nov. 1999) and mandated by SCR 1291 (24 Feb. 2000) to monitor the implementation of the ceasefire agreement between the Democratic Republic of the Congo (DRC), Angola, Namibia, Rwanda, Uganda and Zimbabwe; to supervise and verify the disengagement of forces; to monitor human rights violations; and to facilitate the provision of humanitarian assistance. The operation was given UN Charter Chapter VII powers by SCR 1493 (28 July 2003). SCR 1856 (22 Dec. 2008) mandated the operation to protect civilians, humanitarian personnel and UN personnel and facilities; to assist the disarmament, demobilization and reintegration (DDR) of foreign and Congolese armed groups; to assist security sector reform (SSR) and train and mentor Congolese armed forces; to contribute to the territorial security of the DRC; and to support the strengthening of democratic institutions and the rule of law. SCR 1925 (28 May 2010) transformed the mission into a stabilization operation and renamed it MONUSCO. MONUSCO cooperates with EUPOL RD Congo and EUSEC RD Congo. SCR 1991 (28 June 2011) extended the mandate of MONUSCO until 30 June 2012 and expanded it to include support for the organization and conduct of national, provincial and local elections in Nov. 2011.

Legal instrument/ Deployment date/ Location	Countries contributing	Approved	Actual	Deaths	Cost
SCR 1279	Troops: Bangladesh, Belgium, Benin, China, Egypt, Ghana, Guatemala, <u>India</u>,	19 815	16 854	204	1 429.2
Nov. 1999	Indonesia, Jordan, Morocco, Nepal, Pakistan, Serbia, South Africa, Uruguay	760	703	33	353.3
Democratic Republic	Obs.: *Algeria*, Bangladesh, Belgium, Benin, Bolivia, Bosnia and Herzegovina,	1 441	1 371	(3,17,13,–)	
of the Congo	Burkina Faso, Cameroon, Canada, China, Czech Republic, *Denmark*, Egypt,	1 180	976*		
	France, Ghana, Guatemala, <u>India</u>, Indonesia, Ireland, Jordan, Kenya, Malawi,				

Malaysia, Mali, Mongolia, Morocco, Mozambique, Nepal, Niger, Nigeria, Norway, Pakistan, Paraguay, Peru, Poland, Romania, Russia, Senegal, Serbia, South Africa, Spain, Sri Lanka, Sweden, Switzerland, Tanzania, Tunisia, UK, Ukraine, Uruguay, USA, Yemen, Zambia

Civ. pol.: Bangladesh, **Belgium**, Benin, Burkina Faso, Cameroon, *Canada*, Central African Republic, Chad, Côte d'Ivoire, Egypt, France, Guinea, India, Jordan, Madagascar, Mali, Niger, Nigeria, Romania, Senegal, Sweden, Togo, Turkey, Ukraine, **Uruguay**, Yemen

* The operation is supported by 2865 locally recruited staff and 614 UN volunteers.

UN Mission in Liberia (UNMIL)

UNMIL was established by SCR 1509 (19 Sep. 2003) under UN Charter Chapter VII and mandated to support the implementation of the 2003 Comprehensive Peace Agreement; to assist in matters of humanitarian and human rights; to support SSR; and to protect civilians. SCR 1938 (15 Sep. 2010) authorized the operation to assist the Liberian Government with the 2011 presidential and legislative elections. UNMIL cooperates with UNOCI and UNIPSIL. SCR 2008 (16 Sep. 2011) extended the current mandate until 30 Sep. 2012.

SCR 1509	8 202	7 778	164	524.9
Oct. 2003	133	131	12	55
Liberia	1 375	1 297	(2,3,6,–)	
	544	477*		

Troops: Bangladesh, Benin, Bolivia, Brazil, China, Croatia, Denmark, Ecuador, Ethiopia, Finland, France, Ghana, Jordan, Korea (South), *Mongolia*, Namibia, Nepal, Nigeria, Pakistan, Paraguay, Peru, Philippines, Senegal, Togo, Ukraine, USA, Yemen

Obs.: Bangladesh, Benin, Bolivia, Brazil, Bulgaria, China, Denmark, Ecuador, Egypt, El Salvador, Ethiopia, Gambia, Ghana, Indonesia, Jordan, Korea (South), Kyrgyzstan, Malaysia, **Mali**, Moldova, Montenegro, **Namibia**, Nepal, Niger, Nigeria, Pakistan, Paraguay, Peru, Philippines, Poland, Romania, Russia, Senegal, Serbia, Togo, Ukraine, USA, Zambia, Zimbabwe

Civ. pol.: Argentina, Bangladesh, Bosnia and Herzegovina, China, Czech Republic, Egypt, El Salvador, Fiji, Gambia, Germany, Ghana, India, **Jamaica**, Jordan, Kenya, Kyrgyzstan, Namibia, Nepal, Nigeria, Norway, Pakistan, Philippines, Poland, Russia, Rwanda, Serbia, Sri Lanka, Sweden, Switzerland, Turkey, Uganda, Ukraine, *Uruguay*, USA, Yemen, Zambia, Zimbabwe

* The operation is supported by 991 locally recruited staff and 255 UN volunteers.

UN Operation in Côte d'Ivoire (UNOCI)

Legal instrument/ Deployment date/ Location	Countries contributing troops, observers (Obs.), civilian police (Civ. pol.) and civilian staff (Civ. staff) in 2011	Troops/Obs./ Civ. pol./Civ. staff		Deaths: to date/ 2011/ (by cause^a)	Cost ($ m.): 2011/ unpaid
		Approved	Actual		

UNOCI was established by SCR 1528 (27 Feb. 2004) under UN Charter Chapter VII and mandated to monitor the cessation of hostilities, movement of armed groups and the arms embargo; to support DDR and SSR; to assist with the creation of law and order, human rights and public information; to facilitate humanitarian assistance and rebuild state institutions; and to assist in the holding of free elections. In 2007 the mandate was expanded to support the full implementation of the Ouagadougou Political Agreement (4 Mar. 2007) and of the Supplementary Agreements (28 Nov. 2007). SCR 1933 (30 June 2010) added protection of civilians to the operation's mandate. UNOCI cooperates with UNMIL and Operation Licorne. Following the political crisis after the presidential elections in Nov. 2010, SCR 1951 (24 Nov. 2010) authorized the temporary transfer of units from UNMIL to reinforce UNOCI and SCR 1967 (19 Jan. 2011) authorized the deployment of an additional 2000 troops for UNOCI. SCR 2000 (27 July 2011) extended its mandate until 31 July 2012.

Legal instrument/ Deployment date/ Location	Countries contributing troops, observers (Obs.), civilian police (Civ. pol.) and civilian staff (Civ. staff) in 2011	Approved	Actual	Deaths: to date/ 2011/ (by cause^a)	Cost ($ m.): 2011/ unpaid
SCR 1528 Apr. 2004 Côte d'Ivoire	**Troops:** Bangladesh, Benin, Brazil, Chad, Egypt, France, Ghana, Jordan, **Malawi**, Morocco, Nepal, Niger, **Nigeria**, Pakistan, Paraguay, Philippines, Senegal, Tanzania, Togo, Tunisia, Uganda, Yemen	9 600* 192 1 350 500	9 416 197 1 386 397**	89 18 (–,5,11,–)	565.5 53.6
	Obs.: Bangladesh, Benin, Bolivia, Brazil, Chad, China, Ecuador, El Salvador, Ethiopia, Gambia, Ghana, Guatemala, Guinea, India, Ireland, Jordan, Korea (South), **Malawi**, Moldova, Namibia, Nepal, Niger, Nigeria, Pakistan, Paraguay, Peru, Philippines, Poland, Romania, Russia, Senegal, Serbia, Tanzania, Togo, Tunisia, Uganda, Uruguay, Yemen, Zambia, Zimbabwe				
	Civ. pol.: Argentina, Bangladesh, Benin, Burundi, Cameroon, Canada, Central African Republic, Chad, Congo (Dem. Rep. of), Djibouti, Egypt, France, Ghana, Jordan, **Madagascar**, Niger, **Nigeria**, Pakistan, **Rwanda**, Senegal, *Switzerland*, Togo, Turkey, Ukraine, *Uruguay*, Yemen				

* SCR 1967 (19 Jan. 2011) authorized the deployment of an additional 2000 troops until 30 June 2011. SCR 2000 (27 July 2011) decided that the authorized strength of UNOCI's military component should remain at 9792 personnel, comprising 9600 troops and staff officers, including 2400 additional troops authorized by SCRs 1942 (2010) and 1967 (2011), and 192 military observers and that the authorized strength of UNOCI's police component should remain at 1350 personnel.

** The operation is supported by 743 locally recruited staff and 276 UN volunteers.

UN Stabilization Mission in Haiti (MINUSTAH)

MINUSTAH was established by SCR 1542 (30 Apr. 2004) under UN Charter Chapter VII and mandated to maintain a secure and stable environment to ensure that the peace process is carried forward; to support SSR, including a comprehensive DDR programme, building the capacity of the national police and re-establishing the rule of law; to assist in the holding of free elections; to support humanitarian and human rights activities; and to protect civilians. SCR 1927 (4 June 2010) requested the operation to support the Haitian Government's preparation for municipal and presidential elections scheduled for 2010. SCR 2012 (14 Oct. 2011) extended the mandate until 15 Oct. 2012.

SCR 1542						
June 2004						
Haiti	Troops: Argentina, Bolivia, Brazil, Canada, Chile, Ecuador, France, Guatemala, **Indonesia**, Japan, Jordan, Korea (South), Nepal, Paraguay, Peru, Philippines, Sri Lanka, Uruguay, USA	7 340*	8 065	168	586.8
		3 241	3 546	8	247.5
		534	568**	(–,4,2,2)	
	Civ. pol.: Argentina, Bangladesh, Benin, Brazil, Burkina Faso, Burundi, Cameroon, Canada, Central African Republic, Chad, Chile, China, Colombia, Côte d'Ivoire, Croatia, Egypt, El Salvador, France, Grenada, Guinea, *Guinea-Bissau*, India, Indonesia, Jamaica, Jordan, Kyrgyzstan, Lithuania, Madagascar, Mali, Nepal, Niger, Nigeria, Norway, Pakistan, Philippines, Romania, Russia, Rwanda, Senegal, Serbia, **Sierra Leone**, Spain, Sri Lanka, Sweden, Thailand, Togo, Turkey, Uruguay, USA, Yemen				

* SCR 2012 (14 Oct. 2011) adjusted the operation's overall force level.
** The operation is supported by 1355 locally recruited staff and 236 UN volunteers.

UN Mission in the Sudan (UNMIS)

UNMIS was established by SCR 1590 (24 Mar. 2005) under UN Charter Chapter VII, following the 2005 Comprehensive Peace Agreement, and mandated to monitor the implementation of the peace agreement; to protect and promote human rights; to facilitate the DDR process; and to protect civilians and UN personnel. In 2010 the operation focused on providing stability in preparation for referendums on the independence of southern Sudan and the status of the Abyei Area scheduled for Jan. 2011. Following South Sudan's declaration of independence and the completion of the six-year peace process that began with the signing of the CPA, UNMIS's mandate terminated on 9 July 2011.

Legal instrument/ Deployment date/ Location	Countries contributing troops, observers (Obs.), civilian police (Civ. pol.) and civilian staff (Civ. staff) in 2011	Troops/Obs./ Civ. pol./Civ. staff		Deaths: to date/ 2011/ (by cause^a)	Cost ($ m.): 2011/ unpaid
		Approved	Actual		
SCR 1590	*Troops:* Australia, Bangladesh, Brazil, Cambodia, Canada, China, Croatia,	10 000	9 250	60	537.8
Mar. 2005	*Egypt, Finland, Germany, Greece, Guatemala, India, Japan, Jordan, Kenya,*	525	465	4	147.9
Sudan	*Korea (South), Malaysia, Nepal, Netherlands, New Zealand, Nigeria, Norway,*	715	637	(1,1,2,–)	
	Pakistan, Russia, Rwanda, Sierra Leone, Sweden, Turkey, UK, Yemen, Zambia	1 098	965*		
	Obs.: Australia, Bangladesh, Belgium, Benin, Bolivia, Brazil, Burkina Faso,				
	Cambodia, Canada, China, Denmark, Ecuador, Egypt, El Salvador, Fiji, Finland,				
	Germany, Ghana, Greece, Guatemala, Guinea, India, Indonesia, Iran, Jordan,				
	Kenya, Korea (South), Kyrgyzstan, Malaysia, Mali, Moldova, Mongolia,				
	Namibia, Nepal, Netherlands, New Zealand, Nigeria, Norway, Pakistan,				
	Paraguay, Peru, Philippines, Poland, Romania, Russia, Rwanda, Sierra Leone,				
	Sri Lanka, Sweden, Switzerland, Tanzania, Thailand, Uganda, UK, Ukraine,				
	Yemen, Zambia, Zimbabwe				
	Civ. pol.: Argentina, Australia, Bangladesh, Bosnia and Herzegovina, Brazil,				
	Canada, China, Egypt, El Salvador, Ethiopia, Fiji, Gambia, Germany, Ghana,				
	India, Indonesia, Jamaica, Jordan, Kenya, Kyrgyzstan, Malaysia, Mali,				
	Namibia, Nepal, Netherlands, Nigeria, Norway, Pakistan, Philippines, Russia,				
	Rwanda, Samoa, Sri Lanka, Sweden, Turkey, Uganda, Ukraine, USA, Yemen,				
	Zambia, Zimbabwe				

* The operation was supported by 2803 locally recruited staff and 331 UN volunteers.

UN Integrated Mission in Timor-Leste (UNMIT)

UNMIT was established by SCR 1704 (25 Aug. 2006) and mandated to support the Government of Timor-Leste in post-conflict peacebuilding, capacity building and training of the East Timorese National Police. SCR 1912 (26 Feb. 2010) endorsed the UN Secretary-General's proposal to reconfigure UNMIT's police component after national and municipal elections in 2012. SCR 1969 (24 Feb. 2011) extended the mandate until 26 Feb. 2012. The operation is scheduled to close on 31 Dec. 2012.

SCR 1704	Obs.: Australia, Bangladesh, Brazil, China, Fiji, India, Japan, Malaysia, Nepal,	–	–	12	201.2
Aug. 2006	New Zealand, Pakistan, Philippines, Portugal, Sierra Leone, Singapore	34	33	3	150.8
Timor-Leste	Civ. pol.: Australia, Bangladesh, Brazil, China, Croatia, Egypt, El Salvador, Gambia, India, Jamaica, Jordan, Korea (South), Kyrgyzstan, Malaysia, Namibia, Nepal, New Zealand, Nigeria, Pakistan, Philippines, Portugal, Romania, Russia, Samoa, Senegal, Singapore, Spain, Sri Lanka, Thailand, Turkey, Uganda, Ukraine, Uruguay, Yemen, Zambia, Zimbabwe	1 605	1 183	(-,1,2,-)	
		441	394*		

* The operation is supported by 883 locally recruited staff and 211 UN volunteers.

UN Interim Security Force for Abyei (UNISFA)

UNISFA was established by SCR 1990 (27 June 2011) and mandated to monitor and verify the redeployment of any Sudanese and South Sudanese armed forces from the Abyei Area; to provide demining assistance; to facilitate the delivery of humanitarian aid; to strengthen the capacity of the Abyei Police Service; and to provide security for oil infrastructure in the Abyei Area. SCR 2024 (14 Dec. 2011) broadened its mandate to include assistance in the Sudan–South Sudan border normalization process. SCR 2032 (22 Dec. 2011) extended the mandate until 27 May 2012.

SCR 1990	Troops: Egypt, Ethiopia, Guatemala	4 200	3 724	5	175.5
June 2011	Obs.: Brazil, Ethiopia, Japan, Morocco	–	74	5	..
Abyei		50	20	(-,4,1,-)	
		–			

Legal instrument/ Deployment date/ Location	Countries contributing troops, observers (Obs.), civilian police (Civ. pol.) and civilian staff (Civ. staff) in 2011	Troops/Obs./ Civ. pol./Civ. staff		Deaths: to date/ 2011/ (by cause^a)	Cost ($ m.): 2011/ unpaid
		Approved	Actual		
UN Mission in the Republic of South Sudan (UNMISS)					
	UNMISS was established by SCR 1996 (8 July 2011) for an initial period of one year, mandated to support peace consolidation in order to foster longer-term state building and economic development. It is also mandated to support the South Sudanese Government in conflict prevention, mitigation and resolution; in the protection of civilians; and in providing security, establishing the rule of law and strengthening the security and justice sectors.				
SCR 1996	**Troops: Australia, Bangladesh, Brazil, Cambodia, Canada, China, Egypt, Germany, India, Japan, Jordan, Kenya, Korea (South), New Zealand, Nigeria, Norway, Pakistan, Russia, Rwanda, Sweden, Switzerland, UK, Yemen, Zambia**	7000	4 803	1	722.1
July 2011		–	169	1	..
South Sudan		900	485	(–,–,1,–)	
			697*		
	Obs.: Australia, Bangladesh, Benin, Bolivia, Brazil, Burkina Faso, Cambodia, Canada, China, Denmark, Ecuador, Egypt, El Salvador, Fiji, Germany, Guatemala, Guinea, India, Indonesia, Jordan, Kenya, Korea (South), Kyrgyzstan, Mali, Moldova, Mongolia, Namibia, Nepal, New Zealand, Nigeria, Norway, Papua New Guinea, Paraguay, Peru, Philippines, Poland, Romania, Russia, Rwanda, Sierra Leone, Sri Lanka, Sweden, Switzerland, Tanzania, Timor-Leste, Ukraine, Yemen, Zambia				
	Civ. pol.: Argentina, Australia, Bangladesh, Bosnia and Herzegovina, Canada, China, El Salvador, Ethiopia, Fiji, Gambia, Germany, Ghana, India, Indonesia, Jamaica, Kenya, Kyrgyzstan, Malaysia, Namibia, Nepal, Nigeria, Norway, Philippines, Rwanda, Samoa, Sri Lanka, Sweden, Turkey, Uganda, Ukraine, USA, Zambia, Zimbabwe				

* The operation is supported by 1117 locally recruited staff and 226 UN volunteers.

United Nations political and peacebuilding operations

Total: 4 operations	..	298	353	33	495
		33	21	5	–
		8	8		
		925	863		

UN Assistance Mission in Afghanistan (UNAMA)

UNAMA was established by SCR 1401 (28 Mar. 2002) and mandated to assist with the protection of human rights, the rule of law and gender issues; to support national reconciliation and rapprochement; and to manage humanitarian relief, recovery and reconstruction activities. Its mandate was expanded by SCR 1806 (20 Mar. 2008) to coordinate international assistance; to strengthen cooperation with ISAF; to manage all UN humanitarian relief, recovery and reconstruction activities in Afghanistan; to support efforts to improve governance and the rule of law and to combat corruption; and to promote human rights and provide technical assistance to the electoral process. The operation has 18 regional offices as well as a support office in Kuwait. SRC 1974 (22 Mar. 2011) extended the mandate until 23 Mar. 2012.

SCR 1401	Obs.: Australia, **Czech Republic**, Denmark, Germany, *Italy*, New Zealand,	–	–	20	271.4
Mar. 2002	Norway, Poland, Portugal, Sweden, Uruguay	20	13	4	–
Afghanistan	Civ. pol.: *Jordan, Nepal,* **Netherlands,** Norway, *Turkey*	8	2	(3, –,1,–)	
		425	421*		

* The operation is supported by 1730 locally recruited staff and 77 UN volunteers.

UN Assistance Mission in Iraq (UNAMI)

UNAMI was established by SCR 1500 (14 Aug. 2003) and mandated to support dialogue and national reconciliation; to facilitate humanitarian assistance and the safe return of refugees and displaced persons; to coordinate reconstruction and assistance programmes; to assist in capacity building and sustainable development; and to promote the protection of human rights, judicial and legal reform and strengthen the rule of law. UNAMI cooperates with US Forces–Iraq (formerly the Multinational Force in Iraq), NTM-I and EUJUST LEX. SCR 2001 (28 July 2011) extended the mandate for a period of 12 months.

SCR 1500	Troops: *Fiji,* **Nepal**	298	353	12	193.4
Aug. 2003	Obs.: Australia, Denmark, Jordan, Nepal, New Zealand, *UK, USA*	13	8	1	–
Iraq		–	–	(–, –,1,–)	
		459	391*		

* The operation is supported by 502 locally recruited staff.

Legal instrument/ Deployment date/ Location	Countries contributing troops, observers (Obs.), civilian police (Civ. pol.) and civilian staff (Civ. staff) in 2011	Troops/Obs./ Civ. pol./Civ. staff		Deaths: to date/ 2011/ (by cause[a])	Cost ($ m.): 2011/ unpaid
		Approved	Actual		

UN Integrated Peacebuilding Office in Sierra Leone (UNIPSIL)

UNIPSIL was established by SCR 1829 (4 Aug. 2008) and mandated to monitor and promote human rights, democratic institutions and the rule of law; and to support efforts to identify and resolve potential conflict threats. SCR 1941 (29 Sep. 2010) expanded the mandate to include promoting good governance and supporting the government in preparation for presidential elections in 2012. SCR 2005 (14 Sep. 2011) extended the mandate until 15 Sep. 2012.

		Approved	Actual	Deaths	Cost
SCR 1829	Civ. pol.:..	–	–	1	20.3
Oct. 2008	Civ. staff:..	–	–	–	–
Sierra Leone		–	5		
		41	37*		

* The operation is supported by 29 locally recruited staff and 7 volunteers.

UN Support Mission in Libya (UNSMIL)

UNSMIL was established by SCR 2009 (16 Sep. 2011) and mandated to assist the Libyan authorities with the restoration of public security and the rule of law; the constitution-making and electoral processes; the extension of state authority, through the strengthening of accountable institutions and the restoration of public services; and the promotion of human rights. SCR 2022 (2 Dec. 2011) expanded the mandate to include assisting and supporting national efforts to address the threats of proliferation of arms and related material of all types. The same resolution extended the mandate until 16 Mar. 2012.

		Approved	Actual	Deaths	Cost
SCR 2009	**Civ. pol.:..**	–	–	..	9.9
Sep. 2011	**Civ. staff:..**	–	–	..	–
Libya		–	14		

African Union–United Nations

Total: 1 operation   **52 contributing countries***   19 555   17 778   104   1 748.7
240   262   25   180.2
6 432   4 950
1 524   1 124

* This figure only includes countries deploying uniformed personnel to UNAMID during 2011.

AU/UN Hybrid Operation in Darfur (UNAMID)

UNAMID was established by the AU PSC's 79th Communiqué on the Situation in Darfur (22 June 2007) and by SCR 1769 (31 July 2007) under UN Charter Chapter VII. The operation is mandated to contribute to the restoration of a secure environment, protect the civilian population, facilitate humanitarian assistance, monitor the implementation of related ceasefire agreements, and promote the rule of law and human rights. SCR 2003 (29 July 2011) extended the mandate until 31 July 2012.

SCR 1769		19 555	17 778	104	1 748.7
Oct. 2007		240	262	25	180.2
Sudan		6 432	4 950	(8,1,10,6)	
		1 524	1 124*		

Troops: Bangladesh, Burkina Faso, *Burundi*, Canada, China, Egypt, Ethiopia, Gambia, Germany, Ghana, **Indonesia**, Italy, Jordan, Kenya, Korea (South), Malawi, Malaysia, *Mali*, Mongolia, Namibia, Nepal, Netherlands, <u>Nigeria</u>, Pakistan, **Palau**, Rwanda, Senegal, Sierra Leone, South Africa, Tanzania, Thailand, Yemen, Zambia, Zimbabwe

Obs.: Bangladesh, Burkina Faso, Burundi, Cameroon, *China*, **Ecuador**, Egypt, Ethiopia, *Gambia*, Ghana, Guatemala, Indonesia, **Iran**, Jordan, Kenya, *Lesotho*, Malawi, Malaysia, Mali, Namibia, Nepal, Nigeria, Pakistan, Rwanda, Senegal, Sierra Leone, South Africa, Tanzania, Thailand, Togo, Uganda, <u>Yemen</u>, Zambia, Zimbabwe

Civ. pol.: <u>Bangladesh</u>, Burkina Faso, Burundi, Cameroon, *Canada*, Côte d'Ivoire, Egypt, Fiji, *Finland*, Gambia, *Germany*, Ghana, Indonesia, Jamaica, Jordan, *Kazakhstan*, **Kyrgyzstan**, Madagascar, Malawi, Malaysia, Namibia, Nepal, Niger, Nigeria, *Norway*, Pakistan, *Palau*, Philippines, Rwanda, Senegal, Sierra Leone, South Africa, *Sweden*, Tajikistan, Tanzania, Togo, Turkey, *Uganda*, Yemen, Zambia, *Zimbabwe*.

* The operation is supported by 2904 locally recruited staff and 483 UN volunteers.

Legal instrument/ Deployment date/ Location	Countries contributing troops, observers (Obs.), civilian police (Civ. pol.) and civilian staff (Civ. staff) in 2011	Troops/Obs./ Civ. pol./Civ. staff		Deaths: to date/ 2011/ (by cause^q)	Cost ($ m.): 2011/ unpaid
		Approved	Actual		
African Union (AU) **Total: 1 operation**	**23 contributing countries**	12 000 – 1 680 –	9 796 – 50 50	394 94	152.0 –
PSC 69th Communiqué and SCR 1744 Mar. 2007 Somalia*	Troops: Burundi, **Cameroon**, *Comoros*, Djibouti, **Ethiopia**, *Ghana*, **Kenya**, Senegal, *Sierra Leone*, Uganda, **Zambia** Civ. pol.: **Burundi**, Ghana, Kenya, Nigeria, Sierra Leone, Uganda Civ. staff: Algeria, Benin, Burundi, **Cameroon**, Côte d'Ivoire, Ethiopia, *Ghana*, Kenya, Liberia, **Libya**, Malawi, Mali, Nigeria, Rwanda, *Senegal*, Sierra Leone, **Sudan**, **Swaziland**, Tanzania, Uganda	12 000* – 1 680 –	9 796 – 50** 50	394 94 (..)	152.0*** –

AU Mission in Somalia (AMISOM)

AMISOM was established by the AU PSC's 69th Communiqué (19 Jan. 2007) and endorsed by SCR 1744 (21 Feb. 2007) under UN Charter Chapter VII. It was mandated to support the peace process, humanitarian assistance and overall security in Somalia. In 2008 the mandate was expanded by SCR 1838 (Oct. 2008) to assist implementation of the Djibouti Agreement (19 Aug. 2008), including training of Somali security forces in order to promote security in Mogadishu. UN SCR 1964 (22 Dec. 2010) endorsed an AU proposal to increase the authorized troop level to 12 000. The AU PSC, at its 306th meeting (6 Jan. 2012), decided to increase AMISOM's authorized strength to 17 731, including 5700 Djiboutian and 're-hatted' Kenyan troops and AMISOM's police component. At the same meeting, the PSC extended AMISOM's mandate until 16 Jan. 2013. SCR 2010 (30 Sep. 2011) renewed the UN's endorsement of AMISOM's mandate until 31 Oct. 2012.

* The operation's headquarters are in Nairobi, Kenya.

** The operation is supported by 53 locally recruited staff.

*** The UN has established a trust fund to assist AMISOM's planning and deployment process. Logistical, technical, financial and personnel support are provided by the EU, the Intergovernmental Authority on Development (IGAD), the Arab League and a number of individual countries. This figure is for the period 1 Oct. 2010–30 Sep. 2011.

Arab League
Total: 1 operation   14 contributing countries

166	166	–	..	..	..
–	–	–	–	–	–

Arab League Observer Mission to Syria

The League of Arab States Observer Mission to Syria was was established by Arab League Council Resolution 7439 (16 Nov. 2011). It is mandated to verify implementation of the provisions of the Arab Plan of Action to resolve the Syrian crisis and protect Syrian civilians, adopted on 2 Nov. 2011 by the Arab League Council. These provisions include observing the ceasefire and monitoring violence between all parties to the Syrian crisis; verifying the release of protesters and other detainees; and confirming free media presence in the country. The mission suspended its operations on 28 Jan. 2012 due to an escalation of violence towards civilians and observers.

Arab League Council Resolution 7439 Nov. 2011   **Obs.: Algeria, Bahrain, Egypt, Iraq, Jordan, Kuwait, Mauritania, Morocco, Qatar, Saudi Arabia, Sudan, Tunisia, UAE, Yemen**   Syria*

166	166	–	..	..	..
–	–	–	–	–	–

* The observers were divided into 15 zones covering 20 cities and districts across Syria.

Communauté Économique des États de l'Afrique Centrale (CEEAC)
Total: 1 operation   7 contributing countries

–	498	–	..	..	50.4
–	143	–	..	..	–

Mission for the Consolidation of Peace in the Central African Republic (MICOPAX)

MICOPAX was established by a decision of the 2002 Economic and Monetary Community of Central Africa (CEMAC) Libreville Summit (2 Oct. 2002) in order to secure the border between Chad and the Central African Republic (CAR). The mandate was expanded at the 2003 Libreville Summit (3 June 2003) to include contributing to the overall security environment, assisting in the restructuring of the CAR's armed forces and supporting the transition process. Coinciding with the transfer of authority on 12 July 2008 from CEMAC to CEEAC, the operation's mandate was expanded again to include promotion of political dialogue and human rights. The operation is mandated for 6-month periods, renewable until 2013.

Legal instrument/ Deployment date/ Location	Countries contributing troops, observers (Obs.), civilian police (Civ. pol.) and civilian staff (Civ. staff) in 2011	Troops/Obs./ Civ. pol./Civ. staff		Deaths: to date/ 2011 (by cause[a])	Cost ($ m.): 2011/ unpaid
		Approved	Actual		
MICOPAX continued					
Libreville Summit, 2 Oct. 2002	Troops: Cameroon, Chad, Congo, Congo (Dem. Rep. of), Gabon	–	498*	..	50.4
Dec. 2002	Obs.: *Burundi, Cameroon, Chad, Congo (Rep. of), Equatorial Guinea, Gabon*	–	–	1	–
Central African Republic	Civ. pol.: **Chad**, Equatorial Guinea	–	143	(–,–,1,–)	
		–	–	–	

* The operation was supported by and co-located with a detachment of c. 240 French soldiers (Opération Boali).

Commonwealth of Independent States (CIS)

Total: 1 operation	3 contributing countries	Approved	Actual		
		1 500	1 249	..	..
		–	10	..	..
		–	–		
		–	–		

Joint Control Commission Peacekeeping Force (JCC)

The JCC Peacekeeping Force was established pursuant to the Agreement on the Principles Governing the Peaceful Settlement of the Armed Conflict in the Trans-Dniester region, signed in Moscow by the presidents of Moldova and Russia (21 July 1992). The Joint Control Commission—a monitoring commission comprising representatives of Moldova, Russia and Trans-Dniester—was established to coordinate the activities of the joint force.

Bilateral agreement, 21 July 1992	Troops: Moldova, Russia, (Trans-Dniester)	1 500	1 249	..	..
July 1992	Obs.: *Moldova, Russia, Ukraine*	–	10	..	..
Moldova (Trans-Dniester)		–	–		
		–	–		

European Union (EU)

Total: 11 operations   40 contributing countries

2 647	1 382	28	453.6
323*	134	–	–
2 763**	1 187	–	
70	972		

* The figure for total approved observers applies to EUMM only and includes civilian police and civilian staff.

** The figure for total approved civilian police includes civilian observers and civilian staff.

EU Police Mission in Bosnia and Herzegovina (EUPM)

EUPM was established by CJA 2002/210/CFSP (11 Mar. 2002) and tasked with the establishment—through monitoring, mentoring and inspection—of a sustainable, professional and multi-ethnic police service in Bosnia and Herzegovina under Bosnian ownership. At the request of the Bosnian authorities, the mandate was modified to focus on the police reform process, strengthening of police accountability and efforts to fight organized crime. CJA 2009/906/CFSP (8 Dec. 2009) further strengthened the operation's mandate to include assisting the fight against organized crime and corruption within a broader rule-of-law approach in Bosnia and Herzegovina. Council Decision 2011/781/CFSP (1 Dec. 2011) extended the mandate until 30 June 2012.

CJA 2002/210/CFSP	Civ. pol.: Austria, Belgium, Cyprus, Czech Republic, Estonia, Finland, France,				
Jan. 2003	Germany, Hungary, Ireland, Italy, Malta, Netherlands, Poland, Portugal,	–	–	3	24.5
Bosnia and	Romania, Slovakia, Slovenia, Spain, Sweden, Switzerland, Turkey, Ukraine,	205	83	–	–
Herzegovina	UK	–	34*		
	Civ. staff: Bulgaria, Finland, France, Germany, Ireland, Italy, Netherlands,				
	Portugal, Romania, Spain, Switzerland, Turkey, Ukraine, UK				

* The operation is supported by 156 locally recruited staff.

EU Military Operation in Bosnia and Herzegovina (EUFOR ALTHEA)

EUFOR ALTHEA was established by CJA 2004/570/CFSP (12 July 2004) and was endorsed and given UN Charter Chapter VII powers by SCR 1575 (22 Nov. 2004). It is mandated to maintain a secure environment for the implementation of the 1995 Dayton Agreement; to assist in the strengthening of local policing capacity; and to support Bosnia and Herzegovina's progress towards EU integration. SCR 2019 (16 Nov. 2011) extended the mandate until 16 Nov. 2012.

Legal instrument/ Deployment date/ Location	Countries contributing troops, observers (Obs.), civilian police (Civ. pol.) and civilian staff (Civ. staff) in 2011	Troops/Obs./ Civ. pol./Civ. staff		Deaths: to date/ 2011/ (by cause[a])	Cost ($ m.)/ 2011/ unpaid
		Approved	Actual		
EUFOR ALTHEA continued					
CJA 2004/570/CFSP and SCR 1575 / Dec. 2004 / Bosnia and Herzegovina*	Troops: Albania, Austria, Bulgaria, Chile, Czech Republic, Estonia, Finland, France, Germany, Greece, Hungary, Ireland, Italy, Lithuania, Luxembourg, Macedonia (FYR), Netherlands, Poland, Portugal, Romania, Slovakia, Slovenia, Spain, Sweden, Switzerland, Turkey, UK	2 500	1 291**	21 / 21	29.1 / –

* A multinational manoeuvre battalion (made up of troops from Austria, Hungary and Turkey) is stationed in Sarajevo. Other elements of the operation are the integrated police unit (IPU) and the liaison and observer teams (LOTs), deployed to regional coordination centres.
** The operation is supported by 530 locally recruited staff.

EU Advisory and Assistance Mission for Security Reform in the Democratic Republic of the Congo (EUSEC RD Congo)

EUSEC RD Congo was established by CJA 2005/355/CFSP (2 May 2005). The operation's initial mandate was to advise and assist the DRC authorities, specifically the MOD, on security matters, ensuring that their policies are congruent with international humanitarian law, principles of democratic governance and the rule of law. In 2009 the operation's mandate was broadened to include advising and assisting in SSR by facilitating the implementation of the guidelines adopted by the Congolese authorities in the revised plan for reform of the Congolese armed forces. In carrying out its activities, EUSEC operates in close coordination with MONUSCO and EUPOL RD Congo. Council Decision 2010/565/CFSP (21 Sep. 2010) extended the mandate until 30 Sep. 2012.

| CJA 2005/355/CFSP / June 2005 / Democratic Republic of the Congo | Civ. staff: Austria, Belgium, Finland, France, Germany, Hungary, Italy, Luxembourg, Netherlands, Portugal, Romania, Spain, UK | – | 48* | 2 / – | 17.9 / – |

* The majority of the deployed personnel are military advisers. The operation is supported by 35 locally recruited staff.

EU Integrated Rule of Law Mission for Iraq (EUJUST LEX)

EUJUST LEX was established by CJA 2005/190/CFSP (7 Mar. 2005), in accordance with SCR 1546 (8 June 2004), to strengthen Iraq's criminal justice system through the training of magistrates, senior police officers and senior penitentiary staff. The operation cooperates with NTM-I and UNAMI. Council Decision 2010/330/CFSP (14 June 2010) extended the mandate until 30 June 2012.

CJA 2005/190/CFSP and SCR 1546	Civ. pol.: **Czech Republic, Denmark, France, Sweden**	–	–	31
July 2005	Civ. staff: **Austria**, Belgium, **Bulgaria**, Czech Republic, Denmark, Finland, France, Germany, Hungary, Ireland, Italy, Netherlands, Portugal, Romania,	–	5	
Iraq/Europe	Spain, Sweden, UK	50	41*	

* The operation is supported by 9 locally recruited staff.

EU Border Assistance Mission for the Rafah Crossing Point (EU BAM Rafah)

EU BAM Rafah was established by CJA 2005/889/CFSP (12 Dec. 2005) on the basis of the Agreement on Movement and Access between Israel and the Palestinian Authority (15 Nov. 2005). It is mandated to monitor, verify and evaluate the performance of Palestinian Authority border control, security and customs officials at the Rafah Crossing Point with regard to the 2005 Agreed Principles for Rafah Crossing; and to support the Palestinian Authority's capacity building in the field of border control. Following riots in 2007, the Rafah Crossing Point was closed and only to be opened under exceptional circumstances. However, EU BAM Rafah retained full operational capabilities and it resumed activity when the crossing was reopened on 28 May 2011. Council Decision 2011/857/CFSP (19 Dec. 2011) extended the mandate until 30 June 2012.

CJA 2005/889/CFSP	Civ. pol.: France, Germany, *Hungary*, Italy	–	–	3.1
Nov. 2005	Civ. staff: Finland, France, **Hungary**, Italy, Romania, Spain, UK	–	5	–
Egypt, Palestinian territories (Rafah Crossing Point)		–	8*	

* The operation is supported by 9 locally recruited staff.

EU Coordinating Office for Palestinian Police Support (EUPOL COPPS)

EUPOL COPPS was established by CJA 2005/797/CFSP (14 Nov. 2005). It is mandated to provide a framework for and advice to Palestinian criminal justice and police officials and coordinate EU aid to the Palestinian Authority. CJA 2010/784/CFSP (17 Dec. 2010) decided the operation should be referred to as the EU Coordinating Office for Palestinian Police Support. Council Decision 2011/858/CFSP (19 Dec. 2011) extended the mandate until 30 June 2012.

CJA 2005/797/CFSP	Civ. pol.: *Austria,* Belgium, Canada, **Cyprus**, *Czech Republic, Denmark,* Finland, France, Germany, Italy, Netherlands, Spain, Sweden, UK	–	–	11.5
Jan. 2006		52	20	–
Palestinian territories	Civ. staff: *Austria,* Bulgaria, **Denmark**, Estonia, Finland, **France**, Germany, Ireland, Italy, Lithuania, Netherlands, Romania, Spain, Sweden, UK	–	33*	

* The operation is supported by 37 locally recruited staff.

Legal instrument/ Deployment date/ Location	Countries contributing troops, observers (Obs.), civilian police (Civ. pol.) and civilian staff (Civ. staff) in 2011	Troops/Obs./ Civ.pol./Civ. staff		Deaths: to date/ 2011/ (by cause^a)	Cost ($ m.): 2011/ unpaid
		Approved	Actual		

EU Police Mission in Afghanistan (EUPOL Afghanistan)

EUPOL Afghanistan was established by CJA 2007/369/CFSP (30 May 2007) at the invitation of the Afghan Government. The operation is tasked with strengthening the rule of law by contributing to the establishment of civil policing arrangements and law enforcement under Afghan ownership. CJA 2010/279/CFSP (18 May 2010) extended the mandate until 31 May 2013.

Legal instrument/ Deployment date/ Location	Countries contributing troops, observers (Obs.), civilian police (Civ. pol.) and civilian staff (Civ. staff) in 2011	Approved	Actual	Deaths: to date/ 2011/ (by cause^a)	Cost ($ m.): 2011/ unpaid
CJA 2007/369/CFSP June 2007 Afghanistan	Civ. pol.: **Austria, Bulgaria,** Canada, **Croatia,** Denmark, **Estonia,** Finland, France, Germany, Greece, **Hungary,** *Ireland,* Italy, **Latvia, Lithuania,** Netherlands, **New Zealand,** Norway, **Poland, Romania, Slovakia,** Spain, Sweden, UK	–	–	–	57.1
		–	192	–	–
		400	102*		
	Civ. staff: **Austria, Bulgaria,** Canada, **Croatia,** Denmark, Finland, France, Germany, Greece, **Hungary,** Ireland, Italy, Netherlands, **Poland, Romania, Spain,** Sweden, UK				

* The operation is supported by 208 locally recruited staff.

EU Police Mission in the Democratic Republic of the Congo (EUPOL RD Congo)

EUPOL RD Congo was established by CJA 2007/405/CFSP (12 June 2007). CJA 2009/769/CFSP (19 Oct. 2009) mandated the operation to assist the Congolese authorities in reforming and restructuring the Congolese Police; improving interaction between police and the criminal justice system; supporting efforts against sexual violence; and promoting gender, human rights and children aspects of the peace process. The operation cooperates with EUSEC RD Congo and MONUSCO. Council Decision 2011/537/CFSP (12 Sep. 2011) extended the mandate until 30 Sep. 2012.

Legal instrument/ Deployment date/ Location	Countries contributing troops, observers (Obs.), civilian police (Civ. pol.) and civilian staff (Civ. staff) in 2011	Approved	Actual	Deaths: to date/ 2011/ (by cause^a)	Cost ($ m.): 2011/ unpaid
CJA 2007/405/CFSP July 2007 Democratic Republic of the Congo*	Civ. pol.: Belgium, Finland, France, Italy, Sweden	–	–	–	9.2
	Civ. staff: **Belgium,** *Finland,* France, Germany, Poland, Portugal, Sweden	59	20	–	–
		–	20**		

* With headquarters in Kinshasa, EUPOL also operates in eastern DRC, specifically Goma and Bukavu.
** The operation is supported by 19 locally recruited staff.

EU Rule of Law Mission in Kosovo (EULEX Kosovo)

EULEX Kosovo was established by CJA 2008/124/CFSP (4 Feb. 2008). With certain executive responsibilities, the operation is tasked to monitor, mentor and advise Kosovan institutions in the wider field of the rule of law. It cooperates with UNMIK and OMIK. CJA 2010/619/CFSP (15 Oct. 2010) extended the mandate until 14 June 2012.

CJA 2008/124/CFSP **Feb. 2008** **Kosovo**		–	–	2	224.5

Civ. pol.: Austria, Belgium, Bulgaria, *Canada*, Croatia, Czech Republic, Denmark, Estonia, Finland, France, Germany, Greece, Hungary, Ireland, Italy, Latvia, Lithuania, Luxembourg, Malta, Netherlands, Norway, Poland, Portugal, Romania, Slovakia, Slovenia, *Spain*, Sweden, Switzerland, Turkey, UK, USA — 1 951, 862, 519*

Civ. staff: Austria, Belgium, Bulgaria, *Canada*, Croatia, Czech Republic, Denmark, Estonia, Finland, France, Germany, Greece, Hungary, Ireland, Italy, Latvia, Lithuania, Netherlands, Norway, Poland, Portugal, Romania, Slovakia, Slovenia, Spain, Sweden, Switzerland, Turkey, UK, USA

* The operation is supported by 1150 locally recruited staff.

EU Monitoring Mission in Georgia (EUMM)

EUMM was established by CJA 2008/736/CFSP (15 Sep. 2008) in accordance with an EU–Russia agreement of 8 Sep. 2008, following the conflict in South Ossetia in Aug. 2008. The operation is tasked with monitoring and analysing progress in the stabilization process, focusing on compliance with the six-point peace plan of 12 Aug. 2008, and in the normalization of civil governance; monitoring infrastructure security and the political and security aspects of the return of internally displaced persons and refugees; and supporting confidence-building measures. Council Decision 2011/536/CFSP (12 Sep. 2011) extended the mandate until 14 Sep. 2012.

CJA 2008/736/CFSP **Oct. 2008** **Georgia**		–	–	–	39

Obs.: Austria, Bulgaria, Czech Republic, Denmark, Estonia, Finland, *France*, Germany, Greece, Hungary, *Italy*, Latvia, Lithuania, Luxembourg, Malta, *Netherlands*, Poland, Portugal, Romania, Slovakia, Slovenia, Spain, Sweden, UK — 323, 134, 147*

Civ. staff: Austria, Belgium, **Bulgaria**, Czech Republic, Denmark, **Estonia**, Finland, **France**, Germany, **Greece**, Ireland, Italy, Lithuania, Netherlands, Poland, Romania, **Slovakia**, Spain, Sweden, UK

* The operation is supported by 109 locally recruited staff.

Legal instrument/ Deployment date/ Location	Countries contributing troops, observers (Obs.), civilian police (Civ. pol.) and civilian staff (Civ. staff) in 2011	Troops/Obs./ Civ. pol./Civ. staff		Deaths: to date/ 2011/ (by cause^a)	Cost ($ m.)/ 2011/ unpaid
		Approved	Actual		

EU Training Mission (EUTM) Somalia

EUTM Somalia was established by CJA 2010/197/CFSP (31 Mar. 2010) and is mandated to strengthen the Somali Transitional Federal Government by contributing training and support to Somali security forces. Council Decision 2011/483/CFSP (28 July 2011) extended the mandate until Dec. 2012.

Legal instrument/ Deployment date/ Location	Countries contributing	Approved	Actual	Deaths	Cost
CJA 2010/197/CFSP	Troops: Belgium, *Cyprus*, Finland, *France*, Germany, *Greece*, Hungary, Ireland, Italy, *Luxembourg*, Malta, Portugal, Spain, Sweden, UK	147	91	–	6.7
Mar. 2010		–	–	–	–
Uganda*	Civ. staff: Belgium, France, **Kenya**, **Uganda**, UK	20	20**	–	–

* The training mainly takes place in Uganda.
**The operation is supported by 17 locally recruited staff.

North Atlantic Treaty Organization (NATO) and NATO-led

		Approved	Actual	Deaths	Cost
Total: 3 operations	**51 contributing countries**	10 000	137 363	2 873	667.5
		–	–	543	–
		300	100		

NATO Kosovo Force (KFOR)

KFOR was established by SCR 1244 (10 June 1999). Its mandated tasks include deterring renewed hostilities, establishing a secure environment, supporting UNMIK and monitoring borders. In 2008 NATO expanded the operation's tasks to include efforts to develop a professional, democratic and multi-ethnic security structure in Kosovo. With increased stability, KFOR will continue its gradual drawdown. A positive decision of the UN Security Council is required to terminate the operation.

Legal instrument/ Deployment date/ Location	Countries contributing	Approved	Actual	Deaths	Cost
SCR 1244	Troops: Albania, Armenia, Austria, Bulgaria, Canada, Croatia, Czech Republic, Denmark, Estonia, Finland, France, Germany, Greece, Hungary, Ireland, Italy, Luxembourg, Morocco, Netherlands, Norway, Poland, Portugal, Romania, *Slovakia*, Slovenia, *Spain*, Sweden, Switzerland, Turkey, Ukraine, UK, USA	10 000	5 977	129	28.7
June 1999		–	–	–	–
Kosovo*		–	–		

* The Headquarters of Kosovo Force (HQ KFOR) are located in Pristina and support a NATO-led operation of 2 Multinational Battle Groups (MNBGs) and 5 Joint Regional Detachments. MNBG West, led by Italy, is located in Pec; MNBG East, led by the USA, is located in Urosevac. A Multinational Specialized Unit (MSU) and a Tactical Reserve Manoeuvre Battalion (KTM) are also stationed in Pristina.

International Security Assistance Force (ISAF)

ISAF was established by SCR 1386 (20 Dec. 2001) under UN Charter Chapter VII as a multinational force mandated to assist the Afghan Government to maintain security, as envisaged in Annex I of the 2001 Bonn Agreement. NATO took over command and control of ISAF in Aug. 2003. ISAF has had control of all 28 provincial reconstruction teams (PRTs) in Afghanistan since 2006. SCR 2011 (12 Oct. 2011) extended ISAF's mandate until 13 Oct. 2012.

SCR 1386	Troops: Albania, Armenia, Australia, Austria, Azerbaijan, **Bahrain**, Belgium,	–	131 386**	2 744	621
	Bosnia and Herzegovina, Bulgaria, Canada, Croatia, Czech Republic,	–	–	543	–
Dec. 2001	Denmark, **El Salvador**, Estonia, Finland, France, Georgia, Germany, Greece,	–	–	(481,–,–,	
Afghanistan*	Hungary, Iceland, Ireland, Italy, Korea (South), Latvia, Lithuania,	–	–	–)***	
	Luxembourg, Macedonia (FYR), Malaysia, Mongolia, Montenegro,				
	Netherlands, New Zealand, Norway, Poland, Portugal, Romania, Singapore,				
	Slovakia, Slovenia, Spain, Sweden, **Tonga**, Turkey, Ukraine, UK, USA				

* The territory of Afghanistan is divided into 6 areas of responsibility: Regional Command (RC) Centre (Kabul), currently led by Turkey; RC North (Mazar i Sharif), led by Germany; RC West (Herat), led by Italy; RC South (Kandahar), RC South-West (Lashkar Gah) and RC East (Bagram), all led by the USA.

** The NATO Training Mission in Afghanistan (NTM-A) is included in ISAF personnel figures as it is under ISAF command. It is tasked to mentor and train Afghan police and military personnel. NTM-A has an authorized strength of 2700 troops and police. In Dec. 2011, 2800 were deployed, coming from Albania, Australia, Belgium, Canada, Croatia, Czech Republic, Denmark, Estonia, Finland, France, Germany, Greece, Hungary, Italy, Jordan, Korea (South), Mongolia, Netherlands, Norway, Poland, Portugal, Romania, Singapore, Slovenia, Spain, Sweden, Turkey, UK and USA.

*** In addition, 62 deaths were due to accidents, illnesses or other causes. The breakdown for the 3 latter causes is not available.

NATO Training Mission in Iraq (NTM-I)

NTM-I was established pursuant to SCR 1546 (8 June 2004) and approved by the North Atlantic Council on 17 Nov. 2004. It is mandated to assist in the development of Iraq's security institutions through training and equipment of, in particular, middle- and senior-level personnel from the Iraqi security forces. In 2007 the mandate was revised to focus on mentoring and advising an Iraqi-led institutional training programme.

SCR 1546	Civ. staff: Albania, Bulgaria, *Denmark*, Estonia, *Hungary*, Italy, Lithuania,	–	–	17.8
Aug. 2004	Netherlands, Poland, Romania, Turkey, Ukraine, UK, USA	–	–	–
Iraq		–		–
		300	100	

Legal instrument / Deployment date / Location	Countries contributing troops, observers (Obs.), civilian police (Civ. pol.) and civilian staff (Civ. staff) in 2011	Troops/Obs./ Civ. pol./Civ. staff Approved	Actual	Deaths: to date / 2011 / (by cause[q])	Cost ($ m.): 2011	unpaid
Organization of American States (OAS)						
Total: 1 operation	**15 contributing countries**	–	–	–	**8**	–
		–	–	–		
		–	–			
		–	22			

Mission to Support the Peace Process in Colombia (MAPP/OEA)

MAPP/OEA was established by OAS Permanent Council Resolution CP/RES 859 (1397/04) of 6 Feb. 2004 to support the efforts of the Colombian Government to engage in a political dialogue with the Ejército de Liberación Nacional (ELN, National Liberation Army). It is also mandated to facilitate the DDR process.

CP/RES. 859	Civ. staff: Argentina, *Belgium*, Bolivia, **Bulgaria**, Chile, Ecuador, *Guatemala*,			1	8	
Feb. 2004	Mexico, Netherlands, Nicaragua, Peru, Spain, Sweden, USA, *Venezuela*			1		
Colombia		–	22*	(–, –, 1, –)		

* The operation is supported by 52 locally recruited staff.

Organization for Security and Co-operation in Europe (OSCE)						
Total: 7 operations	**46 contributing countries**	–	–	10	**80.1**	–
		–	–	–		
		–	22			
		350	459			

OSCE Spillover Monitor Mission to Skopje

The OSCE Spillover Monitor Mission to Skopje was established at the 16th Committee of Senior Officials (CSO) meeting (18 Sep. 1992). It was authorized by the Macedonian Government through an exchange of letters on 7 Nov. 1992. Its tasks include monitoring, police training, development and other activities related to the 2001 Ohrid Framework Agreement. PC.DEC/1023 (15 Dec. 2011) extended the mandate until 31 Dec. 2012.

CSO 18 Sep. 1992 — Civ. pol.: **Canada, Estonia, Hungary, Portugal, Romania, Russia, Serbia, Slovenia, Spain,** <u>Turkey</u>**, UK**

Sep. 1992

Former Yugoslav Republic of Macedonia — Civ. staff: Austria, *Belarus,* Bosnia and Herzegovina, Croatia, Czech Republic, *Estonia,* **Finland,** France, Germany, Greece, *Hungary,* Iceland, Ireland, Italy, **Moldova,** Netherlands, *Portugal, Romania, Russia, Serbia, Slovenia,* Spain, *Sweden, Turkey,* UK, USA

* The operation is supported by 126 locally recruited staff.

OSCE Mission to Moldova

The OSCE Mission to Moldova was established at the 19th CSO meeting (4 Feb. 1993) and authorized by the Moldovan Government through an MOU (7 May 1993). Its tasks include assisting the conflicting parties in pursuing negotiations on a lasting political settlement, and gathering and providing information on the situation. PC.DEC/1016 (15 Dec. 2011) extended the mandate until 31 Dec. 2012.

CSO 4 Feb. 1993 — Civ. staff: Bulgaria, **Czech Republic,** Estonia, France, **Germany,** Italy, Latvia, Poland, Russia, Sweden, UK, <u>USA</u>

Apr. 1993

Moldova

* The operation is supported by 41 locally recruited staff.

Personal Representative of the Chairman-in-Office on the Conflict Dealt with by the OSCE Minsk Conference

A Personal Representative on the Conflict Dealt with by the OSCE Minsk Conference was appointed by the OSCE Chairman-in-Office (CIO) on 10 Aug. 1995. The Personal Representative's mandate consists of assisting the CIO in planning a possible peacekeeping operation, assisting the parties in confidence-building measures and humanitarian matters, and monitoring the ceasefire between the parties. The mandate is extended annually as part of the OSCE Unified Budget Approval; in 2011, this decision was PC.DEC/1025 (15 Dec. 2011).

CIO 10 Aug. 1995 — Civ. staff: Bulgaria, *France, Germany,* **Hungary,** *Kazakhstan,* <u>**Lithuania,**</u> **Poland, UK,** *USA*

Aug. 1995

Azerbaijan (Nagorno-Karabakh)

* The operation is supported by 11 locally recruited staff.

Operation					Deaths	Cost
FYR Macedonia (CSO 18 Sep. 1992)	–	22	39*	–	1	9.8
Moldova (CSO 4 Feb. 1993)	13	–	19*	–	–	2.9
Azerbaijan (CIO 10 Aug. 1995)	6	–	6*	–	–	1.6

Legal instrument/ Deployment date/ Location	Countries contributing troops, observers (Obs.), civilian police (Civ. pol.) and civilian staff (Civ. staff) in 2011	Troops/Obs./ Civ. pol./Civ. staff		Deaths: to date/ 2011/ (by cause[a])	Cost ($ m.): 2011/ unpaid
		Approved	Actual		

OSCE Mission to Bosnia and Herzegovina

The OSCE Mission to Bosnia and Herzegovina was established by decision MC(5).DEC/1 of the 5th meeting of the OSCE Ministerial Council (8 Dec. 1995), in accordance with Annex 6 of the 1995 Dayton Agreement. The operation is mandated to assist the parties in regional stabilization measures and democracy building. PC.DEC/1020 (15 Dec. 2011) extended the mandate until 31 Dec. 2012.

Legal instrument/ Deployment date/ Location	Countries contributing troops, observers (Obs.), civilian police (Civ. pol.) and civilian staff (Civ. staff) in 2011	Approved	Actual	Deaths: to date/ 2011/ (by cause[a])	Cost ($ m.): 2011/ unpaid
MC(5).DEC/1 Dec. 1995 Bosnia and Herzegovina	Civ. staff: Armenia, Austria, Belarus, Belgium, Canada, **Croatia**, Czech Republic, Finland, France, Germany, Greece, Hungary, Ireland, Italy, Kyrgyzstan, Netherlands, Norway, **Poland**, Portugal, *Romania*, Russia, Slovakia, *Slovenia*, Spain, Sweden, Tajikistan, Turkey, *Ukraine*, UK, <u>USA</u>	–	65*	– / –	19.6 / –

* The operation is supported by 429 locally recruited staff.

OSCE Presence in Albania

The OSCE Presence in Albania was established by PC.DEC/160 (27 Mar. 1997). In 2003 the operation's mandate was revised to include assisting in legislative, judicial and electoral reform; capacity building; anti-trafficking and anti-corruption activities; police assistance; and good governance. PC.DEC/1019 (15 Dec. 2011) extended the mandate until 31 Dec. 2012.

Legal instrument/ Deployment date/ Location	Countries contributing troops, observers (Obs.), civilian police (Civ. pol.) and civilian staff (Civ. staff) in 2011	Approved	Actual	Deaths: to date/ 2011/ (by cause[a])	Cost ($ m.): 2011/ unpaid
PC.DEC/160 Apr. 1997 Albania	Civ. staff: **Albania**, Austria, Bulgaria, **Canada**, Czech Republic, **France**, Germany, *Latvia*, Lithuania, Montenegro, *Netherlands*, Norway, *Slovenia*, Spain, UK, USA	107	106*	– / –	4.2 / –

* The operation is supported by 84 locally recruited staff.

OSCE Mission in Kosovo (OMIK)

OMIK was established by PC.DEC/305 (1 July 1999). Its mandate includes training police, judicial personnel and civil administrators and monitoring and promoting human rights. The operation is a component of UNMIK. PC.DEC/835 (21 Dec. 2007) extended the mandate until 31 Jan. 2008, after which the mandate is renewed on a monthly basis unless 1 of the participating states objects.

Op. no. / Date / Location	Troops	Mil. obs	Civ. police	Int'l staff	Deaths	Cost ($ m.)
PC.DEC/305 July 1999 Kosovo Civ. staff: Armenia, Austria, Azerbaijan, Belarus, Belgium, Bosnia and Herzegovina, **Bulgaria**, Canada, Croatia, France, Georgia, Germany, Greece, Hungary, Ireland, Italy, Macedonia (FYR), Malta, *Moldova*, Montenegro, Netherlands, Poland, Portugal, Romania, Russia, Slovakia, Spain, Sweden, Turkey, Ukraine, UK, USA, Uzbekistan	–	–	224	189*	9	31.5

* The operation is supported by 479 locally recruited staff.

OSCE Mission to Serbia

The OSCE Mission to Serbia was established by PC.DEC/401 (11 Jan. 2001). It is mandated to advise on the implementation of laws and to monitor the proper functioning and development of democratic institutions and processes in Serbia. It assists in the training and restructuring of law enforcement bodies and the judiciary. PC.DEC/1022 (15 Dec. 2011) extended the mandate until 31 Dec. 2012.

Op. no. / Date / Location	Troops	Mil. obs	Civ. police	Int'l staff	Deaths	Cost ($ m.)
PC.DEC/401 Mar. 2001 Serbia Civ. staff: Austria, Bosnia and Herzegovina, Bulgaria, Canada, Croatia, France, Georgia, Germany, Greece, Hungary, Ireland, Italy, Moldova, Netherlands, Norway, Russia, Slovenia, Spain, Sweden, *Turkey*, Ukraine, UK, USA	–	–	–	35*	–	10.5

* The operation is supported by 141 locally recruited staff.

Ad-hoc coalitions	900	149	273	1 053	105	608
Total: 6 operations 30 contributing countries	2 180	–	–	1 704	4	–

Neutral Nations Supervisory Commission (NNSC)

The NNSC was established by the agreement concerning a military armistice in Korea signed at Panmunjom (27 July 1953). It is mandated with the functions of supervision, observation, inspection and investigation of implementation of the armistice agreement.

Op. / Date / Location				Obs.	Deaths	Cost ($ m.)
Armistice Agreement July 1953 North Korea, South Korea Korea Obs.: Sweden, Switzerland				10	–	1.3*

* This figure reflects only Switzerland's financial contribution to the operation

Multinational Force and Observers (MFO)

The MFO was established on 3 Aug. 1981 by the Protocol to the Treaty of Peace between Egypt and Israel, signed on 26 Mar. 1979. Deployment began on 20 Mar. 1982, following the withdrawal of Israeli forces from the Sinai peninsula, but the mission did not become operational until 25 Apr. 1982, the day that Israel returned the Sinai peninsula to Egyptian sovereignty. The operation is mandated to observe the implementation of the peace treaty and to contribute to a secure environment.

Legal instrument/ Deployment date/ Location	Countries contributing troops, observers (Obs.), civilian police (Civ. pol.) and civilian staff (Civ. staff) in 2011	Troops/Obs./ Civ. pol./Civ. staff		Deaths: to date/ 2011/ (by cause[a])	Cost ($ m.): 2011/ unpaid
		Approved	Actual		
Protocol to Treaty of Peace	Obs.: Australia, Canada, Colombia, Czech Republic, Fiji, France, Hungary, Italy, New Zealand, Norway, Uruguay, <u>USA</u>	–	–	70	78.9
Apr. 1982		2 000	1 656	3	–
Egypt (Sinai)	Civ. staff: Australia, Canada, France, New Zealand, UK, USA	–	59*	(–,1,2,–)	

*The operation is supported by 534 locally recruited staff.

Temporary International Presence in Hebron (TIPH 2)

TIPH 2 was established by the Protocol Concerning the Redeployment in Hebron (17 Jan. 1997) and the Agreement on the Temporary International Presence in Hebron (21 Jan. 1997). It is mandated to contribute to a secure and stable environment and to monitor and report breaches of international humanitarian law. The mandate is renewed every 6 months subject to approval from both the Israeli and Palestinian parties.

Hebron Protocol	Obs.: Denmark, Italy, Norway, Turkey	–	–	2	..
Feb. 1997	Civ. staff: Denmark, Norway, Sweden, Switzerland	180	38	–	–
Palestinian territories (Hebron)		–	39*		

*The operation is supported by 10 locally recruited staff.

Operation Licorne

Operation Licorne was deployed under the authority of SCR 1464 (4 Feb. 2003) and given UN Charter Chapter VII powers to support the ECOWAS mission (2003–2004)—in accordance with UN Charter Chapter VIII—in contributing to a secure environment and, in particular, to facilitate implementation of the 2003 Linas-Marcoussis Agreement. SCR 1528 (27 Feb. 2004) revised the mandate to working in support of UNOCI. SCR 1795 (15 Jan. 2008) expanded the mandate to support implementing the Ouagadougou Political Agreement (4 Mar. 2007) and the Supplementary Agreements (28 Nov. 2007), in particular to assist in the holding of elections. SCR 2000 (27 July 2011) extended the mandate until 30 July 2012.

SCR 1464	Troops: France	900	450*	24	91
Feb. 2003		–	–	–	–
Côte d'Ivoire		–	–	–	–

* The operation is supported by a naval attachment in the Gulf of Guinea (Mission Corymbe).

Regional Assistance Mission to Solomon Islands (RAMSI)

RAMSI was established under the framework of the 2000 Biketawa Declaration (28 Oct. 2000). It is mandated to assist the Solomon Islands Government in restoring law and order and in building up the capacity of the police force.

Biketawa Declaration	Troops: Australia, New Zealand, Papua New Guinea, Tonga	–	143	7	257.5
July 2003	Civ. pol.: Australia, Cook Islands, Fiji, Kiribati, Micronesia, Nauru, New	–	–	–	–
Solomon Islands	Zealand, Niue, Palau, Papua New Guinea, Samoa, Tonga, Tuvalu, Vanuatu	–	149	–	–
	Civ. staff: Australia, Canada, Fiji, India, New Zealand, Nigeria, Papua New	–	175*	–	–
	Guinea, Tonga, UK				

* The operation is supported by a staff of 252 locally recruited professionals.

International Security Forces (ISF)

The ISF was deployed at the request of the Government of Timor-Leste to assist in stabilizing the security environment in the county and endorsed by SCR 1690 (20 June 2006). Its status is defined by status of forces agreement (26 May 2006) between Australia and Timor-Leste and an MOU between Australia, Timor-Leste and the UN (26 Jan. 2007). The operation cooperates with UNMIT.

Legal instrument / Deployment date / Location	Countries contributing troops, observers (Obs.), civilian police (Civ. pol.) and civilian staff (Civ. staff) in 2011	Troops/Obs./ Civ. pol./Civ. staff		Deaths: to date / 2011 / (by cause[a])	Cost ($ m.): 2011 / unpaid
		Approved	Actual		
Bilateral agreement, 25 May 2006, and	Troops: Australia, New Zealand	–	460	2	179.3
SCR 1690		–	–	1	–
May 2006		–	–	(–, 1, –, –)	
Timor-Leste		–	–		

– = not applicable; . . = information not available; CJA = EU Council Joint Action; CP/RES = OAS Permanent Council Resolution; CSO = OSCE Senior Council (previously the Committee of Senior Officials); DDR = disarmament, demobilization and reintegration; ECOWAS = Economic Community of West African States; MC = OSCE Ministerial Council; MOU = Memorandum of Understanding; PC.DEC = OSCE Permanent Council Decision; PSC = AU Peace and Security Council; SCR = UN Security Council Resolution; SSR = security sector reform.

[a] Where cause of death can be attributed, the 4 figures in parentheses are, respectively, deaths due to hostilities, accident, illness and other causes in 2011. As causes of death were not reported for all deaths in the year, these figures do not always add up to the total annual fatality figure.

Source: SIPRI Multilateral Peace Operations Database, <http://www.sipri.org/databases/pko/>.

Sources and methods

Methods

The figures for approved personnel numbers listed are those most recently authorized for 2011. Numbers of locally recruited support staff and volunteers are not included in the table but, where available, are given in the notes. For European Union (EU) operations, the approved total civilian personnel number is given in the civilian police row. Complete information on national contributions to the operations can be found in the SIPRI Multilateral Peace Operations Database, <http://www.sipri.org/databases/pko>. The category 'observers' includes both military and civilian observers.

Personnel fatalities are recorded since the beginning of an operation and in 2011. Known causes of death—whether hostile acts, accidents, illness or other causes—are recorded for fatalities in 2011. As causes of death were not reported for all deaths in the year, these figures do not always add up to the total annual fatality figure. While the United Nations provides data on fatalities of locally recruited staff, other organizations or alliances do not.

Costs are reported in millions of US dollars at 2011 prices. The budget figures are given for the calendar year rather than for financial years. Costs for the calendar year are calculated on the assumption of an even rate of spending throughout the financial year. Budgets set in currencies other than the US dollar are converted based on the International Monetary Fund's aggregated market exchange rates for 2011. The costs recorded for UN and Organization for Security and Co-operation in Europe (OSCE) operations are the amounts budgeted. The figures provided for other operations represent actual spending.

The costs recorded for UN operations are core operational costs, which include the cost of deploying personnel, per diem payments for deployed personnel and direct non-field support costs (e.g. requirements for the support account for peacekeeping operations and the UN logistics base in Brindisi, Italy). The cost of UN peacekeeping operations is shared by all UN member states through a specially derived scale of assessed contributions that takes no account of their participation in the operations. Political and peacebuilding operations are funded through regular budget contributions. UN peacekeeping budgets do not cover programmatic costs, such as those for disarmament, demobilization and reintegration, which are financed by voluntary contributions.

The costs recorded for operations conducted by the North Atlantic Treaty Organization (NATO) only represent common costs. These include mainly the running costs of the NATO headquarters (i.e. costs for civilian personnel and costs for operation and maintenance) and investments in the infrastructure necessary to support the operation. The costs of deploying personnel are borne by individual contributing states and are not reflected in the figures given here.

Most EU operations are financed in one of two ways: civilian missions are funded through the Common Foreign and Security Policy (CFSP) budget, while military operations or operations with a military component are funded by contributions by the participating member states through the Athena mechanism.

For Commonwealth of Independent States (CIS) operations no figures are provided as there is no designated common budget and countries participating in the missions bear the cost of troop deployments.

In operations conducted or led by other organizations, such as by the Organization of American States (OAS) or ad hoc coalitions, budget figures may include resources for programme implementation.

For all these reasons, the budget figures presented in table 3.2 are estimates and the budgets for different operations should not be compared.

Unless otherwise stated, all figures are as of 31 December 2011 or, in the case of operations that were terminated in 2011, the date of closure.

Sources

Data on multilateral peace operations is obtained from the following categories of open source: (*a*) official information provided by the secretariat of the organization concerned; (*b*) information provided by operations themselves, either in official publications or in written responses to annual SIPRI questionnaires; and (*c*) information from national governments contributing to the operation under consideration. In some instances, SIPRI researchers may gather additional information on an operation from the conducting organizations or governments of participating states by means of telephone interviews and email correspondence. These primary sources are supplemented with a wide selection of publicly available secondary sources consisting of specialist journals, research reports, news agencies, and international, regional and local newspapers.

Part II. Military spending and armaments, 2011

Chapter 4. Military expenditure

Chapter 5. Arms production and military services

Chapter 6. International arms transfers

Chapter 7. World nuclear forces

4. Military expenditure

Overview

World military expenditure did not increase in 2011, for the first time since 1998. The world total for 2011 is estimated to have been $1738 billion, representing 2.5 per cent of global gross domestic product or $249 for each person (see section I and the tables in section VII in this chapter). Compared with the total in 2010, military spending remained virtually unchanged in real terms. However, it is still too early to say whether this means that world military expenditure has finally peaked.

The main cause of the halt in military spending growth was the economic policies adopted in most Western countries in the aftermath of the global financial and economic crisis that started in 2008. These policies prioritized the swift reduction of budget deficits that increased sharply following the crisis. In Western and Central Europe in particular, governments enacted austerity measures, including military spending cuts (see section V). In countries such as Greece, Italy and Spain, deficit reduction was given added urgency by acute debt crises where these countries faced being unable to meet their debt obligations, and in some cases required bailouts from the European Union and the International Monetary Fund. The falls in military expenditure brought other policy debates into focus, including long-standing accusations from both sides of the Atlantic that European countries are failing to 'pull their weight' in military affairs, and renewed efforts to promote greater European military cooperation as a way to reduce costs while preserving capabilities.

However, in the United States the administration and the Congress also attempted to agree measures to reduce the soaring US budget deficit, which resulted from tax cuts and the wars in Afghanistan and Iraq, and so preceded the crisis. While these attempts did not lead to substantive cuts in military expenditure, delays in agreeing a budget for 2011 contributed to spending being lower than planned and resulted in a small real-terms fall in US military expenditure (see section III). Alongside these falls, there were increases in military spending in Africa, Asia and Eastern Europe—in Russia in particular. However, even in Asia, where economic growth was still strong, the rate of increase in military spending slowed, which may be partly due to concerns over the impact of the European budget crisis on future economic growth.

One of the dominating factors of the global security environment over the past 10 years, and a key factor influencing military spending in many countries, was the 'global war on terrorism' following the terrorist attacks on the USA of 11 September 2001. The highly militarized policy response to these *attacks chosen by the USA, which included invasions of Afghanistan and Iraq, had cost the USA over $1.2 trillion in additional military expenditure alone by the end of 2011, and may result in total long-term costs of as much as $4 trillion. Much lower, although still substantial, costs had also been incurred by other participants in these wars (see section II). The rapid decade-long increase in US military spending, fuelled by the wars in Afghanistan and Iraq as well as by major ongoing military modernization programmes, appears to be ending. This is the result both of the ending of the Iraq War and the winding down of the Afghanistan War and of budget deficit reduction measures. The exact future direction of US military spending will depend on the outcome of continuing budget discussions between the administration and the Congress. At the same time, the administration has announced plans for reorienting forces and military strategy in the light of tighter budgetary conditions (see section III).*

Africa was the region with the largest increase in military spending in 2011 (see section IV). This was dominated by a massive 44 per cent increase by Algeria, the continent's largest spender. Algeria's continuous increases in recent years were fuelled by increasing oil revenues, and were provided a ready justification by the activities of al-Qaeda in the Islamic Maghreb (AQIM), although regional ambitions may be a more important driver. The terrorist activities of Boko Haram were also a major security concern for Nigeria and the military-led response to these appears to have been one factor in Nigeria's military spending increases. However, the role of oil revenues and other factors should not be ignored.

Against this backdrop, the rate of reporting of military expenditure to the United Nations through its standardized reporting instrument continued to fall, as it has in recent years (see section VI). A UN Group of Governmental Experts reviewed the instrument in 2011, partly with a view to considering ways to improve reporting rates.

SAM PERLO-FREEMAN

I. Global developments in military expenditure

SAM PERLO-FREEMAN AND CARINA SOLMIRANO

Between 1998 and 2010 total world military expenditure increased every year in real terms, but that growth stopped in 2011 as spending reached $1738 billion. The fastest growth was between 2001 and 2009, when the average annual increase was 5 per cent. The rate of growth slowed in 2010 and fell to just 0.3 per cent in 2011, which, given the uncertainties in the estimate, is not significantly different from zero.[1] Military spending in the United States, the main component in global increases since 2001, fell slightly in 2011, for the first time since 1998. Elsewhere, increases in Africa, the Middle East, and Asia and Oceania were countered by falls in Latin America (see table 4.1). In Europe, substantial increases in Eastern Europe—by Azerbaijan and Russia in particular—were offset by a second year of falls in Western and Central Europe.

The list of the top 15 military spenders worldwide in 2011 includes the same countries as in 2010, but the order has changed somewhat (see table 4.2). In contrast to most of the 2000s, the majority—9 of the 15 countries—cut military spending in real terms in 2011. The spending of one, Japan, remained constant, while China, South Korea, Russia, Saudi Arabia and Turkey increased military spending. Over the period 2002–11, however, 10 of the 15 increased military spending, with falls in Japan and most of the European countries: France, Germany, Italy and Turkey. In contrast, military spending as a share of gross domestic product (GDP)—the 'military burden'—fell in 10 of the 15 countries between 2002 and 2011, most notably Turkey, whose military burden fell from 3.9 per cent to 2.3 per cent. Four countries increased their military burdens, with the largest increase being by the USA, from 3.4 per cent to 4.7 per cent. The USA remained by far the world's largest military spender, with military spending roughly equal to that of the next 14 countries combined.

Over the period 2002–11 there were significant increases in military spending in all regions and subregions other than Western and Central Europe, where there was virtually no change. The increases were especially pronounced in North Africa and Eastern Europe. The picture of increases and decreases in 2011 is mixed, both within and between regions (see table 4.3).

Globally, the financial and economic crisis has led to a significant change in military expenditure trends. Between 2002 and 2008, 78 per cent of countries for which data is available increased their military spending, but

---

[1] These uncertainties include estimates for countries with missing data for 2011, the fact that most figures for 2011 are based on budgeted rather than actual expenditure and the fact that the economic data for 2011 used to convert figures into constant (2010) US dollars is provisional.

Table 4.1. Military expenditure by region, by international organization and by income group, 2002–11

Figures for 2002–11 are in US$ b. at constant (2010) prices and exchange rates. Figures for 2011 in the right-most column, marked *, are in current US$ b. Figures do not always add up to totals because of the conventions of rounding.

	2002	2003	2004	2005	2006	2007	2008	2009	2010	2011	2011*
World total	**1 146**	**1 218**	**1 286**	**1 340**	**1 383**	**1 436**	**1 513**	**1 613**	**1 629**	**1 634**	**1 738**
United States	432	492	536	562	571	586	629	680	698	690	711
Rest of the world	713	725	750	777	812	850	884	934	931	945	1 026
Geographical regions											
Africa	19.5	19.4	21.8	22.7	23.7	(24.5)	(27.9)	(28.6)	(29.6)	(32.2)	(34.3)
North Africa	6.3	6.5	7.1	7.3	7.3	8.0	9.4	(10.0)	(10.5)	(13.1)	(13.9)
Sub-Saharan Africa	13.2	12.9	14.8	15.4	16.3	(16.6)	(18.5)	(18.6)	(19.1)	(19.1)	(20.4)
Americas	497	552	600	631	644	664	714	768	791	780	809
Central America and the Caribbean	4.9	4.8	4.4	4.7	5.1	5.7	5.8	6.4	6.5	6.7	7.0
North America	448	508	552	579	588	605	650	701	721	713	736
South America	44.9	40.1	43.1	47.2	51.0	53.5	58.6	60.3	63.6	61.1	66.0
Asia and Oceania	204	213	224	236	249	267	283	317	322	330	364
Central and South Asia	34.5	35.5	40.4	42.8	43.5	44.9	49.3	56.6	57.4	55.9	61.7
East Asia	131	137	143	151	162	175	185	208	212	221	243
Oceania	18.1	18.5	19.2	19.8	20.9	22.2	22.9	24.6	24.9	24.6	28.6
South East Asia	19.9	22.0	21.6	22.0	22.5	25.6	26.2	27.5	27.4	28.2	31.0
Europe	347	352	354	356	365	373	384	392	375	376	407
Eastern Europe	38.7	41.4	43.3	47.9	53.4	58.9	64.9	66.4	65.5	72.1	80.5
Western and Central Europe	308	310	311	308	311	314	319	325	310	304	326
Middle East	78.0	81.5	86.3	94.3	101	107	104	(108)	(111)	(116)	(123)
Organizations											
African Union	22.1	22.1	24.2	25.0	26.1	(26.9)	(29.6)	(30.1)	(30.8)	(33.1)	(35.3)
Arab League	63.0	65.1	71.0	77.0	81.6	91.1	94.3	98.5	102	(109)	(114)
CIS	39.5	42.3	44.4	49.1	54.8	60.8	66.8	67.6	67.0	73.9	82.4

CSTO	36.9	39.3	41.0	45.0	49.5	54.2	59.8	62.3	61.7	67.2	75.1
East African Community	0.9	0.9	0.9	1.0	1.0	1.2	1.2	1.2	1.3	1.1	1.2
ECOWAS	2.8	2.2	2.2	2.2	2.2	2.5	2.9	3.1	3.4	3.5	3.8
European Union	255	259	277	276	278	285	289	294	279	271	293
NATO	728	790	842	866	879	897	947	1 006	1 011	996	1 039
NATO Europe	281	283	290	287	291	293	297	305	290	283	303
OSCE	795	860	908	936	954	980	1 035	1 094	1 098	1 091	1 145
SADC	6.7	7.3	7.4	8.5	9.0	8.7	9.7	9.8	10.0	10.0	10.8
SCO	84.3	90.8	98.1	109	125	141	155	178	182	195	217
Income group											
Low	(4.7)	4.8	(5.1)	(5.2)	(5.5)	(6.0)	(6.2)	(6.3)	(6.7)	(6.8)	(7.4)
Lower middle	112	120	131	141	154	172	189	217	223	232	255
Upper middle	131	128	134	144	156	161	170	176	178	186	202
High	896	965	1 017	1 049	1 067	1 096	1 148	1 214	1 222	1 209	1 274
World military spending per capita (current US$)											
	126	145	162	173	182	200	222	228	236	249	
World military burden (i.e. world military spending as a % of world gross domestic product, both measured in current US$)											
	2.4	2.4	2.4	2.4	2.4	2.4	2.7	2.6	2.5		

( ) = total based on country data accounting for less than 90% of the regional total; .. = available data accounts for less than 60% of the regional total.

Notes: The world total and the totals for regions, organizations and income groups are estimates, based on data in table 4.9 for the countries covered by the SIPRI Military Expenditure Database. When military expenditure data for a country is missing for a few years, estimates are made, most often on the assumption that the rate of change in that country's military expenditure is the same as that for the region to which it belongs (see also 'Sources and methods' below). When no estimates can be made, countries are excluded from the totals. The countries excluded from all totals here are Cuba, Equatorial Guinea, Guyana, Haiti, North Korea, Myanmar, Somalia, Trinidad and Tobago, and Zimbabwe. Totals for regions and income groups cover the same groups of countries for all years. Totals for organizations cover only the member countries in the year given. The coverage of the geographical regions and sub-regions is based on the classification of countries in tables 4.8–4.10.

Sources: Table 4.9; Income groups (based on 2009 gross national income per capita): *World Development Report 2011: Conflict, Security and Development* (World Bank: Washington, DC, 2011); *Population*: UNFPA, *State of World Population 2011: People and Possibilities in a World of 7 Billion* (UNFPA: New York, 2011); and *GDP*: International Monetary Fund (IMF), *World Economic Outlook: Slowing Growth, Rising Risks* (IMF: Washington, DC, Sep. 2011).

Table 4.2. The 15 countries with the highest military expenditure in 2011

Spending figures are in US$, at current prices and exchange rates. Countries are ranked according to military spending calculated using market exchange rates (MER).

Rank			Spending, 2011	Change, 2002–11	Share of GDP (%)[a]		World share,	Spending, 2011
2011	2010	Country	($ b., MER)	(%)	2011	2002	2011 (%)	($ b., PPP)[b]
1	1	USA	711	59	4.7	3.4	41	711
2	2	China	[143]	170	[2.0]	[2.2]	[8.2]	[228]
3	5	Russia	[71.9]	79	[3.9]	[4.5]	[4.1]	[93.7]
4	3	UK	62.7	18	2.6	2.5	3.6	57.5
5	4	France	62.5	−0.6	2.3	2.5	3.6	50.1
Subtotal top 5			**1 051**	..	..	..	**61**	..
6	6	Japan	59.3	−2.5	1.0	1.0	3.4	44.7
7	9	India	48.9	66	2.6	2.9	2.8	117
8	7	Saudi Arabia[c]	48.5	90	8.7	9.8	2.8	58.8
9	8	Germany	[46.7]	−3.7	[1.3]	1.5	[2.7]	[40.4]
10	11	Brazil	35.4	19	1.5	1.9	2.0	33.8
Subtotal top 10			**1 290**	..	..	..	**74**	..
11	10	Italy	[34.5]	−21	[1.6]	2.0	[2.0]	[28.5]
12	12	South Korea	30.8	45	2.7	2.4	1.8	42.1
13	13	Australia	26.7	37	1.8	1.9	1.5	16.6
14	14	Canada	[24.7]	53	[1.4]	1.2	[1.4]	[19.9]
15	15	Turkey	[17.9]	−12	[2.3]	3.9	[1.0]	[25.2]
Subtotal top 15			**1 425**	..	..	..	**82**	..
World			**1 738**	**43**	**2.5**	**2.4**	**100**	..

[ ] = SIPRI estimate; GDP = gross domestic product; PPP = purchasing power parity.

[a] The figures for national military expenditure as a share of GDP are based on estimates for 2011 GDP from the International Monetary Fund (IMF) World Economic Outlook database, Sep. 2011.

[b] The figures for military expenditure at PPP exchange rates are estimates based on the projected implied PPP conversion rates for each country from the IMF World Economic Outlook database, Sep. 2011.

[c] The figures for Saudi Arabia include expenditure on public order and safety and might be slight overestimates.

Sources: SIPRI Military Expenditure Database, <http://www.sipri.org/databases/milex/>; and IMF, World Economic Outlook database, Sep. 2011, <http://www.imf.org/external/pubs/ft/weo/2011/02/weodata/index.aspx>.

for the period 2008–11 this share fell to 56 per cent. In contrast, slow growth or falls in GDP due to the crisis mean that military spending as a share of GDP followed an opposite trend. Between 2002 and 2008, 25 per cent of countries for which data is available increased their military burdens, while 63 per cent reduced them and they stayed constant in 12 per cent. However, between 2008 and 2010, 43 per cent increased their military burdens, 41 per cent reduced them and they remained unchanged in 17 per

Table 4.3. Key military expenditure statistics by region, 2011

Changes are in real terms.

Region/ Subregion	Military expenditure, 2011 (US$ b.)	Change (%) 2010–11	Change (%) 2002–11	Major changes, 2011 (%)[a] Increases		Major changes, 2011 (%)[a] Decreases	
Africa	(34.3)	8.6	65	Zimbabwe	50	Lesotho	−24
North Africa	(13.9)	25	110	Algeria	44	Ghana	−23
Sub-Saharan Africa	(20.4)	−0.1	44	Congo, DR	15	Côte d'Ivoire	−16
				Madagascar	12	Kenya	[−16]
Americas	809	−1.4	57	Paraguay	34	Dominican	−9.4
Central America and Caribbean	7.0	2.7	36	Chile	[12]	Republic	
				Guatemala	7.1	Argentina	[−8.9]
North America	736	−1.2	59	Mexico	5.7	Brazil	−8.2
South America	66.0	−3.9	36			Venezuela	−7.4
Asia and Oceania	364	2.2	61	Afghanistan	36	Philippines	−8.7
Central and South Asia	61.7	−2.7	62	Indonesia	12	Viet Nam	−6.9
				Kazakhstan	[9.7]	Sri Lanka	−6.5
East Asia	243	4.1	69	Malaysia	9.4	Brunei	−4.6
Oceania	28.6	−1.2	36			Darussalam	
South East Asia	31.0	2.7	42				
Europe	407	0.2	8.3	Azerbaijan	89	Bulgaria	−19
Eastern Europe	80.5	10	86	Switzerland	12	Georgia	[−18]
Western and Central Europe	326	−1.9	−1.5	Norway	[11]	Slovakia	−14
				Russia	9.3	Slovenia	−13
Middle East	(123)	4.6	49	Iraq	(55)	Oman	−17
				Bahrain	14	Egypt	−4.2
				Kuwait	9.8	Jordan	−4.2

( ) = uncertain figure; [ ] = SIPRI estimate.

[a] The list shows the largest increases or decreases for each region as a whole, rather than by subregion. Countries with a military expenditure in 2011 of less than $100 m., or $50 m. in Africa, are excluded.

cent. Thus, in the period of generally high world economic growth, most countries increased military spending more slowly than their economies grew, but during the crisis this trend changed.

In Asia and Oceania military spending increased modestly in 2011. The largest national increase was in Afghanistan—36 per cent—due to continued expansion of the Afghan National Army.[2] China's increase of 6.7 per cent in real terms, or $8 billion, was equal to the entire regional increase. Some concerns have been expressed that China's increased military power may be driving a regional arms race.[3] However, a brief survey of military

[2] Afghan Ministry of Finance (MOF), *1390 National Budget* (MOF: Kabul, 2011), pp. 12, 14. The figures do not include military aid from the USA and other international donors.

[3] E.g. Sharma, A. et al., 'Asia's new arms race', *Wall Street Journal*, 12 Feb. 2011.

spending trends shows a mixed picture.[4] India's military spending has increased by 59 per cent since 2002, with rivalry with China as a key driver.[5] Viet Nam has also increased its spending, by 82 per cent since 2003, amid tensions over the South China Sea.[6] However, Japan has cut its military spending by 2.5 per cent since 2002, while Taiwan's increase was just 13 per cent, as relations with China have warmed. The Philippines, which has also had tensions with China over the South China Sea, has made only modest increases. Indeed, some of the largest increases in South East Asia since 2002 are unrelated to China: Indonesia's 82 per cent increase reflects efforts to achieve a 'Minimum Essential Force' to control its vast archipelago, and may also reflect the continued political influence of the military.[7] Increases by Cambodia (70 per cent) and Thailand (66 per cent) are partly related to their border dispute, which saw numerous violent incidents in 2010 and 2011, and in Thailand's case to a long-running insurgency in the south and continuing domestic unrest following the military coup in 2006.[8]

The fall in military spending in South America in 2011 was the first since 2003. This is accounted for by an 8.2 per cent fall in Brazil, which cut its initial discretionary military budget (which includes spending on new equipment, but not, e.g., salaries) by 25 per cent as part of efforts to control inflation.[9] Elsewhere in the region there was a mixture of increases and decreases (see table 4.3). The increase in Central America is largely the result of increasing military involvement in dealing with spiralling armed violence from drug cartels.[10] Mexico in particular increased military spending by 52 per cent in real terms between 2002 and 2011. Partly due to the ineffectiveness and corruption of the police force, 45 000 troops have been deployed nationwide to support law enforcement efforts.[11] The extra spending has been used to increase salaries, to combat high desertion rates

---

[4] For a more extended discussion of trends in East and South East Asia see Perlo-Freeman, S. and Solmirano, C., 'Wettlauf ohne Sieger' [Race without winners], *Welt Sichten*, no. 9-2011 (Sep. 2011), pp. 29–33.

[5] Perlo-Freeman, S. et al., 'Military expenditure', *SIPRI Yearbook 2011*, pp. 166–70.

[6] Data for Viet Nam is not available before 2003. On arms acquisitions by South China Sea littoral states see chapter 6, section III, in this volume.

[7] Anderson, G. and Grevatt, J., 'Island vision', *Jane's Defence Weekly*, 28 Sep. 2011, pp. 28–32.

[8] Chachavalpongpun, P., 'Internal conflicts now shaping defence policy', *South China Morning Post*, 14 Mar. 2011. See also Melvin, N. J., *Conflict in Southern Thailand: Islamism, Violence and the State in the Patani Insurgency*, SIPRI Policy Paper no. 20 (SIPRI: Stockholm, Sep. 2007).

[9] Lima, M. S., 'Goberno oficializa corte de R$ 50 bi no orçamento de 2011' [Government formalizes cut of R$50 billion in the 2011 budget], *Folha* (São Paulo), 9 Feb. 2011.

[10] For lists of recently active conflicts in Central America see chapter 2, section III, in this volume. Aside from Mexico, El Salvador, Guatemala and Honduras have all given the military a role in combating drug-related violence. Infodefensa, 'Militarizacion de la Seguridad Publica en Centroamerica' [Militarization of public security in Central America], 14 Dec. 2011, <http://www.info defensa.com/?opinion=militarizacion-de-la-seguridad-publica-en-centroamerica>.

[11] Fainaru, S. and Booth, W., 'As Mexico battles cartels, the army becomes the law', *Washington Post*, 2 Apr. 2009.

and, to a lesser extent, for new arms acquisitions to support counter-narcotics operations.[12] However, military efforts have not staunched the increase in deaths from armed violence and have led to accusations of human rights abuses.[13]

The estimate for the Middle East in 2011 is highly uncertain, due to the absence of data for key countries, in particular Iran and the United Arab Emirates. Among the countries for which data is available, the largest increase was in Iraq, at 55 per cent. However, in recent years Iraq has consistently underspent its initial military budget, so the actual increase may be considerably smaller. A 2010 US Government Accountability Office (GAO) report found that, from 2005 to 2009, the Iraqi security ministries failed to spend $2.5–5.2 billion of budgeted funds, including $1.2–3.4 billion for arms procurement.[14]

Military spending in the USA, Africa and Europe is discussed in detail in sections III, IV and V, respectively.

---

[12] Guevara Moyano, I., *Adapting, Transforming, and Modernizing under Fire: The Mexican Military 2006–11* (US Army War College, Strategic Studies Institute: Carlisle, PA, Sep. 2011). See also e.g. US Embassy in Mexico City, 'U.S. delivers $43.3 million dollars in equipment support to Mexican Navy as part of Merida Initiative', Press release, 1 Dec. 2011, <http://mexico.usembassy.gov/press-releases/equipment-merida-initiative.html>.

[13] Freedom House, 'Mexico', *Freedom in the World 2011* (Freedom House: Washington, DC, 2011); and Carlsen, L., 'Phase 2 of the drug war', Panama News, 10 Apr. 2010, <http://www.thepanama news.com/pn/v_16/issue_05/opinion_01.html>.

[14] Government Accountability Office (GAO), *Iraqi–U.S. Cost-sharing*, GAO-10-918 (GAO: Washington, DC, Sep. 2010), p. 5.

II. The economic cost of the Afghanistan and Iraq wars

SAM PERLO-FREEMAN AND CARINA SOLMIRANO

The rapid increases in military expenditure worldwide over the past decade have taken place in a global political and security environment shaped by the terrorist attacks on the United States of 11 September 2001. In particular, they have been shaped by the policy responses to these attacks chosen by the USA and its allies, under the rubric of the 'global war on terrorism'. The highly militarized US response included, most notably, major wars in Afghanistan and Iraq.[1]

The two wars have involved—in addition to their great human costs— substantial and continuing economic costs both to Afghanistan and Iraq themselves and to the countries participating in the invasions and subsequent occupations of these countries. A number of studies have tried to establish the extent of these costs, using a range of estimation methods. This section discusses the issues involved in estimating the costs to Afghanistan and Iraq, and surveys available information on the costs to the USA and a number of allied countries.

There is expanding literature in the fields of conflict and development studies on the economic costs of conflict, which attempts to estimate either the cost of individual conflicts or the total cost of conflict worldwide. Methodologies include accounting approaches that attempt to identify all the potential causes of lost income and wealth, and econometric approaches that use statistical methods to estimate loss of gross domestic product (GDP). Such estimates are always subject to major uncertainties, due to the conceptual difficulties in identifying all the causes of costs, as well as the poor quality of data in many cases from countries in conflict and because all such estimates must be relative to a counterfactual of what would have happened in the absence of conflict. A 2010 study by researchers at the German Institute for Economic Research (DIW Berlin) surveyed much of the existing literature and produced an estimate for the total loss of global GDP resulting from all conflict since 1960. It estimated that, had there been no armed conflict since 1960, global GDP in 2007 would have been 14.3 per cent—or $9.1 trillion—higher than it was.[2]

---

[1] The question of whether the war in Iraq should be considered a 'response' to the attacks is debatable, but it arguably could not have taken place were it not for the subsequent political climate.

[2] Bozzoli, C., Brück, T. and de Groot, O. J., 'The global economic costs of conflict', Global Economic Costs of Conflict (GECC) Project Paper, DIW Berlin, Mar. 2010, available on request from the GECC project, <http://www.diw.de/en/diw_01.c.338475.en>. Other papers surveying the cost of conflict literature and discussing the methodological issues involved include Sköns, E., 'The costs of armed conflict', Peace and Security, Expert Papers Series no. 5 (International Task Force on Global Public Goods: Stockholm, 2005); and Brauer, J. and Dunne, J. P., 'On the cost of violence and the benefits of peace', Peace Economics, Peace Science and Public Policy, vol. 16, no. 2 (2011).

The economic costs of a conflict can, conceptually, be divided into three categories. First is the additional resources directly required for a conflict. These include additional military spending by states and human and economic resources used by rebel groups (although the latter is not usually directly measurable). Second is the cumulative loss of national output (GDP) resulting from a conflict. This can be due to many causes, including loss of human capital due to death and disability; disruption of economic activity due to immediate danger from fighting, displacement of people, the laying of mines and other causes; destruction of physical capital and infrastructure; loss of domestic and foreign investment; and loss of revenue from tourism. Many of these effects may continue long after armed conflict ends, due to a continuing legacy of violence and criminality in post-conflict societies, as is the case in Iraq. Third is the cost of reconstruction and rehabilitation: rebuilding physical capital and infrastructure and medical care for victims of conflict. These activities contribute to GDP, but represent resources that could have been devoted to other activities rather than repairing the damage caused by the conflict.

In the cases of Afghanistan and Iraq, few attempts have been made to estimate the costs of the post-September 2001 conflicts. One problem is the lack of available data under the regimes of the Taliban in Afghanistan and Saddam Hussein in Iraq—for example, no military expenditure data is available in either case. Another problem is the choice of counterfactual as Afghanistan was already in conflict before the USA-led war and the Iraqi economy was subject to severe sanctions. One estimate for Iraq, made by Colin Rowat, is that its GDP would have been 40 per cent higher in 2005 were it not for the 2003 invasion.[3]

In both countries, there are many possible sources of economic cost and their full magnitude would be extremely difficult to estimate. Arguably, these are likely to have been especially high in Iraq, as it started from a higher developmental base. First, there is the loss of human capital due to death and disability. A 2008 study by the Iraq Family Health Survey Study Group estimated that there were 151 000 violent deaths in Iraq over the period March 2003–June 2006 alone.[4] Second, there is the disruption of economic activity due to displacement. Over 3 million Iraqi people have been displaced since 2003, either as refugees or internally displaced persons (IDPs), and have not returned home.[5] Third, the war involved

[3] Rowat, C., 'Iraqi GDP since 2003: some simple calculations', *International Journal of Contemporary Iraqi Studies*, vol. 1, no. 2 (2003), pp. 233–45.

[4] Iraq Family Health Survey Study Group, 'Violence-related mortality in Iraq from 2002–2006', *New England Journal of Medicine*, no. 358 (Jan. 2008), pp. 484–93. An earlier study estimated that there had been an additional 655 000 deaths in Iraq during the period Mar. 2003–June 2006. Burnham, G. et al, 'Mortality after the 2003 invasion of Iraq', *The Lancet*, vol. 368, no. 9545 (21 Oct. 2006).

[5] Office of the UN High Commissioner for Refugees (UNHCR), '2012 UNHCR country operations profile—Iraq', <http://www.unhcr.org/pages/49e486426.html>. See also Dewachi, O., 'Insecurity,

major destruction of Iraqi capital and infrastructure. Despite domestic and international reconstruction efforts, the country still experiences disruption to basic services such as electricity. Oil output took several years to return to its pre-war level. Public health, already facing severe difficulties due to sanctions, deteriorated further after the war.[6] Unemployment levels remain high, estimated at 28 per cent in 2011 by the UN, which indicates continuing disruption to normal economic life.[7] Overall, Iraq's GDP per capita has increased since 2003, but this is largely due to increased oil prices and masks poor performance in other sectors.[8]

For Afghanistan, no single total estimate for civilian casualties exists, but in early 2012 the UN Assistance Mission in Afghanistan (UNAMA) reported 11 864 deaths since 2007.[9] In 2011 there were around 500 000 IDPs in Afghanistan. According to the Office of the UN High Commissioner for Refugees (UNHCR), 5.7 million refugees have returned to Afghanistan since 2002, increasing the population by 25 per cent. However, 40 per cent of these have not reintegrated into society.[10] There seems to have been no attempt to estimate the net effect of the conflict on the Afghan economy.

One specific set of costs is that of reconstruction in Afghanistan and Iraq, including of their respective armed forces. These costs have been split between the countries themselves and external actors, especially the USA. According to the US Special Inspector General for Iraq Reconstruction, between 2003 and 2011, $182 billion was made available for the relief and reconstruction of Iraq, comprising $62 billion from the USA, $107 billion of Iraqi funds and $13 billion from other countries.[11] For Afghanistan, international donors provided $8.1 billion in reconstruction aid between 2008 and 2011, including $2.6 billion for the security forces.[12]

For the USA and its allies, the costs of war include budgetary costs to the governments involved and broader economic costs to society as a whole. Some official figures and independent estimates for these various cost elements are available for the countries with the largest involvement in Afghanistan: the USA, the UK, Germany, Canada and France (see table 4.4). Apart from the direct costs of military operations, however, the figures are

displacement and public health impacts of the American invasion of Iraq', Costs of War, 13 June 2011, <http://costsofwar.org/article/refugees-and-health>.

[6] Dewachi (note 5).

[7] Yousif, B., 'The economy of Iraq since 2003: an assessment', Costs of War, 13 June 2011, <http://costsofwar.org/article/economy-iraq>.

[8] Yousif (note 7).

[9] UN Assistance Mission in Afghanistan (UNAMA) and UN Office of the High Commissioner for Human Rights (OHCHR), *Afghanistan Annual Report 2011: Protection of Civilians in Armed Conflict* (UNAMA/OHCHR: Kabul, Feb. 2012).

[10] UNHCR, '2012 UNHCR country operations profile—Afghanistan', <http://www.unhcr.org/pages/49e486eb6.html>.

[11] US Special Inspector General for Iraq Reconstruction (SIGIR), *Quarterly Report to the United States Congress* (SIGIR: Arlington, VA, 30 Oct. 2011), p. 18.

[12] Afghan Ministry of Finance (MOF), *1390 National Budget* (MOF: Kabul, 2011), pp. 17–19.

not directly comparable between countries, as either the figures are not available or they are based on a different definition. For example, the full long-term costs of veteran care and benefits have only been estimated for the USA and Germany.

The budgetary costs include the direct, additional military operational costs of fighting the wars. These are the most frequently quoted figures for the costs of the wars and are available from official sources in most of the countries concerned. In addition, there are direct costs to other government departments, such as to the US Department of State for aid to Afghanistan and Iraq to rebuild their armed forces, and expenditure by foreign governments on civilian reconstruction. These figures are also available from several governments.

The official figures, however, leave out many other costs to the government and society. For some countries, attempts have been made to estimate some elements of these costs. For the USA, the Costs of War website publishes the results of a series of studies by the Brown University Eisenhower Research Project.[13] For Germany, a paper by researchers at DIW Berlin estimates the total cost of German participation in the Afghanistan War.[14] For Canada, the Rideau Institute has produced a study of the costs of the Afghanistan War in 2008.[15]

The additional costs of the wars include a range of items in the short and long terms. First, there may be additional costs to the military itself. The official figures do not include the salaries of soldiers deployed. However, some analysts argue that these should also be counted, at least in cases where the demands of war have led to increases in the size of the armed forces or have prevented decreases. Another potential long-term cost to the military is that of 'resets' (i.e. readjustments) to equipment and force structure following the wars, or for equipment replacement. Both salaries and reset costs are included in the Canadian and German studies. The German study also estimates the future costs of demobilization.

Second, there is the long-term cost of medical treatment and disability benefits for veterans of the wars. In general, there are no official estimates for this cost, but independent estimates have been made for some countries. In particular, Linda Bilmes has estimated the future costs to the US Department of Veterans Affairs resulting from the wars.[16] These figures are

---

[13] Costs of War, <http://www.costsofwar.org>.

[14] Brück, T., De Groot, O. J. and Schneider, F., 'The economic costs of the German participation in the Afghanistan war', Aug. 2010, *Journal of Peace Research*, vol. 48, no. 6 (Nov. 2011).

[15] Macdonald, D. and Staples, S., 'The cost of the war and the end of peacekeeping: the impact of extending the Afghanistan mission', Rideau Institute, Oct. 2008, <http://www.rideauinstitute.ca/2008/10/18/>.

[16] Bilmes, L. J., 'Current and projected future costs of caring for veterans of the Afghanistan and Iraq wars', Costs of War, 13 June 2011, <http://costsofwar.org/article/caring-us-veterans>.

Table 4.4. Estimates of the costs of the Afghanistan and Iraq wars to selected participating states

Figures are in US$ billions.

	USA	UK	Germany	Canada	France
Cost of operations up to 2011[a]	1 208	42	9.7	9	3.6
Estimated cost of future operations	627	13.2	4.2	0	..
Military and other aid[b]	95	..	2.2	2.6	..
Additional military costs[c]	..	..	15.8	8	..
Payments to veterans[d]	589–934	1.6	1.5	1.6	..
Financing costs[e]	1 000	..	10.4–15	..	..
Social costs to veterans[f]	295–400	..	1.9	7.6	..

[a] These are official figures for sums appropriated or spent on military operations, generally referring only to direct, additional costs from the wars, not e.g. salaries of deployed troops.

[b] This is aid for rebuilding the Afghan and Iraqi security forces and for civilian reconstruction. For the USA, figures are up to financial year 2013. For Canada, figures are up to 2011. For Germany, figures are estimated up to 2016.

[c] The figure for Germany refers to the salaries of additional troops required by operations, the depreciation of equipment and demobilization.

[d] For the USA, these are estimates for lifetime medical care and disability payments for disabled veterans, borne by the US Department of Veterans Affairs. For other countries, they refer only to estimates of direct compensation payments to veterans and, for Germany, also to widows or widowers.

[e] These are additional interest payments on national debt due to war spending.

[f] These refer to loss of wages and productivity, and medical care not covered directly by the military or the US Department of Veterans Affairs.

Sources: USA: Belasco, A., *The Cost of Iraq, Afghanistan, and Other Global War on Terror Operations since 9/11*, Congressional Research Service (CRS) Report for Congress RL33110 (US Congress, CRS: Washington, DC, 29 Mar. 2011); US Government budget for financial year 2013; Bilmes, L. J., 'Current and projected future costs of caring for veterans of the Afghanistan and Iraq wars', Costs of War, 13 June 2011, <http://costsofwar.org/article/caring-us-veterans>; and Edwards, R., 'Post-9/11 war spending, debt, and the macroeconomy', Costs of War, 22 June 2011, <http://costsofwar.org/article/macroeconomic-impact-military-spending>. *UK*: Berman, G., 'The cost of international military operations', British House of Commons, Standard Note SN/SG/3139, 26 Sep. 2011, <http://www.parliament.uk/briefing-papers/SN03 139>; British House of Commons, Defence Committee, *Ministry of Defence Main Estimates 2011–12*, Fifth Report of Session 2010–12 (The Stationery Office: London, 19 July 2011); and Docksey, L., 'Lest we forget the true cost of war: the plight of Britain's war veterans', Global Research, 9 Nov. 2011, <http://www.globalresearch.ca/index.php?context=va&aid=27554>. *Canada*: Canadian Government, 'Cost of the Afghanistan mission 2001–2011', Canada's Engagement in Afghanistan, 27 June 2011, <http://www.afghanistan.gc.ca/canada-afghanistan/news-nouvelles/2010/2010_07_09.aspx>; and Macdonald, D. and Staples, S., 'The cost of the war and the end of peacekeeping: the impact of extending the Afghanistan mission', Rideau Institute, Oct. 2008, <http://www.rideauinstitute.ca/2008/10/18/>. *Germany*: Brück, T., De Groot, O. J. and Schneider, F., 'The economic costs of the German participation in the Afghanistan war', Aug. 2010, *Journal of Peace Research*, vol. 48, no. 6 (Nov. 2011). *France*: Hébert, J. P., 'Le coup des OPEX Françaises' [The cost of French OPEX], *Arès XXIII-2*, no. 60 (Dec. 2008); and French Senate, Finance Committee, *Rapport Général sur le project de loi de finances pour 2012*, vol. 3, annex 8, *Défense* [General report on the Finance Bill for 2012, vol. 3, annex 8, defence] (French Senate: Paris, 6 Feb. 2012), pp. 33–38.

uncertain since they depend on future rates of benefits, inflation, the rate of deterioration of disabled veterans and—most uncertain of all—how many more veterans will be disabled in the future. The high projected costs of veterans' care is due to the high proportion of soldiers returning from the wars with mental and physical disabilities, which is partly the result of higher levels of survival from injuries than in previous wars and of higher levels of diagnosis of psychological damage.[17] For other countries, most available estimates relate primarily to direct compensation payments to the more severely wounded soldiers. In European countries, the cost of long-term medical care of veterans will be borne by universal public health care systems, rather than the dedicated veterans' provision in the USA.

Third, there are the additional interest payments on government debt created by war spending. The size of these depends on future interest rates and is thus somewhat uncertain. For the USA, the wars in Afghanistan and Iraq have been unusual compared to previous wars in that they have been financed entirely through borrowing, rather than a mixture of borrowing and additional taxation.[18]

The broader economic costs of the wars—borne by individuals and businesses rather than the government—are even harder to assess and are open to dispute. Most obvious is the loss of earnings and productivity due to the death or injury of soldiers in the wars. In 2008 Joseph Stiglitz and Linda Bilmes suggested that there would also be substantial economic costs due to the Iraq War as a result of higher oil prices.[19] However, in 2011 Ryan Edwards found that there was little evidence of anything but a short-term spike in global oil prices as a result of the war. Edwards also found a mixed result for the macroeconomic effect of the wars on overall GDP levels, where a fiscal stimulus effect is counteracted by higher interest rates (due to higher government debt) reducing the funds available for capital investment. Based on this view, the net macroeconomic impact of the wars on the USA may be small.[20]

[17] Bilmes (note 16), p. 5.

[18] Perlo-Freeman, S. et al., 'Military expenditure', *SIPRI Yearbook 2009*, pp. 184–90.

[19] Stiglitz, J. E. and Bilmes, L. J., *The Three Trillion Dollar War* (W.W. Norton & Company: New York, 2008).

[20] Edwards, R., 'Post-9/11 war spending, debt, and the macroeconomy', Costs of War, 22 June 2011, <http://costsofwar.org/article/macroeconomic-impact-military-spending>.

III. The United States' military spending and the 2011 budget crisis

ELISABETH SKÖNS AND SAM PERLO-FREEMAN

The United States' budget deficit has soared since the global financial crisis in 2008, and the resulting political crisis over how to deal with it had a significant impact on the US debate on military spending in 2011. After a decade of sharp rises in military spending, the debate, particularly in the US Congress, shifted to cuts in military spending. In late July 2011 agreement was reached on legislation to reduce public spending over the next 10 years, which will also have an impact on future US military spending (unless the legislation is repealed in subsequent years).

During the 11 years following September 2001, US federal outlays (i.e. US Government expenditure) on national defence increased by 84 per cent in real terms.[1] This sharp increase in military spending, driven primarily by the wars in Afghanistan and Iraq (see section II above), raised the level of military spending as a share of gross domestic product (GDP) from 3.0 to 4.7 per cent and as a share of total outlays from 16.4 to 20.1 per cent (see table 4.5). The largest increases were in military construction, operations and maintenance, and procurement.

In February 2011 the US administration of President Barack Obama presented a defence budget request for the financial year (FY) 2012, which amounted to $671 billion in budget authority (i.e. authorization to spend) for the Department of Defense (DOD): $553 billion for the base budget and $118 billion for Overseas Contingency Operations (OCOs), that is, for the wars in Afghanistan and Iraq.[2] The OCO portion was $41.5 billion lower than the request for FY 2011, reflecting the planned troop withdrawals from Iraq during the year. However, this budget was soon made obsolete by political controversies over public finance. When the National Defense Authorization Act for FY 2012 was finally passed in December 2011, it allocated $531 billion for the base budget—$22 billion less than the original request and $49 billion less than the FY 2011 budget. The OCO budget was allocated $117 billion—almost the full amount requested.[3]

During 2010 and 2011 the Obama administration came under increasing pressure from the political opposition, the Republican Party, to reduce the annual deficits in the government budget. With an estimated budget deficit

---

[1] SIPRI figures for US military spending include foreign military aid spending by the Department of State in the national defence outlays.

[2] The FY 2012 budget covers the period 1 Oct. 2011–30 Sep. 2012. US Department of Defense (DOD), 'DOD releases fiscal 2012 budget proposal', News release, 14 Feb. 2011, <http://www.defense.gov/releases/release.aspx?releaseid=14263>.

[3] National Defense Authorization Act for Fiscal Year 2012, US Public Law no. 112-81, signed into law 31 Dec. 2011, <http://thomas.loc.gov/cgi-bin/bdquery/z?d112:h.r.01540:>.

of over $1.6 trillion in FY 2011 and federal government debt estimated to exceed 100 per cent of GDP in 2011, the Republican Party requested sharp cuts in spending, while rejecting any proposals to increase revenue (e.g. by removing some of the tax cuts introduced by the previous administration). Proposals by the Obama administration to reduce the deficit by $1.1 trillion over the next 10 years, through expenditure cuts, while making targeted expenditure increases in specific areas, such as education and the environment, were rejected by the opposition.

Finally, on 31 July 2011, a compromise agreement was reached, which on the one hand would increase the government debt ceiling—and thus prevent a default by the US Government—and on the other hand would reduce the growth in government debt. The resulting Budget Control Act, signed into law on 2 August 2011, imposed a set of spending caps, which over the 10-year period 2012–21 would result in total cuts of $917 billion to previously planned expenditure, including $450 billion for military spending.[4] It also established a bipartisan Joint Select Committee on Deficit Reduction (the 'Super Committee'), with the task of identifying ways to further cut the deficit by $1.2–1.5 trillion over the same period. However, the failure of the committee to reach agreement by the deadline of 23 November 2011 triggered a clause in the act providing for automatic spending cuts (so-called sequestration). These automatic cuts, beginning on 2 January 2013 and totalling $1.2 trillion over 10 years, were to be equally split between military and non-military spending. Theoretically, the Congress could change the law before January 2013, and some senators and representatives soon initiated efforts to protect the defence budget from sequestration, while President Obama stated that he would veto any effort to repeal the automatic spending cuts.[5]

The analysis of the need for, and implications of, defence cuts motivated primarily by economic considerations varied widely. While some saw the cuts as having a seriously limiting effect on US military capability, others believed that the cuts did not go far enough, given US national security needs and considering the end of the wars in Afghanistan and Iraq.[6] Gordon Adams, a former senior White House official for national security budgets (1993–97), suggested that planned defence budgets for the period 2012–21 could be reduced by 15 per cent, contributing $1 trillion to deficit reduction and still 'leaving in place a globally operating, dominant military

[4] Budget Control Act of 2011, US Public Law no. 112-25, signed into law 2 Aug. 2011, <http://thomas.loc.gov/cgi-bin/bdquery/z?d112:SN00365:>.

[5] 'Obama pledges to veto effort to undo automatic spending cuts', CBS News, 21 Nov. 2011, <http://www.cbsnews.com/8301-503544_162-57329146-503544/>.

[6] Weisgerber, M., 'Panetta: cuts more than $350b would be dangerous', *Defense News*, 4 Aug. 2011. See also Berteau, D. J. and Crotty, R., 'Super Committee fallout and the implications for defense', Center for Strategic and International Studies (CSIS), 2 Dec. 2011, <http://csis.org/publication/super-committee-fallout-and-implications-defense>.

Table 4.5. US outlays for the Department of Defense and total national defence, financial years 2001, 2005, 2007, 2009 and 2011–13

Figures are in current US\$ b. unless otherwise stated. Years are financial years (starting 1 Oct. of the previous year).

	2001	2005	2007	2009	2011	2012[a]	2013[a]
DOD, military	290.2	474.1	528.5	636.7	678.1	688.3	672.9
Military personnel	74.0	127.5	127.5	147.4	161.6	156.2	155.9
O&M	112.0	188.1	216.6	259.3	291.0	294.5	294.2
Procurement	55.0	82.3	99.6	129.2	128.0	139.9	124.6
RDT&E	40.5	65.7	73.1	79.0	74.9	75.9	71.8
Other DOD military[b]	8.8	10.5	11.6	21.8	22.5	21.8	26.5
Atomic energy, defence	12.9	18.0	17.1	17.6	20.4	19.8	20.7
Other, defence-related	1.6	3.2	5.7	6.8	7.2	8.3	8.2
Total national defence outlays	**304.7**	**495.3**	**551.3**	**661.0**	**705.6**	**716.3**	**701.8**
Outlays at constant (FY 2005) prices	363.0	495.3	509.2	588.2	612.0	610.9	587.9
Outlays as share (%) of GDP	*3.0*	*4.0*	*4.0*	*4.7*	*4.7*	*4.6*	*4.3*
Outlays as share (%) of total government outlays	*16.4*	*20.0*	*20.2*	*18.8*	*19.6*	*18.9*	*18.5*

DOD = Department of Defense; FY = financial year; GDP = gross domestic product; O&M = operations and maintenance; RDT&E = research, development, test and evaluation.

Note: In accordance with the SIPRI definition of military expenditure, SIPRI's figures for total US military expenditure include foreign military aid provided by the US Department of State, in addition to the figures shown here.

[a] Figures for 2012 and 2013 are estimates.

[b] Other spending includes the Office of Management and Budget categories of military construction, family housing and other.

Source: US Office of Management and Budget, *Budget of the United States Government, Fiscal Year 2012: Historical Tables* (Government Printing Office: Washington, DC, 2012), pp. 68–74, 137–38.

capability'.[7] Two examples suggested by Adams of ways to achieve this are the removal of the 92 000 military personnel added over the past 10 years due to the wars in Afghanistan and Iraq; and a reduction of the US ground-force presence in Europe and Asia.

The focus of the debate was how to adjust the US armed forces to the ending of the wars in Afghanistan and Iraq: whether they should be down-sized back to their size before the wars or not. The process of change was to begin with a review of national security and defence strategy, and on 5 January 2012 a Defense Strategic Guidance was presented jointly by the

[7] Adams, G., 'Six ways to save', *New York Times*, 9 May 2011. See also e.g. Dreyfuss, R., 'Panetta's sacred hippopotamus', The Nation blog, 3 Jan. 2012, <http://www.thenation.com/blog/165411/panettas-sacred-hippopotamus>; Taubman, P., 'No need for all these nukes', *New York Times*, 7 Jan. 2012; and Rumbaugh, R., 'Obama's defense cuts are too timid', CNN, 6 Jan. 2012, <http://edition.cnn.com/2012/01/06/opinion/rumbaugh-defense-cutbacks/>.

White House and the DOD.[8] Its stated aim was to identify US strategic interests and guide defence priorities and spending over the decade 2012–21 against the background of the transition from wartime to peacetime and the government spending crisis, requiring a reshaping of the armed forces.

The guidance listed the primary missions of the US armed forces where additional investment was seen as necessary. These included counterterrorism and irregular warfare; deterrence and defence (including being capable of denying the objectives of an aggressor in one region even when engaged in a large-scale operation in another region); power projection capabilities in the face of asymmetric capabilities, such as those used by China and Iran; and advanced and effective operational capabilities in cyberspace and space. In contrast, it included reductions in US conventional ground forces and in major systems designed for the cold war.[9]

The guidance called for a stronger military presence in the Asia–Pacific region in response to China's increasing power, to partner with India and to maintain peace in the Korean Peninsula. The Middle East was identified as another priority area where US defence efforts would 'be aimed at countering violent extremists and destabilizing threats' and where the proliferation of ballistic missiles and weapons of mass destruction was seen as of particular concern to the USA.[10]

While the guidance did not provide information on future military spending trends, President Obama emphasized that even if defence budget growth slows over the next 10 years, it 'will still grow, because we have global responsibilities that demand our leadership'.[11] Making reference to past US experience, he added: 'We can't afford to repeat the mistakes that have been made in the past—after World War II, after Vietnam—when our military was left ill prepared for the future. . . . I will not let that happen again.'[12]

One lesson from the downsizing of US forces after the end of the cold war that independent analysts have pointed to was that the long-term defence plan—for force structure and acquisition programmes—was not downsized as much as the financial plan (i.e. military spending), which caused a mismatch between commitments and budgetary plans. Ultimately, this was only resolved by the large budget increases following 2001.[13] If

---

[8] US Department of Defense (DOD), *Sustaining U.S. Global Leadership: Priorities for 21st Century Defense* (DOD: Washington, DC, Jan. 2012).

[9] US Department of Defense (note 8), pp. 4–5.

[10] US Department of Defense (note 8), p. 2.

[11] White House, 'Remarks by the President on the Defense Strategic Review', 5 Jan. 2012, <http://www.whitehouse.gov/the-press-office/2012/01/05/remarks-president-defense-strategic-review>.

[12] White House (note 11).

[13] See e.g. Gold, D., 'US military expenditure and the 2001 Quadrennial Defense Review', *SIPRI Yearbook 2002*, pp. 309–22.

major acquisition programmes are not cut, there is the risk of a similar mismatch again, which will put upward pressure on the defence budget in the future.[14]

The effects of the Budget Control Act were reflected in the plan included with the FY 2013 budget request, which cut previous plans by $259 billion over the 5-year period FYs 2013–17 and by $487 billion over the 10-year period 2012–21.[15] However, the FY 2013 budget did not take into account the possible further cuts of $600 billion as a result of sequestration. This will be a major issue in the US defence budget debate during 2012 and beyond.

---

[14] On future acquisition plans see chapter 5, section I, in this volume.

[15] US Department of Defense, 'DOD releases fiscal 2013 budget proposal', Press Release no. 098-12, 13 Feb. 2012, <http://www.defense.gov/releases/release.aspx?releaseid=15056>.

IV. Military expenditure in Africa

OLAWALE ISMAIL AND SAM PERLO-FREEMAN

The increase in military expenditure in Africa in 2011 was the largest of any region, at 8.6 per cent in real terms, reaching an estimated $34.6 billion. Over the period 2002–11, African military spending increased by 65 per cent. The regional increase in 2011 was almost exactly equal to the increase of the region's largest spender, Algeria. Its military spending increased by 44 per cent to reach $8.7 billion. The picture in the rest of Africa was mixed, with the spending of another 10 African countries increasing or decreasing by more than 10 per cent in real terms (see tables 4.3 and 4.9). The total for sub-Saharan Africa is estimated to have been unchanged in 2011.

The factors driving military expenditure in Africa include civil conflicts, regional ambitions, economic growth and rising oil revenues. In some parts of the continent, the threat of terrorist activities by Islamist groups has increased, drawing considerable interest from external actors, especially the United States. The most important groups in this regard are Harakat al-Shabab al-Mujahideen (Mujahedin Youth Movement, or al-Shabab) in Somalia, which has also carried out attacks in Kenya and Uganda; al-Qaeda in the Islamic Maghreb (AQIM), operating in Algeria, Mali, Mauritania, Niger and Tunisia; and Boko Haram in Nigeria.[1] The counterterrorism effort in response to each of these groups has largely been led by the military. In most cases, however, it is unclear whether such concerns are acting as a significant driver of military expenditure. In fact, the neighbouring countries most involved in the Somalia conflict—Ethiopia, Kenya and Uganda—have actually cut their reported defence budgets in recent years.[2]

Oil and counterterrorism in Algeria

Algeria has increased its military spending almost continually for two decades but the increase of 44 per cent in 2011—which included a 22 per cent mid-year increase in the defence budget—marked a sharp acceleration of this trend and is likely to leave Algeria with one of the highest military burdens in Africa. Algeria's increases have been fuelled in recent years by

---

[1] On the conflicts in Somalia and the Horn of Africa see chapter 2, section II, in this volume.

[2] Uganda made some significant arms purchases in 2011, several of which were paid for directly with oil. Some payments for arms imports have also been made through supplementary budgets drawn without prior parliamentary approval and it is not certain if these are included in published budget and expenditure figures. 'Uganda receives more SU-30s', Defence Web, 20 Oct. 2011, <http://www.defenceweb.co.za/index.php?option=com_content&view=article&id=20271&catid=74&Itemid=30>. See also Wezeman, P. D., Wezeman, S. T. and Béraud-Sudreau, L., *Arms Flows to Sub-Saharan Africa*, SIPRI Policy Paper no. 30 (SIPRI: Stockholm, Dec. 2011), pp. 22–23.

rising oil revenues, with oil and gas accounting for 70 per cent of public revenues in 2011.[3] Although Algerian oil production has declined slightly since 2008, this has not stopped the rise in military spending.[4]

The activities of AQIM in both Algeria and the wider Sahel region constitute Algeria's most immediate security challenge. The number of terrorist attacks in Algeria increased from 20 in 2001 to 120 in 2006 and 185 in 2009. This trend appears to have continued into 2011. Between July and August 2011, AQIM was responsible for at least 32 attacks against Algerian security forces. Counterterrorism operations by the armed forces of Algeria and neighbouring countries such as Mauritania have subsequently increased.[5] There is also an emerging regional dimension to the response, as countries in the Sahel have established new multilateral military training, cooperation, alliances and joint counterterrorism operations. For example, in 2010 Algeria, Mali, Mauritania and Niger established a joint command centre to coordinate and undertake joint military counterterrorism operations throughout the Sahel.[6] External actors are also involved in the counterterrorism effort. For example, the US-funded Trans-Sahara Counterterrorism Partnership (TSCTP), in which Algeria participates, provides training and other support to counterterrorism activities in the Sahel and the Maghreb.[7]

Nonetheless, it is doubtful that terrorism is the principle driver of Algerian military spending. The mid-year increase in spending in 2011 in particular appears to be linked to concerns over the conflict in neighbouring Libya, in response to which Algeria has opened new military bases near the border.[8] Further, while Algeria has embarked on a major rearmament

---

[3] Alternative Energy Africa, 'Algeria looks to wean its oil revenue dependency', 24 Aug. 2011, <http://ae-africa.com/read_article.php?NID=3212>.

[4] US Energy Information Administration, 'Country Analysis Brief: Algeria', 8 Mar. 2012, <http://www.eia.gov/countries/country-data.cfm?fips=AG&trk=p1>.

[5] Larémont, R. R., 'Al Qaeda in the Islamic Maghreb: terrorism and counterterrorism in the Sahel', *African Security*, vol. 4, no. 4 (2011), pp. 242–268; Leigh, K., 'North Africa's Sahel: the next terrorism hot spot?', *Time*, 12 Sep. 2011; US Department of State, Office of the Co-ordinator for Counterterrorism, *Country Reports on Terrorism 2010* (US Department of State: Washington, DC, 2011), p. 20; and Renard, T., *Terrorism and other Transnational Threats in the Sahel: What Role for the EU?*, Policy Brief (Center on Global Counterterrorism Cooperation: Washington, DC, Sep. 2010), p. 2.

[6] E.g. in Jan. 2012 Algerian forces crossed into Mali to provide assault helicopters, added firepower and other logistics to Malian troops battling AQIM affiliates in northern Mali. Keenan, J., 'A new crisis in the Sahel', Al Jazeera, 3 Jan. 2012, <http://www.aljazeera.com/indepth/opinion/2012/01/2012127444737703.html>.

[7] The TSTCP includes Algeria, Chad, Mali, Mauritania, Morocco, Niger, Nigeria, Senegal and Tunisia. US Africa Command, 'The Trans-Sahara Counterterrorism Partnership', <http://www.africom.mil/tsctp.asp>.

[8] 'L'Algérie révise sa politique de défense face aux menaces en Libye' [Algeria revises its defence policy in the face of threats from Libya], Global Net, 9 Sep. 2011, <http://www.gnet.tn/revue-de-presse-internationale/lalgerie-revise-sa-politique-de-defense-face-aux-menaces-en-libye/id-menu-957.html>; and 'Algérie : la coûteuse sécurité de la crise libyenne' [Algeria: the costly security of the Libyan crisis], *Jeune Afrique*, 3 Oct. 2011. On the conflict in Libya in 2011 see chapter 2, section I, and chapter 3, section II, in this volume.

programme, becoming the seventh largest importer of major conventional weapons worldwide in the period 2007–11, most of this equipment, in particular major naval and air systems, does not relate to counterterrorism.[9] A desire for regional power projection, rivalry with Morocco (which has also increased military spending substantially in recent years) and the political influence of the military may be more important driving factors.[10]

Oil and counterterrorism in Nigeria

In Nigeria, where military spending increased by 11 per cent in 2011, reaching $2.4 billion, oil revenues form a crucial part of government income and drive military expenditure.[11] The country is also facing a major security challenge in the form of escalating violence by the militant Islamist group Boko Haram.[12] The government's adoption of a militarized response to this threat was underlined in September 2011, when it deployed troops to six northern states to address the violent activities of the group, in addition to the existing internal security deployments in the Niger Delta. While the number of troops deployed has not been revealed, one officer suggested that it might amount to a division (10 000–15 000 troops) in one state alone. In many states, soldiers have established roadblocks and checkpoints along highways and have become a common presence on the streets.[13]

Nigeria's approach to counterterrorism is dominated by the military. The office of the National Security Adviser (NSA), which coordinates counterterrorism operations, is headed by a retired army chief; the adviser to the president on terrorism is a serving army general; and the multi-agency Joint Task Force (JTF) deployed for internal security (counterterrorism) operations is dominated, coordinated and headed by the military.[14]

Counterterrorism efforts appear to be shaping the configuration of the armed forces, as reflected in the creation of new antiterrorism units and specialist counterterrorism training. Since 2009, Nigeria has revived or

[9] See also chapter 6, section I, in this volume.

[10] Holtom et al., 'International arms transfers', *SIPRI Yearbook 2010*, pp. 296–301; and Perlo-Freeman et al., 'Military expenditure', *SIPRI Yearbook 2009*, pp. 200–201.

[11] On oil revenues and military spending in Nigeria see Perlo-Freeman et al., 'Military expenditure', *SIPRI Yearbook 2010*, pp. 180–82.

[12] The real name of the group is Jama'atul Ahlus Sunna Li Da'awatis Jihad (JASLIDAT, People Committed to the Propagation of the Prophet's Teachings and Jihad) but it is generally known as Boko Haram ('Western education is forbidden'). It was formed in 2002 in the north-eastern city of Maiduguri and later spread to neighbouring states. 'How we formed Boko Haram, by spokesman', *Vanguard* (Lagos), 27 July 2011.

[13] 'Military in biggest peacetime deployment: investigation', *Daily Trust* (Abuja), 20 Sep. 2011.

[14] Ailemen, T., 'Azazi appointed National Security Advisor', *Daily Champion* (Lagos), 5 Oct. 2010; Ogbu, A. and Shuaibu, I., 'Jonathan fires adviser on counterterrorism', *This Day* (Lagos), 5 Sep. 2011; and Amnesty International, 'Nigeria: unlawful killings by the Joint Military Task Force in Maiduguri must stop', Joint Public Statement, 14 July 2011, <http://www.amnesty.org/en/library/info/AFR44/013/2011/en>.

created the Anti-Terrorism Unit, the Special Warfare Unit, the Mountain Warfare Unit and the Composite Counter Terrorism Unit.[15]

As with AQIM, the activities of Boko Haram have drawn a response involving externals actors, both from West Africa and beyond. In early 2012 Cameroon, Chad, Niger and Nigeria signed a military cooperation and intelligence-sharing pact in relation to Boko Haram.[16] Nigeria has also explored counterterrorism cooperation with the United Kingdom.[17]

The full cost of these counterterrorism efforts is hard to assess but some costs are reported in the government budget. In 2010 a new budget line for the cost of military-led security operations, separate from the regular defence budget, was introduced, amounting to $232 million in 2010 and $137 million in 2011—approximately 12 per cent and 6 per cent of Nigeria's total military spending in 2010 and 2011, respectively.[18] These figures only cover operational costs and therefore may not take account of the costs of changes to force structures due to counterterrorism efforts or of new equipment acquired for these purposes. However, the new budget line does include the cost of operations in the Niger Delta.

The climate of fear and national security emergency generated by terrorism and governments' militarized responses to it makes military spending increases easier to justify domestically. Nigerian President Good-luck Jonathan noted in his 2012 budget speech that providing 'more support for the police, defence and counterterrorism operations' was a key priority in 2012, driving proposed increases in military and counter-terrorism expenditure.[19] Fear of terrorism may also be creating a political climate in which public scrutiny or criticism of military spending or the military in general are increasingly difficult. For example, the Nigerian Government arrested a newspaper columnist in July 2011 for alleged 'subversive' activities following his publication and analysis of the 2011 budgetary allocation to the military, the police and the office of the NSA. Although the columnist was later released without criminal charges, both his arrest and the subsequent deployment of armed soldiers to disperse civil society groups protesting against the removal of petrol subsidies in

---

[15] Soriwei, F., Owuamanam, J. and Adepegba, A., 'Army deploys US-trained Nigerian commandos in the north', The Punch (Lagos), 13 Nov. 2011.

[16] Soriwei, F. and Alechenu, J., 'Nigeria, three others, seal pact against Boko Haram', The Punch (Lagos), 7 Feb. 2012.

[17] 'FG, UK working on counter-terrorism strategy', The Punch (Lagos), 1 Feb. 2012; and British Prime Minister's Office, Transcript of press conference in Lagos, Nigeria, 22 July 2011, <http://www.number10.gov.uk/news/transcript-of-press-conference-in-lagos-nigeria/>.

[18] Nigerian Appropriation (amendment) Act 2011, assented to 26 May 2011, <http://www.nassnig.org/nass2/acts.php>; and Nigerian Appropriation (amendment) Act 2010, assented to 10 Aug. 2010, <http://www.nassnig.org/nass2/acts.php>.

[19] The proposed outlay for national security in 2012 is 920 billion naira ($5.7 billion), including 326 billion naira ($2 billion) for defence, 17 billion naira ($106 million) for internal security operations by the military and 124 billion naira ($773 million) for the NSA, among others. Nigerian Federal Budget Office, '2012 budget speech', 13 Dec. 2011, <http://www.budgetoffice.gov.ng/>, para. 33.

January 2012 suggest increasing militarization in Nigeria.[20] The military, always a strong political actor in Nigeria, is subjected to weak civilian scrutiny. This has encouraged severe corruption in the military sector and wasteful and excessive spending more generally.[21] While the government has made some efforts to tackle this in recent years, for example through greater budget transparency and reforms to military procurement, the climate created by military-led counterterrorism could put such limited gains at risk.[22]

Developments in other countries

The role of oil revenues as a driver, or at least enabler, of military spending increases in many African countries has been noted in previous editions of the SIPRI Yearbook.[23] Angola, now the third largest spender in Africa, is another example. Between the end of the country's civil war in 2002 and 2008, Angola's military spending soared by 148 per cent in conjunction with growth in oil production. Since then, however, military spending has levelled out, possibly linked to a slight dip in oil output.[24] According to official data, the increases in Angola's military budget have largely been directed towards improving the pay and conditions of troops and the creation of a 'professionalization program' for personnel.[25]

South Africa, the largest spender in sub-Saharan Africa and the second largest in Africa after Algeria, resumed its growth in military spending in 2011. After reaching a post-apartheid trough in 1999, spending had increased by 66 per cent by 2005, partly due to a major, corruption-ridden arms acquisition programme; spending then remained relatively constant until 2010.[26] The increase of 4.2 per cent in the budget for 2011, to $5.1 billion, is to be followed with planned increases in the 3 years 2012–14. The

---

[20] Adisa, T., Olatunji, J. S. and Ajayi, W., 'el-Rufai arrested; why he was picked up—SSS; Buhari, Fani-kayode talk tough', *Sunday Tribune* (Ibadan), 3 July 2011.

[21] Nightingale, K., *Shooting Down the MDGs: How Irresponsible Arms Transfers Undermine Development Goals*, Oxfam Briefing Paper no. 120 (Oxfam International: London, Oct. 2008), p. 13; Perlo-Freeman, S. and Perdomo, C., 'The developmental impact of military budgeting and procurement: implications for an arms trade treaty', SIPRI, Apr. 2008, <http://www.sipri.org/research/armaments/milex/publications/unpubl_milex>; and Omitoogun, W. and Tunde Oduntan, T., 'Nigeria', eds W. Omitoogun and E. Hutchful, SIPRI, *Budgeting for the Military Sector in Africa: The Processes and Mechanisms of Control* (Oxford University Press: Oxford, 2006).

[22] Nightingale (note 21).

[23] Perlo-Freeman et al. (note 11).

[24] US Energy Intelligence Administration, 'Country Analysis Brief: Angola', Aug. 2011, <http://www.eia.gov/countries/cab.cfm?fips=AO>.

[25] 'Angola defense budget surges upwards', Forecast International, 19 Aug. 2010, <http://emarketalerts.forecast1.com/mic/eabstract.cfm?recno=176108>; and 'China's visit to Angola raises questions about future arms purchases', Forecast International, 27 May 2010, <http://emarketalerts.forecast1.com/mic/eabstract.cfm?recno=173252>.

[26] See Feinstein, A. et al., 'Corruption and the arms trade: sins of commission', *SIPRI Yearbook 2011*.

increase in 2011 is largely due to a new salary structure but future increases will allow for new equipment purchases.[27]

One of the largest but least remarked upon increases in recent years has taken place in Swaziland, where, despite a slight fall in 2011, military spending has increased by 160 per cent since 2002, reaching $123 million, and has doubled as a share of gross domestic product, to 3.2 per cent in 2010. The increase in spending has occurred despite the fact that 70 per cent of the population earns less than $2 a day. Swaziland also has the world's highest HIV infection rate and faces an economic crisis involving severe cuts to social services. These factors, and the lack of any internal or external military threats, led to increasing criticism in 2011 of the high level of military spending.[28] However, as Swaziland is an absolute monarchy, where parliament is forbidden from debating the defence budget, its high military spending may be in part a matter of poor governance.[29]

[27] Heitman, H., 'S Africa increases defence budget', *Jane's Defence Weekly*, 2 Mar. 2011, p. 19; and South African National Treasury, *Medium Term Budget Policy Statement 2011* (National Treasury: Pretoria, October 2011).

[28] United Nations Development Programme (UNDP), *Human Development Report 2011: Sustainability and Equity—A Better Future for All* (UNDP: New York, 2011), p. 144.

[29] Integrated Regional Information Networks (IRIN), 'Swaziland: opposition to military spending grows', 29 Nov. 2011, <http://www.irinnews.org/Report/94336/SWAZILAND-Opposition-to-military-spending-grows>.

V. Europe and the impact of austerity on military expenditure

SAM PERLO-FREEMAN

As a result of the global financial and economic crisis that started in 2008, budget deficits soared across most of Europe, and in 2011 discussions on military expenditure in Europe were dominated by the impact of the austerity measures enacted by governments in an effort to reduce these deficits. On the one hand, acute debt crises in Greece, Italy and Spain have led to the imposition of particularly severe austerity measures—with major cuts to public spending and increases in taxation—in some cases as a condition of international bailout packages. On the other hand, countries such as the United Kingdom that have not faced such imminent debt problems have also cut public spending, based on the belief that reducing deficits is the overwhelming economic priority following the crisis.

Total military expenditure in Europe in 2011 was, however, essentially unchanged in real terms compared with 2010, at $407 billion. A small reduction of 1.9 per cent in real terms in Western and Central Europe was offset by a 10.2 per cent real increase in Eastern Europe.

The rise in Eastern Europe comes from increases in Russia and Azerbaijan. Russia returned to its long-term trend of rising military expenditure, after a brief dip in 2010. An increase of 9.3 per cent in real terms took Russian military spending to $71.9 billion in 2011, meaning that Russia overtook the UK and France to become the world's third largest spender. Russia plans continued increases in military spending; its draft budget plans include an increase in national defence spending of 53 per cent in real terms between 2011 and 2014.[1] The State Armaments Programme for the period 2011–20—which covers arms procurement and research and development (R&D)—is expected to cost over 20 trillion roubles ($650 billion), with the aim of replacing 70 per cent of Russia's mostly Soviet-era military equipment with modern weaponry by 2020.[2] The planned spending includes 700 billion roubles ($31 billion) for the Russian military-industrial complex to update its equipment and technology.[3] Meanwhile,

---

[1] Cooper, J., 'Military spending in the Russian federal budget, 2010–2014', Research note, 12 Aug. 2011, <http://www.sipri.org/research/armaments/milex/publications/unpubl_milex/>. SIPRI's figures for Russia also include military pensions, expenditure on paramilitary forces and estimates for a number of other small items.

[2] The precise total expenditure for the programme has not yet been determined, with different sources suggesting figures of 19–23 trillion roubles. E.g. Agence France-Presse, 'Putin outlines push for stronger military', *Defense News*, 20 Feb. 2012.

[3] Litovkin, D., 'Triumf and Tsirkon are going into the force: Deputy Defense Minister Vladimir Popovkin explained, how to rearm the army', *Izvestiya*, 11 Mar. 2011, Translation from Russian, Open Source Center.

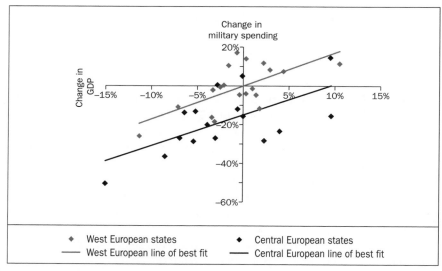

Figure 4.1. Changes in military spending versus gross domestic product, Western Europe and Central Europe, 2008–11

Note: Each country is represented by a point determined by its real-terms change in GDP (horizontal axis) and its real-terms change in military spending (vertical axis) between 2008 and 2011. The lines of best fit show the average relationship between the variables. In both Central and Western Europe, a majority of countries had falling military spending and a positive relationship between changes in the two variables. However, in Central Europe not only were the average falls in GDP higher, but the line of best fit is much lower. Thus, while a West European country with unchanged GDP would, on average, have had unchanged military spending, a Central European country with unchanged GDP would, on average, have cut its military spending by 15%.

Azerbaijan's increase of 89 per cent in real terms was the largest worldwide and took its military spending to $3.1 billion.[4]

Two-thirds of countries in Western and Central Europe have cut military spending since 2008. The size of these cuts shows, unsurprisingly, a strong relationship with trends in gross domestic product (GDP), which has generally fallen. Conversely, many of the countries that have increased military spending—notably Norway, Poland, Sweden, Switzerland and Turkey—have maintained economic growth through the crisis. Perhaps surprisingly, the relationship between changes in military spending and changes in either public debt or public sector deficits as a share of GDP has been much weaker. In comparison with West European countries, the falls in military spending in the former Communist states of Central Europe have been much larger, both absolutely and relative to their GDP growth rates; on average, Central European countries reduced spending by 15 per

---

[4] On arms acquisitions by Armenia and Azerbaijan see chapter 6, section IV, in this volume.

cent more than West European countries, given the same change in GDP (see figure 4.1).[5] The large falls in military spending in Central Europe followed a period of significant increases in military spending by many recent and aspiring members of the North Atlantic Treaty Organization (NATO), which proved unsustainable in the economic crisis. Nonetheless, a few Central European countries (Croatia, Romania and Serbia) are considering making large new purchases of combat aircraft.[6]

The three major spenders in Western Europe—the UK, France and Germany—have made only modest reductions in military spending since 2008, in each case by less than 5 per cent in real terms, although the 2011 figures for the UK are higher due to the cost of the Libya War, which had reached $340 million by September 2011.[7] However, the UK and Germany are planning further cuts: the UK by 7.5 per cent in real terms by financial year 2014/15 compared to financial year 2010/11 and Germany by around 10 per cent by 2015 compared to 2011. France is planning to maintain roughly constant spending in real terms up to 2013.[8]

The crisis countries of Southern Europe

Among West European countries, Greece, Italy, Portugal and Spain in Southern Europe and Ireland have been hardest hit by the economic crisis and have faced acute sovereign debt crises that have called into question governments' abilities to service or refinance their debts. Greece, Ireland and Portugal have required bailouts from the European Union (EU) and the International Monetary Fund (IMF), while rising yields on Italian Government debt—a measure of the perceived risk of lending to the country—contributed to the fall of the Italian Government of Silvio Berlusconi. These countries have introduced particularly severe austerity packages, either as part of conditions attached to bailouts or in order to restore lenders' con-

---

[5] Western Europe includes the 19 states Austria, Belgium, Cyprus, Denmark, Finland, France, Germany, Greece, Ireland, Italy, Malta, Netherlands, Norway, Portugal, Spain, Sweden, Switzerland, Turkey and UK. Iceland and Luxembourg are excluded due to lack of data. Central Europe includes the 16 states Albania, Bosnia and Herzegovina, Bulgaria, Croatia, Czech Republic, Estonia, Hungary, Latvia, Lithuania, FYR Macedonia, Montenegro, Poland, Romania, Serbia, Slovakia and Slovenia.

[6] 'Croatian Gripen offer', *Airforces Monthly*, Dec. 2011, p. 13; 'U.S.–Romania F-16 talks snag', *Defense News*, 6 June 2011, p. 3; and Cvejic, B., 'Combat aircraft due in 2012', *Danas*, 22 Dec. 2011, Translation from Serbian, Open Source Center.

[7] Hammond, P., British Secretary of State for Defence, 'Delivering on the frontline: operational success and sustainable armed forces', Speech, Royal United Services Institute for Defence and Security Studies (RUSI), 8 Dec. 2011, <http://www.rusi.org/events/ref:E4EBAA415CBC7A>.

[8] British Treasury, *Spending Review 2010*, Cm 7942 (The Stationery Office: London, Oct. 2010); Loi de programmation des finances publiques pour les années 2011 à 2014 [Law on the public finance programme for the years 2011 to 2014], French Law no. 2010-1645 of 28 Dec. 2010, <http://www.legifrance.gouv.fr/affichTexte.do?cidTexte=JORFTEXT000023310845>; and Muller, A., 'Germany to boost defense budget by 133m Euros', *Defense News*, 7 Sep. 2011.

fidence.[9] Spain's debt crisis has been less severe, but its economic situation is particularly dire, with unemployment at 22 per cent in January 2012. The Spanish Government has, like other countries, chosen to prioritize deficit reduction.[10] These austerity measures have included military expenditure; the cuts since 2008 of four of these countries—Greece, Ireland, Italy and Spain—were among the largest in Western Europe.

Greece

Assessing trends in Greece's military expenditure is complicated by the fact that the official defence budget does not include all military spending; in particular, military pensions are not included.[11] Figures published by NATO on the military expenditure of member states are more comprehensive, but at the time of writing were only available up to 2010, and the 2010 figure was an estimate that may have been superseded by budget changes.[12] SIPRI's figures for 2010 and 2011 are therefore estimates based on the trend in the defence budget.[13]

Greek military spending actually increased slightly in 2011, but this followed an exceptionally large fall—by almost one-third in real terms—in 2010, when the original budget was greatly reduced during the year. The defence budget for 2012 shows a further 16 per cent fall in nominal terms, with further cuts planned in coming years as part of the austerity package. Included are large cuts to wages and pensions, in common with all public sector employees.[14] The armed forces are also being restructured, with cuts in the number of troops and major equipment. Greece reduced the number of its troop deployed to NATO's Kosovo Force (KFOR) from 711 at the end of 2010 to 215 at the end of 2011.[15] Greece placed no new orders for major arms in 2011, but payments for previous large orders from France and Germany meant that spending on equipment as a share of total military spending spiked in 2009–10.[16] During 2011 there were discussions over the potential purchase of French frigates on a delayed payment basis, but no

---

[9] 'Timeline: the unfolding Eurozone debt crisis', BBC News, 13 Feb. 2012, <http://www.bbc.co.uk/news/business-13856580>.

[10] 'Spain's unemployment total passes 5 million', BBC News, 27 Jan. 2012, <http://www.bbc.co.uk/news/world-16754600>.

[11] This section does not take account of the effects of new austerity measures agreed by the Greek Parliament on 12 Feb. 2012.

[12] North Atlantic Treaty Organization (NATO), 'Financial and economic data relating to NATO defence', 10 Mar. 2011, <http://www.nato.int/cps/en/natolive/news_71296.htm>.

[13] SIPRI figures for Greece also include spending on the coastguard, which operates as a paramilitary force.

[14] 'Greek government austerity measures', BBC News, 19 Oct. 2011, <http://www.bbc.co.uk/news/business-13940431>.

[15] Athanasopoulos, A., 'Fewer generals and camps', To Vima, 5 Dec. 2010, Translation from Greek, Open Source Center; and SIPRI Multilateral Peace Operations Database, <http://www.sipri.org/databases/pko>. See also Valmas, T., 'Greece to reduce Kosovo force as budget cuts bite', Jane's Defence Weekly, 16 June 2010.

[16] North Atlantic Treaty Organization (note 12).

decision had been made by early 2012. In the long term, the 2011–25 Arms Procurement Plan has been reduced by 70 per cent in comparison with the previous 2006–20 plan.[17]

For a long time, Greece has had the highest military burden—military spending as a share of GDP—in the EU, driven by its long-running tensions with Turkey over Cyprus and maritime disputes in the Aegean Sea. The process of cuts to military spending has therefore been made easier by improved relations with Turkey, which announced a 'zero problems with neighbours' strategy in 2010 and removed Greece from a list of countries perceived as a threat. Renewed efforts have also been made to resolve the maritime disputes.[18] Greece's military spending cuts actually took its military burden below that of the UK in 2010, a trend that is likely to persist on the basis of current plans.

Italy

Italy's military spending is also less than fully transparent, in that it is distributed across different departmental budgets. Spending on overseas military operations (in Afghanistan, Kosovo, Lebanon and Libya) is approved by the Italian Parliament separately from the Ministry of Defence budget.[19] Over €1 billion ($1.4 billion) of additional military procurement and R&D spending each year is funded by the Ministry of Economic Development.[20] As was the case for Greece, NATO figures for Italy for 2011 were not available at the time of writing. SIPRI's estimate for Italian military spending in 2011 is thus subject to some uncertainty. Meanwhile, future trends can only be assessed on the basis of the portion of military spending covered by the defence budget.

With this caveat, SIPRI estimates a 16 per cent real-terms drop in Italian military spending between 2008 and 2011. Existing cuts have fallen heavily on operations and maintenance expenditure and were expected to require a freeze on recruitment in 2011.[21] However, despite new austerity packages passed in 2011, including a freeze in public sector wages, the Ministry of Defence budget will actually increase slightly in nominal terms up to 2014,

[17] Müller, A., 'Germany raps French warship deal with Greece', *Defense News*, 18 Oct. 2011; and Dimakas, L., 'An 11% reduction in defense expenditure during 2010', *Ta Nea*, 12 Apr. 2011, Translation from Greek, Open Source Center.

[18] See Perlo-Freeman et al., 'Military expenditure', *SIPRI Yearbook 2011*, pp. 173–76; and Bekdil, B. E. and Eginsoy, U., 'Turks, Greeks seek to end Aegean impasse', *Defense News*, 1 Nov. 2011, p. 11.

[19] Kington, T. 'Italian military hit by 10% budget cut', *Defense News*, 27 May 2010.

[20] D'Agostino G., Di Stefano, L. and Pieroni L., 'Is military burden a stimulus for economic growth? The case of Italy', Paper presented at the 15th Annual International Conference on Economics and Security, 15–16 June 2011; and Kington, T., 'Italy trims defense amid debt crisis', *Defense News*, 18 July 2011, pp. 1, 7.

[21] Kington (note 20); 'Italy's 2011 budget', *Il Foglio*, 23 Oct. 2010, Translation from Italian, Open Source Center; and Bassi, A., 'The Defense Ministry cuts recruitment to zero', *Milano Finanza*, 2 Nov. 2010, Translation from Italian, Open Source Center.

according to the three-year budget plan of October 2011.[22] On the other hand, a major cut of €1.9 billion ($2.6 billion) has been made to the Ministry of Economic Development budget up to 2014, although it was uncertain whether this would affect the military procurement and R&D component.[23] Italy also plans to reduce its overseas military operations, so overall military spending may fall.[24]

Spain

Spain's real-terms increase of 29 per cent in military expenditure over the period 2000–2008 was one of the biggest in Western Europe. However, between the onset of the crisis and 2011, military expenditure fell by 18 per cent and dropped to just 1 per cent of GDP—the third lowest military burden in NATO, after Luxembourg and Hungary.

One consequence of these cuts is that the Spanish Ministry of Defence is now unable to afford repayments of its €26 billion ($36 billion) debts to arms suppliers for 19 major military modernization programmes that were initiated in the 2000s. One temporary solution may be a restructuring of the debts, which the companies would manage by taking loans from the Ministry of Industry—effectively creating an indirect source of extra-budgetary military spending. The acquisition programmes were started during the period of economic growth and increasing military spending but arguably lacked clear strategic justification. Constantino Méndez, Spanish Secretary of State for Defence, admitted in October 2010: 'We should not have acquired systems that we are not going to use, for conflict scenarios that do not exist and, what is worse, with funds that we did not have then and we do not have now'.[25]

The implications of reduced spending

Current and impending military spending cuts have prompted unease in many quarters that European countries risk losing global influence as they fall further behind the United States in military capabilities, while rising powers such as China rapidly catch up and even overtake them. Perennial accusations of free riding on US military power have become more vocal on both sides of the Atlantic.

---

[22] Italian Ministry of Economy and Finance, 'Italy delivers', 15 Sep. 2011, <http://www.mef.gov.it/documenti/open.asp?idd=27880>; Italian Ministry of Economy and Finance (MEF), *Il budget dello stato per il triennio 2011–2013* [The state budget for the period 2011–13] (MEF: Rome, Oct. 2010), pp. 443–69; and Italian Ministry of Economy and Finance (MEF), *Il budget dello stato per il triennio 2012–2014* [The state budget for the period 2012–14] (MEF: Rome, Oct. 2011), pp. 435–63.

[23] Kington (note 20).

[24] Agence France-Presse, 'Italy to scale back overseas military operations', *Defense News*, 6 July 2011.

[25] Gonzales, M., 'Defense Ministry renegotiates debt of 26 billion that it cannot pay', *El País*, 13 Aug. 2011, Translation from Spanish, Open Source Center.

Most prominent among those raising such fears were the NATO Secretary General, Anders Fogh Rasmussen, and the US Secretary of Defense, Robert Gates. Rasmussen, speaking at the Munich Security Conference in February 2011, while recognizing the need for military spending to reflect economic realities, argued that 'Europe simply cannot afford to get out of the security business' and warned that failure to spend enough on the military would lead to a Europe that would be 'divided', 'weaker' and 'increasingly adrift from the United States'.[26] Gates, speaking in Brussels in June 2011, predicted a 'dim and dismal future' for NATO, with the USA losing interest in increasingly irrelevant European allies if the latter continue to reduce military spending.[27]

However, such views are not universally shared among commentators. One US political scientist argued that, far from free riding, European countries were making a rational strategic response in a 'golden age of peace and security', where threats are lower than in any previous era and the ability to achieve goals through military action severely limited; and that arguably, the adjustment was needed by the USA, where the extensive use of military power over the past decade had brought at best dubious results.[28] A similar case was made by a French commentator, who argued that strategic influence had little to do with the share of GDP devoted to military spending, that the threats and risks cited as a consequence of low military spending were generally vague, and likewise the concrete gains that can be made through military force are limited. However, he acknowledged a role for marine power in ensuring the maintenance of vital sea lines of communication, an interest shared by European and Asian states.[29]

Ultimately, the question of what level of military spending is appropriate for European states must come from an overall strategic assessment of what threats there are to security; to what extent military power is an appropriate and effective tool for meeting such threats; what sort of influence the EU, NATO and their member states are seeking to achieve; and in what ways military power can contribute to such influence. The economic crisis has certainly prompted such thinking in a number of

[26] Fogh Rasmussen, A., NATO Secretary General, 'Building security in an age of austerity', Keynote speech, 2011 Munich Security Conference, 4 Feb. 2011, <http://www.nato.int/cps/en/natolive/opinions_70400.htm>.

[27] Gates, R., 'Reflections on the status and future of the transatlantic alliance', Keynote speech, Security and Defence Agenda Conference, Brussels, 10 June 2011, <http://www.securitydefenceagenda.org/Contentnavigation/Activities/Activitiesoverview/tabid/1292/EventType/EventView/EventId/1070/EventDateID/1087/PageID/5141/Reflectionsonthestatusandfutureofthetransatlanticalliance.aspx>.

[28] Fettweis, C. J., 'Free riding or restraint? Examining European grand strategy', *Comparative Strategy*, vol. 30, no. 4 (2011).

[29] Le Guelte, G., 'Le budget d'armement, facteur de puissance?' [The arms budget, a determinant of power?], *Revue Défense Nationale*, no. 737 (Feb. 2011), pp. 23–34.

countries.[30] Meanwhile, the prospect of lower military budgets has led to renewed interest in greater European defence cooperation as a means of obtaining more capability for any given level of spending. Discussion within the EU has focused on the 'pooling and sharing' of capabilities, while NATO has promoted the concept of 'smart defence', which encourages more coordinated prioritization of capabilities and specialization by individual member states as well as greater cooperation through measures such as pooling and sharing.[31] The concept of pooling and sharing was launched at a meeting of EU defence ministers in Ghent, Belgium, in September 2010, where they agreed to draw up a list of suitable projects.[32] As with other European defence cooperation initiatives, questions remain about how far it can be taken given countries' concerns over preserving national sovereignty, but moves such as the major British–French Defence and Security Cooperation Treaty of November 2010 may indicate a greater degree of political commitment.[33] One commentator argues that pooling and sharing is most likely to succeed through promoting 'islands of co-operation' between small groups of like-minded countries on particular areas of defence, rather than attempting more wide-reaching cooperation across a larger 'core group' of EU members.[34]

However, the debate over what military forces, capabilities and levels of spending European countries actually need is strongly conflated with the question of transatlantic cohesion in the face of the spending gap between the USA and Europe. That this gap is the result of US increases, more than European decreases, is rarely highlighted, and the thought that the problem may come from the former rather than the latter is rarely mooted in senior policy circles.

---

[30] E.g. the UK's most recent strategic defence review was prompted by its budget crisis. British Ministry of Defence, *Securing Britain in an Age of Uncertainty: The Strategic Defence and Security Review*, Cm 7948 (The Stationery Office: London, Oct. 2010). In 2011 the French Government also announced that a review of its 2008 Defence and National Security White Paper would take place in 2012. Guibert, N., 'La France va réviser sa stratégie de défense' [France will revise its defence strategy], *Le Monde*, 8 Sep. 2011.

[31] European Defence Agency (EDA), 'EDA's pooling and sharing', Fact sheet, 20 Jan. 2012, <http://eda.europa.eu/publications/12-02-01/Pooling_Sharing_fact_sheet>; and North Atlantic Treaty Organization (NATO), 'Smart defence', 8 Feb. 2012, <http://www.nato.int/cps/en/SID-AF04 C059-D03FE758/natolive/topics_84268.htm?>. On cooperation in arms production see chapter 5, section I, in this volume.

[32] European Defence Agency (note 31).

[33] Treaty between the United Kingdom of Great Britain and Northern Ireland and the French Republic for Defence and Security Co-operation, signed 2 Nov. 2010, Cm 7976 (The Stationery Office: Norwich, 10 Nov. 2010).

[34] Valasek, T., *Surviving Austerity: The Case for a New Approach to EU Military Collaboration* (Centre for European Reform: London, Apr. 2011).

VI. The reporting of military expenditure data to the United Nations, 2002–11

NOEL KELLY

Over the past decade, there has been a general decline in the annual reporting by United Nations member states of their military spending through the use of the UN Standardized Instrument for Reporting Military Expenditures.[1] At the same time, an increasing number of countries have posted information about their military expenditure online, albeit not according to the UN definition or the format of the UN Standardized Instrument. Indeed, of the 79 countries that made no response to the instrument between 2002 and 2008, 61 made at least basic information on their defence budget available online, and 16 of those gave a detailed breakdown of the budget.[2]

While the UN Standardized Instrument represented an important improvement in the availability of data on military spending when it was first introduced in 1981, the gradual decline in reporting has been a matter of concern to many UN member states. It was against this background that, in response to a joint German–Romanian proposal in 2007, a Group of Governmental Experts (GGE) was established in November 2010 to review the operation of the UN Standardized Instrument and its further development. This was the first such review of the instrument, which has remained almost unchanged since its introduction. The aim was to 'strengthen and broaden participation' in the instrument and to 'improv[e] its further development'.[3] The report of the GGE was presented to the UN Secretary-General in June 2011.

This section describes the UN system of reporting, presents trends in reporting for the period 2002–11, and describes the findings and recommendations of the 2011 report by the GGE on the UN Standardized Instrument.

The United Nations reporting system

The UN Standardized Instrument for Reporting Military Expenditures was established in 1980, started its operation in 1981 and is managed by the UN

---

[1] In a Dec. 2011 decision by the UN General Assembly, the name of the instrument was changed to the 'United Nations Report on Military Expenditures'. UN General Assembly Resolution 66/20, 2 Dec. 2011.

[2] United Nations, Office for Disarmament Affairs (UNODA), and SIPRI, *Promoting Further Openness and Transparency in Military Matters: An Assessment of the United Nations Standardized Instrument for Reporting Military Expenditures*, UNODA Occasional Papers no. 20 (United Nations: New York, Nov. 2010), p. 16.

[3] UN General Assembly Resolution 62/13, 5 Dec. 2007.

Table 4.6. Number of countries reporting their military expenditure to the United Nations, 2002 and 2006–11

	2002	2006	2007	2008	2009	2010	2011
No. of UN member states	191	192	192	192	192	192	193
Total no. of reports[a]	**81**	**80**	**78**	**77**	**58**	**60**	**51**
Standardized reports	70	54	48	53	42	41	38
Simplified reports[b]	..	15	18	16	10	12	6
Nil reports[c]	11	11	12	8	6	7	7
Response rate (%)	*42*	*42*	*41*	*40*	*30*	*31*	*26*
Reports from non-UN member states[d]	1	2	1	–	–	–	–

[a] Years are the year of the Secretary-General's request (the deadline of which is 30 Apr. of the following year). Figures for 2011 only include submissions up to 8 Dec. 2011. Some countries may report after this date. Total figures include nil reports.

[b] Countries reporting to the UN with both standardized and simplified reports are listed as standardized reports to avoid double counting.

[c] A nil report is a questionnaire returned to the UN with no data entered, usually submitted by a country that does not maintain regular armed forces.

[d] Reports from non-UN member states are not included in other figures.

Sources: United Nations, General Assembly, 'Objective information on military matters, including transparency of military expenditures', Reports of the Secretary-General, Various dates, 2002–11, <http://www.un.org/disarmament/convarms/Milex/>.

Office for Disarmament Affairs (UNODA).[4] Each year the UN Secretary-General invites all member states (currently 193) through a *note verbale* to report their military expenditure by 30 April for the most recent financial year for which data is available. The basis for this request is a UN General Assembly resolution adopted in 1980.[5] Successive biennial General Assembly resolutions have called for the continued reporting of military expenditure by member states.[6]

In their reports, UN member states are asked to use the UN Standardized Instrument for Reporting Military Expenditures, which has been developed for this purpose, but they can use any other reporting format developed by other international or regional organizations. If appropriate, a state can submit a nil report—a report with no data entered; these are usually submitted by countries with no regular armed forces.[7]

The UN Standardized Instrument is in the form of a matrix with fields for reporting spending by function (e.g. personnel, operations and maintenance, procurement, construction, and research and development, each

[4] UN Office for Disarmament Affairs (UNODA), 'Military spending', <http://www.un.org/disarmament/convarms/Milex/>.

[5] UN General Assembly Resolution 35/142 B, 12 Dec. 1980.

[6] The most recent such resolution is UN General Assembly Resolution 66/20 (note 1).

[7] UN General Assembly Resolution 66/20 (note 1).

broken down into subcategories) and by military service (e.g. air force, army and navy) and to give aggregated totals.[8] In the belief that some countries found this matrix too complicated and to encourage reporting by more countries, the UN introduced an alternative, simplified reporting form in 2002 that requests only aggregate data by service on personnel, operations and procurement. The reported data is included in an annual report to the General Assembly.[9]

The objective of the instrument has evolved over the years. The initial purpose was to use the reporting system as a step towards gradual reductions in military budgets.[10] The justification stated in the most recent resolution is

that the improvement of international relations forms a sound basis for promoting further openness and transparency in all military matters [and] that transparency in military matters is an essential element for building a climate of trust and confidence between States worldwide and that a better flow of objective information on military matters can help to relieve international tension and is therefore an important contribution to conflict prevention.[11]

Trends in reporting, 2002–11

There has been a decrease in reporting to the UN Standardized Instrument during recent years (see table 4.6). The number of countries reporting has dropped from a high of 81 in 2002 to 51 in 2011.

Since 1980, 124 states have submitted a report at least once.[12] Over the period 2002–11 the rate of response to the UN (including nil reports) was 37 per cent, but this fell to 31 per cent in 2010 and to 26 per cent in 2011. The region with the highest overall reporting rate in 2011 was Europe, while the Middle East and Africa had the lowest rates (see table 4.7).[13]

The political sensitivity of military expenditure may be a primary reason for not reporting in some cases. However, this cannot be the reason for the majority of those that do not report as many of them have made their military budgets available to international financial institutions or online to the general public.

---

[8] The Standardized Instrument is available on the UNODA website, <http://www.un.org/disarmament/convarms/Milex/Forms/>.

[9] The most recent report is United Nations, General Assembly, 'Objective information on military matters, including transparency of military expenditures', Report of the Secretary-General, A/66/117, 29 June 2011, and Addendum A/66/117/Add.1, 28 Sep. 2011.

[10] See UNODA and SIPRI (note 2); and Omitoogun, W. and Sköns, E., 'Military expenditure data: a 40-year overview', SIPRI Yearbook 2006, pp. 276–77, 286, 291.

[11] UN General Assembly Resolution 66/20 (note 1).

[12] UNODA and SIPRI (note 2), p. 2.

[13] On reporting rates in Latin America see Bromley, M. and Solmirano, C., Transparency in Military Spending and Arms Acquisitions in Latin America and the Caribbean, SIPRI Policy Paper no. 31 (SIPRI: Stockholm, Jan. 2012).

Table 4.7. Reporting of military expenditure data to the United Nations, by region and subregion, 2011

Region/subregion	No. of countries	Countries reporting to the UN (including nil reports)	Total	Response rate (%)
Africa	54		2	4
North Africa	4	Tunisia[a]	1	
Sub-Saharan Africa	50	Burkina Faso	1	
Americas	35		9	26
Central America and the Caribbean	21	El Salvador[b], Jamaica[b], Mexico, Trinidad and Tobago	4	
North America	2	Canada, USA	2	
South America	12	Argentina, Brazil, Peru	3	
Asia and Oceania	42		8	19
Central and South Asia	12	Kazakhstan	1	
East Asia	5	Japan, South Korea[b],	2	
Oceania	14	Australia, Nauru[a], Samoa[a], Solomon Islands[a]	4	
South East Asia	11	Malaysia[b]	1	
Europe	48		31	65
Eastern Europe	7	Armenia[b], Belarus, Russia	3	
Western and Central Europe	41	Austria, Albania[c], Andorra[c], Bosnia and Herzegovina[c], Bulgaria, Czech Republic[c], Estonia, Finland, Germany, Greece, Iceland[a], Ireland, Latvia, Lithuania, Macedonia (FYR), Monaco[c], Montenegro[c], Netherlands, Norway, Poland, Portugal, Romania[c], Serbia[c], Slovakia, Slovenia, Switzerland, Turkey[c], UK	28	
Middle East	14	Lebanon[b]	1	7
Total	**193**		**51**	**26**

[a] These countries submitted nil reports. [b] These countries reported with the simplified form. [c] These countries reported with both the simplified and the standardized forms.

Sources: United Nations, General Assembly, 'Objective information on military matters, including transparency of military expenditures', Report of the Secretary-General, A/66/117, 29 June 2011, and Addendum A/66/117/Add.1, 28 Sep. 2011.

In general, most countries that have never reported to the UN Standard-ized Instrument tend to make only basic information on military spending available elsewhere (such as a single total figure).[14] Equally, the fact that many countries have responded at least once suggests that they have the capacity and the willingness to report but lack political commitment to respond consistently.

The report of the Group of Governmental Experts

In June 2011 the report of the Group of Governmental Experts on the Oper-ation and Further Development of the United Nations Standardized Instru-ment for Reporting Military Expenditures was presented to the UN Sec-retary-General and submitted to the UN General Assembly.[15]

The GGE suggested that low reporting rates to the UN Standardized Instrument in some regions could be explained by the incompatibility of national accounting systems with the reporting matrix. Other factors men-tioned were the complexity of the standardized reporting form; a lack of political commitment, interest or capacity; the sensitivity of reporting mili-tary expenditures; and a lack of awareness at a sufficiently high political level.

The report emphasized the need for the broadest possible participation in reporting military expenditure and this requirement influenced the recommendations of the GGE. To better accommodate the particularities of national accounting systems and to facilitate and enhance participation in the UN reporting system, the GGE agreed on a common understanding of military expenditure and on a number of modifications to the standardized and simplified reporting forms. It also developed a format for the nil report and proposed a new title for the reporting instrument. The common defin-ition of 'military expenditure' was agreed to be all financial resources that a state spends on the uses and functions of its military forces.[16]

The report suggested that states should be able to choose the most appropriate reporting form (although the standardized form should still be considered the preferred format) and should be encouraged to complement their submissions with explanations, additional materials and document-ation.[17] Given that a simplified version of the UN Standardized Instrument has existed since 2002 it is unlikely that these recommendations alone will lead to increased participation. Nevertheless, recommendations from the report that might lead to increased participation if applied stringently are

[14] UNODA and SIPRI (note 2), p. 22.
[15] United Nations, General Assembly, 'Group of Governmental Experts on the Operation and Further Development of the United Nations Standardized Instrument for Reporting Military Expend-itures', Note by the Secretary-General, A/66/89, 14 June 2011.
[16] United Nations (note 15), p. 21.
[17] United Nations (note 15), p. 2.

improved promotion of the instrument by the UN Secretariat and the offering of practical assistance to member states lacking the capacity to report
data.[18] Such capacity building can take many forms, such as training of key
personnel, online training packages and on-site support.[19]

The GGE report noted the importance of leveraging existing resources of
the UN disarmament machinery to promote the UN Standardized Instrument and encouraged officials at higher levels of the UN Secretariat to
more actively disseminate information on the instrument.[20] To further
efforts at better communication between the Secretariat and member
states, it recommended that national reports include details of the national
contact points.[21] The GGE also called for continued periodic review of the
instrument to ensure continued relevance and operation and suggested the
next review be scheduled in five years.

The report concluded that transparency in military expenditure remains
an essential element for building trust and confidence among states. The
recommendations of the GGE report were endorsed by the First Committee
of the General Assembly and then by the full General Assembly, in each
case without a vote.[22] In doing so, the General Assembly changed the name
of the reporting instrument to the United Nations Report on Military
Expenditures. It will be interesting to see, given the recommendations of
the 2011 GGE report, whether the downward trend in reporting can be
reversed in the coming years.

---

[18] United Nations (note 15), pp. 23–24.
[19] United Nations (note 15), p. 21.
[20] United Nations (note 15), p. 15.
[21] United Nations (note 15), p. 20.
[22] United Nations, General Assembly, First Committee, 'Objective information on military
matters, including transparency of military expenditures', Draft resolution, A/C.1/66/L.35, 17 Oct.
2011; and UN General Assembly Resolution 66/20 (note 1).

VII. Military expenditure data, 2002–11

SAM PERLO-FREEMAN, OLAWALE ISMAIL, NOEL KELLY,
ELISABETH SKÖNS, CARINA SOLMIRANO AND HELEN WILANDH

The following tables contain data on military expenditure in local currency at current prices (table 4.8), constant (2010) US dollars (table 4.9) and as a share of gross domestic product (table 4.10) for the 166 countries covered by the SIPRI Military Expenditure Database, <http://www.sipri.org/data bases/milex/>.

The main purpose of the data on military expenditure is to provide an easily identifiable measure of the scale of resources absorbed by the military. Military expenditure is an 'input' measure, which is not directly related to the 'output' of military activities, such as military capability or military security. Long- and short-term changes in military spending may be signs of a change in military output, but interpretations of this type should be made with caution.

The country data on military expenditure in local currency (table 4.8) is the original data for all the other tables. This data is provided to contribute to transparency and to enable comparison with data reported in government sources and elsewhere. Data in constant dollars is provided to allow for comparison over time (table 4.9) and for calculating world, regional and other totals (see table 4.1). Data in current dollars for 2011 is provided to allow international comparison across countries (table 4.9) and across regions (table 4.1). The current dollar figures also facilitate comparison with other economic indicators, which are often expressed in current dollar terms. Data on military expenditure as a share of GDP is provided (in table 4.10) as an indicator of the proportion of a country's resources used for military activities, that is, as an indicator of the economic burden of military expenditure—the 'military burden'.

Conversion to constant US dollars has been made using market exchange rates. As the base year for conversion to constant US dollars used here is 2010, the figures in table 4.9 are substantially different from those in *SIPRI Yearbook 2011*, where the base year 2009 was used.

Military expenditure data from different editions of the SIPRI Yearbook should not be combined because the data series are continuously revised and updated as new and better data becomes available. This is true in particular for the most recent years as figures for budget allocations are replaced by figures for actual expenditure. Revisions in constant dollar series can also be caused by revisions in the economic statistics used for these calculations. The SIPRI Military Expenditure Database includes consistent series dating back to 1988 for most countries.

Further notes and the sources and methods for the data follow the tables.

Table 4.8. Military expenditure by country, in local currency, 2002–11

Figures are in local currency at current prices. Years are financial years (Jan.–Dec. except where indicated). Countries are grouped by region and subregion.

State	Currency	2002	2003	2004	2005	2006	2007	2008	2009	2010	2011
Africa											
North Africa											
Algeria[1]	b. dinars	168	171	202	214	225	273	334	384	422	631
Libya[‡ ¶ 2]	m. dinars	575	700	894	904	807	807	1 346	..	..	..
Morocco	m. dirhams	16 254	17 418	17 182	18 006	18 775	19 730	22 824	24 615	26 605	27 042
Tunisia	m. dinars	491	525	554	608	662	629	713	763	[805]	[864]
Sub-Saharan Africa											
Angola[|| 3]	b. kwanzas	19.1	50.0	68.3	119	158	156	237	263	322	342
Benin	m. CFA francs	18 122	20 077	22 072	[24 677]	[25 601]	..	[30 330]	..	..	..
Botswana[a]	m. pula	1 451	1 503	1 464	1 446	1 642	1 961	2 372	2 359	2 400	2 581
Burkina Faso[†]	m. CFA francs	24 666	25 571	30 289	33 649	37 081	45 616	55 089	51 948	61 491	65 744
Burundi	b. francs	41.8	47.0	49.4	53.6	46.0	50.1	52.0	..	..	..
Cameroon[§]	b. CFA francs	52.0	110	117	118	134	142	155	162	175	164
Cape Verde	m. escudos	530	565	573	614	614	640	646	667	690	768
Central African Rep.[‡ 4]	m. CFA francs	7 445	8 729	7 979	8 121	..	9 160	14 111	16 995	25 549	..
Chad[5]	b. CFA francs	23.9	23.8	26.7	29.3	..	187	274	206	[112]	[114]
Congo, DRC[6]	b. francs	..	31.9	55.0	78.3	96.0	106	89.5	99.1	166	220
Congo, Republic of[§]	m. CFA francs	35 035	38 728	40 050	41 954	44 070	50 849	63 420	..	66 168	..
Côte d'Ivoire[7]	b. CFA francs	..	124	133	132	140	155	165	198	192	169
Djibouti	m. francs	5 909	7 422	6 639	7 970	[8 800]	6 135	6 447	..	..	..
Equatorial Guinea	m. CFA francs	..	..	..	..	..	..	..	..	..	..
Eritrea	m. nakfa	2 104	2 520	..	..	..	..	..	..	..	..
Ethiopia[b]	m. birr	2 341	2 452	2 920	3 009	3 005	3 453	4 000	4 000	4 581	6 500
Gabon[8]	b. CFA francs	66.0	63.0	65.0	60.0	58.0	(59.0)	..	..	62.0	..
Gambia[‡ 9]	m. dalasis	45.0	57.0	58.0	85.3	78.2	113	..	..	..	..

Country	Currency										
Ghana‖ [10]	m. cedis	29.3	46.2	50.7	58.2	69.4	118	120	159	179	149
Guinea [11]	b. francs	194	167	182	..	..	..	..	..	..	..
Guinea-Bissau‖	m. CFA francs	4 435	4 362	..	6 391	..	..	..	..	..	..
Kenya [b]	m. shillings	17 430	19 921	21 219	26 652	27 540	39 062	41 209	48 520	46 968	[44 720]
Lesotho [a]	m. maloti	209	207	202	218	245	292	204	468	534	374
Liberia [b]	m. dollars	..	104	401	321	126	220	518	336	866	146
Madagascar‖ [12]	b. ariary	78.9	89.8	102	108	116	154	176	139	119	..
Malawi [a]	m. kwacha	1 186	1 309	2 752	4 452	[5 525]	[5 923]	..	..	..	..
Mali [13]	b. CFA francs	45.8	51.6	54.5	63.2	68.9	75.6	77.3	[82.3]	[87.7]	[91.7]
Mauritania‡	b. ouguiyas	9.9	16.4	18.6	17.7	22.0	29.4	29.4	30.1	30.1	..
Mauritius [14]	m. rupees	299	308	293	349	337	392	481	481	444	290
Mozambique‖	m. meticais	1 267	1 422	1 753	1 436	1 459	1 773	2 034	2 320 /	..	..
Namibia [a] [15]	m. dollars	935	994	1 107	1 260	1 382	1 683	2 372	2 593	3 015	3 126
Niger	b. CFA francs	14.4	14.3	16.7	17.3	..	..	24.0	24.0	23.4	..
Nigeria	b. naira	108	75.9	85.0	88.5	99.9	122	192	224	299	369
Rwanda [16]	b. francs	24.3	24.3	23.8	25.1	30.1	30.4	37.0	64.2	44.1	46.4
Senegal‖§¶	m. CFA francs	51 829	56 293	56 819	65 619	77 678	92 407	97 116	98 111	98 838	..
Seychelles	m. rupees	64.1	66.1	87.6	81.0	79.3	102	105	118	108	116
Sierra Leone	b. leones	57.0	66.8	62.0	68.1	[83.7]	[88.0]	[70.3]	[89.7]	[98.2]	[112]
Somalia	shillings	..	..	..	..	..	..	..	..	..	..
South Africa [a]	m. rand	[19 571]	[21 254]	21 326	24 880	25 102	27 764	30 644	34 376	33 748	38 223
South Sudan [17]	m. pounds	..	..	..	..	1 198	1 185	1 874	1 404	1 121	1 600
Sudan‡‖ [18]	m. pounds	1 276	1 039	3 200	2 838	3 338	..	..	..	..	..
Swaziland‡ [a] [19]	m. emalangeni	202	255	283	410	392	451	[584]	[942]	[895]	[895]
Tanzania [b]	b. shillings	125	135	143	172	197	217	247	332	373	430
Togo	m. CFA francs	..	16 757	16 757	17 532	..	..	25 529	..	28 148	27 849
Uganda [b]	b. shillings	267	331	379	393	407	549	[696]	[583]	[638]	[638]
Zambia	b. kwacha	..	..	[490]	626	747	596	1 120	1 068	1 326	1 486
Zimbabwe [20]	m. dollars/m. US$	37.3	136	1 300	2 942	(26 604)	(22 700)	..	..	98.3	153

State	Currency	2002	2003	2004	2005	2006	2007	2008	2009	2010	2011
Americas											
Central America and the Caribbean											
Belize[a]	m. dollars	15.8	17.6	19.4	22.1	25.4	28.2	40.5	32.5	30.1	31.8
Costa Rica[21]	colones	–	–	–	–	–	–	–	–	–	–
Cuba[22]	m. pesos	..	1 259	1 303	1 640	1 695	1 876	2 004	2 083	..	..
Dominican Republic	m. pesos	5 056	4 804	6 436	8 305	8 621	9 153	11 629	11 587	13 239	13 006
El Salvador[23]	m. US dollar	204	166	162	170	185	200	209	215	224	[222]
Guatemala	m. quetzales	1 239	1 420	913	798	993	1 043	1 259	1 203	1 368	1 555
Haiti[a]	gourdes	–	–	–	–	–	–	–	–	–	–
Honduras[24]	m. lempiras	[1 045]	[1 426]	[1 103]	[1 179]	1 428	1 813	2 503	2 963	3 216	3 502
Jamaica[a]	m. dollars	2 936	3 244	3 368	3 804	5 100	6 005	10 677	9 896	8 992	..
Mexico	m. pesos	[33 598]	[35 014]	35 314	39 467	44 496	52 235	54 977	64 348	68 411	74 792
Nicaragua[25]	m. córdobas	496	533	520	655	728	826	849	946	948	1 227
Panama	balboas	–	–	–	–	–	–	–	–	–	–
North America											
Canada[a]	m. dollars	13 379	14 143	14 951	16 001	17 066	19 255	21 100	21 828	24 460	[24 495]
United States[26]	m. dollars	356 720	415 223	464 676	503 353	527 660	556 961	621 138	668 604	698 281	711 421
South America											
Argentina[27]	m. pesos	3 413	3 988	4 285	4 935	5 643	7 109	8 769	11 063	13 541	[13 541]
Bolivia[28]	m. bolivianos	1 153	1 331	1 343	1 368	1 441	1 740	2 371	2 431	2 300	2 438
Brazil	m. reais	28 353	25 922	28 700	33 134	36 117	40 898	46 500	52 322	60 481	59 228
Chile[§ 29]	b. pesos	1 691	1 749	2 032	2 253	2 610	2 766	3 143	2 966	3 357	[3 889]
Colombia[30]	b. pesos	8 383	9 434	10 664	11 405	12 577	14 082	17 810	19 496	19 787	20 197
Ecuador	m. US dollars	505	739	710	954	950	1 310	1 646	1 949	2 094	2 308
Guyana[‡ 31]	m. dollars	2 625	2 697	2 791	3 148	3 267	4 300	5 289	5 798	5 862	6 101
Paraguay[† 32]	b. guaraníes	288	294	364	347	431	476	537	610	730	1 054
Peru[33]	m. nuevos soles	2 982	3 092	3 397	3 820	4 011	3 918	4 057	5 157	5 532	5 777
Uruguay[34]	m. pesos	7 321	7 815	8 269	8 847	9 723	10 106	12 422	14 682	15 807	17 417
Venezuela[‖ 35]	m. bolivares	1 244	1 588	2 740	4 292	6 436	6 377	9 286	8 631	8 683	10 229

Asia and Oceania

Central and South Asia											
Afghanistan[36]	m. afghanis	..	[5 622]	[5 404]	5 544	6 358	11 506	11 471	12 783	29 571	43 273
Bangladesh[b]	m. takas	34 190	38 110	41 150	44 860	53 980	59 510	62 600	87 590	93 180	119 510
India[a 37]	b. rupees	722	774	965	1 035	1 102	1 190	1 518	1 993	2 146	2 330
Kazakhstan	b. tenge	37.7	47.5	58.0	78.7	100	167	185	188	221	[263]
Kyrgyzstan[38]	m. som	2 055	2 408	2 688	3 105	3 606	4 807	6 423	7 080	9 270	..
Nepal[b q]	m. rupees	7 420	8 255	10 996	11 745	11 136	11 389	14 712	17 811	19 491	19 101
Pakistan[b q ‡ 39]	b. rupees	195	220	244	281	292	327	376	448	517	568
Sri Lanka	b. rupees	[54.7]	[52.3]	62.7	64.7	82.2	117	164	175	170	172
Tajikistan	m. somoni	70.7	107	134	..	..	..	..	..	..	..
Turkmenistan	manat	..	..	..	..	..	..	..	..	..	..
Uzbekistan[40]	b. sum	44.5	53.0	..	..	..	..	..	..	..	..
East Asia											
China[41]	b. yuan	[262]	[288]	[331]	[379]	[452]	[546]	[638]	[764]	[820]	[923]
Japan[a † 42]	b. yen	4 956	4 953	4 893	4 870	4 812	4 747	4 769	4 815	4 790	4 775
Korea, North[43]	b. won	(3.3)	(50.8)	(54.4)	(64.5)	(67.1)	(71.3)	(71.3)	(76.3)	(82.6)	(90.0)
Korea, South[44]	b. won	[17 643]	[18 884]	[20 421]	22 694	24 039	25 765	28 733	31 121	31 876	34 113
Mongolia	m. tugriks	28 071	27 899	32 891	35 914	46 232	66 200	77 817	54 110	74 443	103 060
Taiwan	b. dollars	225	238	253	248	235	256	282	298	287	286
Oceania											
Australia[b]	m. dollars	14 739	15 873	16 748	17 921	19 899	21 179	23 249	25 372	25 250	26 560
Fiji[† 45]	m. dollars	67.6	70.7	81.1	72.9	93.6	122	85.4	100	97.0	..
New Zealand[b]	m. dollars	1 419	1 518	1 528	1 645	1 807	1 875	2 083	2 201	2 254	2 284
Papua New Guinea[‡ 46]	m. kina	66.3	68.8	78.7	94.2	93.7	112	100	118	116	145
South East Asia											
Brunei Darussalam[47]	m. dollars	405	530 /	308	449	472	492	520	505	542	514
Cambodia	b. riel	265	270	272	289	328	373	438	837	733	781
Indonesia[48]	b. rupiah	[14 308]	[19 876]	[21 712]	20 829	23 923	30 611	31 349	34 333	42 392	49 984
Laos	b. kip	(115)	(115)	(121)	(125)	(135)	(140)	(150)	(119)	(134)	..

State	Currency	2002	2003	2004	2005	2006	2007	2008	2009	2010	2011
Malaysia	m. ringgit	8 504	10 950	10 728	11 817	11 981	13 649	14 717	13 974	12 429	14 037
Myanmar[a] [49]	b. kyats	76.1	..	..	..	..	..	..	..	..	..
Philippines[50]	b. pesos	[61.9]	70.5	[69.7]	75.6	82.5	93.0	101	101	110	105
Singapore[a]	m. dollars	8 204	8 238	8 620	9 252	9 268	10 009	10 726	11 043	11 455	12 075
Thailand	b. baht	77.2	79.9	74.1	78.1	85.1	115	142	168	154	168
Timor-Leste[51]	m. US dollar	..	..	6.6	9.8	24.4	[11.5]	23.7	36.5	30.8	27.3
Viet Nam	b. dong	..	13 058	14 409	16 278	20 577	28 735	34 848	40 981	49 739	55 100
Europe											
Eastern Europe											
Armenia† [52]	b. drams	36.8	44.3	52.3	64.4	78.3	95.8	121	131	148	[154]
Azerbaijan‖ [53]	m. manats	[136]	[173]	[224]	288	641	812	1 321	1 184	1 185	2 452
Belarus	b. roubles	366	475	679	975	1 355	1 603	1 887	1 887	2 287	2 977
Georgia† [54]	m. lari	74.6	91.5	135	388	720	1 556	1 625	1 008	810	[718]
Moldova†¶ [55]	m. lei	94.7	115	116	151	216	276	383	277	227	245
Russia[56]	b. roubles	[470]	[568]	[656]	[806]	[967]	[1 144]	[1 448]	[1 693]	[1 781]	[2 112]
Ukraine§	m. hryvnias	6 266	7 615	8 963	12 328	15 082	20 685	25 341	[26 077]	[29 445]	[32 496]
Western and Central Europe											
Albania§¶ [57]	m. leks	8 220	9 279	10 373	11 000	13 831	17 619	21 450	23 633	19 749	19 865
Austria	m. euros	1 999	2 111	2 158	2 160	2 105	2 557	2 558	2 495	2 652	[2 577]
Belgium	m. euros	3 344	3 434	3 433	3 400	3 434	3 773	4 298	4 048	3 951	4 016
Bosnia–Herzegovina†¶ [58]	m. marka	501	351	315	273	278	279	311	341	325	346
Bulgaria† [59]	m. leva	[947]	[986]	1 025	1 101	1 171	1 475	1 388	1 355	1 320	1 112
Croatia[60]	m. kunas	[5 775]	[4 757]	4 250	4 323	4 959	5 251	6 396	5 966	5 587	[5 832]
Cyprus†‖	m. euros	[253]	[255]	271	302	304	295	310	339	361	385
Czech Republic[61]	m. koruny	48 924	53 194	52 481	58 445	55 358	54 949	49 827	51 824	47 706	43 874
Denmark	m. kroner	21 269	21 075	21 441	20 800	23 173	22 731	24 410	23 252	25 328	26 091
Estonia‖ [62]	m. euros	130	152	165	214	251	325	346	314	249	[266]
Finland	m. euros	1 712	2 006	2 131	2 206	2 281	2 203	2 468	2 591	2 567	2 856

Country	Unit										
France[63]	m. euros	38 681	40 684	42 690	42 545	43 457	44 273	45 063	48 146	44 619	44 900
Germany	m. euros	31 168	31 060	30 610	30 600	30 365	31 090	32 824	34 166	34 032	[33 563]
Greece	m. euros	5 030	4 462	5 048	5 652	6 064	6 235	7 219	7 612	[5 407]	[5 855]
Hungary	b. forint	280	314	311	319	297	326	321	299	281	[279]
Iceland[64]	m. krónur	–	–	–	–	–	–	688	1 227	:	:
Ireland	m. euros	862	855	887	921	949	1 003	1 081	1 019	962	935
Italy[65]	m. euros	25 887	26 795	27 476	26 959	26 631	[26 275]	[28 156]	[27 578]	[26 827]	[24 772]
Latvia	m. lats	91.0	108	124	154	206	247	280	184	138	148
Lithuania[66]	m. litai	885	967	[936]	[1 040]	[1 174]	[1 355]	[1 571]	1 251	1 068	[1 100]
Luxembourg	m. euros	163	176	189	196	197	209	:	:	:	:
Macedonia, FYR[67]	m. denars	6 841	6 292	6 683	6 259	7 272	7 229	7 000	6 149	6 044	5 860
Malta†‖	m. euros	28.7	30.0	32.5	42.3	35.3	35.8	42.6	55.2	44.3	45.6
Montenegro[68]	m. euros	:	:	:	:	[49.7]	46.9	58.1	55.2	56.8	63.1
Netherlands	m. euros	7 149	7 404	7 552	7 693	8 145	8 388	8 448	8 733	8 514	8 459
Norway	m. kroner	32 461	31 985	32 945	31 471	32 142	34 439	35 932	38 960	38 621	[43 395]
Poland[69]	m. zlotys	15 407	16 141	17 479	19 078	20 541	23 774	[22 190]	[24 701]	[26 475]	[28 757]
Portugal	m. euros	2 765	2 755	2 996	3 248	3 242	3 190	3 285	3 463	3 640	[3 353]
Romania‖	m. lei	3 491	4 151	4 994	5 757	6 324	6 358	7 558	6 785	6 630	6 540
Serbia[70]	m. dinars	43 695	42 070	43 154	41 996	47 342	56 792	61 944	63 841	65 683	69 604
Slovakia†‖	m. euros	662	762	762	848	898	929	994	967	853	760
Slovenia‖	m. euros	328	360	396	413	485	506	566	575	583	514
Spain	m. euros	8 414	8 587	9 132	9 508	11 506	12 219	12 756	12 196	11 132	10 898
Sweden	m. kronor	42 401	42 903	40 527	41 240	41 150	43 163	39 710	38 751	42 423	[44 240]
Switzerland†¶[71]	m. francs	4 493	4 404	4 357	4 339	4 174	4 231	4 439	4 413	4 292	4 827
Turkey‖	m. liras	13 641	15 426	15 568	16 232	19 260	19 528	21 847	24 873	26 527	29 934
United Kingdom[a]	m. pounds	26 991	29 338	29 524	30 603	31 454	33 486	36 431	37 425	37 645	39 606
Middle East											
Bahrain[72]	m. dinars	150	175	180	183	203	222	248	287	292	330
Egypt[b]	m. pounds	13 333	14 563	14 804	15 933	17 922	19 350	21 718	22 831	25 397	25 480
Iran[a]¶[73]	b. rials	19 648	33 998	45 893	65 208	78 611	70 460	(58 135)	:	:	:
Iraq[74]	b. dinars	:	:	(892)	(1 649)	(1 814)	(2 437)	3 428	3 473	4 190	(6 839)

State	Currency	2002	2003	2004	2005	2006	2007	2008	2009	2010	2011
Israel[75]	m. shekels	[51 577]	[51 989]	[49 480]	[48 264]	[52 518]	[51 251]	[51 481]	[53 656]	[53 251]	[58 827]
Jordan	m. dinars	370	434	416	428	497	732	952	997	971	971
Kuwait[a]	m. dinars	882	950	1 039	1 020	1 059	1 219	1 195	1 249	1 388	1 613
Lebanon	b. pounds	1 368	1 392	1 439	[1 451]	[1 521]	[1 737]	1 763	2 150	[2 461]	[2 644]
Oman[‡76]	m. rials	958	1 010	1 144	1 404	1 550	1 663	1 775	1 726	1 882	1 650
Qatar[77]	m. riyals	3 324	3 428	3 374	3 901	4 610	6 391	9 234	:	:	:
Saudi Arabia[§78]	b. riyals	69.4	70.3	78.4	95.1	111	133	143	155	170	182
Syria[79]	b. pounds	55.3	67.1	70.2	75.7	74.9	82.7	86.8	101	109	120
United Arab Emirates[80]	m. dirhams	[22 775]	[24 645]	[27 951]	[27 626]	[30 551]	[36 443]	[49 294]	[57 929]	[58 987]	:
Yemen	b. riyals	130	148	136	156	162	209	239	:	:	:

Notes: See below table 4.10.

Table 4.9. Military expenditure by country, in constant US dollars for 2002–11 and current US dollars for 2011

Figures are in US$ m. at constant (2010) prices and exchange rates for 2002–11 and, in the right-most column, marked * , in current US$ m. for 2011. Years are calendar years except for the USA, where the figures are for financial years. Countries are grouped by region and subregion.

State	2002	2003	2004	2005	2006	2007	2008	2009	2010	2011	2011*
Africa											
North Africa											
Algeria[1]	3 022	2 957	3 364	3 521	3 609	4 235	4 934	5 359	5 671	8 170	8 665
Libya[‡¶2]	557	693	905	892	785	738	1 116	..	..	..	..
Morocco	2 232	2 364	2 298	2 385	2 408	2 479	2 766	2 953	3 161	3 186	3 342
Tunisia	457	475	484	521	542	498	539	556	[563]	[583]	[614]
Sub-Saharan Africa											
Angola[3]	1 354	1 788	1 702	2 411	2 832	2 484	3 363	3 272	3 501	3 281	3 647
Benin	46.8	51.1	55.7	[59.1]	[59.1]	..	[64.0]	..	..	..	..
Botswana	411	396	366	332	327	361	386	372	352	344	371
Burkina Faso[†]	62.0	63.0	74.9	78.2	84.2	104	113	104	124	129	139
Burundi	75.1	78.3	74.4	71.1	59.3	59.7	49.9	..	..	..	..
Cameroon[§]	246	264	281	277	301	316	327	331	354	321	347
Cape Verde	7.7	8.1	8.4	8.9	8.5	8.5	8.0	8.2	8.3	8.8	9.7
Central African Republic[‡4]	19.5	22.0	20.5	20.3	..	21.2	29.9	34.8	51.6	[226]	[242]
Chad[5]	56.5	57.3	67.9	69.0	..	447	595	406	184	211	239
Congo, DRC[6]	..	124	206	242	263	248	178	135	134	..	..
Congo, Republic of[§]	96.1	107	108	110	108	122	141	..	..	..	..
Côte d'Ivoire[7]	..	300	317	303	314	342	343	407	388	325	357
Djibouti	46.3	57.1	49.5	57.6	[61.5]	40.8	38.3	..	..	..	..
Equatorial Guinea	..	..	..	..	..	..	..	..	..	..	..
Eritrea	534	522	..	..	..	..	..	..	..	..	..
Ethiopia	520	427	464	459	414	380	303	300	298	286	328
Gabon[8]	160	149	153	137	134	(130)	..	..	125	..	..

State	2002	2003	2004	2005	2006	2007	2008	2009	2010	2011	2011*
Gambia‡ 9	2.8	3.0	2.7	3.8	3.4	4.6	..	..	..	..	..
Ghana10	63.5	79.0	77.0	76.8	82.6	127	111	123	125	96.0	97.5
Guinea11	137	107	98.8	..	..	..	..	..	..	..	..
Guinea-Bissau	10.7	10.9	..	15.3	..	..	..	..	..	..	..
Kenya	518	523	516	544	538	602	575	589	603	[507]	[516]
Lesotho	45.9	43.2	40.3	41.1	43.3	47.1	34.3	56.8	70.7	53.9	57.0
Liberia	..	..	4.3	10.6	4.9	4.1	4.0	7.4	8.5	..	..
Madagascar12	79.9	92.1	91.7	82.2	79.3	95.5	100	72.6	56.9	63.8	72.0
Malawi	16.6	17.0	28.6	41.7	[47.7]	[49.0]	..	..	..	..	..
Mali13	109	125	136	148	159	172	161	[168]	[177]	[180]	[194]
Mauritania‡	61.8	97.9	101	85.3	99.7	..	116	116	..	..	..
Mauritius14	14.5	14.9	14.1	14.3	14.0	13.7	15.0	..	14.4	8.8	10.1
Mozambique	80.3	79.4	86.9	66.4	59.6	67.0	69.7	76.9	..	..	..
Namibia15	203	200	212	235	247	275	341	362	397	403	427
Niger	36.2	36.6	42.6	40.9	..	..	51.0	..	47.2	..	..
Nigeria	1 795	1 105	1 077	951	991	1 151	1 616	1 695	1 990	2 215	2 410
Rwanda16	84.6	78.9	68.9	66.6	73.4	68.0	71.6	75.1	74.5	74.0	75.4
Senegal§¶	122	133	134	152	176	198	196	201	200	..	..
Seychelles	10.6	10.6	13.5	12.4	12.2	14.8	11.2	9.5	8.9	9.4	9.3
Sierra Leone	35.3	38.5	31.3	30.6	[34.4]	[32.4]	[22.5]	[26.3]	[24.7]	[23.9]	[26.0]
Somalia	..	..	..	..	..	..	..	..	..	..	..
South Africa	[3 982]	[4 165]	4 202	4 576	4 565	4 611	4 566	4 763	4 631	4 827	5 108
South Sudan17										..	597
Sudan‡18	1 152	881	2 507	2 049	2 248						
Swaziland‡19	44.2	51.5	56.8	74.4	74.0	75.3	[84.5]	[122]	[124]	[115]	[123]
Tanzania	169	153	156	168	184	193	196	218	250	253	255
Togo	..	42.2	42.1	41.2	..	..	53.5	..	56.8	54.6	59.0
Uganda	215	232	265	266	257	289	[336]	[305]	[280]	[247]	[253]
Zambia	..	..	[202]	218	238	172	287	242	276	285	306
Zimbabwe20	118	92.4	196	132	107	..	..	..	98.3 ‖	153	153

Americas

Central America and the Caribbean

Belize	9.7	10.3	11.1	12.1	13.3	14.6	18.7	17.4	15.3	15.4	15.7
Costa Rica[21]	-	-	-	-	-	-	-	-	-	-	-
Cuba[22]	..	297	62.0	78.1	75.9	82.7	88.3	91.8	..	..	..
Dominican Republic	376	280	248	307	296	296	340	334	359	325	341
El Salvador[23]	270	215	201	202	211	218	214	218	224	[211]	[222]
Guatemala	255	277	166	134	156	154	165	155	170	182	200
Haiti	-	-	-	-	-	-	-	-	-	-	-
Honduras[24]	[97.3]	[123]	[88.2]	[86.7]	99.5	118	146	164	170	170	185
Jamaica	81.6	85.0	78.9	75.7	90.1	99.8	135	130	106	..	..
Mexico	[3 759]	[3 747]	3 610	3 880	4 221	4 766	4 772	5 304	5 414	5 723	6 022
Nicaragua[25]	46.2	47.2	42.4	48.7	49.6	50.7	43.4	46.7	44.4	53.2	54.7
Panama	-	-	-	-	-	-	-	-	-	-	-

North America

Canada	15 078	15 354	15 935	16 636	17 410	18 980	20 454	21 389	23 109	[23 082]	[24 659]
United States[26]	432 452	492 200	536 459	562 039	570 769	585 749	629 095	679 574	698 281	689 591	711 421

South America

Argentina[27]	1 756	1 808	1 861	1 955	2 015	2 333	2 650	3 146	3 476	[3 167]	[3 295]
Bolivia[28]	256	286	276	267	270	300	358	355	328	316	352
Brazil	26 477	21 101	21 917	23 677	24 772	27 067	29 125	31 244	34 384	31 576	35 360
Chile[§ 29]	4 298	4 324	4 971	5 350	5 993	6 083	6 359	5 901	6 579	[7 392]	[8 040]
Colombia[30]	6 606	6 939	7 406	7 541	7 973	8 458	9 997	10 503	10 422	10 290	10 957
Ecuador	713	967	904	1 187	1 147	1 546	1 792	2 018	2 094	2 209	2 308
Guyana[‡ 31]	20.8	20.1	19.9	21.0	20.5	24.0	27.3	29.1	28.8	28.3	29.9
Paraguay[† 32]	108	96.9	115	103	116	119	122	135	154	206	250
Peru[33]	1 305	1 323	1 402	1 552	1 598	1 533	1 501	1 853	1 958	1 978	2 098
Uruguay[34]	706	631	612	625	646	621	708	781	788	803	902
Venezuela[35]	2 624	2 555	3 622	4 892	6 454	5 388	5 969	4 314	3 363	3 115	2 385

State	2002	2003	2004	2005	2006	2007	2008	2009	2010	2011	2011*
Asia and Oceania											
Central and South Asia											
Afghanistan[36]	..	[186]	[191]	173	188	275	242	305	576	781	878
Bangladesh	861	864	881	893	961	1 011	999	1 166	1 298	1 367	1 436
India[37]	26 658	27 253	31 657	33 690	33 962	34 374	38 987	45 903	46 086	44 282	48 889
Kazakhstan	507	600	686	865	1 012	1 523	1 446	1 364	1 502	[1 648]	[1 794]
Kyrgyzstan[38]	83.6	95.1	102	113	124	150	161	166	202	:	:
Nepal¶	164	183	218	241	226	210	219	244	255	241	259
Pakistan¶‡[39]	4 822	5 149	5 365	5 572	5 636	5 660	5 342	5 504	5 661	5 685	6 282
Sri Lanka	[1 057]	[950]	1 059	980	1 132	1 386	1 587	1 640	1 500	1 403	1 557
Tajikistan	36.7	47.5	55.8	:	:	:	:	:	:	:	:
Turkmenistan	:	:	:	:	:	:	:	:	:	:	:
Uzbekistan[40]	66.3	70.7	:	:	:	:	:	:	:	:	:
East Asia											
China[41]	[47 800]	[52 000]	[57 500]	[64 700]	[76 100]	[87 700]	[96 700]	[116 700]	[121 100]	[129 300]	[142 900]
Japan†[42]	55 938	56 053	55 541	55 330	54 637	53 885	53 159	54 339	54 526	54 529	59 327
Korea, North[43]	:	:	:	:	:	:	:	:	:	:	:
Korea, South[44]	[19 521]	[20 185]	[21 072]	22 791	23 622	24 689	26 297	27 708	27 572	28 280	30 799
Mongolia	44.5	42.1	45.8	44.4	54.4	71.4	67.1	43.9	54.9	69.5	81.4
Taiwan	7 829	8 293	8 680	8 300	7 824	8 380	8 932	9 500	9 067	8 888	9 717
Oceania											
Australia	16 777	17 083	17 788	18 413	19 400	20 591	21 341	22 938	23 221	22 955	26 706
Fiji†[45]	48.9	49.1	54.8	48.1	60.3	74.8	48.7	55.1	50.6	:	:
New Zealand	1 260	1 291	1 306	1 319	1 390	1 445	1 496	1 590	1 606	1 566	1 792
Papua New Guinea‡[46]	37.7	34.1	38.2	44.9	43.7	51.8	41.8	46.0	42.5	49.1	61.1
South East Asia											
Brunei Darussalam[47]	318	332	262	318	357	370	381	374	391	373	414
Cambodia	104	105	102	102	109	115	108	208	175	177	192

Indonesia[48]	[2 866]	[3 736]	[3 841]	3 336	3 387	4 073	3 800	3 971	4 663	5 220	5 709
Laos	(24.3)	(21.0)	(19.9)	(19.3)	(19.5)	(19.3)	(19.3)	(15.3)	(16.3)	..	..
Malaysia	3 178	4 052	3 910	4 183	4 094	4 571	4 674	4 413	3 859	4 223	4 587
Myanmar[49]	..	..	..	..	..	..	..	..	..	..	..
Philippines[50]	[2 071]	2 282	[2 127]	2 145	2 202	2 414	2 391	2 322	2 438	2 225	2 417
Singapore	6 931	6 999	7 132	7 576	7 640	7 935	7 998	8 264	8 323	8 302	9 475
Thailand	3 079	3 131	2 825	2 846	2 966	3 908	4 600	5 485	4 846	5 114	5 521
Timor-Leste[51]	..	..	4.5	11.1	22.1	[27.8]	25.4	39.0	30.8	24.3	27.3
Viet Nam	..	1 366	1 399	1 459	1 718	2 215	2 182	2 397	2 672	2 487	2 675
Europe											
Eastern Europe											
Armenia†[52]	145	167	184	226	267	313	363	378	395	[384]	[414]
Azerbaijan[53]	[332]	[414]	[502]	587	1 205	1 311	1 764	1 558	1 476	2 794	3 104
Belarus	333	337	408	531	689	752	771	682	768	709	598
Georgia†[54]	71.7	83.9	117	311	529	1 047	994	606	454	[371]	[426]
Moldova†¶[55]	16.5	18.0	16.1	18.7	23.8	27.0	33.2	24.0	18.3	18.4	20.8
Russia[56]	[35 780]	[38 064]	[39 599]	[43 190]	[47 264]	[51 275]	[56 892]	[59 565]	[58 644]	[64 123]	[71 853]
Ukraine§	2 009	2 320	2 505	3 034	3 404	4 137	4 048	[3 594]	[3 710]	[3 747]	[4 078]
Western and Central Europe											
Albania§¶[57]	96.0	108	118	122	150	186	219	235	190	185	197
Austria	3 068	3 195	3 201	3 132	3 008	3 577	3 467	3 365	3 513	[3 305]	[3 589]
Belgium	5 223	5 279	5 169	4 981	4 942	5 333	5 814	5 479	5 233	5 136	5 593
Bosnia and Herzegovina†¶[58]	417	290	260	217	209	206	215	236	220	226	246
Bulgaria†[59]	[1 006]	[1 025]	1 002	1 025	1 016	1 181	989	940	894	722	790
Croatia[60]	[1 313]	[1 063]	931	916	1 018	1 048	1 203	1 097	1 016	[1 037]	[1 091]
Cyprus†	[413]	[400]	415	451	443	420	422	460	478	494	537
Czech Republic[61]	3 088	3 355	3 219	3 519	3 251	3 136	2 673	2 752	2 498	2 254	2 479
Denmark	4 418	4 287	4 311	4 108	4 492	4 332	4 499	4 230	4 504	4 515	4 859
Estonia[62]	236	273	288	358	403	488	471	429	330	[336]	[371]
Finland	2 535	2 944	3 122	3 204	3 262	3 074	3 309	3 474	3 400	3 656	3 978

State	2002	2003	2004	2005	2006	2007	2008	2009	2010	2011	2011*
France[63]	58 604	60 385	62 042	60 734	61 058	61 264	60 654	64 747	59 098	58 244	62 535
Germany	46 592	45 955	44 544	43 847	42 835	42 877	44 107	45 769	45 075	[43 478]	[46 745]
Greece	8 612	7 378	8 112	8 772	9 121	9 113	10 131	10 555	[7 162]	[7 502]	[8 155]
Hungary	2 017	2 173	2 011	1 991	1 785	1 819	1 690	1 506	1 351	1 287	1 385
Iceland[64]	..	..	..	..	..	..	6.6	10.6	..	..	..
Ireland	1 327	1 273	1 292	1 309	1 298	1 307	1 354	1 337	1 274	1 207	1 302
Italy[65]	40 333	40 660	40 794	39 247	37 981	[36 831]	[38 151]	[37 087]	[35 532]	[31 946]	[34 501]
Latvia	278	321	346	403	506	552	540	343	260	267	295
Lithuania[66]	449	496	[475]	[514]	[559]	[611]	[638]	487	410	[405]	[444]
Luxembourg	257	272	286	289	283	294	..	..	..	..	..
Macedonia, FYR[67]	176	160	168	157	150	171	158	154	130	121	132
Malta[†]	45.8	47.3	49.9	63.0	51.1	51.2	52.5	57.2	58.7	58.7	63.5
Montenegro[68]	..	..	..	..	[77.8]	70.4	80.1	73.6	75.2	80.5	87.9
Netherlands	10 743	10 896	10 980	10 998	11 513	11 668	11 467	11 714	11 277	10 945	11 781
Norway	6 278	6 035	6 188	5 822	5 811	6 181	6 215	6 596	6 390	[7 083]	[7 744]
Poland[69]	6 275	6 522	6 819	7 289	7 762	8 774	[7 848]	[8 414]	[8 781]	[9 149]	[9 705]
Portugal	4 315	4 164	4 422	4 688	4 554	4 359	4 375	4 651	4 821	[4 285]	[4 670]
Romania	2 084	2 150	2 312	2 446	2 520	2 417	2 664	2 265	2 086	1 945	2 145
Serbia[70]	1 221	1 070	989	828	836	943	915	872	845	805	949
Slovakia[†]	1 211	1 285	1 194	1 293	1 312	1 320	1 351	1 293	1 130	968	1 058
Slovenia	561	584	619	631	723	727	770	776	772	668	715
Spain	13 749	13 618	14 056	14 157	16 550	17 098	17 152	16 465	14 744	13 984	15 178
Sweden	6 521	6 473	6 092	6 172	6 075	6 235	5 545	5 438	5 886	[5 960]	[6 811]
Switzerland[†][¶][71]	4 620	4 500	4 416	4 347	4 138	4 164	4 265	4 261	4 115	4 618	5 436
Turkey	21 207	19 141	17 468	16 537	17 755	16 553	16 767	17 966	17 649	18 687	17 871
United Kingdom	49 088	52 619	53 228	53 676	54 024	55 730	58 217	59 350	58 099	57 875	62 685
Middle East											
Bahrain[72]	485	557	561	555	604	639	691	777	776	883	878
Egypt	4 784	5 012	4 742	4 732	4 842	4 877	4 542	4 408	4 289	4 107	4 285

Iran[q][73]	6 529	7 950	9 777	12 125	13 502	11 096	(7 463)	:	:	:	(5 845)
Iraq[74]	:	:	(1 783)	(2 406)	(1 727)	(2 580)	3 220	3 054	3 581	(5 568)	[16 446]
Israel[75]	[15 971]	[15 982]	[15 275]	[14 704]	[15 668]	[15 213]	[14 610]	[14 737]	[14 242]	[15 209]	1 368
Jordan	760	877	814	809	885	1 236	1 398	1 474	1 367	1 310	5 640
Kuwait	4 136	4 457	4 797	4 642	4 612	4 913	4 526	4 478	4 715	5 178	[1 754]
Lebanon	1 193	1 199	1 219	[1 238]	[1 230]	[1 349]	1 237	1 490	[1 633]	[1 657]	4 291
Oman[‡][76]	3 368	3 543	3 983	4 802	5 134	5 201	4 952	4 633	4 895	4 074	:
Qatar[77]	1 475	1 487	1 370	1 456	1 539	1 875	2 355	:	:	:	48 531
Saudi Arabia[§][78]	24 343	24 522	27 262	32 849	37 420	43 105	42 306	43 477	45 245	46 219	2 495
Syria[79]	2 008	2 302	2 306	2 319	2 086	2 217	2 010	2 282	2 346	2 490	:
United Arab Emirates[80]	[9 964]	[10 455]	[11 289]	[10 506]	[10 632]	[11 412]	[13 752]	[15 913]	[16 062]	:	:
Yemen	1 371	1 415	1 154	1 186	1 110	1 327	1 275	:	:		

Notes: See below table 4.10.

Table 4.10. Military expenditure by country as percentage of gross domestic product, 2002–10

Countries are grouped by region and subregion.

State	2002	2003	2004	2005	2006	2007	2008	2009	2010
Africa									
North Africa									
Algeria[1]	3.7	3.3	3.3	2.8	2.6	2.9	3.0	3.8	3.6
Libya[‡¶2]	2.2	1.9	1.9	1.4	1.0	0.9	1.2	. .	. .
Morocco	3.6	3.7	3.4	3.4	3.3	3.2	3.3	3.3	3.5
Tunisia	1.7	1.7	1.6	1.6	1.6	1.4	1.4	1.4	[1.4]
Sub-Saharan Africa									
Angola[3]	3.8	4.8	4.1	4.5	4.4	3.4	3.7	4.3	4.2
Benin	0.9	0.9	1.0	[1.0]	[1.0]	. .	[1.0]	. .	. .
Botswana	3.7	3.7	3.1	2.8	2.4	2.5	2.5	2.9	2.4
Burkina Faso[+]	1.1	1.0	1.1	1.1	1.2	1.3	1.4	1.3	1.3
Burundi	7.2	7.3	6.6	6.2	4.9	4.7	3.8	. .	. .
Cameroon[§]	1.3	1.4	1.4	1.3	1.4	1.5	1.5	1.6	1.6
Cape Verde	0.7	0.7	0.7	0.7	0.6	0.6	0.5	0.5	0.5
Central African Republic[‡4]	1.1	1.3	1.2	1.1	. .	1.1	1.6	1.8	2.6
Chad[5]	1.7	1.5	1.1	0.9	. .	5.5	7.1	6.2	[2.7]
Congo, DRC[6]	. .	1.4	2.1	2.3	2.4	2.0	1.4	1.0	1.3
Congo, Republic of[§]	1.7	1.9	1.7	1.3	1.1	1.4	1.1	. .	1.1
Côte d'Ivoire[7]	. .	1.5	1.5	1.4	1.5	1.5	1.5	1.7	1.6
Djibouti	6.0	7.2	5.6	6.3	[6.4]	4.1	3.7	. .	. .
Equatorial Guinea	. .	. .	. .	. .	. .	. .	. .	. .	. .
Eritrea	20.7	20.9	. .	. .	. .	. .	. .	. .	. .
Ethiopia	3.4	2.8	2.5	2.3	1.7	1.3	1.1	1.0	. .
Gabon[8]	2.0	1.8	1.7	1.3	1.1	(1.0)	. .	. .	0.9
Gambia[‡9]	1.0	1.1	0.4	0.5	0.4	0.6	. .	. .	0.9

Ghana[10]	0.4	0.4	0.4	0.5	0.4	0.4	0.4	0.5	0.4
Guinea[11]	:	:	:	:	:	:	2.2	2.4	3.1
Guinea-Bissau	:	:	:	:	:	2.1	:	1.6	3.2
Kenya	1.9	1.9	1.9	1.8	1.7	1.7	1.6	1.7	1.6
Lesotho	3.1	2.7	1.7	2.5	2.5	2.5	2.6	2.9	3.0
Liberia	0.9	0.8	0.5	0.5	0.6	1.5	0.7	:	:
Madagascar[12]	0.7	0.8	1.1	1.1	1.0	1.1	1.2	1.3	1.3
Malawi	:	:	:	[1.1]	[1.2]	1.2	0.8	0.5	0.6
Mali[13]	[1.9]	[1.9]	2.0	2.2	2.2	2.2	2.1	2.1	2.1
Mauritania‡	:	3.8	3.4	:	3.0	3.7	4.9	4.9	3.2
Mauritius[14]	0.1	:	0.2	0.1	0.2	0.2	0.2	0.2	0.2
Mozambique	:	0.9	0.8	0.8	0.8	0.9	1.4	1.3	1.3
Namibia[15]	1.5	1.7	2.1	2.9	2.9	3.1	2.9	2.9	2.8
Niger	0.9	:	1.0	:	:	1.0	1.1	0.9	1.0
Nigeria	1.0	0.9	0.8	0.6	0.5	0.6	0.7	0.9	1.5
Rwanda[16]	1.3	1.4	1.4	1.5	1.8	1.7	2.0	2.4	3.0
Senegal[§¶]	1.6	1.6	1.6	1.7	1.6	1.4	1.3	1.4	1.4
Seychelles	1.3	1.5	1.6	2.0	1.9	2.1	2.3	1.7	1.7
Sierra Leone	[1.2]	[1.3]	[1.1]	[1.5]	[1.7]	1.6	1.6	2.0	2.1
Somalia	:	:	:	:	:	:	:	[1.7]	[1.6]
South Africa	1.3	1.4	1.3	1.3	1.4	1.5	1.5	:	:
South Sudan[17]	:	:	:	:	:	:	:	:	:
Sudan‡[18]	:	:	:	:	3.4	3.3	4.7	1.9	2.7
Swaziland‡[19]	[3.0]	[3.2]	[2.1]	1.8	1.9	2.0	1.7	1.6	1.4
Tanzania	1.2	1.2	1.1	1.1	1.1	1.1	1.1	1.2	1.4
Togo	1.7	:	1.7	:	:	1.5	1.5	1.6	:
Uganda	[1.6]	[1.9]	[2.2]	2.0	2.0	2.2	2.3	2.3	2.4
Zambia	1.7	1.7	2.0	1.3	1.9	2.0	[1.9]	:	:
Zimbabwe[20]	1.3	:	:	(1.8)	(2.1)	2.3	5.5	2.5	2.2

State	2002	2003	2004	2005	2006	2007	2008	2009	2010
Americas									
Central America and the Caribbean									
Belize	0.8	0.9	0.9	1.0	1.0	1.1	1.4	1.3	1.1
Costa Rica[21]	–	–	–	–	–	–	–	–	–
Cuba[22]	..	..	..	..	..	..	..	..	..
Dominican Republic	1.1	0.8	0.7	0.8	0.7	0.7	0.7	0.7	0.7
El Salvador[23]	1.4	1.1	1.0	1.0	1.0	1.0	1.0	1.0	1.1
Guatemala	0.8	0.8	0.5	0.4	0.4	0.4	0.4	0.4	0.4
Haiti	–	–	–	–	–	–	–	–	–
Honduras[24]	[0.8]	[1.0]	[0.7]	[0.6]	0.7	0.8	1.0	1.1	1.1
Jamaica	0.6	0.6	0.5	0.5	0.6	0.7	0.9	0.9	0.8
Mexico	[0.5]	[0.5]	0.4	0.4	0.4	0.5	0.5	0.5	0.5
Nicaragua[25]	0.9	0.9	0.7	0.8	0.8	0.8	0.7	0.8	0.7
Panama	–	–	–	–	–	–	–	–	–
North America									
Canada	1.2	1.1	1.1	1.1	1.2	1.2	1.3	1.4	1.5
United States[26]	3.4	3.7	3.9	4.0	3.9	4.0	4.3	4.8	4.8
South America									
Argentina[27]	1.1	1.1	1.0	0.9	0.9	0.9	0.8	1.0	0.9
Bolivia[28]	2.0	2.2	1.9	1.8	1.6	1.7	2.0	2.0	1.7
Brazil	1.9	1.5	1.5	1.5	1.5	1.5	1.5	1.6	1.6
Chile[§ 29]	3.6	3.4	3.5	3.4	3.4	3.2	3.5	3.3	3.2
Colombia[30]	3.4	3.5	3.5	3.4	3.3	3.3	3.7	3.8	3.6
Ecuador	2.0	2.6	2.2	2.6	2.3	2.9	3.0	3.7	3.6
Guyana[‡ 31]	1.9	1.9	1.8	1.9	1.8	2.0	2.2	2.3	2.1
Paraguay[† 32]	1.0	0.8	0.9	0.8	0.8	0.8	0.7	0.9	0.9
Peru[33]	1.5	1.5	1.4	1.5	1.3	1.2	1.1	1.4	1.3
Uruguay[34]	2.8	2.5	2.2	2.1	2.0	1.8	1.9	2.1	2.0
Venezuela[35]	1.2	1.2	1.3	1.4	1.6	1.3	1.4	1.2	0.9

Asia and Oceania

Central and South Asia									
Afghanistan[36]	..	[2.1]	[2.2]	1.8	1.8	2.4	2.2	2.0	3.8
Bangladesh	1.1	1.1	1.1	1.0	1.0	1.0	1.0	1.1	1.1
India[37]	2.9	2.8	2.8	2.8	2.5	2.3	2.6	2.9	2.7
Kazakhstan	1.1	1.1	1.0	1.0	1.0	1.3	1.1	1.1	1.1
Kyrgyzstan[38]	2.7	2.9	2.8	3.1	3.2	3.4	3.4	3.5	4.4
Nepal[¶]	1.3	1.5	1.6	1.7	1.6	1.4	1.3	1.4	1.4
Pakistan[¶ ‡ 39]	3.9	3.7	3.6	3.4	3.3	3.0	2.8	2.8	2.8
Sri Lanka	[3.3]	[2.9]	3.0	2.6	2.8	3.3	3.7	3.6	3.0
Tajikistan	2.1	2.2	2.2	:	:	:	:	:	:
Turkmenistan	:	:	:	:	:	:	:	:	:
Uzbekistan[40]	0.6	0.5	:	:	:	:	:	:	:
East Asia									
China[41]	[2.2]	[2.1]	[2.1]	[2.0]	[2.0]	[2.1]	[2.0]	[2.2]	[2.1]
Japan[† 42]	1.0	1.0	1.0	1.0	1.0	0.9	0.9	1.0	1.0
Korea, North[43]	:	:	:	:	:	:	:	:	:
Korea, South[44]	[2.4]	[2.5]	[2.5]	2.6	2.6	2.6	2.8	2.9	2.7
Mongolia	1.9	1.6	1.5	1.3	1.2	1.4	1.4	1.0	1.1
Taiwan	2.2	2.2	2.2	2.1	1.9	2.0	2.2	2.4	2.1
Oceania									
Australia	1.9	1.8	1.8	1.8	1.8	1.8	1.8	1.9	1.9
Fiji[† 45]	1.7	1.6	1.7	1.4	1.7	2.2	1.5	1.8	1.6
New Zealand	1.1	1.1	1.0	1.0	1.0	1.1	1.1	1.2	1.2
Papua New Guinea[‡ 46]	0.6	0.5	0.6	0.6	0.5	0.6	0.5	0.5	0.4
South East Asia									
Brunei Darussalam[47]	5.3	3.7	2.5	2.6	2.6	2.6	2.5	3.3	3.2
Cambodia	1.6	1.5	1.3	1.1	1.1	1.1	1.0	1.9	1.6
Indonesia[48]	[0.8]	[1.0]	[0.9]	0.8	0.7	0.8	0.6	0.6	0.7
Laos	(0.6)	(0.6)	(0.5)	(0.4)	(0.4)	(0.4)	(0.3)	(0.3)	(0.3)

State	2002	2003	2004	2005	2006	2007	2008	2009	2010
Malaysia	2.2	2.6	2.3	2.3	2.1	2.1	2.0	2.1	1.6
Myanmar[49]	1.3	..	..	..	..	..	..	..	..
Philippines[50]	[1.5]	1.6	[1.4]	1.3	1.3	1.3	1.3	1.3	1.2
Singapore	5.0	4.9	4.5	4.4	4.0	3.7	3.9	4.1	3.7
Thailand	1.4	1.3	1.1	1.1	1.1	1.3	1.6	1.9	1.5
Timor-Leste[51]	..	..	1.1	2.5	5.2	[6.6]	5.3	6.6	4.9
Viet Nam	..	2.1	2.0	1.9	2.1	2.5	2.3	2.5	2.5
Europe									
Eastern Europe									
Armenia[†52]	2.7	2.7	2.7	2.9	2.9	3.0	3.4	4.2	4.2
Azerbaijan[53]	[2.2]	[2.4]	[2.6]	2.3	3.4	2.9	3.3	3.3	2.9
Belarus	1.4	1.3	1.4	1.5	1.7	1.6	1.5	1.4	1.4
Georgia[†54]	1.0	1.1	1.4	3.3	5.2	9.2	8.5	5.6	3.9
Moldova[†¶55]	0.4	0.4	0.4	0.4	0.5	0.5	0.6	0.5	0.3
Russia[56]	[4.4]	[4.3]	[3.8]	[3.7]	[3.6]	[3.5]	[3.5]	[4.3]	[3.9]
Ukraine[§]	2.8	2.8	2.6	2.8	2.8	2.9	2.7	[2.9]	[2.7]
Western and Central Europe									
Albania[§¶57]	1.3	1.3	1.4	1.4	1.6	1.8	2.0	2.1	1.6
Austria	0.9	0.9	0.9	0.9	0.8	0.9	0.9	0.9	0.9
Belgium	1.2	1.2	1.2	1.1	1.1	1.1	1.2	1.2	1.1
Bosnia and Herzegovina[†¶58]	3.9	2.4	1.9	1.5	1.3	1.1	1.1	1.2	1.2
Bulgaria[†59]	[2.9]	[2.8]	2.6	2.4	2.3	2.5	2.0	2.0	1.9
Croatia[60]	[2.8]	[2.1]	1.7	1.6	1.7	1.7	1.9	1.8	1.7
Cyprus[†]	[2.3]	[2.2]	2.1	2.2	2.1	1.9	1.8	2.0	2.1
Czech Republic[61]	2.0	2.1	1.9	2.0	1.7	1.6	1.4	1.4	1.3
Denmark	1.5	1.5	1.5	1.3	1.4	1.3	1.4	1.4	1.5
Estonia[62]	1.7	1.7	1.7	1.9	1.9	2.1	2.1	2.3	1.7
Finland	1.2	1.4	1.4	1.4	1.4	1.2	1.3	1.5	1.4

France[63]	2.5	2.6	2.6	2.6	2.5	2.4	2.3	2.3	2.5	2.3
Germany	1.5	1.4	1.4	1.4	1.4	1.3	1.3	1.3	1.4	1.4
Greece	3.2	2.6	2.6	2.7	2.9	2.9	2.7	3.0	3.2	[2.3]
Hungary	1.6	1.7	1.7	1.5	1.4	1.3	1.3	1.2	1.1	1.0
Iceland[64]	–	–	–	–	–	–	–	0.0	0.1	:
Ireland	0.7	0.6	0.6	0.6	0.6	0.5	0.5	0.6	0.6	0.6
Italy[65]	2.0	2.0	2.0	2.0	1.9	1.8	[1.7]	[1.8]	[1.8]	[1.7]
Latvia	1.6	1.7	1.7	1.7	1.7	1.9	1.7	1.7	1.4	1.1
Lithuania[66]	1.7	1.7	1.7	[1.5]	[1.4]	[1.4]	[1.4]	[1.4]	1.4	1.1
Luxembourg	0.7	0.7	0.7	0.7	0.6	0.6	0.6	0.6	0.7	
Macedonia, FYR[67]	2.8	2.4	2.5	2.5	2.1	1.9	2.0	1.8	1.7	1.4
Malta[†]	0.7	0.7	0.7	0.7	0.9	0.7	0.7	0.7	0.7	0.7
Montenegro[68]	:	:	:	:	:	[2.3]	1.8	1.9	1.9	1.9
Netherlands	1.6	1.6	1.5	1.5	1.5	1.5	1.5	1.4	1.5	1.4
Norway[69]	2.1	2.0	1.9	1.9	1.6	1.5	1.5	1.4	1.7	1.5
Poland[69]	1.9	1.9	1.9	1.9	1.9	1.9	2.0	[1.7]	[1.8]	[1.9]
Portugal	2.0	2.1	2.0	2.0	2.1	2.0	1.9	1.9	2.1	2.1
Romania	2.3	2.1	3.1	2.5	1.8	2.0	1.5	1.5	1.4	1.3
Serbia[70]	4.5	3.7	1.7	1.7	2.4	2.5	2.3	2.3	2.4	2.2
Slovakia[†]	1.8	1.9	1.5	1.4	1.6	1.7	1.5	1.5	1.5	1.3
Slovenia	1.4	1.4	1.1	1.0	1.6	1.4	1.5	1.2	1.6	1.6
Spain	1.2	1.1	1.7	1.5	1.2	1.2	1.2	1.2	1.2	1.0
Sweden	1.7	1.7	1.0	0.9	1.4	1.4	1.4	1.2	1.3	1.3
Switzerland[† q 71]	1.0	1.0	3.4	2.5	0.9	0.9	0.8	0.8	0.8	0.8
Turkey	3.9	3.4	2.8	2.5	2.5	2.5	2.3	2.3	2.6	2.4
United Kingdom	2.5	2.5	2.5	2.4	2.4	2.4	2.3	2.5	2.7	2.6
Middle East										
Bahrain[72]	4.7	4.8	4.3	3.6	3.4	3.2	3.0	3.0	3.9	3.4
Egypt	3.4	3.3	3.0	2.9	2.7	2.5	2.3	2.3	2.1	2.0
Iran[q 73]	2.3	2.7	2.9	3.3	3.4	2.5	2.5	(1.8)	:	:
Iraq[74]	:	:	(1.7)	(2.2)	(1.9)	(2.2)	(1.7)	2.2	2.5	2.4

State	2002	2003	2004	2005	2006	2007	2008	2009	2010
Israel[75]	[9.6]	[9.6]	[8.7]	[8.0]	[8.1]	[7.5]	[7.1]	[7.0]	[6.5]
Jordan	5.4	6.0	5.1	4.8	4.8	6.1	5.9	6.0	5.0
Kuwait	7.4	6.5	5.8	4.3	3.6	3.6	3.0	3.9	3.6
Lebanon	4.7	4.6	4.4	[4.4]	[4.5]	[4.6]	3.9	4.1	[4.2]
Oman[‡][76]	12.4	12.2	12.1	11.8	11.0	10.3	7.6	9.6	8.5
Qatar[77]	4.7	4.0	2.9	2.5	2.1	2.2	2.3	..	..
Saudi Arabia[§][78]	9.8	8.7	8.4	8.0	8.3	9.2	8.0	11.0	10.1
Syria[79]	5.4	6.2	5.5	5.0	4.4	4.1	3.6	4.0	4.1
United Arab Emirates[80]	[8.6]	[7.9]	[7.4]	[5.6]	[5.1]	[5.0]	[5.5]	[7.6]	[6.9]
Yemen	6.0	6.0	4.7	4.3	3.6	4.1	3.9	..	..

.. = not available or not applicable; – = nil or a negligible value; ( ) = uncertain figure; [ ] = SIPRI estimate; / = change of financial year (FY); ||| = series break (figures before this symbol may not be connected to figures after the symbol).

[a] The FY runs from Apr. of the year indicated to Mar. of the following year.

[b] The FY runs from July of the year indicated to June of the following year.

[†] All figures exclude military pensions.

[‡] All figures are for current spending only (i.e. exclude capital spending).

[§] All figures are for the adopted budget, rather than actual expenditure.

[¶] All figures exclude spending on paramilitary forces.

[||] This country changed or redenominated its currency during the period; all figures have been converted to the latest currency.

[1] The figures for Algeria are budget figures from 2004. In July 2006 the Algerian Government issued supplementary budgets increasing total government expenditure by 35%. It is not clear if any of these extra funds were allocated to the military.

[2] The figures for Libya do not include development expenditure, which in 2008 was 1000 million dinars.

[3] The rate of implementation of Angola's budget can vary considerably. Military expenditure for Angola should be seen in the context of highly uncertain economic statistics due to the impact of war on the Angolan economy.

[4] The figures for the Central African Republic do not include investment expenditure, which in 2005 totalled 775 000 CFA francs.

[5] Chad's military expenditure increased sharply after 2005 due to conflict in the east of the country, with exceptional military expenditure financed by oil revenues. Figures for 2006 are not available, but available information suggests a large increase over 2005 followed by a smaller increase between 2006 and 2007.

6 The figures for the Democratic Republic of the Congo (DRC) do not include profits from extensive military-run mining operations.

7 The figures for Côte d'Ivoire for 2003 are for budgeted spending rather than actual expenditure.

8 The figures for Gabon exclude off-budget spending financed by the Provisions pour Investissements Hydrocarbures (PIH), an investment fund based on tax revenues from foreign oil companies active in Gabon.

9 The 2009 budget speech by the Gambian Minister of Finance gave figures for the Ministry of Defence (MOD) budget of 381 million dalasis for 2008 and 189 million dalasis for 2009. However, these figures represent a different definition of military expenditure than earlier figures and would imply a much higher increase in spending in 2008 than is likely to be the case, so they cannot be used to form a consistent series.

10 The figures for Ghana from 2006 are for the adopted budget rather than actual spending.

11 The figures for Guinea might be an underestimate as the IMF reports large extra-budgetary spending for the military.

12 The figures for Madagascar include expenditure for the gendarmerie and the National Police.

13 The figures for Mali are for defence and security.

14 Mauritius changed its FY in 2010 from July–June to Jan.–Dec. A transitional 6-month FY applied from July–Dec. 2009, for which data is not available.

15 The figures for Namibia for 2002 include a supplementary allocation of 78.5 million Namibian dollars.

16 Rwanda changed its FY in 2009 from Jan.–Dec. to July–June. The local currency figure for Rwanda for 2009 is the sum of a special 6-month budget for Jan.–June 2009 (20.6 billion Rwandan francs) and the first full July–June FY of 2009/10 (43.6 billion Rwandan francs). The figures for 2005 and 2006 include allocations for African Union (AU) peace operations.

17 South Sudan became independent from Sudan on 9 July 2011. Between July 2005 and July 2011 southern Sudan was governed by the autonomous Government of Southern Sudan under the terms of the 2005 Comprehensive Peace Agreement. Figures for 2006–10 are the military spending of the Government of Southern Sudan on the Sudan People's Liberation Army (SPLA).

18 The figures for Sudan are for defence and security. The figures for 2006–10 exclude spending by the Government of Southern Sudan. See also note 17.

19 The figures for Swaziland for 2008–11 are based on an estimated share of the Defence, Public Order and Safety budget and are highly uncertain.

20 Zimbabwe abandoned the Zimbabwean dollar in Apr. 2009 and now operates a multiple currency regime, where US dollars, British pounds and South African rands, amongst others, may all be used for transactions. Government budget statistics are provided in US dollars. Local currency figures for Zimbabwe are given in Zimbabwean dollars up to 2007 and in US dollars from 2010. Hyperinflation means that the figures for 2006 and 2007 are highly uncertain and no meaningful price data is available for 2008, so it is not possible to provide a single constant price series. The constant dollar figures are therefore given in constant 2005 US dollars up to 2007, and in constant 2010 US dollars for 2010 and 2011. These two series cannot be joined.

21 Costa Rica has no armed forces. Expenditure for paramilitary forces, border guards, and maritime and air surveillance is less than 0.05% of GDP.

22 Figures for Cuba are for defence and internal order. The figures shown in table 4.9 are for current US dollars, converted at the official exchange rate for each year, instead of constant (2010) US dollars, due to the lack of reliable inflation data for Cuba. Data for military expenditure as a share of GDP is not given due to the lack of reliable GDP data for Cuba.

[23] The figures for El Salvador include military pensions from the Armed Forces Pensions Fund for 2002–10. The figure for 2011 includes an estimate of $75 million for pensions. The pensions figures may be slightly overestimated as they include financial investments by the fund, which was $17 million in 2010.

[24] The figures for Honduras do not include expenditure on arms imports.

[25] The figures for Nicaragua include military aid from Taiwan and the USA for the years 2002–2009 of 12.5, 16.9, 13.6, 11.1, 7.3, 28.8, 12.2 and 11.6 million cordobas, respectively.

[26] All figures for the USA are for FY (1 Oct. of the previous year to 30 Sep. of the stated year), rather than calendar year.

[27] The Argentinian Congress did not approve a budget for 2011. Ministries are therefore officially operating on the 2010 budget and so the SIPRI estimate for 2011 in local currency is identical to the figure for 2010 in current prices. However, expert sources suggest that actual expenditure in 2011 may be considerably higher.

[28] The figures for Bolivia include some expenditure for civil defence.

[29] The figures for Chile include direct transfers from the state-owned copper company Corporacion Nacional del Cobre (CODELCO) for military purchases. Since 2004 the MOD has built up a surplus from unspent portions of these transferred funds, which in 2011 were placed in a Strategic Contingency Fund for future equipment spending. The SIPRI figures continue to count the transfers from CODELCO rather than actual spending.

[30] The figures for Colombia for 2002–2007 include special allocations totalling 2.5 billion pesos from a war tax decree of 12 Aug. 2002. Most of these allocations were spent between 2002 and 2004.

[31] The figures for Guyana do not include capital expenditure, which for 2003–2006 was 147, 154, 155 and 172 million Guyanese dollars, respectively.

[32] The figures for Paraguay in 2003 are for the modified budget, rather than actual expenditure. Spending on military pensions is not included; for the years 2007–11 it was 208, 239.3, 271.7, 293.9 and 340 billion guaranies, respectively.

[33] The figures for Peru from 2005 do not include the transfer of 20% of gas production revenues from the state-owned company CAMISEA for the armed forces and national police.

[34] In previous editions of the SIPRI Yearbook, the figures for Uruguay excluded military pensions. The inclusion of spending on pensions means that the figures presented here are substantially higher than those published in previous editions.

[35] The figures for Venezuela exclude an unknown amount of additional funding from the National Development Fund (FONDEN), created in 2005 and funded by contributions from the Central Bank and the state oil company, PDVSA.

[36] Afghanistan's FY runs from Mar. to Feb. The figures are for core budget expenditure on the Afghan National Army. Military aid from foreign donors—which in 2009 included $4 billion from the USA, 16 times Afghanistan's domestic military expenditure—is not included.

[37] The figures for India include expenditure on the paramilitary forces of the Border Security Force, the Central Reserve Police Force, the Assam Rifles, the Indo-Tibetan Border Police and, from 2007, the Sashastra Seema Bal, but do not include spending on military nuclear activities.

[38] The figures for Kyrgyzstan include spending on internal security, which accounts for a substantial part of total military spending.

[39] The figures for Pakistan do not include spending on paramilitary forces—the Frontier Corps (Civil Armed Forces) and Pakistan Rangers. For 2008, 2009 and 2010, this totalled 16.7, 20.8 and 31.4 billion rupees, respectively. The figures also exclude defence spending in the Public Sector Development Plan, which in 2008–11 was 2.3, 5, 3.9 and 2.1 billion rupees, respectively.

[40] The figures for Uzbekistan expressed in constant US dollars should be seen in the light of considerable differences between the official and the unofficial exchange rates.

[41] The figures for China are for estimated total military expenditure, including estimates for items not included in the official defence budget. They are based on (a) publicly available figures for official military expenditure and for certain other items; (b) estimates based on official data and the methodology of Wang, S., 'The military expenditure of China, 1989–98', SIPRI Yearbook 1999; and (c) for the most recent years, where no official data is available for certain items, either the percentage change in official military expenditure, recent trends in spending in the same category, or, in the case of the commercial earnings of the People's Liberation Army (PLA), on the assumption of a gradual decrease. See 'Sources and methods' below.

[42] The figures for Japan are for the adopted budget before 2004 and for 2010–11. The figures include the budgeted amount for the Special Action Committee on Okinawa (SACO) and exclude military pensions.

[43] The figures for North Korea are as reported by North Korean authorities. They do not include investment in the arms industry and R&D in dual-use technology, or various social welfare services provided through the military sector. Due to lack of a credible exchange rate between the North Korean won and the US dollar, no dollar estimates can be provided.

[44] The figures for South Korea do not include spending on 3 'special funds' for relocation of military installations, relocations of US bases and welfare for troops. These totalled 449.3, 1048.8 and 1285.2 billion won in 2009, 2010 and 2011, respectively.

[45] Fiji's spending on military pensions for 1998–2002 was roughly 3.5% of annual military spending.

[46] Figures for Papua New Guinea are for the recurrent part of the budget. For the years 2008–11, development expenditure was 6, 25.2, 0 and 47 million kina, respectively.

[47] The local currency figure for Brunei Darussalam for 2003 is for a special 15-month FY from Jan. 2003 to Mar. 2004. FYs up to 2002 are Jan.–Dec, those from 2004 onwards are Apr.–Mar.

[48] The figures for Indonesia exclude substantial off-budget expenditure, the size of which is unknown.

[49] The figures for Myanmar are not presented in US dollar terms owing to the extreme variation in stated exchange rate between the kyat and the US dollar.

[50] The figures for the Philippines are slightly overstated as they include spending on Veterans Affairs. Up to 2010 this amounted to no more than c. 1 billion pesos annually, but in 2011 this increased to 13.9 billion pesos.

[51] The local currency figure for Timor-Leste for 2007 is for a special 6-month FY July–Dec. 2007. Previous FYs, up to 2006/2007, are July–June; FYs from 2008 are Jan.–Dec. The figures for military expenditure as a share of GDP are based on GDP data that excludes oil and gas revenues, which in recent years have been several times higher than this measure of GDP.

[52] If the figures for Armenia were to include military pensions they would be 15–20% higher.

[53] The figures for Azerbaijan for 2011 include an allocation of 1087 million manats for 'Special defence projects' in addition to the main defence budget.

54 The budget figures for Georgia for 2003 are believed to be an underestimation of actual spending because of the political turmoil during the year.

55 Adding all military items in Moldova's budget, including expenditure on military pensions and paramilitary forces, would give total military expenditure for 2005, 2006 and 2007 of 343, 457 and 530 million lei, respectively.

56 For the sources and methods of the military expenditure figures for Russia see Cooper, J., 'The military expenditure of the USSR and the Russian Federation, 1987–97', *SIPRI Yearbook 1998*.

57 The figures for Albania prior to 2006 do not fully include pensions. The figures in 2007, 2008 and 2011 are for the modified budget.

58 The figures for Bosnia and Herzegovina from 2005 onwards are for the armed forces of Bosnia and Herzegovina, which was formed in 2005 from the Croat–Bosniak Army of the Federation of Bosnia and Herzegovina and the Bosnian Serb Army of Republika Srpska. The figures prior to 2005 include expenditure for the Army of the Federation of Bosnia and Herzegovina and the Army of Republika Srpska. The figures do not include spending on arms imports.

59 According to NATO figures, Bulgaria's total spending, including pensions, was 1393, 1712 and 1749 million leva in 2006, 2007 and 2008, respectively.

60 The figures for Croatia for 2006–10 include sums allocated from central government expenditure for repayments on a loan for a military radar system. The sums allocated were 147.8, 91.4, 53.2, 54.6 and 55.2 million koruny, respectively. Payments continued in 2011, but figures have not been provided, so an estimate equal to the 2010 figure (55.2 million koruny) has been included.

61 The figures for the Czech Republic do not include military aid to Afghanistan or Iraq. Aid to Afghanistan was 18.7 million koruny in 2004 and 612.6 million koruny in 2007. Aid to Iraq was 1.1 million koruny in 2005.

62 The Estonian Border Guard Service merged with the National Police in 2010, and it is no longer classed as a paramilitary force by SIPRI. This accounts for much of the decrease in Estonian military spending in 2010.

63 The figures for France from 2006 are calculated with a new methodology due to a change in the French budgetary system and financial law.

64 Iceland does not have an army or other military. Until the establishment of the Icelandic Defence Agency in June 2008 there was no budget for defence or military affairs. The Icelandic Defence Agency is responsible for maintaining defence installations such as the Icelandic Air Defence System, intelligence gathering and military exercises.

65 The figures for Italy include spending on civil defence, which typically amounts to about 4.5% of the total.

66 Due to a change in the way Lithuania reports spending on paramilitary forces, it is possible that the figures up to 2003 include spending on some forces not included from 2004.

67 The definition of military expenditure for the Former Yugoslav Republic of Macedonia changed from 2006. Border troops were transferred from the MOD to the Ministry of Interior Affairs and part of the military pensions, previously entirely excluded, are now included.

68 Montenegro declared its independence from the State Union of Serbia and Montenegro on 3 June 2006. See also note 70.

69 The figures for Poland exclude some defence spending in other ministries, and additional domestic defence spending such as the Armed Forces Modernization Fund and some additional defence R&D. Between 2004 and 2011 these additional sums varied between 240 million and 640 million złotys.

70 Montenegro seceded from the State Union of Serbia and Montenegro on 3 June 2006. The figures for Serbia up to 2005 are for Serbia and Montenegro (known as the Federal Republic of Yugoslavia until Feb. 2003) and for 2006 onwards for Serbia alone.

[71] Figures for Switzerland do not include spending by cantons and local government. In 1990–2006, military spending by cantons and local government typically amounted to 5–8% of the central government spending figures.

[72] The figures for Bahrain do not include extra-budgetary spending on defence procurement.

[73] The figures for Iran do not include spending on paramilitary forces such as the Islamic Revolutionary Guards Corps (IRGC).

[74] In recent years, the Iraqi MOD has substantially underspent its budget. The figures for Iraq for 2011 should therefore be treated with caution. The figures up to 2007 are uncertain due to the high rate of inflation.

[75] The figures for Israel include supplemental budgets for operations in the Palestinian territories and elsewhere and an estimate for the paramilitary Border Police.

[76] The figures for Oman are for expenditure on defence and national security. In 2011 the government enacted a supplemental budget of 1000 million rials, equal to 12% of the original total budget, but it is not known if any of this additional allocation went to military spending.

[77] The figures for Qatar are for expenditure on defence and security.

[78] The figures for Saudi Arabia are for expenditure on defence and security.

[79] The figures for Syria in US dollars have been converted from local currency using the market exchange rate for the base year of 2010 of $1 = 46.422 Syrian pounds. Previously, Syria operated an official exchange rate of $1 = 11.225 Syrian pounds, which was used in editions of the SIPRI Yearbook up to 2009. Syria abolished the official rate in 2007, moving to the parallel market rate that had previously operated unofficially.

[80] The military expenditure of the United Arab Emirates is uncertain and lacking in transparency. The only available sources of data are IMF Staff Country Reports and the IMF's *Government Finance Statistics*. The Country Reports include 2 lines relating to military expenditure: the Goods and Services expenditure of the Defence and Interior ministries (which does not include military wages, salaries and pensions), and Abu Dhabi Federal Services, which the reports say are mainly defence and security expenditure. *Government Finance Statistics* gives only the Goods and Services figures. The SIPRI figures are estimated as 80% of the Abu Dhabi Federal Services item, plus 100% of the Goods and Services figures. The latter item is estimated for 2006–10 assuming a constant real value.

Sources and methods

The definition of military expenditure

The guideline definition of military expenditure used by SIPRI includes expenditure on the following actors and activities: (*a*) the armed forces, including peacekeeping forces; (*b*) defence ministries and other government agencies engaged in defence projects; (*c*) para-military forces, when judged to be trained and equipped for military operations; and (*d*) military space activities. It includes all current and capital expenditure on (*a*) military and civil personnel, including retirement pensions of military personnel and social services for personnel; (*b*) operations and maintenance; (*c*) procurement; (*d*) military research and development; and (*e*) military aid (in the military expenditure of the donor country). It does not include civil defence and current expenditure for past military activities, such as for veterans' benefits, demobilization, conversion and weapon destruction. While this definition serves as a guideline, in practice it is often difficult to adhere to due to data limitations.

Limitations of the data

There are three main types of limitation of the data: reliability, validity and comparability.

The main problems of reliability are due to the less than comprehensive coverage of official military expenditure data, the lack of detailed information on military expenditure and the lack of data on actual, rather than budgeted, military expenditure. In many countries the official data covers only a part of total military expenditure. Important items can be hidden under non-military budget headings or can even be financed entirely outside the government budget. Many such extra-budgetary and off-budget mechanisms are employed in practice.

The validity of expenditure data depends on the purpose for which it is used. Since expenditure data is a measure of monetary input, its most valid use is as an indicator of the economic resources consumed for military purposes. For the same reason, its utility as an indicator of military strength or capability is limited. While military expenditure does have an impact on military capability, so do many other factors such as the balance between personnel and equipment, the technological level of military equipment, and the state of maintenance and repair, as well as the overall security environment in which the armed forces are to be employed.

The comparability of the data is limited by two different types of factor: the varying coverage (or definition) of the data and the method of currency conversion. The coverage of official data on military expenditure varies significantly between countries and over time for the same country. For the conversion into a common currency, the choice of exchange rate makes a great difference in cross-country comparisons (see below). This is a general problem in international comparisons of economic data and is not specific to military expenditure. However, since international comparison of military expenditure is often a sensitive issue, it is important to bear in mind that the interpretation of cross-country comparisons of military expenditure is greatly influenced by the choice of exchange rate.

Methods

SIPRI data is based on open sources and reflects the official data reported by governments. However, the official data does not always conform to the SIPRI definition of military expenditure. Nor is it always possible to recalculate data according to the definition, since this would require detailed information about what is included in the official defence budgets and about extra-budgetary and off-budget military expenditure items. In many cases SIPRI is confined to using the data provided by governments, regardless of definition. If several data series are available, which is often the case, SIPRI chooses the data series that corresponds most closely to the SIPRI definition of military expenditure. Nevertheless, priority is given to choosing a uniform time series for each country, in order to achieve consistency over time, rather than to adjusting the figures for individual years according to a common definition. In addition, estimates have to be made in specific cases.

Estimation. Estimates of military expenditure are predominantly made (*a*) when the coverage of official data diverges significantly from the SIPRI definition or (*b*) when no complete consistent time series is available. In the first case, estimates are made on the basis of an analysis of primarily official government budget and expenditure accounts. The most comprehensive estimates of this type are for China (as presented in *SIPRI Yearbook 1998* and updated in *SIPRI Yearbook 2011*) and Russia (as presented in *SIPRI Yearbook 1999*). In the second case, when only incomplete times series are available, the figures from the data series which corresponds most closely to the SIPRI definition are used for the years covered by that series. Figures for the missing years are then estimated by applying the percentage change between years in an alternative series to the data in the first series, in order to achieve consistency over time.

All estimates are based on official government data or other empirical evidence from open sources. Thus, no estimates are made for countries that do not release any official data, and no figures are displayed for these countries.

SIPRI estimates are presented in square brackets in the tables. Round brackets are used when data is uncertain for reasons beyond SIPRI's control, for example, when the data is based on a source of uncertain reliability and in cases when data expressed in constant dollars or as shares of GDP is uncertain due to uncertain economic data.

The data for the most recent years includes two types of estimate, which apply to all countries. First, figures for the most recent years are for adopted budget, budget estimates or revised estimates, the majority of which will be revised in subsequent years. Second, in table 4.9 the deflator used for the final year in the series is an estimate based on part of a year or as provided by the International Monetary Fund (IMF). Unless exceptional uncertainty is involved, these estimates are not bracketed.

The totals for the world, regions, organizations and income groups in table 4.1 are estimates because data is not available for all countries in all years. In cases where data for a country is missing at the beginning or end of the series, these estimates are made on the assumption that the rate of change for that country is the same as the average for the region to which it belongs. In cases where data is missing in the middle of the series, the estimates are made on the assumption of an even trend between the end values. When no estimate can be made, countries are excluded from all totals.

Calculations. The original country data is provided in local currency at current prices (table 4.8) for financial years. Those countries with financial years that do not coincide with calendar years are indicated in table 4.8. In all but one such case, the figure shown for a given year is for the financial year *beginning* in that calendar year. The exception is the USA, where each figure is for the financial year beginning on 1 October of the year previous to that indicated. A few countries changed their financial year during the period 2002–11. These cases are indicated in footnotes.

Figures in constant US dollars and as a share of GDP (tables 4.9 and 4.10) are displayed on a calendar year basis, which makes it necessary to convert financial year figures to calendar year figures for some countries. These calculations are made on the assumption of an even rate of expenditure throughout the financial year. Local currency data is then converted to US dollars at constant prices and exchange rates (table 4.9) using the national consumer prices index (CPI) for the respective country and the annual average market exchange rate (MER).

The use of CPIs as deflators means that the trend in the SIPRI military expenditure for each country (in constant dollars) reflects the real change in its purchasing power for country-typical baskets of civilian consumer goods. A military-specific deflator would be a more appropriate choice, but these are unavailable for most countries.

GDP-based purchasing power parity (PPP) exchange rates would be an alternative to MERs. PPP rates better represent the volume of goods and services that can be purchased with a given sum of money in each country than do MERs. However, they are not necessarily a better measure than MERs of the volume of *military* goods and services that may be obtained (as discussed in detail in *SIPRI Yearbook 2006*). In particular, PPP rates are unlikely to reflect the relative costs of advanced weapons technology and systems in each country. In fact, military spending figures, whatever exchange rate is used, do not directly measure military capability. PPP rates thus do not give a 'better' indication of what a country is 'really' spending; rather, they measure what alternative volume of goods and services could be bought within the country in question if the money was used for other purposes. MERs on the other hand measure what the military spending could purchase on international markets. In addition to these issues, as PPP rates are estimates, they are less reliable than MERs. Thus, SIPRI uses market exchange rates to convert military expenditure data into US dollars, despite their limitations, as the simplest and most objective measure for comparing international spending levels.

Sources

The sources for military expenditure data are, in order of priority, (*a*) primary sources, that is, official data provided by national governments, either in their official publications or in response to questionnaires; (*b*) secondary sources that quote primary data; and (*c*) other secondary sources.

The first category consists of national budget documents, defence white papers and public finance statistics as well as responses to a SIPRI questionnaire that is sent out annually to the finance and defence ministries, central banks, and national statistical offices of the countries in the SIPRI Military Expenditure Database. It also includes government responses to questionnaires about military expenditure sent out by the United Nations and, if made available by the countries themselves, the Organization for Security and Co-operation in Europe (OSCE).

The second category includes international statistics, such as those of the North Atlantic Treaty Organization (NATO) and the IMF. The data for the 16 pre-1999 NATO member states has traditionally been taken from military expenditure statistics published in a number of NATO sources. The introduction by NATO of a new definition of military expenditure in 2005 has made it necessary to rely on other sources for some NATO countries for the most recent years. The data for many developing countries is taken from the IMF's *Government Finance Statistics Yearbook*, which provides a defence heading for most IMF member countries, and from country reports by IMF staff. This category also includes publications of other organizations that provide references to the primary sources used, such as the Country Reports of the Economist Intelligence Unit.

The third category of sources consists of specialist journals and newspapers.

The main sources for economic data are the publications of the IMF: *International Financial Statistics*, *World Economic Outlook* and country reports by IMF staff.

The SIPRI Military Expenditure Network

Contribution of military expenditure data, estimates and advice are gratefully acknowledged from Julian Cooper (University of Birmingham, Centre for Russian and East European Studies), Dimitar Dimitrov (University of National and World Economy, Sofia), Iñigo Guevara y Moyano (Colectivo de Análisis de la Seguridad con Democracia, Querétaro), Gülay Günlük-Şenesen (Istanbul University), Iduvina Hernández (Asociación para el estudio y la promoción de la seguridad en democracia, Guatemala City), Shir Hever (Alternative Information Center, Jerusalem), Pavan Nair (Jagruti Seva Sanstha, Pune), Elina Noor (Institute of Strategic and International Studies Malaysia, Kuala Lumpur), Tamara Pataraia (Caucasus Institute for Peace, Democracy and Development, Tbilisi), Thomas Scheetz (Lincoln University College, Buenos Aires), Nerhan Yentürk (Istanbul Bilgi Universty), Tasheen Zayouna (International IDEA, Stockholm) and Ozren Zunec (University of Zagreb).

5. Arms production and military services

Overview

The public spending crisis in the Global North has not yet had a large overall impact on the major companies in the arms production and military services industry ('the arms industry'). Sales of arms and military services by the largest arms-producing companies—the SIPRI Top 100—continued to increase in 2010 to reach $411.1 billion, although at 1 per cent in real terms the rate of increase was slower than in 2009 (see section IV in this chapter). Between 2002 and 2010 arms sales of companies in the Top 100 rose by 60 per cent.

The most likely reason for this lack of major change is that the impact of the world financial slowdown is being delayed by the structure of the arms industry (as discussed in SIPRI Yearbook 2011). One factor contributing to the overall slowdown in 2010 was the United States' drawdown from Iraq and anticipated lower US military demand there.

The economic and spending uncertainties in both the USA and Western Europe will have general implications for the way in which weapon programmes are developed and implemented, and so have contributed to uncertainty as to whether arms sales will be maintained or increase at the same rate as in the past. The impact of this uncertainty on arms producers based in the USA and Western Europe is illustrated by the US National Defense Authorization Act (NDAA) for 2012 and discussions on arms industry production cooperation in Western Europe (see section I).

The NDAA has sent a mixed message about the US arms industry. On the one hand, it maintains many of the USA's largest, most costly weapons programmes, such as the F-35 (Joint Strike Fighter) combat aircraft. Authorization to continue spending on these costly programmes indicates that arms sales in the US market are likely to continue largely unchanged from current levels. On the other hand, new contract rules on risk sharing between the US Government and the companies winning arms contracts mean that a potentially heavier burden will fall on the industry as these programmes develop.

The financial crisis has seeped into the discussions on arms industry cooperation in Western Europe, although these discussions have not yet resulted in widespread increased cooperation. West European countries have discussed and begun to implement cooperative development and production strategies for unmanned aerial systems (UASs) and in June 2011 the European Commission initiated a process for developing and producing UASs. However, these projects have not yet come to fruition, as seen in the stagnation of the Talarion project.

Some key military services sectors—such as maintenance, repair and overhaul (MRO), systems support, logistics, and training of foreign militaries—

have been more resistant to the impact of the drawdown from Iraq and to the global financial instability. Their long-term growth can be attributed to a variety of post-cold war changes, including structural transformation of military needs and the decrease in in-house capabilities for ever more complex systems. It seems that increased pressure on public spending, which has raised the possibility that military spending will fall, will contribute to an increase in demand for outsourced services, for example for weapon systems MRO (see section II). In addition to an increased focus on military services, companies are relying on other business strategies in an effort to maintain their bottom lines. A notable development has been the growth in acquisitions of specialist cybersecurity firms as the largest arms-producing companies attempt to shield themselves from potential cuts in military spending and move into adjacent markets (see section I).

Many countries outside the Global North are attempting to develop a self-sustaining national arms industry. India's efforts to modernize, upgrade and maintain the equipment of its armed forces and to expand its military capabilities have made it the largest importer of major arms. Its domestic arms industry is also attempting to meet this demand—for example by increasing levels of technology through technology transfer—but the Indian defence industrial policy requires major reform (see section III).

Companies based in the USA remained at the top of the SIPRI Top 100 arms-producing and military services companies for 2010 and were responsible for over 60 per cent of the arms sales in the SIPRI Top 100 (see section IV). The number of West European companies in the list declined to 30, while the Brazilian company Embraer entered the Top 100. Russia's continued arms industry consolidation added another parent corporation to its top arms producers—United Shipbuilding Corporation.

SUSAN T. JACKSON

I. Key developments in the main arms-producing countries

SUSAN T. JACKSON

The ongoing consequences of the global financial and economic crisis have led to many countries in the Global North discussing and implementing substantial spending cuts to reduce deficits in government finances. These proposed cuts to current and future public expenditure have generally included military expenditure, and could thus have an impact on the arms-producing and military services industry.[1]

In the United States in particular political disagreement about how to reduce the budget deficit along with the drawdown and eventual withdrawal from Iraq and the planned withdrawal from Afghanistan have created a highly unpredictable situation for US military expenditure, and thus for the global arms industry. Cuts in military expenditure as part of deficit-reduction efforts in Western Europe also have potential implications for how weapon programmes are developed and implemented. These developments are reducing the rate of increase of the arms sales of the SIPRI Top 100 arms-producing and military services companies: it peaked at 13 per cent in 2003 and continued at a lower level between 2006 and 2009 but fell to 1 per cent in 2010 (see table 5.1).

Initial reports of arms sales in 2011 have been mixed. In some cases, sales fell, as expected, following completion of a contract. For example, BAE Systems of the United Kingdom reported reduced 2011 half-year figures due to lower volume in its Land and Armaments unit and to completion of its part of the F-22 programme.[2] Other companies reported higher sales as the programmes they worked on continued. In its financial report for the third quarter of 2011, the US company Lockheed Martin estimated that its total sales in 2011 would reach $47 billion, with increases in three of its four business units and little change in the fourth.[3] Similarly, the total sales of Aselsan of Turkey in the first nine months of 2011 were 33 per cent higher than in the same period in 2010.[4] Still others had sales increases that can in part be attributed to acquisitions, as with the French company Safran's purchase of small- and medium-sized enterprises.[5]

---

[1] On changes in military spending see chapter 4, sections I, III and V, in this volume.

[2] BAE Systems, *Half-yearly Report and Presentation 2011* (BAE Systems: London, 2011).

[3] Lockheed Martin, 'Lockheed Martin announces third quarter 2011 results', Press release, 26 Oct. 2011, <http://www.lockheedmartin.com/us/news/press-releases/2011/october/3Q-2011-earnings.html>.

[4] Aselsan, '30 Eylul 2011 tarihinde sona eren dokuz aylik ara doneme ait ozet konsolide finansal tablolar', [Consolidated financial statements for the period ended 30 September 2011], <http://www.aselsan.com.tr/Content.aspx?mid=119&oid=934>.

[5] Safran, 'Safran reports improved half-year results for 2011 with a recurring operating margin of nearly 10% of revenue', Press release, 28 July 2011, <http://www.safran-group.com/site-safran-en/finance-397/financial-publications/financial-press-releases/2011-727/>.

Table 5.1. Arms sales of companies in the SIPRI Top 100 arms-producing and military services companies, 2002–10

	2002	2003	2004	2005	2006	2007	2008	2009	2010	2002–10
Arms sales at constant (2010) prices and exchange rates										
Total ($ b.)	257	279	317	325	340	356	379	406	411	
Change (%)		*13*	*10*	*2*	*5*	*5*	*6*	*7*	*1*	*60*
Arms sales at current prices and exchange rates										
Total ($ b.)	196	235	274	289	312	347	385	399	411	
Change (%)		*20*	*17*	*5*	*8*	*11*	*12*	*4*	*3*	*110*

Note: The figures in this table refer to the companies in the SIPRI Top 100 in each year, which means that they refer to a different set of companies each year, as ranked from a consistent set of data. In particular, the figures shown above for 2009 differ from those in table 5.4.

Source: Table 5.5; and the SIPRI Arms Industry Database.

Many countries outside Western Europe and North America, such as India and some countries in the Middle East, are maintaining large arms procurement projects and as a result many West European and North American companies are adopting strategies that prioritize marketing of their arms in these countries.[6] Similarly, Japan's announcement in late 2011 that it is to lift its ban on arms exports—in part to support its domestic arms industry and potentially lower costs per unit—is indicative of increasing prioritization of arms exports in the Global North.[7] Overall, the budget uncertainty that persists in many places contributes to general uncertainty regarding future arms sales.

The US National Defense Authorization Act for 2012

The National Defense Authorization Act (NDAA) for financial year 2012, which was passed by the US Congress in December 2011, gives an indication of what to expect in the short term in the US arms market.[8] While discussions on this document have tended to focus on the level of US military spending, a major role of the NDAA is to authorize annual funding for equipment purchases, and it therefore has implications for the arms industry.

---

[6] See e.g. BAE Systems, *Annual Report 2010: Total Performance Across Our Markets* (BAE Systems: London, [2011]), p. 4; and Harris Corporation, *When It Matters Most, Who Can You Trust? 2010 Annual Report* (Harris Corporation: Melbourne, FL, 2010), p. 17.

[7] Dawson, C., 'Japan lifts decades long ban on export of weapons', *Wall Street Journal*, 28 Dec. 2011; and Japanese Ministry of Defense, 'Press conference by the defense minister', 27 Dec. 2011, <http://www.mod.go.jp/e/pressconf/2011/12/111227.html>.

[8] National Defense Authorization Act for Fiscal Year 2012, US Public Law no. 112-81, signed into law 31 Dec. 2011, <http://thomas.loc.gov/cgi-bin/bdquery/z?d112:h.r.01540:>. On the US budget debate and US military spending see also chapter 4, section III, in this volume.

Although the public spending crisis is growing in some sectors of US Government spending, the 2012 NDAA demonstrates that many large weapon producers are currently experiencing less pressure. It contains no significant large-scale equipment funding cuts, indicating that spending on arms in the world's largest arms market will continue at near-current levels. Nonetheless, one key justification cited as the basis for company strategies and decisions on job cuts or mergers and acquisitions is a perceived decrease in arms spending in the USA as a result of the public spending crisis.

Among programmes for which spending is maintained by the 2012 NDAA are the Ground Combat Vehicle (GCV), tactical wheeled vehicle and C/MV-22 aircraft programmes.[9] Despite significant cost and delivery overruns, the NDAA also authorizes continued spending on the F-35 (Joint Strike Fighter) programme.[10] It is the most expensive and perhaps the most controversial weapon-procurement programme in US history, costing the USA a projected $382 billion for 2443 aircraft.[11] Led by Lockheed Martin, the programme joins companies in nine partner countries in the development and production of the fifth generation fighter. While it is in no danger of deep cuts in the short term, the NDAA requires the US Undersecretary of Defense for Acquisition, Technology and Logistics to implement the 2009 Weapon Systems Acquisition Reform Act for the F-35 programme, in part to better assess the project's costs.[12] In addition, the NDAA requires future low-rate, initial production (LRIP) lots—which allow equipment to be tested prior to mass production and purchase of the system—to be fixed-price contracts, with Lockheed Martin agreeing to take full responsibility for cost overruns.[13] This is a significant change from the earlier contract, in which the government agreed to pay cost overruns.

[9] US House of Representatives, Armed Services Committee, 'The National Defense Authorization Act for FY 2012: highlights of the conference report', 12 Dec. 2011, <http://armedservices.house.gov/index.cfm?p=ndaa-conference-report-highlights>.

[10] US House of Representatives (note 9); US Government Accountability Office (GAO), *Joint Strike Fighter*, GAO-10-382 (GAO: Washington, DC, Mar. 2010); and Dunn, M. M., 'Washington perspective: FY12 NDAA', Air Force Association Blog, 16 Dec. 2011, <http://airforceassociation.blog spot.com/2011/12/washington-perspective-fy12-ndaa.html>.

[11] This figure does not include the lifetime expense to the USA of operating and maintaining the aircraft, as pointed out by the Department of Defense, meaning that costs could surpass $1 trillion. US Department of Defense (DOD), *Selected Acquisition Report (SAR): F-35* (DOD: Washington, DC, 31 Dec. 2010), p. 53; and Thierney, D., 'The F-35: a weapon that costs more than Australia', *The Atlantic*, Mar. 2011. On recalculation of the figures see Gertler, J., *F-35 Joint Strike Fighter (JSF) Program: Background and Issues for Congress*, Congressional Research Service (CRS) Report for Congress RL30563 (US Congress, CRS: Washington, DC, 26 Apr. 2011).

[12] This law reformed how the US Department of Defense purchases and contracts for major weapon systems and requires, e.g., analysis of the cost of new projects and more weapon testing before production runs begin. Weapon Systems Acquisition Reform Act of 2009, US Public Law no. 111-23, signed into law 22 May 2009, <http://thomas.loc.gov/cgi-bin/bdquery/z?d111:s.00454:>; and Tirpak, J. A., 'Make or break time for the F-35', *Airforce Magazine*, Aug. 2011.

[13] Levin, C. (Senator), 'Senate Armed Services Committee completes conference on National Defense Authorization Act for FY12', Press release, 12 Dec. 2011, <http://levin.senate.gov/news

While the US Department of Defense (DOD) and the US Congress agree that the impact on the USA's defence industrial and technological base should be considered when making spending cuts and that the arms industry's profit should be safeguarded, the change to the F-35 contract is one of a number of cases where the DOD has proposed amendments to its contracts with arms-producers that aim to allocate some of the cost risk to the industry side.[14] In November 2011, in a joint letter coordinated by the Aerospace Industries Association, over 100 US executives from the aerospace and defence industry commented on the DOD's proposed amendments to contracts.[15] They warned the US Secretary of Defense, Leon Panetta, that the increased risk built into contracts would lead to the proposed amendments decreasing competition and thereby contributing to lower innovation, increased costs and employee lay-offs.

Other sections of the 2012 NDAA that are not related to funding also affect the arms industry.[16] Provisions on political influence mean that arms producers are no longer required to disclose political contributions before participating in DOD tenders. Provisions on counterfeit parts task the DOD and the arms industry with developing mechanisms for tracking, stemming and penalizing those who traffic in and use counterfeit parts in US weapon systems.[17]

Acquisitions, spin-offs and sell-offs in the United States

Arms-producing companies can choose from a variety of strategies in response to budgetary pressures, including consolidation of military businesses, diversification into commercial (i.e. non-military) activities and

room/press/release/senate-armed-services-committee-completes-conference-on-national-defense-authorization-act-for-fy12>.

[14] Panetta, L., 'Defense priorities: today and tomorrow', Lee H. Hamilton Lecture, Woodrow Wilson Center, Washington, DC, 11 Oct. 2011, <http://www.wilsoncenter.org/event/defense-priorities-today-and-tomorrow-secretary-leon-panetta>; Carter, A., 'The defense industry enters a new era', Prepared remarks, Cowen Investment Conference, New York, 9 Feb. 2011; US Department of Defense, 'Contracts', no. 1010-11, 9 Dec. 2011, <http://www.defense.gov/contracts/contract.aspx?contractid=4681>; Adler, L., 'Pentagon open to mergers, but not at the very top', Reuters, 9 Feb. 2011, <http://www.reuters.com/article/2011/02/09/>; Shalal-Esa, A., 'Pentagon vows to keep defense industry healthy', 2 Dec. 2011, <http://in.reuters.com/article/2011/12/01/pentagon-industry-idINDE7B00O020111201>; and Moore, J., 'Sharing the pain & gain of a multimillion-dollar contract', GovConExec, 2 May 2011, <http://www.govconexec.com/2011/03/02/sharing-the-pain-the-gain-of-a-multimillion-dollar-contract/>.

[15] The letter, which was not released, is summarized in Shalal-Esa, A., 'U.S. defense firms blast Pentagon on contract changes', Reuters, 6 Dec. 2011, <http://www.reuters.com/article/2011/12/07/us-pentagon-industry-idUSTRE7B608O020111207>.

[16] US House of Representatives (note 9); and Levin (note 13).

[17] Levin (note 13); and Corrin, A. and Weigelt, M., 'Counterfeit parts, fixed-price contracts, contactor pay rules and SBIR addressed in Senate Defense Authorization bill', Georgia Institute of Technology, Contracting Education Academy, 2 Sep. 2011, <http://contractingacademy.gatech.edu/2011/12/counterfeit-parts-fixed-price-contracts-contractor-pay-rules-and-sbir-addressed-in-senate-defense-authorization-bill/>.

streamlining by spinning off non-core businesses. Developments in mergers and acquisitions in the USA give some indication of the strategies that are being pursued.

While welcoming mergers and acquisitions in the arms industry more broadly, in February 2011 the US DOD reiterated its policy of discouraging mergers and acquisitions between the largest arms-producing and military services companies. Referring to the 1993 'last supper' speech, which promoted arms industry consolidation, the US Undersecretary of Defense for Acquisitions, Technology and Logistics, Ashton Carter, stated that today's environment is different and mergers among the largest companies are discouraged by the DOD. As for spin-offs, Carter questioned the long-term survival of the resulting new companies.[18] Later in 2011 another DOD official stated that, while there are no set rules, it would 'take some convincing' for mergers and acquisitions among the upper tier of US arms-producing companies to gain approval.[19] However, if spending cuts significantly decrease demand for certain weapon systems, it is possible that the DOD will reconsider its opposition to large-scale company acquisitions.[20] These disparate messages make it unclear whether the US Government supports major mergers and acquisitions in the arms industry and what the implications might be.

Many arms-producing and military services companies have large cash reserves and are interested in moving into adjacent commercial sectors via acquisitions, some large-scale.[21] In September 2011 United Technologies Corporation (UTC) agreed to acquire Goodrich Corporation, an aerospace manufacturing company, for approximately $18.4 billion (including $16.5 billion in cash).[22] According to UTC, the deal will strengthen its position in the aerospace and defence industry by increasing the range of commercial services offered at a time when production in the commercial aerospace industry is increasing. It will also contribute to UTC's military-related sales.[23] This transaction is by far the largest deal in the global arms industry in recent years and may reflect a move towards large-scale deals among arms-producing and military services companies, at least in the USA.

[18] Adler (note 14). On the 'last supper' see Dunne, J. P. and Surry, E., 'Arms production', *SIPRI Yearbook 2006*, pp. 399–401.

[19] Shalal-Esa (note 14).

[20] Shalal-Esa, A., 'Bigger firms seen in the next US defense consolidation', Reuters, 20 Sep. 2011, <http://www.reuters.com/article/2011/09/20/us-defense-consolidation-idUSTRE78J4MY20110920>.

[21] Shalal-Esa (note 20).

[22] United Technologies Corporation, 'United Technologies to acquire Goodrich Corporation: complements and strengthens position in aerospace and defense industry', Press release, 21 Sep. 2011, <http://utc.com/News/Press+Releases/>. UTC is ranked 10th and Goodrich 41st in the SIPRI Top 100 for 2010. See section IV below.

[23] Lerner, J., 'UTC to acquire Goodrich for $16.5bn', *Financial Times*, 22 Sep. 2011.

Other companies intend to streamline their businesses by spinning off non-core and underperforming units in order to prepare for what they anticipate will be a tightening market.[24] ITT Corporation split into three separate companies in 2011, including ITT Exelis, the former ITT Defense and Information Systems unit. This spin-off was reportedly initiated largely based on the flat performance of ITT Defense and Information Systems and the anticipation that military spending cuts will create more competition for contracts in the areas in which ITT Exelis operates.[25]

In July 2011 L-3 Communications Holding announced that it was to spin off businesses from its Government Solutions unit into a publicly traded government services company, Engility Corporation, which will focus on a variety of services for the US DOD, civilian US Government agencies and international customers. In addition, L-3 will combine its cyber, intelligence and security solutions businesses into a new unit named National Security Solutions in order to focus on DOD, intelligence and global security customers. According to L-3's management, the spin-off is the result of a lengthy strategy review that addresses changing dynamics in the industry and the need to refocus on those technology-based solutions that the company considers to be its strengths.[26]

The debate on arms industry cooperation in the European Union

The debate on the public spending crisis includes renewed discussion of the potential for deeper and wider cross-border cooperation in weapon production in the European Union (EU), especially Western Europe. Calls for cooperation are partially motivated by the duplication in infrastructure and equipment, and the subsequent higher costs, that result from multiple weapon programmes with similar output. The prospect of coordination leading to cheaper military services—including combined equipment repair and maintenance and testing and evaluation—is also a motivating factor.

---

[24] The spin-offs in the arms-production and military services industry may indicate a wider trend in the corporate world to rationalize business and streamline activities. See Thomas, H., 'Rise in spin-offs as groups focus on valuation', *Financial Times*, 4 July 2011.

In addition to the deals covered here, another notable spin-off in early 2011 was Northrop Grumman's spin-off of its shipbuilding unit as Huntington Ingalls Industries. Northrop Grumman, 'Northrop Grumman completes spin-off of Huntington Ingalls Industries, Inc.', Press release, 31 Mar. 2011, <http://investor.northropgrumman.com/phoenix.zhtml?c=112386&p=irol-newsArticle&ID=1544584>.

[25] Potter, M., 'ITT Exelis lays off workers as SINGCARS production ends', Defense Procurement News, 17 Nov. 2011, <http://www.defenseprocurementnews.com/2011/11/17/itt-exelis-lays-offs-workers-as-singcars-production-ends/>.

[26] L-3 Communications, 'L-3 announces plan to spin-off a new publicly traded government services company', Press release, 28 July 2011, <http://l-3com.com/media-center/press-releases.html?pr_id=1589960>.

These concerns predate the public spending crisis but are considered to be especially salient now.[27]

The prestige associated with retaining national arms industries acts as a barrier to cooperative arms production.[28] In the European context, multiple producers in the same market create more competition for both national government funds and export markets. As an example, even though demand is lower than in previous decades and export competition is fiercer, companies in France, Germany and Poland offer at least four competing designs for armoured vehicles.[29]

However, certain characteristics need to be fostered before European arms production cooperation can become commonplace, including a shared regional identity; trust and confidence in partners; a level playing field for European arms producers; and low levels of corruption.[30] Overall, current and potential arms industry cooperation in Europe involves an ever more complicated set of bilateral relationships. As this trend continues, the industry's role will strengthen in relation to government, and achieving any change will require more than just political will: it will take coordination among a variety of actors from government, industry and civil society as well as the ambition to move from bilateral to multilateral cooperation and towards a level playing field.[31]

Some European states have agreed to bilateral arms industry cooperation. In their 2010 Treaty for Defence and Security Co-operation, France and the United Kingdom agreed to develop joint arms production in some areas.[32] A December 2011 summit to further this cooperation, including on a joint unmanned aerial system (UAS) programme, was delayed so that the two countries could focus on the continuing public spending crisis and the related euro monetary issues.[33] At a meeting held in November 2011 in response to the British–French treaty, the German and Italian defence

---

[27] Velasek, T., *Surviving Austerity: The Case for a New Approach to EU Military Collaboration* (Centre for European Reform: London, Apr. 2011); Rizzi, A., 'Crisis boosts European military cooperation', Presseurop, 12 Aug. 2010, <http://www.presseurop.eu/en/content/article/314541-crisis-boosts-european-military-cooperation>; and chapter 4, section V, in this volume.

[28] See Jackson, S. T., 'Arms production', *SIPRI Yearbook 2011*, pp. 233–36.

[29] See Dickow, M. et al., *Weimar Defence Cooperation: Projects to Respond to the European Imperative*, German Institute for International and Security Affairs (SWP) Working Paper FG03-WP no. 06 (SWP: Berlin, Nov. 2011).

[30] O'Hagan, P., Gaebel, C. and Crawford, C., 'The prospect for further European defence cooperation', Konrad-Adenauer-Stiftung, 22 June 2011, <http://www.kas.de/grossbritannien/en/publications/23523/>.

[31] Chick, C., '2011 FBC annual defence conference report', Franco-British Council, 31 Mar. 2011, <http://www.francobritishdefence.org/conferences.php?id=37>.

[32] Treaty between the United Kingdom of Great Britain and Northern Ireland and the French Republic for Defence and Security Co-operation, signed 2 Nov. 2010, Cm 7976 (The Stationery Office: Norwich, 10 Nov. 2010). See also Jackson (note 28), p. 233.

[33] International Institute for Strategic Studies (IISS). Dec. 2011. 'Anglo-French defence: "Entente Frugale plus"', *IISS Strategic Comments*, vol. 17, no. 47 (Dec. 2011), <http://www.iiss.org/publications/strategic-comments/past-issues/volume-17-2011/december/>.

ministers issued a letter of intent on cooperation in arms production.[34] This was followed by an industry association memorandum of understanding on the formation of the German–Italian Defence Industry Cooperation Group to support a dialogue between the German and Italian arms industries and to make recommendations to their respective governments on developing and sustaining industrial cooperation in arms production.[35] In addition, Germany is arguing for closer ties with France, especially in UAS projects (see below). Under Nordic Defence Cooperation (NORDEFCO), Denmark, Finland, Iceland, Norway and Sweden have agreed to promote the competitiveness of their arms industries and have made efforts to increase Nordic industrial cooperation.[36] However, despite the increased rhetoric about cooperation, large-scale European cooperative arms production is not expected in the short term.

West European arms producers are trying to compete in the US- and Israeli-dominated market for UASs.[37] Not only is the global UAS market expected to expand in the short and medium terms—especially in terms of demand for reconnaissance, intelligence and surveillance UASs—there is also pressure on Europe to fill a gap in its capabilities that was exposed during air operations against Libya in 2011.[38] At present there are two main avenues of UAS development in Western Europe: the British–French Telemos programme of BAE Systems and Dassault and EADS's Talarion programme supported by Germany, France and Spain, although the latter programme has stalled. In another illustration of how bilateral cooperative relationships are becoming increasingly complicated, in January 2012 Cassidian, an EADS subsidiary, formed a partnership with Rheinmetall to

[34] Kington, T. and Müller, A., 'Italy, Germany make their own pacts', *Defense News*, 19 Dec. 2011.

[35] Memorandum of Understanding between AIAD, the Italian Industries Federation for Aerospace Defence and Security, and BDSV, the Federation of German Security and Defence Industries Association, 16 Dec. 2011, <http://www.aiad.it/aiad/en/aiad_mou.wp>.

[36] Memorandum of Understanding on Nordic Defence Cooperation (NORDEFCO), signed 4 Nov. 2009, <http://www.norden.org/da/om-samarbejdet/aftaler/aftaler/forsvarsspoergsmaal/>; Norwegian Ministry of Defence, 'Nordic Defence Cooperation: NORDEFCO', <http://www.regjeringen. no/en/?id=532212>; and NORDEFCO, *Military Level Annual Report 2010* (Norwegian Armed Forces Media Centre: Oslo, Feb. 2011). On Nordic cooperation programmes that were a prelude to the formation of NORDEFCO see Kiss, P., 'Eastern European defense review: defense cooperation within the Visegrad Group. Unexplored opportunities?', Center for Strategic and International Studies, 25 Feb. 2011, <http://csis.org/blog/eastern-european-defense-review-defense-cooperation-within-visegrad-group-unexplored-opportunit>; and Hagelin, B., 'Hardware politics, "hard politics" or "where, politics?": Nordic defence equipment cooperation in the EU context', eds A. J. K. Bailes, G. Herolf and B. Sundelius, SIPRI, *The Nordic Countries and the European Security and Defence Policy* (Oxford University Press: Oxford, 2006).

[37] An unmanned aerial system is the larger system, including e.g. control systems and data links, that includes an unmanned aerial vehicle (UAV).

[38] 'NATO allies to hold talks on Libya, Afghanistan wars', Al Arabiya News, 5 Oct. 2011, <http://www.alarabiya.net/articles/2011/10/05/170293.html>. See also chapter 2, section I, and chapter 3, section II, in this volume.

develop and produce Rheinmetall's UASs.[39] While each of these projects might seem to be cost-saving to their respective partner countries, the duplicate research and development (R&D) being carried out by the large European UAS programmes is likely to contribute to overall cost increases at a time when West European countries are likely to face budget cuts. According to an official with the German Ministry of Defence, not only are the costs of the Telemos and Talarion programmes too high, they will also be competing with each other in export markets.[40] A number of European countries are also engaged in unmanned combat air vehicle (UCAV) projects. Since R&D for UCAVs is particularly expensive, potential cost savings may become an incentive for increased cooperation.[41]

In June 2011 the European Commission initiated a process for developing and producing UASs in the EU. A principal purpose of this process is to develop a civil UAS strategy that takes advantage of the exponential growth in military applications of UASs. The Commission scheduled five workshops for 2011–12, with the first, in July 2011, focusing on the UAS industry and market. It primarily received input from company and industry representatives on how to manage and increase UAS development and production in the EU as well as the EU's share of the global UAS market. In line with the purpose of the overall process, many of the workshop comments and recommendations focused on the dual-use potential of UASs.[42]

Within the UAS market as a whole, countries and companies seek to increase their market share, while arms producers are looking beyond military applications to civilian sectors for medium- and long-term growth in sales.[43] This illustrates the wider debate on coordinating military and civil capabilities in dual-use markets, which in turn highlights issues concerning the arms industry's influence on broader security discussions.[44]

---

[39] EADS, 'Cassidian and Rheinmetall pool their unmanned aerial systems activities', Press release, 20 Jan. 2012, <http://www.eads.com/eads/int/en/news/press.20120120_cassidian_rheinmetall_uas.html>.

[40] Beemelmans, S., '"Il faut reconcevoir le marche europeen de la defense"' ['We must redesign the European market for defence'], La Tribune, 23 Nov. 2011; and 'Germany calls for Franco-German UAV cooperation', Security & Defence Agenda, 29 Nov. 2011, <http://www.securitydefenceagenda.org/Contentnavigation/Library/Libraryoverview/tabid/1299/articleType/ArticleView/articleId/2991/Germany-calls-for-FrancoGerman-UAV-cooperation.aspx>.

[41] International Institute for Strategic Studies (note 33).

[42] European Commission, Directorate General Enterprise and Industry, 'Strategy for unmanned aircraft systems in the European Union', <http://ec.europa.eu/enterprise/sectors/aerospace/uas/>.

[43] Aerospace and Defence Association of Europe, UAS Working Group, 'Industry & market issues', Written contribution, UAS Industry and Market Workshop, 15 July 2011, <http://ec.europa.eu/enterprise/sectors/aerospace/uas/>.

[44] Boulanin, V. and Bellais, R., 'Towards high-tech "Limes" on the edges of Europe? Managing the external borders of the European Union', Paper presented at conference 'Fences, Walls and Borders: State of Insecurity?', Montreal, 17 May 2011.

Table 5.2. Selected cybersecurity acquisitions by OECD arms-producing and military services companies, 2011

The table lists major acquisitions in the arms industries of member states of the Organisation for Economic Co-operation and Development (OECD) that were announced or completed between 1 Jan. and 31 Dec. 2011. It is not an exhaustive list but gives an overview of strategically significant and financially noteworthy transactions. Figures for deal value and revenue are in US $m., at current prices. Companies are US-based unless indicated otherwise.

Buyer company (country)	Acquired company (country)	Seller company (country)	Deal value ($ m.)	Revenue or employees[a]
Avnet	Pinnacle Data Systems	Publicly listed	22.0	..
BAE Systems (UK)	Intelligence Services Group	L-1 Identity Solutions	297.0	1000 employees
BAE Systems (UK)	Norkom Group (Ireland)	Publicly listed	287.0	350 employees
BAE Systems (UK)[b]	Stratsec (Australia)	Privately owned	23.0	70 employees
Boeing	Solutions Made Simple	Privately owned	..	c. 60 employees
CACI International	Advance Programs Group	Privately owned	..	110 employees
CACI International	Pangia Technologies	Privately owned	..	$18.5 m.
CACI International	Paradigm Holdings	Publicly listed	61.5	c. 185 employees
Camber Corp.	Defense Security and Systems Solutions	EADS (trans-European)[c]	..	..
General Dynamics	Network Connectivity Solutions	Privately owned	..	160 employees
Jacobs Engineering	Unique World	Privately owned	..	c. 50 employees
Kratos Defense and Security Solutions	SecureInfo Corp.	Insight Venture Partners	17.5	$2.5 m.
Raytheon	Henggeler Computer Consultants	Privately owned	..	142 employees
ManTech	TranTech	Privately owned	21.6	$40 m.
ManTech	Worldwide Information Network Systems	Privately owned	90.0	c.150 employees
National Security Partners	Summit Solutions	Privately owned	..	$17 m.
Raytheon	Applied Signal Technology	Publicly listed	490.0	c. 800 employees
Raytheon	Pikewerks Corp.	Privately owned	..	c. 33 employees
Sotera Defense Solutions	Potomac Fusion	Privately owned	..	$40 m.
Sotera Defense Solutions	Software Process Technologies	Privately owned	..	$35 m.
Ultra Electronics (UK)	3e Technologies International	EF Johnson Technologies	30.0	$29.1 m.
Ultra Electronics (UK)	Special Operations Technology	Privately owned	38.4	130 employees
Ultra Electronics (UK)	Zu Industries	Privately owned	76.6	20 employees

[a] Since companies do not always disclose the values of transactions, the acquired company's annual revenue is listed where known (either actual revenue for 2010 or expected revenue for 2011 or 2012). Where information is not available for the acquired company's revenue, the acquired company's number of employees is shown, where known.

[b] Stratsec was bought by BAE Systems Australia, rather than directly by the parent company.

[c] Defense Security and Systems Solutions was sold by EADS North America, rather than directly by the parent company.

Diversification into cybersecurity

While arms production and military services companies continued major acquisitions in the industry in order to streamline and increase military specialization, many of these companies' mergers and acquisitions in 2011 were outside of traditional arms production and military services areas. One noticeable area for acquisitions was in cybersecurity, as companies looked to shield themselves from potential cuts in military spending on arms acquisitions and move into adjacent markets that also have civilian applications (see table 5.2).[45]

While a majority of the company press releases announcing cyber-security-related acquisitions cite mixed motivations, many include either starting sales or increasing products offered to civilian US Government agencies, especially for intelligence and homeland security. It seems that these acquisitions bridge the civilian and military sectors of government. A few of the acquisitions are even commercial (i.e. non-military) in focus, being marketed at the financial sector, for example, or for the protection of critical infrastructure.

Individual company motivations included broadening military product offerings (e.g. Ultra Electronics); increasing access to the intelligence market (e.g. ManTech); strengthening 'home market' positions (e.g. BAE Systems); improving positions in US civilian government markets, including intelligence (e.g. CACI International); and securing supply chains (e.g. Boeing). In making acquisitions outside the arms industry, arms producers have found themselves competing with other companies for position in the cybersecurity market (e.g. IBM, which acquired i2 in 2011).[46]

---

[45] The term cybersecurity is often used but left undefined. From an industry perspective it might include 'protection against [threats] deriving from the unauthorised use of digital information and communications systems'. Finmeccanica, *2010 Consolidated Financial Statements* (Finmeccanica: Rome, 2011), p. 36.

[46] Bell, M., 'IBM extends cyber footprint with i2 purchase', *Jane's Defence Industry*, 2 Sep. 2011.

II. The military services industry

SUSAN T. JACKSON

Military services are military-specific services—such as research and analysis, technical services, operational support, and armed force—that were once undertaken by military establishments but have been outsourced to private companies.[1] The private military services industry has grown substantially over the past two decades. The SIPRI Top 100 arms-producing and military services companies for 2010 includes 20 companies categorized as primarily military services providers; their combined military-related sales in 2010 totalled $55 billion (see table 5.3). This is a 147 per cent real-terms increase in sales since 2002, when the SIPRI Top 100 included 20 military services companies with combined military sales of $22 billion (in constant 2010 dollars).[2] While this was a major increase, the annual rate of growth in sales of these military services slowed in 2009 and 2010.

The increase in privatized military services began as a result of post-cold war restructuring in the United States and Western European arms industries. The concentration and specialization in arms production during the consolidation of the 1990s included expansion into military services, as part of the longer-running trend to privatize (or outsource) government services.[3] Justifications for outsourcing (in both the private and the public sectors) include cost savings, quality improvement, access to new knowledge, expertise and skills, and risk management, as well as greater flexibility and 'on-time' deliveries.[4]

The growth in the military services industry has been most obvious in the USA.[5] In 2010 the US Department of Defense's annual expenditure on services (including non-military services) accounted for half of the $400 billion it spent on procurement.[6] Furthermore, the current trend for US arms-

---

[1] Perlo-Freeman, S. and Sköns, E., 'The private military services industry', SIPRI Insights on Peace and Security no. 2008/1, Sep. 2008, <http://books.sipri.org/product_info?c_product_id=361>. Military services do not include generic services, such as peacetime provision of health care and cleaning. As well as military services outsourced by armed forces or defence ministries, military services include those services that are military in nature and purchased by other parts of government and by clients in the private sector.

[2] Figures for the 2002 SIPRI Top 100 are drawn from the SIPRI Arms Industry Database. Consistent SIPRI data for these companies is only available since 2002.

[3] Singer, P. W., *Corporate Warriors: The Rise of the Privatized Military Industry* (Cornell University Press: Ithaca, 2003).

[4] Perlo-Freeman and Sköns (note 1); and Singer (note 3).

[5] Although public–private partnership programmes also grew in Western Europe during this period, this section focuses on the USA.

[6] US Department of Defense, 'DOD news briefing with Under Secretary Carter with opening remarks by Secretary Gates from the Pentagon', News transcript, 14 Sep. 2010, <http://www.defense.gov/transcripts/transcript.aspx?transcriptid=4684>.

producing companies to shift into military services is likely to continue.[7] On the one hand, the shift is part of strategies to maintain sales in anticipation of cuts in armaments programmes. On the other hand, companies are moving into military services (*a*) to take advantage of general government cost-savings efforts, (*b*) to protect themselves from the reduction in projects that had become expected to rotate among the prime contractors as a means of maintaining the financial health of the arms industry (known as Kurth's 'follow-on' imperative), and (*c*) to take advantage of governments' general willingness to decrease the number of new programmes and extend the in-service time of existing platforms.[8] For instance, even before the global financial and economic crisis set in, the US military was planning to move to a commercial maintenance, repair and overhaul (MRO) model for air systems. This 'through-life' approach aims to reduce the costs of aircraft acquisition as well as support for equipment already in service.[9]

Military services companies in the SIPRI Top 100

Of the 20 military services companies in the Top 100 for 2010, 16 are based in the USA, with total military services sales of $47 billion. A further three are based in the United Kingdom, with total sales of $6.6 billion, and one is based in Kuwait, with sales of $1.3 billion (see table 5.3).[10]

While the composition of the military services companies in the SIPRI Top 100 has been largely stable, there have been some notable changes since 2002.[11] In addition to sales increases from military services contracts related to the wars in Afghanistan and Iraq and the subsequent emergence of some top military services providers, changes in the composition of the Top 100 can also be attributed to acquisitions and divestment of specifically military services companies. In 2003 General Dynamics acquired Signal Corporation, which had bought Veridian in 2002, and in 2006 acquired Anteon, removing all three of the smaller companies from the SIPRI

---

[7] Shalal-Esa, A., 'Bigger firms seen in the next US defense consolidation', Reuters, 20 Sep. 2011, <http://www.reuters.com/article/2011/09/20/us-defense-consolidation-idUSTRE78J4MY20110920>.

[8] Kurth, J. R., 'The political economy of weapons procurement: the follow-on imperative', *American Economic Review*, vol. 62, nos 1–2 (Mar. 1972).

[9] Magelhaes, M., 'Military aircraft maintenance, repair and overhaul: wake-up call to a silent revolution?', Frost & Sullivan, 8 Mar. 2004, <http://www.frost.com/prod/servlet/market-insight-top.pag?docid=10899576>.

[10] The military services sales of the Kuwaiti company, Agility, decreased by 47% in 2010 due to a contract ending and because the company was suspended from bidding on US Government contracts pending the outcome of ongoing legal cases in the USA. In 2010 Agility transitioned the remainder of its last US Government contract to Anham, a company based in the United Arab Emirates, which was subsequently awarded a contract worth $2.16–6.47 billion to provide food services to the US military and non-military personnel in Iraq, Jordan and Kuwait. As a result of the ongoing cases in the USA, Agility is refocusing its business on civilian logistics. On the legal cases see Jackson, S. T., 'The SIPRI Top 100 arms-producing companies, 2009', *SIPRI Yearbook 2011*, p. 252. See also Anham, 'Selected contracts', <http://www.anham.com/Contracts.aspx>.

[11] On companies active in military services provision see Perlo-Freeman and Sköns (note 1).

Table 5.3. Military services companies in the SIPRI Top 100 for 2010

Figures are in constant (2010) US$ m. Companies are those in the Top 100 that specialize in military services; other companies in the Top 100 may also sell military services.

Rank in Top 100				Sales of military services (US$ m.)	
2010	2002	Company	Country	2010	2002
9	9	L-3 Communications	USA	13 070	3 660
12	13	SAIC	USA	8 230	3 640
14	17	Computer Sciences Corp.	USA	5 940	2 400
23	–	KBR^a	USA	3 310	..
29	74	Babcock International Group	UK	2 770	540
32	–	Hewlett-Packard^b	USA	2 570	..
33	76	ManTech International Group	USA	2 490	520
38	24	DynCorp International	USA	2 390	1 650
39	75	CACI International	USA	2 320	520
43	62	Serco	UK	2 130	670
50	40	QinetiQ	UK	1 730	1 150
58	–	Agility	Kuwait	1 310	..
59	–	Fluor	USA	1 300	..
67	67	Jacobs Engineering Group	USA	1 020	600
78	–	Shaw Group	USA	810	..
81	95	Cubic Corp.	USA	810	380
86	–	Alion Science and Technology	USA	770	..
88	77	Mitre	USA	740	510
93	–	VSE Corp.	USA	680	..
98	–	AAR Corp.	USA	650	..

^{a} In 2002 KBR was a subsidiary of Halliburton, which was ranked 39 with sales of $930 million. Halliburton divested KBR in 2006; the company entered the Top 100 in 2007.

^{b} Hewlett-Packard entered the Top 100 in 2008 when it acquired EDS. EDS was ranked 58 in 2002 with sales of $570 million.

Source: SIPRI Arms Industry Database.

Top 100. L-3 Communications increased its military services portfolio in 2003 with its acquisition of Vertex Aerospace and in 2005 with its acquisition of Titan.[12] After Halliburton divested KBR in 2006, the former parent company left the Top 100; KBR entered the Top 100 as a military services company in 2007. Hewlett-Packard entered the Top 100 when it acquired EDS in 2008. In late 2009 VT Group divested its shipbuilding business to become a services-only company; in turn, it was acquired in 2010 by Babcock International, increasing the latter's share in the military services market.[13]

[12] After Raytheon divested the company in 2001 and until 2003, Vertex Aerospace was known as Raytheon Aerospace.

[13] Acquisition and divestment data is based on the SIPRI Arms Industry Database. On the military services sales related to the wars in Afghanistan and Iraq see Jackson, S. T., 'Arms production', *SIPRI Yearbook 2010*.

The military services industry is much larger than the data above suggests, since the data covers only companies categorized as predominantly military services providers. In addition to these 20 companies, a large number of companies in the Top 100 that are not categorized as military services companies nevertheless generate significant sales from military services. Although most of these companies with mixed portfolios generally do not provide separate figures for their service revenues in their financial reporting, some do. For example, 48 per cent of BAE Systems' total reported sales in 2010 were generated in the services market, including 42 per cent for 'readiness and sustainment' services and 6 per cent for cybersecurity and intelligence.[14] Sikorsky, a subsidiary of UTC, reported a 2 per cent increase in sales of aftermarket support in 2010. It stated that this increase was due primarily to higher military sales and more aircraft modernizations.[15]

Developments in selected military services sub-sectors

There are four main categories of military services: (a) research and analysis; (b) technical services (e.g. informational technology services, system support, and MRO); (c) operational support (e.g. logistics and training); and (d) armed force.[16] To show where and how some of the core aspects of military technical and operational support activities have shifted to the private sector, four sub-sectors are examined here: military aircraft MRO; systems support for unmanned aerial systems (UASs); logistics support during the Iraq War and for United Nations peace operations; and training for stability and UN peace operations. These have been less systematically examined than more controversial sectors, such as armed force, and represent some of the more discreet ways in which governments are outsourcing services with little debate.

Maintenance, repair and overhaul: military aircraft services

There has been general growth in aftermarket sales of maintenance and upgrading of in-service weapon systems. This growth has an impact on the structure of the MRO sector as large systems integrators and original equipment manufacturers (OEMs) rethink how they supply MRO and restructure their businesses in order to raise the priority of MRO to match

---

[14] BAE Systems, *Annual Report 2010: Total Performance Across Our Markets* (BAE Systems: London, [2011]), p. 4.

[15] United Technologies Corporation, *Form 10-K Annual Report under Section 13 or 15(d) of the Securities and Exchange Act of 1934 for the Fiscal Year Ended December 31, 2010* (US Securities and Exchange Commission: Washington, DC, 10 Feb. 2011), p. 16.

[16] Perlo-Freeman and Sköns (note 1).

that of systems production.[17] With the general push to privatize government services, industry has viewed military maintenance as being a relatively stable market (compared, e.g., to commercial aircraft maintenance) in
the unstable economic environment of recent years. Because military maintenance contracts are made with governments, which have long-term
budget commitments, military maintenance is generally less susceptible to
fluctuations in the global political economy.[18]

The growth in global MRO in the first decade of the 21st century was particularly noticeable in military aircraft services, sales of which reached
$59.8 billion in 2010, a 2 per cent decrease from $61.1 billion in 2009 but
still higher than the $58.6 billion in 2008.[19] Sales of military aircraft MRO
reached $31.1 billion in North America (primarily the USA) in 2010, nearly
double MRO sales in Europe. The overall increase in military aircraft MRO
sales since the early 2000s indicates one way in which arms-producing
companies are diversifying in order to counter anticipated military budget
cuts in equipment acquisition.

Countries that do not have the industrial capability to produce military
aircraft are building up their military aircraft MRO sectors instead. For
example, the aerospace division of the Singaporean company ST Engineer
provides MRO not only for the Singaporean Air Force but also for Brazil,
Indonesia and the USA.[20]

Systems support: unmanned aerial systems

Growth in services for systems support is occurring in many sectors
including helicopters and military communications systems. This trend is
largely due to a diminishing military workforce and increasingly complex
systems. These systems require a more specialized workforce and longer
periods of support activities, which has led to a rebalancing of companies'
production and services portfolios.

Unmanned aerial systems provide a clear illustration of the growth in
systems support services.[21] The increasing use of UASs, their growing technological sophistication and a shortage of trained military personnel have
led to greater use of civilian personnel in their operation. Notably—and
contrary to the argument typically used to justify the outsourcing of

---

[17] Michaels, K., 'Outlook for the aerospace MRO market', Gerson Lehrman Group, 28 Aug. 2007,
<http://www.glgresearch.com/glgi-presentations/Kevin Michaels/>.
[18] '737 maintenance: supporting a bestseller', *Aircraft Technology Engineering & Maintenance*,
Farnborough Air Show 2010 Special Edition (July 2010), pp. 48–59.
[19] AeroWeb, 'Military aircraft MRO', version 1.96, Barr Group Aerospace, <http://www.bga-aero
web.com/Military-MRO.html>; and PricewaterhouseCoopers and Confederation of Indian Industry,
Changing Dynamics: India's Aerospace Industry (PricewaterhouseCoopers: New Delhi, 2009), p. 25.
[20] Grevatt, J., 'Singapore's defence industrial capabilities', *Jane's Defence Industry*, 6 Dec. 2011.
[21] Jackson (note 13), pp. 259–60.

military services—the more civilians that are involved in operating a UAS, the more expensive the service becomes.[22]

In many cases, the military services companies provide services such as maintenance and systems training for military personnel. For example, General Atomics provides UAS training for the British Royal Air Force and it has employees based in the Middle East who provide air system maintenance, technical support and pilots for the US Army.[23] As with other types of military service, large systems integrators provide multiple levels of service. For example, Boeing provides not only traditional military equipment and related MRO and training but, through its subsidiary Insitu, also offers field, training and demonstration services for UASs and related equipment, which have been in more demand since September 2001.[24]

Operational support: logistics for wars and peace operations

The majority of the analytical literature on privatized military support services has centred on logistics companies working in the wars in Afghanistan and Iraq. The focus on contractors in these wars can be partly explained by their being integral to the wars' conduct. For example, contractors collectively were the second biggest contributors to the 'coalition of the willing' in the Iraq War, and in Afghanistan in March 2010 there were, for the first time, more contractors than US troops in a US war.[25]

These wars have contributed significantly to sales in military services. For example, KBR's military services sales increased by 433 per cent between 2002 and 2009, and by 2009 it had $4.8 billion in sales from the Logistics Civilian Augmentation Program (LOGCAP) of the US Department of Defense. KBR's sales decreased slightly in 2010 due to the completion of LOGCAP III and shared participation in LOGCAP IV.[26] The US Department of State will continue to use the LOGCAP provisions to maintain private sector logistical support in Iraq following the pull-out of US troops. Although the number of foreign military contractors in Iraq decreased during the drawdown in 2011, 5500 security contractors were expected to remain in Iraq to protect US Department of State personnel.[27] This deployment of private security contractors where US troops can no longer be

---

[22] Sweetman, B., 'Contractors make UAV ops happen', *Aviation Week*, 1 Dec. 2009.

[23] Sweetman (note 22).

[24] Insitu, 'Family of UAS', <http://www.insitu.com/uas>.

[25] Huskey, K. A., *The American Way: Private Military Contractors & US Law after 9/11*, 2010 update, PRIV-WAR Report, National Reports Series no. 03/10 (PRIV-WAR: Florence, 1 Oct. 2010), p. 6.

[26] Sales figures are from the SIPRI Arms Industry Database. In 2001 KBR was the sole recipient of contracts for LOGCAP III, and in 2007 was 1 of 3 companies awarded contracts for LOGCAP IV. US Army, Army Sustainment Command, 'Army segues from LOGCAP III to IV', 27 Mar. 2009, <http://www.army.mil/article/18864/>. On LOGCAP in 2010 see section IV below.

[27] US Senate, Committee on Foreign Relations, *Iraq: The Transition from a Military Mission to a Civilian-led Effort* (US Government Printing Office: Washington, DC, 31 Jan. 2011), p. 10.

deployed raises the question of the role these contractors are playing in US foreign policy and what the implications are for the US State Department as a diplomatic entity.[28]

Despite their prominence, the provision of military services in the wars in Afghanistan and Iraq are outlier examples. There has been a longer presence of military services companies in UN peace operations, which has implications for peace management in post-conflict settings. Every UN-led multilateral peace operation since 1990 has included private security companies.[29] For example, private companies actively support many peace and stability operations in Africa, including support for logistics, training and development.[30] Demand for these types of service in UN peace operations has grown because of the higher number of operations over the past 15 years and their growing complexity. While this has created a need for more highly trained personnel, the number of skilled personnel contributed by the militaries of the Global North has simultaneously decreased.[31]

During this period some companies have rebranded themselves from companies providing private military capabilities and protective services to include human rights training, democratic transition services and other non-arms related services.[32] For example, in 2011 Academi—which was previously known as Xe Services and, before that, Blackwater—announced that it would shift its focus from security provision to training.[33] Even with these elements of rebranding and diversification, many private military companies continue to provide traditional services for conflict and war situations. Even the largest weapon systems integrators promote their service divisions for peace and stability operations. For example, on the website of the International Stability Operations Association, BAE Systems lists its services as aviation logistics and maintenance; communications and

[28] Strobel, W. P., 'State Dept. planning to field a small army in Iraq', 21 July 2010, McClatchy Washington Bureau, <http://www.mcclatchydc.com/2010/07/21/97915/state-dept-planning-to-field-a.html>.

[29] Avant, D. D., *The Market for Force: The Consequences of Privatizing Security* (Cambridge University Press: Cambridge, 2005), p. 7.

[30] Gichanga, M., Roberts, M. and Gumedze, S., *The Involvement of the Private Security Sector in Peacekeeping Missions*, Conference report (Institute for Security Studies: Nairobi, 21–22 July 2010); and Serafino, N., *The Global Peace Operations Initiative: Background and Issues for Congress*, Congressional Research Service (CRS) Report for Congress RL32773 (US Congress, CRS: Washington, DC, 8 Feb. 2006).

[31] Østensen, Å. G., *UN Use of Private Military and Security Companies: Practices and Policies*, SSR Paper no. 3 (Geneva Centre for the Democratic Control of Armed Forces: Geneva, 2011), p. 39. On trends in peace operations see chapter 3 in this volume. On the involvement of the Global South in UN peace operations see Tardy, T., 'Peace operations: the fragile consensus', *SIPRI Yearbook 2011*.

[32] Østensen (note 31), p. 36.

[33] Academi, 'Leading training and security services provider Xe Services announces name change to Academi', Press release, 12 Dec. 2011, <http://academi.com/press_releases/1>; and Sizemore, B., 'Past lingers for company formerly called Blackwater', *Virginia-Pilot*, 3 Jan. 2012.

tracking; information technology; intelligence services and analysis; logistics, freight and supply; security; and training.[34]

Operational support: training of foreign military personnel and peacekeeping and security sector reform programmes

Since the Balkan wars of the 1990s, in addition to becoming more involved in the provision of logistical and MRO support services in conflict and post-conflict environments, military services companies have become more entrenched in the provision of other types of operational support service, including training. The presence of these companies in training operations in post-conflict settings marks a new international trend in security policies. Many programmes funded by governments and organizations in a variety of contexts rely on private companies to provide such services. One example is the Global Peace Operations Initiative (GPOI), a multilateral programme established in 2004 to train military troops for peace operations. Under the GPOI the US Department of State spent an estimated $100 million in financial years 2010 and 2011 on training local forces in Africa for peace operations.[35] Beyond companies primarily categorized as military services companies, large systems integrators also participate in these types of programme, for example by providing military training for security sector reform programmes or, as in the case of Northrop Grumman, for the Africa Contingency Operations Training and Assistance (ACOTA) programme.[36] These firms are even involved in advising on the structure of joint African security forces, for example with advice on the 'logistic design and concept' of the African Standby Force of the African Union (AU) and the AU/UN Hybrid Operation in Darfur (UNAMID).[37]

For reasons similar to the growth in the use of private military services in peace operations, sponsoring governments and organizations are likely to continue to increase their use of private companies in security sector reform and other types of operational support service. As for peace operations, the falling size of standing militaries means that fewer skilled military personnel are available to send on these training missions.[38] The chal-

---

[34] International Stability Operations Association, 'BAE Systems', <http://stability-operations.org/BAE Systems>.

[35] US Department of State, 'Global Peace Operations Initiative (GPOI)', <http://www.state.gov/t/pm/ppa/gpoi/>; US Department of State, *Congressional Budget Justification*, vol. 2, *Foreign Operations Fiscal Year 2011* (Department of State: Washington, DC, 1 Feb. 2010); and Isenberg, D., 'Africa: the mother of all PMC', Huffington Post, 22 Mar. 2010, <http://www.huffingtonpost.com/david-isenberg/africa-the-mother-of-all_b_509111.html>.

[36] Northrop Grumman, 'U.S. Department of State awards Northrop Grumman African training contract', Press release, 6 July 2010, <http://investor.northropgrumman.com/phoenix.zhtml?c=112386&p=irol-newsArticle&ID=1444523>.

[37] Gumedze, S., 'Introduction to the SSG project on private military/security companies', Gichanga, Roberts and Gumedze (note 30), p. 5.

[38] Østensen (note 31), p. 39.

lenge will be to regulate these companies as few countries have general regulations concerning the conduct of private military service personnel and there are no uniform regulations on the export of these services from sponsoring countries.[39]

Conclusions

In the short term, growth in military services sales is likely to slow. This can be attributed to market saturation caused by rapid increases in sales in earlier years and the continuing decrease in the USA's military activities in Afghanistan and Iraq, although the US Department of State's continuing presence in Iraq will require some private military services. However, the decreases have not been, and are unlikely to be, uniform across companies, especially as military services sales in other areas such as aircraft maintenance, repair and overhaul have increased.

There is a general assumption that private companies provide services more cheaply and efficiently than government agencies. This suggests that outsourcing of military services—both through direct government contracts with 'prime contractors' and through third-party contracts from prime contractors—is likely to continue in the short-to-medium term. In addition to potential impacts on costs, these companies are having an impact on security discourse and practice, for example in how equipment maintenance and systems support are provided, what kinds of capabilities countries have in conflict settings and how countries' armed forces are structured and trained.[40]

---

[39] See Badong, P., 'Keeping the peace: private military and security companies in peacekeeping operations in Africa', Gichanga, Roberts and Gumedze (note 30); and Holmqvist, C., *Private Security Companies: The Case for Regulation*, SIPR Policy Paper no. 9 (SIPRI: Stockholm, 2005).

[40] Leander, A., 'The power to construct international security: on the significance of private military companies', *Millennium Journal of International Studies*, vol. 33, no. 3 (June 2005).

III. The Indian arms-production and military services industry

SUSAN T. JACKSON AND MIKAEL GRINBAUM

Having tried for more than a decade to develop a self-sufficient indigenous arms industry, in January 2011 the Indian Government announced its first official defence production policy.[1] This long-term process had been prompted by a national security review that followed the 1999 Kargil conflict with Pakistan. Indeed, the bulk of India's arms acquisitions have been motivated by perceived external threats from Pakistan and China as well as India's ambitions to become a regional power in competition with China.[2]

Over the next decade, India plans to spend an estimated $150 billion on modernizing, upgrading and maintaining military equipment for its armed forces, with some estimates predicting that this upward spending trend will continue until 2040.[3] However, it is unlikely to meet demand via domestic production alone, with the general consensus being that Indian defence industry policy requires major reforms in the areas of research and development (R&D) and acquisitions.[4] In addition, India faces the cost burden of developing and maintaining a private arms industry that has only existed since 2001, a late start when compared to countries with similar levels of military expenditure and domestic arms industry ambitions.[5]

It is widely thought that state-owned facilities will be unable to meet India's military equipment demands.[6] By the government's own reckoning, half of the domestically produced equipment is obsolete and only 15 per cent is considered state-of-the-art.[7] According to one estimate, in order to achieve a reversal of the current situation, in which 70 per cent of all arms and military services are foreign-sourced, the Indian arms industry would need to double its production output every year for five years.[8] This annual doubling is unlikely to be achieved due to the expense of building and

---

[1] Indian Ministry of Defence, *Defence Production Policy* (Department of Defence Production: New Delhi, 1 Jan. 2011). See also Smith, C., SIPRI, *India's Ad Hoc Arsenal: Direction or Drift in Defence Policy?* (Oxford University Press: Oxford, 1994), pp. 204–20.

[2] Holtom, P. et al., 'International arms transfers', *SIPRI Yearbook 2011*, pp. 278–83.

[3] Agency for the Dissemination of Technology Information (ADIT), *Who's Who: Key Decision Makers of the Indian Defense Sector* (ADIT: Paris, 2009), p. 22. See also Confederation of Indian Industry, 'Defence sector', <http://www.cii.in/Sectors.aspx?SectorID=S000000003>.

[4] Deloitte and Confederation of Indian Industry, *Prospects for Global Defence Export Industry in Indian Defence Market* (Deloitte: New Delhi, 2010), p. 98.

[5] Indian Ministry of Defence, 'Defence production: supplies wing', <http://mod.nic.in/product&supp/welcome.html>. On cost burden see Jackson, S. T., 'Arms production', *SIPRI Yearbook 2011*, pp. 233–36.

[6] Agency for the Dissemination of Technology Information (note 3), p. 20.

[7] Indian Department of Industrial Policy and Promotion (DIPP), *Foreign Direct Investment (FDI) in Defence Sector* (DIPP: New Delhi, 17 May 2010), p. 2.

[8] Deloitte and Confederation of Indian Industry (note 4), p. 13.

maintaining a domestic arms industry and external barriers to transfer of knowledge and technology by foreign arms exporters.[9] Nevertheless, pressures on global arms producers to find export markets, especially at a time of reduced public spending in the Global North, give India growing leverage in negotiating purchasing conditions and more opportunities to offer economic incentives for foreign technology transfers.[10]

India's arms industry structure

One of the conclusions of the national security review that followed the 1999 Kargil conflict was that India needed to rebuild its arms industry in order to, in particular, facilitate arms acquisition and domestic arms production.[11] Arms production and military services were formerly under the purview of the Indian Government. Since May 2001 the government has allowed the private sector to participate in the arms industry on the condition that companies obtain a licence from the Department of Industrial Policy and Promotion (DIPP) in cooperation with the Ministry of Defence (MOD).[12] The current policy allows for 100 per cent private ownership by Indian companies and up to 26 per cent foreign ownership via foreign direct investment (FDI).[13] The government has discussed privatizing Hindustan Aeronautics Limited (HAL) and is planning an initial public offering (IPO), although a timeframe has not been set.[14]

The Indian arms industry is dominated by state-owned companies: Indian Ordnance Factories' 39 factories and the 8 Defence Public Sector Undertakings (DPSUs). Of the 30 per cent of Indian arms procurement that comes from domestic sources, 21 per cent is procured from state-owned businesses and 9 per cent is procured directly from the private sector.[15] Ordnance Factories and the DPSUs accounted for approximately 386 billion rupees ($8.4 billion) in turnover in 2010, according to official figures.[16] While it is more difficult to obtain figures for the private sector, this part of the Indian arms industry is growing as major industrial conglomerates diversify into the military sector. For example, Tata Group, Mahindra Group, Kirloskar Group, and Larsen and Toubro are forming joint ventures

---

[9] Deloitte and Confederation of Indian Industry (note 4), p. 36.

[10] Holtom et al. (note 2), p. 280. See also section I above.

[11] Agency for the Dissemination of Technology Information (note 3), p. 14.

[12] Indian Ministry of Defence (note 5).

[13] Indian Ministry of Defence (MOD), *Annual Report 2010–2011* (MOD: New Delhi, 2011), p. 55; and Indian Department of Industrial Policy and Promotion (note 7), p. 3.

[14] The IPO is likely to amount to 10% of the company's value, or an estimated $400 million. Grevatt, J., 'Banks line up to lead Hindustan Aeronautics IPO', *Jane's Defence Industry*, 11 Nov. 2011.

[15] KPMG and Confederation of Indian Industry, *Opportunities in the Indian Defence Sector: An Overview* (KPMG: New Delhi, 2010), p. 21; and Indian Department of Industrial Policy and Promotion (note 7), p. 2.

[16] Indian Ministry of Defence (note 13), p. 56.

with both Indian and foreign companies.[17] In addition to these large companies, there are also a number of small and medium-sized enterprises (SMEs). Ordnance Factories and the DPSUs outsource 20–25 per cent of their orders to these companies.[18]

Three Indian companies appear in the SIPRI Top 100 arms-producing and military services companies for 2010: Bharat Electronics Limited (BEL), HAL and Ordnance Factories (see section IV below). HAL, the largest of the DPSUs, derives 90 per cent of its sales from the Indian armed forces.[19] With arms sales of $2.48 billion in 2010, it ranked 34th in the SIPRI Top 100. Ordnance Factories' arms sales of $1.96 billion in 2010 ranked it at 46th, while BEL, another DSPU, with sales of $971 million, ranked at 71st in the SIPRI Top 100. Both Ordnance Factories and BEL attribute 80 per cent of their sales to the Indian MOD. Over the period 2002–10, HAL's arms sales increased by 383 per cent, Ordnance Factories' by 69 per cent and BEL's by 138 per cent. Over this period, arms sales figures for both HAL and BEL have increased continually, while there were minor fluctuations in Ordnance Factories' overall growth. Between 2002 and 2010, HAL's arms sales as a share of total sales ranged between 80 and 90 per cent, while Ordnance Factories' ranged between 73 and 82 per cent, and BEL's ranged between 76 and 85 per cent.

While FDI is currently capped at 26 per cent, there is an ongoing, and often heated, debate over the appropriate level of foreign investment in the Indian arms industry. Some argue for maintaining the current level, others support a maximum limit of 49 per cent and still others have advocated a 74 per cent limit.[20] Proponents of increasing FDI argue that it would lead to higher incentives to transfer technology and for foreign original equipment manufacturers (OEMs) to invest; the MOD argues that such an increase would jeopardize local industry and possibly threaten national security interests.[21]

According to the latest official figures, in 2009 India exported arms worth a total of $70 million.[22] However, India exports few finished weapons systems; instead, it exports parts and components.[23] In contrast, India was

[17] KPMG and Confederation of Indian Industry (note 15), p. 21. See also 'Government to encourage private shipyards for increasing the submarine building capacity', Defence Now, 24 May 2011, <http://www.defencenow.com/news/179/government-to-encourage-private-shipyards-for-increasing-the-submarine-building-capacity.html>.

[18] KPMG and Confederation of Indian Industry (note 15), p. 22.

[19] Indian Ministry of Defence (note 13), p. 59.

[20] Industry supports an increase to 49%, while the DIPP advocates 74%. Indian Department of Industrial Policy and Promotion (note 7), p. 9.

[21] The 26% limit is often cited as having a deterrent effect on foreign investment in the arms industry. Behera, L., 'India's defence offset policy', Strategic Analysis, vol. 33, no. 2 (Mar. 2009), p. 246.

[22] See chapter 6, section VI, in this volume. The figure is in constant (2010) US dollars.

[23] See e.g. Boeing, 'Boeing teams with Hindustan Aeronautics Limited for P-81 weapons bay doors', Press release, 11 Feb. 2010, <http://boeing.mediaroom.com/index.php?s=43&item=1073>.

the largest importer of major conventional weapons in the period 2007–11, with the vast majority coming from Russia.[24]

India's arms production framework

The Indian Government's 2011 arms production policy integrates policies that had previously been articulated in a variety of statements and procedures and outlines the government's agenda for developing and maintaining a domestic arms industry.[25] Its stated objectives are (a) achieving a high level of self-reliance within as short a time as possible; (b) creating the conditions necessary for private industry participation; (c) increasing the role of SMEs in the weapon indigenization process; and (d) broadening the industry's R&D base.[26] It also lays out a procurement procedure reiterating policies on offsets (i.e. the necessary involvement of a local joint venture partner or local supplier) and industrial licencing (requiring companies entering arms production to obtain a licence).[27] One potential barrier in the licencing regime is the stipulation that foreign companies can only choose partners that already have (or are likely to receive) licences. It therefore becomes difficult to formulate an offset strategy if a company is unsure whether it can licence its products.[28]

Two of the Indian MOD's four departments have a direct impact on the structure and output of the Indian arms industry. Established in 1962, the Department of Defence Production (DDP) manages general arms production issues (such as indigenization of imported equipment) and also plans for and controls Ordnance Factories and the DPSUs. Since 1958 the Department of Defence Research and Development (DDRD) has overseen the Defence Research and Development Organisation (DRDO); advised the MOD on scientific aspects of military equipment and logistics; and provided input on the research, design and development of equipment for the armed forces.[29]

There are other key players outside the MOD. Within the Ministry of Commerce and Industry, for example, the DIPP is tasked with FDI policy formulation, approval and promotion, including facilitating and increasing

[24] See chapter 6, section I, in this volume.

[25] Ben-Ari, G. and Lombardo, N., 'India's military modernization', Centre for Strategic and International Studies, 1 Apr. 2011, <http://csis.org/publication/indias-military-modernization>.

[26] Indian Ministry of Defence (note 1), p. 1.

[27] Indian Department of Industrial Policy and Promotion (note 7), pp. 3–4.

[28] Behera (note 21), p. 246.

[29] Indian Ministry of Defence, 'About the ministry', <http://mod.nic.in/aboutus/welcome.html>; Indian Ministry of Defence, 'Defence production: overview', <http://mod.nic.in/product&supp/welcome.html>; and Indian Defence Research and Development Organisation, 'Genesis & growth', <http://drdo.gov.in/drdo/English/index.jsp?pg=genesis.jsp>.

the flow of FDI to the arms industry.[30] The industry itself is represented by a number of associations including the Confederation of Indian Industry (CII) and the Federation of Indian Chambers of Commerce and Industry.[31]

The Defence Acquisition Council (DAC) is charged with advising on and approving capital acquisitions in the Long-Term Integrated Perspective Plan (LTIPP). Under the LTIPP, the DAC designates capital acquisitions according to five categories: (a) 'Buy' (an outright purchase of equipment); (b) 'Buy and Make (India)' (a purchase from an Indian company in a production arrangement with a foreign OEM); (c) 'Buy and Make (global)' (purchases from a foreign vendor with a licence agreement for local content); (d) 'Make' (indigenous production of highly technological systems); and (e) 'Upgrade' (for any category of in-service equipment).[32]

While offset policies were introduced in India in the 1960s, they were not officially formulated until 2005, when the Indian MOD added an offset clause to its arms procurement guidelines. The clause was clarified in 2006 and again in 2008.[33] The DDP's Defence Offset Facilitation Agency (DOFA)—a body with representatives from the armed forces, the DRDO, industry associations, Ordnance Factories and the DPSUs—is responsible for facilitating implementation of offset policies.[34] Projects valued at 3 billion rupees ($65 million) or more are required to include 30 per cent defence-specific offsets, although the government reserves the right to increase the percentage on a case-by-case basis.[35]

The DRDO has set up four research boards covering both military and civilian research areas. The boards bring together academia, R&D centres and industry and provide grants-in-aid for collaborative projects on defence-related forward-focused research.[36] The R&D sector has been criticized for its lack of ability to absorb technology transfers, which contributes to the high level of obsolete equipment produced by the Indian arms industry.[37] At the same time, in 2009–10 India spent 84.8 billion rupees ($1.85 billion)—7 per cent of its military budget—on R&D, while it

---

[30] Indian Department of Industrial Policy and Promotion, 'Role and functions of the Department of Industrial Policy & Promotion', <http://dipp.nic.in/English/AboutUs/Roles.aspx>.

[31] Confederation of Indian Industry (note 3); and Federation of Indian Chambers of Commerce and Industry, 'Defence', <http://www.ficci.com/sector.asp?secid=9>.

[32] Indian Ministry of Defence (MOD), *Defence Procurement Procedure: Capital Procurement* (MOD: New Delhi, 2011).

[33] Behera (note 21), pp. 242–43.

[34] Indian Defence Offset Facilitation Agency, 'Vision statement', <http://mod.nic.in/DOFA.htm>. It has been argued that DOFA cannot manage its workload. See e.g. Behera (note 21), p. 244.

[35] Indian Defence Offset Facilitation Agency (note 34). As with FDI, there are complaints over India's offset policy. See e.g. Komradin quoted in Anderson, G., 'Eurocopter, HAL collaboration targets international markets', *Jane's Defense Industry*, 22 July 2011.

[36] Indian Defence Research and Development Organisation, 'Research boards', <http://drdo.gov.in/drdo/English/index.jsp?pg=researchboards.jsp>.

[37] Indian Department of Industrial Policy and Promotion (note 7), p. 3.

has budgeted 103 billion rupees ($2.25 billion) for 2011–12.[38] In addition, in order to encourage domestic and foreign private sector investment in R&D, the government has offered to share development costs by contributing 80 per cent of project funding.[39] It has also begun to fund private industry R&D, although at much lower levels.[40]

Individual DPSUs also maintain R&D centres. In addition to production facilities, HAL operates 10 R&D centres that work on design and production infrastructure for military aircraft and avionic systems, among other things. Ordnance Factories runs 12 development centres working in a variety of areas including night vision thermal imaging, vehicle armour and ammunition. BEL has three central R&D laboratories that focus on technology such as surveillance software and missile simulation. Between 2008 and 2010 BEL's R&D funding grew by 25 per cent, while its turnover in the same period grew by only 10 per cent.[41]

India's military services industry

A number of arms producers in India have been expanding their military services portfolios. To support these efforts, the DRDO focuses on a number of services-oriented projects and programmes. One example is a computerized war-gaming system (Sangram-II), which is used for tactical training, planning and strategy development. The DRDO is also conducting research on net-centric operations and communication secrecy systems.[42]

On the company side, 80 to 85 per cent of HAL's overhaul and services sales come from the Indian armed forces.[43] HAL provides a variety of services for military aircraft including overhaul, general maintenance, repair and overhaul (MRO), logistics management, on-site repair, product training and design support.[44] Among other companies, BEL provides maintenance and training services in electronics, while Hindustan Shipyard and Goa Shipyard provide some similar services for ships and submarines.[45]

---

[38] Indian Ministry of Defence (note 13), p. 14; and Behera, L., Institute for Defence Studies and Analyses (IDSA), New Delhi, Communication with author, 7 Jan. 2012.

[39] PricewaterhouseCoopers and Confederation of Indian Industry, *Changing Dynamics: India's Aerospace Industry* (PricewaterhouseCoopers: New Delhi, 2009), p. 32.

[40] An estimated 1.18 billion rupees ($26 million) has been made available for financial year 2011/12 for prototype development under the 'Make' procedure described above. Behera (note 21).

[41] Indian Ministry of Defence (note 13), pp. 57, 59, 63.

[42] Indian Ministry of Defence (note 13), p. 90.

[43] Behera (note 21), p. 245.

[44] Anderson (note 35). See also Hindustan Aeronautics Ltd, 'Accessories Division Lucknow: our services', <http://www.hal-india.com/Accessories/services.asp>; and Hindustan Aeronautics Ltd, 'Aircraft Division Nasik: our services', <http://www.hal-india.com/AircraftNasik/services.asp>.

[45] Indian Ministry of Defence (note 13), pp. 62, 66. See also Hindustan Shipyard Ltd, 'Ship Repairs Division', <http://www.hsl.nic.in/sr.html>.

Military services are covered by India's offset regulations.[46] Foreign companies are seen as integral to improving India's competencies in military services, just as they are seen to improve competencies in arms production. For example, in February 2011 Tata Industrial Services (part of Tata Group) teamed up with QinetiQ of the UK. The intention of the partnership is for Tata Industrial Services to identify Indian manufacturers and undertake programme management and other related tasks in order for major foreign companies to meet their offset and supply requirements.[47] At least part of the partnership will focus on military services. India is now a 'home market' for BAE Systems and, through partnerships with Indian companies, provides aerospace software and engineering services.[48]

Indian companies are also forming joint ventures and international partnerships, in particular for the servicing of military aircraft. In 2009 India and Russia renewed their military cooperation commitment for another 10 years in a series of agreements, including one that specifically covers after-sales support for military equipment of Russian origin.[49] One example of this cooperation is Integrated Helicopter Services, a joint venture between Vectra Group India and Vertolety Rossii. The joint venture, which will commence with civilian aircraft maintenance and expand into military helicopters, will be Vertolety Rossii's first service centre in India.[50] However, questions remain regarding Russia's overall ability to maintain military aircraft serviceability, which might require India to source equipment from elsewhere. Services would also have to shift to cover that equipment, and this could also include offsets for Indian industry.[51] Another example of foreign partnership in military aircraft service is HAL's agreement with Dassault of France to perform major inspections of Dassault's Mirage 2000 combat aircraft.[52] HAL is the largest provider of MRO to the

---

[46] For this purpose, services are defined as 'maintenance, overhaul, upgradation, life extension, engineering, design, testing of eligible products and related software or quality assurance services . . . and training'. Indian Ministry of Defence (note 32), p. 45.

[47] 'Tata Industrial Services, QinetiQ tie up for military robotics, UAVs, space exploration', India Defence, 10 Feb. 2011, <http://www.india-defence.com/reports-5010>.

[48] BAE Systems, *Annual Report 2010: Total Performance Across Our Markets* (BAE Systems: London, [2011]), p. 30. Home markets are discussed in Jackson, S. T., 'Arms production', *SIPRI Yearbook 2010*, p. 253fn.

[49] Anand, 'India, Russia Military Technical Cooperation Agreement to be extended till 2020', Machinist.in, 20 Oct. 2009, <http://machinist.in/index.php?option=com_content&task=view&id=2398>; and Kashani, S., 'Military pact with Russia will boost defence capability: India', Thaindian News, 8 Dec. 2009, <http://www.thaindian.com/newsportal/world-news/military-pact-with-russia-will-boost-defence-capability-india_100285828.html>.

[50] Vertolety Rossii, 'Indo-Russian company Integrated Helicopter Services Pvt. Ltd. opens Russian rotorcraft service centre in India', Press release, 7 Feb. 2011, <http://www.rus-helicopters.ru/en/news/index.php?ELEMENT_ID=1874>.

[51] 'Features', Indian Aviation, [n.d.], <http://www.indianaviationnews.com/indian-aviation-archievenews.asp?id=26&NID=260>.

[52] Hindustan Aeronautics Ltd, 'Our services', <http://www.hal-india.com/Overhaul/services.asp>.

Indian military.[53] The increase in military aircraft in India and the required minimum offset of 30 per cent could translate into additional military MRO in India.[54]

Conclusions

India, as with other countries with similar security situations and ambitions, sees the development and maintenance of a domestic arms industry as a way to protect itself while also projecting power and displaying prestige.[55] Other world powers encourage this perspective when they equate regional influence with military might.[56] India's attempts to introduce more sophisticated defence technologies have been far less successful than the government and industry had hoped, in part due to an inability to integrate foreign technology transfers into domestic production capacity. In the future, India hopes to expand its military services industry, especially MRO, both through foreign companies establishing themselves in India and through increased sales of services to other countries in the region.

[53] PricewaterhouseCoopers and Confederation of Indian Industry (note 39), p. 8.

[54] Moser, R., von der Gracht, H. and Gnatzy, T., *The Indian Aerospace Industry 2019: An Analysis of the Political, Technological and Economic Conditions* (Supply Chain Management Institute, EBS Business School: Wiesbaden, 2010). On India's combat aircraft procurement plans see chapter 6, section I, in this volume.

[55] Jackson, S. T., 'Arms production', *SIPRI Yearbook 2011*, pp. 233–34.

[56] E.g. the United States tends to conflate India's military equipment with added regional security in the Indian Ocean. See US Department of Defense (DOD), *Quadrennial Defense Review Report* (DOD: Washington, DC, Feb. 2010), p. 60.

IV. The SIPRI Top 100 arms-producing and military services companies, 2010

SUSAN T. JACKSON*

The SIPRI Top 100 lists the world's 100 largest arms-producing and military services companies (excluding Chinese companies), ranked by their arms sales in 2010. Sales of arms and military services by companies in the SIPRI Top 100 increased to $411.1 billion in 2010. This was a 1 per cent real-terms increase over 2009 and a 60 per cent increase since 2002 (see table 5.1 above).

Companies based in the United States remained at the top of the SIPRI Top 100 for 2010, although the 44 US companies in the list increased their arms sales by only 1 per cent in real terms (see table 5.4). Even so, US-based companies made over 60 per cent of the arms and military services sales in the SIPRI Top 100 for 2010. Lower ranked US-based companies (e.g. ARINC and the Aerospace Corporation) left the Top 100 as other US companies moved in (e.g. Hawker Beechcraft and Triumph Group, the latter due to its 2010 acquisition of Vought Aircraft Industries). The number of West European companies in the Top 100 declined from 33 in 2009 to 30 in 2010, in part due to the slightly lower arms sales of Italy's Avio and Fiat (which thus both left the Top 100 in 2010) and because of the re-entry into the Top 100 of the Brazilian company Embraer.[1]

Russia's continued arms industry consolidation added another parent corporation—United Shipbuilding Corporation—to its top arms producers, resulting in eight Russian arms producers in the SIPRI Top 100 for 2010.[2] Vertolety Rossii's sales increased by 135 per cent due in part to the sale of Mi-8/17 transport helicopters to the Russian armed forces and to Afghanistan, Azerbaijan and Iraq.[3]

The wars in Afghanistan and Iraq had mixed impacts on companies' arms sales, even with the drawdown in Iraq that started in 2010. The transition

---

[1] Although the number of Italian companies in the SIPRI Top 100 fell from 4 in 2009 to 2 in 2010, the increase in the arms sales of Finmeccanica and Fincantieri was great enough to increase Italy's total Top 100 arms sales.

[2] Jackson, S. T., 'The SIPRI Top 100 arms-producing companies, 2009', *SIPRI Yearbook 2011*, p. 253.

[3] Vasilyev, D., 'Ranking of top Russian defense companies in 2010', *Moscow Defense Brief*, vol. 3, no. 25 (2011), p. 16.

* Arms industry data was supplied by the SIPRI Arms Industry Network: Vincent Boulanin (École des hautes études en sciences sociales, Paris), Gülay Günlük-Şenesen (Istanbul University), Shinichi Kohno (Mitsubishi Research Institute, Tokyo), Valerie Miranda (Istituto Affari Internazionali, Rome), Pere Ortega (Centre d'Estudis per la Pau J. M. Delàs, Barcelona) and Paek Jae Ok (Korea Institute for Defense Analyses, Seoul).

Table 5.4. Regional and national shares of arms sales for the SIPRI Top 100 arms-producing and military services companies, 2010 compared to 2009[a]

Arms sales figures are in US$ b., at current prices and exchange rates. Figures do not always add up to totals because of the conventions of rounding.

Number of companies	Region/ country[b]	Arms sales ($ b.)		Change in arms sales, 2009–10 (%)		Share of total Top 100 arms sales, 2010 (%)
		2010	2009[c]	Nominal[d]	Real[e]	
45	**North America**	**250.2**	**243.7**	**3**	**1**	**60.9**
44	United States	249.4	243.0	3	1	60.7
1	Canada	0.8	0.7	18	5	0.2
30	**Western Europe**	**120.4**	**117.6**	**2**	**3**	**29.3**
10	United Kingdom	49.7	48.4	3	0	12.1
6	France	23.0	23.0	0	3	5.6
1	Trans-European[f]	16.4	15.9	3	6	4.0
2	Italy	15.4	14.1	9	12	3.7
5	Germany	7.4	8.1	–8	–4	1.8
2	Spain	2.8	2.9	–5	–2	0.7
1	Sweden	2.8	2.6	5	–2	0.7
1	Norway	1.5	1.1	38	29	0.4
1	Switzerland	0.8	0.7	14	8	0.2
1	Finland	0.7	0.7	0	4	0.2
8	**Eastern Europe**	**14.6**	**9.7**	**51**	**36**	**3.6**
8	Russia	14.6	9.7	51	36	3.6
11	**Other OECD**	**16.7**	**15.8**	**6**	**–2**	**4.1**
5	Japan[g]	7.5	6.9	8	2	1.8
3	Israel	6.4	6.3	1	–7	1.6
2	South Korea	2.1	1.9	9	–4	0.5
1	Turkey	0.8	0.6	19	6	0.2
6	**Other non-OECD**	**9.1**	**8.9**	**3**	**–9**	**2.2**
3	India[h]	5.4	4.5	21	2	1.3
1	Kuwait	1.3	2.5	–47	–49	0.3
1	Singapore	1.8	1.5	21	10	0.4
1	Brazil	0.7	0.5	43	19	0.2
100	**Total**	**411.1**	**395.7**	**4**	**2**	**100**

OECD = Organisation for Economic Co-operation and Development.

[a] Although it is known that several Chinese arms-producing enterprises are large enough to rank among the SIPRI Top 100, a lack of comparable and sufficiently accurate data makes it impossible to include them. There are also companies in other countries, such as Kazakhstan and Ukraine, that could be large enough to appear in the SIPRI Top 100 list if data were available, but this is less certain.

[b] Figures for a country or region refer to the arms sales of the Top 100 companies headquartered in that country or region, including those in its foreign subsidiaries. They do not reflect the sales of arms actually produced in that country or region.

[c] Arms sales figures from 2009 refer to companies in the SIPRI Top 100 for 2010 and not to the companies in the Top 100 for 2009.

[d] This column gives the change in arms sales between 2009 and 2010 in current US dollars.

e This column gives the change in arms sales between 2009 and 2010 in constant (2009) US dollars.

f The company classified as trans-European is EADS.

g Figures for Japanese companies are based on contracts with the Japanese Ministry of Defense.

h Figures for India include a rough estimate for Ordnance Factories.

Source: Table 5.5.

from the sole-source contract for the third round of the Logistics Civilian Augmentation Program (LOGCAP III) to the multi-source contract for the fourth round (LOGCAP IV) contributed to KBR's decrease in sales in 2010 compared to 2009, while both Fluor's and ITT Corporation's revenues increased because of LOGCAP IV contracts (see also section II above). KBR's overall sales decreased by $2 billion (17 per cent) and Fluor increased its government segment sales by 53 per cent in 2010.[4] Navistar's sales decreased 16 per cent due to decreases in purchases of military vehicles.[5] BAE Systems also experienced a decrease in sales of the Bradley Family of Medium Tactical Vehicles (FMTV).[6] At the same time, Oshkosh's sales increased by 87.4 per cent in 2010, primarily due to winning a US contract to build the M-ATV mine-resistant ambush-protected (MRAP) vehicle.[7]

Some companies' arms sales increased significantly in 2010. Kongsberg's 37 per cent increase in sales was related in particular to major contracts from Finland, Norway, Poland and the USA.[8] Hawker Beechcraft had a 29.3 per cent increase as a result of higher sales in trainer and attack aircraft.[9] Lockheed Martin's F-35 (Joint Strike Fighter) contract contributed to its $2.3 billion increase, as did deliveries and support activities in its C-130 Hercules transport aircraft programmes, support activities for the F-16 combat aircraft, and increases in its 'readiness and stability' oper-

---

[4] KBR, *Form 10-K Annual Report under Section 13 or 15(d) of the Securities and Exchange Act of 1934 for the Fiscal Year Ended December 31, 2010* (US Securities and Exchange Commission: Washington, DC, 23 Feb. 2011), p. 26; and Fluor, *Form 10-K Annual Report under Section 13 or 15(d) of the Securities and Exchange Act of 1934 for the Fiscal Year Ended December 31, 2010* (US Securities and Exchange Commission: Washington, DC, 23 Feb. 2011), p. 36.

[5] Navistar, *Form 10-K Annual Report under Section 13 or 15(d) of the Securities and Exchange Act of 1934 for the Fiscal Year Ended October 31, 2010* (US Securities and Exchange Commission: Washington, DC, 22 Dec. 2010), p. 28.

[6] BAE Systems, *Annual Report 2010: Total Performance Across Our Markets* (BAE Systems: London, [2011]), p. 66.

[7] Oshkosh, *Form 10-K Annual Report under Section 13 or 15(d) of the Securities and Exchange Act of 1934 for the Fiscal Year Ended September 30, 2010* (US Securities and Exchange Commission: Washington, DC, 18 Nov. 2010), p. 32.

[8] Kongsberg, *2010 Annual Report* (Konsberg Gruppen: Kongsberg, 2011), p. 8.

[9] Hawker Beechcraft, *Form 10-K Annual Report under Section 13 or 15(d) of the Securities and Exchange Act of 1934 for the Fiscal Year Ended December 31, 2010* (US Securities and Exchange Commission: Washington, DC, 25 Feb. 2010), p. 27.

ations.[10] Northrop Grumman's $1.1 billion increase was attributed to increases across its businesses.[11]

Acquisitions continue to contribute to large increases in arms and military services sales. Hewlett-Packard's acquisition of EDS in 2008 contributed to a 62.7 per cent increase in its military-related sales in 2010 due to on-going contracts that it absorbed through the acquisition.[12] The acquisition of VT Group in 2010 was a key factor in Babcock's 37.8 per cent sales increase in 2010.[13] ManTech attributed its 28.9 per cent ($2.6 billion) increase over 2009 to contracts that the company absorbed through the acquisition of Sensor Technologies Incorporated (STI) in January 2010.[14] AgustaWestland's acquisition of PZL-Świdnik was one factor in Finmeccanica's increase of $1.1 billion.

The SIPRI Top 100 for 2010 appears in table 5.5. The companies in the SIPRI Top 100 account for the majority of the global financial value of sales of military goods and services, in particular, high-technology systems and services. Because of a lack of comparable financial data, the SIPRI Top 100 does not cover all arms-producing countries. However, with a few exceptions, the volume of arms production in omitted countries is believed to be relatively small. Chinese companies would almost certainly appear in the Top 100 (and probably in the top 50) if satisfactory data were available. Apart from the omission of China, analysis of the companies in the Top 100 is sufficient to capture the major trends in the global arms industry.

[10] Lockheed Martin, *2010 Annual Report* (Lockheed Martin: Bethesda, MA, 2011), p. 5.

[11] Northrop Grumman, *Form 10-K Annual Report under Section 13 or 15(d) of the Securities and Exchange Act of 1934 for the Fiscal Year Ended December 31, 2010* (US Securities and Exchange Commission: Washington, DC, 9 Feb. 2010), pp. 44, 47, 48.

[12] Hewlett-Packard, *2010 HP Annual Report* (Hewlett-Packard: Palo Alto, CA, 2011), p. 48.

[13] Babcock International, *Trusted to Deliver: Annual Reports and Accounts 2011* (Babcock International: London, [2011]), p. 3.

[14] ManTech, *Form 10-K Annual Report under Section 13 or 15(d) of the Securities and Exchange Act of 1934 for the Fiscal Year Ended December 31, 2010* (US Securities and Exchange Commission: Washington, DC, 25 Feb. 2011), p. 35.

Table 5.5. The SIPRI Top 100 arms-producing and military services companies in the world excluding China, 2010[a]

Figures for arms sales, total sales and profit are in US$ million. Dots (..) indicate that data is not available. Sector abbreviations are explained below.

Rank[b]		Company[c]	Country	Sector	Arms sales		Total sales, 2010	Arms sales as % of total sales, 2010	Total profit, 2010	Total employment, 2010
2010	2009				2010	2009				
1	1	Lockheed Martin	USA	Ac El Mi Sp	35 730	33 430	45 803	78	2 926	132 000
2	2	BAE Systems	UK	Ac A El Mi MV SA/A Sh	32 880	32 540	34 609	95	1 671	98 200
3	3	Boeing	USA	Ac El Mi Sp	31 360	32 300	64 306	49	3 307	160 500
4	4	Northrop Grumman	USA	Ac El Mi Sh Sp	28 150	27 000	34 757	81	2 053	117 100
5	5	General Dynamics	USA	A El MV SA/A Sh	23 940	23 380	32 466	74	2 624	90 000
6	6	Raytheon	USA	El Mi	22 980	23 080	25 183	91	1 879	72 400
S	S	BAE Systems Inc. (BAE Systems, UK)	USA	A El MV SA/A	17 900	19 280	17 903	100	1 966	46 900
7	7	EADS	Trans-Eur.	Ac El Mi Sp	16 360	15 930	60 599	27	732	121 690
8	8	Finmeccanica	Italy	Ac A El Mi MV SA/A	14 410	13 280	24 762	58	738	75 200
9	9	L-3 Communications	USA	El Ser	13 070	13 010	15 680	83	955	63 000
10	10	United Technologies	USA	Ac El Eng	11 410	11 110	54 326	21	4 711	208 220
11	11	Thales	France	A El Mi MV SA/A Sh	9 950	10 200	17 384	57	60	63 730
12	12	SAIC	USA	Ser Comp(MV)	8 230	8 030	11 117	74	618	43 400
13	27	Oshkosh Truck	USA	MV	7 080	2 770	9 842	72	790	12 400
14	13	Computer Sciences Corp.	USA	Ser	5 940	6 050	16 042	37	759	91 000
15	14	Honeywell	USA	El	5 400	5 380	33 370	16	2 022	130 000
16	16	Safran	France	El	4 800	4 740	14 252	34	673	54 260
S	S	Sikorsky (United Technologies)	USA	Ac	4 530	3 980	6 684	68	..	18 000
17	19	Rolls-Royce	UK	Eng	4 330	4 260	16 794	26	839	38 900
18	18	General Electric	USA	Eng	4 300	4 700	150 211	3	11 644	287 000
S	S	Pratt & Whitney (United Technologies)	USA	Eng	4 080	3 940	12 935	32	..	35 000
19	17	ITT Corp.	USA	El	4 000	4 730	10 995	36	654	40 000
20	22	Almaz-Antei[d]	Russia	Mi	3 950	3 260	4 436	89	24	88 700
S	S	MBDA (BAE Systems, UK/EADS, trans-European/Finmeccanica, Italy)	Trans-Eur.	Mi	3 710	3 610	3 709	100	219	10 010

Rank[b]		Company[c]	Country	Sector	Arms sales		Total sales, 2010	Arms sales as % of total sales, 2010	Total profit, 2010	Total employment, 2010
2010	2009				2010	2009				
21	28	United Aircraft Corp.[d]	Russia	Ac	3 440	2 710	4 222	82	-639	95 900
22	21	DCNS	France	Sh	3 320	3 340	3 315	100	181	12 500
23	15	KBR[e]	USA	Ser	3 310	4 990	10 099	33	327	35 000
24	26	URS Corp.	USA	El	3 030	2 770	9 177	33	288	47 000
25	24	Mitsubishi Heavy Industries[f]	Japan	Ac Mi MV Sh	2 960	2 810	33 080	9	343	68 820
S	S	Eurocopter Group (EADS, trans-Eur.)	France	Ac	2 940	3 050	6 397	46	..	16 760
S	S	AgustaWestland (Finmeccanica)	Italy	Ac	2 920	2 800	4 827	61	273	13 570
26	23	Alliant Techsystems	USA	SA/A	2 870	2 810	4 842	59	313	15 000
27	33	Rockwell Collins	USA	El	2 860	2 580	4 665	61	561	20 000
28	31	Saab	Sweden	Ac El Mi	2 780	2 640	3 390	82	63	12 540
29	42	Babcock International Group	UK	Ser Sh Oth	2 770	2 010	4 475	62	162	27 340
30	34	Textron	USA	Ac El Eng MV	2 740	2 570	10 525	26	86	32 000
31	32	Rheinmetall	Germany	A El MV SA/A	2 660	2 640	5 283	50	230	19 980
32	51	Hewlett-Packard	USA	Ser	2 570	1 580	126 033	2	8 761	324 600
33	47	ManTech International Corp.	USA	Ser	2 490	1 920	2 604	96	125	10 100
34	38	Hindustan Aeronautics	India	Ac Mi	2 480	2 130	2 756	90	..	..
35	29	Elbit Systems	Israel	El	2 480	2 700	2 607	95	183	12 320
S	S	EADS Astrium (EADS, trans-Eur.)	France	Sp	2 450	2 400	6 626	37	..	15 340
36	25	Navistar	USA	MV	2 410	2 800	12 145	20	223	18 700
37	41	Israel Aerospace Industries	Israel	Ac El Mi	2 400	2 030	3 150	76	94	16 000
38	30	DynCorp International (Cerberus Capital)[g]	USA	Ser	2 390	2 650	3 387	71	-9	23 000
39	40	CACI International	USA	Ser	2 320	2 080	3 149	74	107	13 100
40	36	Cobham	UK	Comp(Ac El)	2 260	2 260	2 941	77	298	11 640
41	44	Goodrich	USA	Comp(Ac)	2 230	2 010	6 967	11	579	16 300
42	37	CEA	France	Oth	2 200	2 160	5 485	40	90	15 850
S	S	MBDA France (MBDA, trans-Eur.)	France	Mi	2 190	1 740	2 187	100	219	4 300
43	48	Harris	USA	El	2 130	1 900	5 206	41	562	15 800

		Company	Country	Sector						
44	39	Serco	UK	Ser	2 130	2 110	6 688	32	243	70 000
45	45	Navantia	Spain	Sh	2 010	1 980	2 102	96	-61	5 230
46	55	Indian Ordnance Factories[h]	India	A SA/A	1 960	1 440	2 451	80	..	..
S	S	Alenia Aeronautica (Finmeccanica)	Italy	Ac	1 920	1 810	2 861	67	58	10 050
47	73	Vertolety Rossii (OPK Oboronprom)[d]	Russia	Ac	1 910	810	2 677	71	204	38 490
48	20	AM General[i]	USA	MV	1 900	3 720	..	..	..	2 500
49	53	ST Engineering (Temasek)	Singapore	Ac El MV SA/A Sh	1 750	1 450	4 384	40	360	6 570
50	49	QinetiQ	UK	Ser	1 730	1 770	2 512	69	-98	13 080
51	–	United Shipbuilding Corp.[d]	Russia	Sh	1 650	..	2 359	70	..	71 280
52	50	Krauss-Maffei Wegmann[j]	Germany	MV	1 590	1 630	1 693	94	391	..
53	62	Kongsberg Gruppen	Norway	El Mi SA/A	1 500	1 090	2 564	58	248	5 680
54	53	Rafael	Israel	Ac Mi SA/A Oth	1 470	1 570	1 500	98	..	6 500
55	57	Nexter	France	A MV SA/A	1 430	1 230	1 425	100	217	2 700
S	S	BAE Systems Australia (BAE Systems, UK)	Australia	Ac Sh	1 380	1 090	1 376	100	..	6 500
S	S	Sukhoi (United Aircraft Corp.)[d]	Russia	Ac	1 360	1 440	1 466	93	53	26 900
56	44	ThyssenKrupp	Germany	Sh	1 340	1 980	56 452	2	1 228	177 350
S	S	Irkut Corp. (United Aircraft Corp.)[d]	Russia	Ac	1 330	1 060	1 548	86	56	14 030
57	–	IHI Group[f]	Japan	Eng Sh	1 330	280	13 526	10	339	26 040
58	36	Agility	Kuwait	Ser	1 310	2 480	5 596	23	87	22 000
59	89	Fluor[k]	USA	Ser	1 300	710	20 849	6	358	39 230
60	59	Samsung	S. Korea	A El Eng MV Sh	1 290	1 170	133 756	1	13 967	344 000
61	55	Groupe Dassault	France	Ac	1 270	1 360	5 546	23	523	11 490
62	91	United Engine Corp.[d]	Russia	Eng	1 250	680	2 805	44	92	69 580
S	–	Sevmash (United Shipbuilding Corp.)[d]	Russia	Sh	1 240	530	1 381	90	-23	..
63	64	Diehl	Germany	Mi SA/A	1 210	1 070	3 609	34	29	13 570
64	46	Mitsubishi Electric[f]	Japan	El Mi	1 160	1 950	41 528	3	1 419	114 440
65	–	Triumph Group	USA	Ac Comp(Oth) Ser	1 080	480	2 905	37	150	12 100
S	S	Thales Nederland (Thales, France)	Netherlands	El	1 060	880	1 062	100	52	..
66	60	GKN	UK	Comp(Ac)	1 050	1 110	8 391	13	502	39 900
S	S	Samsung Techwin (Samsung)	S. Korea	A El Eng MV	1 030	930	2 249	46	..	..
67	69	Jacobs Engineering Group[l]	USA	Ser	1 020	880	9 915	10	246	38 500

Rank[b]		Company[c]	Country	Sector	Arms sales		Total sales, 2010	Arms sales as % of total sales, 2010	Total profit, 2010	Total employment, 2010
2010	2009				2010	2009				
68	59	Kawasaki Heavy Industries[f]	Japan	Ac Eng Mi Sh	1 020	1 110	13 978	7	296	32 710
69	68	TRV Corp.[d]	Russia	Mi	1 010	910	1 120	90	62	..
70	77	NEC[f]	Japan	El	980	770	35 491	3	-143	115 840
71	67	Bharat Electronics	India	El	970	920	1 214	80	..	11 100
72	66	Moog	USA	Comp(El Mi)	960	920	2 114	46	108	10 120
73	71	Fincantieri	Italy	Sh	940	860	3 809	25	-164	10 210
S	S	IHI Marine United (IHI Group)[f]	Japan	Sh	890	..	2 163	41	15	..
74	80	Chemring Group	UK	SA/A	890	750	923	96	103	4 280
75	74	Ultra Electronics	UK	El	880	810	1 097	80	102	4 150
76	87	CAE	Canada	El	840	710	1 582	53	165	7 500
77	84	RUAG	Switzerland	Ac A Eng SA/A	830	730	1 722	48	88	7 720
S	S	Selex Galileo (Finmeccanica)	Italy	El	820	770	899	91	45	2 690
78	61	Shaw Group[m]	USA	Ser	810	1 100	7 001	12	93	27 000
79	81	LIG Nex1	S. Korea	El	810	750	822	99	35	..
80	70	Precision Castparts Corp.	USA	Comp(Ac)	810	880	6 220	13	1 015	18 300
81	86	Cubic Corp.	USA	Comp(El) Ser	810	710	1 194	68	71	6 100
82	75	Meggitt	UK	Comp(Ac El) Oth	780	810	1 796	44	215	7 370
83	–	Hawker Beechcraft	USA	Ac	780	600	2 805	28	-304	6 800
84	65	Indra	Spain	El	780	940	3 387	23	249	28 610
85	79	Curtiss-Wright Corp.	USA	Comp(Ac Sh)	780	760	1 893	41	107	7 600
86	83	Alion Science and Technology	USA	Ser	770	740	834	93	-15	3 100
87	95	Aselsan	Turkey	El	760	640	792	97	160	4 010
S	S	Selex Communications (Finmeccanica)	Italy	Comp(El Oth)	750	810	943	80	30	4 140
88	90	Mitre[n]	USA	Ser	740	700	1 310	57	..	7 540
89	76	Uralvagonzavod[d]	Russia	MV	730	800	1 814	40	188	27 930
90	78	SRA International	USA	El	700	760	1 667	42	18	7 100
91	98	Esterline Technologies	USA	Comp(A Ac SA/A Sh)	690	640	1 527	45	142	8 980
92	–	MMPP Salut[d]	Russia	Comp(Ac)	690	490	721	95	..	..

		Company	Country	Sector						
S	S	Thales Australia (Thales, France)	Australia	A El Mi MV SA/A Sh	680	630	681	*100*	..	3 300
93	72	VSE Corp.	USA	Ser	680	840	866	*78*	24	2 900
94	–	Embraer	Brazil	Ac	670	470	5 364	*12*	346	17 150
95	85	Teledyne Technologies	USA	El	670	720	1 644	*41*	121	9 200
96	93	Patria	Finland	Ac MV SA/A	660	660	747	*88*	5	3 400
97	64	Force Protection	USA	MV	660	980	656	*100*	15	1 280
98	99	AAR Corp.	USA	Ser	650	610	1 352	*48*	45	5 800
99	100	GenCorp	USA	El Eng	650	610	838	*77*	7	3 140
S	S	MBDA Italia (MBDA, trans-European)	Italy	Mi	640	610	644	*100*	7	1 260
100	82	MTU Aero Engines	Germany	Eng	640	740	3 586	*18*	188	7 670
S	S	Raytheon Australia (Raytheon, USA)	Australia	Comp(Ac) Ser	640	490	641	*100*	..	1 350

A = artillery; Ac = aircraft; El = electronics; Eng = engines; Mi = missiles; MV = military vehicles; SA/A = small arms/ammunition; Ser = services; Sh = ships; Sp = space; Oth = other; Comp() = components, services or anything else less than final systems in the sectors within the parentheses—used only for companies that do not produce final systems.

a Although several Chinese arms-producing enterprises are large enough to rank among the SIPRI Top 100, it has not been possible to include them because of lack of comparable and sufficiently accurate data. In addition, there are companies in other countries, such as Kazakhstan and Ukraine, that could also be large enough to appear in the SIPRI Top 100 list if data were available, but this is less certain.

b Companies are ranked according to the value of their arms sales in 2010. An S denotes a subsidiary company. A dash (–) indicates that the company did not rank among the SIPRI Top 100 for 2009. Company names and structures are listed as they were on 31 Dec. 2010. Information about subsequent changes is provided in these notes. The 2009 ranks may differ from those published in *SIPRI Yearbook 2011* owing to continual revision of data, most often because of changes reported by the company itself and sometimes because of improved estimations. Major revisions are explained in these notes.

c For subsidiaries and operational companies owned by a holding or investment company, the name of the parent company is given in parentheses along with its country, where it differs.

d This is the 9th year in which Russian companies have been covered by the SIPRI Top 100. There may be other Russian companies that should be in the list but for which insufficient data is available. Figures for Russian companies are from the Centre for Analysis of Strategies and Technologies (CAST), Moscow.

Vertolety Rossii has since 2005 operated as a subsidiary of OPK Oboronprom. However, since comparable financial data for Oboronprom for 2010 are not currently available, Vertolety Rossii is reported in the Top 100 as a parent company. This is the first year in which United Shipbuilding Corporation (USC)— the new main Russian state-owned conglomerate in 2010—reported parent company figures and subsidiary figures. In previous years, these figures were reported separately for each subsidiary or not reported at all. This year, figures for Sevmash are reported as a subsidiary of USC. For more on Russian arms industry consolidation see Jackson, S. T., 'The SIPRI Top 100 arms-producing companies, 2009', *SIPRI Yearbook 2011*, p. 253; Jackson, S. T., 'Arms production', *SIPRI Yearbook 2010*, p. 263; and Perlo-Freeman, S. et al., 'The SIPRI Top 100 arms-producing companies, 2007', *SIPRI Yearbook 2009*, pp. 286–87.

[e] The arms sales figures for KBR are an estimate based on payments from the US Department of Defense (DOD) for LOGCAP III and IV contracts and payments by the British Ministry of Defence (MOD).

[f] Arms sales figures for Japanese companies represent new military contracts rather than arms sales.

[g] Veritas Capital sold its shares in DynCorp to Cerberus Capital Management in 2010. The arms sales figure for DynCorp is an estimate based on pro forma revenues reported in financial statement of Delta Tucker Holdings (Cerberus Capital's technical reporting parent for DynCorp) for the 9-months from the company's inception until 31 Dec. 2010.

[h] All figures for Indian Ordnance Factories are estimates.

[i] Limited financial data is available for AM General. The SIPRI estimate of arms sales is based on a 2-year average of US DOD prime contract awards.

[j] The arms sales figures for Krauss-Maffei Wegmann are based on a small estimate of the company's non-military sales.

[k] The arms sales figures for Fluor are based on US DOD LOGCAP IV contracts.

[l] The arms sales figures for Jacobs Engineering Group are based on a 3-year average of US DOD prime contract awards.

[m] The arms sales figures for Shaw Group are based on a 2-year average of US DOD prime contract awards.

[n] The arms sales figures for Mitre are based on a 5-year average of US DOD prime contract awards.

Sources and methods

Selection criteria and sources of data

The SIPRI Arms Industry Database includes public and private companies but excludes manufacturing or maintenance units of the armed services. Only companies with operational activities in the field of military goods and services are included, holding or investment companies are not.

The sources of data on the companies include company annual reports and websites, and news published in the business sections of newspapers, in military journals and by Internet news services specializing in military matters. Press releases, marketing reports, government publications of contract awards and country surveys are also consulted. Publicly available information on financial and employment data on the arms industry worldwide are limited. The scope of the data and the geographical coverage are largely determined by the availability of information.

SIPRI data on arms-producing and military services companies is revised on an on-going basis as improved data becomes available. For this reason, it is not possible to make a strict comparison between editions of the SIPRI Yearbook. In addition, coverage may differ because of problems with obtaining data to make satisfactory estimates for all companies every year.

Definitions

Arms and military services sales ('arms sales') are defined by SIPRI as sales of military goods and services to military customers, including sales for both domestic procurement and export. Military goods and services are those that are designed specifically for military purposes and include the technologies related to these goods and services. Military goods are military-specific equipment and do not include general-purpose goods, such as oil, electricity, office computers, uniforms and boots. Military services are also military-specific. They include technical services, such as information technology, maintenance, repair and overhaul, and operational support; services related to the operation of the armed forces, such as intelligence, training, logistics and facilities management; and armed security in conflict zones. They do not include the peacetime provision of purely civilian services—such as health care, cleaning, catering and transportation—but supply services to operationally deployed forces are included.

The SIPRI definition of arms sales serves as a guideline; in practice it is difficult to apply. Nor is there any good alternative, since no generally agreed standard definition exists. In some cases, the data on arms sales reflects only what a company considers to be the defence share of its total sales. In other cases, SIPRI uses the figure for the total sales of a 'defence' division, although the division may also have some civil sales.

When the company does not report a sales figure for a defence division or similar entity, arms sales are sometimes estimated by SIPRI. Such estimates are based on data on contract awards, information on the company's current arms production and military services programmes, and figures provided by company officials in media or other reports. For all these reasons, the comparability of the company arms sales figures given in table 5.5 is limited.

Data on total sales, profit and employment is for entire companies, not for arms-producing and military services activities alone. All data is for consolidated sales, that is, including those of domestic as well as foreign subsidiaries. The data on profit represents profit after taxes. Employment data represents year-end figures except for those companies that publish only a yearly average. All data is presented on the financial year basis reported by the company in its annual report.

Calculations

All data is collected in local currency and at current prices. For conversion from local currencies to US dollars, SIPRI uses the International Monetary Fund (IMF) annual average of market exchange rates provided in *International Financial Statistics*. The data in table 5.5 is provided in current dollars. Changes between years in this data are difficult to interpret because the change in dollar values is made up of several components: the change in arms and military services sales; the rate of inflation; and, for sales conducted in local currency, fluctuations in the exchange rate. Sales on the international arms market are often conducted in dollars. Fluctuations in exchange rates thus do not have an impact on the dollar values but affect instead the value in local currency. Calculations in constant dollar terms are difficult to interpret for the same reasons. Without knowing the relative shares of arms and military services sales derived from domestic procurement and from arms exports, it is impossible to interpret the exact meaning and implications of the arms sales data. This data should therefore be used with caution. This is particularly true for countries with strongly fluctuating exchange rates.

6. International arms transfers

Overview

The volume of international transfers of major conventional weapons grew by 24 per cent between 2002–2006 and 2007–11. The five largest suppliers in 2007–11—the United States, Russia, Germany, France and the United Kingdom—accounted for three-quarters of the volume of exports. Among other suppliers, China and Spain recorded significant increases in the volume of deliveries during 2007–11. While China's exports are likely to continue to grow, Spain's order book for ships—which account for the bulk of its exports—indicates that it will not maintain its volume of exports (see section I in this chapter).

The first year of the Arab Spring provoked debate about the policies of major arms suppliers on exports to states in the Middle East and North Africa (see section II). Russian officials saw no reason to halt deliveries to any state in the region not subject to a United Nations arms embargo. In contrast, the USA and several major European suppliers to the region revoked or suspended some export licences to the region and in certain cases undertook reviews of their arms export policies. However, strategic and economic concerns continued to play a central role in all states' decision-making on arms exports to the region. The impact of the Arab Spring on arms export policies is thus likely to be limited.

States in Asia and Oceania received nearly half of all imports of major conventional weapons in 2007–11. Moreover, the five largest recipients of major conventional weapons were all located in Asia and Oceania: India, South Korea, Pakistan, China and Singapore. Major importers are taking advantage of the competitive arms market to seek attractive deals in terms of financing, offset arrangements and the transfer of technology (see section I). India, which received 10 per cent of all imports in 2007–11, is likely to remain the largest recipient of major conventional weapons in the coming years.

The volume of arms transfers to South East Asia increased threefold between 2002–2006 and 2007–11. Naval equipment and aircraft with maritime roles accounted for a significant share of deliveries and outstanding orders by Brunei Darussalam, Indonesia, Malaysia, the Philippines, Singapore and Viet Nam. Determinants of the types and volumes of weapons sought by these states include piracy, illegal fishing and terrorism. However, defence white papers, the types of weapons acquired in 2007–11 and, in particular, low-level maritime confrontations in disputed waters suggest that territorial disputes in the South China Sea play the most important role in procurement decisions (see section III). States in the region are also making efforts to secure transfers of technology and diversify their sources of supply. Suppliers *are increasingly willing to meet the demands of South East Asian states for extensive technology transfers in arms deals or partnerships to develop new weapon systems.*

Recent acquisitions, orders and procurement plans by Armenia and Azerbaijan have the potential to increase the risk of renewed conflict over the disputed region of Nagorno-Karabakh. Azerbaijan has significantly increased its volume of arms imports against a backdrop of bellicose rhetoric on the use of force to settle the conflict over Nagorno-Karabakh. There is limited public information on Armenian arms imports in recent years but during 2010 and 2011 it announced plans to procure more advanced weapon systems in connection with the Azerbaijani procurement drive. Each of the two states has been quick to draw attention to the acquisitions and military spending of the other and to label its opponent's actions as those of a state intent on pursuing an arms race. While a voluntary Organization for Security and Co-operation in Europe (OSCE) arms embargo is in force, there are different interpretations of its status by OSCE participating states and arms continue to be supplied to both sides (see section IV). Russia is a major supplier to both parties, although Azerbaijan has recently concluded significant licensed production arrangements and deals with Israel, South Africa and Turkey as it seeks to use foreign technology to develop an indigenous arms industry.

The number of states reporting their arms imports and exports to the United Nations Register of Conventional Arms (UNROCA) increased in 2011 to 85, from an all-time low of 72 states in 2010. There was a notable increase in the Americas, but only one African state reported, the lowest number since UNROCA was created. An increasing number of governments have published national reports on arms exports, including Poland, which published its first reports in 2011 (see section V). While SIPRI data on international arms transfers do not represent their financial value, a number of states also publish figures on the financial value of their arms exports (see section VI).

PAUL HOLTOM

I. Developments in arms transfers in 2011[1]

PAUL HOLTOM, MARK BROMLEY, PIETER D. WEZEMAN AND
SIEMON T. WEZEMAN

The volume of international arms transfers in the period 2007–11 was 24 per cent higher than in 2002–2006 (see figure 6.1).[2] While the five largest suppliers of arms remained unchanged, China and Spain emerged as significant suppliers during 2007–11. India established its position as the largest recipient of arms, while China continued to fall down the ranking in the list of recipients.

Major supplier developments

The five largest suppliers in 2007–11—the United States, Russia, Germany, France and the United Kingdom—accounted for 75 per cent of the volume of exports of major conventional weapons, down from 78 per cent in 2002–2006 (see tables 6.1 and 6.2).

The United States

The USA was the largest exporter of major conventional weapons in the period 2007–11, accounting for 30 per cent of all transfers. The volume of US arms exports increased by 16 per cent between 2002–2006 and 2007–11 but its share of international arms exports stayed the same. Existing contracts combined with those signed or agreed in 2011 indicate that the USA will maintain its position as the largest exporter in the coming years. As with other states, US arms exports are influenced by a mixture of strategic and economic concerns.

Asia and Oceania received 45 per cent of US deliveries of major conventional weapons in 2007–11, followed by the Middle East and Europe (see

---

[1] Except where indicated, the information on arms deliveries and contracts referred to in this chapter is taken from the SIPRI Arms Transfers Database, <http://www.sipri.org/databases/arms transfers>. The database contains data on transfers of major conventional weapons between 1950 and 2011. The data for 2007–11 and for 2011, on which most of this chapter is based, is given in the 'Register of major conventional weapon transfers, 2011' and the 'Register of major conventional weapon transfers, 2007–11', which are available at <http://www.sipri.org/databases/armstransfers/ recent_trends>. The data on which this chapter is based is valid as of 13 Feb. 2012. The figures in this chapter may differ from those in previous editions of the SIPRI Yearbook because the SIPRI Arms Transfers Database is updated annually.

[2] SIPRI data on arms transfers refers to actual deliveries of major conventional weapons, including sales, licences, aid, gifts and leases. SIPRI uses a trend-indicator value (TIV) to compare the data on deliveries of different weapons and to identify general trends. TIVs give an indication only of the volume of international arms transfers—based on an assessment of the arms' capabilities—and not of their financial values. Since year-on-year deliveries can fluctuate, a 5-year moving average is employed to provide a more stable measure for trends in international transfers of major conventional weapons. For a description of the TIV and its calculation see below.

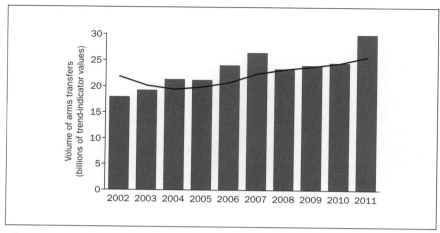

Figure 6.1. The trend in international transfers of major conventional weapons, 2002–11

Note: The bar graph shows annual totals and the line graph shows the five-year moving average (plotted at the last year of each five-year period). See 'Sources and methods' below for an explanation of the SIPRI trend-indicator value.

Source: SIPRI Arms Transfers Database, <http://www.sipri.org/databases/armstransfers/>.

table 6.1). Moreover, of the five largest recipients of US arms in the period—South Korea (13 per cent of US deliveries), Australia (10 per cent), the United Arab Emirates (UAE, 7 per cent), Pakistan (6 per cent) and Singapore (6 per cent)—four are in Asia and Oceania. Deliveries to South Korea in 2011 included the first 2 of a total order of 4 B-737AEW airborne early-warning (AEW) aircraft and 11 of a planned 21 F-15E combat aircraft. Deliveries to Australia in 2011 included 9 of 24 F/A-18E combat aircraft on order, 2 B-737AEW AEW aircraft and the first of an order of 2 C-17A transport aircraft. Despite strains in Pakistani–US relations, deliveries to Pakistan continued in 2011, including 1 Perry frigate and 2 P-3C anti-submarine warfare (ASW) aircraft.

In recent years the USA has focused attention on strategic priorities in Asia and has identified India as a long-term strategic partner in the region. At the same time, it has signalled an interest in acquiring a share of India's substantial spending on arms imports.[3] In 2011 the US–Indian arms transfer relationship developed further with the delivery of the first 6 of 12 ordered C-130J transport aircraft and an order for 10 C-17 transport aircraft. In the case of Taiwan, security and economic concerns sometimes come into conflict. Despite the significant economic benefits at stake, in

[3] US Department of Defense (DOD), *Report to Congress on U.S.–India Security Cooperation* (DOD: Washington, DC, Nov. 2011); and US Department of Defense, *Sustaining U.S. Global Leadership: Priorities for 21st Century Defense* (DOD: Washington, DC, Jan. 2012), p. 2.

August 2011 the US Government decided to refuse—for the time being—a sale of 66 new F-16 combat aircraft to Taiwan, largely to avoid straining ties with China.[4] Instead, the USA agreed to negotiate a deal in which Taiwan's existing fleet of 145 F-16s would be extensively upgraded to the latest standards.[5]

In the Middle East, US arms supplies to member states of the Gulf Cooperation Council (GCC) are an integral part of US security policy—including countering al-Qaeda and a perceived threat from Iran—and, by generating revenue for US industry, they advance US economic policy.[6] In 2011 US deliveries to the UAE—the third largest recipient of US major arms during 2007–11—included 4 C-17 transport aircraft, 15 UH-60 transport helicopters, 20 M-142 High Mobility Artillery Rocket System (HIMARS) multiple rocket launchers and a large number of guided weapons for its aircraft. The most significant deal concluded by the UAE with the USA in 2011 was an order for two Terminal High Altitude Area Defense (THAAD) anti-tactical ballistic missile systems. This was the first export order for the THAAD system.

The single largest arms order placed in 2011 was placed by Saudi Arabia for 154 F-15SA combat aircraft, worth $29.4 billion. The US Government stated that the deal would 'support more than 50 000 American jobs … providing $3.5 billion in annual economic impact to the US economy', without indicating the period covered by the deal.[7] Saudi Arabia also ordered other US weapons, including 36 AH-64D combat helicopters. Other major new contracts concluded with countries in the Middle East during 2011 included an order from Iraq for 18 F-16C combat aircraft, an order from Oman for 12 F-16Cs and an order from Egypt for 125 M-1A1 tanks.

Sales of the F-35 (Joint Strike Fighter) combat aircraft will have a strong influence on long-term developments in US arms exports. Turkey confirmed its commitment to the programme by placing an initial order for 2 F-35s, of a planned total of 100, and Japan announced that it will order 42. By early 2012, nine states had ordered or were planning to order a total of over 700 F-35s in addition to US plans.

Russia

Russia accounted for 24 per cent of the volume of international arms exports in the period 2007–11. The volume of Russia's arms exports increased by 12 per cent between 2002–2006 and 2007–11 but its share of

---

[4] Minnick, W., 'U.S. to deny Taiwan new jets', *Defense News*, 15 Aug. 2011, p. 1.

[5] Enav, P., 'U.S. "no" on Taiwan F-16 bid reveals China sway', *Air Force Times*, 21 Sep. 2011.

[6] For a brief description and list of members of the GCC see annex B in this volume.

[7] White House, 'Statement by Principal Deputy Press Secretary Joshua Earnest on U.S. sale of defense equipment to Saudi Arabia', 29 Dec. 2011, <http://www.whitehouse.gov/the-press-office/2011/12/29/statement-principal-deputy-press-secretary-joshua-earnest-us-sale-defens>.

Table 6.1. The 10 largest suppliers of major conventional weapons and their destinations, by region, 2007–11

Figures are the percentage shares of the supplier's total volume of exports delivered to each recipient region. Figures may not add up because of the conventions of rounding. For the states in each region and subregion see page xx.

Recipient region	Supplier									
	USA	Russia	Germany	France	UK	China	Spain	Netherlands	Italy	Israel
Africa	2	17	9	10	4	9	2	5	6	4
North Africa	2	14	–	9	2	0	–	5	3	–
Sub-Saharan Africa	0	2	9	1	3	8	2	–	3	4
Americas	7	8	12	6	28	6	30	24	19	22
South America	3	8	7	3	7	6	17	20	12	19
Asia and Oceania	45	63	27	51	25	73	9	25	28	31
Central Asia	0	2	0	–	–	–	–	–	1	1
East and South East Asia	25	27	24	39	8	5	9	21	8	9
Oceania	10	–	1	8	2	–	–	2	0	2
South Asia	10	34	3	4	15	68	–	1	20	19
Europe	18	3	41	21	13	–	60	37	33	19
European Union	17	0	40	19	10	–	10	37	31	18
Middle East	27	10	11	12	30	12	1	10	13	23
International organizations	1	–	–	–	–	–	–	–	–	1
Total	**100**	**100**	**100**	**100**	**100**	**100**	**100**	**100**	**100**	**100**

– = nil; 0 = <0.5.

Source: SIPRI Arms Transfers Database, <http://www.sipri.org/databases/armstransfers/>.

total exports fell by 2 percentage points. Asia received 63 per cent of Russian exports, followed by Africa and the Middle East (see table 6.1). The largest individual recipients of Russian weapons in the period were India (33 per cent of Russian deliveries), China (16 per cent), Algeria (14 per cent), Venezuela (7 per cent) and Viet Nam (4 per cent).

In 2011 Russia continued deliveries to India of complete systems, kits and components for assembly under licence, including an estimated 25 Su-30MKI and 12 MiG-29K combat aircraft, the first 10 of a planned 80 Mi-17 helicopters and 100 T-90S tanks. In early 2012 India commissioned a Project-971 nuclear submarine that has been supplied by Russia on a 10-year lease.[8] Although Russia's MiG-35 was not shortlisted for India's Medium Multi-Role Combat Aircraft (MMRCA) programme for the acquisition of 126 combat aircraft, in late 2011 Russia secured an order for the licensed production of 42 more Su-30MKI combat aircraft.

While China was Russia's second largest recipient of major conventional weapons in 2007–11, deliveries of a number of large-ticket items such as combat aircraft, surface-to-air missiles (SAMs) and ships were completed in 2009. China remains interested in buying Russian aircraft engines, SAMs, helicopters, transport and tanker aircraft, and naval technology, but Russia may be reluctant to provide its technology to a potential competitor for arms sales (see below).[9] China's neighbours in South East Asia, in particular Viet Nam, have emerged as major recipients of Russian combat aircraft and naval equipment (see section III below).

Russian weapons received by Algeria in 2011 include the first 8 of an order of 16 Su-30MKA combat aircraft, the first export deliveries of 10 of 16 Yak-130 trainer/light combat aircraft and the second of 2 S-300PMU-2 SAM systems. In 2011 Russia delivered to Uganda the first 4 of a planned 6 Su-30MK2 combat aircraft and it emerged that Uganda had also ordered T-90S tanks as part of a $740 million deal agreed in 2010.[10]

Weapons that Venezuela received from Russia during 2011 included T-72M1M tanks and S-125 Pechora-2M SAM systems ordered in 2010. Russia and Venezuela also agreed a $4 billion line of credit for arms purchases in 2012 and 2013.[11]

During 2011 Russia resisted pressure to end arms deliveries to Syria and back the imposition of sanctions, including an arms embargo, by the United

[8] 'Russia hands over Nerpa nuclear sub to India', RIA Novosti, 23 Jan. 2012, <http://en.rian.ru/mlitary_news/20120123/170896950.html>.

[9] Jakobson, L. et al., *China's Energy and Security Relations with Russia: Hopes, Frustrations and Uncertainties*, SIPRI Policy Paper no. 29 (SIPRI: Stockholm, July 2011), pp. 21–22.

[10] On the decision to buy the combat aircraft see Wezeman, P. D., Wezeman, S. T. and Béraud-Sudreau, L., *Arms Flows to Sub-Saharan Africa*, SIPRI Policy Paper no. 30 (SIPRI: Stockholm, Dec. 2011), pp. 22–23.

[11] Gabuev, A., [Business in a hat with Venezuela], *Kommersant*, 26 Aug. 2011 (in Russian); and 'Russia to lend Venezuela $4 bln to pay for arms deals', RIA-Novosti, 7 Oct. 2011, <http://en.rian.ru/world/20111007/167461572.html>.

Table 6.2. The 50 largest suppliers of major conventional weapons, 2007–11

Ranking is according to the volume of major conventional weapons exported in 2007–11. Figures are SIPRI trend-indicator values (TIVs). Figures may not add up because of the conventions of rounding.

Rank 2007–11	Rank 2002–2006[a]	Supplier	Volume of exports (TIV, millions)						Share (%), 2007–11
			2007	2008	2009	2010	2011	2007–11	
1	1	United States	7 919	6 463	6 656	8 111	9 984	39 133	30
2	2	Russia	5 496	5 980	5 287	5 881	7 874	30 517	24
3	4	Germany	3 234	2 383	2 494	2 476	1 206	11 794	9
4	3	France	2 400	2 048	2 037	856	2 437	9 778	8
5	5	United Kingdom	1 008	998	1 027	1 133	1 070	5 236	4
6	7	China	434	593	1 018	1 335	1 356	4 736	4
7	12	Spain	594	610	997	280	927	3 408	3
8	6	Netherlands	1 235	512	517	440	538	3 242	3
9	8	Italy	691	406	505	594	1 046	3 241	3
10	9	Israel	511	318	814	528	531	2 703	2
11	10	Sweden	348	430	370	653	686	2 488	2
12	11	Ukraine	732	367	385	488	484	2 455	2
13	14	Switzerland	302	482	256	182	297	1 519	1
14	13	Canada	337	230	183	236	292	1 277	1
15	20	South Korea	219	78	163	97	225	782	1
16	18	South Africa	165	161	186	123	61	696	1
17	19	Belgium	19	221	233	8	111	592	0
18	23	Norway	55	108	147	141	108	559	0
19	25	Belarus	6	226	42	160	59	493	0
20	32	Brazil	53	92	37	184	27	394	0
21	15	Poland	175	75	81	8	8	347	0
22	30	Australia	1	8	57	98	126	290	0
23	16	Uzbekistan	–	–	90	90	90	270	0
24	24	Finland	47	67	41	46	47	248	0
25	29	Austria	97	14	29	34	30	204	0
26	27	Turkey	38	61	43	45	6	193	0
27	44	Jordan	13	12	60	91	–	176	0
28	–	Portugal	–	99	46	–	0	145	0
29	43	Montenegro	109	–	–	14	–	123	0
30	58	Bosnia and Herzegovina	–	–	–	–	119	119	0
31	26	Czech Republic	31	34	21	3	11	100	0
32	65	Chile	–	100	–	–	–	100	0
33	–	Libya	10	18	32	28	–	87	0
34	69	Serbia	4	45	1	30	4	85	0
35	36	Moldova	19	29	20	–	–	68	0
36	40	India	21	11	23	4	8	67	0
37	23	Denmark	6	17	14	10	20	66	0
38	41	Singapore	–	–	31	27	4	63	0
39	49	Saudi Arabia	–	–	–	1	58	59	0
40	33	Iran	–	2	5	5	45	57	0
41	60	Syria	–	–	25	25	–	50	0
42	48	United Arab Emirates	3	–	–	38	3	44	0

Rank 2007–11	Rank 2002–2006[a]	Supplier	Volume of exports (TIV, millions)						Share (%), 2007–11
			2007	2008	2009	2010	2011	2007–11	
43	54	Venezuela	–	3	40	–	–	43	0
44	–	Japan	40	–	–	–	–	40	0
45	47	Romania	32	–	2	1	1	36	0
46	28	Bulgaria	9	3	14	4	–	31	0
47	39	Slovakia	20	8	–	–	–	28	0
48	–	Brunei Darussalam	–	–	–	–	24	24	0
49	–	Nigeria	–	–	–	–	19	19	0
50	35	Kyrgyzstan	–	14	–	–	–	14	0
..	..	Unknown suppliers	0	35	13	24	8	80	0
..	..	Others	13	2	2	1	6	25	0
Total			**26 448**	**23 362**	**24 044**	**24 535**	**29 954**	**128 343**	

0 = <0.5.

Note: The SIPRI data on arms transfers relates to actual deliveries of major conventional weapons. To permit comparison between the data on such deliveries of different weapons and to identify general trends, SIPRI uses a trend-indicator value. This value is only an indicator of the volume of international arms transfers and not of the financial values of such transfers. Thus, it is not comparable to economic statistics such as gross domestic product or export/import figures. The method for calculating the trend-indicator value is described in 'Sources and methods' below.

[a] The rank order for suppliers in 2002–2006 differs from that published in *SIPRI Yearbook 2007* because of subsequent revision of figures for these years.

Source: SIPRI Arms Transfers Database, <http://www.sipri.org/databases/armstransfers/>.

Nations Security Council (see section II below).[12] During 2007–11, 78 per cent of Syria's imports of major conventional weapons came from Russia, while Syria was Russia's seventh largest recipient, accounting for 3 per cent of its exports. During 2011 Russia completed delivery of Yakhont anti-ship missiles and Pantsir-S1 and Buk-M1 SAM systems. Twenty-four MiG-29M combat aircraft were on order but had not yet been delivered. In December 2011 Syria signed a contract worth $550 million for 36 Yak-130 trainer/combat aircraft.[13]

Other major suppliers

Between 2002–2006 and 2007–11 Germany's arms exports increased by 37 per cent and it rose from being the fourth largest exporter to third place (see table 6.2). Other states in Europe received 41 per cent of German arms exports in 2007–11, followed by Asia and Oceania and the Americas (see table 6.1). In June 2011 the German Federal Security Council approved the

[12] On moves to impose a UN arms embargo on Syria see also chapter 10, section III, in this volume.
[13] Safronov, I., [Syria has secured the next Yak-130], *Kommersant*, 23 Jan. 2012 (in Russian).

potential sale of at least 200 Leopard 2A7+ tanks to Saudi Arabia.[14] Saudi Arabia is believed to have requested versions of the Leopard tank since the 1980s but has always been refused. News of the approval sparked a wide-ranging debate in Germany, largely because it came soon after Saudi Arabia had deployed armoured vehicles in support of Bahrain's crackdown on demonstrators.[15] There was a similar response to the news that Germany had approved the potential sale of TPz-1 armoured personnel carriers, frigates and other equipment to Algeria worth up to €10 billion ($14.5 billion).[16] During 2011 Germany approved a subsidy of €135 million ($180 million)—one-third of the total price—for Israel's purchase of a sixth Dolphin submarine.[17]

While the volume of France's exports of major conventional weapons rose by 12 per cent between 2002–2006 and 2007–11, it fell from being the third largest exporter to fourth place. Asia and Oceania received 51 per cent of the volume of French arms exports, followed by Europe and the Middle East. During 2011 France failed in its efforts to secure the first export order for Rafale combat aircraft. It did not secure an expected order from the UAE for 60 aircraft because of the 'uncompetitive and unworkable' commercial terms of the proposed deal, and the UAE issued requests for alternate proposals to other manufacturers.[18] In addition, the Swiss Government opted for the JAS-39 combat aircraft from Sweden over the Rafale.[19] However, in January 2012 the Indian Government announced that the Rafale had won the competition for the MMRCA programme thanks to Dassault's low tender.[20] Significant orders for French arms in 2011 included an Indian order for the rebuilding of 51 Mirage 2000 combat aircraft as Mirage 2000-5s and a deal with Russia for 2 Mistral amphibious assault ships. Russia and France signed a contract in December 2011 for the construction under licence of 2 more Mistrals.[21]

The volume of the United Kingdom's exports of major conventional weapons rose by 2 per cent between 2002–2006 and 2007–11 and it maintained its position as the 5th largest exporter. The Middle East received 30 per cent of the volume of British arms exports, closely followed by the

---

[14] 'Germany wants to supply battle tanks to Saudi Arabia', Spiegel Online, 4 July 2011, <http://www.spiegel.de/international/germany/0,1518,772177,00.html>.

[15] German Bundestag, Stenographic report, 119th meeting, Plenarprotokoll 17/119, 6 July 2011. See also section II below and chapter 2, section I, in this volume.

[16] 'Deutschland gibt Rüstung für Algerien frei' [Germany approves arms to Algeria], Handelsblatt, 3 July 2011.

[17] Opall-Rome, B., 'Germany redoubles support for Israel', Defense News, 5 Dec. 2012.

[18] Tran, P., 'UAE says France's Rafale deal "unworkable"', Defense News, 16 Nov. 2011.

[19] 'Swiss Air Force to get Swedish jets', swissinfo.ch, Swiss Broadcasting Corporation, 1 Dec. 2011, <http://www.swissinfo.ch/eng/politics/internal_affairs/?cid=31673198>.

[20] Kumar, M., 'French Rafale favoured for huge India warplane deal', Reuters, 31 Jan. 2012, <http://www.reuters.com/article/2012/01/31/us-india-defence-idUSTRE80U24620120131>.

[21] 'Russia to build hulls for 2 Mistral-class warships', RIA Novosti, 2 Dec. 2011, <http://en.rian.ru/world/20111202/169255665.html>.

Americas and Asia and Oceania. The most significant deal signed by British companies in 2011 was a $73 million contact for the provision of air-to-air refuelling systems for the US Air Force's KC-46 tanker aircraft. Although this contract is relatively small in value, it is likely to lead to additional orders for air-to-air refuelling systems for all 179 KC-46 tankers that the USA intends to acquire.[22]

While the USA, Russia, Germany, France and the UK have been the five largest arms exporters since the end of the cold war, several states just outside the top 5 significantly increased the volume of deliveries between 2002–2006 and 2007–11. China's share of the volume of international arms exports rose from 2 per cent to 4 per cent. This reflected an increase of 95 per cent in its exports of major conventional weapons and meant that it rose from being the seventh largest exporter to sixth place. Other states in Asia and Oceania received 73 per cent of the volume of Chinese arms exports, followed by the Middle East and Africa. The main recipient of China's exports was Pakistan, with 64 per cent of transfers, thanks primarily to deliveries of MBT-2000 tanks, JF-17 combat aircraft and F-22P frigates. Pakistan is likely to remain the largest recipient of Chinese arms due to ongoing deliveries of these systems as well as outstanding orders for other weapons including two Azmat fast-attack craft and six newly developed submarines.

Spain's exports of major conventional weapons increased by 165 per cent between 2002–2006 and 2007–11 and it rose from being the 12th largest exporter to 7th place. Other states in Europe accounted for 67 per cent of the volume of Spanish deliveries, followed by the Americas and Asia and Oceania. The majority—67 per cent—of Spain's exports during the period 2007–11 were of ships. At the end of 2011 only a limited number of Spain's ship orders remained uncompleted—including three Hobart destroyers and two BPE amphibious assault ships, which are due to be delivered to Australia in 2014–17. Spain had not received a major contract for the export of ships since 2007.

Recipient developments

In the period 2007–11, 44 per cent of imports of major conventional weapons were made by states in Asia and Oceania. The next largest recipient region was Europe (19 per cent), followed by the Middle East (17 per cent), the Americas (11 per cent) and Africa (9 per cent).

The five largest recipients of major conventional weapons—India, South Korea, Pakistan, China and Singapore (see tables 6.3 and 6.4)—were all in

---

[22] Cobham, 'Cobham awarded USAF KC-46 tanker engineering subcontracts in excess of US $73 million', Press release, 26 July 2011, <http://www.cobham.com/media/news.aspx>.

Table 6.3. The 10 largest recipients of major conventional weapons and their suppliers, 2007–11

Figures are the percentage shares of the recipient's total volume of imports received from each supplier. Only suppliers with a share of 1 per cent or more of total imports of any of the 10 largest recipients are included in the table. Smaller suppliers are grouped together under 'Other suppliers'. Figures may not add up because of the conventions of rounding.

Supplier	Recipient									
	India	South Korea	Pakistan	China	Singapore	Australia	Algeria	USA	UAE	Greece
Australia	–	–	–	–	1	..	–	2	–	–
Canada	–	0	–	–	0	–	–	17	1	–
China	–	–	42	..	–	–	0	–	–	–
France	1	7	5	12	39	15	3	5	15	22
Germany	1	17	2	0	8	3	–	11	1	35
Israel	4	0	–	–	4	1	–	1	–	–
Italy	3	1	2	–	–	–	1	4	1	2
Netherlands	0	–	–	–	–	–	–	–	–	2
Norway	–	–	–	–	–	0	–	10	–	–
Russia	80	–	2	78	–	–	93	0	14	–
South Africa	0	–	–	–	–	–	0	9	0	–
Spain	–	–	–	–	2	0	–	5	–	–
Sweden	–	1	5	–	2	0	–	0	2	3
Switzerland	–	–	2	5	2	–	1	9	2	–
Ukraine	0	–	4	2	–	–	1	–	–	–
United Kingdom	6	–	–	–	–	2	2	25	–	2
United States	3	74	36	–	43	79	0	..	62	32
Uzbekistan	2	–	–	–	–	–	–	–	–	–
Other suppliers	–	0	0	3	1	–	–	2	2	2
Total	**100**	**100**	**100**	**100**	**100**	**100**	**100**	**100**	**100**	**100**

– = nil; 0 = <0.5.

Source: SIPRI Arms Transfers Database, <http://www.sipri.org/databases/armstransfers/>.

Asia and Oceania. Moreover, some of the largest increases in the volume of arms imports between 2002–2006 and 2007–11 were made by states in South East Asia (see section III below). A range of security, political and economic factors explain the increase in the volume of deliveries to Asian recipients. Several major importers in Asia are seeking to develop their own arms industries and decrease reliance on external sources of supply.[23] However, they continue to rely on external suppliers for designs, technologies and components for the production of arms and military equipment. Licensed production thus represents a considerable share of the volume of deliveries to many of these major recipients. However, China has rapidly developed an indigenous arms industry to meet its needs and this is one of the main factors behind the decline in the volume of deliveries to China in recent years: between 2002–2006 and 2007–11, its imports of major arms decreased by 58 per cent.

There was a notable increase in the volume of deliveries to North Africa between 2002–2006 and 2007–11.[24] The volume of deliveries to Algeria increased by 307 per cent, and it rose from being 24th largest recipient to 7th place (see table 6.4). Morocco rose from 51st place to 25th, with an increase of 440 per cent in deliveries. There were also big increases in imports by Afghanistan and Iraq as they rebuilt their armed forces with supplies from major arms suppliers in North America and Europe. The volume of deliveries to Iraq increased by 301 per cent between 2002–2006 and 2007–11, moving it from 40th place to 19th.[25] The volume of deliveries to Afghanistan increased more dramatically, by 2000 per cent, as it rose from 78th place to 24th.

---

[23] On efforts to establish or maintain national arms industries, and the examples of India and South Korea, see chapter 6, section III, in this volume; and Jackson, S. T., 'Arms production', *SIPRI Yearbook 2011*, pp. 233–36, 240–44.

[24] See also Holtom, P. et al., 'International arms transfers', *SIPRI Yearbook 2010*, pp. 296–302.

[25] See also Holtom et al. (note 24), pp. 302–305.

Table 6.4. The 50 largest recipients of major conventional weapons, 2007–11

Ranking is according to the volume of major conventional weapons imported in 2007–11. Figures are SIPRI trend-indicator values (TIVs). Figures may not add up because of the conventions of rounding.

Rank 2007–11	Rank 2002–2006[a]	Recipient	Volume of imports (TIV, millions)						Share (%), 2007–11
			2007	2008	2009	2010	2011	2007–11	
1	2	India	2 213	1 804	2 200	2 851	3 582	12 650	10
2	5	South Korea	1 767	1 710	874	1 320	1 422	7 093	6
3	11	Pakistan	636	1 037	1 124	2 450	1 675	6 923	5
4	1	China	1 758	1 683	1 054	718	1 112	6 325	5
5	22	Singapore	384	1 178	1 697	946	921	5 126	4
6	8	Australia	640	385	649	1 386	1 749	4 808	4
7	24	Algeria	489	1 444	1 093	836	783	4 644	4
8	10	United States	818	880	947	881	946	4 473	3
9	3	United Arab Emirates	970	762	565	569	1 444	4 309	3
10	4	Greece	1 708	521	1 230	664	177	4 299	3
11	12	Saudi Arabia	195	369	818	1 025	1 095	3 502	3
12	9	Turkey	613	583	642	390	1 010	3 238	3
13	28	Malaysia	568	540	1 577	404	14	3 102	2
14	13	United Kingdom	740	550	496	601	412	2 800	2
15	46	Venezuela	785	743	357	207	560	2 652	2
16	35	Norway	552	612	570	168	650	2 551	2
17	7	Egypt	678	247	174	676	545	2 321	2
18	16	Chile	697	407	339	480	323	2 246	2
19	40	Iraq	269	380	402	455	722	2 228	2
20	15	Japan	517	641	392	370	254	2 174	2
21	20	Poland	987	601	157	135	144	2 023	2
22	25	South Africa	880	486	128	174	175	1 842	1
23	6	Israel	859	653	153	43	76	1 784	1
24	78	Afghanistan	41	152	344	371	835	1 743	1
25	51	Morocco	29	47	39	63	1 558	1 735	1
26	45	Portugal	60	145	414	978	115	1 711	1
27	37	Indonesia	576	238	461	228	201	1 704	1
28	23	Canada	463	458	107	270	342	1 641	1
29	18	Spain	342	370	273	304	248	1 537	1
30	32	Viet Nam	2	166	56	152	1 009	1 385	1
31	17	Italy	498	192	90	73	311	1 165	1
32	29	Brazil	204	193	169	289	266	1 120	1
33	68	Syria	–	253	192	299	291	1 035	1
34	48	Colombia	236	112	310	202	155	1 015	1
35	36	Jordan	176	161	237	114	263	952	1
36	31	Netherlands	260	146	233	156	145	939	1
37	64	Austria	306	220	330	5	6	867	1
38	53	Azerbaijan	211	30	147	147	277	812	1
39	19	Iran	385	79	79	94	94	732	1
40	70	Belgium	174	204	94	33	22	526	0
41	21	Yemen	151	40	5	234	77	507	0
42	43	Thailand	8	13	37	82	360	499	0

Rank 2007–11	Rank 2002–2006[a]	Recipient	Volume of imports (TIV, millions)						Share (%), 2007–11
			2007	2008	2009	2010	2011	2007–11	2007–11
43	103	Qatar	–	–	285	26	181	491	0
44	44	Finland	115	157	43	79	97	491	0
45	26	Germany	81	103	122	66	112	484	0
46	77	Kuwait	279	5	20	73	58	435	0
47	34	Peru	172	–	139	46	74	431	0
48	50	Myanmar	7	45	1	38	331	423	0
49	72	NATO	–	–	420	–	–	420	0
50	33	Sudan	33	106	77	137	63	415	0
..	..	Others	1 951	1 623	1 763	2 366	2 745	10 438	8
..	..	Unknown recipients	–	12	–	8	5	25	0
Total			**26 448**	**23 362**	**24 044**	**24 535**	**29 954**	**128 343**	

0 = <0.5; NATO = North Atlantic Treaty Organization.

Note: The SIPRI data on arms transfers relates to actual deliveries of major conventional weapons. To permit comparison between the data on such deliveries of different weapons and to identify general trends, SIPRI uses a trend-indicator value. This value is only an indicator of the volume of international arms transfers and not of the financial values of such transfers. Thus, it is not comparable to economic statistics such as gross domestic product or export/import figures. The method for calculating the trend-indicator value is described in 'Sources and methods' below.

[a] The rank order for recipients in 2002–2006 differs from that published in *SIPRI Yearbook 2007* because of subsequent revision of figures for these years.

Source: SIPRI Arms Transfers Database, <http://www.sipri.org/databases/armstransfers/>.

Sources and methods

The SIPRI Arms Transfers Database, <http://www.sipri.org/databases/armstransfers/>, contains information on deliveries of major weapons to states, international organizations and non-state armed groups from 1950 to 2011. Data collection and analysis are continuous processes: the database is updated as new data becomes available and a new set of data is published annually. Revisions of coverage are applied retroactively for the whole period covered by the database. Data from several editions of the SIPRI Yearbook or other SIPRI publications cannot be combined or compared. Readers who require time-series TIV data for years prior to 2007 should contact the SIPRI Arms Transfers Programme via the above URL.

Sources and estimates

Data on arms transfers are collected from a wide variety of sources. The common criterion for all these sources is that they are open; that is, published and available to the public. Such open information cannot, however, provide a comprehensive picture of world arms transfers. Sources often provide only partial information, and substantial disagreement between them is common. Since publicly available information is inadequate for the tracking of all weapons and other military equipment, SIPRI covers only what it terms major conventional weapons. Order and delivery dates and the exact numbers (or even types) of weapons ordered and delivered, or the identity of suppliers or recipients, may not always be clear. Exercising judgement and making informed cautious estimates are therefore important elements in compiling the SIPRI Arms Transfers Database.

Types of transfer

SIPRI's definition of an arms transfer includes sales of weapons, including manufacturing licences, as well as aid, gifts, and most loans or leases. The recipient of the arms must be the armed forces, paramilitary forces or intelligence agencies of another country, a non-state armed group, or an international organization. In cases where deliveries are identified but it is not possible to identify either the supplier or the recipient with an acceptable degree of certainty, transfers are registered as coming from an 'unknown supplier' or going to an 'unknown recipient'.

Types of weapon: major conventional weapons

The SIPRI Arms Transfers Database only includes 'major conventional weapons', which are defined as (a) most aircraft (including unmanned), (b) most armoured vehicles, (c) artillery over 100 millimetres in calibre, (d) sensors (radars, sonars and many passive electronic sensors), (e) air defence missile systems and larger air defence guns, (f) guided missiles, torpedoes, bombs and shells, (g) most ships, (h) engines for combat-capable aircraft and other larger aircraft, for combat ships and larger support ships, and for armoured vehicles, (i) most gun or missile-armed turrets for armoured vehicles and ships, (j) reconnaissance satellites, and (k) air refuelling systems.

The transferred item must have a military purpose. In cases where a sensor, turret or refuelling system (items d, i and k) is fitted on a platform (vehicle, aircraft or ship), the transfer only appears as a separate entry in the database if the item comes from a different supplier than that of the platform.

The SIPRI trend indicator

SIPRI has developed a unique system to measure the volume of transfers of major conventional weapons using a common unit, the trend-indicator value (TIV). The TIV is based on the known unit production costs of a core set of weapons and is intended to represent the transfer of military resources rather than the financial value of the transfer. Weapons for which a production cost is not known are compared with core weapons based on size and performance characteristics (weight, speed, range and payload); type of electronics, loading or unloading arrangements, engine, tracks or wheels, armament and materials; and, finally, the year in which the weapon was produced. A weapon that has been in service in another armed force is given a value of 40 per cent of that of a new weapon; a used weapon that has been significantly refurbished or modified by the supplier before delivery is given a value of 66 per cent of the value when new.

SIPRI calculates the volume of transfers to, from and between all parties using the TIV and the number of weapon systems or subsystems delivered in a given year. This quantitative data is intended to provide a common unit to allow the measurement of trends in the flow of arms to particular countries and regions over time. Therefore, the main priority is to ensure that the pricing system remains consistent over time, and that any changes introduced are backdated.

SIPRI TIV figures do not represent sales prices for arms transfers. They should therefore not be compared with gross domestic product (GDP), military expenditure, sales values or the financial value of export licences in an attempt to measure the economic burden of arms imports or the economic benefits of exports. They are best used as the raw data for calculating trends in international arms transfers over periods of time, global percentages for suppliers and recipients, and percentages for the volume of transfers to or from particular states.

II. Policies on exports of arms to states affected by the Arab Spring

MARK BROMLEY AND PIETER D. WEZEMAN

The violent reaction to the Arab Spring in 2011—in particular the deaths of anti-government protesters in Bahrain, Egypt, Tunisia and Yemen and the more intense armed conflicts in Libya and Syria—involved the use of major conventional weapons and small arms and light weapons acquired from a number of supplier states.[1] While the United Nations imposed an arms embargo on Libya and the European Union (EU) and the Arab League imposed arms embargoes on Syria, no other multilateral restraints were imposed on arms transfers to states affected by the Arab Spring.[2]

This section describes the immediate reactions of major suppliers to the Arab Spring and the debates on whether their governments had struck the right balance between security, commercial and human rights concerns when deciding whether to permit or deny arms exports. Despite widespread criticism by civil society and parliamentarians within many Western states and discussions between states, the impact of the Arab Spring on states' arms export policies appears to have been limited.

Russia has been a significant supplier to four of the states most affected by the Arab Spring: Egypt, Libya, Syria and Yemen (see table 6.5). It is the only major supplier discussed here that did not publicly announce a review of its arms export policy or a suspension of arms deliveries to the region. In March 2011 Anatoly Isaikin, the Director of Rosoboronexport—the agency responsible for managing the Russian arms trade—stated that the Arab Spring would not have a serious effect on Russia's arms exports, since Russia did not have any deals in place 'with the countries hit by the rioting' and he saw no reason to suspend ongoing Russian transfers to Egypt.[3] However, one Russian source has estimated that the Arab Spring could lead to Russia losing $10 billion worth of arms sales in the Middle East and North Africa.[4] For example, it has been suggested that the imposition of the UN arms embargo on Libya in February 2011, which Russia supported, resulted in Russia losing contracts worth $4 billion.[5] During 2011 there were limited

---

[1] On developments in these countries in 2011 see chapter 2, section I, and chapter 3, section II, in this volume. See also Vranckx, A., Slijper, F. and Isbister, R., *Lessons from MENA: Appraising EU Transfers of Military and Security Equipment to the Middle East and North Africa* (Academia Press: Gent, Nov. 2011).

[2] On these multilateral arms embargoes see chapter 10, section III, in this volume.

[3] Oleg, N., 'Mideast unrest won't affect Russia's arms exports', Voice of Russia, 9 Mar. 2011, <http://english.ruvr.ru/2011/03/09/47162396.html>.

[4] 'Russia risks losing $10 bn' arms sales from Arab unrest', Middle East Online, 22 Feb. 2011, <http://www.middle-east-online.com/english/?id=44527>.

[5] 'Russia could "lose $4 bn" in Libya arms deals', Agence France-Presse, 27 Feb. 2011.

Table 6.5. Suppliers of major conventional weapons to states affected by the Arab Spring, 2007–11

Recipient	Share of global arms transfers (%)	Main suppliers (share of recipient's transfers, %)		
		1st	2nd	3rd
Bahrain	0.10	USA (73%)	Belgium (12%)	United Arab Emirates (11%)
Egypt	1.81	USA (52%)	Russia (28%)	China (6%)
Libya	0.05	Russia (63%)	Italy (22%)	France (15%)
Syria	0.81	Russia (78%)	Belarus (17%)	Iran (5%)
Tunisia	0.01	USA (100%)	–	–
Yemen	0.40	Belarus (37%)	Ukraine (23%)	Russia (18%)

Source: SIPRI Arms Transfers Database, <http://www.sipri.org/databases/armstransfers>.

signs that Russia might benefit from the imposition of constraints on transfers to states affected by the Arab Spring by US and West European governments.

During 2011 Russia opposed US, West European and Arab League calls for the imposition of UN sanctions, including an arms embargo, on Syria.[6] One of the main reasons given to explain this position is the Russian view that UN Security resolutions 1970 and 1973 on Libya laid the foundations for regime change and contributed to regional instability and that UN sanctions on Syria would produce the same results.[7] Further, Syria's hosting of Russia's only military base outside the territory of the former Soviet Union, at the port of Tartous, and the arms deals that the two countries have concluded (see section I) are important signals of the Russian–Syrian strategic partnership.

The USA has been a major supplier of arms to three of the states most affected by the Arab Spring: Bahrain, Egypt and Tunisia (see table 6.5). After initially supporting the existing regimes in Egypt and Tunisia, the USA expressed support for pro-democracy movements and led calls for the imposition of multilateral arms embargoes on Libya and Syria.[8] In early 2011, when political pressure groups and members of the US Congress called for arms transfers and military aid to Arab states to be contingent on respect for human rights, the US Government indicated that it had sus-

---

[6] See chapter 10, section III, in this volume.

[7] Meyer, H., 'Russia warns Assad ouster may trigger collapse, Mideast unrest', Bloomberg, 23 Aug. 2011, <http://www.bloomberg.com/news/2011-08-23/russia-warns-assad-ouster-may-trigger-collapse-mideast-unrest.html>.

[8] See e.g. White House, 'Remarks by the President on the Middle East and North Africa', 19 May 2011, <http://www.whitehouse.gov/the-press-office/2011/05/19/remarks-president-middle-east-and-north-africa>. The USA has maintained a unilateral arms embargo on Syria since 1979 based on its assessment that Syria had been a sponsor of terrorist activities. Sharp, J. M. and Blanchard, C. M., *Unrest in Syria and U.S. Sanctions against the Asad Regime*, Congressional Research Service (CRS) Report for Congress RL33487 (US Congress, CRS: Washington, DC, 9 Nov. 2011), p. 13.

pended a number of arms transfers and that it was reviewing its arms export and military aid policies.[9] By the end of the year this review had resulted in more restrictive policies towards some states (e.g. Bahrain) and more limited changes in other cases (e.g. Egypt).

In the case of Bahrain, the USA was willing to reconsider arms sales despite the two countries' long-standing military relations. Bahrain hosts the headquarters of the US Fifth Fleet and has been designated a major non-NATO ally.[10] It has received military aid from the USA and has bought US military equipment for several decades. A review of US arms supplies to Bahrain reportedly began immediately after political violence started there in February 2011.[11] However, in September 2011 the US Department of Defense (DOD) announced a plan to sell 44 M-1151A1B2 light armoured vehicles armed with anti-tank missiles to Bahrain, arguing that these weapons were needed for Bahrain's external defence, particularly against Iran.[12] Civil society and members of the US Congress criticized this plan and the deal was delayed by the government pending the outcome of Bahraini investigations into alleged human rights abuses by Bahraini Government forces.[13]

The USA has maintained strong military relations with Egypt since the Egyptian–Israeli peace agreement of 1979 and was by far its largest arms supplier during the period 1979–2011. In February 2011 the DOD indicated that, although it had reviewed arms supplies to Egypt, it did not plan to stop them.[14] Throughout 2011 the USA continued to ship arms, including riot control ammunition, and approved the sale of 125 M-1A1 tanks to Egypt.[15] The US administration stressed the strategic importance of Egyptian–US military relations and argued that the Egyptian Army had played a stabilizing role during 2011.[16] In December 2011 President Barack

[9] Saine, C., 'Experts say US should link military aid to Egypt to democratic transition', Voice of America, 9 Feb. 2011, <http://www.voanews.com/english/news/middle-east/Experts-say-US-Should-Link-Military-Aid-to-Egypt-to-Democratic-Transition-115664839.html>; Entous, A., 'U.S. reviews arms sales amid turmoil', Wall Street Journal, 23 Feb. 2011; Brannen, K., 'U.S. rethinks Mideast arms sales', Defense News, 12 May 2011; and Shapiro, A. J., Assistant Secretary, US Department of State, Bureau of Political-Military Affairs, 'Defense trade advisory group plenary', Remarks, 3 May 2011, <http://www.state.gov/t/pm/rls/rm/162479.htm>.

[10] Katzman, K., Bahrain: Reform, Security, and U.S. Policy, Congressional Research Service (CRS) Report for Congress 95-1013 (US Congress, CRS: Washington, DC, 29 Dec. 2011), pp. 18–24.

[11] Entous (note 9).

[12] US Department of State, 'Daily press briefing', 14 Oct. 2011, <http://www.state.gov/r/pa/prs/dpb/2011/10/175530.htm>.

[13] Katzman (note 10), pp. 22–23.

[14] 'No plans to halt US military aid to Egypt: Pentagon', Agence France-Presse, 3 Feb. 2011.

[15] 'USA repeatedly shipped arms supplies to Egyptian security forces', Amnesty International, 7 Dec. 2011, <http://www.amnesty.org/en/news/usa-repeatedly-shipped-arms-supplies-egyptian-security-forces-2011-12-06>.

[16] Clinton, H. R., US Secretary of State, 'Remarks with Egyptian foreign minister Mohamed Kamel Amr after their meeting', 28 Sep. 2011, <http://www.state.gov/secretary/rm/2011/09/174550.htm>.

Obama signed into law an act granting Egypt up to $1.3 billion in Foreign Military Financing (FMF) aid in US financial year 2012 on the condition that Egypt holds free and fair elections and protects due process and freedom of expression and association.[17]

During 2011 the media, civil society and parliamentarians criticized several EU member states for their arms exports to states affected by the Arab Spring. These debates were largely framed by questions about how states were implementing the 2008 EU Common Position on arms exports, which is intended to harmonize member states' arms export policies in line with agreed minimum standards, including in the fields of human rights and international humanitarian law.[18] The Council of the EU imposed arms embargoes on two of the states affected by the Arab Spring: Libya and Syria.[19] During 2011 EU member states also discussed arms exports to states affected by the Arab Spring in all meetings of the Council Working Group on Conventional Arms Exports (COARM)—the forum in which states discuss implementation of the EU Common Position.[20]

At the national level, EU member states implemented different policies, with a number of states suspending or revoking export licences for particular deals or end-users. By 3 March 2011, the British Government had revoked 122 licences for arms exports to Bahrain (23 licences), Egypt (36 licences), Libya (62 licences) and Tunisia (1 licence).[21] France suspended the issuing of licences for export of military equipment to Egypt in January and to Bahrain and Libya in February and stated that all shipments of law-enforcement and explosive materials had been halted.[22] In March 2011 Germany suspended the issuing of export licences for transfers of military equipment to Bahrain, Libya and Tunisia.[23] Like a number of other EU countries, Germany lacks the necessary powers in its national legis-

---

[17] Sharp, J. M., *Egypt in Transition*, Congressional Research Service (CRS) Report for Congress RL33003 (US Congress, CRS: Washington, DC, 18 Nov. 2011), p. 20; 'Egypt risks losing military aid after conducting raids on international NGOs', Agence France-Presse, 31 Dec. 2011; and Consolidated Appropriations Act, 2012, US Public Law 112-74, signed into law 23 Dec. 2011, <http://thomas.loc.gov/cgi-bin/bdquery/z?d112:HR02055:>.

[18] Council Common Position 2008/944/CFSP of 8 December 2008 defining common rules governing control of exports of military technology and equipment, *Official Journal of the European Union*, L335, 8 Dec. 2008. See also Bromley, M., 'The review of the EU Common Position on arms exports: prospects for strengthened controls', Non-proliferation Papers no. 7, EU Non-proliferation Consortium, Jan. 2012, <http://www.nonproliferation.eu/activities/activities.php>, pp. 12–13.

[19] See chapter 10, section III, in this volume.

[20] Bromley (note 18), p. 13.

[21] British House of Commons, 'Arms trade: exports', Written answers, *Hansard*, 9 Mar. 2011, column 1173W.

[22] 'Les ventes d'armes françaises à l'Egypte sont suspendues depuis le 27 janvier, selon Matignon [French arms sales to Egypt have been suspended since January 27, according to Matignon]', *Le Monde*, 5 Feb. 2011; and 'France: export of weapons to Libya and Bahrain suspended', ANSAmed, 18 Feb. 2011, <http://ansamed.biz/en/francia/news/ME.XEF57063.html>.

[23] 'EU schickt Erkundungsteam nach Libyen [EU sends assessment team to Libya]', Welt Online, 6 Mar. 2011, <http://www.welt.de/politik/ausland/article12710946/EU-schickt-Erkundungsteam-nach-Libyen.html>.

lation to suspend or revoke licences.[24] However, according to one official, Germany asked companies holding relevant licences for export to countries in the region not to use them until they had been reviewed in the light of the current situation.[25]

Events in the Middle East and North Africa also prompted several EU member states to reassess aspects of their arms export procedures. The British Government declared its intention to create new powers that will allow for export licensing to be suspended for countries 'experiencing a sharp deterioration in security or stability' as well as new systems for collecting information for export licence risk assessments.[26] However, weapon exports continued to be licensed to destinations where abuses had taken place, such as Bahrain.[27] Thus, as with Russia and the USA, there were few signs that EU member states with significant arms exports to the Middle East and North Africa—such as France and the United Kingdom—were willing to affect these interests by applying criteria on human rights and international humanitarian law more stringently.

The rapidly developing Turkish arms industry has been actively pursuing arms sales to the Middle East and North Africa.[28] During 2007–11 Turkish companies upgraded hundreds of Saudi Arabian M-113 armoured personnel carriers and supplied rocket launchers to the United Arab Emirates and armoured vehicles to Bahrain. In 2011 Turkey cut its previously friendly relations with Syria and took a leading role in denouncing the Syrian Government's use of violence to suppress demonstrations and pushing for a change of government. In August 2011 Turkey suspended the supply of military equipment to Syria, including the planned sale of military radios and small patrol boats.[29] In November it confirmed the embargo and banned all transfers of weapons to Syria via Turkey.[30] It did not change its arms export policy with respect to other recipients in the region.[31]

[24] Bromley (note 18), p. 14.
[25] German official, Interview with author, 2 Dec. 2011.
[26] British House of Commons, 'FCO review of export policy', Written ministerial statements, *Hansard*, 13 Oct. 2011, columns 41WS–42WS.
[27] 'Bahrain receives military equipment from UK despite violent crackdown', *The Guardian*, 14 Feb. 2012.
[28] On the Turkish arms industry see Jackson, S. T., 'Arms production', *SIPRI Yearbook 2011*, pp. 244–47.
[29] Şık, B., 'Ankara projeleri donduruyor' [Ankara freezes projects], *Cumhuriyet*, 17 Aug. 2011.
[30] 'Turkey announces economic sanctions package against Syria', *Today's Zaman*, 30 Nov. 2011.
[31] Enginsoy, U. and Bekdil, B. E., 'Business as usual for Turkish firms in Mideast', *Defense News*, 7 Mar. 2011, p. 7.

III. The maritime dimension of arms transfers to South East Asia, 2007–11

SIEMON T. WEZEMAN

The volume of arms transfers to South East Asia in the period 2007–11 was almost 200 per cent higher than in 2002–2006, a significantly bigger rise than the global average increase of 24 per cent. The volume of imports in the region during 2007–11 was the highest for any five-year period since the end of the Second Indochina War (Viet Nam War) in 1975. The increase in the volume of imports was particularly significant for Indonesia, Malaysia, Singapore and Viet Nam (see table 6.6), all of which acquired or ordered quantitatively or qualitatively significant naval platforms and advanced combat aircraft in 2007–11. This section focuses on imports and orders placed with foreign suppliers by these four countries and two other states on the South China Sea—Brunei Darussalam and the Philippines—related to maritime security, first by examining the background to and motives for the acquisitions and then by detailing acquisitions in 2007–11.[1]

Naval weapons accounted for the bulk of the arms acquisitions by these six states: ships and other weapons with a maritime role accounted for 52 per cent of the total volume of their deliveries in the period 2007–11. Deliveries of aircraft, associated missiles and radars intended for maritime as well as overland roles accounted for a further 37 per cent. Often these newly acquired weapons are advanced systems with substantially longer combat ranges than those that had been in service until recently. Equipment with maritime roles also dominates outstanding orders and announced plans for arms acquisitions. Indonesia, the Philippines and Viet Nam have substantial inventories of obsolete and sometimes worn-out weapons and have announced plans for replacements.[2] The types of weapon acquired in 2007–11 therefore suggest that maritime security concerns are the most important determinant of the types and volumes of weapons sought by states around the South China Sea.

Maritime security in South East Asia

The motives for arms acquisitions of most countries in South East Asia are often not well explained, even where official documents on defence policy

---

[1] This section does not discuss imports by Cambodia, Laos, Myanmar, Thailand and Timor-Leste.

[2] E.g. 9 of the 12 frigates and offshore patrol vessels in the Philippine Navy are over 75 years old and in 2008 over 50% of the Indonesian Navy was in need of urgent repairs to remain operational. Saunders, S. (ed.), *Jane's Fighting Ships 2011–2012* (Jane's Information Group: London, 2011), pp. 612–14; and Supriyanto, R. A., 'Naval modernisation: a sea change for Indonesia', *The Nation* (Bangkok), 30 Jan. 2012.

Table 6.6. Suppliers of major conventional weapons to Brunei Darussalam, Indonesia, Malaysia, the Philippines, Singapore and Viet Nam, 2007–11

Recipient	Share of global arms transfers (%)	Change (%) in volume of deliveries, 2002–2006 to 2007–11	Main suppliers, 2007–11 (share of recipient's transfers, %)		
			1st	2nd	3rd
Brunei Darussalam	0.2	10 333	Germany (82%)	France (6%)	Denmark (4%), Netherlands (4%)
Indonesia	1.3	144	Netherlands (35%)	Russia (26%)	South Korea (22%)
Malaysia	2.4	281	Russia (42%)	Germany (21%)	France (12%)
Philippines	0.1	20	USA (90%)	Italy (4%)	UK (3%)
Singapore	4.0	293	USA (62%)	France (39%)	Germany (8%)
Viet Nam	1.1	80	Russia (97%)	Ukraine (1%)	Romania (<0.5%)

Source: SIPRI Arms Transfers Database, <http://www.sipri.org/databases/armstransfers>.

or military budgets are published. This is to be expected when drivers include the political influence of the military (in Indonesia and probably also in Viet Nam), national pride and rivalry with other South East Asian countries.[3] However, defence and security policy documents and statements by officials tend not to identify any particular country as a major threat or driver for arms acquisitions. Recent defence white papers produced by Brunei, Indonesia and Viet Nam stress maritime security concerns relating to piracy, illegal fishing and terrorism.[4] Indonesia's and Malaysia's acquisitions of patrol crafts for maritime policing purposes can also be linked to such concerns. However, defence white papers and policy statements also highlight competing sovereignty claims over islands and islets and maritime rights in the South China Sea, which also involve China and Taiwan (see figure 6.2). The salience of these disputes is increased by the presence of oil and natural gas in the disputed areas and the expectations of further large finds.[5] There have already been numerous low-level maritime confrontations between navies, coastguards and civilian vessels in

[3] McBeth, J., 'Arms-wrestling in Indonesia', Asia Times Online, 28 Jan. 2012, <http://www.atimes.com/atimes/Southeast_Asia/NA28Ae01.html>; and Anderson, G., 'Growing and evolving', *Jane's Defence Weekly*, 18 Jan. 2012, pp. 28–32.

[4] See e.g. Bruneian Ministry of Defence (MOD), *Defence White Paper 2011* (MOD: Bolkiah Garrison, 2011); Indonesian Ministry of Defence, *Buku Putih Pertahanan Indonesia 2008* [Indonesia defence white paper 2008] (MOD: Jakarta, 2008); and Vietnamese Ministry of National Defence (MND), *Vietnam National Defence* (MND: Hanoi, Dec. 2009).

[5] Estimates of oil reserves in the South China Sea range from 28 billion barrels to 213 billion barrels. US Energy Information Administration, 'South China Sea', Analysis brief, Mar. 2008, <http://www.eia.gov/countries/regions-topics.cfm?fips=SCS>. One small section of sea claimed by both Brunei and Malaysia is estimated to contain 1–4 billion barrels of oil, worth possibly more than $100 billion. 'Tempest in the South China Sea', Asia Sentinel, 14 June 2010, <http://www.asiasentinel.com/index.php?option=com_content&task=view&id=2530>.

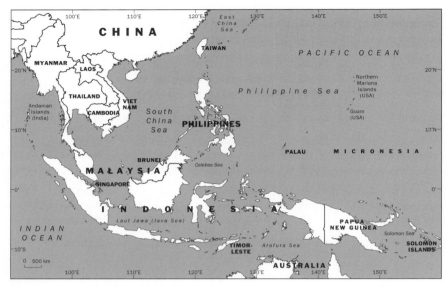

Figure 6.2. Map of South East Asia

disputed waters in the region, including incidents between China and Indonesia, the Philippines and Viet Nam in 2010 and 2011.[6]

While all the governments involved in such confrontations stress the need for peaceful solutions, much of their military modernizations would allow them to negotiate maritime claims from a position of some strength. These acquisitions are linked to military modernizations across Asia, led by China. Simultaneously, the interest and presence of Australia, Japan, India, South Korea and the United States in South East Asia is increasing. These factors are raising concerns about the increased potential for incidents at sea, both unintended and otherwise, between increasingly better-armed stakeholders. Although there are platforms for regional dialogue, including those provided by the Association of Southeast Asian Nations (ASEAN), there are few effective agreements on preventing small incidents that could escalate into unplanned armed confrontations.[7]

In themselves, the arms acquisitions and the resulting increases in military capabilities in South East Asia are not dramatic. Many countries in the region are large and so, it can be argued, need substantial military forces to patrol and defend their territories. Yet the armed forces of South East Asian

[6] Jamaluddin, J. M., 'US reinforce Asia–Pacific presence', *Asian Defence Journal*, Dec. 2011, p. 5; Associated Press, 'US assures Manila of 2nd warship amid Spratys row', *Philippine Daily Inquirer*, 17 Nov. 2011; and Supriyanto (note 2).

[7] E.g. China and the ASEAN member states agreed the non-binding Declaration on the Conduct of Parties in the South China Sea, signed 4 Nov. 2002, <http://www.asean.org/13163.htm>. See also Jamaluddin (note 6). For brief descriptions and lists of members of ASEAN, the ASEAN Regional Forum, ASEAN Plus Three and the East Asia Summit see annex B in this volume.

states are relatively small. For example, Indonesia has 31 combat ships with a displacement of over 500 tonnes (with a total displacement of 38 000 tonnes) and 50 combat aircraft to patrol and protect its approximately 18 000 islands spread over an area as large as Europe.[8] By way of comparison, the Netherlands, a small European country, has 10 combat ships (with a total displacement of 30 000 tonnes) and 72 combat aircraft, all of which are much more advanced than most of Indonesia's ships and aircraft.[9]

Arms transfers related to maritime security

The USA is the largest supplier of arms to South East Asia. It has increased its contacts with states in the region and has shown a greater willingness to sell or even give weapons to allies there. This has been interpreted as being related to its focus on the Asia–Pacific region and the growing military power of China.[10] Other supplier states appear to have more limited strategic goals in providing arms to the region; instead they see developments in South East Asia as presenting sales opportunities. Suppliers are increasingly willing to meet the demands of South East Asian states for extensive technology transfers in arms deals or partnerships to develop new weapon systems.[11]

Singapore was the region's largest importer of major weapons in 2007–11 (see table 6.6)—indeed, it was the fifth largest importer worldwide—and it has the best-equipped and most capable forces in the region. During 2007–11 it imported 6 La Fayette frigates from France; 4 G-550 airborne early-warning aircraft from Israel; 6 SH-60B anti-submarine warfare (ASW) helicopters and 19 of an order of 24 F-15E combat aircraft and associated advanced air-to-air and air-to-surface missiles from the USA; and the first of 2 Västergotland submarines from Sweden. In 2011 Singapore announced plans to acquire 40 new combat aircraft, potentially the F-35A supplied by the USA, 4 submarines and surveillance aircraft.

---

[8] Saunders (note 2), pp. 353–69; and International Institute for Strategic Studies (IISS), *The Military Balance 2011* (Routledge: London, 2011), pp. 244.

[9] ed. Saunders (note 2), pp. 549–61; and International Institute for Strategic Studies (note 8), p. 131.

[10] The USA announced a 'rebalance' of US military forces toward the Asia–Pacific region in Jan. 2012. US Department of Defense (DOD), *Sustaining U.S. Global Leadership: Priorities for 21st Century Defense* (DOD: Washington, DC, Jan. 2012), p. 2; and Billo, A., 'The risks of America's Asia strategy', CNN, 6 Jan. 2012 <http://edition.cnn.com/2012/01/06/opinion/billo-asia-us/index.html>.

[11] Grevatt, J., 'France, Germany, UK seek more defence ties with Southeast Asia', *Jane's Defence Weekly*, 30 Nov. 2011, p. 19; 'Indonesia boosting international defense cooperation', Antara News, 21 Sep. 2011 <http://www.antaranews.com/en/news/75872/indonesia-boosting-international-defense-cooperation>; 'Vietnam, Singapore hold 4th defense dialogue', Talk Vietnam, <http://talkvietnam.com/2012/01/vietnam-singapore-hold-4th-defense-dialogue/>; Anderson, G., 'Growing and evolving', *Jane's Defence Weekly*, 18 Jan. 2012, pp. 28–32; and Grevatt, J., 'Malaysia plans export promotion agency in UKTI mould', *Jane's Defence Weekly*, 19 Oct. 2011, p. 20.

During 2007–11 Malaysia received 18 Su-30 combat aircraft with advanced air-to-air and air-to-surface missiles from Russia, 6 MEKO A-100 frigates from Germany, and 2 Scorpene submarines jointly supplied by France and Spain. In 2010 Malaysia placed an order for two offshore patrol vessels (OPVs) with South Korea. The country's planned acquisitions are also related to maritime roles. In 2011 it confirmed a planned acquisition of six frigates; by the end of 2011 the French Gowind seemed to have been selected.[12] It also confirmed a plan to acquire 12–18 combat aircraft with a dual land and sea attack capability.[13] Malaysia also has plans to acquire up to 30 naval helicopters, additional submarines and six frigates.[14] However, Malaysia's plans may not all be realized. For example, in 2012 the Malaysian armed forces were expected to receive only 30 per cent of the requested procurement budget.[15]

Indonesia received four SIGMA-90 frigates from the Netherlands, four LPD-122m amphibious assault ships from South Korea and six Su-27 and Su-30MK combat aircraft from Russia during 2007–11. It also received Yakhont anti-ship missiles from Russia for modernization of six frigates, and C-705 and C-802 anti-ship missiles from China for locally produced fast attack craft (FAC). A SIGMA-105 frigate is on order from the Netherlands for production in Indonesia, probably to be followed by up to 16 more.[16] In 2011 an order was signed for three Type-209 submarines from South Korea and for six Su-30MK2 combat aircraft—a version optimized for a maritime strike role—from Russia. In recent years Indonesia has announced substantial plans for the procurement of new weapons but many of these have been delayed due to funding issues.[17] Others are simply unrealistic, such as plans to acquire over 100 combat ships and over 150 patrol and support ships to be in service by 2024 or 180 Su-27 and Su-30 combat aircraft.[18] However, military spending on procurement is to be increased significantly from 2010.[19] After Indonesia ordered 16 T-50 trainer/combat aircraft from South Korea, the two countries signed an agreement in 2011 to cooperate in the development of the KFX combat air-

[12] Mahadzir, D., 'Acquisition strategy', *Jane's Defence Weekly*, 23 Nov. 2011, pp. 30–32; and 'Des Gowind bientôt commandées par la Malaisie? [Gowinds soon ordered by Malaysia?], Mer & Marine, 9 Dec. 2011.

[13] Mahadzir (note 12); and Waldron, G., 'LIMA: Eurofighter, Rafale raise stakes in Malaysian fighter contest', *Flight International*, 6 Dec. 2011.

[14] 'Interview: Admiral Tan Sri Abdul Aziz Jaafar, Chief of Navy, RMN', *Asian Defence Journal*, Dec. 2011, pp. 12–16.

[15] Mahadzir (note 12), p. 30.

[16] Supriyanto (note 2).

[17] 'TNI to modernize its main armament system', Antara News, 20 Sep. 2011, <http://portal.antara.co.id/en/news/75825/tni-to-modernize-its-main-armament-system>; and Anderson, G. and Grevatt, J., 'Island vision', *Jane's Defence Weekly*, 28 Sep. 2011, p. 30.

[18] Anderson, G., 'Growing and evolving', *Jane's Defence Weekly*, 18 Jan. 2012, pp. 28–32; and Supriyanto (note 2).

[19] Anderson and Grevatt (note 17), pp. 28–32; and Anderson (note 18).

craft, of which Indonesia would buy 50.[20] The two countries signed a similar agreement for the joint development of a large FAC.[21] In a sign of improved relations, in 2011 the USA offered Indonesia 24 second-hand F-16C combat aircraft.

Almost all the major weapons that Viet Nam imported in 2007–11 came from Russia (see table 6.6), including two Gepard frigates, two Project-12418 FACs, eight Su-30MK2 combat aircraft and two Bastion coast defence systems. Up to eight more Project-12418 FACs are being produced under licence, and six Project-636 submarines, 12 Su-30MK2 and two additional Gepard frigates (with increased ASW capabilities) are on order from Russia. Negotiations with Russia for additional Bastion systems and Kh-35 anti-ship missiles were under way in late 2011.[22] However, Viet Nam also hopes to diversify its sources of supply. At the end of 2011 it was reportedly negotiating the acquisition of up to four SIGMA frigates from the Netherlands and to be interested in buying P-3 ASW aircraft from the USA.[23]

Brunei Darussalam and the Philippines are also acquiring naval vessels, albeit at a much lower level than neighbouring states. Brunei received three OPV-80 corvettes from Germany during 2007–11, while the Philippines received a second-hand Hamilton OPV from the USA and has been promised a second second-hand Hamilton OPV. During 2011 the Philippines announced urgent plans to acquire a third Hamilton OPV, other patrol ships, maritime patrol aircraft and up to 12 second-hand US F-16 combat aircraft.[24]

[20] 'RI sending KFX jet-fighter production team to South Korea', Antara News, 11 July 2011, <http://www.antaranews.com/en/news/73621/ri-sending-kfx-jet-fighter-production-team-to-south-korea>.

[21] 'RI, Korea hammer out deal to develop tanks', Jakarta Post, 10 Sep. 2011.

[22] 'Việt Nam mua thêm Bastion-P và phát triển tên lửa hành trình' [Viet Nam to buy more Bastion-P and cruise missile development], Vietnam Defence, 16 Feb. 2012, <http://quocphong.vn/Home/tintuc/vietnam/Viet-Nam-mua-them-BastionP-va-phat-trien-ten-lua-hanh-trinh/20122/51363.vnd>.

[23] Steketee, M., 'Vietnam bestelt vier korvetten bij Damen' [Viet Nam orders four corvettes from Damen], NRC (Rotterdam), 3 Oct. 2011, pp. 26–27; and Francis, L., 'SE Asian nations seek improved ASW, AEW', Aviation Week, 17 Feb. 2012.

[24] Romero, A., 'Submarine for Navy? Noy bares AFP shop list', Philippine Star, 24 Aug. 2011; Romero, A., 'DND eyes 3 more Hamilton-class ships', Philippine Star, 14 Dec. 2011; 'Philippines eyes US materiel', Jane's Defence Weekly, 18 Jan. 2012, p. 18; Pazzibugan, D. Z., 'P70B in contracts up for grabs in AFP', Philippine Daily Inquirer, 28 Jan. 2012; and Evangelista, K., 'Philippines eye submarines to boost navy', Philippine Daily Inquirer, 17 May 2011.

IV. Arms transfers to Armenia and Azerbaijan, 2007–11

PAUL HOLTOM

There have been regular warnings since the 1994 ceasefire about the prospect of a renewal of the 1992–94 war between Armenia and Azerbaijan over Nagorno-Karabakh, an Armenian-populated region of Azerbaijan (see figure 6.3). In 2011 several observers noted particular pressures in the two countries that could push them into war in the near future.[1] Armenia and Azerbaijan have both identified the settlement of the Nagorno-Karabakh conflict as a key national security priority.[2] While both sides stress a commitment to a peaceful resolution of the conflict, each accuses the other of violating the 1990 Treaty on Conventional Armed Forces in Europe (CFE Treaty) and of pushing them into an arms race.[3] In military parades held in 2011 both states displayed new and previously unseen military equipment in obvious shows of strength.[4]

Azerbaijan had the largest real-terms increase in military expenditure between 2010 and 2011, while in 2010 Armenia spent a larger proportion of its gross domestic product (GDP) on military expenditure than any other state in Europe.[5] Between 2002–2006 and 2007–11 Azerbaijan increased its volume of imports of major conventional weapons, and it rose to become the 38th largest recipient, up from 53rd in 2002–2006, while Armenia's imports fell and it dropped from 71st place to 84th. While in 2002–2006 Azerbaijan imported 2.5 times the volume of major conventional weapons imported by Armenia, by 2007–11 the gap had widened, with Azerbaijan importing 7.5 times more arms than Armenia (see table 6.7). However, during 2010–11 Armenia made declarations that indicate that it is seeking to procure greater quantities of weapons in response to Azerbaijan's arms

---

[1] E.g. International Crisis Group (ICG), *Armenia and Azerbaijan: Preventing War*, Europe Briefing no. 60 (ICG: Tbilisi, 8 Feb. 2011); 'The Nagorno-Karabakh conflict: still just about frozen', *The Economist*, 7 May 2011; and Babayan, A., [According to Russian experts, the Karabakh conflict sides are actively preparing for war], Radio Azatutyun, 1 Aug. 2011, <http://rus.azatutyun.am/content/article/24283732.html> (in Russian).

[2] Armenian National Security Council, 'National Security Strategy of the Republic of Armenia', 26 Jan. 2007, annex to Presidential Decree no. NH-37-N, 7 Feb. 2007, <http://www.mil.am/1320693 104>, p. 4; Armenian Ministry of Defence, 'Military doctrine of the Republic of Armenia', 2007, <http://www.mil.am/1320693242>, p. 4; and President of Azerbaijan, 'National Security Concept of the Republic of Azerbaijan', Instruction no. 2198, 23 May 2007, <http://www.un.int/azerbaijan/pdf/National_security.pdf>, p. 6.

[3] US Mission to the OSCE, '27 January Plenary—Azerbaijan, Armenia trade charges on Russian arms transfers', Cable to US Department of State, no. 09USOSCE15, 2 Feb. 2009, <http://www.wikileaks.org/cable/2009/02/09USOSCE15.html>. On developments related to the CFE Treaty see chapter 10, section IV, in this volume. For a summary and other details of the treaty see annex A.

[4] Holdanowicz, G., 'Armenia displays surface-to-surface missile system hardware during anniversary parade', *Jane's Missiles and Rockets*, Nov. 2011, p. 11; and Holdanowicz, G., 'Azerbaijan shows new equipment at parade', *Jane's Defence Weekly*, 6 July 2011, p. 8.

[5] See chapter 4, section VII, in this volume.

Figure 6.3. Map of Armenia and Azerbaijan

Table 6.7. Suppliers of major conventional weapons to Armenia and Azerbaijan, 2007–11

Recipient	Share of global arms transfers (%)	Main suppliers (share of recipient's transfers, %)		
		1st	2nd	3rd
Armenia	0.1	Russia (95%)	Ukraine (4%)	Belarus (1%)
Azerbaijan	0.6	Russia (55%)	Ukraine (34%)	Belarus (5%)

Source: SIPRI Arms Transfers Database, <http://www.sipri.org/databases/armstransfers>.

procurement. Further details of Armenia's and Azerbaijan's arms acquisitions in the period 2007–11 and the stated policies underlying those acquisitions appear below.

Although both countries are the subjects of a voluntary Organization for Security and Co-operation in Europe (OSCE) arms embargo, a number of OSCE participating states—including Belarus, Russia, Turkey, Ukraine and the United States—supplied major conventional arms during 2007–11.[6] Among these suppliers, Russia's role is particularly important as it

[6] In 1992 the OSCE's predecessor, the Conference on Security and Co-operation in Europe (CSCE), requested that its participating states impose an embargo on deliveries of arms to forces engaged in combat in the Nagorno-Karabakh area. Although it is not a mandatory embargo, several OSCE participating states have denied licences to export arms and military equipment to Armenia and Azerbaijan on the grounds that it would violate the embargo. Conference on Security and Co-operation in Europe, Committee of Senior Officials, annex 1 to Journal no. 2 of the Seventh Meeting of the Committee, Prague, 27–28 Feb. 1992. For a brief description and list of states participating in the OSCE see annex B in this volume.

co-chairs the OSCE's Minsk Group—a forum for negotiations on a peaceful settlement of the conflict. But instead of pushing for a peaceful resolution of the conflict, Russia appears to have helped preserve the status quo, and at the same time it has emerged as a major supplier of arms to both sides.[7]

Armenia

Armenia's military expenditure in 2011 was $414 million. Although this was 2.8 per cent lower in real terms than in 2010 (when military spending represented 4.2 per cent of GDP), over the decade 2002–11 spending increased by 165 per cent. However, it has been argued that to gain a fuller understanding of Armenian military expenditure (and the military balance with Azerbaijan), spending by the self-proclaimed Republic of Nagorno-Karabakh should also be considered.[8] According to one estimate, total military spending by Armenia and Nagorno-Karabakh in 2011 was at least $600 million.[9]

There is little public information on international transfers of major conventional weapons to Armenia in recent years. According to SIPRI data, the volume of deliveries of conventional weapons during 2007–11 was 11 per cent lower than in 2002–2006, although the overall volume for both periods is low. Russia is Armenia's largest arms supplier by far (see table 6.7). The most significant known delivery from Russia in this period was of S-300PMU (SA-10C) surface-to-air missile (SAM) systems, which Armenia revealed for the first time in late 2010. Ukraine delivered two second-hand L-39C trainer aircraft. Several European Union (EU) member states have reported issuing export licences for a small quantity of military equipment during 2007–10.[10] Montenegro has reported issuing licences worth €2.9 million ($3.8 million) and exporting mainly small arms and light weapons (SALW) and ammunition worth €1.3 million ($1.7 million) in 2009.[11]

In August 2010 an Armenian Government ad hoc task force recommended measures for the modernization of the Armenian armed forces, focusing on arms acquisitions and development of the domestic arms

---

[7] The Minsk Group was established by the CSCE in 1992 to encourage Armenia and Azerbaijan to reach a peaceful, negotiated resolution to the conflict over Nagorno-Karabakh. France, Russia and the USA are co-chairs, but in recent years Russia has played a leading role. For a full list of members see annex B in this volume.

[8] Mukhin, V., [Commonwealth of militarized states], *Nezavisimaya Gazeta*, 17 Mar. 2010 (in Russian).

[9] Mukhin (note 8).

[10] Council of the European Union, 10th–13th EU annual reports on arms exports, <http://www.consilium.europa.eu/eeas/foreign-policy/non-proliferation,-disarmament-and-export-control-/security-related-export-controls-ii?lang=en>.

[11] Montenegrin Ministry of Economy, *2009 Annual Report on Foreign Trade in Controled Goods* (Ministry of Economy: Podgorica, 2010), p. 35.

industry. The Defence Minister, Seyran Ohanyan, explained that the Armenian Government planned to acquire long-range, precision-guided weapons and did not deny that Armenia's planned acquisitions are related to Azerbaijan's acquisitions and orders.[12] In December 2010 Armenian President Serzh Sargsyan and the National Security Council approved the State Programme of Developing Weaponry and Military Hardware in 2011–15, which drew on the findings of the task force.[13] There is little public information on the systems to be procured under this programme, although in June 2011 officials of Russia's Rosoboronexport announced Armenian interest in acquiring BM-30 Smerch multiple rocket launchers (MRLs).[14] The Strategic Defence Review 2011–15 called for 'an integrated system of radar and air surveillance assets, linked to a modernized ground-based air defense system'.[15]

Two reasons explain Russia's dominant supplier relationship with Armenia. First, Armenia's membership of the Collective Security Treaty Organization (CSTO) and bilateral agreements with Russia relating to its military base at Gyumri, in north-west Armenia, mean that Armenia can acquire arms from Russia cheaply or for free.[16] In August 2010 Russia provided security guarantees to Armenia and extended a commitment to provide arms and military equipment as military aid in return for Armenia's agreement to extend Russia's use of the base at Gyumri until 2044.[17] Second, Armenia has a limited pool of potential suppliers due to the OSCE arms embargo, conflict concerns and pressure from Azerbaijan on potential suppliers. EU member states denied 22 of the 30 reported licence applications for the export of arms and military equipment to Armenia during 2007–10; 21 of these denials cited criterion 1 of the EU Common Position on arms exports as grounds for denial, which includes consideration of OSCE arms embargoes.[18]

The political sensitivities of supplying weapons to Armenia were underlined in September 2011 when the Moldovan Ministry of Defence announced that it had sold 'obsolete ammunition' to Armenia via a Latvian

---

[12] 'Armenia seeking long-range weapons', Radio Free Europe/Radio Liberty, 10 Aug. 2010, <http://www.rferl.org/articleprintview/2124214.html>.

[13] Danielyan, E., 'Armenia displays sophisticated air defence systems', *Eurasia Daily Monitor*, 19 Jan. 2011.

[14] 'Armenian military "interested" in acquiring Russian rocket artillery', Radio Free Europe/Radio Liberty, 9 June 2011, <http://www.rferl.org/articleprintview/24230218.html>.

[15] Armenian Ministry of Defence (MOD), *Strategic Defense Review 2011–2015, Public Release* (MOD: Yerevan, [n.d.]), p. 13.

[16] For a brief description and list of members of the CSTO see annex B in this volume.

[17] President of Russia, 'Ratification of Protocol No. 5 between Russia and Armenia', 27 June 2011, <http://eng.kremlin.ru/news/2477>.

[18] Council of the European Union (note 10); and Council Common Position 2008/944/CFSP of 8 Dec. 2008 defining common rules governing control of exports of military technology and equipment, *Official Journal of the European Union*, L335, 13 Dec. 2008.

company.[19] It emerged that Moldova had agreed to supply 60 tonnes of anti-tank missiles and launchers and MRL systems and munitions, with 40 tonnes delivered in September 2011. According to the Latvian Ministry of Foreign Affairs, the Latvian company involved in the transaction did not have a licence to conduct this deal, while the Moldovan Parliament investigated the deal due to concerns that the surplus arms were being sold too cheaply.[20] Moldova decided to freeze the deal; in doing so, it is likely to have been influenced by Azerbaijani pressure, as the Moldovan ambassador to Baku declared the deal an 'unfortunate mistake' that had damaged relations with Azerbaijan.[21]

Azerbaijan

Azerbaijan's military expenditure in 2011 was $3.1 billion, a real-terms increase of 89 per cent since 2010 and of 742 per cent since 2002. In 2010 military expenditure represented 2.9 per cent of GDP, down from 3.3 per cent in 2008 and 2009. In late 2010 the Azerbaijani Government announced that it planned to spend 20 per cent of the 2011 national budget on military expenditure, to pay for modern weapons and military reform.[22] Azerbaijan's 2011 military budget of $3.1 billion, announced in October 2010 shortly after the Armenian Government had proposed a total budget of $2.8 billion, included budget lines for state prosecutors and the courts, suggesting that the military budget was padded with non-military spending items.[23] It can be questioned whether Azerbaijan's military expenditure will translate into increased military capabilities. Some sceptical observers have highlighted the impact of corruption on military spending or suggested that military expenditure has been inflated to ensure that President Ilham Aliyev could fulfil his 2007 promise that Azerbaijan's military spending would be larger than the total budget of Armenia.[24]

The volume of deliveries of conventional weapons to Azerbaijan in 2007–11 was 164 per cent higher than in 2002–2006. Russia, Ukraine and Belarus were the main suppliers of arms in 2007–11 (see table 6.7), but

[19] Moldovan Ministry of Defence, 'Sale of ammunition considered legal', 21 Sep. 2011, <http://www.army.md/?lng=3&action=show&cat=122&obj=871>.

[20] Kudryavtsev, N., [The case of the arms supplier Latspeceksports: 5 million were lost in the course of the transaction], kriminal.lv, 28 Oct. 2010, <http://www.kriminal.lv/news/delo-postavshtika-oruzhiya-latspeceksports-po-hodu-sd> (in Russian).

[21] 'Moldova nixes arm sale to Armenia', Radio Free Europe/Radio Liberty, 11 Nov. 2011, <http://www.rferl.org/articleprintview/24388532.html>.

[22] Manafov, R. and Khalilov, Dzh., [In 2011 expenditure on defence to double], Echo, 13 Oct. 2010, <http://www.echo-az.com/archive/2010_10/2388/politica01.shtml> (in Russian).

[23] Sanamyan, E., 'Tight leash: Azerbaijan–Armenia arms race accelerates', *Jane's Intelligence Review*, Mar. 2011, pp. 22–23.

[24] International Crisis Group (ICG), *Nagorno-Karabakh: Risking War*, Europe Report no. 187 (ICG: Tbilisi, 14 Nov. 2007), p. 6; and International Crisis Group (ICG), *Azerbaijan: Defence Sector Management and Reform*, Europe Briefing no. 50 (ICG: Baku, 29 Oct. 2008), pp. 7–8.

Israel, South Africa and Turkey also supplied major conventional arms. Imports of aircraft accounted for 55 per cent of the volume of Azerbaijan's imports, armoured vehicles for 19 per cent, missiles for 12 per cent, air defence systems for 7 per cent and artillery for 7 per cent. The Czech Republic and Romania granted exported licences worth €6.4 million ($8.3 million) and €12 million ($15.6 million), respectively, and delivered €4 million ($5.2 million) and €6.6 million ($8.6 million) worth of various arms, components and military equipment during 2007–11.[25]

In 2011 Azerbaijan took delivery from Russia of the first of a planned 2 S-300PMU-2 (SA-20B) SAM systems, 4 of a planned 24 Mi-35M combat helicopters and 15 of a planned 60 Mi-17 helicopters, all ordered in 2010. Israel delivered the first Hermes-450 unmanned aerial vehicle (UAV), which was ordered in 2008, and the first Aerostar UAVs produced under licence in Azerbaijan were also delivered. Deliveries of 25 Marauder and 25 Matador armoured personnel carriers (APCs) from South Africa, which were assembled in Azerbaijan, were completed in 2011. Turkey began deliveries of 60 Cobra APCs and 30 Roketsan 107-mm self-propelled MRLs.

Since the establishment of the Ministry of Defence Industry in December 2005, the Azerbaijani Government has stressed its desire to develop indigenous arms production capabilities both to equip its own armed forces and for export.[26] The capabilities of the local arms industry are currently limited to assembly and some production under licence. During 2011 Azerbaijan announced several deals for SALW, armoured vehicles, artillery rockets and UAVs that included arrangements for production under licence or assembly in Azerbaijan. In February 2011 Azerbaijan confirmed that it had a licence from Russia to produce 12 000 AK-74M 5.45-mm assault rifles annually.[27] Cooperation between Azerbaijani and Turkish arms producers is also developing, on the stable base provided by the close bilateral political ties. In 2011 Azerbaijan announced joint production arrangements with Turkish companies for 40-mm grenade launchers, MP5 sub-machine guns and Roketsan 107-mm and 122-mm rockets.[28] In 2011 Azerbaijan also announced an order for 30 more Marauder and 30 Matador APCs from

[25] Czech Ministry of Industry and Trade (MPO), *Annual Report on the Czech Republic's Control of the Export of Military Equipment and Small Arms for Civilian Use*, 2007–10 edns (MPO: Prague, 2008–11); and Romanian Ministry of Foreign Affairs (MFA), *National Agency for Export Controls, Arms Export Controls Annual Report*, 2007–10 edns (MFA: Bucharest, 2008–11).

[26] 'Azerbaijan to export military hardware of its make in 2–3 years', ITAR-TASS, 20 Nov. 2007; and 'Azeri paper questions need for Defence Industry Ministry', *Baku Zerkalo*, 19 Feb. 2008, Translation from Russian, World News Connection.

[27] Suleymanov, R., 'Azerbaijan starts serial production of AK-74M assault rifles basing on Russian license', Azeri Press Agency, 7 July 2011, <http://www.en.apa.az/print.php?id=151080>.

[28] Suleymanov, R., 'Azerbaijan and Turkey to jointly produce grenade launcher and submachine gun', Azeri Press Agency, 21 Feb. 2011, <http://en.apa.az/print.php?id=141182>; and Suleymanov, R., 'Turkish company to begin delivering missiles to Azerbaijani Armed Forces in early 2012', Azeri Press Agency, 19 Oct. 2011, <http://en.apa.az/news.php?id=157658>.

South Africa, to be assembled in Azerbaijan, and placed orders for the licensed production of Ukrainian–Belarusian Skif (R-2) anti-tank missiles for Azerbaijani border troops and upgraded Mi-24G combat helicopters.

During 2011 there was a lot of visible activity by Azerbaijani UAVs along the line of contact (see figure 6.3), and on 12 September 2011 Nagorno-Karabakh armed forces reported the first downing of an Azerbaijani UAV.[29] Azerbaijan obtained a small number of UAVs from Israel prior to 2011. Cooperation developed in 2011 when Azerbaijan's Azad Systems Company and the Israeli company Aeronautics established a joint venture to produce 60 Orbiter and Aerostar UAVs. Israel looks set to emerge as a major supplier of arms and military equipment to Azerbaijan, as it was revealed in February 2012 that Israel has concluded deals worth $1.6 billion with Azerbaijan for UAVs, SAM systems and air surveillance radar systems.[30]

In 2010 Azerbaijan expressed interest in procuring the Chinese–Pakistani JF-17 combat aircraft, and talks continued with Pakistan Aeronautical Complex during 2011.[31] Azerbaijan's Minister of Defence Industry, Yavar Jamalov, also announced in May 2011 that Azerbaijan was negotiating with Chinese companies for long-range surface-to-surface missiles.[32]

EU member states denied 36 applications for licences to export arms and military equipment to Azerbaijan during 2007–10, with 35 of the denials citing criterion 1 of the EU Common Position as the grounds for denial.[33] In 2010 the Czech Republic announced that it had reconsidered its policy towards both Armenia and Azerbaijan and would 'only [grant] approvals to permits related to the export of non-weaponized and non-lethal-type military equipment'.[34] The position of some EU member states also has implications for other suppliers willing to provide military equipment to Azerbaijan. For example, Turkey is seeking to supply T-155 Fırtına self-propelled howitzers, but the German company MTU has reportedly refused to provide the necessary engines because of the Nagorno-Karabakh conflict.[35] Turkish companies are therefore trying to either obtain engines from another country or produce them in Turkey.

[29] 'Azerbaijani drone reportedly downed over Nagorno-Karabakh', Radio Free Europe/Radio Liberty, 14 Sep. 2011, <http://www.rferl.org/articleprintview/24328599.html>.

[30] Teibel, A., 'Israel inks 1.6 billion arms deal with Azerbaijan', Associated Press, 26 Feb. 2012.

[31] 'Azerbaijan interested in purchase of JF-17 Thunder fighters', News.Az, 9 Aug 2010, <http://www.news.az/articles/20583/print>; and Suleymanov, R., [Azerbaijan announced its intention to purchase combat aircraft co-produced by Pakistan and China], Azeri Press Agency, 15 Nov. 2011, <http://www.ru.apa.az/print.php?id=207656> (in Russian).

[32] Holdanowicz, G., 'Azerbaijan shows off its improved missile and rocket-artillery power during parade', *Jane's Missiles and Rockets*, Aug. 2011, p. 13.

[33] Council of the European Union (note 10).

[34] Czech Ministry of Industry and Trade, 2009 report (note 25), p. 11.

[35] Suleymanov, R., 'Turkey insists on selling T-155 Fırtına self-propelled howitzer to Azerbaijan', Azeri Press Agency, 14 Oct. 2011, <http://en.apa.az/news.php?id=157324>.

V. Transparency in arms transfers

PAUL HOLTOM AND MARK BROMLEY

Official and publicly accessible data on arms transfers is important for assessing states' arms export and arms procurement policies. However, publishing data on arms sales and acquisitions is a sensitive issue for nearly all states. This section analyses recent developments in official international, regional and national reporting mechanisms that aim, in whole or in part, to increase the quality and quantity of publicly available information on international arms transfers. This includes the United Nations Register of Conventional Arms (UNROCA) as well as national and regional reports on arms exports.[1]

The United Nations Register of Conventional Arms

UNROCA, which was established in 1991, is the key international mechanism for official transparency on arms transfers. Each year all UN member states are requested to report information to UNROCA on the export and import of seven categories of conventional weapons in the previous calendar year.[2] States are also invited to provide information on their international transfers of small arms and light weapons (SALW) and their holdings and procurement from domestic production of major conventional weapons.

The level of reporting in 2011 increased from an all-time low in 2010 (see figure 6.4). As of December 2011, 85 states had submitted reports on their arms transfers during 2010 (including 35 nil reports, i.e. reports indicating no imports or exports of major conventional weapons). There was a notable increase in reporting by states in the Americas, with a number of states reporting in 2011 for the first time in several years (see table 6.8). For example, the Dominican Republic reported for the first time since 2002, Uruguay for the first time since 2003, Ecuador and Guyana for the first time since 2006, and Trinidad and Tobago for the first time since 2007.[3]

---

[1] This section does not address confidential intergovernmental exchanges of information on arms transfers, such as those that occur within the Organization for Security and Co-operation in Europe, the Organization of American States and the Wassenaar Arrangement. Another source of information on the international arms trade is the customs data of the UN Commodity Trade Statistics Database (Comtrade). Comtrade data is not discussed here because it is neither intended nor designed to be a tool for increasing the amount of publicly available information on international arms transfers. Comtrade data is included in the Norwegian Initiative on Small Arms Transfers (NISAT) Small Arms Trade Database, <http://www.prio.no/NISAT/Small-Arms-Trade-Database/>.

[2] These categories are battle tanks, armoured combat vehicles, large-calibre artillery systems, combat aircraft, attack helicopters, warships and missiles or missile launchers.

[3] See also Bromley, M. and Solmirano, C., *Transparency in Military Spending and Arms Acquisitions in Latin America and the Caribbean*, SIPRI Policy Paper no. 31 (SIPRI: Stockholm, Jan. 2012).

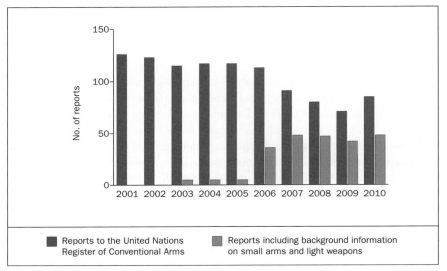

Figure 6.4. Reports submitted to the United Nations Register of Conventional Arms, 2001–10

Years refer to the year covered by the report, not the year of its submission.

Source: UNROCA database, <http://www.un-register.org/>.

Table 6.8. Reports submitted to the United Nations Register of Conventional Arms, by region, 2006–10

Years refer to the year covered by the report, not the year of its submission. Figures in brackets are numbers of nil reports.

Region	2006	2007	2008	2009	2010
Africa	15 (12)	8 (7)	4 (3)	4 (3)	1 (0)
Americas	22 (16)	13 (6)	15 (9)	10 (2)	19 (10)
Asia and Oceania	27 (18)	21 (12)	19 (7)	17 (9)	19 (11)
Europe	47 (15)	46 (13)	40 (10)	39 (15)	44 (13)
Middle East	2 (1)	3 (1)	2 (1)	2 (1)	2 (1)
Total	**113 (62)**	**91 (39)**	**80 (30)**	**72 (30)**	**85 (35)**

Source: UNROCA database, <http://www.un-register.org/>.

South Africa was the only African state to report to UNROCA during 2011. The Republic of the Congo, in its submission to the UN Secretary-General on conventional arms control at the regional and subregional levels, highlighted several factors that limited African participation in UNROCA, including the omission of light weapons from the scope of UNROCA's seven categories, the 'excessive use of the designation of "classified information"' by African states, and the need for 'international aid to contribute to disarmament in Africa through the establishment of related cooperation mechanisms'.[4] Considering the increase in participation by states in the Americas and the various arms control arrangements in that region, it is noteworthy that the Republic of the Congo referred to the experience of the Americas as a positive example for African states interested in pursuing conventional arms control.[5]

Of the 85 states that provided information to UNROCA in 2011, 49 provided background information on international transfers of SALW, including 8 nil reports. Austria, Grenada, Guyana, Iceland and Mongolia provided background information on international transfers of SALW for the first time. So far, nine states have submitted views on the inclusion of SALW in UNROCA since being invited to do so by the UN General Assembly at the end of 2009. In 2011 Burkina Faso and the Netherlands expressed their support for the expansion of UNROCA to include SALW.[6]

During 2011 information was only made available on 64 of the 85 states that had reported to UNROCA on transfers carried out in 2010.[7] The delay in publishing an addendum report containing information on the 21 states that reported after mid-July may have been linked to the unveiling in October 2011 of a new map interface for the publicly accessible online UNROCA database by the UN Office of Disarmament Affairs (UNODA).[8] Although the aim of the new database was to increase transparency, at the time of its launch it had a number of flaws. For example, it does not provide a comprehensive overview of all submissions, as was previously the case; it was launched before all of the information provided by UN member states during 2011 had been entered and, as of December 2011, it remained incomplete; and, moreover, its introduction seems to have delayed the public release of these states' reports. It is hoped that some of these problems will be addressed during 2012. The UNODA intends to use the new interface to enable states to report electronically, with a trial planned for 2012.

In December the UN General Assembly confirmed that a group of governmental experts (GGE) will be convened in 2012 to review the con-

---

[4] United Nations, General Assembly, 'Conventional arms control at the regional and subregional levels', Report of the Secretary-General, A/66/154, 15 July 2011, pp. 5–6.

[5] On transparency in Latin America see Bromley and Solmirano (note 3).

[6] United Nations, General Assembly, 'United Nations Register of Conventional Arms', Report of the Secretary-General, A/66/127, 12 July 2011. Burkina Faso did not report to UNROCA during 2011 Its support for an 8th, SALW category is contained in United Nations, General Assembly, 'The arms trade treaty', Report of the Secretary-General, 13 Dec. 2011, p. 3. On reporting on SALW to UNROCA see Holtom, P., *Transparency in Transfers of Small Arms and Light Weapons: Reports to the United Nations Register of Conventional Arms, 2003–2006*, SIPRI Policy Paper no. 22 (SIPRI: Stockholm, July 2008); and Holton, P., 'Reporting transfers of small arms and light weapons to the United Nations Register of Conventional Arms, 2007', SIPRI Background Paper, Feb. 2009, <http://books.sipri.org/product_info?c_product_id=373>.

[7] United Nations, General Assembly, 'United Nations Register of Conventional Arms', Report of the Secretary-General, A/66/127, 12 July 2011.

[8] UNROCA database, <http://www.un-register.org/>.

tinuing operation and further development of UNROCA.[9] However, in contrast to previous GGEs, whose sessions took place during a single calendar year, the new GGE will convene in November 2012 and during the first half of 2013. The GGE's report will be presented at the UN General Assembly's 68th session, in 2013. The decision to begin the GGE in late 2012 was taken primarily to accommodate the UN conference on an arms trade treaty (ATT), which will take place in July 2012, since the scope of and ways of reporting under an ATT are often discussed in connection with UNROCA.[10]

National and regional reports on arms exports

Since the early 1990s an increasing number of governments have published national reports on arms exports.[11] As of January 2012, 35 states had published at least one national report on arms exports since 1990, including 32 that had done so since 2009.[12] Of the 32 states, 27 included information in their reports on arms export licences granted and 23 included information on actual arms exports (see table 6.9).

One state, Poland, published its first two national reports on arms exports during 2011, providing information on arms exports in 2008–2009 and in 2010.[13] The reports contained information on the number and value of arms export licences issued and the European Union (EU) Common Military List category of the goods involved, broken down by destination. Canada produced its first national report on arms exports since 2009, providing data on exports in 2007, 2008 and 2009.[14] The report provided the financial value of goods exported broken down by destination and control list category. As in previous editions, the Canadian report did not include information on transfers to the USA, which—the report states—accounted for more than half of Canada's exports of military goods and technology.[15] Ireland published its first national report on arms exports for over 10 years,

---

[9] UN General Assembly Resolution 66/39, 2 Dec. 2011.

[10] See chapter 10, section II, in this volume.

[11] A database of the published reports is maintained by SIPRI at <http://www.sipri.org/research/armaments/transfers/transparency/national_reports>. See also Weber, H. and Bromley, M., 'National reports on arms exports', SIPRI Fact Sheet, Mar. 2011, <http://books.sipri.org/product_info?c_product_id=423>.

[12] The 3 states that have produced a report since 1990 but not since 2009 are Australia, Belarus and the Former Yugoslav Republic of Macedonia.

[13] Polish Ministry of Foreign Affairs (MFA), *Exports of Arms and Military Equipment from Poland: Report for the Years 2008–2009* (MFA: Warsaw, 2010); and Polish Ministry of Foreign Affairs, *Exports of Arms and Military Equipment from Poland: Report for 2010* (MFA: Warsaw, 2011).

[14] Canadian Department of Foreign Affairs and International Trade (DFAIT), Trade Controls and Technical Barriers Bureau, Export Controls Division, *Report on Exports of Military Goods from Canada 2007–2009* (DFAIT: Ottawa, 2011). Canada's previous national report, published in 2009, covered exports during 2006.

[15] Canadian Department of Foreign Affairs and International Trade (note 14), pp. 5, 7.

providing information on arms exports during 2008, 2009 and 2010.[16] The report contained information on the number and value of arms export licences issued and the EU Common Military List category of the goods, broken down by destination.

Trends in the level of detail that states include in their national reports on arms exports are mixed. In 2011 Albania published its third annual report on arms exports, detailing transfers in 2010.[17] The report provided information that was not present in previous editions, including descriptions of the goods transferred and their number or weight. Croatia published its second annual report on arms exports, detailing transfers in 2010.[18] Again, the report provided information that was not present in the first edition, including details of actual exports—the first edition only covered export licences granted—and either the number or weight of the goods transferred. In contrast, the latest edition of the '655 Report' published by the United States Department of State, which provides information on goods licensed for export and exported under the Direct Commercial Sales (DCS) programme, contained less detail than in previous years.[19] While the report was published 6 months earlier than previous editions, information was disaggregated by US Military List category as opposed to US Military List subcategory, as was the case in previous editions.[20]

The EU Common Position defining common rules governing the control of exports of military technology and equipment requires EU member states to exchange data on the financial values of their export licence approvals and actual exports along with information on their denials of arms export licences.[21] The Council of the EU compiles and publishes this data in an annual report. The 13th annual report, published in December 2011, covers transfers during 2010. Seventeen of the 27 EU member states provided full submissions to both the 12th and 13th annual reports—that is, they provided data on the financial value of both arms export licences and actual arms exports, broken down by both destination and EU Military List

---

[16] Irish Department of Jobs, Enterprise and Innovation (DJE), *Annual Report under the Control of Exports Act 2008 Covering the Period 2008–2010* (DJE: Dublin, 2011). Prior to this report, the most recent data available covered licences granted during Jan. 1998.

[17] Albanian State Export Control Authority, *Annual Report on Export Control for 2010* (Ministry of Defence: Tirana, 2011).

[18] Croatian Ministry of Economy, Labour and Entrepreneurship (MELE), *Annual Report on Export and Import of Military Goods and Non-Military Lethal Goods for 2010* (MELE: Zagreb, [2011]).

[19] US Department of State, 'Direct Commercial Sales authorizations for fiscal year 2010', Report pursuant to Section 655 of the Foreign Assistance Act, [n.d.], <http://www.pmddtc.state.gov/reports/655_intro.html>.

[20] See also Bromley, M., 'The financial value of states' arms exports, 2000–2009', *SIPRI Yearbook 2011*, pp. 306–307.

[21] Council Common Position 2008/944/CFSP of 8 Dec. 2008 defining common rules governing control of exports of military technology and equipment, *Official Journal of the European Union*, L335, 13 Dec. 2008

category—down from 19 states for the 11th annual report.[22] Several states— including France, Germany and the UK, the EU's three largest arms exporters—continue to have difficulties collecting and submitting data on actual arms exports disaggregated by EU Common Military List category.[23] Poland—another state that does not submit data on actual exports—noted that one way to generate data on actual arms exports would be to require companies to report on the use of the export licences that they have been issued.[24]

[22] Council of the European Union, Thirteenth Annual Report according to Article 8(2) of Council Common Position 2008/944/CFSP defining common rules governing control of exports of military technology and equipment, *Official Journal of the European Union*, C382, 30 Dec. 2011; Council of the European Union, Twelfth Annual Report according to Article 8(2) of Council Common Position 2008/944/CFSP defining common rules governing control of exports of military technology and equipment, *Official Journal of the European Union*, C9, 13 Jan. 2011; and Council of the European Union, Eleventh Annual Report according to Article 8(2) of Council Common Position 2008/944/CFSP defining common rules governing control of exports of military technology and equipment, *Official Journal of the European Union*, C265, 6 Nov. 2010.

[23] Weber and Bromley (note 11).

[24] Polish Ministry of Foreign Affairs, *Report for 2010* (note 13), p. 15.

Table 6.9. States participating in international, regional and national reporting mechanisms on arms transfers, 2009–11

An x denotes that the state published or submitted a report at least once in the period 2009–11. In the cases of UNROCA and the OAS, 'nil' indicates a nil report. In the case of the EU, an asterisk, '*', denotes a complete data set (see note c below).

| State | UNROCA | | Regional reports | | National reports | |
	Exports or imports	Background information on SALW	EU[a]	OAS[b]	Export licences[c]	Arms exports[d]
Albania	x (nil)	x	–	–	x	–
Andorra	x (nil)	x	–	–	–	–
Antigua and Barbuda	x (nil)	x (nil)	–	–	–	–
Argentina	x	x (nil)	–	–	–	–
Armenia	x (nil)	x	–	–	–	–
Australia	x	x	–	–	–	–
Austria	x	x	x*	–	x	x
Azerbaijan	x	–	–	–	–	–
Bangladesh	x	x	–	–	–	–
Belarus[e]	x	–	–	–	–	–
Belgium	x	x	x	–	x[f]	–
Belize	x (nil)	–	–	–	–	–
Bhutan	x (nil)	–	–	–	–	–
Bolivia	x (nil)	x	–	x (nil)	–	–
Bosnia and Herzegovina	x	x	–	–	x	–
Brazil	x	–	–	x	–	–
Bulgaria	x	x	x*	–	x	x
Burundi	x (nil)	–	–	–	–	–
Cambodia	x (nil)	–	–	–	–	–
Canada	x	x	–	–	–	x
Chile	x	x	–	x	–	–
China	x	–	–	–	–	–
Colombia	x	x	–	–	–	–
Comoros	x (nil)	x (nil)	–	–	–	–
Cook Islands	x (nil)	–	–	–	–	–
Costa Rica	x (nil)	–	–	–	–	–
Croatia	x	x	–	–	x	x
Cyprus	x	x (nil)	x*	–	–	–
Czech Republic	x	x	x*	–	x	x
Denmark	x	x	x	–	x	–
Dominican Republic	x	–	–	–	–	–
Ecuador	x	–	–	x	–	–
El Salvador	x (nil)	x (nil)	–	x (nil)	–	–
Estonia	x	–	x*	–	x	–
Finland	x	–	x*	–	x	x
France	x	x	x	–	x	x
Germany	x	x	x	–	x	x
Greece	x	x	x*	–	–	–
Grenada	x (nil)	x	–	–	–	–
Guatemala	–	–	–	x (nil)	–	–
Guyana	x (nil)	x	–	–	–	–

State	UNROCA Exports or imports	UNROCA Background information on SALW	Regional reports EU[a]	Regional reports OAS[b]	National reports Export licences[c]	National reports Arms exports[d]
Hungary	x	x	x*	–	x	x
Iceland	x (nil)	x	–	–	–	–
India	x	–	–	–	–	–
Indonesia	x	x	–	–	–	–
Ireland	x	x	x*	–	x	–
Israel	x	–	–	–	–	–
Italy	x	x	x	–	x	x
Japan	x	x (nil)[g]	–	–	–	–
Kazakhstan	x	x	–	–	–	–
Korea, South	x	x	–	–	–	–
Kyrgyzstan	x (nil)	–	–	–	–	–
Laos	x (nil)	–	–	–	–	–
Latvia	x	x	x*	–	–	–
Lebanon	x (nil)	x (nil)	–	–	–	–
Liechtenstein	x (nil)	x	–	–	–	–
Lithuania	x	x	x*	–	–	–
Luxembourg	–	–	x*	–	–	–
Malaysia	x	–	–	–	–	–
Macedonia, FYR	x (nil)	x	–	–	–	–
Malta	x (nil)	x (nil)	x*	–	–	–
Mauritius	x (nil)	–	–	–	–	–
Mexico	x	x	–	x (nil)	–	–
Moldova	x (nil)	x	–	–	–	–
Monaco	x (nil)	–	–	–	–	–
Mongolia	x (nil)	x	–	–	–	–
Montenegro	x	x	–	–	x	x
Nauru	x (nil)	–	–	–	–	–
Netherlands	x	x	x*	–	x	–
New Zealand	x	x	–	–	–	–
Norway	x	x	–	–	–	x
Pakistan	x	–	–	–	–	–
Palau	x (nil)	–	–	–	–	–
Panama	x (nil)	x	–	–	–	–
Peru	x	x	–	x	–	–
Philippines	x (nil)	x	–	–	–	–
Poland	x	x	x	–	x	–
Portugal	x	x	x*	–	x	x
Romania	x	x	x*	–	x	x
Russia	x	–	–	–	–	–
Saint Vincent and the Grenadines	x (nil)	x	–	–	–	–
Samoa	x (nil)	–	–	–	–	–
San Marino	x (nil)	x	–	–	–	–
Serbia	x	x	–	–	x	x
Seychelles	x (nil)	–	–	–	–	–
Singapore	x	–	–	–	–	–
Slovakia	x	x	x*	–	x	x

State	UNROCA		Regional reports		National reports	
	Exports or imports	Background information on SALW	EU[a]	OAS[b]	Export licences[c]	Arms exports[d]
Slovenia	x	x	x*	–	x	x
Solomon Islands	x (nil)	–	–	–	–	–
South Africa	x	–	–	–	–	x
Spain	x	x	x*	–	x	x
Suriname	x (nil)	–	–	–	–	–
Swaziland	x (nil)	x (nil)	–	–	–	–
Sweden	x	x[h]	x	–	x	x
Switzerland	x	x	–	–	–	x
Tajikistan	x (nil)	–	–	–	–	–
Thailand	x	x	–	–	–	–
Trinidad and Tobago	x (nil)	x (nil)	–	–	–	–
Tunisia	x (nil)	–	–	–	–	–
Turkey	x	x	–	–	–	–
Turkmenistan	x (nil)	–	–	–	–	–
Ukraine	x	x	–	–	–	x
United Kingdom	x	x	x	–	x	–
United States	x	–	–	–	x	x
Uruguay	x (nil)	–	–	–	–	–
Viet Nam	x (nil)	–	–	–	–	–
Total: 106 states	**104** **(43 nil)**	**68** **(10 nil)**	**27** **(19*)**	**8** **(4 nil)**	**27**	**23**

EU = European Union; OAS = Organization of American States; SALW = small arms and light weapons; UNROCA = United Nations Register of Conventional Arms.

[a] The EU Common Position defining common rules governing the control of exports of military technology and equipment requires EU member states to exchange data on the financial values of their export licence approvals and actual exports along with information on their denials of arms export licences. This data is published in an annual report. A country is marked as providing a complete data set to the EU annual report if it provided data on the financial value of both arms export licences and actual arms exports, broken down by both destination and EU Military List category.

[b] The 1999 Inter-American Convention on Transparency in Conventional Weapons Acquisitions (OAS Transparency Convention) was modelled on UNROCA. It requires the governments of states parties to submit annual reports on all imports and exports of the 7 UNROCA categories of major conventional weapons.

[c] A country is marked as providing information on arms export licences in its national report if it identifies the destinations for which arms export licences have been granted.

[d] A country is marked as providing information on arms exports in its national report if it identifies the destinations to which arms have been exported.

[e] In May 2009 Belarus published a report on its export controls and arms exports in 2008, but this report does not provide information on export licences, licence denials, etc.

[f] Since 2003 the 3 regional governments of Belgium (Brussels, Flanders and Wallonia) have been responsible for issuing export licences. Each region produces its own report on arms exports, each of which contains more detail than the Belgian national report.

[g] Japan submitted background information to UNROCA on the procurement of SALW through national production in 2009 and 2010.

[h] Sweden did not submit information on the number of SALW imported and exported in 2009 and 2010, only the categories of weapon systems and the origin or destination.

Sources: UNROCA database, <http://www.un-register.org/>; Council of the European Union, 11th–13th annual reports according to Article 8(2) of Council Common Position 2008/944/ CFSP defining common rules governing control of exports of military technology and equipment, <http://www.consilium.europa.eu/eeas/foreign-policy/non-proliferation,-disarma ment-and-export-control-/security-related-export-controls-ii>; Organization of American States, Catalogue of Member States Reports Presented in Compliance with General Assembly Resolutions on Hemispheric Security Issues, <http://www.apps.oas.org/cshdocs/>; and national reports collected at <http://www.sipri.org/research/armaments/transfers/trans parency/national_reports>.

VI. The financial value of states' arms exports, 2001–10

MARK BROMLEY

Table 6.10 presents official data on the financial value of states' arms exports in the years 2001–10. The countries included in the table are those that provide official data on the financial value of 'arms exports', 'licences for arms exports' or 'arms export agreements' for at least 6 of the 10 years and for which the average of the values given exceeds $10 million.

In all cases, the stated data coverage reflects the language used in the official publication from which the data has been extracted. National practices in this area vary, but 'arms exports' generally refers to the financial value of arms actually exported, 'licences for arms exports' generally refers to the financial value of licences for arms exports issued by the national export licensing authority, and 'arms export agreements' refers to the financial value of agreements signed for arms exports. The arms export data for the different states in table 6.10 is not necessarily comparable and may be based on significantly different definitions and methodologies.

Conversion to constant (2010) US dollars is made using the market exchange rates of the reporting year and the US consumer price index (CPI).

Table 6.10. The financial value of states' arms exports according to national government and industry sources, 2001–10

Figures are in US$ m. at constant (2010) prices. Years are calendar years, unless otherwise stated.

State	2001	2002	2003	2004	2005	2006	2007	2008	2009	2010	Stated data coverage
Austria	..	50	155	6	157	197	178	312	491	494	Arms exports
Belgium	425	267	329	23	355	415	1 985	1 403	3 177	2 342	Arms export licences
Bosnia and Herzegovina	936	1 307	891	780	355	1 193	1 295	1 981	1 556	1 328	Arms export licences
Brazil	..	..	..	50	89	68	55	86	66	..	Arms export licences
Bulgaria	357	202	58	329	318	381	168	223	205	342	Arms exports
Canada	471	524	613	571	443	596	544	705	446	392	Arms export licences[a]
Czech Republic	67	88	111	129	297	343	319	530	482	287	Arms exports[a]
Denmark	..	..	142	178	122	126	250	282	247	..	Arms exports
Finland	85	129	107	145	168	247	687	315	551	597	Arms export licences
France	44	62	66	60	124	176	282	242	356	498	Arms export licences
Germany	41	67	136	470	143	72	108	138	123	78	Arms exports
Greece	3 489	5 054	5 746	10 209	5 296	5 474	6 535	4 707	5 261	5 010	Arms export licences
Hungary	4 454	4 284	5 644	4 846	5 713	7 808	8 147	9 768	11 527	6 778	Arms exports
India	404	363	1 783	1 618	2 263	1 864	2 173	2 117	1 891	2 806	Arms export licences
Ireland	4 061	3 717	6 507	5 457	5 854	5 684	5 280	8 587	7 121	6 296	Arms export licences
Israel	56	59	150	22	40	119	47	71	321	391	Arms exports
Italy	..	..	15	13	17	22	24	22	24	25	Arms export licences[c]
Korea, South	..	..	66	57	44	84	138	177	179	183	Arms export licences
Lithuania	60	28	112	81	65	102	87	200	70	32	Arms export licences
	611	41	47	39	42	62	47	46	64	..	Arms export licences[c]
	3 102	4 878	3 556	4 271	3 908	5 300	5 889	6 407	7 013	7 200	Arms export agreements
	611	556	843	688	1 154	1 316	1 824	2 636	3 113	816	Arms exports
	951	1 050	1 715	2 136	1 890	2 974	6 828	8 398	9 450	4 306	Arms export licences
	246	170	284	485	290	270	888	1 043	1 189	1 190	Arms exports
	–	16	..	4	7	11	91	70	112	30	Arms export licences

Country	Category										
Netherlands	Arms exports	..	..	..	..	947	1 096	1 258	742	801	895
	Arms export licences	717	513	1 540	894	1 632	1 527	1 032	1 866	1 857	1 209
Norway	Arms exports	219	349	506	345	426	492	574	699	734	592
Poland	Arms export licences	..	..	245	377	403	373	413	546	1 964	605
Portugal	Arms exports	12	7	33	17	10	1	..	105	23	26
	Arms export licences	21	..	41	24	17	1	39	113	40	28
Romania	Arms exports	31	53	82	48	51	108	88	123	138	163
	Arms export licences	42	..	..	..	111	119	178	177	233	201
Russia	Arms exports	4 563	5 843	6 638	6 673	6 840	7 031	7 782	8 457	8 639	10 000
Slovakia	Arms exports	..	..	..	29	29	43	53	56	62	20
	Arms export licences	..	..	51	93	69	87	107	105	151	77
South Africa	Arms export licences	248	295	485	489	..	463	597	723	937	1 138
Spain	Arms exports	255	314	512	582	582	1 147	1 344	1 386	1 902	1 494
	Arms export licences	376	646	357	631	1 708	1 759	2 824	3 747	4 508	2 964
Sweden	Arms exports	365	428	950	1 145	1 289	1 521	1 494	1 951	1 801	1 907
	Arms export licences	2 849	732	1 322	1 020	2 263	2 204	1 063	1 476	1 474	1 835
Switzerland	Arms exports	188	216	334	373	231	343	407	675	680	614
Turkey	Arms exports	165	301	392	226	376	381	442	583	681	634
Ukraine	Arms exports	616	606	593	..	..	..	736	810	813	957
United Kingdom	Arms exports[d]	7 474	7 486	8 796	10 911	9 190	9 348	11 519	..	..	..
	Arms export orders[d]	7 375	9 159	9 448	9 609	8 098	11 000	20 309	8 112	11 481	9 007
United States	Arms export licences	..	3 647	6 005	4 264	4 188	3 235	1 888	3 658	4 888	3 757
	Arms exports	11 253	11 812	12 855	13 408	13 148	13 326	12 944	12 075	14 540	12 189
	Arms export agreements	13 965	15 655	16 934	14 286	14 062	16 731	25 129	37 186	22 640	21 255

[a] These figures exclude exports to the USA.

[b] These figures cover only exports of 'war weapons' as defined by German national legislation.

[c] Figures for India for 2001–2008 are for the period 1 Apr.–31 Mar. The figure for 2009 covers the period 1 Apr.–31 Dec. 2009.

[d] These figures cover exports of defence equipment and additional aerospace equipment and services.

Sources: Published information or direct communication with governments or official industry bodies. For a full list of sources and all available financial data on arms exports see <http://www.sipri.org/research/armaments/transfers/measuring/financial_values>.

7. World nuclear forces

Overview

At the start of 2012 eight states possessed approximately 4400 operational nuclear weapons. Nearly 2000 of these are kept in a state of high operational alert. If all nuclear warheads are counted—operational warheads, spares, those in both active and inactive storage, and intact warheads scheduled for dismantlement—the United States, Russia, the United Kingdom, France, China, India, Pakistan and Israel together possess a total of approximately 19 000 nuclear weapons (see table 7.1).

All five legally recognized nuclear weapon states, as defined by the 1968 Treaty on the Non-Proliferation of Nuclear Weapons (Non-Proliferation Treaty, NPT)—China, France, Russia, the UK and the USA—appear determined to remain nuclear powers for the indefinite future. Russia and the USA have major modernization programmes under way for nuclear delivery systems, warheads and production facilities (see sections I and II in this chapter). At the same time, they continue to reduce their nuclear forces through the implementation of the bilateral 2010 New START treaty, which entered into force in 2011, as well as through unilateral force reductions. Since Russia and the USA possess by far the two largest nuclear weapon arsenals, one result has been that the total number of nuclear weapons in the world has been declining. The nuclear arsenals of the other three legally recognized nuclear weapon states are considerably smaller, but all are either deploying new weapons or have announced their intention to do so (see sections III–V). China is the only legally recognized nuclear weapon state that appears to be expanding the size of its nuclear forces.

The availability of reliable information about the nuclear weapon states' arsenals varies considerably. France, the UK and the USA have recently disclosed important information about their nuclear capabilities. In contrast, transparency in Russia has decreased as a result of its decision not to publicly release detailed data about its strategic nuclear forces under New START, even though it shares the information with the USA. China remains highly non-transparent as part of its long-standing deterrence strategy, and little information is publicly available about its nuclear forces and weapon production complex.

Reliable information on the operational status of the nuclear arsenals and capabilities of the three states that have never been party to the NPT—India, Israel and Pakistan—is especially difficult to find. In the absence of official declarations, the available information is often contradictory or incorrect. India and Pakistan are expanding their nuclear strike capabilities, while Israel appears to be waiting to see how the situation in Iran develops (see

Table 7.1. World nuclear forces, January 2012

All figures are approximate.

Country	Year of first nuclear test	Deployed warheads[a]	Other warheads[b]	Total inventory
United States	1945	2 150[c]	5 850	~8 000[d]
Russia	1949	1 800[e]	8 200[f]	~10 000[g]
United Kingdom	1952	160	65	225
France	1960	290	10	~300
China	1964	..	200[h]	~240
India	1974	..	80–100[h]	80–100
Pakistan	1998	..	90–110[h]	90–110
Israel	..	..	~80[h]	~80
North Korea	2006	..	..	?[i]
Total		**~4 400**	**~14 600**	**~19 000**

[a] 'Deployed' means warheads placed on missiles or located on bases with operational forces.

[b] These are warheads in reserve, awaiting dismantlement or that require some preparation (e.g. assembly or loading on launchers) before they become fully operationally available.

[c] In addition to strategic warheads, this figure includes c. 200 non-strategic (tactical) nuclear weapons deployed in Europe.

[d] The US Department of Defense nuclear stockpile contains c. 4900 warheads. Another c. 3100 retired warheads are scheduled to be dismantled by 2022.

[e] These are warheads earmarked for delivery by deployed strategic launchers (intercontinental ballistic missiles, submarine-launched ballistic missiles and long-range bombers).

[f] This figure up to 4000 non-strategic (tactical) nuclear weapons for use by short-range naval, air force and air defence forces. In 2010 the Russian Government declared that all tactical nuclear weapons were in storage and not deployed.

[g] This includes a military stockpile of c. 4500 nuclear warheads and another c. 5500 retired warheads await dismantlement.

[h] The nuclear stockpiles of China, India, Pakistan and Israel are not thought to be fully deployed.

[i] North Korea conducted nuclear test explosions in 2006 and 2009, but there is no public information to verify that it possesses operational nuclear weapons.

sections VI–VIII). A ninth state—the Democratic People's Republic of Korea (DPRK, or North Korea)—has demonstrated a military nuclear capability. However, there is no public information to verify that it possesses operational nuclear weapons (see section IX).

The raw material for nuclear weapons is fissile material, either highly enriched uranium (HEU) or separated plutonium. The five nuclear weapon states have produced both HEU and plutonium. India, Israel and North Korea have produced mainly plutonium, and Pakistan mainly HEU for weapons (see section X).

The figures presented on nuclear forces in this chapter are estimates based on public information and contain some uncertainties, as reflected in the notes to the tables.

SHANNON N. KILE

I. US nuclear forces

SHANNON N. KILE, PHILLIP SCHELL AND HANS M. KRISTENSEN

As of January 2012 the United States maintained an estimated arsenal of approximately 2150 operational nuclear warheads, consisting of roughly 1950 strategic and 200 non-strategic warheads (see table 7.2). In addition to this operational arsenal, about 2750 warheads are held in reserve, for a total stockpile of approximately 4900 warheads. Another 3100 retired warheads are awaiting dismantlement for a total inventory of roughly 8000 warheads.

The operational force level is comparable to the estimate presented in *SIPRI Yearbook 2011.*[1] The slight reduction in the total stockpile is due to the ongoing retirement of excess W76 warheads.

The USA has released the full unclassified data for its strategic nuclear forces pursuant to implementation of the 2010 Russian–US Treaty on Measures for the Further Reduction and Limitation of Strategic Offensive Arms (New START), including a breakdown of deployed and non-deployed missiles and bombers at individual bases as well as the warheads attributed to them.[2] As of 1 September 2011, the USA deployed a total of 697 land- and sea-based ballistic missiles and 125 heavy bombers; another 485 non-deployed missiles and 25 bombers were in storage. Combined, the deployed forces were attributed a total of 1790 warheads. Since each of the deployed bombers is only attributed 1 warhead, the ballistic missiles therefore carried 1665 warheads.[3]

The USA will only have to offload 100 additional warheads over the next seven years to meet the New START limit by February 2018. However, it will have to dismantle 243 launchers to meet the limit of no more than 700 deployed and 100 non-deployed launchers.

Nuclear modernization

In parallel with implementing the modest nuclear force reductions under New START, the USA plans to modernize nuclear delivery vehicles, warheads and warhead production facilities. Over the next decade, as much as

---

[1] Kile, S. N. et al., 'World nuclear forces', *SIPRI Yearbook 2011*, pp. 319–53.

[2] US Department of State, Bureau of Arms Control, Verification and Compliance, 'New START Treaty aggregate numbers of strategic offensive arms', Fact sheet, 1 Dec. 2011, <http://www.state.gov/t/avc/rls/178058.htm>. For a summary and other details of New START see annex A in this volume. On developments in 2011 see chapter 8, section I, in this volume.

[3] For analysis of the US unclassified New START data see Kristensen, H., 'US releases full New START data', FAS Strategic Security Blog, Federation of American Scientists, 9 Dec. 2011, <http://www.fas.org/blog/ssp/2011/12/newstartnumbers.php>.

Table 7.2. US nuclear forces, January 2012

Type	Designation	No. deployed[a]	Year first deployed	Range (km)[b]	Warheads x yield	No. of warheads
Strategic forces						~1 950
Bombers		*111/60*				*300*
B-52H	Stratofortress	91/44	1961	16 000	ALCM 5–150 kt	200[c]
B-2	Spirit	20/16	1994	11 000	B61-7, -11, B83-1 bombs	100[d]
ICBMs		*714/500*				*500[e]*
LGM-30G	Minuteman III					
	Mk-12A	250	1979	13 000	1–3 x 335 kt	250
	Mk-21 SERV	250	2006	13 000	1 x 300 kt	250
SSBNs/SLBMs[f]		*410/288*				*1 152*
UGM-133A	Trident II (D5)[g]					
	Mk-4	..	1992	>7 400	4 x 100 kt	468
	Mk-4A	..	2008	>7 400	4 x 100 kt	300
	Mk-5	..	1990	>7 400	4 x 475 kt	384
Non-strategic forces						**200**
B61-3, -4 bombs		..	1979	..	0.3–170 kt	200[h]
RGM/UGM-109A/TLAM/N		(0)	1984	2 500	1 x 5–150 kt	(0)[i]
Total deployed warheads						~2 150[j]

.. = not available or not applicable; ( ) = uncertain figure; ALCM = air-launched cruise missile; ICBM = intercontinental ballistic missile; kt = kiloton; SERV = security-enhanced re-entry vehicle; SLBM = submarine-launched ballistic missile; SLCM = sea-launched cruise missile; SSBN = nuclear-powered ballistic missile submarine.

[a] The first figure in the 'No. deployed' column is the total number in the inventory, including those for training, test and reserve. The second figure is the number of these that are operational delivery vehicles assigned for nuclear missions. It is not calculated according to New START's counting rules and so differs from the treaty data.

[b] Aircraft range is for illustrative purposes only; actual mission range will vary according to flight profile and weapon loading.

[c] The B-52H can also deliver B61-7 and B83-1 gravity bombs, but the aircraft serves mainly as a carrier of ALCMs. The total ALCM inventory has been reduced to 528, of which an estimated 200 are deployed. Under New START, each nuclear bomber is only attributed 1 weapon although many more may be stored at bomber bases.

[d] Operational gravity bombs are only counted for the B-2A bomber. The B-52H can also deliver bombs, but its nuclear mission is thought to be focused on ALCMs since the bomber is not capable of penetrating modern air defence systems.

[e] The 2010 Nuclear Posture Review (NPR) decided to download each ICBM to carry a single warhead in the near future and also to retain an upload capability to re-MIRV (i.e. fit with a multiple independently targetable re-entry vehicle, MIRV) the W78 portion of the force if necessary. The download is scheduled for 2013–17.

[f] Of 14 SSBNs, 2 or more are normally undergoing overhaul at any given time. Their missiles and warheads are not included in the deployed total.

[g] Although D5 missiles were counted under START as carrying 8 warheads each, the US Navy is estimated to have downloaded each missile to an average of 4–5 warheads to meet the SORT-mandated warhead ceiling. Delivery of the W76-1 warhead began in Oct. 2008.

h Since 2001 the number of B61 bombs deployed in Europe has been unilaterally reduced by almost two-thirds from 480 to *c*. 180. Additional warheads remain in reserve.

i The Tomahawk Land Attack Cruise Missile/Nuclear (TLAM/N) sea-launched cruise missile has been retired in accordance with the 2010 NPR.

j Including the additional *c*. 2750 warheads in reserve, the total stockpile is *c*. 4900 warheads. Another *c*. 3100 warheads await dismantlement for a total inventory of *c*. 8000 warheads. A further *c*. 15 000 plutonium pits are stored at the Pantex Plant in Texas.

Sources: US Department of Defense, various budget reports and press releases; US Department of Energy, various budget reports and plans; US Department of Defense, various documents obtained under the Freedom of Information Act; US Air Force, US Navy and US Department of Energy, personal communication; 'Nuclear notebook', *Bulletin of the Atomic Scientists*, various issues; and authors' estimates.

$214 billion will be spent on designing a new class of ballistic missile submarines and a new dual-role (nuclear and conventional) long-range bomber; studying options for the next-generation land-based intercontinental ballistic missile; deploying a new nuclear-capable combat aircraft; producing enhanced or modernized nuclear warheads; and building new nuclear weapon production facilities.

All existing US warhead types are scheduled to undergo extensive life-extension and modernization programmes over the next decades. Full-scale production of approximately 1200 W76-1 warheads for the Trident II (D5) submarine-launched ballistic missile (SLBM) is well under way, providing the nuclear-powered ballistic missile submarine (SSBN) fleet with improved targeting capabilities. Production of the B61-12—a consolidation of the B61-3/4/7/10 bombs—is scheduled to follow in 2017–21.

The 2010 Nuclear Posture Review (NPR) of the US Department of Defense (DOD) pledged that the USA 'will not develop new nuclear warheads' but consider the 'full range' of life-extension programme options, including 'refurbishment of existing warheads, reuse of nuclear components from different warheads, and replacement of nuclear components'.[4] This was intended to preclude resumption of nuclear explosive testing and enable US adherence to the 1996 Comprehensive Nuclear-Test-Ban Treaty (CTBT). The NPR also decided that any life-extension programme 'will use only nuclear components based on previously tested designs, and will not support new military . . . capabilities'.[5] However, this will depend on how such capabilities are defined, since the installation of a new arming, fusing and firing unit, for example, can significantly enhance a warhead's ability to destroy certain types of target.[6]

[4] US Department of Defense (DOD), *Nuclear Posture Review Report* (DOD: Washington, DC, Apr. 2010), p. xiv.

[5] US Department of Defense (note 4).

[6] Kristensen, H. M., 'Small fuze—big effect', FAS Strategic Security Blog, Federation of American Scientists, 14 Mar. 2007, <http://www.fas.org/blog/ssp/2007/03/small_fuze_-_big_effect.php>.

Nuclear strategy and planning

In 2011 the administration of President Barack Obama ordered a review of US nuclear targeting plans and alert postures in preparation for future arms reduction agreements with Russia.[7] The initial inter-agency phase was completed in early 2012 and is expected to lead to changes in guidance on how the military should plan for the potential use of nuclear weapons, including the US strategic war plan—OPLAN (Operations Plan) 8010-08 Strategic Deterrence and Global Strike.[8]

To exercise that plan, Strategic Command (STRATCOM) in October 2011 conducted the worldwide Global Thunder nuclear exercise to test the readiness of intercontinental ballistic missiles (ICBMs), SLBMs, long-range bombers, refuelling aircraft, and command and control to carry out the strategic nuclear mission.

Land-based ballistic missiles

The USA has 450 Minuteman III ICBMs deployed in silos at three bases: Malmstrom Air Force Base (AFB) in Montana, Minot AFB in North Dakota, and F. E. Warren AFB in Wyoming. The New START data listed 448 deployed ICBMs as of 1 September 2011, with another 324 non-deployed ICBMs (266 Minuteman and 58 Peacekeeper missiles) held in storage.[9]

Most of the deployed ICBMs carry a single warhead, but a small number still have multiple warheads, thus yielding an estimated total of 500 warheads. The NPR decided to complete the process initiated during the administration of President George W. Bush to download all ICBMs to single warhead configuration.[10] The multiple independently targetable re-entry vehicle (MIRV) capability of the ICBMs will be retained, if necessary, with hundreds of warheads kept in storage.

A multi-year multi-billion dollar modernization programme is in its final phase to extend the service life of the Minuteman III missile to 2030.[11] The NPR decided that an initial study will begin in 2011–12 to consider a range

[7] US Mission Geneva, 'Remarks as prepared for delivery by Tom Donilon, National Security Advisor to the President, Carnegie International Nuclear Policy Conference', 29 Mar. 2011, <http://geneva.usmission.gov/2011/03/31/donilon-future-nuclear-policy/>.

[8] For a description of the review see Kristensen, H. M. and Norris, R., 'Reviewing nuclear guidance: putting Obama's words into action', Arms Control Today, vol. 41 (Nov. 2011), pp. 12–19.

[9] The non-deployed ICBMs are not intended for redeployment but for spares and missile flight tests. The Peacekeeper missiles were withdrawn from service in 2003–2005 and their silos will be destroyed.

[10] For a description of the warhead download programme see Kile, S. N., Fedchenko, V. and Kristensen, H. M., 'World nuclear forces, 2007', SIPRI Yearbook 2007, pp. 517–19.

[11] 'Missile envy: modernizing the US ICBM force', Defense Industry Daily, 14 Mar. 2011, <http://www.defenseindustrydaily.com/Missile-Envy-Modernizing-the-US-ICBM-Force-06059>.

of deployment options for a replacement missile. This will involve exploring 'new modes of ICBM basing that could enhance survivability and further reduce any incentives for prompt launch. Such an assessment will be part of the Department of Defense's study of possible replacements for the current ICBM force.'[12]

Ballistic missile submarines

The US Navy operates a fleet of 14 Ohio class SSBNs, each equipped with 24 Trident II (D5) SLBMs. Normally, 12 of the 14 SSBNs are considered operational with a total of 288 D5 SLBMs, each of which is estimated to carry an average of 4 warheads for a total of about 1152 warheads.[13] The number of operational submarines can fluctuate considerably, however, and the New START data shows that, as of 1 September 2011, only 10 of the 14 SSBNs were loaded, with a total of 249 SLBMs (3 SSBNs were empty and 1 partially loaded). By increasing the warhead loading of each missile, the fluctuation can be offset; the New START data indicates that the 10 'deployed' submarines carried a total of roughly 1200 warheads, or an average of 4–5 per missile.

On average, 64 per cent of the SSBNs (eight or nine boats) are at sea at any given time, with each boat normally conducting three 70–100-day patrols each year in an operational tempo comparable to that of the cold war. Up to five of those SSBNs are on 'hard alert', with 120 missiles carrying an estimated 540 warheads.

The US Navy is designing a new SSBN class to begin replacing the Ohio class SSBN in 2029. The new class, currently known as SSBN(X), will include 12 boats, each equipped to carry 16 Trident II (D5) SLBMs. The Congressional Budget Office (CBO) projected in 2010 that $100 billion will be required to develop and build the new class. In approving the defence budget for financial year 2012, the US Congress required the DOD to consider alternative SSBN design options to save money.[14]

Non-strategic nuclear weapons

As of January 2011 the USA retained approximately 760 non-strategic nuclear warheads. This included nearly 200 B61 gravity bombs deployed in Europe and 300 reserve bombs in the USA. Some 260 warheads for the Tomahawk Land-Attack Cruise Missile (TLAM/N) are scheduled to be retired in the near future.

---

[12] US Department of Defense (note 4), pp. 23, 27.
[13] The 48 missiles and 192 warheads for the two SSBNs in overhaul are not included in the total.
[14] On the US military budget see chapter 4, section III, in this volume.

The B61 bombs are deployed at six airbases in five European member states of the North Atlantic Treaty Organization (NATO): Belgium, Germany, Italy, the Netherlands and Turkey.[15] Approximately half of the bombs are earmarked for delivery by US F-15E and F-16 combat aircraft. The aircraft of non-nuclear weapon NATO countries that are assigned nuclear strike missions with US nuclear weapons include Belgian, Dutch and Turkish F-16 combat aircraft and German and Italian Tornados.

The NPR decided to equip a portion of the F-35 (Joint Strike Fighter) Block IV aircraft with nuclear capability but did not explicitly state that nuclear weapons should be deployed in Europe. The F-35s will carry the new B61-12, a modified version of the B61-3/4/10 and -7 bombs.

The B61-12 bomb will bring significant new military capabilities to Europe when deployment begins in 2018. It will use the nuclear explosive package of the B61-4, which has a maximum yield of approximately 50 kilotons. However, since the B61-12 also has to meet the mission requirements of the more powerful strategic B61-7 (360-kt maximum), it will be equipped with a $700 million guided tail kit to increase its accuracy. This will give the B61-12 an improved capability to destroy underground targets and enable strike planners to select lower yields for other targets to reduce collateral damage.[16]

---

[15] During a NATO briefing on the NPR in Sep. 2009, the US Principal Under Secretary of Defense for Policy, James Miller, mentioned '180 NATO sub-strategic warheads'. He may have been referring to the number of weapons listed in the US deployment authorization plan for Europe. The plan allows for a deviation of ±10% from the authorized warhead number. US Mission to NATO, 'PDUSDP Miller consults with allies on Nuclear Posture Review', Cable to US State Department, no. 09USNATO378, 4 Sep. 2009, <http://wikileaks.org/cable/2009/09/09USNATO378.html>, para. 17.

[16] For a description of the B61-12 and its implications see Kristensen, H. M., 'B61 LEP: increasing NATO nuclear capability and precision low-yield strikes', FAS Strategic Security Blog, Federation of American Scientists, 15 June 2011, <http://www.fas.org/blog/ssp/2011/06/b61-12.php>.

II. Russian nuclear forces

SHANNON N. KILE, VITALY FEDCHENKO, PHILLIP SCHELL AND
HANS M. KRISTENSEN

As of January 2012 Russia maintained an arsenal of approximately 1800 deployed nuclear warheads, all of which were either placed on long-range strategic missiles or located on bases with operational forces (see table 7.3). This represents a decrease from the figure published in *SIPRI Yearbook 2011* and reflects a recalculation based on New START aggregate data and adjustment of the bomber weapon count. In addition, Russia possessed a sizable stockpile of non-deployed nuclear warheads, consisting of approximately 2000 non-strategic (tactical) nuclear warheads held in storage, and another 5500 warheads that were retired and awaiting dismantlement.

In 2011 Russia and the United States completed two exchanges of data on the numbers, locations and technical characteristics of their strategic nuclear forces that are subject to New START.[1] As of 1 September 2011, Russia deployed a total of 1566 warheads attributed to 516 treaty-account-able strategic launchers—intercontinental ballistic missiles (ICBMs), sub-marine-launched ballistic missiles (SLBMs) and heavy bombers.[2] This meant that Russia was already close to meeting the New START ceiling of 1550 deployed warheads that is to be achieved by the 2018 deadline for implementing the treaty. Russia has refused to publicly release the full unclassified data exchanged under New START, including a breakdown of deployed and non-deployed missiles and bombers at individual bases as well as the warheads attributed to them.

The modest arms reductions mandated by New START codified existing trends in Russian strategic forces. These forces have continued to decline as Soviet-era missiles and bombers have reached the end of their service lives. Because of technical and financial constraints, Russia has not intro-duced new or modernized delivery systems at nearly the same rate as it has retired the older systems.

The force reductions have been accompanied by a doctrinal shift away from the Soviet requirement of 'nuclear parity' with all potential adver-saries towards a posture of minimal deterrence vis-à-vis the USA. Russia's national security strategy, approved in 2009, states that Russia will

---

[1] On New START's provisions see chapter 8, section I, and annex A in this volume.

[2] See chapter 8, section I, table 8.2, in this volume. Under New START, each heavy bomber is counted as carrying only 1 warhead, even though the aircraft can carry larger payloads of nuclear-armed cruise missiles or nuclear gravity bombs. US State Department, Bureau of Arms Control, Verification and Compliance, 'New START Treaty aggregate numbers of strategic offensive arms', Fact sheet, 25 Oct. 2011, <http://www.state.gov/t/avc/rls/176096.htm>.

Table 7.3. Russian nuclear forces, January 2012

Type/Russian designation (NATO designation)	No. deployed	Year first deployed	Range (km)[a]	Warhead loading	No. of warheads[b]
Strategic offensive forces					~1 510/2 430
Bombers	72				72/820[c]
Tu-95MS6 (Bear-H6)	28	1981	6 500– 10 500	6 x AS-15A ALCMs, bombs	28/168
Tu-95MS16 (Bear-H16)	31	1981	6 500– 10 500	16 x AS-15A ALCMs, bombs	31/496
Tu-160 (Blackjack)	13	1987	10 500– 13 200	12 x AS-15B ALCMs or AS-16 SRAMs, bombs	13/156
ICBMs	322				1 087
RS-20V (SS-18 Satan)	50	1992	11 000– 15 000	10 x 500–800 kt	500
RS-18 (SS-19 Stiletto)	48	1980	10 000	6 x 400 kt	288
RS-12M Topol (SS-25 Sickle)	135	1985	10 500	1 x 800 kt	135
RS-12M2 Topol-M (SS-27)	56	1997	10 500	1 x 800 kt	56
RS-12M1 Topol-M (SS-27)	18	2006	10 500	1 x (800 kt)	18
RS-24 Yars (SS-27 Mod 2)	15	2010	10 500	6 x (100? kt)	90
SLBMs	144				352/528[d]
RSM-50 Volna (SS-N-18 M1 Stingray)	48	1978	6 500	3 x 50 kt	96/144
RSM-54 Sineva (SS-N-23 Skiff)	96	1986/2007	9 000	4 x 100 kt	256/384
RSM-56 Bulava (SS-NX-32)	(32)	(2011)	>8 050	6 x (100? kt)	(192)
Non-strategic forces					(~2 000)*
ABM, air/coastal defence[e]	~1 100				(~425)*
53T6 (SH-08, Gazelle)	68	1986	30	1 x 10 kt	(68)*
S-300/S-400 (SA-10/12/20/21)	1 000	1980	..	1 x low kt	(~340)*
SSC-1B (Sepal)	34	1973	500	1 x 350	(~17)*
Air force weapons[f]	430				(~730)*
Tu-22M3 (Backfire-C)	150	1974	..	3 x ASM, bombs	(~450)*
Su-24M/M2 (Fencer-D)	264	1974	..	2 x bombs	
Su-34 (Fullback)	16	2006	..	2 x bombs	
Army weapons[g]	164				(~164)*
SS-21 Tochka (Scarab)	150	1981	120	(1 x 10 kt)	(~150)*
SS-26 Iskander (Stone)	24	2005	500	(1 x 10 kt)	(~24)*
Navy weapons					(~700)*
SLCM, ASW, SAM, depth bombers, torpedoes[h]					
Total deployed/assigned warheads					~1 800/4 430[i]

.. = not available or not applicable; ( ) = uncertain figure; ABM = anti-ballistic missiles; ALCM = air-launched cruise missile; ASM = air-to-surface missile; ASW = anti-submarine warfare; ICBM = intercontinental ballistic missile; kt = kiloton; NATO = North Atlantic Treaty Organization; SAM = surface-to-air missile; SLBM = submarine-launched ballistic missile; SLCM = sea-launched cruise missile; SRAM = short-range attack missile.

* According to the Russian Government, all non-strategic nuclear warheads are in storage, and are therefore not counted in the total number of deployed warheads. In addition to the 2000 warheads available for non-strategic nuclear-capable forces listed in the table, another 2000 warheads are estimated to have been retired and awaiting dismantlement.

a Aircraft range is for illustrative purposes only; actual mission range will vary according to flight profile and weapon loading.

b For strategic warhead estimates with two figures, the number on the left is the estimated count under New START for deployed warheads, while the number on the right is the total number of warheads estimated to be assigned to the delivery system. The table does not count so-called phantom aircraft, bombers that are not assigned a nuclear mission but still carry electronic equipment that make them accountable under the treaty.

c Of the 820 weapons that are estimated to be assigned to long-range bombers, only 300 are thought to be present at the bomber bases. The remaining weapons are thought to be stored at central storage facilities.

d Two or three of the SSBNs are in overhaul at any given time and do not carry their assigned nuclear missiles and warheads.

e The 51T6 (SH-11 Gorgon) is no longer operational. The S-300P (SA-10 Grumble, SA-12 Gargoyle), S-300V (SA-12A Gladiator, SA-12B Giant) and S-400 (SA-21 Growler) may have some capability against some ballistic missiles. Only about one-third of the 1000 deployed air-defence launchers are counted as having nuclear capability.

f These figures assume that only half of land-based strike aircraft have nuclear missions.

g According to NATO's International Military Staff, the Russian Zapad and Ladoga exercises held in Aug.–Sep. 2009 included 'missile launches, some of which may have simulated the use of tactical nuclear weapons'. Daalder, I., US Ambassador to NATO, 'NATO–Russia: NAC discusses Russian military exercises', Cable to SIPDIS, USNATO546, 23 Nov. 2009, <http://www. aftenposten.no/spesial/wikileaksdokumenter/article4028273.ece>.

h Surface ships are not believed to have been assigned nuclear torpedoes.

i The left-hand number is the number of warheads estimated to be counted by New START plus *c*. 300 bomber weapons that are thought to be present at bomber bases. Another 700 strategic warheads are estimated to be in reserve for SSBNs and bombers, and *c*. 2000 non-strategic warheads are thought to be in central storage. In addition, *c*. 5500 retired warheads are thought to be in queue for dismantlement for a total inventory of *c*. 10 000 warheads.

Sources: Russian Ministry of Defence press releases; US Department of State, START Treaty Memoranda of Understanding, 1990–July 2009; New START aggregate data releases, 2012; US Air Force, National Air and Space Intelligence Center (NASIC), *Ballistic and Cruise Missile Threat* (NASIC: Wright-Patterson Air Force Base, OH, June 2009); World News Connection, National Technical Information Service (NTIS), US Department of Commerce, various issues; Russian news media; Russian Strategic Nuclear Forces, <http://www.russianforces.org/>; International Institute for Strategic Studies, *The Military Balance 2010* (Routledge: London, 2010); Cochran, T. B. et al., *Nuclear Weapons Databook*, vol. 4, *Soviet Nuclear Weapons* (Harper & Row: New York, 1989); *Jane's Strategic Weapon Systems*, various issues; *Proceedings*, US Naval Institute, various issues; 'Nuclear notebook', *Bulletin of the Atomic Scientists*, various issues; and authors' estimates.

maintain parity with the USA's offensive strategic weapons in the most cost-effective way.[3] According to senior military experts, Russia's strategic nuclear forces can guarantee 'minimally sufficient' (*garantirovanno dostat-ochnyi*) deterrence under current arms control limitations but need quali-

---

[3] [National security strategy of the Russian Federation for the period until 2020], Presidential Decree no. 537, 12 May 2009, <http://www.scrf.gov.ru/documents/99.html>.

tative improvements to enhance their survivability for an assured second-strike capability and their ability to penetrate missile defences.[4]

Russia's strategic force modernization plans have prioritized the deployment of a new road-mobile ICBM and the development of a new silo-based heavy ICBM. Russia is also pressing ahead with the introduction into service of a new generation of strategic submarines and SLBMs, as well as the overhaul of its long-range bomber force.

Strategic bombers

Russia's Long-range Aviation Command includes 13 Tu-160, 31 Tu-95MS16 and 28 Tu-95MS6 bombers. In 2011 the command conducted 50 strategic bomber patrols, continuing the practice that was suspended in 1992 and resumed in 2007.[5] In order to maintain the pace of long-range patrols, Russia has initiated a programme to upgrade and extend the service life of its ageing heavy bomber force. However, Russia's strategic aviation units have reportedly experienced problems with overhaul and maintenance, which have precluded any increase in patrol activity. A shortage of aerial refuelling aircraft (Il-78), necessary for long-range missions, has also been reported.[6]

In 2011 the Tupolev Design Bureau continued to develop the new strategic bomber, known as the PAK DA (Advanced Aviation Complex for Long-Range Aviation). The current plans include building the first PAK DA prototype by 2020, and the aircraft is expected to enter service by 2030.[7]

Land-based ballistic missiles

As of January 2012 Russia's Strategic Rocket Forces (SRF) consisted of three missile armies, with 12 missile divisions, deploying a total of 322 ICBMs of different types.[8] The RS-20V (SS-18) and RS-18 (SS-19) liquid-fuelled, silo-based ICBMs date from the Soviet era and are expected

---

[4] Umnov, S., [Russia's SNF: building up ballistic missile defence penetration capacities], *Voenno-Promyshlennyi Kur'er*, 8–14 Mar. 2006; and Esin, V., [The United States: in pursuit of a global missile defence], *Voenno-Promyshlennyi Kur'er*, 25–31 Aug. 2010.

[5] President of Russia, 'Press statement and responses to media questions following the Peace Mission 2007 counterterrorism exercises and the Shanghai Cooperation Organisation Summit', 17 Aug. 2007, <http://archive.kremlin.ru/eng/speeches/2007/08/17/2033_type82915_141812.shtml>; and [Long-range aviation day is celebrated by the Air Force], ITAR-TASS, 23 Dec. 2011, <http://www.itar-tass.com/c9/304603.html>.

[6] Stukalin, A., 'Bears and Blackjacks are back: what's next?', *Moscow Defense Brief*, no. 4 (22), 2010.

[7] [Long-range aviation day is celebrated by the Air Force], ITAR-TASS, 23 Dec. 2011, <http://www.itar-tass.com/c9/304603.html>.

[8] [RVSN will keep three armies and 12 divisions until 2016], RIA Novosti, 6 May 2011, <http://ria.ru/defense_safety/20110506/371480435.html>.

to be taken out of service around 2020.[9] On 27 December 2011 an RS-18 was launched from the Baikonur space launch facility in Kazakhstan as part of a programme to extend the missiles' service life three times longer than originally planned.[10] In 2011 the Ministry of Defence announced that it had selected the Makeyev Design Bureau—traditionally a developer of SLBMs—to begin design and development work on a new silo-based heavy ICBM to replace the RS-20V and the RS-18.[11]

The solid-fuelled, road-mobile RS-12M Topol (SS-25) ICBM is undergoing a service-life extension programme. Based on the results of two test launches conducted in 2011, the SRF announced that the RS-12M missile would remain on combat duty until 2019. In 2011 two test launches were conducted as part of the service-life extension programme. Based on the results of the tests, the SRF announced that the service life of the RS-12M missile would be extended until 2019.[12] One of the tests, on 3 September 2011, involved trials of a 'prospective combat payload', which some experts interpreted as referring to missile defence penetration aids.[13]

The RS-12 Topol-M (SS-27) has been developed in both road-mobile (RS-12M1) and silo-based (RS-12M2) versions.[14] In 2010 the SRF abandoned production of the RS-12M1 in favour of a MIRVed variant, the RS-24 (SS-27 Mod 2), which can carry up to three warheads. The deployment of the first regiment, consisting of nine RS-24s, was completed in August 2011.[15] Another six RS-24 missiles were deployed in December 2011.[16]

Ballistic missile submarines and sea-launched ballistic missiles

As of January 2012 the Russian Navy operated a total of 10 nuclear-powered ballistic missile submarines (SSBNs), six of which were operation-

[9] Isby, D. C., 'Russia to develop new heavy ICBM', *Jane's Missiles and Rockets*, vol. 15, no. 5 (May 2011), p. 16.

[10] Russian Ministry of Defence, Information and Public Relations Service, [The RS-18 ICBM launched from Baikonur], 27 Dec. 2011, <http://www.function.mil.ru/news_page/country/more. htm?id=10865745@egNews>; and 'RS-18 ICBM to serve three times the planned operational life', *Jane's Missiles and Rockets*, vol. 15, no. 10 (Oct. 2011), p. 6.

[11] Litovkin, V., [The military is waiting for the 5th generation missiles], *Izvestiya*, 13 May 2011; and Kovalenko, D., [Against the BMD], *Vzglyad*, 16 Dec. 2011.

[12] Russian Ministry of Defence, Information and Public Relations Service, [A successful test launch of the RS-12M 'Topol' missile was conducted from Plesetsk], 2 Sep. 2011, <http://www. structure.mil.ru/structure/forces/strategic_rocket/news/more.htm?id=10679038@egNews>; and 'Topol ballistic missiles may stay in service until 2019', RIA Novosti, 28 Oct. 2011, <http://en.rian.ru/ mlitary_news/20111028/168206957.html>.

[13] 'Old Topol is tested with a new warhead', Russian Strategic Nuclear Forces Blog, 3 Sep. 2011, <http://russianforces.org/blog/2011/09/old_topol_is_tested_with_a_new.shtml>.

[14] Lennox, D. (ed.), *Jane's Strategic Weapon Systems* (IHS Global Limited: Coulsdon, 2011), p. 175.

[15] Richardson, D., 'Russia places first RS-24 Yars ICBM unit on combat alert', *Jane's Missiles and Rockets*, vol. 15, no. 10 (Oct. 2011), p. 6.

[16] Russian Ministry of Defence, Information and Public Relations Service, [Two more divisions will be equipped with the state-of-the-art 'Yars' missile complex], 19 Dec. 2011, <http://www. structure.mil.ru/structure/forces/strategic_rocket/news/more.htm?id=10854015@egNews>.

ally deployed. Three Delta III class (Project 667BDR Kalmar) submarines, each carrying 16 RSM-50 SLBMs, were assigned to the Pacific Fleet, and six Delta IV class (Project 667BDRM Delfin) submarines, each carrying 16 RSM-54 SLBMs, were assigned to the Northern Fleet. On 29 December 2011, one of the Delta IV Class SSBNs, the K-84 *Ekaterinburg*, caught fire in its floating dry dock during maintenance. The fire damage was not expected to be repaired before mid-2014.[17] As of January 2012, two other Delta IV class submarines were undergoing overhauls. In addition, one Typhoon class (Project 941 Akula) submarine was being kept for use as a test platform.[18]

Successful launches of the new R-29RMU2.1 'Liner' SLBM, a variant of the RSM-54 Sineva (SS-N-23 Skiff) SLBM, were conducted on 20 May by K-84 *Ekaterinburg* and on 29 September 2011 by K-114 *Tula*. The new missile reportedly can carry up to 10 warheads of different yields as well as missile defence countermeasures.[19]

Russia is pressing ahead with the introduction into service of a new class of SSBN, the Project 955 Borei. The lead boat in the class, the *Yurii Dolgorukii*, successfully finished sea trials in December 2011 and is expected to enter service in 2012. The second boat in the class, the *Aleksandr Nevskii*, will continue its trials in 2012.[20]

Each of the Borei class submarines will carry 16 SLBMs of a new type, the three-stage, solid-fuelled RSM-56 Bulava. Serious technical problems related to the poor quality of missile components led to an administrative reorganization of the Bulava's development programme in 2009–10. In 2011 the Russian Navy conducted four successful flight tests of the Bulava, including a salvo launch in the White Sea of two missiles on 23 December 2011.[21] After the successful salvo launch, the Bulava missile was officially approved for service with the Russian Navy.[22]

---

[17] There were conflicting reports about whether the submarine's reactors had been shut down and its ballistic missiles removed prior to the fire. Safronov-Jr., I., [The "Ekaterinburg" submarine is promised to be back in service by 2014], *Kommersant*, 13 Jan. 2012, <http://www.kommersant.ru/doc-y/1849693>.

[18] 'Russia set to keep Typhoon class nuclear subs until 2019—Navy', RIA Novosti, 7 May 2010, <http://en.rian.ru/mlitary_news/20100507/158917310.html>.

[19] 'Liner SLBM explained', Russian Strategic Nuclear Forces Blog, 4 Oct. 2011, <http://russianforces.org/blog/2011/10/liner_slbm_explained.shtml>; and Richardson, D., 'Liner SLBM completes its trials programme', *Jane's Missiles and Rockets*, vol. 15, no. 12 (Dec. 2011), p. 5.

[20] [The 'Yurii Dolgorukii' submarine is about to enter service with the Russian strategic nuclear Navy], ARMS-TASS, 11 Jan. 2012, <http://www.arms-tass.su/?page=article&aid=102458&cid=44>.

[21] 'Yuri Dolgoruky launches its first Bulava missile', *Jane's Missiles and Rockets*, vol. 15, no. 8 (Aug. 2011), p. 9; 'Russians practice submerged salvo launch of Bulava missile from *Yuri Dolgoruky*', *Jane's Missiles and Rockets*, vol. 16, no. 1 (Jan. 2012), p. 3; and Kramnik, I., 'Russia completes Bulava missile testing', Voice of Russia, 29 Dec. 2011, <http://english.ruvr.ru/2011/12/ 29/63127625.html>.

[22] 'Bulava missile completes flight tests, ready to deploy', RIA Novosti, 27 Dec. 2011, <http://en.rian.ru/mlitary_news/20111227/170516131.html>.

Non-strategic nuclear weapons

There is considerable uncertainty about the size and location of Russia's non-strategic nuclear inventory, which continues to be characterized by a high degree of secrecy and a lack of transparency. Estimates about the size of the Soviet inventory of non-strategic nuclear weapons in 1991 ranged from approximately 15 000 to 21 700.[23] Since the end of the cold war, Russia has significantly reduced its inventory of non-strategic nuclear weapons.[24] In November 2011 a senior US Department of Defense official testified before the US Congress that Russia possessed approximately 2000–4000 non-strategic nuclear weapons.[25] This number is somewhat lower than the '3000–5000 plus' range given during a NATO briefing on the USA's 2010 Nuclear Posture Review in September 2009.[26]

Based on an analysis of Russia's remaining nuclear-capable naval, air force and air defence delivery systems and their nominal warhead capacity, it is estimated here that Russia has available approximately 2000 non-strategic nuclear warheads for these systems.[27] Another 2000 warheads are estimated to have been retired and awaiting dismantlement.

[23] For an estimated range see Norris, R. S. and Arkin, W. M., 'Nuclear notebook: estimated Soviet nuclear stockpile (July 1991)', *Bulletin of the Atomic Scientists*, vol. 47, no. 6 (July/Aug. 1991), p. 48; and Arbatov, A., 'Deep cuts and de-alerting: a Russian perspective', ed. H. A. Feiveson, *The Nuclear Turning Point: A Blueprint for Deep Cuts and De-Alerting of Nuclear Weapons* (Brookings Institution Press: Washington, DC, 1999), p. 320.

[24] The Russian Government declared in 2010 that it had reduced the number of non-strategic nuclear weapons by approximately 75% since 1991. See 2010 NPT Review Conference, Delegation of the Russian Federation, 'Practical steps of the Russian Federation in the field of nuclear disarmament', Statement, New York, 3–28 May 2010, p. 8.

[25] Miller, J., Principal Deputy Under Secretary of Defense for Policy, Statement before the US House of Representatives, Armed Services Committee, 2 Nov. 2011, <http://armedservices.house.gov/index.cfm/2011/11/the-current-status-and-future-direction-for-u-s-nuclear-weapons-policy-and-posture>, p. 2.

[26] Kile, S. N. et al., 'World nuclear forces', *SIPRI Yearbook 2011*, p. 334; and US Mission to NATO, 'PDUSDP Miller consults with allies on Nuclear Posture Review', Cable to US State Department, no. 09USNATO378, 4 Sep. 2009, <http://wikileaks.org/cable/2009/09/09USNATO378.html>.

[27] Kristensen, H. M., *Non-Strategic Nuclear Weapons*, Federation of American Scientists (FAS) Special Report no. 3 (FAS: Washington, DC, May 2012), p. 52.

III. British nuclear forces

SHANNON N. KILE, PHILLIP SCHELL AND HANS M. KRISTENSEN

The United Kingdom's nuclear deterrent consists exclusively of a sea-based component: Vanguard class Trident nuclear-powered ballistic missile submarine (SSBNs), Trident II (D5) submarine-launched ballistic missiles (SLBMs) and associated warheads, and support infrastructure. The UK possesses an arsenal of about 160 operational nuclear warheads that are available for use by a fleet of four Trident SSBNs (see table 7.4). The UK leases the Trident II (D5) SLBMs from the US Navy under a system of 'mingled asset ownership'.

Each Vanguard class SSBN is equipped with 16 Trident II (D5) missiles carrying up to 48 warheads (i.e. up to 3 per missile). The warhead is similar to the US W76 warhead and has an explosive yield of about 100 kilotons. It is being upgraded with the US-produced arming, fusing and firing system for the Mk-4A re-entry vehicle. It is believed that a number of the D5 missiles are deployed with only one warhead, possibly with a reduced explosive yield, instead of three.[1] The reduced force-loading option reflects a decision by the Ministry of Defence (MOD) in 1998 to give a 'sub-strategic', or limited-strike, role to the Trident fleet aimed at enhancing the credibility of the British deterrent.[2]

In a posture known as Continuous at Sea Deterrence (CASD), one British SSBN is on patrol at all times.[3] While the second and third SSBNs can be put to sea rapidly, not enough missiles have been leased from the US Navy to simultaneously arm the fourth British submarine. Since the end of the cold war, the SSBN on patrol has been kept at a level of reduced readiness with its missiles de-targeted and a 'notice to fire' measured in days.

In the 2010 Strategic Defence and Security Review (SDR) the British Government made a commitment to retain a submarine-based nuclear deterrent force for the indefinite future. The MOD has plans to replace the four Vanguard class SSBNs, which will reach the end of their service lives from 2024. The new submarines will be based on the current Trident system and equipped with the modified Trident II (D5) SLBM developed under the US Navy's D5 Life Extension (LE) programme. As a cost-saving

---

[1] Quinlan, M., 'The future of United Kingdom nuclear weapons: shaping the debate', *International Affairs*, vol. 82, no. 4 (July 2006).

[2] British Ministry of Defence, *The Strategic Defence Review: Modern Forces for the Modern World*, Cm 3999 (The Stationery Office: Norwich, July 1998), para. 63. An addendum in 2002 extended the role of nuclear weapons to include deterring 'leaders of states of concern and terrorist organisations'. British Ministry of Defence, *The Strategic Defence Review: A New Chapter*, Cm 5566, vol. 1 (The Stationery Office: Norwich, July 2002), para. 21.

[3] British Ministry of Defence and British Foreign and Commonwealth Office, *The Future of the United Kingdom's Nuclear Deterrent*, Cm 6994 (The Stationery Office: Norwich, Dec. 2006), p. 27.

measure, they will have a smaller missile compartment, designed jointly with the US Navy, that will carry 12 launch tubes rather than the 16 carried by the Vanguard class submarines. The maximum number of nuclear warheads carried on each submarine will decrease from 48 to 40.[4]

In May 2011 the MOD announced the completion of the 'initial gate' phase for the replacement submarine programme. This involved decisions about the broad design parameters for the new SSBN, including the choice of reactor propulsion systems.[5] The SDR delayed the 'main gate' decision—when the detailed acquisition plans, design and number of submarines are to be finalized—until 2016. As a result, the first of the new generation of SSBNs is not scheduled to enter service until 2028. The service lives of the Vanguard submarines are to be further prolonged in accordance with the government's commitment to reliably sustain the CASD posture.

The 2010 SDR revealed plans for cutting the size of the British nuclear arsenal. The stockpile of operational nuclear warheads will be reduced from fewer than 160 at present to no more than 120. Likewise, the overall size of the nuclear stockpile, including non-deployed weapons, will decrease from the current 225 warheads to 'not more than 180 by the mid 2020s'.[6]

In announcing the results of the SDR, the British Government said it would defer a decision about whether to refurbish or replace the nuclear warhead carried on the Trident II (D5) SLBM until the next parliament (i.e. after May 2015).[7] However, in 2011 there were reports, based on a publication from the US Sandia National Laboratory, indicating that the Royal Navy has decided to procure the W76-1 warhead that is currently in production in the USA.[8] The warhead is an enhanced version of the US W76 warhead and will make Trident missiles more accurate and more effective against hardened targets.[9] Together with the modified D5LE SLBMs, the new warhead will extend the service life of the Trident missile system into the 2040s.

The UK has launched a long-term investment programme aimed at sustaining key skills and facilities at the Atomic Weapons Establishment at Aldermaston. In 2011 the MOD confirmed that it plans to build a new

[4] British Ministry of Defence, *Securing Britain in an Age of Uncertainty: The Strategic Defence and Security Review*, Cm 7948 (The Stationery Office: London, Oct. 2010), para. 3.11, p. 38.

[5] British Ministry of Defence (MOD), *The United Kingdom's Future Nuclear Deterrent: The Submarine Initial Gate Parliamentary Report* (MOD: London, May 2011), p. 5.

[6] British Ministry of Defence (note 4), para. 3.11, p. 39; and Norton-Taylor, R., 'Britain's nuclear arsenal is 225 warheads, reveals William Hague', *The Guardian*, 26 May 2010.

[7] British Ministry of Defence (note 4), para. 3.9, p. 39.

[8] Kristensen, H. M., 'British submarines to receive upgraded US nuclear warhead', FAS Strategic Security Blog, Federation of American Scientists, 1 Apr. 2011, <http://www.fas.org/blog/ssp/2011/04/britishw76-1.php>.

[9] Norton-Taylor, R., 'Trident more effective with US arming device, tests suggest', *The Guardian*, 6 Apr. 2011.

324 MILITARY SPENDING AND ARMAMENTS, 2011

Table 7.4. British nuclear forces, January 2012

Type	Designation	No. deployed	Year first deployed	Range (km)[a]	Warheads x yield	Warheads in stockpile
Submarine-launched ballistic missiles						
D5	Trident II	48	1994	>7 400	1–3 x 100 kilotons	225[b]

[a] Range is for illustrative purposes only; actual mission range will vary according to flight profile and weapon loading.

[b] Fewer than 160 warheads are operationally available, c. 144 to arm 48 missiles on 3 of 4 nuclear-powered ballistic missile submarines (SSBNs). Only 1 SSBN is on patrol at any time, with up to 48 warheads. In 2010 it was decided that the number of operational warheads will be reduced to a maximum of 120 within the next few years, of which 40 will be on patrol at any given time. The stockpile will be reduced to no more than 180 by the mid-2020s.

Sources: British Ministry of Defence, white papers, press releases and website, <http://www.mod.uk/>; British House of Commons, *Parliamentary Debates (Hansard)*, various issues; Norris, R. S. et al., *Nuclear Weapons Databook*, vol. 5, *British, French, and Chinese Nuclear Weapons* (Westview: Boulder, CO, 1994), p. 9; 'Nuclear notebook', *Bulletin of the Atomic Scientists*, various issues; and authors' estimate.

facility at Aldermaston to store and handle enriched uranium components for nuclear warheads and reactor fuel for nuclear-powered submarines. It is intended to replace an ageing facility built in the 1950s that does not meet modern safety design standards.[10]

The British–French nuclear cooperation agreement

On 2 November 2010 France and the UK signed an agreement for technical cooperation and the exchange of classified information in the areas of nuclear weapon safety, and security and stockpile certification. The agreement entered into force in July 2011 and entails the establishment of 'joint radiographic/hydrodynamics facilities', one in France and one in the UK, to conduct computer-based testing of nuclear weapon components to ensure their safety and reliability in the absence of explosive testing of nuclear weapons.[11] Both countries, however, emphasized that they will continue to maintain independent nuclear deterrent forces under the agreement.

[10] '£750m spend on AWE enriched uranium facility revealed', BBC News, 10 Oct. 2011, <http://www.bbc.co.uk/news/uk-england-berkshire-15189981>.

[11] Joint Anglo-French communiqué, Présidence de la République/Cabinet Office, 8 July 2011, <https://update.cabinetoffice.gov.uk/resource-library/joint-french-anglo-communiqué>; and Treaty between the United Kingdom of Great Britain and Northern Ireland and the French Republic relating to Joint Radiographic/Hydrodynamics Facilities, signed 2 Nov. 2010, Cm 7975 (The Stationery Office: Norwich, 10 Nov. 2010).

IV. French nuclear forces

SHANNON N. KILE, PHILLIP SCHELL AND HANS M. KRISTENSEN

France's nuclear forces consist of aircraft and nuclear-powered ballistic missile submarines (SSBNs), carrying a total of about 300 warheads (see table 7.5). The backbone of the French nuclear deterrent consists of four Triomphant class SSBNs. The newest boat in the class, *Le Terrible*, is equipped with 16 M51.1 submarine-launched ballistic missiles (SLBMs).[1] The M51.1 is a three-stage, solid-fuelled missile that can carry up to six TN-75 warheads. The other three Triomphant class SSBNs will be rearmed with the M51.1 by 2017, replacing the M45 SLBM.[2] The upgrade of *Le Vigilant* was expected to be completed in 2011, and those of *Le Triomphant* and *Le Téméraire* in 2012 and 2017, respectively.[3] An improved version of the M51.1, the M51.2, is designed to carry the new Tête Nucléaire Océanique (TNO, Oceanic Nuclear Warhead) with selectable yields of up to 150 kilotons, which is believed to be housed in a new re-entry vehicle and will replace the M51.1 after 2015.[4]

By the end of 2011 the aircraft component of the French nuclear forces consisted of two land- and one sea-based nuclear-capable aircraft squadrons, comprised of Mirage and Rafale combat aircraft.[5] The Mirage 2000N aircraft of the 3/4 Limousin Fighter Squadron will be replaced by Rafales in 2018. The aircraft are equipped with the Air-Sol Moyenne Portée–Améliorée (ASMP-A, medium-range air-to-surface–improved) missile.[6] The ASMP-A cruise missiles carry the Tête Nucléaire Aeroportée (TNA, Airborne Nuclear Warhead), which is a new thermonuclear warhead that is reported to have a selectable yield of 20 kt, 90 kt and 300 kt. A new TNO warhead with selectable yields up to 150 kt will become operational around 2015.[7]

---

[1] French Navy, '*Le Terrible* livré à la marine' [*Le Terrible* delivered to the navy], Press release, 4 Oct. 2010, <http://www.defense.gouv.fr/marine/actu-marine/le-terrible-livre-a-la-marine>.

[2] Richardson, D., 'France tests M51 SLBM under operational conditions', *Jane's Missiles and Rockets*, vol. 14, no. 9 (Sep. 2010), p. 6; and Richardson, D., 'M51 SLBM performs fourth test-flight', *Jane's Missiles and Rockets*, vol. 14, no. 3 (Mar. 2010), p. 3.

[3] Lennox, D. (ed.), *Jane's Strategic Weapon Systems*, no. 54 (IHS Global Limited: Coulsdon, 2011), p. 51.

[4] Lennox, ed. (note 3), p. 50.

[5] French Senate, *Avis présenté au nom de la commission des affaires étrangères, de la défense et des forces armées (1) sur le projet de loi de finances pour 2012*, vol. 6, *Défense: Equipement des forces* [Opinions submitted on behalf of the Committee on Foreign Affairs, Defence and Armed Forces (1) on the finance bill for 2012, vol. 6, Defence: Equipping the forces], no. 102 (French Senate: Paris, 17 Nov. 2011), chapter II, section I. B.

[6] French Ministry of Defense, 'Le missile ASMPA' [The ASMPA missile], 16 June 2011, <http://www.defense.gouv.fr/dga/equipement/dissuasion/le-missile-asmpa>.

[7] Lennox, ed. (note 3), p. 48.

Table 7.5. French nuclear forces, January 2012

Type	No. deployed	Year first deployed	Range (km)[a]	Warheads x yield	Warheads in stockpile
Land-based aircraft					
Mirage 2000N	~20	1988	2 750	1 x up to 300 kt TNA	~20
Rafale F3	~20	2010–11	2 000	1 x up to 300 kt TNA	~20
Carrier-based aircraft					
Rafale MK3	~10	2010–11	2 000	1 x up to 300 kt TNA	~10
Submarine-launched ballistic missiles[b]					
M45	32	1996	6 000[c]	4–6 x 100 kt TN-75	160[d]
M51.1	16	2010–11	6 000	4–6 x 100 kt TN-75	80
M51.2	0	(2015)	6 000	4–6 x TNO	0
Total					**~300[e]**

( ) = uncertain figure; kt = kiloton; TNA = Tête Nucléaire Aéroportée (Airborne Nuclear Warhead); TNO = Tête Nucléaire Océanique (Oceanic Nuclear Warhead).

[a] Aircraft range is for illustrative purposes only; actual mission range will vary according to flight profile and weapon loading.

[b] France transitioned to a posture of 4 SSBNs in the mid-1990s, which meant having enough SLBMs to equip 3 operational SSBNs, with the 4th being overhauled.

[c] The range of the M45 is listed as only 4000 km in a 2001 report from the French National Assembly's National Defence Commission.

[d] The missile upgrade that started with the *Le Vigilant* submarine does not affect its warheads, which will be fitted back to the new M51.1 missiles.

[e] France does not have a reserve but may have a small inventory of spare warheads for a total stockpile of *c.* 300 warheads.

Sources: Sarkozy, N., French President, Speech on defence and national security, Porte de Versailles, 17 June 2008, <http://www.elysee.fr/president/les-dossiers/defense/livre-blanc/paris-17-juin-2008/livre-blanc-sur-la-defense-et-la-securite.6651.html>; Sarkozy, N., French President, 'Presentation of SSBM "Le Terrible"', Speech, Cherbourg, 21 Mar. 2008, <https://pastel.diplomatie.gouv.fr/editorial/actual/ael2/bulletin.gb.asp?liste=20080331.gb.hml>; French Ministry of Defence, various publications, <http://www.defense.gouv.fr/>; French National Assembly, various defence bills; Norris, R. S. et al., *Nuclear Weapons Databook*, vol. 5, *British, French, and Chinese Nuclear Weapons* (Westview: Boulder, CO, 1994), p. 10; *Air Actualités*, various issues; *Aviation Week & Space Technology*, various issues; 'Nuclear notebook', *Bulletin of the Atomic Scientists*, various issues; and authors' estimates.

V. Chinese nuclear forces

SHANNON N. KILE, PHILLIP SCHELL AND HANS M. KRISTENSEN

China is gradually expanding its nuclear arsenal as part of a long-term modernization programme aimed at developing a more survivable force and strengthening its nuclear retaliatory capabilities. China's nuclear forces have long been the least transparent among the legally recognized nuclear weapon states. China is estimated to have an arsenal of approximately 200 operational nuclear weapons for delivery mainly by ballistic missiles (see table 7.6). A small number of gravity bombs are believed to be available for delivery by aircraft. Additional warheads may be in reserve, giving a total stockpile of about 240 warheads.

The Chinese Communist Party's Central Military Commission (CMC) maintains strict control over China's operational nuclear warheads through a centralized system managed by the Second Artillery of the People's Liberation Army (PLA). The Second Artillery's missile units appear to be organized into six geographically dispersed bases and one central storage facility.[1] It is believed that China stores its nuclear warheads in storage facilities separate from their delivery vehicles and not ready for immediate launch.[2]

In March 2011 the Chinese Government released the latest of its biennial defence white papers.[3] The document reiterated China's commitment to the policy of no-first-use of nuclear weapons and its intention to limit its nuclear capabilities to the minimum level required for national security. However, the white paper provided no information about the size or structure of China's nuclear forces.

China is estimated to possess the smallest inventories of military highly enriched uranium (HEU) and plutonium of the legally recognized nuclear weapon states (see section X below). Although China has never officially declared a formal moratorium on fissile material production for weapon purposes, it is believed to have ceased military HEU production at some time between 1987 and 1989 and military plutonium production in 1991. The current inventories mean that China could not significantly expand its nuclear warhead stockpile without restarting military plutonium production. There are no credible reports indicating that the size of the Chinese nuclear weapon stockpile has changed significantly in recent years.[4]

---

[1] Stokes, M. A., *China's Nuclear Warhead Storage and Handling System* (Project 2049 Institute: Arlington, VA, 12 Mar. 2010), p. 7.

[2] Lewis, J., *The Minimum Means of Reprisal: China's Search for Security in the Nuclear Age* (MIT University Press: Cambridge, MA, 2007), pp. 111–35.

[3] Chinese State Council, *China's National Defense in 2010* (Information Office of the Chinese State Council: Beijing, Mar. 2011).

[4] In 2011 one US academic speculated that China's nuclear arsenal could be much larger than previously estimated because it may have hidden warheads and missiles in underground facilities. See

Table 7.6. Chinese nuclear forces, January 2012

Type/Chinese designation (US designation)	No. deployed	Year first deployed	Range (km)[a]	Warhead loading	No. of warheads
Land-based missiles[b]	~130				~130
DF-3A (CSS-2)	~16	1971	3 100[c]	1 x 3.3 Mt	~16
DF-4 (CSS-3)	~12	1980	5 500	1 x 3.3 Mt	~12
DF-5A (CSS-4)	20	1981	13 000	1 x 4–5 Mt	20
DF-21 (CSS-5)	~60	1991	2 100[d]	1 x 200–300 kt[e]	· ~60
DF-31 (CSS-10 Mod 1)	10–20	2006	>7 200	1 x 200–300 kt[e]	10–20
DF-31A (CSS-10 Mod 2)	10–20	2007	>11 200	1 x 200–300 kt[e]	10–20
SLBMs	(48)				(48)
JL-1 (CSS-N-3)	(12)	1986	>1 770	1 x 200–300 kt	(12)
JL-2 (CSS-NX-14)[f]	(36)	..	>7 400	1 x 200–300 kt[e]	(36)
Aircraft[g]	>20				(40)
H-6 (B-6)	~20	1965	3 100	1 x bomb	(~20)
Cruise missiles	150–350				..
DH-10	150–350	2007	>1 500	1 x ..	..[h]
Total					(~240)[i]

.. = not available or not applicable; ( ) = uncertain figure; kt = kiloton; Mt = Megaton; SLBM = submarine-launched ballistic missile.

[a] Aircraft range is for illustrative purposes only; actual mission range will vary.

[b] China defines missile ranges as short-range (<1000 km), medium-range (1000–3000 km), long-range (3000–8000 km) and intercontinental range (>8000 km).

[c] The range of the DF-3A may be greater than is normally reported.

[d] The DF-21A (CSS-5 Mod 2) variant is believed to have a range of up to 2500 km.

[e] The DF-31 and DF-31A intercontinental ballistic missiles and the JL-2 SLBM may use the same warhead design as the DF-21, although this has not been confirmed.

[f] A US Defense Intelligence Agency report projected in Feb. 2012 that the JL-2 would reach initial operational capability around 2014.

[g] Figures for aircraft are for nuclear-configured versions only.

[h] There are conflicting US Government reports about whether the DH-10 has a nuclear capability.

[i] Additional warheads are thought to be in storage to arm future DF-31, DF-31A and JL-2 missiles. The total stockpile is believed to comprise c. 240 warheads.

Sources: US Department of Defense, *Military Power of the People's Republic of China*, various years; US Air Force, National Air and Space Intelligence Center (NASIC), various documents; US Central Intelligence Agency, various documents; Kristensen, H. M., Norris, R. S. and McKinzie, M. G., *Chinese Nuclear Forces and U.S. Nuclear War Planning* (Federation of American Scientists/Natural Resources Defense Council: Washington, DC, Nov. 2006); Norris, R. S. et al., *Nuclear Weapons Databook*, vol. 5, *British, French, and Chinese Nuclear Weapons* (Westview: Boulder, CO, 1994); 'Nuclear notebook', *Bulletin of the Atomic Scientists*, various issues; Google Earth; and authors' estimates.

Land-based ballistic missiles

The Second Artillery, which operates China's land-based ballistic missiles, is modernizing its missile force. This involves replacing ageing liquid-fuelled missiles with newer solid-fuelled models. In recent years the Second Artillery has also prioritized deploying mobile medium- and long-range ballistic missile systems, which are more able to survive an attack than silo-based missiles. This has become an increasingly important consideration for Chinese planners in assuring the credibility of the country's nuclear retaliatory capabilities.[5]

China's nuclear-capable ballistic missile arsenal consists of approximately 130 missiles.[6] The road-mobile, solid-fuelled, two-stage DF-21 medium-range ballistic missile is replacing China's oldest missile, the liquid-fuelled, single stage DF-3A intermediate-range ballistic missile and acts as a regional nuclear deterrent. Additionally, China fields the liquid-fuelled, two-stage DF-4 intercontinental ballistic missiles (ICBM), which is being gradually replaced by the solid-fuelled, three-stage, road-mobile DF-31 ICBM, which is capable of targeting the western USA, Russia and Europe.

Only the liquid-fuelled, two-stage, silo-based DF-5A and the solid-fuelled, three-stage, road-mobile DF-31/DF-31A ICBMs have a true intercontinental range of over 5500 kilometres. It remains unclear whether the Second Artillery will replace the ageing DF-5A with the DF-31A or maintain both missile systems.[7]

Both the DF-31 and the longer-range DF-31A have shortened launch preparation times compared to previous generations of long-range missiles. This reflects the Second Artillery's emphasis on increasing the survivability of the new missiles by prioritizing mobility over the silo-based DF-5A's greater range and warhead loading.[8] However, the Second Artillery has relatively limited experience in managing mobile missile patrols. According to the US Department of Defense (DOD), this could pose serious challenges for China's current command and control structures.[9]

Wan, W., 'Georgetown students shed light on China's tunnel system for nuclear weapons,' *Washington Post*, 30 Nov. 2011; and Kristensen, H. M., 'No, China does not have 3,000 nuclear weapons', FAS Strategic Security Blog, Federation of American Scientists, 3 Dec. 2011, <http://www.fas.org/blog/ssp/2011/12/chinanukes.php>.

[5] Li Bin, 'Tracking Chinese strategic mobile missiles,' *Science & Global Security*, vol. 15, no. 1 (2007), pp. 4–5.

[6] Although China has its own system for defining missile ranges, the US DOD definitions are used here: short range = <1100 km; medium range = 1100–2750 km; intermediate range = 2750–5500 km; and intercontinental range = >5500 km.

[7] Kristensen, H. M. and Norris, R. S., 'Chinese nuclear forces 2011', *Bulletin of the Atomic Scientists*, vol. 67, no. 6 (Nov./Dec. 2011), p. 82.

[8] Li Bin (note 5), p. 26.

[9] US Department of Defense (DOD), *Military and Security Developments Involving the People's Republic of China 2011*, Annual Report to Congress (DOD: Washington, DC, Aug. 2011) p. 34.

Ballistic missile submarines

China has had difficulty in developing a sea-based nuclear deterrent. China's 2011 Defence White Paper reiterated the PLA Navy's possession of a nuclear capability stating that 'the PLA Navy ... enhances its capabilities in strategic deterrence and counterattack'.[10] However, the status and envisioned strategy of its current and future nuclear-powered ballistic missile submarines (SSBNs), once they become operational, remain unclear.[11]

China built a single Xia class (Type 092) SSBN armed with 12 solid-fuelled, two-stage JL-1 (Ju Lang, or Great Wave) submarine-launched ballistic missiles (SLBMs). The submarine has never conducted a deterrent patrol and is thought not to be fully operational, despite several refits.

The PLA Navy has developed a successor SSBN, the Jin class (Type 094) submarine. Conflicting reports exist as to the number of submarines that have been constructed.[12] According to the US DOD, the first Jin class SSBN appears to be ready for deployment.[13] A second submarine may be at a similar stage of readiness, while the status of a third submarine under construction remains unclear.[14] There is also uncertainty about the total number of submarines that China plans to build.[15] The US DOD had previously estimated that China would be likely to require five Jin class SSBNs in order to maintain one or two boats on deterrence patrols; however, no such estimate was made in its latest report.[16]

Each Jin class SSBN will carry 12 three-stage, solid-fuelled SLBMs, the JL-2, which is a sea-based derivative of the DF-31 ICBM. The JL-2 programme has encountered several setbacks due to technical difficulties. It remains uncertain when the combination of Jin class SSBNs and JL-2 SLBMs will be fully operational. The US DOD reported in 2011 that the date when the JL-2 would reach initial operational capability remained uncertain but that the missile is likely to continue flight tests.[17] According to press reports, the PLA Navy conducted a series of six JL-2 flight tests in late December 2011 or early January 2012.[18]

---

[10] Chinese State Council (note 3).

[11] Wu Riqiang, 'Survivability of China's sea-based nuclear forces,' *Science & Global Security*, vol. 19, no. 2 (2011), pp. 94–96.

[12] Kristensen, H. M., 'Chinese Jin-SSBNs getting ready?', FAS Strategic Security Blog, Federation of American Scientists, 2 June 2011, <http://www.fas.org/blog/ssp/2011/06/jin2011.php>.

[13] US Department of Defense (note 9), p. 34.

[14] Kristensen (note 12).

[15] Kristensen and Norris (note 7), p. 84.

[16] US Department of Defense (note 9).

[17] US Department of Defense (note 9), p. 34.

[18] Richardson, D., 'Chinese navy conducts series of Julang-2 SLBM firings,' *Jane's Missiles and Rockets*, vol. 16, no. 3 (Mar. 2012), p. 10.

Aircraft and cruise missiles

The PLA Air Force is believed to maintain a small number of gravity bombs to be delivered by the H-6 fighter-bomber and possibly a more modern combat aircraft. The PLA Air Force is not believed to have units whose primary mission is to deliver nuclear bombs.[19]

The US DOD stated in 2011 that China is deploying several new types of cruise missile.[20] Only one type, the DH-10 (Donghai-10 or East Sea 10), also designated CJ-10 (Changjian-10 or Long Sword 10), has been reported as being possibly nuclear capable. Relatively little is publicly known about the DH-10's technical characteristics, and claims about the missile's derivation and classification are inconsistent.[21] The US Air Force listed the DH-10 as 'conventional or nuclear', which is the same designation it uses for other dual-capable cruise missiles such as the Russian AS-4. The US DOD, however, lists the DH-10 as part of China's 'conventional precision strike' capabilities.[22] China is also developing an air-launched version of the DH-10, possibly for delivery by an upgraded version of the H-6 aircraft.

[19] US National Security Council, 'Report to Congress on status of China, India and Pakistan nuclear and ballistic missile programs', 28 July 1993, obtained under the US Freedom of Information Act by the Federation of American Scientists, <http://fas.org/irp/threat/930728-wmd.htm>.

[20] In 2009 the US DOD estimated that 150–300 DH-10 cruise missiles had been deployed, increasing its assessment to 200–500 in 2010. US Department of Defense (DOD), *Military and Security Developments Involving the People's Republic of China 2010*, Annual Report to Congress (DOD: Washington, DC, 2010), pp. 2, 66.

[21] Easton, I., 'The assassin under the radar, China's DH-10 cruise missile program', Futuregram no. 09-005, Project 2049 Institute, 1 Oct. 2009, <http://project2049.net/publications.html>.

[22] US Department of Defense (note 9), p. 30.

VI. Indian nuclear forces

SHANNON N. KILE, PHILLIP SCHELL AND HANS M. KRISTENSEN

India is estimated to have an arsenal of 80–100 nuclear weapons. This figure is based on calculations of India's inventory of weapon-grade plutonium as well as the number of operational nuclear-capable delivery systems.

India's nuclear weapons are believed to be plutonium-based. As of 2011 India's military plutonium stockpile was estimated to be between 0.38 and 0.66 tonnes (see section X below). The plutonium was produced by the 40-megawatt-thermal (MW(t)) heavy water CIRUS reactor, which was shut down at the end of 2010, and the 100-MW(t) Dhruva heavy water reactor. Both are located at the Bhabha Atomic Research Centre near Mumbai, Maharashtra. India has plans to build six fast breeder reactors, which will significantly increase its capacity to produce plutonium for weapons. A 1250 MW(t) prototype fast breeder reactor is nearing completion at Kalpakkam, Tamil Nadu, which also houses a reprocessing facility that is not subject to International Atomic Energy Agency (IAEA) safeguards. The reactor is scheduled to be commissioned in June 2012.[1] At 75 per cent operating capacity, it could potentially produce around 140 kilograms of weapon-grade plutonium per year, or enough for 28–35 weapons depending on bomb design and fabrication skills.[2]

India continues to enrich uranium at the centrifuge facility at Rattehalli Rare Materials Plant near Mysore, Karnataka, to produce highly enriched uranium (HEU) for use as naval reactor fuel. The Indian Atomic Energy Commission has announced plans to build a 'special material enrichment facility', at a site in Chitradurga district, Karnataka, which potentially could be used to produce HEU for weapons, among other purposes.[3]

India's nuclear doctrine is based on the principle of a minimum credible deterrent and no-first-use of nuclear weapons.[4] There have been no official statements specifying the size of the arsenal required for 'minimum credible deterrence' but, according to the Indian Ministry of Defence (MOD), it involves 'a mix of land-based, maritime and air capabilities'.[5] In May 2011 the Indian Prime Minister, Manmohan Singh, convened a meeting of

---

[1] Kanavi, S., 'Why India's fast breeder programme is cutting edge', Rediff.com, 13 June 2011, <http://www.rediff.com/news/slide-show/slide-show-1-why-indias-fast-breeder-programme-is-cutting-edge/20110613.htm>.

[2] Cochran, T. B. et al., *Fast Breeder Reactor Programs: History and Status* (International Panel on Fissile Materials: Princeton, NJ, Feb. 2010), pp. 41, 45.

[3] Jha, S., 'Enrichment capacity enough to fuel nuke subs', IBNLive, 26 Nov. 2011, <http://ibnlive.in.com/news/enrichment-capacity-enough-to-fuel-nuke-subs/206066-61.html>.

[4] Indian Ministry of External Affairs, 'Draft report of National Security Advisory Board on Indian nuclear doctrine', 17 Aug. 1999, <http://www.mea.gov.in/mystart.php?id=51515763>.

[5] Indian Ministry of Defence (MOD), *Annual Report 2004–05* (MOD: New Delhi, 2005) p. 14.

India's Nuclear Command Authority (NCA), the body responsible for over-seeing the country's nuclear arsenal, to assess progress towards the goal of achieving an operational 'triad' of nuclear forces.[6]

Strike aircraft

Aircraft constitute the most mature component of India's nuclear strike capabilities (see table 7.7). The Indian Air Force (IAF) has reportedly certified the Mirage 2000H multi-role combat aircraft for delivery of nuclear gravity bombs. The IAF's Jaguar IS Shamsher and Sukhoi Su-30MKI combat aircraft have also been mentioned as having a possible nuclear role.[7] The Indian Strategic Forces Command (SFC) has reportedly submitted a proposal to the MOD for setting up two dedicated squadrons of fighter aircraft for the nuclear delivery role under its command.[8]

Land-based missiles

The Prithvi short-range ballistic missile was India's sole operational ballistic missile for many years. The 150 kilometre-range Prithvi I is a single-stage, road-mobile, liquid-fuelled missile that was inducted into Indian Army service in 1994. A number of Prithvi I missiles are widely believed to have been modified for a nuclear delivery role, although this has never been officially confirmed. The Prithvi II is a longer-range variant that is rumoured to also have a nuclear role. In 2011 the SFC conducted three successful launches of Prithvi II missiles—on 11 March, 9 June and 26 Sep-tember—during routine exercises.[9] Pakistan complained that India had failed to inform it in advance about the March test launch, as required under a 1991 bilateral agreement on missile test notifications.[10]

Indian defence sources indicate that the family of longer-range Agni ballistic missiles, which are designed to provide a quick-reaction nuclear

[6] The NCA comprises the political council, chaired by the prime minister, and the executive coun-cil, chaired by the national security adviser to the prime minister. The NCA's directives are oper-ationalized by a Strategic Forces Command under the control of a commander-in-chief. Pandit, R., 'Manmohan Singh takes stock of country's nuclear arsenal', Times of India, 17 May 2011.

[7] Naik, P. V., 'IAF aiming for diverse capabilities, says vice chief of air staff, Air Marshall P. V. Naik in his keynote address on fighter technology and advance systems', India Strategic, 26 Sep. 2008, <http://www.indiastrategic.in/topstories178.htm>.

[8] Press Trust of India, 'Strategic Command to acquire 40 nuclear capable fighters', Hindustan Times, 12 Sep. 2010.

[9] 'Prithvi-II ballistic missile test-fired successfully', Indian Express, 26 Sep. 2011; Mallikarjun, Y., 'Prithvi-II successfully flight-tested', The Hindu, 9 June 2011; and 'Prithvi II, Dhanush test-fired successfully', Times of India, 11 Mar. 2011.

[10] 'Pakistan test-fires Abdali missile', Dawn, 26 Mar. 2011.

Table 7.7. Indian nuclear forces, January 2012

Type	Range (km)[a]	Payload (kg)	Status
Aircraft[b]			
Mirage 2000H Vajra	1 850	6 300	Has reportedly been certified for delivery of nuclear gravity bombs
Land-based ballistic missiles[c]			
Prithvi I/II	150/250	800/500	Prithvi I entered service in 1994; Prithvi I reportedly had a nuclear capability and Prithvi II also is widely rumoured to have nuclear capability, but any nuclear role is probably diminishing with the introduction of the Agni; fewer than 50 launchers deployed; most recent test flight on 26 Sep. 2011
Agni I[d]	~700	1 000	Most recent Indian Army operational test on 1 Dec. 2011
Agni II	2 000	1 000	Successful test launch on 30 Sep. 2011; operational status uncertain
Agni III	~3 000	1 500	In production and inducted into army service
Agni IV[e]	>3 000	1 000	Under development; test launched to 3000 km on 15 Nov. 2011
Agni V	>5 000	1 000	Under development; test launch planned for 2012
Sea-based ballistic missiles			
Dhanush	350	500	Test-launched on 11 Mar. 2011; induction under way but not thought to be operational
K-15[f]	700	500–600	Under development; test-launched from a submerged pontoon on 26 Feb. 2008
K-4	3 500	1 000	Developmental tests of gas booster reportedly carried out in Jan. 2010

[a] Aircraft range is for illustrative purposes only; actual mission range will vary according to flight profile and weapon loading. Missile payloads may need to be reduced in order to achieve maximum range.

[b] The Jaguar IS Shamsher and Sukhoi Su-30MKI combat aircraft have also been mentioned as having a possible nuclear delivery role.

[c] India has also begun developing a subsonic cruise missile with a range of 1000 km, known as the Nirbhay (Fearless), which may have a nuclear capability.

[d] The original Agni I, now known as the Agni, was a technology demonstrator programme that ended in 1996. The Indian Ministry of Defence refers to Agni I as A1.

[e] A previous version was known as the Agni II Prime.

[f] A land-based version of the K-15, known as the Shourya, was test-launched for the first time on 12 Nov. 2008 and again on 24 Sep. 2011.

Sources: Indian Ministry of Defence, annual reports and press releases; International Institute for Strategic Studies, *The Military Balance 2010* (Routledge: London, 2010); US Air Force, National Air and Space Intelligence Center (NASIC), *Ballistic and Cruise Missile Threat* (NASIC: Wright-Patterson Air Force Base, OH, June 2009); Indian news media reports; 'Nuclear notebook', *Bulletin of the Atomic Scientists*, various issues; and authors' estimates.

capability, has largely taken over the Prithvi's nuclear delivery role. Like the Prithvi, the Agni was developed by India's Defence Research and Development Organisation (DRDO) as a part of its problem-plagued integrated guided missile development programme.[11] The 700-km-range Agni I (designated the A1 by the Indian MOD) is a single-stage, solid-fuelled missile that is deployed with the Indian Army's 334 Missile Group. On 1 December 2011 an Agni I missile was test-fired from a road-mobile launcher during an army training exercise.[12] The Agni II is a two-stage solid-fuelled missile that can deliver a 1000-kg payload to a maximum range of 2000 km. On 30 September 2011 the SFC successfully launched an Agni II from the Wheeler Island complex on the Orissa coast. This marked the second successful test launch of the missile following two failures in 2009.[13]

The DRDO has been developing a variant of the Agni II, known previously as the Agni II Prime but redesignated as the Agni IV. According to DRDO officials, the two-stage Agni IV incorporates several technological advances, including composite rocket engines, improved stage separation and a state-of-the-art navigational system.[14] On 15 November 2011 an Agni IV was successfully launched from the Wheeler Island complex and travelled 3000 km to a target zone in the Bay of Bengal.[15] The DRDO plans for the Agni IV to be inducted into army service in 2014, following two to four more flight tests.[16]

The DRDO has also developed the Agni III, a two-stage, solid-fuelled missile capable of delivering a 1500-kg payload to a range of 3000–3500 km. In June 2011 Vijay Kumar Saraswat, the director-general of the DRDO, said that the missile had been inducted into army service and was in production.[17]

The DRDO has prioritized the development of the three-stage, road-mobile Agni V. With a range of 5000 km, the missile will be capable of reaching targets throughout most of China. The first test launch of the Agni V had been expected by the end of 2011 but did not take place until 19 April 2012.[18]

[11] Verma, B., 'How DRDO failed India's military', Rediff, 15 Jan. 2008, <http://www.rediff.com/news/2008/jan/15guest.htm>.

[12] Indian Ministry of Defence, Press Information Bureau, 'Army conducts successful flight test of missile Agni A1-06', 1 Dec. 2011, <http://pib.nic.in/newsite/erelease.aspx?relid=77985>.

[13] Subramanian, T. S., and Mallikarjun, Y., 'Agni-II soars in success', The Hindu, 30 Sep. 2011.

[14] Pandit, R., 'With China in mind, India tests new-generation Agni missile with high "kill efficiency"', Times of India, 16 Nov. 2011.

[15] Subramanian, T. S., 'Agni-IV test-flight a "stupendous success"', The Hindu, 15 Nov. 2011.

[16] Shukla, A., 'DRDO plans early entry of Agni-4 into arsenal', Business Standard, 17 Dec. 2011.

[17] Press Trust of India, 'India to test fire Agni-V by year-end', The Hindu, 3 June 2011.

[18] Pandit, R., 'Eyeing China, India to enter ICBM club in 3 months', Times of India, 17 Nov. 2011.

Sea-based missiles

The DRDO has tested components of an underwater missile launch system and is developing a two-stage ballistic missile that can be launched from a submerged submarine using a gas-charged booster.[19] Indian MOD statements have designated the missile as the K-15 or B-05, although other sources have referred to it as Sagarika (Oceanic), which is the name of the DRDO development project.[20] The new nuclear-capable missile will be able to deliver a 500-kg payload to a distance of up to 700 km. A land-based variant of the K-15, called the Shourya, was successfully test-launched for the third time on 24 September 2011.[21]

The DRDO is also developing a new submarine-launched ballistic missile, known as the K-4, which may have a range of up to 3500 km.[22] The K-4 will eventually replace the K-15 missile in arming an indigenously constructed nuclear-powered ballistic missile submarine that is the product of India's Advanced Technology Vessel (ATV) programme. The first of the submarines, the INS *Arihant*, was launched in 2009 and is expected to begin sea trials in 2012. The new submarine can carry either 12 K-15 or 4 K-4 missiles.[23]

India also continues to work on the Dhanush missile, a naval version of the Prithvi II, which is launched from a stabilization platform mounted on a surface ship. It can reportedly carry a 500-kg warhead to a maximum range of 350 km and is designed to be able to hit both sea- and shore-based targets. A Dhanush was successfully test-launched from an Indian Navy ship, the INS *Suvarna*, off the coast of Orissa on 11 March 2011.[24]

[19] Unnithan, S., 'The secret "K" missile family', *India Today*, 20 Nov. 2010; and Subramanian, T. S., 'DRDO plans another K-15 missile launch', *The Hindu*, 28 Jan. 2011.

[20] Subramanian (note 19).

[21] Subramanian, T. S. and Mallikarjun, Y., 'India successfully test-fires Sourya missile', *The Hindu*, 24 Sep. 2011.

[22] Unnithan (note 19).

[23] Press Trust of India, 'Nuclear sub Arihant to start sea trials in some months: Verma', IBN Live, 2 Dec. 2011, <http://ibnlive.in.com/generalnewsfeed/news/nuclear-sub-arihant-to-start-sea-trials-in-some-months-ver ma/921449.html>; and 'India to achieve N-arm triad in February', *Times of India*, 2 Jan. 2012.

[24] Shukla, A., 'Strategic Forces Command tests Prithvi and Dhanush missiles', Indian Military.org, 12 Mar. 2011, <http://www.indian-military.org/news-archives/indian-air-force-news/1428-strategic-forces-command-test-prithvi-and-dhanush-missiles.html>.

VII. Pakistani nuclear forces

SHANNON N. KILE, PHILLIP SCHELL AND HANS M. KRISTENSEN

Pakistan is estimated to possess 90–110 nuclear weapons that can be delivered by aircraft and missiles (see table 7.8). Pakistan's current warhead designs are believed to use highly enriched uranium (HEU), but there is evidence that it is moving towards an arsenal based on plutonium. Warheads using plutonium could be lighter and more compact than those using HEU to achieve the same yield. Some experts have estimated that Pakistan's nuclear stockpile could double within a decade based on increased military plutonium-production capabilities.[1]

Pakistan is expanding its plutonium-production capabilities at the nuclear complex at Khushab, Punjab. The complex currently consists of three heavy water nuclear reactors and a heavy water production plant. A fourth heavy water reactor is under construction. All four reactors appear to be capable of generating the same amount of power.[2] Its first plutonium production reactor, the 40–50-megawatt-thermal Khushab-I, is estimated to produce 5.7–11.5 kilograms of plutonium annually, depending on operational efficiency, enough for 1–3 nuclear weapons, depending on weapon design and fabrication skills.[3] A second plutonium production reactor, Khushab-II, may have commenced operation in late 2009 or 2010.[4] The first weapon-grade plutonium from Khushab-II could have become available in 2011.[5] Construction work on a third reactor at the Khushab site began in 2006 and seems to have been completed in late 2011, based on recent open source satellite imagery. Satellite imagery also indicates that work on a fourth reactor also started in late 2010.[6] Rumours of possible Chinese assistance in building the fourth reactor appear to have been unfounded.[7] The Khushab nuclear complex, combined with the annual HEU production, could increase Pakistan's annual nuclear warhead production capacity several-fold. This will depend, however, on the country

---

[1] Norris, R. S. and Kristensen, H. M., 'Nuclear notebook: Pakistan's nuclear forces, 2011', *Bulletin of the Atomic Scientists*, vol. 67, no. 4 (July 2011), p. 91.

[2] International Panel on Fissile Materials (IPFM), *Global Fissile Material Report 2011: Nuclear Weapon and Fissile Material Stockpiles and Production* (IPFM: Princeton, NJ, Jan. 2012), p. 19.

[3] International Panel on Fissile Materials (IPFM), *Global Fissile Material Report 2010: Balancing the Books: Production and Stocks* (IPFM: Princeton, NJ, Dec. 2010), p. 132.

[4] Brannan, P., 'Steam emitted from second Khushab reactor cooling towers; Pakistan may have started operating second reactor', Institute for Science and International Security (ISIS) Report, 24 Mar. 2010, <http://isis-online.org/isis-reports/category/pakistan/>.

[5] International Panel on Fissile Materials (note 3).

[6] Albright, D. and Brannan, P., 'Pakistan appears to be building a fourth military reactor at the Khushab nuclear site', Institute for Science and International Security (ISIS) Report, 9 Feb. 2011, <http://isis-online.org/isis-reports/category/pakistan/>.

[7] Hibbs, M., 'Chinese help on Khushab-4?', Arms Control Wonk, 22 Feb. 2011, <http://hibbs.arms controlwonk.com/archive/162/>. See also chapter 8, section V, in this volume.

Table 7.8. Pakistani nuclear forces, January 2012

Type	Range (km)[a]	Payload (kg)	Status
Aircraft			
F-16A/B	1 600	4 500	Currently undergoing mid-life upgrades, to be completed 2013–14
Mirage III/V	2 100	4 000	Used to test launch dual-capable Ra'ad cruise missile
Land-based ballistic missiles			
Abdali (Hatf-2)	~180	200–400	Under development; test-launched on 11 Mar. 2011
Ghaznavi (Hatf-3)[b]	290	500	Entered service with the Pakistani Army in 2004; fewer than 50 launchers deployed; most recent test launch on 8 May 2010
Shaheen I (Hatf-4)[c]	650	750–1 000	Entered service with the Pakistani Army in 2003; fewer than 50 launchers deployed; most recent test launch on 8 May 2010
Shaheen II (Hatf-6)	2 500	(~1 000)	Under development; expected to become operational soon
Ghauri I (Hatf-5)	>1 200	700–1 000	Entered service with the Pakistani Army in 2003; fewer than 50 launchers deployed; most recent test-launch on 20 Dec. 2010
Nasr (Hatf-9)	~60	..	Under development; first test launch on 19 Apr. 2011
Cruise missiles			
Babur (Hatf-7)[c]	600	400–500	Under development; most recent test-launch on 28 Oct. 2011
Ra'ad (Hatf-8)	350	..	Under development; air-launched; most recent test launch on 29 Apr. 2011

.. = not available; ( ) = uncertain figure.

[a] Aircraft range is for illustrative purposes only; actual mission range will vary according to flight profile and weapon loading. Missile payloads may need to be reduced in order to achieve maximum range.

[b] The Hatf-3 is believed to be a copy of the M-11 missile acquired from China in the 1990s.

[c] An extended-range version, the Shaheen IA, is under development.

[d] Sea- and air-launched versions are reportedly also under development.

Sources: US Air Force, National Air and Space Intelligence Center (NASIC), *Ballistic and Cruise Missile Threat* (NASIC: Wright-Patterson Air Force Base, OH, June 2009); US Central Intelligence Agency, 'Unclassified report to Congress on the acquisition of technology relating to weapons of mass destruction and advanced conventional munitions, 1 January through 30 June 2002', Apr. 2003, <https://www.cia.gov/library/reports/archived-reports-1/>; US National Intelligence Council, 'Foreign missile developments and the ballistic missile threat through 2015' (unclassified summary), Dec. 2001, <http://www.dni.gov/nic/special_missile threat2001.html>; International Institute for Strategic Studies, *The Military Balance 2006–2007* (Routledge: London, 2007); 'Nuclear notebook', *Bulletin of the Atomic Scientists*, various issues; and authors' estimates.

having sufficient capacity to reprocess spent fuel as well as an adequate supply of uranium to fuel the reactors at Khushab.[8]

[8] Albright, D. and Brannan, P., 'Commercial satellite imagery suggests Pakistan is building a second much larger plutonium production reactor: is South Asia headed for a dramatic buildup in

As of 2011 Pakistan was estimated to have a stockpile of 2.35–3.15 tonnes of 90 per cent HEU (see section X below). The enrichment is believed to be taking place at the uranium centrifuge facilities at Kahuta and Gadwal.

Strike aircraft

The Pakistani Air Force (PAF) is believed to have previously given a nuclear delivery role to some of the F-16A/B combat aircraft supplied by the USA in the 1980s.[9] It is unclear whether the aircraft are currently assigned nuclear missions. The PAF also operates Mirage III and V combat aircraft, which have been upgraded with new avionics to augment their strike capabilities and could have a nuclear delivery role. The range of the Mirage aircraft has been extended by the PAF's development of an aerial refuelling capability using Il-78 aircraft.

Pakistan is also developing an air-launched cruise missile, known as the Ra'ad (Hatf-8), which will have a range of 350 kilometres. The latest test launch was conducted on 29 April 2011. According to the Pakistani Inter Services Public Relations, the Ra'ad is a dual-capable cruise missile with 'stealth capabilities' that 'enabled Pakistan to achieve greater strategic stand off capability on land and at sea'.[10]

Land-based missiles

Pakistan's operational nuclear-capable ballistic missile arsenal is of three types. The Ghaznavi (Hatf-3) is a solid-fuelled, road-mobile short-range ballistic missile (SRBM) that was inducted into service with the Pakistani Army in 2004. The solid-fuelled Shaheen I (Hatf-4) SRBM entered into service in 2003. The liquid-fuelled Ghauri I (Hatf-5), which is based on the North Korean Nodong missile, is Pakistan's only operational medium-range ballistic missile (MRBM).

Pakistan's National Defence Complex is developing additional types of nuclear-capable ballistic missile: the medium-range Shaheen IA and Shaheen II (Hatf-6) and the short-range Abdali (Hatf-2) and Nasr (Hatf-9). The Shaheen IA is an extended-range version of the Shaheen I. The Shaheen II is a two-stage, solid-fuelled, road-mobile missile that may eventually replace the Ghauri MRBM. It has been under development for more than a decade and may soon become operational.

nuclear arsenals', Institute for Science and International Security (ISIS) Report, 24 July 2006, <http://isis-online.org/isis-reports/category/pakistan/>.

[9] US National Security Council, 'Report to Congress on status of China, India and Pakistan nuclear and ballistic missile programs', 28 July 1993, obtained under the US Freedom of Information Act by the Federation of American Scientists, <http://fas.org/irp/threat/930728-wmd.htm>, p. 7.

[10] Pakistani Inter Services Public Relations, Press Release no. PR104/2011-ISPR, 29 Apr. 2011, <http://www.ispr.gov.pk/front/main.asp?o=t-press_release&date=2011/4/29>.

On 11 March 2011 Pakistan conducted a test launch of the Abdali (Hatf-2) SRBM. The purpose of the test was to validate 'technical improvements' to the missile.[11] The Abdali programme began in the 1980s but was terminated in 1994. In 1997 Pakistan restarted work on a new design for the missile with a reduced range. The missile, which was first flight-tested in 2002, may have a nuclear capability.[12]

On 19 April 2011 Pakistan conducted the first flight test of the nuclear-capable Nasr (Hatf-9) SRBM.[13] The Nasr is as a road-mobile, solid-fuelled missile that appears to be designed to carry a new, highly compact nuclear warhead suitable for battlefield use.[14] Khalid Ahmed Kidwai, Director of the Strategic Plans Division, described the test as consolidating Pakistan's strategic deterrence capability 'at all levels of the threat spectrum', providing a 'short range missile capability in addition to the already available medium and long range ballistic missiles and cruise missiles'.[15]

On 28 October 2011 Pakistan conducted the latest in a series of flight tests of the Babur (Hatf-7), a nuclear-capable ground-launched cruise missile. The 600 km-range missile was launched from a new three-tube, road-mobile missile launch vehicle that is designed for enhanced 'target employment and survivability'.[16] Pakistan's missile development organization, the National Engineering and Scientific Commission (NESCOM), is reportedly working to extend the range of the missile to up to 1000 km.[17]

Pakistan's development of new types of nuclear-capable cruise missiles and SRBMs may be an indication of its growing concern about being able to counter India's superior conventional forces and its nascent ballistic missile defences. The Abdali and Nasr missile programmes further suggest that Pakistan's strategic planning has evolved to include a wider range of contingencies for the use of nuclear weapons. According to some Pakistani defence experts, the country has been forced to develop battlefield nuclear weapons in response to the Indian Army's Cold Start doctrine, under which India is prepared to carry out rapid but limited conventional attacks on Pakistani territory using forward-deployed mechanized forces.[18]

---

[11] Pakistani Inter Services Public Relations, Press Release no. PR62/2011-ISPR, 11 Mar. 2011, <http://www.ispr.gov.pk/front/main.asp?o=t-press_release&id=1689>.

[12] Lennox, D. (ed.), *Jane's Strategic Weapon Systems*, no. 54 (IHS Global Limited: Coulsdon, 2011) p. 120.

[13] Pakistani Inter Services Public Relations, Press Release no. PR94/2011-ISPR, 19 Apr. 2011, <http://www.ispr.gov.pk/front/main.asp?o=t-press_release&id=1721>.

[14] Ansari, U., 'Pakistan tests "nuke-capable" short-range missile', *Defense News*, 20 Apr. 2011.

[15] Pakistani Inter Services Public Relations (note 13).

[16] Pakistani Inter Services Public Relations, Press Release no. PR256/2011-ISPR, 28 Oct. 2011, <http://www.ispr.gov.pk/front/main.asp?o=t-press_release&date=2011/10/28>.

[17] Associated Press of Pakistan, 'Government has prepared comprehensive plan to equip armed forces: Musharraf', 30 May 2008, <http://www.app.com.pk/en_/index.php?option=com_content& task=view&id=9898&Itemid=2>.

[18] Ansari (note 14); Reuters, 'Pakistan builds low yield nuclear capability', *Dawn*, 15 May 2011; and 'Hatf- IX test-fired', *The Nation*, 20 Apr. 2011.

VIII. Israeli nuclear forces

SHANNON N. KILE, PHILLIP SCHELL AND HANS M. KRISTENSEN

Israel continues to maintain its long-standing policy of nuclear opacity, neither officially confirming nor denying that it possesses nuclear weapons.[1] However, Israel is widely believed to have used the heavy-water research reactor at the Negev Nuclear Research Center, near Dimona, to produce plutonium for a nuclear weapon arsenal. There is little publicly available information about the Dimona reactor's operating history. According to one estimate, it could have produced 690–950 kilograms of weapon-grade plutonium as of 2011 (see section X below). Only part of this plutonium may have been used to produce weapons.

It is estimated here that Israel has approximately 80 intact nuclear weapons, of which 50 are warheads for delivery by ballistic missiles and the remainder are bombs for delivery by aircraft (see table 7.9). Israel may have produced non-strategic nuclear weapons, including artillery shells and atomic demolition munitions, but this has never been confirmed.

Israel continues to develop advanced long-range ballistic missiles capable of delivering nuclear warheads. On 2 November 2011 it conducted a test launch of a multi-stage ballistic missile from Palmachim Airbase.[2] While not providing details about the missile, the Israeli Ministry of Defence stated that the purpose of the launch had been to test the missile's propulsion system.[3] Foreign analysts identified the missile as most likely being an improved version of the Jericho III intermediate-range ballistic missile, which was first flight-tested in January 2008.[4]

There has been considerable speculation that Israel may have developed a nuclear-capable sea-launched cruise missile for its current fleet of three Type 800 Dolphin class diesel-electric submarines that were purchased from Germany.[5] Israel has steadfastly denied these reports. Israel has since purchased from Germany two additional boats of the same class, which were under construction during 2011 at the Howaldtswerke-Deutsche Werft AG shipyard, near Kiel.[6]

---

[1] On the role of this policy in Israel's national security decision making see Cohen, A., 'Israel', eds H. Born, B. Gill and H. Hänggi, SIPRI, *Governing the Bomb: Civilian Control and Democratic Accountability of Nuclear Weapons* (Oxford University Press: Oxford, 2010).

[2] Williams, D., 'Israel test-fires missile as Iran debate rages', Reuters, 2 Nov. 2011, <http://www.reuters.com/article/2011/11/02/us-israel-missile-idUSTRE7A11BR20111102>.

[3] Pfeffer, A. and Reuters, 'IDF test-fires ballistic missile in central Israel', *Haaretz*, 2 Nov. 2011.

[4] Richardson, D., 'Israel tests ballistic missile', *Jane's Missiles and Rockets*, vol. 16, no. 1 (Jan. 2012).

[5] 'Germany sells Israel more Dolphin subs', Defense Industry Daily, 6 Feb. 2012, <http://www.defenseindustrydaily.com/germany-may-sell-2-more-dolphin-subs-to-israel-for-117b-01528/>; and Williams, D., 'Admiral stirs question on Israel's "nuclear" subs', Reuters, 22 Sep. 2010, <http://www.reuters.com/article/2010/09/22/nuclear-israel-submarines-idUSLDE68L12T20100922>.

[6] On Israel's purchase of Dolphin submarines see also chapter 6, section I, in this volume.

Table 7.9. Israeli nuclear forces, January 2012

Type	Range (km)[a]	Payload (kg)	Status
Aircraft[b]			
F-16A/B/C/D/I Falcon	1 600	5 400	205 aircraft in the inventory; some are believed to be certified for nuclear weapon delivery
Ballistic missiles[c]			
Jericho II	1 500– 1 800	750– 1 000	c. 50 missiles; first deployed in 1990; test-launched on 27 June 2001
Jericho III	>4 000	1 000– 1 300	Test-launched on 17 Jan. 2008 and 2 Nov 2011; status unknown

[a] Aircraft range is for illustrative purposes only; actual mission range will vary. Missile payloads may need to be reduced in order to achieve maximum range.

[b] Some of Israel's 25 F-15I aircraft may also have a long-range nuclear delivery role.

[c] The Shavit space launch vehicle, if converted to a ballistic missile, could deliver a 775-kg payload to a distance of 4000 km.

Sources: Cohen, A., *The Worst-Kept Secret: Israel's Bargain with the Bomb* (Columbia University Press: New York, 2010); Cohen, A. and Burr, W., 'Israel crosses the threshold', *Bulletin of the Atomic Scientists*, vol. 62, no. 3 (May/June 2006); Cohen, A., *Israel and the Bomb* (Columbia University Press: New York, 1998); Albright, D., Berkhout, F. and Walker, W., SIPRI, *Plutonium and Highly Enriched Uranium 1996: World Inventories, Capabilities and Policies* (Oxford University Press: Oxford, 1997); Fetter, S., 'Israeli ballistic missile capabilities', *Physics and Society*, vol. 19, no. 3 (July 1990)—for an updated analysis see unpublished 'A ballistic missile primer', <http://www.publicpolicy.umd.edu/Fetter/Publications>; 'Nuclear notebook', *Bulletin of the Atomic Scientists*, various issues; and authors' estimates.

IX. North Korea's military nuclear capabilities

SHANNON N. KILE, PHILLIP SCHELL AND HANS M. KRISTENSEN

The Democratic People's Republic of Korea (DPRK, or North Korea) demonstrated a military nuclear capability by carrying out underground nuclear test explosions in October 2006 (with an estimated yield of less than 1 kiloton) and May 2009 (estimated yield of about 2–3 kt).[1] In both tests the estimated yield of the explosions was much lower than the yields of the initial nuclear tests conducted by other states. The US intelligence community called the 2006 test a failure and considered that the 2009 test 'was apparently more successful than the 2006 test'.[2] One expert has hypothesized, based on radionuclide signatures that were collected by monitoring stations in Japan, South Korea and Russia in May 2010, that North Korea may have carried out two very low yield nuclear test explosions during that month.[3]

At the end of 2010 North Korea was estimated to have roughly 30 kilograms of plutonium separated from the spent fuel of its 5-megawatt-electric graphite-moderated research reactor at Yongbyon (see section X below).[4] This would be sufficient to construct up to eight nuclear weapons, assuming that each weapon used 4–5 kg of plutonium and depending on North Korea's design and engineering skills. North Korea may have obtained weapon design assistance from the A. Q. Khan network.[5]

According to a leaked report prepared in 2011 by the United Nations Security Council's panel of experts on North Korea, the country has pursued a uranium enrichment programme 'for several years or even decades'.[6] In November 2010 a visiting delegation of US scientists was shown a previously undisclosed centrifuge enrichment facility, located in a former metal fuel rod fabrication building at Yongbyon.[7] According to the

---

[1] See Fedchenko, V., 'North Korea's nuclear test explosion, 2009', SIPRI Fact sheet, Dec. 2009, <http://books.sipri.org/product_info?c_product_id=397>.

[2] 'Annual threat assessment of the US intelligence community for House Permanent Select Committee on Intelligence: Dennis C. Blair, Director of National Intelligence', Statement for the record, 3 Feb. 2010, <http://dni.gov/testimonies_2010.htm>, p. 14.

[3] The analysis suggested that North Korea may have tested materials and techniques intended to boost the yield of its fission devices. De Geer, L.-E., 'Radionuclide evidence for low-yield nuclear testing in North Korea in April/May 2010', Science & Global Security, vol. 20, no. 1 (2012).

[4] Hecker, S. S., 'A return trip to North Korea's Yongbyon nuclear complex', Center for International Security and Cooperation, 20 Nov. 2010, <http://cisac.stanford.edu/publications/north_koreas_yongbyon_nuclear_complex_a_report_by_siegfried_s_hecker/>.

[5] On the Khan network, led by Pakistani scientist Abdul Qadeer Khan, see Fitzpatrick, M. (ed.), Nuclear Black Markets: Pakistan, A. Q. Khan and the Rise of Proliferation Networks, International Institute for Strategic Studies (IISS) Strategic Dossier (Routledge: Abingdon, 2007).

[6] Panel of experts established pursuant to Resolution 1874 (2009), Report, p. 20. The leaked report is available at <http://www.scribd.com/doc/55808872/UN-Panel-of-Experts-NORK-Report-May-2011>.

[7] Hecker (note 4).

UN panel of experts' report, it was 'highly likely that one or more parallel covert facilities capable of LEU [low-enriched uranium] or HEU [highly enriched uranium] production exist elsewhere' in the country.[8] The panel also judged that North Korea was likely to possess other covert facilities for processing and converting uranium feedstock to a form usable in gas centrifuges as well as for manufacturing the centrifuges. It is not known whether North Korea has produced HEU for use in nuclear weapons.

[8] Panel of experts established pursuant to Resolution 1874 (note 6), p. 20.

X. Global stocks and production of fissile materials, 2011

ALEXANDER GLASER AND ZIA MIAN
INTERNATIONAL PANEL ON FISSILE MATERIALS

Materials that can sustain an explosive fission chain reaction are essential for all types of nuclear explosives, from first-generation fission weapons to advanced thermonuclear weapons. The most common of these fissile materials are highly enriched uranium (HEU) and plutonium of almost any isotopic composition. This section gives details of current stocks of HEU (table 7.10) and separated plutonium (table 7.11), including in weapons, and details of the current capacity to produce these materials (tables 7.12 and 7.13, respectively). The information in the tables is based on new estimates prepared for the *Global Fissile Material Report 2011.*[1]

The production of HEU and plutonium both start with natural uranium.[2] Natural uranium consists almost entirely of the non-chain-reacting isotope U-238, with about 0.7 per cent U-235, but the concentration of U-235 can be increased through enrichment—typically using gas centrifuges. Uranium that has been enriched to less than 20 per cent U-235 (typically, 3–5 per cent)—known as low-enriched uranium—is suitable for use in power reactors. Uranium that has been enriched to contain at least 20 per cent U-235—known as HEU—is generally taken to be the lowest concentration practicable for use in weapons. However, in order to minimize the mass of the nuclear explosive, weapon-grade uranium is usually enriched to over 90 per cent U-235. Plutonium is produced in nuclear reactors through the exposure of U-238 to neutrons and is subsequently chemically separated from spent fuel in a reprocessing operation. Plutonium comes in a variety of isotopic mixtures, most of which are weapon-usable. Weapon designers prefer to work with a mixture that predominantly consists of Pu-239 because of its relatively low rate of spontaneous emission of neutrons and gamma rays and the low generation of heat through this radioactive decay. Weapon-grade plutonium typically contains more than 90 per cent of the isotope Pu-239. The plutonium in typical spent fuel from power reactors (reactor-grade plutonium) contains 50–60 per cent Pu-239 but is weapon-usable, even in a first-generation weapon design.

The five nuclear weapon states party to the 1968 Non-Proliferation Treaty—China, France, Russia, the UK and the USA—have produced both HEU and plutonium. India, Israel and North Korea have produced mainly plutonium, and Pakistan mainly HEU for weapons. All states with a civilian nuclear industry have some capability to produce fissile materials.

---

[1] International Panel on Fissile Materials (IPFM), *Global Fissile Material Report 2011: Nuclear Weapon and Fissile Material Stockpiles and Production* (IPFM: Princeton, NJ, Jan. 2012).

[2] For full details see International Panel on Fissile Materials (note 1), appendix B.

Table 7.10. Global stocks of highly enriched uranium (HEU), 2011

State	National stockpile (tonnes)[a]	Production status	Comments
China	16 ± 4	Stopped 1987–89	
France[b]	31 ± 6	Stopped 1996	Includes 4.6 tonnes declared civilian
India[c]	2.0 ± 0.3	Continuing	
Israel[d]	0.3	–	
Pakistan	2.75 ± 0.4	Continuing	
Russia[e]	666 ± 120	Stopped 1987–88	Includes 50 tonnes assumed to be reserved for naval and research reactor fuel; does not include 71 tonnes to be blended down
UK[f]	21.2 (declared)	Stopped 1962	Includes 1.4 tonnes declared civilian
USA[g]	510 (declared)	Stopped 1992	Includes 130 tonnes reserved for naval reactor fuel and 20 tonnes for other HEU reactor fuel; does not include 100 tonnes to be blended down or for disposal as waste
Non-nuclear weapon states[h]	~20		
Total	**~1270[i]**		**Does not include 171 tonnes to be blended down**

[a] Most of this material is 90–93% enriched uranium-235, which is typically considered as weapon-grade. Important exceptions are noted where required. Blending down (i.e. reducing the concentration of U-235) of excess Russian and US weapon-grade HEU up to late 2011 and mid-2011, respectively, has been taken into account.

[b] France declared 4.6 tonnes of civilian HEU to the International Atomic Energy Agency (IAEA) as of the end of 2010; it is assumed here to be weapon-grade, 93% enriched HEU, even though some of the material is in irradiated form. The uncertainty in the estimate applies only to the military stockpile of 26 tonnes and does not apply to the declared stock of 4.9 tonnes.

[c] It is believed that India is producing HEU (enriched to 30–45%) for use as naval reactor fuel. The estimate is for HEU enriched to 30%.

[d] Israel may have acquired c. 300 kg of weapon-grade HEU from the USA in or before 1965.

[e] As of 31 Dec. 2011, 442 tonnes of Russia's weapon-grade HEU had been blended down. The estimate given for the Russian reserve for naval reactors is the authors' estimate based on the size of the Russian fleet.

[f] The UK declared a stockpile of 21.9 tonnes of HEU as of 31 Mar. 2002, the average enrichment of which was not given. An estimated 0.7 tonnes may have been consumed since then in naval reactor fuel. The UK declared a stock of 1.4 tonnes of civilian HEU to the IAEA as of the end of 2010.

[g] The amount of US HEU is given in actual tonnes, not 93% enriched equivalent. As of 30 Sep. 1996 the USA had an inventory of 741 tonnes of HEU containing 620 tonnes of U-235. To date, the USA has earmarked 233 tonnes of HEU for blending down. As of mid-2011 it had blended down 135 tonnes of this; however, little if any of this HEU was weapon-grade. An additional at least 100 tonnes is in the form of irradiated naval fuel.

[h] The 2010 IAEA Annual Report lists 230 significant quantities of HEU under comprehensive safeguards. In order to reflect the uncertainty in the enrichment levels of this material, mostly in research reactor fuel, a total of 20 tonnes of HEU is assumed. About half of this is in Kazakhstan and has been initially irradiated slightly higher than 20%-enriched fuel.

[i] This total is rounded to the nearest 5 tonnes.

Table 7.11. Global stocks of separated plutonium, 2011

State	Military stocks as of 2011 (tonnes)	Military production status	Civilian stocks as of 2011, unless indicated (tonnes)[a]
China	1.8 ± 0.8	Stopped in 1991	0.01
France	6 ± 1.0	Stopped in 1992	56 (does not include 24.2 foreign owned)
Germany	–	–	7.6 (in France, Germany and the UK)
India[b]	0.52 ± 0.14	Continuing	4.44 (includes 4.2 outside safeguards)
Israel[c]	0.82 ± 0.13	Continuing	–
Japan	–	–	44.9 (including a total of 35 in France and the UK)
Korea, North[d]	0.03	Resumed in 2009	–
Pakistan[e]	0.11 ± 0.02	Continuing	–
Russia[f]	128 ± 8 (34 declared excess)	Effectively stopped in 1997	48.4
UK[g]	7.6 (4.4 declared excess)	Stopped in 1995	86.8 (includes 0.9 abroad but not 28.0 foreign owned)
USA[h]	92 (53.9 declared excess)	Stopped in 1988	–
Totals	**~237 (92 declared excess)**		**~248**

[a] Some countries own civilian plutonium that is stored overseas, mostly in France and the UK, but do not submit an IAEA INFCIRC/549 declaration. This includes Italy, which has 5.8 tonnes of plutonium, and the Netherlands, which has 0.3 tonnes of plutonium, all at La Hague, France.

[b] India produced weapon-grade plutonium from the CIRUS and Dhruva reactors until CIRUS closed at the end of 2010. As part of the 2005 Indian–US Civil Nuclear Cooperation Initiative, India has included in the military sector much of the plutonium separated from its spent power-reactor fuel. While it is labelled civilian here since it is intended for breeder reactor fuel, this plutonium was not placed under safeguards in the 'India-specific' safeguards agreement signed by the Indian Government and the IAEA on 2 Feb. 2009.

[c] Israel is believed to still be operating the Dimona plutonium production reactor but may be using it primarily for tritium production.

[d] North Korea is reported to have declared plutonium production of 31 kg in June 2008; to have carried out nuclear tests in 2006 and 2009; and to have resumed production in 2009, adding 8–10 kg.

[e] Pakistan is estimated to be producing c. 20 kg a year of weapon-grade plutonium from its Khushab-1 and -2 reactors. Two additional plutonium production reactors are under construction at the same site.

[f] Russia does not include its plutonium declared as excess in its INFCIRC/549 statement.

[g] The UK declared 86 tonnes of civilian plutonium (not including 28 tonnes of foreign-owned plutonium in the UK). This includes 4.4 tonnes of military plutonium declared excess and placed under European Atomic Energy Community (Euratom) safeguards and designated for IAEA safeguarding. It is included in the civilian stocks. The UK declared in 1995 that it had stopped fissile material production for weapons; this was the last year in which the UK's Atomic Weapons Establishment at Aldermaston received plutonium from the Sellafield reprocessing plant.

[h] In its IAEA INFCIRC/549 statement, the USA declared 53.9 tonnes of plutonium as excess for military purposes.

Sources for table 7.10: International Panel on Fissile Materials (IPFM), *Global Fissile Material Report 2011: Nuclear Weapon and Fissile Material Stockpiles and Production* (IPFM: Princeton, NJ, Jan. 2012), figure 1, p. 10; *Israel*: Myers, H., 'The real source of Israel's first fissile material', *Arms Control Today*, vol. 37, no. 8 (Oct. 2007), p. 56; see also Gilinsky, V. and Mattson, R. J., 'Revisiting the NUMEC affair', *Bulletin of the Atomic Scientists*, vol. 66, no. 2 (Mar./Apr. 2010); *Russia*: United States Enrichment Corporation, 'Megaton to megawatts', <http://www.usec. com/>; *UK*: British Ministry of Defence, 'Historical accounting for UK defence highly enriched uranium', Mar. 2006, <http://www.mod.uk/DefenceInternet/AboutDefence/Corp oratePublications/HealthandSafetyPublications/DepletedUranium/>; International Atomic Energy Agency (IAEA), Communication received from the United Kingdom of Great Britain and Northern Ireland concerning its policies regarding the management of plutonium, INFCIRC/549/Add.8/14, 28 June 2011; *USA*: US Department of Energy (DOE), *Highly Enriched Uranium, Striking a Balance: A Historical Report on the United States Highly Enriched Uranium Production, Acquisition, and Utilization Activities from 1945 through September 30, 1996* (DOE: Washington, DC, 2001); George, R. and Tousley, D., DOE, 'US highly enriched uranium disposition', Presentation to the Nuclear Energy Institute Nuclear Fuel Supply Forum, Washington, DC, 24 Jan. 2006; George, R., 'U.S. HEU disposition program', Institute of Nuclear Materials Management 50th Annual Meeting, Tucson, AZ, 13–19 July 2009; and Person, G. A., 'Future surplus HEU disposition in the U.S.', Institute of Nuclear Materials Management 52nd Annual Meeting, Palm Desert, CA, July 2011; *Non-nuclear weapon states*: IAEA, *Annual Report 2010* (IAEA: Vienna, 2011), table A4.

Sources for table 7.11: International Panel on Fissile Materials (IPFM), *Global Fissile Material Report 2011: Nuclear Weapon and Fissile Material Stockpiles and Production* (IPFM: Princeton, NJ, Jan. 2012), figure 4, p. 17; US Department of Energy (DOE), 'U.S. removes nine metric tons of plutonium from nuclear weapons stockpile', Press release, 17 Sep. 2007, <http://www. energy.gov/nationalsecurity/5500.htm>; *Civilian stocks (except for India)*: declarations by countries to the International Atomic Energy Agency (IAEA) under INFCIRC/549, <http:// www.iaea.org/Publications/Documents/>; *North Korea*: Kessler, G., 'Message to U.S. preceded nuclear declaration by North Korea', *Washington Post*, 2 July 2008; *Russia*: Russian–US Agreement concerning the Management and Disposition of Plutonium Designated as No Longer Required for Defense Purposes and Related Cooperation (Russian–US Plutonium Management and Disposition Agreement), signed 29 Aug. and 1 Sep. 2000, amended Apr. 2010, and entered into force July 2011, <http://www.state.gov/t/isn/trty/>; *UK*: 2010 Non-Proliferation Treaty Review Conference, Delegation of the United Kingdom, Statement, 19 May 2010, <http://www.un.org/en/conf/npt/2010/statements/statements_day_19may.shtml>.

Table 7.12. Significant uranium enrichment facilities and capacity worldwide, as of December 2011

State	Facility name or location	Type	Status	Enrichment process[a]	Capacity (thousands SWU/yr)[b]
Argentina	Pilcaniyeu	Civilian	Resuming operation	GD	20–3 000
Brazil	Resende Enrichment	Civilian	Under construction	GC	115–200
China	Lanzhou 2	Civilian	Operational	GC	500
	Lanzhou (new)	Civilian	Operational	GC	500
	Shaanxi	Civilian	Operational	GC	1 000
France	Eurodif	Civilian	Operational	GD	10 800
	Georges Besse II	Civilian	Operational	GC	7 500–11 000
Germany	Urenco Gronau[c]	Civilian	Operational	GC	2 200–4 500
India	Rattehalli	Military	Operational	GC	15–30
Iran	Natanz	Civilian	Under construction	GC	120
	Qom	Civilian	Under construction	GC	5–10
Japan	Rokkasho[d]	Civilian	Temporarily shut down	GC	<1 050
Korea, North	Yongbyon	..	..	GC	8[e]
Netherlands	Urenco Almelo	Civilian	Operational	GC	5 000–6 000
Pakistan	Gadwal	Military	Operational	GC	..
	Kahuta	Military	Operational	GC	15–45
Russia	Angarsk (formerly Angarsk-10)	Civilian	Operational	GC	2 200–5 000
	Novouralsk (formerly Sverdlovsk-44)	Civilian	Operational	GC	13 300
	Seversk (formerly Tomsk-7)	Civilian	Operational	GC	3 800
	Zelenogorsk (formerly Krasnoyarsk-45)	Civilian	Operational	GC	7 900
UK	Capenhurst	Civilian	Operational	GC	5 000
USA	Areva Eagle Rock	Civilian	Planned	GC	3 300–6 600
	Paducah	Civilian	To be shut down	GD	11 300
	Piketon, Ohio	Civilian	Planned	GC	3 800
	Urenco Eunice	Civilian	Operating	GC	5 900

[a] The gas centrifuge (GC) is the main isotope-separation technology used to increase the percentage of U-235 in uranium, but a few facilities continue to use gaseous diffusion (GD).

[b] SWU/yr = Separative work units per year: a SWU is a measure of the effort required in an enrichment facility to separate uranium of a given content of uranium-235 into 2 components, 1 with a higher and 1 with a lower percentage of uranium-235.

[c] Expansion is under way.

[d] The Rokkasho centrifuge plant was shut down in Dec. 2010; it is being refitted with new centrifuge technology.

[e] On North Korea's Yongbyon facility see section IX above.

Sources: Enrichment capacity data is based on International Atomic Energy Agency (IAEA), Integrated Nuclear Fuel Cycle Information Systems (INFCIS), <http://www-nfcis.iaea.org/>; International Panel on Fissile Materials (IPFM), *Global Fissile Material Report 2011: Nuclear Weapon and Fissile Material Stockpiles and Production* (IPFM: Princeton, NJ, Jan. 2012); and Citizens' Nuclear Information Center (CNIC), 'Uranium enrichment plant turns into a big waste dump', *Nuke Info Tokyo*, no. 140 (Jan./Feb. 2011), pp. 3–4.

Table 7.13. Significant reprocessing facilities worldwide, as of December 2011

All facilities process light water reactor (LWR) fuel, except where indicated.

State	Facility name or location	Type	Status	Design capacity (tHM/yr)[a]
China	Lanzhou pilot plant	Civilian	Operational	50–100
France	La Hague UP2	Civilian	Operational	1 000
	La Hague UP3	Civilian	Operational	1 000
India[b]	Kalpakkam (HWR fuel)	Dual-use	Operational	100
	Tarapur-I (HWR fuel)	Dual-use	Operational	100
	Tarapur-II (HWR fuel)	Dual-use	Operational	100
	Trombay (HWR fuel)	Military	Operational	50
Israel	Dimona (HWR fuel)	Military	Operational	40–100
Japan	JNC Tokai	Civilian	Temporarily shut down	200
	Rokkasho	Civilian	Starting up	800
Korea, North	Yongbyon	Military	On standby	100–150
Pakistan	Chashma (HWR fuel?)	Military	Under construction	50–100
	Nilore (HWR fuel)	Military	Operational	20–40
Russia	Mayak RT-1, Ozersk (formerly Chelyabinsk-65)	Civilian	Operational	200–400
	Seversk (formerly Tomsk 7)	Military	To be shut down	6 000
	Zheleznogorsk (formerly Krasnoyarsk-26)	Military	To be shut down	3 500
UK	BNFL B205 Magnox	Civilian	To be shut down	1 500
	BNFL Thorp, Sellafield	Civilian	Operational	1 200
USA	H-canyon, Savannah River Site	Civilian	Operational	15

HWR = Heavy water reactor.

[a] Design capacity refers to the highest amount of spent fuel the plant is designed to process and is measured in tonnes of heavy metal per year (tHM/yr), tHM being a measure of the amount of heavy metal—uranium in these cases—that is in the spent fuel. Actual throughput is often a small fraction of the design capacity. E.g. Russia's RT-1 plant has never reprocessed more than 130 tHM/yr and France, because of the non-renewal of its foreign contracts, will soon only reprocess 850 tHM/yr. LWR spent fuel contains about 1% plutonium, and heavy-water- and graphite-moderated reactor fuel about 0.4%.

[b] As part of the 2005 Indian–US Civil Nuclear Cooperation Initiative, India has decided that none of its reprocessing plants will be opened for IAEA safeguards inspections.

Sources: Data on design capacity is based on International Atomic Energy Agency (IAEA), Integrated Nuclear Fuel Cycle Information Systems (INFCIS), <http://www-nfcis.iaea.org/>; and International Panel on Fissile Materials (IPFM), *Global Fissile Material Report 2011: Nuclear Weapon and Fissile Material Stockpiles and Production* (IPFM: Princeton, NJ, Jan. 2012).

Part III. Non-proliferation, arms control and disarmament, 2011

Chapter 8. Nuclear arms control and non-proliferation

Chapter 9. Reducing security threats from chemical and biological materials

Chapter 10. Conventional arms control

8. Nuclear arms control and non-proliferation

Overview

The year 2011 saw continued political momentum behind treaty-based approaches to arms control and disarmament as well as multilateral initiatives to prevent the spread of weapons of mass destruction and capabilities to produce them. It was highlighted by the entry into force of the Russia–United States New START treaty, which mandated additional reductions in the two parties' strategic offensive nuclear forces (see section I in this chapter). The parties implemented on schedule the inspections, data exchanges, notifications and other measures set out in the treaty's cooperative monitoring and verification regime. This regime represents one of the main achievements of New START because it preserves and extends previous treaty arrangements for increasing the transparency and predictability of the former cold war adversaries' nuclear forces. In establishing this regime, New START continued an arms control process through which Russia and the USA have redefined their strategic relationship.

International efforts to prevent the spread of nuclear weapons remained a top priority in 2011. Two states—Iran and Syria—came under intensified scrutiny during the year for allegedly concealing military nuclear activities, in contravention of their commitments under the 1968 Non-Proliferation Treaty (NPT). A three-year investigation by the International Atomic Energy Agency (IAEA) concluded that a building in Syria destroyed by an Israeli air strike in 2007 was 'very likely' to have been a nuclear reactor that should have been declared to the agency (see section II). The IAEA reported that it had credible evidence that Iran had pursued nuclear weapon-related activities in the past and said that some of the activities might still be continuing (see section III). The difficulties encountered by inspectors in both countries led to renewed calls to expand the IAEA's legal powers to investigate NPT states parties suspected of violating their treaty-mandated safeguards agreements, even beyond those set out in the Model Additional Protocol.

The unresolved Iranian and Syrian nuclear controversies raised further doubt about the efficacy of international legal approaches, in particular the role of the United Nations Security Council, in dealing with suspected or known cases of states violating important arms control treaty obligations and norms. During 2011 Iran continued to defy five Security Council resolutions, adopted since 2006, demanding that it suspend all uranium enrichment and other sensitive nuclear fuel cycle activities. A divided Security Council failed to take action on Syria's nuclear file after the IAEA Board of Governors had declared the country to be non-compliant with its safeguards agreement. In the view of some observers, the lack of action set the stage for future controversies about the suitability of extra-legal measures, including the pre-emptive use of military force, in addressing proliferation concerns.

In East Asia, the diplomatic impasse over the fate of the nuclear programme of North Korea remained unresolved (see section IV). Preliminary discussions aimed at restarting the suspended Six-Party Talks on the denuclearization of North Korea made little progress, despite renewed contacts between North Korean and US diplomats. The legal and normative challenges posed by North Korea to the global non-proliferation regime were underscored by reports that the country had been involved in covert transfers of nuclear and ballistic technologies to third countries on a larger scale than previously suspected.

In an important development in long-running efforts to strengthen supply-side controls on the transfer of sensitive nuclear fuel cycle technologies, in June the Nuclear Suppliers Group reached a controversial consensus agreement to tighten its transfer guidelines for uranium-enrichment and plutonium-reprocessing equipment and technology (see section V).

The risks of nuclear terrorism and the illicit diversion of nuclear materials continued to be the focus of high-level political attention around the globe. Several measures were adopted to strengthen or enhance existing legal and regulatory arrangements aimed at increasing the security of nuclear materials and facilities worldwide (see section VI). Among these was an agreement by the Group of Eight (G8) to extend the 2002 Global Partnership against the Spread of Weapons and Materials of Mass Destruction—an initiative which has supported cooperative projects aimed at addressing non-proliferation, disarmament and nuclear security issues. In addition, the UN Security Council adopted Resolution 1977, which extended by 10 years the mandate of the committee established under Resolution 1540 to monitor and facilitate states' compliance with their obligations under the resolution.

As 2011 ended, the prospects for making new advances on the arms control and disarmament agenda remained unclear. Much unfinished business remained on that agenda, in particular the opening of the long-stalled negotiations on a fissile material cut-off treaty and the bringing into force of the 1996 Comprehensive Nuclear-Test-Ban Treaty. There were also questions about the next steps in Russian–US arms control after New START. Both sides acknowledged that making further cuts in their nuclear arsenals would require expanding the bilateral agenda to address tactical nuclear weapons and non-deployed warheads as well as broader strategic stability issues. The most prominent of the latter related to ballistic missile defence, which was the focus of an intensifying dispute between Russia and the USA in 2011. There was also recognition that deeper cuts in their respective strategic nuclear arsenals would require bringing the other NPT-recognized nuclear weapon states into a multilateral nuclear arms-reduction process.

SHANNON N. KILE

I. Russian–US nuclear arms control

SHANNON N. KILE

A new chapter in strategic nuclear arms control and Russian–US relations was opened on 5 February 2011, when the Russian Foreign Minister, Sergei Lavrov, and the US Secretary of State, Hillary Rodham Clinton, exchanged the ratification documents to bring into force the 2010 Treaty on Measures for the Further Reduction and Limitation of Strategic Offensive Arms (New START).[1]

The new treaty mandated modest reductions in the numbers of strategic nuclear warheads deployed by Russia and the United States below the limits imposed by two existing treaties: the 1991 Treaty on the Reduction and Limitation of Strategic Offensive Arms (START) and the 2002 Treaty on Strategic Offensive Reductions (SORT, or Moscow Treaty).[2] It also imposed numerical limits on the parties' deployed and non-deployed strategic nuclear delivery vehicles—intercontinental ballistic missiles (ICBMs), submarine-launched ballistic missiles (SLBMs) and long-range heavy bombers (see table 8.1). The delivery vehicles will be treaty-accountable until they are converted or eliminated according to the provisions described in a protocol.[3]

One of New START's main achievements was to extend the verification regime established by START. Both countries had emphasized that this was an indispensable step for maintaining transparency and predictability in their strategic nuclear force postures. The New START verification regime is built around an extensive database that identifies the numbers, locations and technical characteristics of weapon systems and facilities limited by the treaty. It provides for notifications, inspections and exhibitions to confirm information in the database and to monitor treaty-limited forces. Among other measures, the treaty requires each party to place a 'unique identifier' (an alphanumeric tag) on all missiles, associated launchers and bombers, which is to be used in notifying the other party when they are moved between declared facilities or change status. In addition, New START allows for Russia and the USA to continue to use national technical

---

[1] 'New START Treaty "lays foundation" for Russia-U.S. cooperation—Lavrov', RIA Novosti, 5 Feb. 2011, <http://en.rian.ru/russia/20110205/162466422.html>. The US Senate had provided its advice and consent to ratification of New START on 22 Dec. 2010. The Russian State Duma and Federation Council ratified the treaty on 25 Jan. 2011 and 26 Jan. 2011, respectively. For a summary and other details of New START see annex A in this volume. For a summary of the Russian and US ratification debates see Kile, S. N., 'Nuclear arms control and non-proliferation', *SIPRI Yearbook 2011*, pp. 370–71.

[2] US Department of State, Bureau of Verification, Compliance and Implementation, 'Comparison of the START Treaty, Moscow Treaty, and New START Treaty', Fact sheet, 8 Apr. 2010 <http://www.state.gov/t/avc/rls/139901.htm>. For summaries and other details of START and SORT see annex A in this volume.

[3] For a description of New START's central limits see Kile (note 1), pp. 365–68.

Table 8.1. Russian–US nuclear arms reduction treaties' force limits

Treaty	Date of signature	Date of entry into force	Total treaty-accountable nuclear warheads	Total strategic nuclear delivery vehicles[a]	Expiration date
START	31 July 1991	5 Dec. 1994[b]	6000	1600	5 Dec. 2009
SORT	24 May 2002	1 June 2003	1700–2200	. .[c]	. .[d]
New START	8 Apr. 2010	5 Feb. 2011	1550	800[e]	5 Feb. 2021

START = Treaty on the Reduction and Limitation of Strategic Offensive Arms; SORT = Treaty on Strategic Offensive Reductions (Moscow Treaty)

[a] These are intercontinental ballistic missiles (ICBMs), submarine-launched ballistic missiles (SLBMs) and heavy bombers

[b] In May 1992 Belarus, Kazakhstan and Ukraine became parties to START alongside Russia (as the legally recognized successor state to the Soviet Union) and the USA.

[c] SORT did not impose a numerical limit on total strategic nuclear delivery vehicles

[d] SORT, which was scheduled to expire on 31 Dec. 2012, was superseded by New START.

[e] No more than 700 may be deployed

Source: US Department of State, Bureau of Verification, Compliance and Implementation, 'Comparison of the START Treaty, Moscow Treaty, and New START Treaty', Fact sheet, 8 Apr. 2010, <http://www.state.gov/t/avc/rls/139901.htm>.

means (NTM), such as satellites and remote sensing equipment, to gather data about each other's strategic forces. It also provides for the parties to exchange telemetry data from up to five missile flight tests annually as a transparency and confidence-building measure.

New START's inspection provisions were simplified compared to those in START in order to reduce implementation costs. One result was that the total number of permitted annual inspections decreased under the new accord. However, individual inspections can be more comprehensive—in some cases gathering data that would have required multiple inspections under START. Under the new treaty, there are two types of short-notice on-site inspection compared to the nine different types of inspection specified in START. Each side may conduct Type 1 inspections up to 10 times annually, and Type 2 inspections up to 8 times annually, to confirm the accuracy of declared data on launchers, missiles, bombers and related facilities subject to the treaty. Type 1 inspections focus on sites with deployed and non-deployed strategic systems; Type 2 inspections focus on sites with only non-deployed strategic systems.[4] Type 1 inspections are also used to confirm that the number of warheads carried on deployed ICBMs and SLBMs is consistent with the numbers listed in the database. This objective reflects an important change in warhead attribution rules under New START: it permits the parties to count—through direct observation—the actual number of warhead re-entry vehicles on deployed missiles ran-

---

[4] For detail of the 2 types of inspection see Kile (note 1), pp. 366–67.

Table 8.2. Russian and US aggregate numbers of strategic offensive arms under New START, as of 5 February 2011 and 1 September 2011

	Russia		United States	
Category of data	Feb. 2011	Sep. 2011	Feb. 2011	Sep. 2011
Deployed ICBMs, SLBMs and heavy bombers	521	516	882	822
Warheads on deployed ICBMs and SLBMs, and warheads counted for heavy bombers[a]	1 537	1 566	1 800	1 790
Deployed and non-deployed launchers of ICBMs, SLBMs and heavy bombers	865	871	1 124	1 043

ICBM = intercontinental ballistic missile; SLBM = submarine-launched ballistic missile.

[a] Each heavy bomber, whether equipped with nuclear-armed cruise missiles or nuclear gravity bombs, is counted as carrying only 1 warhead, even though the aircraft can carry larger weapon payloads.

Source: US Department of State, Bureau of Arms Control, Verification and Compliance, 'New START Treaty aggregate numbers of strategic offensive arms', Fact Sheet, 1 June 2011 and 25 Oct. 2011, <http://www.state.gov/t/avc/rls/164722.htm> and <http://www.state.gov/t/avc/rls/176096.htm>.

domly selected for inspection. START had attributed a fixed number of warheads to each ICBM and SLBM—in most cases equal to the maximum number of re-entry vehicles that the missile had been tested with—regardless of whether an individual missile carried fewer warheads.

Implementation of data exchanges, notifications and inspections

On 22 March 2011 Russia and the USA completed the initial exchange of data, which was required no later than 45 days after New START entered into force, on numbers, locations and technical characteristics of the strategic arms subject to the treaty. The parties subsequently released to the public the total number of nuclear warheads carried on their respective treaty-accountable strategic nuclear delivery vehicles as well as the aggregate numbers of their deployed and non-deployed delivery vehicles (see table 8.2).

The summary of the aggregate data from the parties' second biannual exchange was publicly released in October 2011. The new data showed that the USA continued to make modest reductions in its treaty-limited forces under New START. It also revealed that Russia was already close to meeting the New START ceiling of 1550 deployed warheads to be achieved by the 2018 deadline for implementing the treaty.[5] However, the data did

[5] Some US critics of New START have argued that the treaty disproportionately favoured Russia since it planned to reduce its strategic nuclear forces with or without a new treaty. See e.g. Payne, K. B., 'Postscript on New START', *National Review*, 18 Jan. 2011.

not provide information about specific changes in the Russian force structure.[6]

The release of the aggregate treaty data highlighted a potential shortcoming in New START: the information that the parties are required to make public about their respective strategic nuclear forces is more limited, in terms of scope and level of detail, than that provided under START. The new treaty permits Russia and the USA to release detailed information about changes in their own force structures but, unlike the earlier treaty, one party may not release information on the other's strategic forces going beyond the summary of aggregate data without consent.[7] Following the second exchange of data the USA declassified and published information about its numbers of specific types of delivery vehicle and their locations. Russia has not indicated whether it plans to release additional data or allow the USA to do so. Several non-governmental analysts and former US defence officials have expressed concern that the restrictive public data-sharing provision in New START represents a setback for efforts to promote international nuclear transparency and to build the requisite confidence for advancing a multilateral arms-reduction process.[8]

During 2011 the parties fulfilled other New START inspection and monitoring requirements in accordance with the schedule set out in the treaty's protocol and annexes. In March Russia showed US inspectors for the first time its new multiple-warhead RS-24 ICBM and road-mobile launcher at the production plant in Votkinsk, Udmurtia.[9] During the same month the USA conducted similar one-time exhibitions of its B-2A and B-1B bombers. The USA's B-1B bombers have all been converted to carry only conventional weapons. Following the exhibition to demonstrate that the bombers were not capable of employing nuclear armaments, they no longer counted against the New START limits on US forces.[10]

As of 5 February 2012 Russia and the USA had each conducted 18 Type 1 and Type 2 inspections—the maximum number permitted on an annual basis—at ICBM, SLBM and heavy bomber bases, storage facilities, conversion and elimination facilities, and test ranges. The Type 1 inspections

---

[6] For detail of the changes in Russian and US strategic nuclear forces see chapter 7, sections I and II, in this volume.

[7] Russia and the USA have the right to release to the public data and information obtained during the implementation of the treaty following agreement within the Bilateral Consultative Commission. New START (note 1), Article VII, para. 5.

[8] Kristensen, H. M., 'New START aggregate numbers released: first round slim picking', Federation of American Scientists (FAS), FAS Strategic Security Blog, 1 June 2011, <http://www.fas.org/blog/ssp/2011/06/aggregatedata.php>.

[9] 'U.S. and Russia know location of each other's missile silos–RSVN commander', Interfax, 16 Dec. 2011.

[10] US Department of State, Bureau of Verification, Compliance and Implementation, 'New START Treaty implementation update', Fact sheet, 5 Feb. 2012, <http://www.state.gov/t/avc/rls/183335.htm>.

used for the first time the procedures specified in the New START protocol to confirm the actual number of warheads placed on randomly selected missiles. In addition, the parties' nuclear risk-reduction centres had exchanged over 1800 notifications, including those related to the production, conversion, elimination and movement of launchers and delivery vehicles based on the 'unique identifiers' assigned to treaty-limited items.[11]

The notification process was also used for convening the initial meetings of the Bilateral Consultative Commission (BCC), which is the treaty's principal implementation and compliance body. The BCC has a mandate similar to that of the Joint Compliance and Inspection Commission (JCIC) under START. It is intended to resolve questions relating to treaty compliance and to adopt 'such additional measures as may be necessary to improve the viability and effectiveness of the treaty'; the BCC has the authority to amend the protocol, or its annexes, as long as the changes do not affect substantive rights or obligations under the treaty.[12]

Russia and the USA held the first regular biannual meeting of the BCC from 28 March to 8 April 2011.[13] The representatives issued two joint statements that addressed technical procedures to be used during the on-site inspection process.[14] The BCC's second meeting for the year was held from 19 October to 2 November 2011.[15] Among other topics, the two sides reportedly discussed Russia's concerns about the procedures by which the USA had converted its B-1B bombers so that the aircraft could only carry conventional weapons.[16]

New START and missile defence

The implementation of New START proceeded apace against the background of the ongoing dispute between Russia and the USA over US plans to develop and deploy a new missile defence architecture that will include radar and missile interceptors sites in Europe. Russia has expressed con-

[11] US Department of State (note 10).

[12] New START (note 1), protocol, part VI; and US Department of State, Bureau of Verification, Compliance and Implementation, 'Bilateral Consultative Commission', Fact sheet, 11 Aug. 2011, <http://www.state.gov/t/avc/rls/145830.htm>.

[13] Russian Ministry of Foreign Affairs, 'On the first session of the Bilateral Consultative Commission under the new START Treaty', Press release, 11 Apr. 2011, <http://www.mid.ru/brp_4.nsf/0/4e6295f7991faabac325786800493b29>.

[14] US Department of Defense (DOD), Office of the Undersecretary of Defense for Acquisition, Technology and Logistics, 'New START BCC joint statements', 8 Apr. 2011, <http://www.acq.osd.mil/tc/treaties/NST/BCC_statements.htm>.

[15] US Department of State, 'U.S.–Russia Bilateral Consultative Commission on the New START Treaty', Media note, 2 Nov. 2011, <http://www.state.gov/r/pa/prs/ps/2011/11/176586.htm>.

[16] Misasnikov, E., 'Developing approaches toward resolving the issue of nonstrategic nuclear weapons', Centre for Arms Control, Energy and Environmental Studies, Paper prepared for the Roundtable 'Improving transparency on tactical nuclear weapons: building blocks for a NATO–Russia dialogue', Berlin, 17–18 Nov. 2011, <http://www.armscontrol.ru/pubs/en/em231111.html>.

cern that the USA's European Phased Adaptive Approach (EPAA) to missile defence would increase the capabilities of US and North Atlantic Treaty Organization (NATO) missile defences in a way that could threaten Russia's strategic nuclear deterrent.[17] The EPAA envisions the deployment, in four phases, of approximately 500 interceptor missiles on more than 40 ships and at two European land bases (one in Poland and one in Romania), as well as a radar based in Turkey, by the beginning of the 2020s.[18] The USA has insisted that the system's architecture is designed to provide protection for US forces, allies and partners in Europe against ballistic missile threats from the Middle East, in particular from Iran, and is not directed against Russia.

During 2011 the discussions between Russia and the USA and its NATO allies on missile defence cooperation made little progress. At a meeting of the heads of state and government of the NATO–Russia Council held in November 2010, NATO and Russia had agreed to pursue missile defence cooperation, including a joint missile threat assessment.[19]

Russia proposed establishing a sector-based joint missile defence system in which each side (Russia and NATO) would be fully responsible for its own zone and would have control over any decision to launch interceptor missiles.[20] In contrast, the USA and its NATO allies favoured the creation of two independent missile interceptor systems that could form the basis for Russian–NATO cooperation. The proposed cooperation could include exchanging missile early-warning and tracking information and setting up a joint data 'fusion' centre. The new body would allow NATO and Russian officers to have simultaneous access to missile launch data from sensors in NATO countries and Russia.[21]

Following NATO's rejection of its proposal, Russia intensified its call for the USA to provide legally binding guarantees that the EPAA system would not be directed against Russia's strategic nuclear forces. Russia also reportedly wanted an agreement that would limit the total number of new missile interceptors as well as place restrictions on the speed and deployment locations of the interceptors. Russian officials warned that the unrestrained qualitative and quantitative build-up of Western missile defences could be

---

[17] For a technical assessment of the EPAA's implications for Russia's strategic deterrent see Butt, Y. and Postol, T., *Upsetting the Reset: The Technical Basis of Russian Concern over NATO Missile Defense*, Federation of American Scientists (FAS) Special Report no. 1 (FAS: Washington, DC, Sep. 2011.

[18] See Arms Control Association, 'The phased adaptive approach at a glance', Fact sheet, June 2011, <http://www.armscontrol.org/factsheets/Phasedadaptiveapproach>.

[19] NATO–Russia Council, Joint statement, Lisbon, 20 Nov. 2011, <http://www.nato.int/cps/en/natolive/news_68871.htm>.

[20] Bogdanov, K., 'European missile defenses and Russia's last warning', RIA Novosti, 7 Oct. 2011, <http://en.rian.ru/analysis/20111007/167474493.html>.

[21] Collina, T. Z., 'Missile defense cooperation stalls', *Arms Control Today*, vol. 41, no. 5 (July/Aug. 2011).

regarded by Russia as an exceptional event under Article 14 of New START, whereby Russia has the right to withdraw from the treaty.[22]

The parties made little progress during the year towards reaching a compromise formula for settling the missile defence dispute. On 23 November Russian President Dmitry Medvedev warned in a nationally televised speech that Russia was losing patience with the impasse in bilateral and multilateral talks on missile defence and reserved 'the right to discontinue further disarmament and arms control measures'.[23] He also outlined a number of possible Russian military and diplomatic responses if the USA and NATO moved forward with plans for a missile defence system that did not adequately address Russia's concerns. At a meeting of the NATO–Russia Council held on 8 December 2011 and attended by NATO foreign ministers and their Russian counterpart, the officials showed little willingness to modify their established positions on missile defence in order to break the diplomatic impasse.[24]

Next steps after New START

In addition to the long-running dispute over missile defence, Russia and the USA continued to disagree about the focus and timing of the next steps in bilateral arms control. These disagreements primarily concerned two categories of nuclear weapon that are not subject to constraints under New START or other legally binding instruments: non-strategic (or tactical) nuclear weapons and warheads that are held in storage or otherwise not deployed.

During 2011 the USA renewed its call for the two sides to begin new talks aimed at limiting their non-strategic nuclear weapon inventories. Russia is believed to maintain a considerably larger stockpile of such weapons than the USA. On 3 February US President Barrack Obama informed the US Senate, pursuant to a provision added to the New START ratification resolution by Republican senators, that the administration's next arms control goal was to begin talks with Russia within one year on limiting stockpiles of non-strategic nuclear weapons.[25] US officials emphasized that addressing tactical nuclear weapons would require close coordination with

---

[22] 'Russia "disappointed" by U.S. failure to provide missile guarantees', RIA Novosti, 16 May 2011, <http://en.rian.ru/russia/20110516/164052008.html>.

[23] Office of the President of Russia, 'Statement in connection with the situation concerning the NATO countries' missile defence system in Europe', 23 Nov. 2011, <http://eng.kremlin.ru/news/3115>.

[24] Presto, S., 'NATO, Russia remain at odds over missile shield', Voice of America, 8 Dec. 2011, <http://www.voanews.com/english/news/europe/NATO-Russia-Still-at-Odds-Over-Missile-Shield-135258238.html>.

[25] US Senate, Resolution of advice and consent to ratification, Senate Treaty Document 111-5, 22 Dec. 2010, <http://www.state.gov/t/avc/rls/153910.htm>.

allies in NATO as well as deeper engagement with Russia on a range of security issues.[26]

Russia showed little interest in US proposals for discussing measures to reduce or regulate non-strategic nuclear weapon stockpiles, at least in the near term.[27] Lavrov emphasized that Russia would not take part in any such discussions before the USA had withdrawn its non-strategic nuclear weapons from Europe and irreversibly dismantled the infrastructure for their deployment.[28] In addition, Russian officials continued to link the opening of negotiations on tactical nuclear arms reductions to progress on other issues affecting strategic stability. These included limits on US ballistic missile defences, long-range conventional strike weapons and weapons in space.[29]

As the year ended, senior US officials acknowledged that new talks on non-strategic nuclear weapons were unlikely to get under way soon. The Assistant Secretary of State for Verification, Compliance, and Implementation, Rose Gottemoeller, explained that the USA was currently in a 'homework period' to prepare a way forward for new talks leading to cuts in non-strategic nuclear weapons and warheads in storage.[30] She suggested that the two sides could already begin to discuss technical and definitional issues related to non-strategic weapons as a preliminary step towards the eventual opening of negotiations.[31]

[26] Benitez, J., 'US consults with NATO allies on reducing tactical nuclear weapons', NATO Source, Atlantic Council, 17 Feb. 2011, <http://www.acus.org/natosource/us-consults-nato-allies-reducing-tactical-nuclear-weapons>. In the Strategic Concept adopted on 19–20 Nov. 2010, the NATO member states agreed to continue the discussion of the role of defence and deterrence in NATO's strategy, including its nuclear posture. NATO, *Active Engagement, Modern Defence: Strategic Concept for the Defence and Security of the Members of the North Atlantic Treaty Organization* (NATO: Brussels, Nov. 2010).

[27] For Russian views on reducing tactical nuclear weapons see Misasnikov (note 16).

[28] Russian Ministry of Foreign Affairs, 'Statement by H.E. Mr Sergey Lavrov, Minister of Foreign Affairs of the Russian Federation, at the Plenary meeting of the Conference on Disarmament, Geneva, 1 Mar. 2011', 1 Mar. 2011, <http://www.mid.ru/brp_4.nsf/0/2de66a92e764dbb8c325784600 4dfd44>.

[29] Miasnikov (note 16); and Sokov, N., 'Medvedev's statement on missile defense might mean Russia postpones further dialogue until 2013', James Martin Center for Non-Proliferation Studies (CNS), 2 Dec. 2011, <http://cns.miis.edu/stories/111202_medvedev_statement.htm>.

[30] 'Rose Gottemoeller: getting to yes', *Bulletin of the Atomic Scientists*, vol. 67, no. 6 (Nov./Dec. 2011), p. 5.

[31] 'U.S. preparing for tactical nuclear cuts in future arms deal with Russia', RIA Novosti, 27 Dec. 2011, <http://en.rian.ru/mlitary_news/20111227/170513651.html>.

II. Syria and nuclear proliferation concerns

SHANNON N. KILE

In 2011 Syria came under renewed international scrutiny by refusing to dispel suspicions that it had carried out work on a suspected undeclared nuclear facility. The suspicions centred on a facility located at al-Kibar, a remote site in Deir Ez-Zor governorate in eastern Syria. The site was destroyed by an Israeli air strike in September 2007. The Israeli and US governments alleged that Syria had been secretly constructing, with technical assistance from North Korea, a nuclear reactor similar to the reactor that North Korea used to produce plutonium for nuclear explosive devices. The Syrian Government has stated that the building was a disused military facility that had no connection to nuclear activities, and that it had no nuclear cooperation with North Korea.[1]

On 25 February 2011 the Director General of the International Atomic Energy Agency (IAEA), Yukiya Amano, reported to the IAEA Board of Governors that Syria's lack of cooperation since June 2008 in providing access and requested information meant that the agency was unable to confirm Syria's statements about the non-nuclear nature of the Deir Ez-Zor site.[2] Among other failures, Syria had declined to provide information about its procurement of material and equipment that the IAEA believed could be used for building a reactor. Syria had also continued to deny inspectors access to three other locations inside the country that were suspected of being 'functionally related' to the activities at Deir Ez-Zor.[3]

In a subsequent report to the board, issued on 24 May 2011, Amano stated that the IAEA had assessed that the building destroyed at the Deir Ez-Zor site was 'very likely a nuclear reactor and should have been declared by Syria' under its comprehensive safeguards agreement with the agency.[4] The report outlined the evidence that had led inspectors to conclude that Syria had been building a covert nuclear reactor. It noted that the dimensions of the destroyed building were similar to the dimensions of the plutonium

---

[1] For more on the controversy over the alleged undeclared nuclear reactor in Syria see Kile, S. N., 'Nuclear arms control and non-proliferation', *SIPRI Yearbook 2009*, pp. 402–405.

[2] IAEA, Board of Governors, 'Implementation of the NPT safeguards agreement in the Syrian Arab Republic', Report by the Director General, GOV/2011/8, 25 Feb. 2011, p. 3.

[3] IAEA, GOV/2011/8 (note 2), p. 2.

[4] IAEA, Board of Governors, 'Implementation of the NPT safeguards agreement in the Syrian Arab Republic', Report by the Director General, GOV/2011/30, 24 May 2011, p. 8. A comprehensive safeguards agreement (CSA) between a non-nuclear weapon state and the IAEA places safeguards on all peaceful nuclear activities and all nuclear material on the territory of the state in order to verify that they are not misused for military purposes. Such agreements provide the legal basis for the IAEA's system of nuclear material accountancy, which is designed to verify that a state's declarations of nuclear material subject to safeguards are correct. The 1968 Non-Proliferation Treaty obliges all non-nuclear weapon states parties to conclude a CSA with the IAEA. For a list of states that have safeguards agreements in force with the IAEA see annex A in this volume.

production reactor at Yongbyon, North Korea. The report also stated that imagery of the building after the bombing showed features 'corresponding' to a containment structure, heat exchangers and a spent fuel pond, among other things, which were characteristic of that type of reactor. In addition, there had been suspected concealment activity at the site after the bombing, including Syrian efforts 'to recover equipment and material from the destroyed building prior to its complete demolition and burial'.[5]

On 9 June 2011 the IAEA Board of Governors adopted a resolution stating that Syria's failure to declare the construction of a nuclear reactor at Deir Ez-Zor constituted 'non-compliance with its obligations under its Safeguards Agreement with the Agency'.[6] It called on Syria to give the IAEA access to all information, sites, material and persons necessary for the agency to resolve the outstanding safeguards compliance questions and urged Syria to bring into force and implement an additional protocol to its comprehensive safeguards agreement.[7] The resolution instructed the Director General, pursuant to the IAEA Statute, to report Syria's non-compliance to the UN Security Council for its consideration and possible action.[8]

The resolution was approved by a deeply divided Board of Governors, with fewer than half of the 35 member states voting in favour; 6 states—including China and Russia—voted against and 11 others abstained.[9] One authoritative observer suggested that the use of the phrase 'maintenance of international peace and security' in the resolution's preamble—reminiscent of Chapter VII of the UN Charter, which authorizes the Security Council to use non-military and military means 'to maintain or restore international peace and security'—had been problematic for a number of board members.[10] In addition, officials from some abstaining countries indicated that the IAEA's assessment that the Deir Ez-Zor facility was 'very likely' to be a reactor was not sufficiently convincing to warrant referral to the Security Council.[11]

---

[5] IAEA, GOV/2011/30 (note 4), p. 4. On another compliance question, the report noted that the particles of anthropogenic (man-made) uranium found at the miniature neutron source reactor (MNSR) facility near Damascus would be further considered by the agency as a routine safeguards issue.

[6] IAEA, Board of Governors, 'Implementation of the NPT safeguards in the Syrian Arab Republic', Resolution, GOV/2011/41, 9 June 2011, p. 2.

[7] An additional protocol to a safeguards agreement (see note 4) is designed to enhance the IAEA's capability to detect and deter undeclared nuclear material or activities. It requires a state party to give the IAEA information on all aspects of its nuclear fuel cycle-related activities and provides the IAEA with new or expanded investigatory powers.

[8] IAEA, GOV/2011/41 (note 6), p. 2.

[9] Crail, P., 'IAEA sends Syria case to UN', *Arms Control Today*, vol. 41, no. 5 (July/Aug. 2011). One country was absent from the vote.

[10] Hibbs, M., 'A bridge too far? Syria & GOV/40', Arms Control Wonk, 11 June 2011, <http://hibbs.armscontrolwonk.com/archive/192/>.

[11] Crail (note 9).

In the wake of the vote, Western diplomats acknowledged that the UN Security Council was unlikely to censure Syria for its non-compliance or impose sanctions against the country in light of opposition from China, Russia and some countries of the Non-Aligned Movement (NAM). Russian officials said that Russia had opposed referring Syria to the Security Council because its destroyed nuclear programme no longer posed a threat to international peace and security.[12] There was also little prospect that Amano would call for the agency to carry out a special inspection in Syria, as had earlier been advocated by some non-governmental experts, in light of the lack of strong political support on the board for doing so.[13]

The approval of the board resolution had no immediate effect on the stalemate between the IAEA and Syria over the unresolved safeguards compliance questions. On 17 November 2011 Amano reported that the agency had made no progress in obtaining requested information from Syria.[14] The board subsequently decided to defer discussion of the issue because of the intensifying civil unrest inside Syria.[15]

The Syrian case highlighted the growing difficulty experienced by the IAEA Board of Governors over the past decade in reaching a consensus among the members. The board's decision making has increasingly pitted the Western industrial countries against the NAM countries; the latter have become more proactive in asserting the right of non-nuclear weapon states parties to the 1968 Non-Proliferation Treaty to pursue nuclear programmes for peaceful purposes.[16] At the same time, some observers hailed the board's referral of Syria to the Security Council as having set an important precedent. It demonstrated that a country could not prevent the IAEA from drawing informed conclusions about its nuclear activities simply by refusing to cooperate. This in turn had important implications for the agency's handling of the Iran case (see section III below).[17]

[12] Charbonneau, L., 'Q & A: what will U.N. council do on Syria's nuclear program'?, Reuters, 9 June 2011, <http://uk.reuters.com/article/2011/06/09/uk-syria-nuclear-un-idUKTRE75863820110 609>.

[13] See Acton, J. M., Fitzpatrick, M., and Goldschmidt, P., 'The IAEA should call for a special inspection in Syria', Proliferation Analysis, Carnegie Endowment for International Peace, 26 Feb. 2009, <http://carnegieendowment.org/2009/02/26/iaea-should-call-for-special-inspection-in-syria/4x2>.

[14] IAEA, Board of Governors, 'Introductory Statement to the Board of Governors by IAEA Director General Yukiya Amano', 17 Nov. 2011, <http://www.iaea.org/newscenter/statements/2011/amsp2011n030.html>.

[15] On the conflict in Syria in 2011 see chapter 2, section I, and chapter 3, section II, in this volume.

[16] Hibbs, M., 'Reaching consensus at the IAEA', Q&A, Carnegie Endowment for International Peace, 13 Sep. 2010, <http://carnegieendowment.org/2010/09/13/reaching-consensus-at-iaea/58p>.

[17] Mark Fitzpatrick, former US Deputy Assistant Secretary of State for Non-Proliferation, in Borger, J., 'Syria referred to UN security council over suspected nuclear programme', The Guardian, 9 June 2011.

III. Iran and nuclear proliferation concerns

SHANNON N. KILE

The international controversy over the scope and nature of Iran's nuclear programme intensified following the release in November 2011 of the most comprehensive review and assessment to date by the International Atomic Energy Agency (IAEA) of information about Iranian nuclear research and development activities with 'possible military dimensions'. There was also growing international concern about Iran's expansion of its uranium enrichment capabilities, in continued defiance of the United Nations Security Council's demands, set out in five resolutions, that it suspend all enrichment and other sensitive nuclear fuel cycle activities.[1]

The IAEA's assessment of alleged Iranian military nuclear activities

On 8 November 2011 the IAEA Director General, Yukiya Amano, issued the latest in the series of regular reports to the IAEA Board of Governors on safeguards implementation in Iran.[2] A 15-page annex described the results of the agency's analysis of the information available to it regarding indicators of clandestine nuclear-related activities in Iran, including weaponization. The report attracted considerable attention because the Director General stated, for the first time, that the agency assessed that Iran had carried out activities directly related to the development of a nuclear explosive device and that it might be continuing to pursue some of the activities.[3] The report did not address the question of whether Iran had decided to build a nuclear weapon.

The report stated that most of Iran's alleged weapon-related work took place prior to 2003. Information provided by IAEA member states indicated that nuclear research and development activities had been conducted in different military and academic institutions, assisted by advisory bodies, that were linked together in the late 1990s under an administrative umbrella called the 'AMAD Plan'. The consolidated programme was headed by a physicist named Mohsen Fakhrizadeh, and other 'senior Iranian figures featured' in the command structure of the plan 'at least for some significant period of time'.[4]

---

[1] UN Security Council resolutions 1737, 23 Dec. 2006; 1747, 24 Mar. 2007; 1803, 3 Mar. 2008; 1835, 27 Sep. 2008; and 1935, 9 June 2010.

[2] IAEA, Board of Governors, 'Implementation of the NPT safeguards agreement and relevant provisions of the Security Council resolutions in the Islamic Republic of Iran', Report by the Director General, GOV/2011/65, 8 Nov. 2011.

[3] 'UN nuclear agency IAEA: "Iran studying nuclear weapons"', BBC News, 9 Nov. 2011, <http://www.bbc.co.uk/news/world-middle-east-15643460>.

[4] IAEA, GOV/2011/65 (note 2), Annex, para. 18.

Alleged weaponization activities

According to the report's findings, the weapon-related activities that Iran allegedly pursued under the AMAD Plan involved all of the key technologies needed to develop an implosion-type nuclear explosive device fuelled by highly enriched uranium (HEU). The main activities included the following.

1. *Uranium conversion experiments.* Iran carried out work on the conversion of uranium dioxide into uranium tetrafluoride ('green salt') as part of a larger programme to obtain an autonomous source of uranium feedstock suitable for use at an undeclared enrichment plant.[5]

2. *Experiments with detonating high explosives.* Iran developed exploding bridgewire detonators and conducted experiments with multipoint initiation systems for the symmetrical detonation of a hemispherical high-explosive charge. This work, which has direct application for an implosion-type nuclear weapon, was allegedly assisted by a former Soviet scientist.[6]

3. *Hydrodynamic testing.* Iran made preparations for high-explosives tests using surrogate nuclear material designed to simulate the initial stages of a nuclear explosion. It also constructed a high-explosives test-containment chamber at the Parchin military complex in which to conduct hydrodynamic experiments to test the validity of warhead designs.[7]

4. *Missile payload design and integration.* As part of the so-called Project 111, Iran conducted computer modelling and engineering studies to examine how to integrate a new spherical payload, which was the size and shape of a nuclear weapon, into a re-entry vehicle for the Shahab-3 ballistic missile. Also under Project 111, Iran carried out development work on a prototype firing, arming and fusing system for a missile warhead.[8]

The report stated that most of the alleged weaponization activities were 'stopped rather abruptly pursuant to a "halt order"' by the Iranian leadership in late 2003. The decision may have been motivated by 'growing concerns about the international security situation in Iraq and neighbouring countries at that time'.[9]

According to the report, after 2003 Iran may have resumed some of the work carried out under the AMAD Plan, albeit in a less structured manner under different military and academic institutions.[10] There were indi-

[5] IAEA, GOV/2011/65 (note 2), Annex, paras 21–22.
[6] Warrick, J., 'Russian scientist Vyacheslav Danilenko's aid to Iran offers peek at nuclear program', *Washington Post*, 12 Nov. 2011.
[7] IAEA, GOV/2011/65 (note 2), Annex, paras 47–51.
[8] IAEA, GOV/2011/65 (note 2), Annex, paras 59–63.
[9] IAEA, GOV/2011/65 (note 2), Annex, para. 23.
[10] IAEA, GOV/2011/65 (note 2), Annex, para. 24.

cations that since 2006 Iran had conducted work to validate the design of a device to produce a burst of neutrons that could initiate a fission chain reaction.[11] There were also indications that Iran had carried out modelling studies on nuclear warhead design in 2008 and 2009 as well as experimental research on scaling down and optimizing a high-explosives package that could be relevant for a nuclear explosive device.[12] The report acknowledged, however, that the IAEA's ability 'to construct an equally good understanding of activities in Iran after the end of 2003' was 'reduced' owing to the more limited information provided by member states.[13]

Assessing the IAEA's assessment

One section of the report's annex was devoted to describing, in general terms, the sources on which the IAEA had based its analysis and conclusions. It emphasized that the agency had received information from 'a wide variety of independent sources', including from 'more than ten' states.[14] In addition, the agency's assessments were based on the results of its own investigations; information provided by Iran; and discussions with members of the nuclear trafficking network led by the Pakistani nuclear engineer Abdul Qadeer Khan. Overall, the agency deemed the information contained in the annex to be credible and 'consistent in terms of technical content, individuals and organizations involved, and time frames'.[15]

However, some government officials and non-governmental analysts pointed out that the IAEA's description of alleged nuclear weapon-related activities undertaken by Iran prior to the end of 2003 relied heavily on well-known material drawn from more than 1000 pages of documents contained on an Iranian defector's laptop computer. The so-called 'alleged studies' documents were supplied to the IAEA by a US intelligence agency, and their authenticity has been frequently questioned.[16] Robert Kelley, a former IAEA safeguards inspector, criticized the IAEA report for its lack of new information and for relying on documents whose 'provenance could not be established'.[17] Kelley and other experts also expressed doubts about specific claims made in the IAEA report.[18]

[11] IAEA, GOV/2011/65 (note 2), Annex, paras. 55–56.

[12] IAEA, GOV/2011/65 (note 2), Annex, paras. 44–45, 52.

[13] IAEA, GOV/2011/65 (note 2), Annex, para. 18.

[14] IAEA, GOV/2011/65 (note 2), Annex, paras 12–16.

[15] IAEA, GOV/2011/65 (note 2), para. 8.

[16] See e.g. Lewis, J., 'Is the laptop of death bogus?', Arms Control Wonk, 23 Feb. 2007, <http://lewis.armscontrolwonk.com/archive/1409/is-the-laptop-of-death-bogus>.

[17] Quoted in Hersh, S. M., 'Iran and the IAEA', Daily Comment, New Yorker, 18 Nov. 2011, <http://www.newyorker.com/online/blogs/comment/2011/11/iran-and-the-iaea.html>. See also Salami, I., 'IAEA report thrives on laptop of lies', Press TV, 8 Nov. 2011, <http://presstv.ir/detail/209074.html>.

[18] Porter, G., 'Ex-inspector rejects IAEA claims', Asia Times Online, 22 Nov. 2011 <http://www.atimes.com/atimes/Middle_East/MK22Ak02.html>.

Iran promptly rejected the report's findings and continued to categorically deny that it had ever worked on nuclear weapons. Iranian officials either dismissed documents pertaining to the alleged studies as forgeries and fabrications or, where they acknowledged the factual basis of some of the information, insisted that the work had nothing to do with a military programme.[19] Iranian officials also questioned the Director General's motives for preparing the 15-page annex to the report. Iran's ambassador to the IAEA, Ali Asgahr Soltanieh, described it as 'unbalanced, unprofessional and prepared with political motivation and under political pressure mostly by the United States'.[20]

New US National Intelligence Estimate on Iran

The general conclusions and timelines contained in the IAEA report were consistent with official testimony about the findings of the most recent US National Intelligence Estimate (NIE) on Iran's nuclear programme. The updated NIE was completed, after lengthy delay, in early 2011 and reflected the consensus views of 16 US intelligence agencies. It reportedly concluded that Iran was continuing to take steps towards developing a nuclear weapon capability, although not on the same scale and in a less structured manner than prior to the autumn of 2003.[21] This represented something of a shift from the main conclusion of the controversial 2007 NIE on Iran. The earlier document had concluded 'with high confidence' that Iran had halted its weaponization research in the autumn of 2003 and assessed with 'moderate confidence' that it had not resumed work on nuclear weapons as of mid-2007.[22]

According to testimony given to the US Senate in February 2011 by James Clapper, the Director of National Intelligence, the US intelligence community assessed that Iran was 'keeping open the option to develop nuclear weapons in part by developing various nuclear capabilities that better position it to produce such weapons' and to reduce the time frame needed to do so.[23] However, he confirmed that the intelligence community still had

---

[19] 'US dictated new IAEA report to Amano', Press TV, 8 Nov. 2011, <http://www.presstv.ir/detail/209020.html>; and 'IAEA report is unbalanced, politically motivated: Iran envoy', *Tehran Times*, 10 Nov. 2011.

[20] 'Iranian envoy criticizes IAEA conduct', Press TV, 22 Nov. 2011, <http://www.presstv.ir/detail/211406.html>.

[21] Miller, G., and Warrick, J., 'U.S. report finds debate in Iran on building nuclear bomb', *Washington Post*, 19 Feb. 2011. The 2011 NIE was not released in an unclassified form.

[22] US Director of National Intelligence, 'Iran: nuclear intentions and capabilities', National Intelligence Estimate, Nov. 2007, <http://www.dni.gov/press_releases_2007.htm>, pp. 6–8; and Kile, S. N., 'Nuclear arms control and non-proliferation', *SIPRI Yearbook 2008*, pp. 348–49.

[23] Clapper, J. R., Director of National Intelligence, 'Worldwide threat assessment of the U.S. Intelligence Community', Statement for the record for the US Senate Select Committee on Intelligence, 16 Feb. 2011, <http://www.dni.gov/testimonies.htm>, pp. 4–5.

a high level of confidence that Iran had not yet made a decision to restart its nuclear weapon programme. Clapper added that Iran's decision making on the nuclear issue was 'guided by a cost–benefit approach, which offers the international community opportunities to influence Tehran'.[24]

IAEA Board of Governors resolution on Iran

On 18 November 2011 the IAEA Board of Governors adopted a new resolution on Iran.[25] The resolution expressed 'deep and increasing concern about the unresolved issues regarding the Iranian nuclear program, including those which need to be clarified to exclude the existence of possible military dimensions'. It stressed the need for Iran to provide the IAEA with 'access to all relevant information, documentation, sites, material, and personnel' as part of an intensified dialogue to resolve the outstanding issues relating to Iran's nuclear work. The resolution also called on Iran 'to engage seriously and without preconditions in talks aimed at restoring international confidence in the exclusively peaceful nature of Iran's nuclear program'.[26]

The new resolution, which was submitted by the five permanent members of the UN Security Council (China, France, Russia, the United Kingdom and the United States) and Germany (the P5+1 states), did not directly censure Iran or call for additional punitive steps to be taken against it. Russia and China, along with some Non-Aligned Movement countries on the board, reportedly ruled out measures that, in their view, would lead to the further isolation of Iran.[27] Russia's ambassador to the IAEA, Grigory Berdennikov, had warned before the vote that the Director General's latest report 'in effect, has been transformed into a new source of rising tensions over Iran's nuclear program' by a 'well-orchestrated media campaign, aimed at the further aggravation' of the controversy.[28] China had urged a cautious approach, with a Foreign Ministry spokesperson emphasizing that the nuclear controversy should be 'addressed through dialogue and cooperation'.[29]

---

[24] Clapper (note 23), p. 5.

[25] IAEA, Board of Governors, 'Implementation of the NPT safeguards agreement and relevant provisions of United Nations Security Council resolutions in the Islamic Republic of Iran', Resolution, GOV/2011/69, 18 Nov. 2011. The resolution was approved by a vote of 32–2, with Cuba and Ecuador rejecting it and Indonesia abstaining.

[26] IAEA, GOV/2011/69 (note 25), paras 2, 4.

[27] Dahl, F. and Westall, S., 'U.N. nuclear watchdog board rebukes defiant Iran', Reuters, 18 Nov. 2011, <http://www.reuters.com/article/2011/11/18/us-nuclear-iran-iaea-idUSTRE7AG0RP20111118>.

[28] 'Publication of speculations about Iran's alleged research untimely: Russia', ITAR-TASS, 19 Nov. 2011, <http://pda.itar-tass.com/en/c154/276160.html>.

[29] Chinese Ministry of Foreign Affairs, 'Foreign Ministry spokesperson Hong Lei's regular press conference on November 9, 2011', 10 Nov. 2011, <http://www.fmprc.gov.cn/eng/xwfw/s2510/t876741.htm>.

Status of Fordow enrichment plant

In 2011 international tensions over Iran's nuclear programme were heightened by new developments at the enrichment facility being built by the Atomic Energy Organization of Iran (AEOI) in an underground tunnel complex on a military base at Fordow, near the city of Qom. The Fordow Fuel Enrichment Plant (FFEP) had become the subject of controversy in 2009, when Iran acknowledged that it was building the previously undeclared facility. At the time Iran had explained that the site was being prepared as a 'contingency' plant so that enrichment activities would not be halted in the case of military attacks on Iran's pilot- and commercial-scale centrifuge plants at Natanz.[30]

According to the IAEA Director General's report of 8 November 2011, Iran had revised the information it provided to the IAEA about planned enrichment operations at the Fordow facility. In 2009 Iran had stated that the purpose of the FFEP was to produce low-enriched uranium (LEU), enriched up to 5 per cent in the isotope uranium-235 (U-235), for use as nuclear fuel.[31] In June 2011 Iran informed the IAEA that the plant would instead produce LEU enriched 'up to 20 per cent' to be fabricated into fuel to replenish the Tehran Research Reactor (TRR).[32] The production of 20 per cent LEU would be moved to Fordow from the pilot fuel-enrichment plant at Natanz, under IAEA supervision, and the total output of 20 per cent LEU would be tripled at the new plant, using advanced centrifuges.[33] In September 2011 there were contradictory signals from the Iranian leadership about whether it would be willing to hold talks on a revived nuclear fuel exchange deal with the USA under which Iran would halt production of the 20 per cent LEU.[34]

On 9 January 2012 Iran announced that it had begun enriching uranium at the FFEP.[35] Iranian officials stressed that the Fordow plant was subject to

[30] IAEA, Board of Governors, 'Implementation of the NPT safeguards agreement and relevant provisions of Security Council resolutions 1737 (2006), 1747 (2007), 1803 (2008) and 1835 (2008) in the Islamic Republic of Iran', Report by the Director General, GOV/2009/74, 16 Nov. 2009, para. 12. See also Kile, S. N., 'Nuclear arms control and non-proliferation', *SIPRI Yearbook 2010*, pp. 385–88.

[31] IAEA GOV/2009/74 (note 30), para. 7.

[32] The TRR is a 5-megawatt-thermal research reactor that is used to produce medical isotopes. Iran has undertaken to produce fuel plates for the reactor after it exhausts the fuel supplied by Argentina in 1993.

[33] 'Iran to triple production of 20% enriched uranium', *Tehran Times*, 9 June 2011; and Pomeroy, R. and Amiri, M., 'Defiant Iran plans rise in nuclear enrichment', Reuters, 9 June 2011, <http://www.reuters.com/article/2011/06/08/us-iran-nuclear-enrichment-idUSTRE7572R620110608>.

[34] 'Ahmadinejad and Abbasi-Davani at odds on enrichment claims', Institute for Science and International Security (ISIS), Iran in Brief, 14 Sep. 2011, <http://isis-online.org/isis-reports/detail/ahmadinejad-and-abbasi-davani-at-odds-on-enrichment-claims/>. On previous fuel exchange proposals see Kile (note 30), pp. 385–88; and Kile, S. N., 'Nuclear arms control and non-proliferation', *SIPRI Yearbook 2009*, pp. 388–89.

[35] 'Iran enriching uranium at Fordo plant near Qom', BBC News, 10 Jan. 2012, <http://www.bbc.co.uk/news/world-middle-east-16470100>

IAEA safeguards and that the enrichment operations were intended to produce fuel that would enable the TRR to continue to produce medical isotopes. They also insisted that Iran would not give up its legitimate right under the 1968 Non-Proliferation Treaty to pursue uranium enrichment for peaceful purposes.[36]

Iran's announcement elicited strong criticism from France, Germany and the UK (the 'EU-3') as well as from the USA.[37] They denounced the Iranian move as a provocation and a step intended to bring Iran closer to achieving a so-called 'breakout' capability that would enable it to make enough weapon-grade uranium for a nuclear weapon in a short period of time.[38] The British Foreign Secretary, William Hague, pointed out that Iran had already accumulated several year's worth of LEU enriched to nearly 20 per cent but still lacked the technical ability to manufacture the fuel plates for the TRR.[39]

European Union (EU) and US officials pledged to intensify sanctions aimed at forcing Iran to return to negotiations about its nuclear activities.[40] On 23 January 2012 the Council of the European Union imposed an embargo that prohibited the 'import, purchase or transport of Iranian crude oil and petroleum products' by EU member states.[41] The Council also imposed a freeze on the assets of the Central Bank of Iran within the EU.[42] Iran had earlier threatened to block the Strait of Hormuz if Western countries attempted to enforce an embargo on Iranian petroleum exports, which reportedly prompted a sharp warning from the USA.[43]

The intensified Western sanctions against Iran over its nuclear programme led to renewed fears about a possible armed conflict. Tensions were heightened on 10 January 2012, when an Iranian nuclear scientist was assassinated in a bomb attack that Iran claimed was part of a foreign-

---

[36] 'Iran N-activities totally transparent', Press TV, 10 Jan. 2012, <http://www.presstv.ir/detail/220360.html>.

[37] 'Iran enriching uranium at Fordo plant near Qom' (note 35).

[38] Enrichment from natural uranium to 3.5% U-235, which is typical of reactor fuel, is significantly more time consuming and resource intensive than subsequent enrichment to the weapon-grade uranium (typically enriched above 90%) required for a nuclear weapon.

[39] Schneeweiss, Z., 'U.K.'s Hague 'disappointed' by Iran's provocative enrichment', Bloomberg, 9 Jan. 2012, <http://www.bloomberg.com/news/2012-01-09/u-k-s-hague-disappointed-by-iran-s-provocative-enrichment.html>.

[40] Hafezi, P. and Dahl, F., 'EU ministers plan Iran oil embargo, IAEA team to visit', Reuters, 10 Jan. 2011, <http://www.reuters.com/article/2012/01/10/us-iran-idUSTRE8090ZL20120110>.

[41] Council Decision 2012/35/CFSP of 23 Jan. 2012 amending Decision 2010/413/CFSP concerning restrictive measures against Iran, *Official Journal of the European Union*, L19, 24 Jan. 2012.

[42] US sanctions on financial institutions that dealt with the Central Bank of Iran were included in the National Defense Authorization Act for Fiscal Year 2012, US Public Law no. 112-81, signed into law 31 Dec. 2011, <http://thomas.loc.gov/cgi-bin/bdquery/z?d112:h.r.01540:>, section 1245. See also 'Obama signs US sanctions bill into law', BBC News, 31 Dec. 2011, <http://www.bbc.co.uk/news/world-us-canada-16376072>.

[43] 'U.S. message on Strait of Hormuz conveyed through 3 officials: Iran', *Tehran Times*, 15 Jan. 2012.

orchestrated sabotage campaign aimed at slowing its nuclear programme.[44] There was also mounting speculation that Israeli political leaders were considering pre-emptive military action against Iran's nuclear facilities.[45]

With its diplomatic and economic isolation deepening, Iran showed signs of adopting a more conciliatory approach to the nuclear issue. On 18 January 2012, the Iranian Foreign Minister, Ali Akbar Salehi, said during a visit to Turkey that Iran would resume talks with the P5+1 group about its nuclear programme.[46] Iran also confirmed that, prior to the talks reconvening, it would host a visit by the IAEA at the end of the January 2012.[47]

[44] 'Iran car explosion kills nuclear scientist in Tehran', BBC News, 11 Jan. 2012, <http://www.bbc.co.uk/news/world-middle-east-16501566>. Three similar attacks against Iranian nuclear scientists had been carried out by unknown assailants since Jan. 2010.

[45] Bergman, R., 'Will Israel attack Iran?', New York Times, 25 Jan. 2012.

[46] 'Iran: talks with P5+1 may be in Turkey', Press TV, 18 Jan. 2012, <http://www.presstv.ir/detail/221782.html>. On previous negotiations between Iran and the P5+1 states see Kile (note 30), pp. 388–89; and Kile, S. N., 'Nuclear arms control and non-proliferation', SIPRI Yearbook 2009, pp. 389–92.

[47] 'IAEA inspectors due in Iran in January', Press TV, 13 Jan. 2012, <http://www.presstv.ir/detail/220856.html>.

IV. North Korea's nuclear programme

SHANNON N. KILE

During 2011 the Six-Party Talks on the nuclear programme of the Democratic People's Republic of Korea (DPRK, or North Korea) remained blocked by disagreement over the terms for restarting negotiations.[1] North Korea repeatedly stated its willingness to return to the talks but emphasized that it would not accept any preconditions for doing so.[2] South Korean and US officials insisted that North Korea must first halt its uranium-enrichment programme and impose a moratorium on nuclear weapon and missile tests before negotiations could resume. North Korea rejected this demand in separate meetings held in July 2011 with South Korea's chief nuclear negotiator, Wi Sung-lac, and with the special US envoy on North Korean affairs, Glyn Davies.[3] However, on 24 August, after a meeting between Russian President Dmitry Medvedev and the North Korean leader, Kim Jong-il, North Korea reportedly indicated that it would be willing to observe a moratorium on the production and testing of nuclear weapons and missiles in the context of resumed talks.[4]

On 17 December 2011 there were unconfirmed media reports that North Korea had agreed to suspend its uranium-enrichment programme in exchange for food aid from the United States.[5] US officials had previously denied that there was any linkage between the issue of food aid deliveries to North Korea and progress in bilateral discussions of nuclear issues.[6] The planned US announcement of the decision to resume food aid reportedly had to be postponed, however, following the announcement on 19 December of the death of Kim Jong-il.[7] As the year ended, the uncertainties created by Kim's death appeared to halt, at least for the time being, further North Korean–US talks.

During the year there were renewed questions and concerns about the scope of North Korea's nuclear programme and its possible connection

---

[1] The Six-Party Talks began in Aug. 2003 as a Chinese diplomatic initiative to reach a deal under which international aid would be provided to North Korea in return for North Korea verifiably giving up its nuclear weapon capabilities. In addition to China and North Korea, the other parties are Japan, the Republic of Korea (South Korea), Russia and the United States.

[2] 'North Korea ready to discuss nuclear enrichment', BBC News, 15 Mar. 2011, <http://www.bbc.co.uk/news/world-asia-pacific-12742016>.

[3] Mydans, S. and Choe, S., 'North Korea is said to weigh nuclear test moratorium', New York Times, 25 Aug. 2011.

[4] Dyomkin, D., 'North Korea ready to discuss nuclear moratorium: Kremlin', Reuters, 24 Aug. 2011.

[5] 'U.S., N. Korea agree on 240,000 tons of food assistance: source', Yonhap, 17 Dec. 2011.

[6] US Department of State, 'Remarks by Special Representative Davies in Beijing, China', 15 Dec. 2011, <http://www.state.gov/p/eap/rls/rm/2011/12/178875.htm>.

[7] Rogin, J., 'Kim's death thwarts Obama's North Korean engagement attempts', The Cable, Foreign Policy, 19 Dec. 2011, <http://thecable.foreignpolicy.com/posts/2011/12/19/kim_s_death_thwarts_obama_s_north_korean_engagement_attempts>.

with the A. Q. Khan network. These had to do with the previously undeclared centrifuge enrichment plant, located at the Yongbyon nuclear site, that North Korea had shown to a visiting US scientific delegation in November 2010. North Korea claimed that the purpose of the enrichment plant was to produce low-enriched uranium for use as fuel in two light-water power reactors. A leaked report prepared by the United Nations Security Council's panel of experts on North Korea said that the enrichment plant and reactor projects constituted serious violations of the sanctions imposed by the Security Council on North Korea after its 2006 and 2009 nuclear tests.[8]

There was an emerging consensus among experts that the enrichment plant revealed in 2010 had been built with assistance from the Khan network. A report on North Korea issued in September 2011 by the IAEA Director General, Yukiya Amano, noted that the design and physical characteristics of the plant's centrifuge cascade were 'broadly consistent with a design' that had been disseminated through the network.[9] It also stated that 'information available to the agency' indicated that North Korea had attempted to procure material and equipment suitable for use in an enrichment programme from a wide range of suppliers. According to the UN panel's leaked report, in the 1990s the Khan network had supplied North Korea with a 'starter kit' of centrifuges that included first-generation (P-1) and second-generation (P-2) centrifuges based on Pakistani designs.[10]

There was also evidence to support speculation that North Korea had covertly transferred to other states material, equipment and technology of relevance for the development of nuclear weapons and their means of delivery. The IAEA report concluded that uranium hexafluoride found in a cylinder shipped to Libya by the Khan network in 2001 was 'very likely' to have originated in North Korea.[11] The UN panel concluded that North Korea had routinely shared prohibited 'ballistic missile-related items' with Iran in breach of UN sanctions on North Korea.[12] The transfers were believed to have taken place on regular scheduled flights 'through a neighboring third country', which several UN diplomats identified as China.[13]

---

[8] Panel of experts established pursuant to Resolution 1874 (2009), Report, p. 19. The leaked report is available at <http://www.scribd.com/doc/55808872/UN-Panel-of-Experts-NORK-Report-May-2011>. The sanctions were imposed by UN Security Council resolutions 1718, 14 Oct. 2006; and 1874, 12 June 2009. On the sanctions see also chapter 10, section III, in this volume.

[9] IAEA, Board of Governors and General Conference, 'Application of safeguards in the Democratic People's Republic of Korea', Report by the Director General, GOV/2011/53-GC(55)/24, 2 Sep. 2011, p. 8. The report did not indicate on what basis the IAEA had made this assessment.

[10] Panel of experts established pursuant to Resolution 1874 (note 8), p. 20. See also Pollack, J., 'The secret treachery of A. Q. Khan', Playboy, Jan./Feb. 2012.

[11] IAEA, GOV/2011/53-GC(55)/24 (note 9), p. 10. The IAEA thus assessed that North Korea had an undeclared uranium conversion capability prior to 2001.

[12] Panel of experts established pursuant to Resolution 1874 (note 8), p. 40.

[13] Bilefsky, D., 'China delays report suggesting North Korea violated sanctions', New York Times, 14 May 2011.

V. Developments in the Nuclear Suppliers Group

SIBYLLE BAUER

Many of the states that produce items that can be used in weapon of mass destruction (WMD) programmes cooperate on strategic trade controls in informal, non-legally binding, multilateral trade-control regimes with limited memberships.[1] In the case of nuclear material, equipment and technology, the relevant regime is the Nuclear Suppliers Group (NSG).[2] Its 46 participating states, along with the European Commission and the chair of the Zangger Committee as permanent observers, meet annually in a consensus-based, decision-making plenary in addition to intersessional preparatory and technical meetings.[3]

At the 2011 NSG plenary meeting, held on 23–24 June, in Noordwijk, the Netherlands, the participating states discussed and revised the NSG guidelines and debated its relationships with India, among other things. The revised guidelines imposed additional conditions on the transfer of sensitive nuclear fuel cycle materials, equipment and technologies for use in uranium enrichment and reprocessing of spent fuel (ENR) to states that do not already possess them.

Revision of the guidelines for export of sensitive technology

The origins of the discussion and key points of contention

The NSG first publicly released its guidelines in 1978, via the International Atomic Energy Agency (IAEA), and since then has revised them several times.[4] The guidelines require suppliers to base decisions on the export of

---

[1] The term 'strategic trade controls' is often defined as including conventional arms as well as dual-use items including software and technology. In strategic trade controls, the term 'dual-use' refers to items that may be used in WMD (nuclear, biological and chemical weapons) or their means of delivery. In the nuclear context, including in the NSG guidelines, dual-use items are defined differently as those with both nuclear and non-nuclear applications.

[2] The other regimes are the Australia Group, the Missile Technology Control Regime (MTCR), and the Wassenaar Arrangement on Export Controls for Conventional Arms and Dual-Use Goods and Technologies. For brief descriptions and lists of the participants in these regimes and the Zangger Committee see annex B in this volume. On developments in 2011 in the MTCR and the Wassenaar Arrangement see chapter 10, section II, in this volume. For earlier developments see previous editions of the SIPRI Yearbook and, specifically on the NSG, see Anthony, I., Ahlström, C. and Fedchenko, V., *Reforming Nuclear Export Controls: The Future of the Nuclear Suppliers Group*, SIPRI Research Report no. 22 (Oxford University Press: Oxford, 2007).

[3] The Zangger Committee was established to discuss export control issues related to the 1968 Non-Proliferation Treaty (NPT) and to find a common interpretation of Article III.2 of the treaty, including of the term 'equipment or material especially designed and prepared for the processing, use or production of special fissionable material'. See Anthony et al. (note 2), pp. 13–16.

[4] IAEA, Communication received from certain member states regarding guidelines for the export of nuclear material, equipment or technology, INFCIRC/254, Feb. 1978. Prior to the 2011 revision the most recent version of the NSG guidelines was in IAEA, Communication received from the Per-

specified nuclear and nuclear-related items on certain conditions. The recipient should guarantee that the items will not be used for a nuclear explosive device (paragraph 2) and it should implement a comprehensive safeguards agreement with the IAEA. The supplier should make provisions regarding future arrangements for the physical protection of nuclear materials and facilities and regarding re-transfer controls, and it should be 'satisfied that the transfers would not contribute to the proliferation of nuclear weapons or other nuclear explosive devices' or be 'diverted to acts of nuclear terrorism' (paragraph 10). Suppliers should also have 'in place legal measures to ensure the effective implementation of the Guidelines, including export licensing regulations, enforcement measures, and penalties for violations' (paragraph 11). The guidelines include control lists of items to which specific restrictions apply and 'catch-all' controls for unlisted items with a nuclear end-use. A 'safety clause' states that transfers may be made to a non-nuclear weapon state without a safeguards agreement with the IAEA 'only in exceptional cases when they are deemed essential for the safe operation of existing facilities' (paragraph 4). In these cases, the nuclear supplier should 'inform and, if appropriate, consult in the event that they intend to authorize or to deny such transfers'.

The NSG guidelines are not legally binding and are thus only enforceable if a participating state integrates them into national law; they leave scope for national interpretation, in particular regarding certain subjective criteria.[5] Importantly, the guidelines present a minimum standard, and national governments may impose stricter conditions of supply.

The debate on revising the NSG guidelines regarding ENR can be traced back to a US initiative in 2001, in response to Russia's controversial invoking of the safety clause when exporting nuclear fuel to India.[6] However, the clause was not affected by the 2011 guideline revision as the discussion changed course.[7]

---

manent Mission of Brazil regarding certain member states' guidelines for the export of nuclear material, equipment and technology, INFCIRC/254/Rev.9/Part 1, 7 Nov. 2007; and IAEA, Communication received from certain member states regarding guidelines for transfers of nuclear-related dual-use equipment, material, software and related technology, INFCIRC/254/Rev.8/Part 2, 30 June 2010. Part 2 was not revised in 2011.

[5] The EU Dual-use Regulation 428/2009, which is directly applicable law within the EU, refers to EU member states' commitments and obligations as members of export control regimes, including the NSG, thus making the guidelines a legal obligation. Council Regulation (EC) no. 428/2009 of 5 May 2009 setting up a Community regime for the control of exports, transfer, brokering and transit of dual-use items, *Official Journal of the European Union*, L134, 29 May 2009. See also Wetter, A., *Enforcing European Union Law on Exports of Dual-use Goods*, SIPRI Research Report no. 24 (Oxford University Press: Oxford, 2009).

[6] Anthony, I., 'Multilateral export controls', *SIPRI Yearbook 2002*, pp. 752–55.

[7] Viski, A., 'The revised Nuclear Suppliers Group guidelines: a European Union perspective', Non-proliferation Papers no. 15, EU Non-proliferation Consortium, May 2012, <http://www.nonprolifer ation.eu/activities/activities.php>.

The public disclosure in 2003 of the A. Q. Khan network, which had sold uranium enrichment technology, gave a strong impetus to the debate on ENR export restrictions. In 2004 US President George W. Bush proposed that the NSG should ban the spread of ENR capacity to countries that do not already possess it.[8] This proposal failed to find consensus within the NSG, but it did prompt the group to begin discussions on revising its ENR guidelines, and a draft revision was circulated in 2008.[9]

Agreeing a list of specific criteria that countries would have to meet to be eligible to receive ENR transfers proved difficult. The biggest controversies revolved around an objective criterion—a requirement that the recipient had agreed an additional safeguards protocol with the IAEA—and certain subjective criteria. Subjective criteria in the draft included a requirement for suppliers to 'exercise vigilance' and to consider such factors as (a) 'Whether the recipient has a credible and coherent rationale' for pursuing ENR capability 'in support of civil nuclear power generation programmes', (b) 'Whether the transfer would have a negative impact on the stability and security of the recipient state', and (c) 'General conditions of stability and security'.[10] The United States proposed three additional subjective criteria designed to prevent non-nuclear weapon states from replicating sensitive nuclear technology.[11] One of these was a 'black box approach' that would prevent recipients from gaining access to sensitive technology, which the USA referred to as 'standard commercial practice'.[12]

The proposed 'objective' requirement for an additional safeguards protocol proved to be particularly contentious. Argentina, Brazil and South Africa objected to it, although on different grounds. South Africa argued that, as a matter of principle, voluntary agreements such as an additional safeguards protocol should not be made a requirement.[13] Neither Argentina

---

[8] The White House, 'President announces new measures to counter the threat of WMD', Remarks at the National Defense University, Washington, DC, 11 Feb. 2004, <http://georgewbush-whitehouse. archives.gov/news/releases/2004/02/20040211-4.html>; and Hibbs, M., *The Future of the Nuclear Suppliers Group* (Carnegie Endowment for International Peace: Washington, DC, 2011), p. 29.

[9] The draft 'Revised Paragraph 6 and 7 of INFCIRC 254/Part I', 20 Nov. 2008, is published in McGoldrick, F., *Limiting Transfers of Enrichment and Reprocessing Technology: Issues, Constraints, Options* (Harvard Kennedy School, Belfer Center for Science and International Affairs: Cambridge, MA, May 2011), appendix 2.

[10] 'Revised Paragraph 6 and 7 of INFCIRC 254/Part I' (note 9), p. 62.

[11] Anthony, I. and Bauer, S., 'Controls on security-related international transfers', *SIPRI Yearbook 2009*, p. 467.

[12] US Embassy in Buenos Aires, 'Argentina shares concerns over proposed NSG restrictions of enrichment and reprocessing technology transfers with visiting DOE NNSA Administrator D'Agostino', Cable to US State Department, no. 08BUENOSAIRES1552, 13 Nov. 2008, <http://wiki leaks.org/cable/2008/11/08BUENOSAIRES1552.html>.

[13] Hibbs, M., 'New global rules for sensitive nuclear trade', Nuclear Energy Brief, Carnegie Endowment for International Peace, 28 July 2011, <http://carnegieendowment.org/2011/07/28/ new-global-rules-for-sensitive-nuclear-trade/4atv>; and US Embassy in Pretoria, 'South Africa: amending NSG guidelines', Cable to the US State Department, no. 09PRETORIA2, 2 Jan. 2009, <http://wikileaks.org/cable/2009/01/09PRETORIA2.html>.

nor Brazil has signed an additional protocol with the IAEA; instead, the Brazilian–Argentine Agency for Accounting and Control of Nuclear Materials (Agencia Brasileño-Argentina de Contabilidad y Control de Materiales Nucleares, ABACC) is based on a safeguards agreement signed by the agency, the two countries and the IAEA, which Argentina and Brazil insisted made signing of an additional protocol unnecessary.[14]

Several countries, including South Africa, were concerned that some proposed criteria might limit their option to develop a civil nuclear programme in the future.[15] A number of countries, including Canada, the Netherlands, South Africa and Turkey, voiced objections to the subjective criteria in the draft.[16] Canada was also among those that objected to the USA's black box proposal.[17]

A fundamental underlying issue is the justification for limiting ENR supplies and the scope for allowing legitimate civilian uses of highly enriched uranium (HEU) and plutonium. There are currently four legitimate uses of HEU: fast neutron reactors, nuclear-powered submarines, research reactors, and medical diagnosis and treatment. Plutonium has fewer civilian applications, including use in mixed oxide (MOX) fuel, but poses a particular proliferation risk due to the small quantity required for a nuclear weapon.

The revised guidelines of 2011

At the 2011 NSG plenary, participating states could not agree on language for the imposition of the subjective criteria. They therefore settled on conditioning the transfer of nuclear technology on signing an additional safeguards protocol and on the importing state being in full compliance with its IAEA obligations. The concluding statement of the 2011 plenary referred to the decision to strengthen the guidelines, and the updated text was published one month later, in a *note verbale* to the IAEA.[18]

The 2011 revision focused on paragraph 6 ('Special controls on sensitive exports') and paragraph 7 ('Special arrangements for export of enrichment facilities, equipment and technology'). The previous version of paragraph 7

[14] Agreement between the Republic of Argentina, the Federal Republic of Brazil, the Brazilian–Argentine Agency for Accounting and Control of Nuclear Materials and the International Atomic Energy Agency for the Application of Safeguards (Quadripartite Agreement), signed 13 Dec. 1991, <http://www.abacc.org.br/?page_id=150&lang=en>; and Viski (note 7).

[15] Hibbs (note 13).

[16] Viski (note 7).

[17] US Embassy in Rome, 'G-8 nonproliferation directors group meeting', Cable to US State Department, no. 09ROME1240, 10 Nov. 2011, <http://wikileaks.org/cable/2009/11/09ROME1240.html>; and US Embassy in Buenos Aires (note 12).

[18] Nuclear Suppliers Group, 'NSG public statement', NSG Plenary, Noordwijk, 23–24 June 2011, <http://www.nuclearsuppliersgroup.org/Leng/05-pubblic.htm>; and IAEA, Communication received from the Permanent Mission of the Netherlands regarding certain member states' guidelines for the export of nuclear material, equipment and technology, INFCIRC 254/Rev.10/Part I, 26 July 2011.

required the recipient to seek the consent of the supplier before using the transferred facility or technology to enrich uranium beyond 20 per cent. Apart from requesting suppliers to 'encourage ... supplier involvement and/or other appropriate multinational participation', the previous version only required suppliers to 'exercise restraint in the transfer of sensitive facilities, technology and material usable for nuclear weapons or other nuclear explosive devices' but did not define the term 'restraint'.[19] The 2011 revision for the first time further specifies conditions for the transfer of ENR technology, both regarding the decision on whether such a transfer can take place, and if so, how.

According to the new version of paragraphs 6 and 7, the decision on whether a transfer of ENR facilities, equipment or technology can take place is to be based on the following minimum objective criteria.

1. The recipient is party to and 'in full compliance' with the 1968 Treaty on the Non-proliferation of Nuclear Weapons (Non-Proliferation Treaty, NPT).[20]

2. The recipient has not been identified in a report by the IAEA Secretariat as currently being in breach of its safeguards obligations.

3. The recipient adheres to NSG guidelines and has reported to the UN Security Council that it implements 'effective export controls as identified in' UN Security Council Resolution 1540.[21]

4. The recipient has 'concluded an inter-governmental agreement with the supplier including assurances regarding non-explosive use, effective safeguards in perpetuity, and retransfer'.

5. The recipient has 'made a commitment to the supplier to apply mutually agreed standards of physical protection based on current international guidelines'.

6. The recipient has 'committed to IAEA safety standards and adheres to accepted international safety conventions'.

7. The recipient 'has brought into force a Comprehensive Safeguards Agreement, and an Additional Protocol ... or, pending this, is implementing appropriate safeguards agreements in cooperation with the IAEA, including a regional accounting and control arrangement for nuclear materials, as approved by the IAEA Board of Governors'.[22]

---

[19] IAEA, INFCIRC/254/Rev.9/Part 1 (note 4), paras 6, 7.

[20] For a summary and other details of the NPT see annex A in this volume.

[21] UN Security Council Resolution 1540, 28 Apr. 2004. Resolution 1540 obliges all states to, among other things, refrain from supporting by any means non-state actors from developing, acquiring, manufacturing, possessing, transporting, transferring or using nuclear, biological or chemical weapons and their delivery systems. It imposes binding obligations on all states to establish domestic controls to prevent the proliferation of such weapons, including by establishing appropriate controls over related materials.

[22] IAEA, INFCIRC 254/Rev.10/Part I (note 18), para. 6.

The revised text on safeguards provides a compromise. While an additional safeguards protocol is not an absolute condition of supply, the text indicates that efforts to sign an additional safeguards protocol should be evident even where a regional safeguards agreement is in place. The ABACC, however, issued a statement interpreting the language as beginning to recognize the Argentine–Brazilian–IAEA agreement 'as an alternative criterion to the Additional Protocol'.[23]

The subjective criteria were kept rather vague. The revised guidelines require NSG suppliers to take 'into account at their national discretion, any relevant factors as may be applicable'. The term 'restraint' was maintained, while adding that this should apply in particular to countries that include entities subject to active denials relating to Part 2 of the guidelines (on nuclear-related dual-use goods) from more than one NSG participant.[24]

The new version of paragraph 7 reinforces previous provisions. Suppliers should now seek a 'legally-binding undertaking' from the recipient state that transferred ENR facilities, equipment or technology not be used or modified for enrichment beyond 20 per cent. An additional new requirement placed on suppliers is to 'seek to design and construct' facilities and equipment in a way that precludes the possibility of enrichment beyond 20 per cent 'to the greatest extent practicable'.

While the revised text encourages states to go as far as they can to ensure that sensitive technologies are not replicated, it falls short of the black box proposals advocated by the USA. The new version of paragraph 7 provides that the transfer of 'enabling design and manufacturing technology' should be avoided and specifies that suppliers should seek acceptance from recipients of transfer conditions that 'do not permit or enable replication of the facilities'. However, an exception permitting cooperation to develop potential new enrichment technologies is included.[25]

Other Nuclear Supplier Group discussions during 2011

During its 2011 plenary the NSG 'discussed brokering and transit issues and agreed to consider options [for] how to best reflect these matters in the guidelines'.[26] This reflects developments in national and international strategic trade controls, where discussions, decisions and implementation efforts have broadened from the traditional focus on controlling exports to encompass a wider range of activities, including the control of transit, trans-shipment, financing and brokering. These developments are in

---

[23] ABACC, 'Nuclear Suppliers Group (NSG) recognizes the Quadripartite Agreement as an alternative criterion to the Additional Protocol', 28 June 2011, <http://www.abacc.org.br/?p=3846>. The ABACC statement quotes a note from the Brazilian Foreign Ministry.

[24] IAEA, INFCIRC 254/Rev.10/Part I (note 18), para. 6.

[25] IAEA, INFCIRC 254/Rev.10/Part I (note 18), para. 7.

[26] Nuclear Suppliers Group (note 18), p. 2.

response to the evolving nature of procurement for nuclear weapon programmes, technological developments, changes in global trade patterns, the increased availability of non-listed dual-use items and the requirements of UN Security Council Resolution 1540.[27]

Other issues discussed at the 2011 plenary included adherence to the additional safeguards protocol and ongoing efforts to review the control lists of both trigger and dual-use items.[28] In the opening speech by the hosts of the plenary, the Netherlands announced 'outreach missions to the non-NPT countries and to various regions of interest' and 'to potential new Participating Governments'.[29] The plenary later discussed a report on outreach to non-NSG countries and announced the development of guidelines.

As in previous years, participating governments also exchanged information on countries and regions of proliferation concern. In this context, Iran and North Korea were specifically named. Notably, Syria was not mentioned in the public statement, although concerns about IAEA observations of non-compliance had been included in the opening speech.[30] Moreover, the NSG guidelines require an extraordinary plenary meeting to take place within one month of the IAEA Board of Governors finding a recipient to be in non-compliance with its safeguards obligations, 'at which suppliers will review the situation, compare national policies and decide on an appropriate response'.[31] However, such a meeting did not take place following the resolution on Syrian non-compliance adopted by the board on 9 June 2011 (see section II above).[32]

The NSG's relationship with India

As expected, a key issue discussed at the 2011 plenary was the NSG's relationship with India, specifically whether the revised guidelines affected India's eligibility to receive ENR transfers and its possible membership of the NSG.

The NSG's relationship with India has been a key factor driving and shaping supplier cooperation, discussion and action. The first Indian nuclear explosive test, in 1974, provided the *raison d'être* for the creation of

---

[27] See Bauer, S., Dunne, A. and Mićić, I., 'Strategic trade controls: countering the proliferation of weapons of mass destruction', *SIPRI Yearbook 2011*. 'Non-listed' dual-use items do not appear in national or international control lists but can also be controlled if their intended use is in a WMD or missile programme.

[28] Trigger list items are defined as 'especially designed or prepared' for nuclear use. IAEA, INFCIRC 254/Rev.10/Part I (note 18). On dual-use items see note 1.

[29] Kronenburg, E., Secretary General of the Dutch Ministry of Foreign Affairs, Opening speech, NSG Plenary, Noordwijk, 23 June 2011, <http://www.rijksoverheid.nl/ministeries/bz/documenten-en-publicaties/toespraken/2011/06/24opening-speech-by-ed-kronenburg-secretary-general>.

[30] Kronenburg (note 29).

[31] IAEA, INFCIRC 254/Rev.10/Part I (note 18), para. 16(e).

[32] IAEA, Board of Governors, 'Implementation of the NPT safeguards in the Syrian Arab Republic', Resolution, GOV/2011/41, 9 June 2011; and Official from an NSG country, Communication with author, Mar. 2012.

the NSG. Based on India's non-membership of the NPT and its refusal to allow comprehensive IAEA safeguards covering all of its nuclear activities and facilities, NSG participants agreed not to supply India with nuclear materials, equipment, facilities and technology. This agreement in principle lasted until 2008 when, in a move spearheaded by the USA following the Indian–US Civil Nuclear Cooperation Agreement, the NSG agreed a country-specific exemption from the guidelines.[33] India's re-entry into international nuclear commerce has resulted in it reaching bilateral agreements with, among others, Canada, France, Russia, the UK, the USA and, most recently, South Korea.[34] India has an interest both in receiving equipment and technology from advanced nuclear suppliers to implement its ambitious nuclear energy expansion programme and in offering equipment and expertise to countries seeking to begin or to expand nuclear energy production, including countries such as Namibia that can offer uranium in return.[35]

Indian observers have complained that the 2011 revisions to the NSG guidelines effectively eliminated the 'clean waiver' that India claimed to have received in 2008. Specifically, in 2008 the NSG waived the full-scope safeguards requirement of paragraph 4 of its guidelines and expressly allowed ENR exports, subject to paragraphs 6 and 7. Consternation has been expressed in India that, under the revised 2011 guidelines, it may not be eligible to receive enrichment and reprocessing technology since it is not a party to the NPT.[36]

During his November 2010 visit to India, US President Barack Obama announced his support for Indian membership of the NSG and the other export control regimes, thus initiating an international debate on the issue. This was further discussed during a visit by the US Secretary of State, Hillary Rodham Clinton, to India in February 2011.[37] In a 'food for thought

[33] Nuclear Suppliers Group, 'Statement on Civil Nuclear Cooperation with India', Extraordinary Plenary Meeting, 6 Sep. 2008, Attachment to IAEA, INFCIRC/734 (Corrected), 19 Sep. 2008; and Agreement for cooperation between the Government of India and the Government of the United States of America concerning peaceful uses of nuclear energy, signed 10 Oct. 2008, entered into force 6 Dec. 2008, <http://www.state.gov/s/l/treaty/tias/2008/>. On the Indian–US Civil Nuclear Cooperation Initiative, initiated in 2005, see previous editions of the SIPRI Yearbook. On the 2008 NSG decision see Anthony and Bauer (note 11), pp. 467–71. Prior to this, Russia had already provided nuclear fuel to India under the safety clause. See above; and Anthony (note 6).

[34] The Indian–South Korean Civil Nuclear Cooperation Agreement was signed on 25 July 2011. Baruah, P., 'India–ROK nuclear cooperation: is it a win–win situation?', Institute of Peace and Conflict Studies, 16 Aug. 2011, <http://www.ipcs.org/article/india/india-rok-nuclear-cooperation-is-it-a-win-win-situation-3439.html>.

[35] Hibbs (note 8), p. 11; and Rajiv, S. S. C., 'India's accommodation in multi-lateral export control regimes', Political and Defence Weekly (New Delhi), 9 Nov. 2011.

[36] Varadarajan, S., 'NSG ends India's "clean waiver"', The Hindu, 24 June 2011; and Varadarajan, S., 'Challenges ahead for India's nuclear diplomacy', The Hindu, 1 Nov. 2011.

[37] The White House, 'Joint statement by President Obama and Prime Minister Singh of India', 8 Nov. 2010, <http://www.whitehouse.gov/the-press-office/2010/11/08/joint-statement-president-

paper' of 23 May 2011 circulated by the USA to other NSG members, two options for pursuing Indian membership were presented: either revising the membership criteria 'in a manner that would accurately describe India's situation' or 'recognize' that not all of the criteria published as 'Factors taken into account for [NSG] participation' have to be met.[38]

No decision was taken on Indian membership during the 2011 NSG plenary, although the concluding statement refers to discussions on the issue. Public proponents include France and Russia.[39] A number of countries are reported to oppose the move, but have not done so publicly.[40] The issue is likely to be discussed again during the 2012 plenary, to be held in the USA, and to fuel the broader discussion on membership criteria and decision-making modalities.[41]

Chinese supplies to Pakistan

Some observers have expressed concern that the NSG's exemption for India had set a precedent for other countries—in particular, that it had paved the way for further nuclear cooperation between China and Pakistan—which threatens to further erode the credibility of the NSG.[42]

In 2010 China indicated that it would proceed with the supply of two new civil nuclear power reactors to Pakistan (Chashma-3 and -4).[43] The reactors are to be supplied under a bilateral agreement concluded in 2003, about which China informed the NSG when it joined the group in 2004. China claims that implementation of the 2003 deal did not need NSG approval since China did not join the NSG until 2004. While some NSG participants agreed with this, the USA maintained that this so-called grandfather clause is not applicable based on the information China provided to the NSG at accession.[44] Options for NSG responses include (*a*) tacit per-

obama-and-prime-minister-singh-india>; Rajiv (note 35); and Nayar, K. P., 'US push for nuclear club entry', *The Telegraph* (Kolkata), 17 Feb. 2011.

[38] Horner, D., 'NSG revises rules on sensitive exports', *Arms Control Today*, vol. 41, no. 6 (July/Aug. 2011). The factors 'taken into account' when admitting a state to the NSG are listed in IAEA, Communication of 1 October 2009 received from the Resident Representative of Hungary to the Agency on behalf of the participating governments of the Nuclear Suppliers Group, INFCIRC/539/Rev.4, 5 Nov. 2009.

[39] 'France not bound by new NSG restrictions on nuclear sales to India', *The Hindu*, 24 Oct. 2011; and Radyuhin, V., 'Russia assures India on ENR', *The Hindu*, 15 July 2011.

[40] Krishnan, A., 'China calls for dialogue on India's NSG entry', *The Hindu*, 18 Nov. 2011.

[41] Hibbs (note 8), pp. 23–28.

[42] Hibbs, M., 'The breach', *Foreign Policy*, 4 June 2010.

[43] Dyer, G., Bokhari, F. and Lamont, J., 'China to build reactors in Pakistan', *Financial Times*, 28 Apr. 2010. China had previously supplied 2 reactors (Chashma-1 and Chashma-2) to Pakistan under a bilateral civil nuclear cooperation agreement concluded in 1991. Miglani, S., 'China pursues Pakistan nuclear deal; dilemma in West', Reuters, 15 Dec. 2010, <http://af.reuters.com/article/energy OilNews/idAFL3E6NF08Q20101215>; and Hibbs (note 8), pp. 2, 16.

[44] Hibbs (note 8), p. 15. Germany is one of those that agrees with China's interpretation. Meier, O., 'Germany opposes United States on China–Pakistan nuclear deal', Arms Control Now, Arms Control Association, 21 June 2011, <http://armscontrolnow.org/2011/06/21/germany-opposes-united-states-on-china-pakistan-nuclear-deal/>.

mission, (b) the recording of objections but taking no action, (c) explicit recognition of the validity of the grandfather clause in this case, (d) agreement with China to proceed with the transaction but to refrain from exporting further reactors, (e) insistence that China must receive an explicit exemption, based on the precedent of the Indian waiver, or (f) urging China to suspend the export until specific conditions of supply to Pakistan are agreed.[45] This debate illustrates both ambiguities in the grandfather clause and the general difficulty of enforcing voluntary NSG provisions.

The debate on these issues has been further ignited by reports, which had not been confirmed by the Chinese Government, of discussions with China to supply a Chashma-5 plant and two further nuclear reactors (Kanupp-2 and -3).[46]

The future of nuclear export controls

While the establishment of effective export control systems is a necessary foundation for slowing down or preventing proliferation, it is only one element of an effective non-proliferation approach. It must always be seen as complementary to the NPT, as well as to other non-proliferation approaches such as efforts to develop and supply proliferation-resistant nuclear technologies. An issue at the very heart of nuclear non-proliferation is the relationship between the NSG suppliers and those states with nuclear weapons that are outside of the framework of the NPT and the NSG. A crucial and closely related issue is credibility, not only in the relationship between the five nuclear weapon states and the rest of the world, but in the balancing of non-proliferation and commercial interests.

A factor to consider in future will be the expected wider availability of nuclear materials and technology due to increasing reliance on nuclear energy, and the probable resulting demands for an increase in NSG membership. With the notable exception of Germany, which has returned to an earlier decision to give up nuclear energy altogether, it remains to be seen to what extent national nuclear energy plans have been affected by the disaster at Japan's Fukushima Daiichi nuclear power plant in 2011.

While advanced nuclear technology has been within the control of a small number of suppliers for many years, this exclusivity has been continually eroded. In addition to the emergence of new countries with

---

[45] Hibbs (note 8), p. 15.

[46] Krishnan, A., 'Pakistan eyeing China's new 1000-MW reactor', *The Hindu*, 15 Nov. 2011. In Nov. 2010 the Pakistani Atomic Energy Commission was reported to have signed a construction agreement with China National Nuclear Corporation (CNNC) for a 5th unit at Chashma. The status of the planned Kanupp-2 and Kanupp-3 reactors is uncertain. World Nuclear Association, 'Nuclear power in Pakistan', Aug. 2011, <http://www.world-nuclear.org/info/inf108.html>; and 'Pakistan signs accord for fifth Chinese reactor at Chashma', *Nucleonics Week*, 18 Nov. 2010.

nuclear weapon capabilities, the modus operandi of illicit procurement networks has adapted to restrictions on the direct export of dual-use items from producing countries by using increasingly complex transactions and by increasing use of non-listed, often suboptimal, items. Consequently, in line with broader counter-proliferation activities, decisions and participation in nuclear export controls will have to further adjust to consider relations with non-NSG members and the full range of nuclear trade activities, including brokering, transit, trans-shipment and finance as well as intangible transfers of technology.

VI. International cooperation on non-proliferation, arms control and nuclear security

SHANNON N. KILE

UN Security Council Resolution 1977

On 20 April 2011 the UN Security Council unanimously adopted Resolution 1977, which extended by 10 years the mandate of the committee established to monitor and facilitate states' compliance with Resolution 1540.[1] Since its adoption in 2004, Resolution 1540 has gained legitimacy as the legal basis for a range of national and multilateral non-proliferation and counter-terrorism activities, including export and trans-shipment controls to prevent trafficking in items related to weapons of mass destruction (WMD).[2] The 10-year extension of the 1540 Committee was reportedly a compromise between Security Council members seeking to permanently institutionalize the body and those preferring a more limited extension.[3] Under Resolution 1977, the 1540 Committee will conduct a comprehensive review of its operations after five years and another prior to the renewal of its mandate in 2021. In its reports on these reviews, the committee can make recommendations to the Security Council for 'adjustments' to its mandate.[4]

Resolution 1977 affirmed that the 1540 Committee should prioritize efforts to enhance the capacities of states to implement Resolution 1540, rather than highlight compliance shortcomings. The committee could do this by providing resources, training and technical support to states that encountered difficulties in drafting or implementing legal and regulatory measures aimed at preventing proliferation of WMD. The new resolution also requested the committee to 'identify effective practices, templates and guidance' in the areas covered by Resolution 1540, as well as to produce a technical reference guide, in order to assist states in their implementation efforts.[5] To facilitate these activities, the committee was authorized to establish a working group on technical issues consisting of up to eight experts. It was also encouraged to engage with relevant international and regional organizations and to urge such organizations to appoint a coordinator or point of contact.

---

[1] UN Security Council resolutions 1540, 28 Apr. 2004; and 1977, 20 Apr. 2011.

[2] For a legal assessment of the resolution, see Åhlström, C., 'United Nations Security Council Resolution 1540: non-proliferation by means of international legislation', *SIPRI Yearbook 2007*, pp. 460–73.

[3] Crail, P., 'UN bolsters WMD nonproliferation body', *Arms Control Today*, vol. 41, no. 4 (May 2011). The Security Council had previously extended the 1540 Committee's mandate for 2 years in 2006 and 3 years in 2008. UN Security Council resolutions 1673, 27 Apr. 2006; and 1810, 25 Apr. 2008.

[4] UN Security Council Resolution 1977 (note 1), para. 3.

[5] UN Security Council Resolution 1977 (note 1), para. 12.

Extension of the Group of Eight's Global Partnership programme

Concern about the risk of nuclear material falling into the hands of non-state actors who could use it for terrorist purposes has impelled leading industrialized countries to invest resources in strengthening selected countries' national measures for protecting nuclear materials and facilities. This concern was evident in the decision taken at the 2002 Group of Eight (G8) summit, held in Kananaskis, Canada, to create the Global Partnership against the Spread of Weapons and Materials of Mass Destruction.[6] The Global Partnership was established to support cooperative projects aimed at addressing non-proliferation, disarmament, counterterrorism and nuclear safety issues. The partner countries pledged to provide up to $20 billion for such efforts over 10 years.

On 27 May 2011, at a summit meeting held in Deauville, France, the heads of state and government of the G8 countries announced that they had agreed to extend the Global Partnership for an unspecified period beyond its 2012 expiration and would encourage additional countries to participate in its activities.[7] The extended programme would continue to focus on the threat-reduction priorities adopted at the 2008 G8 summit.[8] These concentrated on activities for enhancing nuclear and radiological security, ensuring biosecurity and facilitating national implementation of export controls under UN Security Council Resolution 1540.[9] At the same time, the leaders reaffirmed their commitment to completing priority projects in Russia.[10]

The G8 leaders did not pledge a specified amount of money to support the extended Global Partnership. Instead, the 23 states currently participating in the initiative would discuss assistance needs and additional threat-reduction projects, and the partners would later 'decide on funding of such projects on a national, joint, or multilateral basis'.[11]

[6] G8 Kananaskis Summit 2002, 'The G8 Global Partnership against the Spread of Weapons and Materials of Mass Destruction', 27 June 2002. For a brief description and list of members of the G8 see annex B in this volume.

[7] G8 Deauville Summit 2011, 'Report on the G8 Global Partnership against the Spread of Weapons and Materials of Mass Destruction', 26–27 May 2011.

[8] G8 Deauville Summit 2011, 'G8 Global Partnership: assessment and options for future programming', 26–27 May 2011.

[9] G8 Hokkaido Summit 2008, 'Report on the G8 Global Partnership', 8 July 2008, <http://www.g8.utoronto.ca/summit/2008hokkaido/2008-gp.pdf>, para. 33.

[10] Global Partnership project activities initially focused on 5 priority activities, primarily in Russia: (*a*) constructing chemical weapon destruction facilities; (*b*) dismantling decommissioned Russian nuclear submarines; (*c*) redirecting employment of scientists formerly working on WMD-related activities to peaceful civilian endeavours; (*d*) disposing of weapon-usable fissile material; and (*e*) improving the physical protection of facilities and enhancing the custodial security of nuclear material.

[11] G8 Deauville Summit 2011, 'G8 Declaration: renewed commitment for freedom and democracy', 26–27 May 2011, para. 78; and G8 Deauville Summit 2011, 'Declaration on non-proliferation and disarmament', 26–27 May 2011, para. 25.

The P5 states' discussion of multilateral arms control

From 30 June to 1 July 2011, officials from the five permanent members of the UN Security Council (the P5 states: China, France, Russia, the UK and the USA), which are also the legally recognized nuclear weapon states under the 1968 Treaty on the Non-proliferation of Nuclear Weapons (Non-Proliferation Treaty, NPT), met in Paris, France, to consider how to follow through with the commitments they made at the 2010 NPT Review Conference and to discuss cooperative approaches to nuclear transparency and confidence-building measures (CBMs).[12] The P5 states had convened a similar 'Conference on Confidence Building Measures towards Nuclear Disarmament and Non-proliferation' in London in 2009.[13] The representatives issued a joint statement reaffirming their states' determination to take concrete steps to reduce the number and role of nuclear weapons in the world and to increase the transparency of their stockpiles, pursuant to their commitments under the action plan agreed in the final document of the 2010 NPT Review Conference.[14]

In addition, the representatives pledged to establish a regular multilateral dialogue among the P5 states on nuclear transparency, verification and CBMs. As an initial step, they exchanged information on nuclear doctrine and capabilities and approved the creation of a working group on nuclear definitions and terminology. They also discussed technical challenges associated with verifying nuclear disarmament and agreed to hold additional expert-level consultations on this subject. They decided to hold a third P5 conference on nuclear transparency and CBMs in the context of the NPT Preparatory Committee meeting in April–May 2012.[15]

[12] First P5 Follow-up Meeting to the NPT Review Conference, Final Joint Press Statement, Paris, 1 July 2011, <http://www.mid.ru/brp_4.nsf/0/2886687EC0070109C32578C00058F9B5>. For a summary and other details of the NPT see annex A in this volume.

[13] British Foreign and Commonwealth Office, 'P5 statement on disarmament and non-proliferation issues', 9 Sep. 2009, <http://www.fco.gov.uk/en/news/latestnews/?view=News&id=208 04873>.

[14] 2010 NPT Review Conference, Final Document, NPT/CONF.2010/50 (Vol. I), 28 May 2010, <http://www.un.org/en/conf/npt/2010/confdocs.shtml>, pp. 19–29.

[15] Kimball, D. G., 'Nuclear-weapon states meet in Paris', Arms Control Today, vol. 41, no. 6 (July/ Aug. 2011).

9. Reducing security threats from chemical and biological materials

Overview

At the international, national and regional levels in 2011 states continued to develop strategies to prevent and remediate the effects of the possible misuse of toxic chemical and biological materials.

The Seventh Review Conference of the States Parties to the 1972 Biological and Toxin Weapons Convention (BTWC) agreed to conduct a third intersessional meeting process that will 'discuss, and promote common understanding and effective action' on cooperation and assistance, the review of relevant developments in science and technology, and the strengthening of, among other things, national implementation of the convention. Despite the expectations of many states and analysts that the BTWC would somehow be 'bolstered' (e.g. by taking additional steps with respect to institutional strengthening and various operational-level or 'practical' measures), the political conditions at the conference inhibited taking decisions to establish an intersessional process that is more 'action-' and decision-oriented. Thus, the regime is evolving incrementally and is focused on process (see section I in this chapter).

The 16th Conference of the States Parties to the 1993 Chemical Weapons Convention (CWC) witnessed exchanges between Iran and the United States that partly reflected wider international tension regarding the nature and purpose of Iran's nuclear activities (see section II). Russia and the USA confirmed that they would be unable to complete the destruction of their chemical weapon stockpiles by the final CWC-mandated deadline of 29 April 2012 but would nevertheless undertake to complete the destruction expeditiously. In the case of Iraq, the Organisation for the Prohibition of Chemical Weapons (OPCW) concluded that progress has been made in razing chemical weapon production facilities. An advisory panel to the OPCW's Director-General submitted its final report after reviewing the implementation of the CWC with a focus on how the convention's activities should be structured after the destruction of chemical weapon stockpiles ends, sometime after 2012. The Director-General, together with the states parties and the OPCW Executive Council, used the process of formulating the report as a means to develop agreed policy guidance for future OPCW priorities and programmes in the lead-up to the Third CWC Review Conference, which will be held in 2013. The report therefore presented options and activities that had been subjected to political and technical review, which the Director-General may use to inform the balance and focus of future activities by the OPCW Technical Secretariat. The report also reflects the CWC regime's continuing transition towards other priorities that will become more apparent once chemical weapon stockpiles are eliminated.

During the Libyan civil war concern was expressed that the regime of Muammar Gaddafi would employ a stock of residual sulphur mustard against anti-government protestors and armed rebel groups. Similar concerns were expressed regarding the nature and fate of possible chemical and biological weapons in Syria over the course of the country's civil unrest and tension (see section III). The OPCW sent a special inspection team to Libya in November to investigate reports of undeclared chemical weapons and it was confirmed that the Gaddafi regime had not declared a secret chemical weapon stockpile. The fact that the OPCW did not uncover Libya's deceptive declarations prior to the 2011 overthrow of Gaddafi raised questions about the organization's ability to detect violations more generally and prompted calls to review the CWC's verification regime, although little discussion occurred on how to link this problem to the convention's challenge inspection request provisions.

Science and technology and related research can strongly affect chemical and biological warfare prevention, response and remediation efforts (see section IV). Research on avian influenza in particular has raised a number of policy implications, such as whether it is preferable to describe scientific research on its merits for peaceful purposes and to avoid characterizing it in terms of potential security threats. The debate also affects research funding, publication policies (e.g. lack of common international standards), agreed principles in research oversight and differences in approach on agreeing and implementing appropriate safety and security standards.

JOHN HART

I. Biological weapon arms control and disarmament

JOHN HART

The principal activity in 2011 in biological arms control was the Seventh Review Conference of the 1972 Biological and Toxin Weapons Convention (BTWC) in December and preparation for it, which included considering and structuring relevant topics and drafting background text. Much of this activity was procedural and referred to long-standing implementation principles contained in the various articles of the convention, such as those dealing with the strengthening of national implementation and economic cooperation and development. Lack of consensus continued to affect the parties' ability to consider possible specific compliance concerns regarding past, current or planned activity by states, or specific consideration of known or suspected bioterrorist activity. The parties also remained divided on the question of whether and how to put in place permanent or legally binding mechanisms to encourage a more substantive exchange of views on such concerns. The review conference nevertheless continued to provide the parties with a framework in which to exchange views and experience on the implementation of the convention, and the Seventh Review Conference agreed that another intersessional programme should continue this practice. Two new parties joined the BTWC in 2011: Burundi and Mozambique. A further 12 states had signed but not ratified the convention.[1]

Before the Seventh Review Conference the Implementation Support Unit (ISU) collated support documentation and various analyses and proposals concerning biosecurity and biosafety, science and technology (S&T), disease and health surveillance, dual-use issues, the intersessional meeting process, confidence-building measures (CBMs), education and awareness, and non-state actor threats.[2] The BioWeapons Prevention Project (BWPP), a coalition of non-governmental organizations, developed a list of 12 topics, each introduced by a briefing paper, to discuss prior to the review conference: (*a*) exploring the influence of technological developments on the BTWC; (*b*) ascertaining whether verification is needed and its nature; (*c*) determining the requirements for reporting; (*d*) implementing Article X successfully; (*e*) studying how countering bioterrorism and the BTWC

---

[1] For a summary and list of parties and signatories of the Convention on the Prohibition of the Development, Production and Stockpiling of Bacteriological (Biological) and Toxin Weapons and on Their Destruction see annex A in this volume. The states that had signed but not ratified the BTWC were Central African Republic, Côte d'Ivoire, Egypt, Guyana, Haiti, Liberia, Malawi, Myanmar, Nepal, Somalia, Syria and Tanzania. The states that had neither signed nor ratified the convention were Andorra, Angola, Cameroon, Chad, Comoros, Djibouti, Eritrea, Guinea, Israel, Kiribati, Marshall Islands, Mauritania, Micronesia, Namibia, Nauru, Niue, Samoa, South Sudan and Tuvalu.

[2] UN Office at Geneva, 'Disarmament: think zone for the Seventh Review Conference', <http://www.unog.ch/bwc/thinkzone>.

relate to each other; (*f*) establishing how national implementation, or its absence, affects the strength of the BTWC; (*g*) educating life scientists, including how to conduct that process and its content; (*h*) determining the place of public health issues in bioweapon control forums; (*i*) ensuring global accountability of biodefence activities; (*j*) learning how existing United Nations investigation mechanisms can be used to fortify the convention; (*k*) ascertaining the role that biosecurity plays in preventing bioweapon development; and (*l*) assessing the effectiveness of the intersessional process in strengthening the BTWC.[3] Together with their associated comments, the BWPP-moderated discussion presents an up-to-date review of the various political and legal nuances associated with the BTWC.

In the lead-up to the review conference many parties signalled their expectations for preferred outcomes. The common position of the European Union (EU) called for 'examining annual CBM declarations as the regular national declaration tool on implementation and compliance and developing them further with this objective in mind'.[4] In its opening statement, Iran cautioned that CBMs, while important, 'shall not constitute a mechanism for verification of compliance'.[5] The United States stated that it viewed the review conference 'as an opportunity to bolster' the convention, 'to take on the challenge of encouraging scientific progress, but constraining the potential for misuse of science'.[6] The US representative went on to say that:

We will ask for member states to come together and focus on new ways to enhance confidence in compliance through richer transparency, more effective implementation, an improved set of confidence building measures, and cooperative use of the BWC's consultative provisions. We need to work together, moreover, on measures to counter the threat of bioterrorism, and to detect and respond effectively to an attack should one occur.[7]

Russia criticized the US focus on 'raising the so-called transparency of bioresearch' and said it was no 'substitute for full verification'.[8] Some of the

---

[3] BioWeapons Prevention Project, 'Civil society preparations for the 7th BWC Review Conference 2011', [n.d.], <http://www.bwpp.org/revcon.html>.

[4] Council Decision 2011/429/CFSP of 18 July 2011 relating to the position of the European Union for the Seventh Review Conference of the States Parties to the Convention on the prohibition of the development, production and stockpiling of bacteriological (biological) and toxin weapons and on their destruction (BTWC), *Official Journal of the European Union*, L188, 19 July 2011, p. 44.

[5] Seventh BTWC Review Conference, Statement by H. E. Mr. Mohammed Reza Sajjadi, Permanent Representative of Iran, 7 Dec. 2011.

[6] Gottemoeller, R., US Department of State, 'Remarks by delegation of the United States of America First (Disarmament and International Security) Committee', 4 Oct. 2011, <http://www.state.gov/t/avc/rls/175000.htm>.

[7] Gottemoeller (note 6).

[8] Russian Ministry of Foreign Affairs, 'Russian MFA Press and Information Department comment in relation to the publication of the US State Department reports on adherence to and compliance with arms control, non-proliferation and disarmament agreements and commitments', Press Release

other parties to the convention remain, at the margins (i.e. informally), interested in learning further details of the fate of the former Soviet offensive biological weapon programme. However, such consultation has been largely absent during the past decade.[9] Finally, the parties broadly supported another intersessional process and the inclusion of S&T in it.[10]

Ambassador Paul van den IJssel of the Netherlands chaired the Seventh Review Conference, which considered the legal and political implications associated with efforts to achieve universal membership for the convention and what constitutes 'full' and 'balanced' implementation of its provisions under the chairman's theme of 'ambitious realism'. In the final two days it became evident that a number of political markers, indicated earlier in the conference, were in fact firm 'red lines' not to be crossed, including no decision-making power for the intersessional programme meetings and minimization of further transparency measures via CBMs. Five delegations notably coordinated their positions during the conference: China, India, Iran, Pakistan and Russia.

The review conference agreed to conduct an intersessional meeting process, the third such process, which will explicitly consider cooperation and assistance, S&T review, and strengthening national implementation.[11] Annual meetings of the parties and annual meetings of experts will be held in 2012–15 until the Eight Review Conference, to be held in 2016. The review conference also agreed modified formats for CBMs, including more detailed reporting of disease outbreaks. The existing three-person ISU will support the new process and remain the same size (the non-expansion reflects political constraints and ongoing international financial uncertainty). The ISU will compile a database of information relevant to economic and technological development to assist in strengthening cooperation and assistance under Article X of the BTWC, which calls for the convention to be implemented in a manner that avoids hampering economic and technological development while facilitating the exchange of information, material and equipment for peaceful purposes. Text that allowed for conceptual discussion on verification and compliance with the BTWC was dropped from the final review conference document because some states had proposed alternative text that diverged from an essentially conceptual exchange of views. The parties were generally aware that such a

---

1292-02-09-2011, 2 Sep. 2011, <http://www.ln.mid.ru/brp_4.nsf/0/f53d23a14bf702b8c32579010047c468>. Available in Russian at <http://www.ln.mid.ru/brp_4.nsf/0/C2356A2C34FC35A6C32578FF005CA2E9>.

[9] See Kelly, D. C., 'The trilateral agreement: lessons for biological weapons proliferation', eds T. Findlay and O. Meier, *Verification Yearbook 2002* (Verification Research, Training and Information Centre (VERTIC): London, 2002), pp. 93–109.

[10] E.g. 'Proposal for structured and systematic review of science and technology developments under the convention: submitted by India', Working paper, Think Zone for the Seventh BTWC Review Conference, 2011, <http://www.unog.ch/bwc/thinkzone>.

[11] Seventh BTWC Review Conference, Final Document, Advance copy, 22 Dec. 2011, p. 19.

shift would risk US rejection.[12] The new intersessional process will consist of an exchange of views and best practice among the parties. Notably, the parties will consider S&T developments systematically for the first time since the 1992–93 Ad Hoc Group of Governmental Experts to Identify and Examine Potential Verification Measures from a Scientific and Technical Standpoint (VEREX) meetings on the BTWC.

[12] BioWeapons Prevention Project, 'The Seventh BWC Review Conference: outcome and assessment', RevCon Report no. 16, 31 Dec. 2011, <http://http://www.bwpp.org/reports.html>, p. 2.

II. Chemical weapon arms control and disarmament

JOHN HART

As of 31 December 2011, 188 states had ratified or acceded to the 1993 Chemical Weapons Convention (CWC), the principal international legal instrument against chemical warfare; a further two states had signed but not ratified it; and six states had neither signed nor ratified the convention.[1] No state joined the convention in 2011. The activity of the Organisation for the Prohibition of Chemical Weapons (OPCW) in 2011 was, with the notable exception of the Director-General's advisory panel report, largely process-oriented.

The 16th Conference of the States Parties (CSP) agreed a 2012 budget of €70 561 800 ($94 million) of which €33 296 600 ($44 million) is allocated for verification-related costs and €37 265 200 ($50 million) for administrative and other costs; this represents a 5.4 per cent reduction compared to the 2011 budget.[2] In a unique, non-precedent setting measure, the CSP gave the Director-General, Ahmet Üzümcü, the authority to grant contract extensions or renewals to staff (who may not work longer than 10 years) with expertise applicable to the 'operational requirements of verification and inspection of destruction-related activities' until 29 April 2016.[3]

The 2012 regular budget consists of (a) administration (21 per cent), (b) executive management (12 per cent), (c) external relations (3 per cent), (d) support for the OPCW's policymaking organs (7 per cent), (e) international cooperation and assistance (10 per cent), (f) inspections (35 per cent), and (g) verification (12 per cent).[4] The inspection component of the budget will decline by a little over 5 percentage points for 2012. Reduced inspections reflect the April 2012 deadline for the destruction of chemical weapon stockpiles. Since the CWC's entry into force, approximately 85 per cent of the inspection resources of the OPCW have been devoted to verifying chemical weapon destruction.[5] Although the overall inspection effort is declining, the chemical weapon destruction deadline will not be met by

---

[1] For a summary and a list of parties and signatories of the Convention on the Prohibition of the Development, Production, Stockpiling and Use of Chemical Weapons and on Their Destruction see annex A in this volume. The states that had not signed or ratified the CWC were Angola, Egypt, North Korea, Somalia, South Sudan and Syria. Israel and Myanmar had signed but not ratified the CWC.

[2] OPCW, Conference of the States Parties, 'Programme and budget of the OPCW for 2012', Decision C-16/DEC.12, 2 Dec. 2011, pp. 2, 9. In each of the previous 6 years the OPCW had nominal zero growth budgets.

[3] OPCW, Conference of the States Parties, 'Future implementation of the tenure policy of the OPCW', Decision C-16/DEC.9, 30 Nov. 2011.

[4] OPCW, C-16/DEC.12 (note 2), p. 11.

[5] Üzümcü, A., OPCW Director-General, Statement to the United Nations, General Assembly, First Committee (Disarmament and International Security), 12 Oct. 2011, p. 1.

Libya, Russia and the United States. It is noteworthy that the number of future inspections is determined primarily by the number of active destruction facilities, which will drop in 2012, before increasing somewhat when the final two US chemical weapon destruction facilities are commissioned.

The CSP also established an international support network for victims of chemical weapons along with a voluntary trust fund; among other activities, the OPCW Technical Secretariat will administer the fund, and coordinate and facilitate the establishment of contacts and appropriate information.[6] The CSP undertook further efforts to achieve universal membership of the CWC.[7]

The Director-General established an advisory panel in order to help clarify how the OPCW's focus on chemical weapon destruction can best be shifted to a broader objective of sustained chemical weapon disarmament. The report emphasized that the OPCW, among other functions, should 'remain the global repository of knowledge and expertise' on chemical weapon disarmament as well as on the verification of the non-possession and non-use of such weapons.[8] The delegations praised the report, which presented a menu of options and associated principles that could serve to validate the balance and scope of activity that the Director-General wishes the Technical Secretariat to implement over the coming years. For example, Pakistan stated that the report correctly assigns priority to completion of chemical weapon destruction and strikes a proper balance between regulatory aspects (industry, verification and national implementation) and international cooperation in chemistry.[9] The Director-General stated that effective industry verification and data monitoring are the 'bedrock' for the prevention of the re-emergence of chemical weapons.[10]

Mexico expressed dissatisfaction with the manner in which the OPCW's policymaking organs have functioned since the CWC entered into force, stating that adjustments should be made to administration practice and asking whether it is 'appropriate to place the weight of decisions lengthy and intensively negotiated on the discussions of report language during the

---

[6] OPCW, Conference of the States Parties, 'The establishment of the international support network for victims of chemical weapons and the establishment of a voluntary trust fund for this purpose', Decision C-16/DEC.13, 2 Dec. 2011.

[7] For a summary of universality efforts in Africa see the newsletter of the South African Institute for Security Studies. Broodryk, A. and Stott, N., 'Enhancing the role of the OPCW in building Africa's capacity to prevent the misuse of toxic chemicals', *Africa's Policy Imperatives*, no. 6 (May 2011).

[8] OPCW, Technical Secretariat, 'Report of the advisory panel on future priorities of the Organisation for the Prohibition of Chemical Weapons', Note by the Director-General, S/951/2011, 25 July 2011, para. 35.

[9] OPCW, Conference of the States Parties, Statement by Ambassador Aizaz Ahmad Chaudhry, Leader of Pakistani Delegation, 28 Nov.–2 Dec. 2011, p. 3.

[10] OPCW, Conference of the States Parties, Opening statement by the Director-General, C-16/DG.18, 28 Nov. 2011, para. 21.

adoption of the final report, many times reflecting occurrences that did not take place or decisions that were not taken during the formal sessions?'[11]

Destruction of chemical weapons

As of 30 November 2011, of 71 195 agent tonnes of declared chemical weapons, 50 619 agent tonnes had been verifiably destroyed; of 8.67 million declared items and chemical weapon containers, 3.95 million had been destroyed.[12] As of November 2011, 13 states had declared 70 former chemical weapon production facilities, of which 43 had been destroyed and 21 converted to peaceful purposes.[13] The states that had declared chemical weapon stockpiles to the OPCW are Albania, India, Iraq, South Korea, Libya, Russia and the USA. Albania, India and South Korea had destroyed all of their declared chemical weapons, and all declared Category 3 chemical weapons had also been destroyed.[14] The OPCW estimates that approximately three-quarters of the declared chemical weapon stockpiles were to be destroyed by the extended (and final) CWC deadline of 29 April 2012.[15]

Iraq

Iraq continued to explore and develop options for the OPCW-verified destruction of chemical weapons in bunkers 13 and 41 at Al Muthanna in the south of the country.[16] Iraqi authorities have deemed physical entry to bunker 41 possible, while bunker 13 is still too hazardous to enter.[17] Iraq is committed to destroying the contents of bunker 41 and rendering harmless the contents of bunker 13 by encapsulating it in concrete.[18] The files of the UN Special Commission on Iraq (UNSCOM) and those of its successor, the UN Monitoring, Verification and Inspection Commission (UNMOVIC), remain sealed and thus largely unavailable to the OPCW Executive Council.[19] Technical meetings involving representatives of Iraq, Germany, the United Kingdom, the USA and the OPCW have been held to discuss base-

[11] OPCW, Conference of the States Parties, Statement by Ambassador Jorge Lomónaco, Permanent Representative of Mexico, C-16/NAT.23, 28 Nov. 2011, p. 2.

[12] OPCW, 'Demilitarisation', <http://www.opcw.org/our-work/demilitarisation/>.

[13] OPCW, C-16/DG.18 (note 10), para. 52.

[14] The CWC's Annex on Chemicals comprises 3 'schedules'. Schedule 1 chemicals consist of chemicals and their precursors judged to have few, if any, peaceful applications. Chemicals listed in schedules 2 and 3 have wider peaceful, including commercial, applications. The definition of chemical weapon categories, which is partly based on what schedule a chemical may be listed under, is given in CWC (note 1), Verification Annex, Part IV(A), para. 16.

[15] OPCW, C-16/DG.18 (note 10), para. 5.

[16] The other bunkers have been ascertained to be either empty or containing only conventional munitions.

[17] Al Sharaa, M., Director General, Iraqi National Monitoring Directorate, 'Al Muthanna bunkers decommissioning project', Slide presentation at the 14th Annual International Chemical Weapons Demilitarisation Conference (CWD 2011), Interlaken, 23–26 May 2011, p. 16.

[18] Al Sharaa (note 17), p. 15.

[19] Al Sharaa (note 17), p. 16.

line data on the contents of the storage bunker ('containers and munitions ... too volatile to attempt to destroy')—characterized by former UNSCOM Deputy Chairman Charles Duelfer as reminding him of the 'Great Pyramid at Giza'—and the extent to which the verification of any destruction of the contents of the bunkers should be non-intrusive (i.e. remote sampling, analysis and verification) or intrusive (i.e. involving physical entry).[20]

In May the OPCW also conducted a low-altitude aerial inspection of Iraq's former chemical weapon production and storage facilities, using UN Assistance Mission in Iraq (UNAMI) helicopters. The visual inspection and overhead imagery from these flyovers confirmed that Iraq has made progress in razing chemical weapon production facilities and that the two storage bunkers at Al Muthanna appear to remain undisturbed and intact.[21] Iraq has approved $55 million for the decommissioning project.[22] Bunker 13 appears to contain (a) approximately 2500 partially destroyed 122-mm chemical rockets, (b) approximately 180 tonnes of sodium cyanide, (c) approximately 1.75 tonnes of 'potassium cyanides', (d) 75 kilograms of arsenic trichloride, and (e) 170 one-tonne containers that were previously used to hold tabun. Bunker 41 is believed to hold (a) approximately 2000 empty 155-mm artillery shells, (b) 605 one-tonne sulphur mustard containers, which originally held residues of polymerized sulphur mustard, (c) incinerator equipment, (d) about 200 one-litre barrels that contain waste material from decontamination, and (e) 'heavily contaminated construction material scrap'; bunker 41 also suffers from 'serious' contamination from chemical weapon precursor barrel leakage.[23] An Iraqi Experts Technical Committee (established by the head of Iraq's Ministry of Science and Technology) has issued a report that outlines possible solutions to these problems. After Iraq's Council of Ministers approves the committee's recommendations, the Ministry of Science and Technology will 'take the necessary measures to start the Decomissioning project'.[24]

Libya

During the war in Libya concern was expressed that a stock of residual sulphur mustard might be used by forces loyal to Muammar Gaddafi against anti-government protestors and armed rebel groups.[25]

---

[20] Al Sharaa (note 17), p. 8; and Duelfer, C., *Hide and Seek: The Search for the Truth in Iraq* (Public-Affairs: New York, 2009), pp. 96–97.

[21] OPCW, C-16/DG.18 (note 10), para. 48; and OPCW, Conference of the States Parties, Statement on behalf of the European Union by H. E. Mara Marinaki, Managing Director for Global and Multilateral Issues, European External Action Service, C-16/NAT.25, 28 Nov.–2 Dec. 2011, p. 4.

[22] Al Sharaa (note 17), p. 13.

[23] Al Sharaa (note 17), p. 4.

[24] Al Sharaa (note 17), p. 12.

[25] US House of Representatives, Permanent Select Committee on Intelligence, 'Chairman Rogers comments regarding recent developments in Libya', Press release, 22 Aug. 2011, <http://intelligence.house.gov/press-release/chairman-rogers-comments-regarding-recent-developments-libya>. Simi-

The OPCW had verified that Libya had destroyed 54.4 per cent of its declared stockpile of Schedule 1 chemical weapons as of 8 February 2011, when destruction operations were stopped because of the need to demolish a heating unit at the destruction facility.[26] On 1 September the Executive Council convened an informal meeting to discuss the situation in Libya and the unspecified 'delivery of assistance' that had been provided by the Office of the Director-General.[27] On 22 September, representatives of the new Libyan Government stated that its forces had captured a sulphur mustard depot in the Al Jufra area (the so-called Ruwagha depot, located 700 kilometres south-east of Tripoli).[28] On 3 October the Libyan Under-Secretary for Foreign Affairs sent a note to the Director-General 'confirming ... and reiterating' the importance of sending an OPCW inspection team to Libya to inventory and verify the status of the country's chemical weapon stockpiles, to confirm that they are secure and to prepare for the resumption of destruction operations 'at the appropriate time'; on 4 October the Libyan representative to the Executive Council stated that the new government had secured the chemical weapon storage sites at Ruwagha.[29]

On 2 November an OPCW inspection team visited Libya to verify the status of a temporary chemical weapon holding facility at the Ruwagha Hydrolysis and Neutralisation System to confirm whether sulphur mustard and two chemical weapon precursors had been diverted (the previous inspection had taken place in February when destruction operations were stopped).[30] The inspection was financed by Germany's Federal Foreign Office with further support provided by the UN Department of Safety and Security.[31] The one-day inspection examined the chemical weapons stockpiled at the Ruwagha depot and was meant to verify whether Libya's chemical weapon stocks remained intact and, if so, that they were properly secured in the aftermath of the country's civil conflict.[32] The team confirmed that the facility's stock of sulphur mustard and chemical weapon precursors had not been diverted.[33] On 28 November Libya provided a revised declaration to the OPCW that presents information on previously

lar concerns have been expressed regarding the nature and fate of possible CBW in Syria over the course of the country's civil unrest and tension. On the conflicts in Libya and Syria see chapter 2, section I, and chapter 3, section II, in this volume.

[26] OPCW, C-16/DG.18 (note 10), para. 34.

[27] OPCW, Executive Council, Statement by the Libyan delegation, EC-66/NAT.17, 4 Oct. 2011, p. 2.

[28] Black, I., 'Libyan rebels discover Gaddafi's chemical weapons', The Guardian, 22 Sep. 2011.

[29] OPCW, Libya, EC-66/NAT.17 (note 27), p. 2.

[30] OPCW, C-16/DG.18 (note 10), para. 39.

[31] German Federal Foreign Office, 'Securing Libya's chemical weapons', Press release, 4 Nov. 2011, <http://www.auswaertiges-amt.de/EN/Aussenpolitik/Laender/Aktuelle_Artikel/Libyen/111104-OVCW-Inspektion-node.html>; and OPCW, C-16/DG.18 (note 10), para. 13. Germany is also cooperating with Libya to remove small arms and landmines in Libya.

[32] German Federal Foreign Office (note 31).

[33] OPCW, 'OPCW inspectors return from Libya', Press release, 4 Nov. 2011, <http://www.opcw.org/news/article/opcw-inspectors-return-to-libya/>.

undeclared chemical weapons (known and suspected).[34] However, Libya will be unable to complete the destruction of its stockpile by 29 April 2012.[35] The UN Security Council has called on Libya to 'continue . . . close coordination' with the OPCW to destroy its chemical weapons.[36] The new government reiterated that the country remains committed to 'all international conventions and treaties it has signed', including the CWC.[37] The OPCW will undertake a full determination of the status of the previously undeclared chemical weapons (mainly artillery shells) in 2012.

Russia

In 2011 chemical weapon destruction operations were carried out at four facilities in Russia: Leonidovka (c. 6000 tonnes of chemical weapon agent, 87 per cent of the total facility stockpile), Maradykovsky (c. 5600 tonnes, 82 per cent of the facility stockpile), Pochep (c. 1800 tonnes, 24 per cent of the facility stockpile) and Shchuchye (c. 2500 tonnes, 47 per cent of the facility stockpile).[38] The seventh and final chemical weapon destruction facility is scheduled to start operating at Kizner in 2012 (Russia had earlier completed destruction operations at Gorny and Kambarka).[39] As of 31 October Russia had 'destroyed and withdrawn' 57 per cent (22 714 tonnes) of its Category 1 chemical weapons.[40]

The United States

As of November 2011 the USA had spent $23.7 billion on destroying its chemical weapon stockpiles.[41] It completed destruction operations at Anniston, Alabama (22 September 2011); Umatilla, Oregon (25 October 2011); and at Tooele, Utah (21 January 2012). The remaining stockpile is located at Blue Grass, Kentucky, and Pueblo, Colorado. Of the total original chemical weapon stockpile, 1.7 per cent is located at Blue Grass (consisting of sarin, VX and sulphur mustard), and 8.5 per cent is located at Pueblo (consisting of sulphur mustard). A neutralization-based destruction technology will be used at both sites, although the time frame to complete operations at these two sites is uncertain.[42] The USA will also continue to

---

[34] OPCW, C-16/DG.18 (note 10), para. 40.

[35] OPCW, C-16/DG.18 (note 10), para. 13.

[36] UN Security Council Resolution 2017, 31 Oct. 2011.

[37] OPCW, Libya, EC-66/NAT.17 (note 27), p. 2.

[38] OPCW, Conference of the States Parties, Statement by V. I. Kholstov, Acting Head of the Russian Delegation, C-16/NAT.12, 28 Nov. 2011, pp. 1–2.

[39] OPCW, Russia, C-16/NAT.12 (note 38), p. 2.

[40] OPCW, C-16/DG.18 (note 10), para. 41. Russia has now destroyed all of its Category 2 chemical weapons (10 616 tonnes) and its Category 3 chemical weapons.

[41] OPCW, Conference of the States Parties, Statement by Ambassador Robert P. Mikulak, US Permanent Representative, C-16/NAT.31, 29 Nov. 2011, p. 2.

[42] Weber, A. C., 'United States chemical demilitarization program', PowerPoint presentation to the 16th session of the Conference of the States Parties, OPCW, The Hague, Nov. 2011, p. 5; and OPCW, USA, C-16/NAT.31 (note 41), p. 1.

destroy non-stockpiled chemical munitions as they are discovered in coming years (other parties to the CWC will continue to face this problem).

Abandoned chemical weapons and old chemical weapons

As of December 2011, 4 countries had declared that abandoned chemical weapons (ACWs) are present on their territories, and 15 had declared that they have possessed old chemical weapons (OCWs) since the convention's entry-into-force.[43] OCW destruction operations in 2011 were carried out in Belgium, Italy, Japan, Germany, Switzerland and the UK, while France continued to develop a comprehensive OCW destruction programme.[44]

Destruction operations for ACWs in China continued.[45] ACW sites are clustered in five, geographically distinct projects.[46] As of 30 September 2011, 35 203 ACWs had been destroyed at Nanjing, Jiangsu province: this represents 99 per cent of the declared ACWs at that location and 75 per cent of the declared ACWs in China.[47] Two mobile destruction chambers were scheduled to be used in Haerbaling, Jilin province, and in the northern part of China. As of October, Japan had shipped one destruction chamber.[48] Japan provided further information on its destruction operations in Nanjing, which began on 12 October 2010.[49]

[43] The 4 countries that have declared ACWs to the OPCW are China, Iran, Italy and Panama. The Technical Secretariat determined the ACW munitions declared by Iran to be conventional. The 15 countries that have declared OCWs to the OPCW are Austria, Australia, Belgium, Canada, France, Germany, Italy, Japan, Poland, Russia, Slovenia, Solomon Islands, Switzerland, the UK and the USA. ACWs are defined as chemical weapons that were abandoned by a state after 1 Jan. 1925 on the territory of another state without the permission of the latter. CWC (note 1), Article II, para. 6. OCWs are defined as chemical weapons that were produced before 1925 or chemical weapons produced between 1925 and 1946 that have deteriorated to such an extent that they are no longer usable in the manner in which they were designed. CWC (note 1), Article II, para. 5. For information on countries not discussed here see CBW chapters in previous editions of the SIPRI Yearbook.

[44] OPCW, C-16/DG.18 (note 10), para. 51.

[45] On World War II-era chemical weapons see Tu, A. T., 'Chemical weapons abandoned by the Imperial Japanese Army in Japan and China at the end of World War II', *Toxin Reviews*, vol. 30, no. 1 (Feb. 2011), pp. 1–5.

[46] The projects are (*a*) Mobile Destruction Facility (MDF)-South at Nanjing and Wuhan; (*b*) MDF-North at Shijiazhuang and Haerbin; (*c*) Haerbaling; (*d*) 'activities at other burial sites' at Jiamusi, Heilongjiang province; Hunchun, Jilin province; Lianhuapao, Jilin province; and Guangzhou, Guangdong province; and (*e*) identification operations at Anqing, Bengbu, Hangzhou, Shijiazhuang, Shouyang, Wuhan and Xinyang. Fujiwara, H., Deputy Director-General, Abandoned Chemical Weapons Office, Japanese Cabinet Office, 'Japan's ACWs in China', PowerPoint presentation at 14th Annual International Chemical Weapons Demilitarisation Conference (CWD 2011), Interlaken, 23–26 May 2011, slide 5.

[47] OPCW, Executive Council, Statement by H. E. Ambassador Takashi Koezuka, Permanent Representative of Japan, EC-66/NAT.8, 4 Oct. 2011, p. 1; OPCW, C-16/DG.18 (note 10), para. 50; and OPCW, Correspondence with author, May 2012.

[48] OPCW, Japan, EC-66/NAT.8 (note 47).

[49] Fujiwara (note 46), slide 4.

Political tension

The CSP was marked by political tension between Iran and (mainly) the USA. The Iranian representative stated that 'The former regime of Iraq in its aggression against Iran, deployed chemical weapons against the innocent people of my country, which had been provided to that regime by the United States of America and its western allies'. He also stated that it is 'unfortunate' that the USA 'has explicitly stated that it cannot meet the [chemical weapon destruction] deadline, which is a clear-cut case of non-compliance' that should therefore be referred to the United Nations. Iran also called on the persons and companies that supplied Saddam Hussein with chemical weapon-related 'equipment' to be sued and stated that Israel possesses 'weapons of mass destruction' and therefore poses 'the most dangerous threat against the regional peace and security'.[50]

The US representative replied that the USA has not deliberately failed to destroy its chemical weapon stockpiles by the April 2012 deadline and has no intention of retaining such stockpiles. The delay rather reflected exigencies of its destruction programme over previous years. He stated that 'A delay in destroying one's stockpile, even though we are destroying it as rapidly as practicable, is not a deliberate attempt to illicitly retain chemical weapons.'[51] The US representative also denied that the USA had provided the Iraqi regime under Saddam Hussein with chemical weapons.[52]

At the end of the CSP Iran cast the sole vote against an OPCW decision on the final extended deadline for chemical weapon destruction.[53] It requested the OPCW to sanction the USA (but not Russia, which will also fail to meet its April 2012 chemical weapon destruction deadline).[54] Discussions by the Executive Council and the CSP centred on the language used by the chemical weapon possessor states to reiterate their unequivocal

---

[50] OPCW, Conference of the States Parties, Statement by H. E. Kazem Gharib Abadi, Permanent Representative of Iran, 28 Nov.–2 Dec. 2011. Israel attended the CSP as an observer and, for the first time, addressed the meeting from the floor. Although it expressed support for the object and purpose of the CWC, Israel stated that it was unable to join the regime at present given the current broader geopolitical circumstances in the Middle East—arguing that a broader peaceful accommodation must be reached among the states in the region prior to any accession to the various arms control and disarmament regimes.

[51] OPCW, Conference of the States Parties, Supplemental US statement distributed as an official document, The Hague, 29 Nov. 2011, p. 1.

[52] OPCW, USA (note 51).

[53] OPCW, Conference of the States Parties, 'Final extended deadline of 29 April 2012', Decision C-16/DEC.11, 1 Dec. 2011. Previously, CSP decisions had almost always been taken by consensus, with the notable exception of the vote to end the tenure of the second OPCW Director-General in 2002. See Hart, J., Kuhlau, F. and Simon, J., 'Chemical and biological weapon developments and arms control', *SIPRI Yearbook 2003*, pp. 651–52.

[54] OPCW, Conference of the States Parties, 'Explanation of vote on the draft decision on the final extended deadline of 29 April 2012', Statement by H. E. Kazem Gharib Abadi, Permanent Representative of Iran, 28 Nov.–2 Dec. 2011. The document was circulated at the CSP.

commitment to destroying their stockpiles in the shortest time and to submit further details to the OPCW of their destruction programmes.

The OPCW has continued to make special visits to destruction sites in Russia and the USA; the visits serve to underline the political commitment of both states to destroy their chemical weapon stockpiles as soon as is practical. The CSP decision requires future meetings to undertake an annual review of the progress of chemical weapon destruction by those parties that have not met their April 2012 deadline and sets aside a specially designated meeting at the 2017 CSP to consider this matter.[55] Previous discussions on setting a new chemical weapon destruction deadline will thus be superseded by a process of annual information submission, verification and review by the parties that will probably continue for at least five more years.

[55] OPCW, C-16/DEC.11 (note 53), para. 3(f).

III. Allegations of chemical and biological weapon programmes

JOHN HART

Allegations of activity related to chemical and biological weapons (CBW) continued in 2011 with little official or otherwise authoritative reporting to clarify these contentions.

A report written by a doctor for the World War II Japanese military, which was uncovered in October 2011 in 'a local office' of the National Diet Library in Kyoto Prefecture, states that 25 946 people were infected by the Japanese military's biological weapons during the 1937–45 Second Sino-Japanese War. The report states that the Imperial Japanese Army's Unit 731 released plague-infected fleas in six operations between 1940 and 1942 in several provinces including Jiangxi, Jilin and Zhejiang.[1]

North Korea

In May 2011 China voted not to allow the UN Security Council to release a report on sanctions on the Democratic People's Republic of Korea (DPRK, or North Korea) under Security Council Resolution 1874.[2] According to the leaked text of the report, North Korea is 'suspected to possess a large stockpile of chemical weapons, and of maintaining a biological weapons programme to independently cultivate and produce agents such as the bacteria of anthrax, smallpox and cholera since the 1980s'.[3] It also stated that 'it is broadly believed' that North Korea possesses 2500–5000 tonnes of chemical weapons, including phosgene, sarin, sulphur mustard, tabun, unspecified blood agents and other persistent organophosphorus nerve agents; and that North Korea has at least eight chemical weapon production facilities, including at the Chungsu and the Eunduk chemical plants.[4] An unnamed UN member state told the panel that the Second Economic Committee of the National Defence Commission (via its Fifth Machine Industry Bureau and the Second Academy of Natural Sciences) are 'believed to play leading roles in activities related to the production, import and export' of North

---

[1] 'Report shows Japanese Imperial Army used bioweapons during Sino War', Jiji Press, 15 Oct. 2011. For background see Harris, S., *Factories of Death: Japanese Biological Warfare, 1932–1945, and the American Cover-up*, revised edn (Routledge: London, 2002).

[2] Kan, S. A., *China and Proliferation of Weapons of Mass Destruction and Missiles: Policy Issues*, Congressional Research Service (CRS) Report for Congress RL31555 (US Congress: Washington, DC, 9 Nov. 2011), p. 29. See also chapter 8, section IV, and chapter 10, section III, in this volume.

[3] Panel of experts established pursuant to Resolution 1874 (2009), Report, para. 74. The leaked report is available at <http://www.scribd.com/doc/55808872/UN-Panel-of-Experts-NORK-Report-May-2011>. The report was partly informed by South Korean Ministry of National Defense (MND), *2010 Defense White Paper* (MND: Seoul, 2011).

[4] Panel of experts established pursuant to Resolution 1874 (note 3), para. 75.

Korea's CBW programme. The panel also stated that the Green Pine Associated Company is 'deeply engaged in the illicit procurement of chemical material and other specialty items abroad'.[5]

Additionally, in 2011 diplomats were quoted as saying that in 2009 Greece had seized almost 14 000 chemical protection suits from a North Korean ship that was possibly headed for Syria. The UN Security Council considered the information on the seizure during its deliberations on ongoing sanctions against North Korea in 2011.[6]

Iran and Libya

The United States reportedly investigated whether Iran had supplied the Libyan regime of Muammar Gaddafi with 'hundreds of special artillery shells for chemical weapons that Libya kept secret for decades'. The suspected shells were filled with sulphur mustard and were those uncovered by Libyan rebel forces in late 2011 (see section II above).[7] The former Libyan regime had declared air bombs as the only chemical munitions in its stockpile.

Donald A. Mahley, a retired US Army colonel and State Department official who was involved in the discussions in 2003 between Libya, the United Kingdom and the USA on the modalities for Libya to verifiably renounce nuclear and chemical weapons and long-range ballistic missiles and who also served as head of the US delegation that negotiated a draft protocol to the Biological and Toxin Weapons Convention in the 1990s, stated that 'we will have to think very seriously about finding inspectors with a different skill set, and about more intelligence-sharing, and about looking widely, not just at declared sites'.[8]

The Iranian Ministry of Foreign Affairs denied that Iran had provided such shells and attributed motivation for the story to a form of 'soft warfare'.[9] The Organisation for the Prohibition of Chemical Weapons (OPCW) did not publicly react on the matter. The ability of the OPCW to verify locations outside declared facilities is partly dependent on the willingness of the parties to implement the 1993 Chemical Weapons Con-

[5] Panel of experts established pursuant to Resolution 1874 (note 3), para. 76.

[6] Agence France-Presse, 'Greece seizes N. Korea chemical weapons suits: diplomats', *Korea Herald*, 17 Nov. 2011.

[7] Smith, R. J., Warrick, J. and Lynch, C., 'Iran may have sent Libya shells for chemical weapons', *Washington Post*, 21 Nov. 2011. In Jan. 2012 an OPCW official erroneously stated that the shells were not filled. The OPCW subsequently issued a clarification to the effect that they were.

[8] See Hart, J. and Kile, S. N., 'Libya's renunciation of NBC weapons and longer-range missile programmes', *SIPRI Yearbook 2005*, pp. 629–48. For Mahley's remarks see Smith et al. (note 7).

[9] 'Iran denies claims of supplying chemical weapon parts to Al-Qadhafi regime', Islamic Republic of Iran News Network Television, 22 Nov. 2011, 9:33:05, Open Source Center transcript. The media does not appear to have addressed the question of whether the shells, whatever their origin, were empty when (or if) shipped to Libya.

vention's challenge inspection procedures (which have not been used).[10] The OPCW nevertheless continues to train to carry out such an inspection should one be requested.

Syria

US intelligence services reportedly believe that Syria possesses sarin, VX and sulphur mustard, as well as missile and artillery shells for their delivery.[11] Anonymous current and former US officials have been cited as saying that Syria has 'at least five sites where it produces chemical-weapons agents, including mustard gas, Sarin and VX'.[12] The officials stated that these facilities are located in Aleppo, Damascus, Hamah and Lattakia, among other places, and that some chemical weapon production facilities are located at military sites that also store Scud missiles.[13] In response to the question of whether Syria possesses such weapons, the US Department of State stated:

We have long called on the Syrian Government to give up its chemical weapons arsenal and to join the Chemical Weapons Convention . . . we do believe that Syria's chemical stockpile remains under government control and that there is no change in the lockdown status of those weapons. Syria has a stockpile of nerve agent and some mustard gas, and we will continue to work closely with likeminded countries to ensure that there is no proliferation of that material.[14]

---

[10] See Chemical Weapons Convention, Article IX, paras 8–25; and Verification Annex, parts X–XI.
[11] Solomon, J., 'U.S., Israel monitor suspected Syrian WMD', *Wall Street Journal*, 27 Aug. 2011.
[12] Solomon (note 11).
[13] Solomon (note 11).
[14] US Department of State, 'Daily press briefing', 30 Aug. 2011, <http://www.state.gov/r/pa/prs/dpb/2011/08/171281.htm>.

IV. Chemical and biological warfare prevention and response

JOHN HART

In 2011 further details regarding the 'anthrax letter' investigation in the United States, which began in October 2001 and was conducted by the US Federal Bureau of Investigation (FBI), were released.[1] Discussions focused on how the Department of Justice had determined that Bruce E. Ivins, a US Army scientist, was responsible for the letters and acted alone. The Department of Justice found that Ivins's psychiatric history provides 'considerable additional circumstantial evidence' that he was guilty. However, the US National Academy of Sciences issued a report that concluded 'It is not possible to reach a definitive conclusion about the origins of the *Bacillus anthracis* in the mailings based on the available scientific evidence alone'.[2] The US Congress will continue to consider this matter in 2012.

In 2011 the United Nations Office for Disarmament Affairs and the UN Secretary-General concluded a memorandum of understanding (MOU) with the World Health Organization (WHO) concerning the the Secretary-General's authority to investigate alleged use of chemical and biological weapons (CBW).[3] Other MOUs with the World Organisation for Animal Health (OIE) and the Organisation for the Prohibition of Chemical Weapons were still being negotiated.

In August 2011 the Working Group on Preventing and Responding to Weapons of Mass Destruction Attacks, which had taken on some of the activities of the Counter-Terrorism Implementation Task Force in support of the 2006 UN Global Counter-Terrorism Strategy, called for enhancing coordination between all relevant international actors and strengthening response capacities at regional, national and local levels.[4] The report concluded that, while lead international agencies for dealing with nuclear and

---

[1] Guillemin, J., *American Anthrax: Fear, Crime, and the Investigation of the Nation's Deadliest Bioterror Attack* (Times Books: New York, 2011).

[2] Amerithrax Expert Behavioral Analysis Panel, *Report of the Expert Behavioral Analysis Panel* (Research Strategies Network: Vienna, VA, 2011), p. 2; and National Research Council, *Review of the Scientific Approaches Used during the FBI's Investigation of the 2001 Anthrax Letters* (National Academies Press: Washington, DC, 2011), p. 4. See also US Public Broadcasting Service, 'The anthrax files', *Frontline*, 11 Oct. 2011, <http://www.pbs.org/wgbh/pages/frontline/anthrax-files/>.

[3] United Nations, Counter-Terrorism Implementation Task Force (CTITF), *Interagency Coordination in the Event of a Terrorist Attack using Chemical or Biological Weapons or Materials* (United Nations: New York, Aug. 2011), para. 152; and United Nations, Office for Disarmament Affairs, 'Memorandum of Understanding between the World Health Organization and the United Nations concerning WHO's support to the Secretary-General's mechanism for investigation of the alleged use of chemical, biological or toxin weapons', 31 Jan. 2011, <http://www.un.org/disarmament/WMD/Secretary-General_Mechanism/>.

[4] The UN Global Counter-Terrorism Strategy and its Plan of Action are contained in UN General Assembly Resolution 60/288, 20 Sep. 2006.

radiological threats are readily identifiable, organizations with responsibility for CBW threats are more diffuse and characterized by having 'partial mandates' in the various activities associated with prevention, preparedness and response.[5]

In 2011 the US Trade & Aid Monitor blog released primary documents and information on planned environmental remediation activity to clean up the after-effects of the US use of defoliants in Viet Nam in the 1960s and early 1970s.[6]

Scientific research

In late 2011 two research groups, one in the USA and the other in the Netherlands, released preliminary results of work to modify the virulence of the A(H5N1) strain of the avian influenza virus. Biosafety and biosecurity concerns led the US National Science Advisory Board for Biosecurity (NSABB) to request, for the first time since the body began to meet in 2005, that the researchers withhold part of their research findings from publication.[7] The NSABB's authority in the matter derives from the fact that both research groups have received funding from the US National Institutes of Health.

At the Fourth European Scientific Working Group on Influenza (ESWI) in September 2011, Dr Ron Fouchier of the Dutch Erasmus Medical Centre, who leads one of the two research groups, presented findings that show how a modified avian influenza virus strain became readily transmissible among ferrets, the animal model that Fouchier was using to study human infections.[8] The second research group is led by Dr Yoshihiro Kawaoka of the University of Wisconsin and the University of Tokyo. Fouchier's group submitted its research to *Science*, while Kawaoka's group submitted its work to *Nature*. The editorial board of *Nature* indicated that it would consult with the researchers concerning the NSABB's request.

This research exemplifies the growing ability of scientists to manipulate and create pathogens with novel characteristics. The NSABB reviewed the draft research and stated that neither manuscript should be published in its

[5] United Nations, Counter-Terrorism Implementation Task Force (note 3).

[6] 'Da Nang Agent-Orange/dioxin technical documents obtained', US Trade & Aid Monitor blog, 23 May 2011, <http://www.tradeaidmonitor.com/2011/05/da-nang-agent-orangedioxin-technical-documents-obtained.html>.

[7] As of 5 Jan. 2012, 576 cases of A(H5N1) infection had been reported to the WHO since 2003, and 339 of those infected had died. The mortality rate, c. 50%, is perhaps too high because it is possible that some proportion of those infected went unreported, partly because they recovered without being tested. World Health Organization (WHO), 'Cumulative number of confirmed human cases for avian influenza A(H5N1) reported to WHO, 2003–2011', <http://www.who.int/influenza/human_animal_interface/H5N1_cumulative_table_archives/en/index.html>.

[8] European Scientific Working Group on Influenza (ESWI), Fourth ESWI Influenza Conference, Malta, 11–14 Sep. 2011, <http://www.eswiconference.org/>.

entirety 'with complete data and experimental details', and that text should be added to describe, among other things, (*a*) the goals of the research, (*b*) the potential health benefits, (*c*) the risk assessments carried out prior to the start of the research, (*d*) the biosafety oversight and related measures, (*e*) the biosecurity practices and the facilities' 'adherence to select agent regulation', and (*f*) text 'addressing biosafety, biosecurity, and occupational health [that] is part of the responsible conduct of all life sciences research'. It is less clear how the adherence of facilities to select agent regulation would apply to non-US entities that receive US grants. However, the harmonization of such standards internationally is a broader policy objective within, for example, the framework of the Australia Group. The NSABB also stated that the US Government should 'encourage the authors to submit a special communication/commentary letter' to the journals 'regarding the dual use research issue'.[9]

The WHO stated that it was 'deeply concerned about the potential negative consequences' of the research.[10] In January 2012 it requested a 60-day moratorium to suspend such research during which time the WHO member states were asked to consider what approaches and decisions (if any) should be taken. Some observers and analysts have expressed concern that such work unnecessarily risks the accidental release from a laboratory of a modified virus, or that such work might suggest to states and non-state actors unorthodox avenues for biological weapon attack. Conversely, observers and analysts have argued that it is important to better understand the mechanisms by which influenza viruses become readily transmissible among humans.[11] There were further disagreements regarding whether and how the research proposal could have been modified to make it less 'proliferation sensitive'.

DNA recovery and sequencing from deteriorated ('ancient') and novel specimens are becoming increasingly common, mainly due to rapidly improving capabilities to extract, duplicate and sequence minute and ancient DNA samples. Such work yields greater insight into the function of pathogens and the nature of associated virulence factors. On 12 October 2011, *Nature* published a draft genome of *Yersinia pestis* (the causative agent of plague) that was derived from victims of the Black Death, dating

---

[9] US National Science Advisory Board for Biosecurity (NSABB), 'National Science Advisory Board for Biosecurity Recommendations', 21 Nov. 2011, <http://www.aaas.org/news/releases/2012/0120sp_flu.shtml>.

[10] World Health Organization (WHO), 'WHO concerned that new H5N1 influenza research could undermine the 2011 Pandemic Influenza Preparedness Framework', Press statement, 30 Dec. 2011, <http://www.who.int/mediacentre/news/statements/2011/pip_framework_20111229/en/index.html>.

[11] In birds, the A(H5N1) strain is principally a gut disease that is shed through faeces, while in humans the strain is principally found in the lungs, nose, and throat and shed through mucous and saliva. Scientists have found that a change in the PB2 gene facilitated virus reproduction at a temperature 4 degrees Celsius lower than the temperature in the guts of birds. Birds and humans also share similar cell receptors (alpha 2,3 and alpha 2,6, respectively).

from a strain associated with plague deaths in London in 1348–50. The samples were taken from the teeth of victims, and DNA from current *Y. pestis* strains was used as a complementary template to the historical strain. Analysis of the genetic structure of the strain, including its phylogeny, 'reveal[s] no unique derived positions' as compared to those currently found in nature and, thus, 'factors other than microbial genetics, such as environment, vector dynamics and host susceptibility' should be the focus for analysis of the epidemiology of the bacterium.[12] The researchers sought to understand why the strain that caused the Black Death was so virulent. The possible reasons include (*a*) yet to be understood aspects of how the genes are structured in the chromosomes, (*b*) the possible greater susceptibility of the population of 14th century Europe to the bacterium, and (*c*) a combination of environmental factors—including extended periods of warmer, wet weather, as well as the proximity of humans to rodents and unsanitary living conditions, both of which were more common at the time. One of the principal researchers, Dr Hendrick Poinar, underlined the fast pace of change in science and technology (S&T) by observing that scientists would have been 'unlikely' to be able to extract the genome in 2009.[13]

Future implications of science and technology

The current and future S&T environment poses several difficult questions for CBW arms control, including what is an 'activity of concern'; what is the appropriate policy response with respect to both general S&T trends and developments and possible future specific activities that may require regulation and other governance responses; and what is the expected operating environment of the 1972 Biological and Toxin Weapons Convention (BTWC) and the 1993 Chemical Weapons Convention (CWC) in the coming 10–20 years?[14]

Many S&T advances have increased the knowledge, material and technologies that could be misused if science were to be applied for hostile purposes. Yet, on their own, they do not lead to the emergence of new warfare options. What matters is rather the context in which these scientific activ-

---

[12] Schuenemann, V. J. et al., 'Targeted enrichment of ancient pathogens yielding the pPCP1 plasmid of *Yersinia pestis* from victims of the Black Death', *Proceedings of the National Academy of Sciences*, vol. 108, no. 38 (20 Sep. 2011), pp. E746–E752; and Bos, K. I. et al., 'A draft genome of *Yersinia pestis* from victims of the Black Death', *Nature*, vol. 478 (27 Oct. 2011), pp. 506–10.

[13] US Public Broadcasting Service, 'Reconstructing Black Death: why was plague microbe so deadly?', Interview of Hendrick Poinar by Ray Suarez, *Newshour*, 13 Oct. 2011, <http://www.pbs.org/newshour/bb/health/july-dec11/blackdeath_10-13.html>.

[14] Partly based on Hart, J. and Trapp, R., 'Science and technology and their impacts on the Biological and Toxin Weapons Convention: a synthesis report on preparing for the Seventh Review Conference and future challenges', SIPRI, Dec. 2011, <http://www.sipri.org/research/disarmament/bw/publications/btwc111212.pdf>. See also UN Office at Geneva, 'Disarmament: think zone for the Seventh Review Conference', <http://www.unog.ch/bwc/thinkzone>.

ities are carried out. For example, threat assessment and biodefence programmes (depending on how they are structured and implemented) can, if conducted with a lack of sufficient transparency, raise concerns among other states or actors regarding their legitimacy or intent. This, in turn, can destabilize the BTWC and the CWC regimes. However, it is not the nature of the research itself that should be the focus of clarification and evaluation by states. While monitoring scientific activities can assist in the identification of new discoveries or research activity, what is most important is an in-depth evaluation of their implications for the convention regimes. In particular, states should understand whether these new scientific activities and discoveries could lead to paradigm shifts and, therefore, call for new approaches and responses in CBW arms control. This can be done by states (both individually and collectively) in the context of the BTWC and the CWC regime meetings. Any S&T evaluation mechanisms should be systematic and participatory in nature.

With regard to policy responses to S&T trends, the nature of science calls for a combination of top-down regulation based on the principles and norms of the BTWC and the CWC, and a bottom-up approach of self-regulation and voluntary measures to increase transparency and strengthen responsible conduct in research and development activity. Interaction between governments and regulators, on the one hand, and science and industry, on the other hand, is also important. Scientists need to have the freedom to carry out research and publish new discoveries and methods. Industry requires a predictable and fair environment in which to conduct science while complying with the BTWC and the CWC norms and the various relevant mechanisms to resolve compliance issues vis-à-vis other parties to these conventions. The entire exercise is both multidisciplinary and driven by the overlapping interests and responsibilities of governments, private enterprise and the science community. Effective chemical and biological arms control calls for a combination of a traditional regulatory approach and the more fluid networking solutions that bring together a wide range of actors.

It is difficult to predict the future operating environment of the two conventions. The focus of concerned practitioners and policy analysts should be on major trends and 'drivers', many or most of which can be readily identified today. For example, as the cost of key enabling technologies (e.g. computing, synthesis and screening) drops and the international capacity to utilize them increases, traditional distinctions between 'donors' and 'recipients' of technology transfer will become increasingly irrelevant. The world is already living in a 'post-proliferation' environment that is characterized less by the spread of weapons, and more by increasing accessibility to and capacity for work in S&T.

Despite the inherently subjective (qualitative) nature of CBW threat assessments, scientists and technical experts working for states, in principle, understand such threats—provided their national structures are oriented to take such threats into account. Non-state actors—'terrorists' and the proverbial garage science operators—lack institutional depth and capacity to achieve similar levels of sophistication or output. Another key ('chicken and egg') conundrum is whether threat pronouncements—often made by those who are not conducting scientific research and development—prompt al-Qaeda affiliates (or their equivalent) to consider or to pursue the acquisition of chemical and biological weapons.[15]

Broader challenges include the extent to which threat perceptions are driven by actual interest and activity by non-state actors; whether and how the deliberate spread of disease constitutes a weapon of mass destruction; and whether states can achieve absolute security, or rather prioritize the attention and resources devoted to a variety of threats (qualitatively or quantitatively) according to a 'reasoned and balanced' hierarchy of risk. Prioritization implies that decision makers and policymakers (and the public more broadly) can tolerate a degree of ambiguity.

[15] Stenersen, A., *Al-Qaida's Quest for Weapons of Mass Destruction: The History behind the Hype* (VDM Verlag Dr Müller: Saarbrücken, 2008), p. 29.

10. Conventional arms control

Overview

While states are continuously concerned with whether or not their national military potential is properly matched to vulnerabilities (actual or perceived), they have also been willing to discuss restraints on military capabilities with one another. With the exception of some promising progress in South America and in South Eastern Europe, in 2011 most developments in conventional arms control were discouraging as states were not willing to modify national positions in order to facilitate agreement, either globally or regionally.

Three background factors have contributed to the difficulty of developing conventional arms control. First, the huge and sustained investment that the United States has made in its military power has made it impossible to find solutions based on balance. Moreover, the strategic direction of US military development, with an increased emphasis on flexible force projection, challenges regional arms control. Second, technological developments have blurred the picture of which capabilities will confer military power now and in the future. The potential impacts of, for example, cyberweapons and missile defences have made it harder to define the scope of arms control as countries try to understand the implications of any limits they might accept. Third, the lack of agreed rules about the use of force—which may be for ostensibly constructive purposes and not only a defensive response to aggression—makes countries reluctant to give up military capabilities even if there is a humanitarian argument in favour of restraint.

For some weapons—such as anti-personnel mines and cluster munitions—states have found it difficult to balance their military security objectives and humanitarian concerns. The 1997 Anti-Personnel Mines Convention and the 2008 Convention on Cluster Munitions (CCM) are examples of agreements based on the principle that, even if a given weapon delivers some military advantage, it should still be limited or banned because the humanitarian consequences of use outweigh any military benefit. While the parties to these two conventions continued their implementation in 2011, the parties to the 1981 Certain Conventional Weapons Convention failed to agree on a protocol defining rules for the use of cluster munitions and banning those with particularly harmful effects (see section I in this chapter). The international community is now polarized between a group of states that have committed themselves to a total ban on cluster munitions through a separate convention negotiated among themselves—the CCM—and a group of states that are not bound by any shared rules at all, apart from the laws of war.

The Vientiane Action Plan, adopted in 2010 to guide implementation of the CCM, is an example of another approach, sometimes labelled 'practical dis-

armament', intended to assist the transition to peace in post-conflict locations by ensuring that weapons are held under proper custody or by collecting and destroying weapons that are considered surplus or that pose an unacceptable risk to civilians and block economic recovery in post-conflict locations.

Some processes seek to control the military capability of other states by making it illegal to export specified military items without a prior risk assessment of the given transfer by the responsible authorities in the exporting state. Efforts to improve the technical efficiency of export control continued in 2011 in global and regional organizations and in the informal regimes of the Missile Technology Control Regime and the Wassenaar Arrangement (see section II). However, a common approach to assessing acceptable risk remains elusive, beyond general guidelines agreed in the 1990s.

Export controls do not presume denial of a transfer (in fact denials are rare), and even when a given transaction is denied the decision need not signal disapproval aimed at the denied party. In contrast, arms embargoes—broad restrictions imposed on the supply to or receipt of specified items from a designated party—are restrictive measures that signal disapproval or aim to modify the behaviour of the target. The United Nations Security Council imposed one new arms embargo—binding on all states—in 2011, on Libya, but could not agree on an embargo on Syria (see section III). The Arab League did impose an arms embargo on Syria, its first ever, as did the European Union.

The most highly developed conventional arms control regime is in Europe, where it acts as a self-restraint measure intended to help achieve strategic stability and maintain a military balance in a defined region. In addition to the important impact on the size and composition of armed forces during the post-cold war period, the arms control regime provided the framework in which European countries could discuss the military-technical dimensions of security in Europe. Decisions in 2011 signalled that the main actors—in the North Atlantic Treaty Organization (NATO) as well as in Russia—no longer believe that the implications of modern military-technical developments can be discussed regionally (see section IV). However, they have not yet agreed on whether or how to move this discussion into a bilateral framework.

Finally, there are measures intended to restrict the operational activities of armed forces, or to make those activities transparent, in order to enhance stability and predictability. While these measures do not impose limits on the size or structure of armed forces, they can act as important confidence- and security-building measures (CSBMs). Most activity in this field in 2011 took place in Europe, where states agreed on an updated version of the Vienna Document on CSBMs, and South America, where states have agreed to a series of CSBMs intended to support their wider objective of building a common and cooperative security system in the region (see section V).

IAN ANTHONY

I. Limiting conventional arms for humanitarian reasons: the case of cluster munitions

LINA GRIP

Several years of international negotiations on imposing greater controls on cluster bombs reached a climax in 2011 when states parties to the 1981 Certain Conventional Weapons (CCW) Convention convened to negotiate a draft protocol on cluster munitions in the convention's Fourth Review Conference.[1] The weapon category 'cluster munitions' lacks an internationally agreed legal definition, but in general terms a cluster munition can be defined as a canister that breaks apart prior to detonation, releasing multiple individual sub-munitions. These weapons can be delivered from aircraft or land- or sea-based systems against moving or fixed targets—including people, vehicles or infrastructure such as airfield runways. The individual sub-munitions may be difficult or impossible to target precisely, and a certain proportion may not detonate immediately. There is a risk that the use of these weapons will fail to discriminate between military targets and protected civilians and that unexploded ordnance will continue to pose a threat beyond the duration of the conflict in which they were used. For these reasons there have been efforts to restrict or entirely prohibit cluster munitions.

The CCW Convention was the first treaty under international law with provisions to address cluster munitions, and discussions to expand restrictions on these weapons by introducing a specific CCW protocol on cluster munitions have been ongoing in the CCW regime since 2003.[2] In 2006, at the Third CCW Review Conference, six countries submitted a proposal for a mandate to negotiate a CCW protocol on cluster munitions.[3] At the same conference, 25 states parties issued a declaration that called for an agreement—not necessarily within the CCW regime—that would prohibit the 'use of cluster munitions within concentrations of civilians', ban the 'development, production, stockpiling, transfer and use of cluster munitions that pose serious humanitarian hazards because they are for example

---

[1] On this process see Lachowski, Z., 'Conventional arms control', *SIPRI Yearbook 2008*, pp. 488–90. For a summary and other details of the Convention on Prohibitions or Restrictions on the Use of Certain Conventional Weapons which may be Deemed to be Excessively Injurious or to have Indiscriminate Effects (CCW Convention) and its protocols see annex A in this volume.

[2] Protocol V to the CCW Convention, which was adopted on 28 Nov. 2003 and entered into force on 12 Nov. 2006, includes obligations on states to remove or destroy explosive remnants of war on their territory, including unexploded cluster munitions. CCW Convention (note 1), Protocol V, Article 3. As of 1 Jan. 2012, 76 of the 114 parties to the CCW Convention were parties to Protocol V.

[3] Third CCW Review Conference, 'Proposal for a mandate to negotiate a legally-binding instrument that addresses the humanitarian concerns posed by cluster munitions', Presented by Austria, the Holy See, Ireland, Mexico, New Zealand and Sweden, CCW/CONF.III/WP.1, 25 Oct. 2006. Documents relating to the CCW Convention are available at <http://www.unog.ch/ccw/>.

unreliable and/or inaccurate', require the destruction of stockpiles of such cluster munitions and establish forms of cooperation and assistance to achieve this destruction.[4]

The states parties were unable to agree on a way forward in 2006. Instead, they convened an intersessional group of governmental experts (GGE) meeting to 'consider further the application and implementation of existing international humanitarian law to specific munitions that may cause explosive remnants of war, with particular focus on cluster munitions'. This meeting was also opened to information and input from non-governmental sources, including expert reports produced under the auspices of the International Committee of the Red Cross (ICRC).[5] In 2008 the states parties agreed to negotiate a draft sixth protocol to the CCW, on cluster munitions, partly spurred by rapid progress in a parallel process taking place outside the framework of the CCW.

In December 2006 Norway had invited all 'countries that are ready to explore ways to address this pressing humanitarian issue in a determined and an effective manner and are prepared to develop a new legally binding international instrument on cluster munitions' to a conference in Oslo in early 2007.[6] The letter of invitation was explicit about the intention to address the issue outside the CCW framework—thus avoiding the need to build consensus among the parties to the CCW Convention—and that the terms of reference for the exercise included a ban, rather than restrictions, on identified cluster munitions. Norway also invited relevant United Nations agencies, the ICRC and non-governmental organizations (NGOs) from the Cluster Munitions Coalition 'that have been central in bringing attention to the problem'. The 'Oslo Process' launched at the conference on 22–23 February 2007 later resulted in the adoption of the 2008 Convention on Cluster Munitions (CCM)—a far-reaching treaty imposing a complete ban on cluster munitions.[7] While the CCM had 67 parties as of 1 January 2012 (including 18 that ratified it in 2011), states such as China, India, Israel, Pakistan, Russia and the United States that are critically relevant to the control of cluster munitions are strongly opposed to a outright ban on these weapons.

---

[4] Third CCW Review Conference, 'Declaration on cluster munitions', Presented by Austria, Belgium, Bosnia and Herzegovina, Croatia, Costa Rica, the Czech Republic, Denmark, Germany, the Holy See, Hungary, Ireland, Liechtenstein, Lithuania, Luxembourg, Malta, Mexico, New Zealand, Norway, Peru, Portugal, Serbia, Slovakia, Slovenia, Sweden and Switzerland, CCW/CONF.III/WP.18, 20 Nov. 2006.

[5] Third CCW Review Conference, Final document, Part II, Final declaration, CCW/CONF.III/11 (Part II), 17 Nov. 2006, p. 6.

[6] Støre, J. G., Norwegian Minister of Foreign Affairs, Letter of invitation to the Oslo meeting on cluster munitions, Dec. 2006, <http://www.regjeringen.no/en/dep/ud/selected-topics/humanitarian-efforts/clusterinitiative/conference.html>.

[7] For a summary and other details of the Convention on Cluster Munitions see annex A in this volume.

It was against this background that the Fourth CCW Review Conference met to consider a draft protocol on cluster munitions.

The Fourth Review Conference of the Certain Conventional Weapons Convention

The mandate of the GGE that prepared the Fourth CCW Review Conference was to negotiate a draft protocol on cluster munitions 'to address urgently the humanitarian impact of cluster munitions, while striking a balance between military and humanitarian considerations'.[8] Within the GGE the states that are primarily motivated by the humanitarian aspects of the issue argued for the CCW protocol to include a ban on cluster munitions to mirror the provisions of the CCM. Their main concerns were that, if the CCW Convention were to maintain states' rights to produce and use some types of cluster munition, it would lead to their active use in future conflicts, and thus impede the building of a norm against cluster munitions.[9] In other words, the acceptance of some cluster munitions would create loopholes in the legal framework for weapons that are known to cause unacceptable harm to civilians. States not party to the CCM focused their attention on the conditions for the legal use of cluster munitions considered necessary for national defence. The users and producers of cluster munitions commonly put two main arguments forward. First, several states cited their 'legitimate defence interests' based on the unmatched strategic role of cluster munitions in their national defence. Second, some states claimed that the humanitarian risks posed by cluster munitions would be reduced through technical improvement, for example by making them more precise or adding self-destruction mechanisms, and that the risks would be further mitigated by stopping the use of cluster munitions by non-state actors and in civilian areas.[10]

The GGE's draft protocol on cluster munitions, which was used as the basis for negotiations at the review conference, would prohibit the use, acquisition, stockpiling or retention of cluster munitions produced prior to 1980 and would impose restriction on cluster munitions manufactured in or after 1980.[11] It would permit the continued use of all cluster munitions produced in or after 1980 for up to 12 years after the protocol's entry into force; after that point, only the use of a restricted class of cluster munitions

---

[8] Meeting of the High Contracting Parties to the CCW Convention, Final report, CCW/MSP/2010/5, 10 Feb. 2011, p. 7.

[9] In the case of landmines, e.g., an explanation that has been put offered for the successful reduction of their use in conflict is that they are now considered to be 'weapons of another era'.

[10] See e.g. Fourth CCW Review Conference, Statement by Mr Wu Haitao, Head of the Chinese Delegation, 14 Nov. 2011, pp. 3–4.

[11] Group of Governmental Experts of the High Contracting Parties to the CCW Convention, 'Draft protocol on cluster munitions', 26 Aug. 2011, articles 4 and 5.

would be permitted.[12] The draft protocol would ban the sale of cluster munitions to non-state actors and to states not party to the CCW Convention.[13]

According to the USA, the CCM's combined impact on all of its states parties would be exceeded by the draft protocol's impact on cluster munition stockpiles in the USA alone.[14] In fact, the GGE's draft protocol mirrored existing US law in key aspects, for example by requiring low failure rates, and would impose few new conditions on the USA.[15] States such as Brazil and India supported the text, with Brazil highlighting its 'unequivocal potential to make a difference on the ground' and stating that 'a protocol based on the [GGE draft] would be better than the alternative of having no obligations at all'.[16] Several European Union member states, including Ireland and Poland, expressed the opinion that even an imperfect protocol would have value.[17] Although Germany criticized the GGE draft (based on the ICRC's concerns about such humanitarian aspects as safeguard mechanisms), it also underlined the need to recognize the fundamental differences between the CCW and CCM processes and noted that a CCW protocol must be seen as an intermediate step towards a future ban on the use of cluster munitions.[18]

While most states known to be users or producers of cluster munitions were in favour of the GGE's draft protocol, the USA was the most active supporter. It called the draft protocol 'the only chance' to bring major producing and using states 'into a legally binding set of prohibitions and regulations' on cluster munitions.[19] Other such states objected to certain provisions in the draft. Pakistan was the most sceptical, raising the concern

[12] Group of Governmental Experts of the High Contracting Parties to the CCW Convention (note 11), Article 5 and Technical Annex B.

[13] Group of Governmental Experts of the High Contracting Parties to the CCW Convention (note 11), articles 7(4c). Non-state armed groups have used cluster munitions in Afghanistan (the Northern Alliance), Bosnia and Herzegovina (a Serb militia), Croatia (a Serb militia) and Israel (Hezbollah). Landmine and Cluster Munition Monitor, *Cluster Munition Monitor 2011* (Mines Action Canada: Ottawa, Oct. 2011), p. 15.

[14] Fourth CCW Review Conference, Opening statement by Phillip Spector, Head of the US Delegation, 14 Nov. 2011, p. 2.

[15] The US Department of Defense's June 2008 policy on cluster munitions served as the basis for the US position in the negotiations. It bans use of cluster munitions in civilian areas and the procurement and use of cluster munitions with a failure rate of more than 1%. US Department of Defense, 'DoD policy on cluster munitions and unintended harm to civilians', 19 June 2008, <http://www.defense.gov/releases/release.aspx?releaseid=12049>.

[16] Fourth CCW Review Conference, Statement by Mr Neil Benevides, Deputy Permanent Representative of Brazil to the Conference on Disarmament, 14 Nov. 2011, p. 3; and Fourth CCW Review Conference, Statement by Ambassador Sujata Mehta, Permanent Representative of India to the Conference on Disarmament, 14 Nov. 2011.

[17] Fourth CCW Review Conference, Statement by Gerard Corr, Permanent Representative of Ireland to the UN in Geneva, 15 Nov. 2011; and Fourth CCW Review Conference, Statement by Dr Cezary Lusinski, Deputy Permanent Representative of Poland to the UN in Geneva, 14 Nov. 2011.

[18] Fourth CCW Review Conference, General statement, Ambassador Hellmut Hoffmann, Ambassador of Germany for Global Disarmament Affairs, 15 Nov. 2011, pp. 3–4.

[19] Fourth CCW Review Conference (note 14), p. 2.

that the choices of technical provisions for permitted cluster munitions and of the cut-off date of 1 January 1980 could favour the cluster munitions produced by certain countries and might give them commercial advantages.[20]

The strongest opposition to the draft came from parties to the CCM, which had objected to the text throughout the preparatory process.[21] They objected to the CCW proposals on the grounds that the CCM has established a legal norm that the possession and use of cluster munitions is prohibited while the protocol to the CCW Convention would permit their use, and so the two would be incompatible.[22] For example, South Africa, one of the many states that rejected the draft protocol, was 'uncertain about the real impact of these measures' and stated that the draft was 'fundamentally flawed', that it would have 'a detrimental impact on the CCM and the credibility of the CCW' and that the draft 'fall[s] short of urgently addressing the humanitarian impact' of cluster munitions and therefore 'does not give effect to the mandate given to the GGE'.[23] Some non-CCM parties argued that no norm had been established and that without a CCW protocol they would be under no obligation with respect to cluster munitions other than the general rules of international humanitarian law.[24]

More than 50 of the CCW Convention's parties expressed opposition to the proposal on the last day of the conference. The conference did not lead to an agreement and negotiations within the CCW framework on a protocol on cluster munitions were thus postponed for at least five years, until the next review conference.[25]

The important role played by NGOs in CCW deliberations was noteworthy. In particular, Jakob Kellenberger, president of the ICRC, circulated his statement on the draft protocol to all CCM states parties prior to the review conference.[26] A number of NGOs and UN agencies presented their criticisms of the draft protocol in statements to the conference.[27] This

---

[20] Fourth CCW Review Conference, Statement by Ambassador Zamir Akram, Permanent Representative of Pakistan to the UN, 15 Nov. 2011.

[21] Austria, Mexico and Norway had submitted an alternative draft text in Aug. 2011 that followed the structure of the CCM but without any legal obligations or a definition of a cluster munition. Group of Governmental Experts of the High Contracting Parties to the CCW Convention, 'Draft alternative protocol on cluster munitions (draft protocol VI to the CCW)', Working Paper submitted by Austria, Mexico and Norway, CCW/GGE/2011-III/WP.1/Rev.1, 26 Aug. 2011.

[22] See e.g. Fourth CCW Review Conference, Norwegian Delegation, General exchange of views, 15 Nov. 2011.

[23] Fourth CCW Review Conference, Statement by South Africa, 14–25 Nov. 2011, p. 2.

[24] See e.g. Fourth CCW Review Conference, Statement by Tamar Rahamimoff-Honing, Counsellor, Representative of Israel, 14 Nov. 2011, p. 5.

[25] Zughni, F., 'Cluster munitions protocol fails', *Arms Control Today*, vol. 41, no. 10 (Dec. 2011).

[26] Kellenberger, J., President of the International Committee of the Red Cross, Statement to the Fourth CCW Review Conference, 15 Nov. 2011, <http://www.icrc.org/eng/resources/documents/statement/ccw-statement-2011-11-15.htm>.

[27] See e.g. Fourth CCW Review Conference, Statement by United Nations agencies and other organizations involved in humanitarian action, Delivered by Navanethem Pillay, United Nations High Commissioner for Human Rights, 14 Nov. 2011.

criticism was echoed in conference statements made by smaller states that had not been affected by cluster munitions.[28] The role of the ICRC as not just an observer but an assertive actor in the CCW review conference produced a strong reaction from some states parties. For example, India stated that the NGOs 'should continue to contribute as in the past to enhancing our understanding of and sensitivity to [international humanitarian law] issues in a neutral and apolitical manner'.[29] In light of the fact that the conference ultimately failed, at least one participant at the review conference has expressed concerns that NGO participation in future disarmament negotiations could be limited or even prevented.[30]

The Convention on Cluster Munitions

Seven of the eight states parties to the CCM that have completed the destruction of their stockpiles are European.[31] The largest remaining stockpiles subject to the CCM are also European: Germany (which had declared 67 million sub-munitions) and the United Kingdom (which had declared 39 million sub-munitions) had each destroyed more than half of their stockpiles by mid-2011.[32]

The model for the CCM was the 1997 Anti-Personnel Mines (APM) Convention, which has provided the framework for a sustained practical disarmament effort that has led to the demining of large areas of contaminated territory and the destruction of large numbers of landmines.[33] In June 2011 Iraq became the 87th state to declare that it had completed destruction of its stockpiles of landmines falling within the scope of the treaty and Nigeria became the 18th state to report completion of its obligation to clear APMs in known mined areas.[34] While the convention has been highly successful in preventing the use of and trade in landmines, there seems to have been a loss of momentum in certain aspects of its implementation. According to the *Landmine Monitor 2011*, 'the rate of compliance with submitting annual transparency reports is at an all-time low' and 'clearance deadline extension requests are becoming the norm rather than the exception'.[35]

---

[28] See e.g. Fourth CCW Review Conference, Statement by Jones Applerh, Executive secretary, Ghana National Commission on Small Arms, 14 Nov. 2011.

[29] Fourth CCW Review Conference, Statement by Ambassador Sujata Mehta (note 16), p. 5.

[30] CCW state party official, Interview with author, 9 Dec. 2011.

[31] Austria, Belgium, Ecuador, Moldova, Montenegro, Norway, Portugal and Spain have completed destruction of their stockpiled cluster munitions.

[32] Landmine and Cluster Munition Monitor (note 13), pp. 19–20.

[33] For a summary and other details of the Convention on the Prohibition of the Use, Stockpiling, Production and Transfer of Anti-Personnel Mines and on their Destruction see annex A in this volume.

[34] International Campaign to Ban Landmines, *Landmine Monitor 2011* (Mines Action Canada: Ottawa, Oct. 2011), p. 2.

[35] International Campaign to Ban Landmines (note 34), pp. 2, 30.

After the entry into force of the CCM in 2010, the first meeting of states parties took place in November 2010 in Vientiane, Laos (the country most contaminated with cluster munitions). At the conference, the states parties agreed on an action plan to guide implementation of the CCM's provisions on stockpile destruction, clearance and victim assistance, among other things.[36] In order to monitor progress, consensus was reached on the submission of annual updates of the initial national transparency reports as required by Article 7 of the convention.[37] In 2011 a total of 43 states parties submitted such a report, which provide valuable information on, for example, land contamination and bilateral assistance programmes.[38]

The second meeting of states parties to the CCM took place in Beirut, Lebanon (a country also badly affected by cluster munitions), on 12–16 September 2011. The meeting focused on the national implementation of the CCM, including in legislation.

Prospects and challenges

With the failure of negotiations on a cluster munitions protocol to the CCW Convention it will be difficult to sustain political engagement in discussing future prospects and challenges. The main priority within the CCM is likely to be ensuring compliance with stockpile destruction timetables and mobilizing support for countries that need assistance with land clearance. The CCM prohibits assistance in the use, production, transfer and stockpiling of cluster munitions. However, there are different views on what constitutes 'assistance', with some parties (e.g. Norway) taking a restrictive approach and others (e.g. the UK) taking a less restrictive approach. Questions such as how to manage stockpiles on the territory of a CCM party that are owned by a non-party and the transit, trans-shipment, financing or export of explosives or other components necessary to produce banned munitions have been addressed in the CCM and are likely to be future topics of discussion.

Of the 28 states that are heavily contaminated by cluster munition remnants, 8 have ratified the CCM and a further 8 have signed but not yet ratified it.[39] Bringing such countries as Cambodia, Serbia and Viet Nam that are seriously affected by cluster munitions into the CCM is likely to be a priority for the parties to the convention.

The wider normative effect of the CCM is difficult to assess. Production and marketing of cluster munitions is ongoing. Some trade in cluster muni-

---

[36] 'CCM Vientiane Action Plan', 12 Nov. 2010, <http://www.clusterconvention.org/documents/action-plan/>.

[37] 'CCM Vientiane Action Plan' (note 36), Action 59.

[38] United Nations Office at Geneva, 'Article 7 database', <http://www.unog.ch/80256EE600585943/(httpPages)/84610CE6A9FDDACDC1257823003BBC39>.

[39] Landmine and Cluster Munition Monitor (note 13), p. 5.

tions was reported in 2011: the Republic of Korea (South Korea) allegedly sold munitions to Pakistan; and in 2010–11 the USA approved potential deals for CBU-105 sales to Saudi Arabia and Taiwan.[40] Yet the strong reactions to Spain's confirmation that it had sold 1055 cluster munitions to Libya in 2006 and 2008, some of which were used in 2011, suggests that a norm-building process is under way, even if it is still in its early stages.[41] Singapore has unilaterally imposed a moratorium on the export of cluster munitions to parties 'who might use them in an irresponsible and indiscriminate manner' and the USA has suspended all exports of cluster munitions with a failure rate of more than 1 per cent; neither is a party to the CCM.[42] South Korea, which is a party to neither the CCM nor the CCW Convention, has restricted its acquisitions of cluster munitions to those that have self-destruct mechanisms and a failure rate of 1 per cent or lower.[43]

These developments suggest that, at a minimum, the discussion of cluster munitions has been the catalyst for a dialogue at the national level on a responsible approach.

[40] Amnesty International, IPIS and TransArms, *Deadly Movements: Transportation Controls in the Arms Trade Treaty* (Amnesty International: London, July 2010), p. 11; and Landmine and Cluster Munition Monitor (note 13), p. 17.

[41] Landmine and Cluster Munition Monitor (note 13), pp. 168–69.

[42] Landmine and Cluster Munition Monitor (note 13), pp. 307, 330.

[43] Landmine and Cluster Munition Monitor (note 13), p. 280.

II. Limiting the military capabilities of others: developments in arms export control

MARK BROMLEY AND GLENN MCDONALD

During 2011 efforts to improve controls over the export of items specially designed, developed or modified for military use included those in the Missile Technology Control Regime (MTCR) and the Wassenaar Arrangement on Export Controls for Conventional Arms and Dual-use Goods and Technologies as well as in the European Union (EU). Meanwhile, ongoing efforts to reduce the risks associated with the proliferation of small arms and light weapons (SALW)—including attempts to improve export controls—continued in the Organization of American States (OAS), the Organization for Security and Co-operation in Europe (OSCE) and at the United Nations.

Also during 2011 discussions continued in the UN on the creation of a legally binding arms trade treaty (ATT), prior to the negotiating conference to be held in July 2012.[1] Hopes were raised that China and Russia—which had been relatively passive in discussions—were becoming more engaged in the process when the five permanent members of the UN Security Council (China, France, Russia, the United Kingdom and the United States) issued a joint statement in July 2011 that expressed support for 'efforts aimed at establishing an international instrument on the transfer of conventional weapons'.[2] There was a further positive sign on 2 December 2011, when China and Russia voted for the UN General Assembly decision to hold the final session of the ATT Preparatory Committee, having abstained from all previous ATT votes.[3] Nonetheless, discussions at the Preparatory Committee meetings during 2011 demonstrated significant differences between states over the content and purpose of a future treaty.

Export control regimes

During 2011 the two informal, non-legally binding, multilateral export control regimes that focus in part on conventional arms transfers—the Mis-

---

[1] Attention at the July 2011 meeting of the ATT preparatory committee focused on how any treaty would be implemented. Holtom, P. and Bromley, M., *Implementing an Arms Trade Treaty: Lessons on Reporting and Monitoring from Existing Mechanisms*, SIPRI Policy Paper no. 28 (SIPRI: Stockholm, July 2011).

[2] Third Preparatory Committee on an Arms Trade Treaty, P5 Statement, 12 July 2011, <http://www.un.org/disarmament/convarms/ATTPrepCom/Statements.html>.

[3] United Nations, General Assembly, First Committee, 'The arms trade treaty', Draft resolution, A/C.1/66/L.50, 14 Oct. 2011; and Reaching Critical Will, 'Draft resolutions and decisions, voting results, and explanations of vote from First Committee 2011', <http://www.reachingcriticalwill.org/political/1com/1com11/resolutions.html>.

sile Technology Control Regime and the Wassenaar Arrangement—continued their work.[4] No new members were admitted to either in 2011.[5]

At the MTCR Plenary Meeting in Buenos Aires, Argentina, in April 2011 discussions covered transit and trans-shipment controls as a means of preventing proliferation as well as the risks posed by countries with weak export controls. States exchanged information on the ongoing missile programmes of states in the Middle East, North East Asia and South Asia, including Iran and the Democratic People's Republic of Korea (DPRK, or North Korea).[6]

During 2011 the states participating in the Wassenaar Arrangement continued to update and improve its joint military list. They also adopted two new best practice guidelines, including one on re-export controls for conventional weapon systems, and updated others.[7] In addition, the Wassenaar Arrangement carried out its fourth assessment and evaluation of the overall functioning of the regime and its 'contribution to regional and international security and stability', the first since 2007. Several initiatives were launched and completed while others continued beyond the conclusion of the assessment period.[8]

The European Union

The 2008 EU Common Position defining common rules governing control of exports of military technology and equipment aims to harmonize the national arms export policies of EU member states in line with agreed minimum standards.[9] Prior to 2011, meetings of the Council of the EU's Working Party on Conventional Arms Exports (COARM)—where states discuss implementation of the EU Common Position—were chaired by the state holding the rotating Council presidency. COARM meetings are now chaired by a representative of the new European External Action Service (EEAS).[10] In line with Article 15 of the Common Position, a review of the

---

[4] The MTCR and the Wassenaar Arrangement also cover transfers of so-called dual-use goods. On their work in these areas see previous editions of the SIPRI Yearbook. On the activities of the Nuclear Suppliers Group (NSG) to coordinate national transfer controls on nuclear materials see chapter 8, section V, in this volume. See also annex B, section III, in this volume.

[5] However, Mexico was admitted to the Wassenaar Arrangement on 25 Jan. 2012.

[6] Missile Technology Control Regime, 25th Plenary Meeting, Press release, Buenos Aires, 13–15 April 2011, <http://www.mtcr.info/english/press.html>.

[7] Wassenaar Arrangement on Export Controls for Conventional Arms and Dual-Use Goods and Technologies, 2011 Plenary Meeting, Public statement, Vienna, 14 Dec. 2011, <http://www.wassenaar.org/publicdocuments/index_PS_PS.html>.

[8] Official from Wassenaar Arrangement participating state, Communication with author, 12 Apr. 2012.

[9] Council Common Position 2008/944/CFSP of 8 Dec. 2008 defining common rules governing control of exports of military technology and equipment, *Official Journal of the European Union*, L335, 13 Dec. 2008

[10] Treaty of Lisbon amending the Treaty on European Union and the Treaty establishing the European Community, signed 13 Dec. 2007, entered into force 1 Dec. 2009, <http://europa.eu/

instrument was initiated in 2011. The EEAS sought member states' views on the potential scope and coverage of the review to be conducted during 2012.[11]

During 2011 EU member states also proceeded with transposing the European Commission directive on intra-community transfers of defence-related products (ICT Directive) into their national legislation on arms transfer controls.[12] The directive obliges EU member states to introduce simplified procedures for licensing the export of military equipment to other EU member states. It forms part of a wider package of Commission efforts aimed at reducing barriers to intra-EU cooperation in the defence industry.[13] EU member states were given until 30 June 2011 to transpose the directive and until 30 June 2012 to apply it.[14] As of December 2011, 19 states had informed the Commission that they had transposed the directive.[15]

Regional efforts to control small arms and light weapons in the Americas and Europe

Since the late 1990s, many—but not all—regions have adopted legally or politically binding instruments on small arms. Implementation efforts continued in 2011. This section focuses on two regional organizations: the OAS and the OSCE.

The Organization of American States was the first organization to take concrete steps at the regional level to curb the illicit small arms trade by improving controls on the movement of these weapons. The Inter-American Convention against the Illicit Manufacturing of and Trafficking in Firearms, Ammunition, Explosives, and Other Related Materials (CIFTA) was adopted on 14 November 1997 and entered into force on 1 July 1998.[16] Through its Department of Public Security, the OAS assists states

---

lisbon_treaty/>. See also Grip, L., 'Mapping the European Union's institutional actors related to WMD non-proliferation', Non-proliferation Papers no. 1, EU Non-proliferation Consortium, May 2011, <http://www.nonproliferation.eu/activities/activities.php>, pp. 6–7.

[11] Della Piazza, F., Chair of COARM, Presentation to the European Parliament Subcommittee on Security and Defence, 5 Dec. 2011, <http://www.europarl.europa.eu/ep-live/EN/committees/video?event=20111205-1500-COMMITTEE-SEDE>. See also Bromley, M., 'The review of the EU Common Position on arms exports: prospects for strengthened controls', Non-proliferation Papers no. 7, EU Non-proliferation Consortium, Jan. 2012, <http://www.nonproliferation.eu/activities/activities.php>.

[12] Directive 2009/43/EC of the European Parliament and of the Council of 6 May 2009 simplifying terms and conditions of transfers of defence-related products within the Community, *Official Journal of the European Union*, L146, 10 June 2009.

[13] Anthony, I. and Bauer, S., 'Controls on security-related international transfers', *SIPRI Yearbook 2009*, pp. 476–78. See also chapter 5, section I, in this volume.

[14] European Commission, Directorate-General for Enterprise and Industry, 'Defence industries: reference documents', 2 Feb. 2012, <http://ec.europa.eu/enterprise/sectors/defence/documents/index_en.htm>.

[15] Hale, J., '19 EU countries OK defense product transfers law', *Defense News*, 13 Jan. 2012.

[16] For a summary and other details of CIFTA see annex A in this volume.

parties to implement the convention and, more broadly, tackle the problem of firearms trafficking. During 2011 the OAS focused on three specific areas: legislative assistance; marking, record keeping and tracing; and stockpile management and surplus destruction.[17]

The effectiveness of a multilateral instrument depends, in the first instance, on appropriate national legislation and administrative procedures, and on their enforcement. The OAS offers legislative assistance to its member states in implementation of CIFTA. In 2011 the OAS conducted an analysis of legislation on firearms trafficking in Central American states, coupled with an assessment of their level of implementation of the convention. The OAS plans to expand this initiative to all Spanish-speaking member states in 2012. In addition, a project for the preparation of model legislation, covering all CIFTA issue areas, neared completion in 2011, with approval of the last sets of model legislation expected in late 2012.

CIFTA's marking requirements, subsequently developed in both the 2001 UN Firearms Protocol and the 2005 International Tracing Instrument (ITI), underpin the prosecution of firearms trafficking through tracing.[18] With funding from the USA, the OAS is providing its member states with marking machines, training in their use and associated record keeping equipment. In 2011, 16 OAS member states signed a cooperation agreement with the OAS to participate in the programme and received the equipment and training.[19] As of early January 2012 the project had trained approximately 120 governmental personnel in the use of the marking equipment.

In response to the fact that 'the excessive and destabilizing accumulation and uncontrolled spread of small arms ... pose a threat and a challenge to peace', the states participating in the Organization for Security and Co-operation in Europe adopted the OSCE Document on Small Arms and Light Weapons in November 2000.[20] The document outlines a range of commitments for states in many aspects of SALW control, including in areas relating to transfer controls. Since 2000 it has been supplemented

[17] Information on OAS activities is derived from correspondence with the OAS Department of Public Security, Jan. 2012.

[18] Protocol against the Illicit Manufacturing of and Trafficking in Firearms, their Parts and Components and Ammunition, supplementing the United Nations Convention against Transnational Organized Crime (UN Firearms Protocol), adopted 31 May 2001, entered into force 3 July 2005, *United Nations Treaty Series*, vol. 2326 (2007); and International Instrument to Enable States to Identify and Trace, in a Timely and Reliable Manner, Illicit Small Arms and Light Weapons (International Tracing Instrument, ITI), adopted by the UN General Assembly in Decision 60/519, 8 Dec. 2005, <http://www.poa-iss.org/InternationalTracing/InternationalTracing.aspx>. On the Firearms Protocol and the ITI see below.

[19] These states are the Bahamas, Barbados, Belize, Costa Rica, Ecuador, El Salvador, Grenada, Guatemala, Guyana, Honduras, Paraguay, Saint Kitts and Nevis, Saint Lucia, Saint Vincent and the Grenadines, Trinidad and Tobago, and Uruguay. As of 1 Jan. 2012, all but one—Saint Vincent and the Grenadines—were parties to CIFTA.

[20] OSCE, Forum for Security Co-operation, OSCE Document on Small Arms and Light Weapons, 24 Nov. 2000, <http://www.osce.org/fsc/20783>, section I, para. 1.

and strengthened by the adoption of a series of politically binding decisions on export control as well as the creation of several best practices documents and the exchange of information between states.[21]

During 2011 the OSCE continued to assist participating states to improve their controls over international transfers of SALW. This included conducting a survey of how states were implementing the OSCE Principles on the Control of Brokering in Small Arms and Light Weapons and the development of an electronic end-user certificate template.[22] The OSCE also initiated a series of regional workshops for export licensing officials and customs agencies dealing with controls on the export of military and dual-use goods. The first workshop, for states in South Eastern Europe, was held in Zagreb, Croatia, in October 2011. Follow-on events were held in early 2012 in Valletta, Malta, and in Ashgabat, Turkmenistan.[23] Future events are planned in Eastern Europe and the Caucasus.

The United Nations Programme of Action on small arms and light weapons

From 9 to 13 May 2011 an open-ended meeting of governmental experts (MGE) convened in New York to discuss implementation of the 2001 UN Programme of Action to Prevent, Combat and Eradicate the Illicit Trade in Small Arms and Light Weapons in All Its Aspects (the Programme of Action, POA).[24] On the basis of consultations conducted by the meeting

[21] See OSCE, *Handbook of Best Practices on Small Arms and Light Weapons* (OSCE: Vienna, 2003); OSCE, Forum for Security Co-operation, 'Standard elements of end-user certificates and verification procedures for SALW exports', Decision no. 5/04, FSC.DEC/5/04, 17 Nov. 2004; OSCE, Forum for Security Co-operation, 'Updating the OSCE principles for export controls of man-portable air defence systems', Decision no. 5/08, FSC.DEC/5/08, 26 May 2008; and OSCE, Forum for Security Co-operation, 'Information exchange with regard to sample formats of end-user certificates and relevant verification procedures', Decision no. 12/08, FSC.DEC/12/08, 12 Nov. 2008.

[22] OSCE, Forum for Security Co-operation, 'OSCE principles on the control of brokering in small arms and light weapons', Decision no. 8/04, FSC.DEC/8/04, 24 Nov. 2004; OSCE, Conflict Prevention Centre, 'Summary report on replies provided by participating States on the one-off information exchange with regard to OSCE Principles on the Control of Brokering in Small Arms and Light Weapons', FSC.GAL/95/11, 1 Sep. 2011; OSCE, Ministerial Council, 'The continuing implementation of the OSCE Document on Small Arms and Light Weapons', FSC Chairperson's progress report, MC.GAL/2/11, 14 Nov. 2011; and OSCE, Conflict Prevention Centre, 'OSCE helps control export of small arms and light weapons', News, [n.d.], <http://www.osce.org/cpc/83173>.

[23] OSCE, Forum for Security Co-operation, 'OSCE holds a workshop for customs and licensing authorities with Mediterranean Partners on military and dual-use goods', Jan. 2012, <http://www.osce.org/fsc/87153>.

[24] United Nations, General Assembly, Programme of Action to Prevent, Combat and Eradicate the Illicit Trade in Small Arms and Light Weapons in All Its Aspects, A/CONF.192/15, 20 July 2001, pp. 7–22. On the 2011 MGE see <http://www.poa-iss.org/MGE/>. In the UN context, 'open-ended' indicates that all member states are invited to participate. For a fuller account of the MGE see McDonald, G., 'Precedent in the making: the UN meeting of governmental experts', Small Arms Survey Issue Brief no. 5, Mar. 2012, <http://www.smallarmssurvey.org/publications/by-type/issue-briefs.html>.

Chair, Ambassador Jim McLay of New Zealand, small arms marking, record keeping and tracing were selected as the themes for the MGE.[25]

The durable marking of weapons, coupled with adequate record keeping and cooperation between and within countries, allows for the tracing of SALW from the time of manufacture or last legal import to the point of their diversion to the illicit sphere. In practice, the reference point for the discussion of marking, record keeping and tracing was not the POA, but a spin-off measure, the 2005 International Tracing Instrument, which covers the area in much greater detail.

While no substantive outcome was negotiated at the MGE, it did provide a space for focused discussion of technical issues by governmental experts. The discussion covered some current sticking points in ITI implementation.[26] For example, since the ITI and the UN Firearms Protocol were adopted, the manufacture of polymer-frame firearms has become more widespread, especially for the civilian market. In contrast to metal-frame firearms, it is relatively difficult to put a durable mark on a polymer-frame weapon, especially after it has been manufactured (e.g. on import into a second country). MGE delegates highlighted this problem and discussed various solutions to it. In the same way, they considered 'implementation challenges and opportunities' arising in all of the areas under discussion, which, besides marking, were record keeping, cooperation in tracing, national frameworks, regional cooperation, and international assistance and capacity building.[27]

It is clear that some of the discussions held during the MGE, including those conducted in the margins of the main session, will yield concrete improvements in implementation of the ITI. For example, one critical aspect of ITI implementation is the nomination of one or more national points of contact for tracing requests and broader information-exchange functions. As of mid-January 2011, the website of the UN Office for Disarmament Affairs listed ITI-specific points of contact for only 18 of the UN's 192 member states. By 12 May, the penultimate day of the MGE, that figure had increased to 67.[28]

---

[25] See New Zealand Permanent Mission to the United Nations, Letter dated 13 December 2010 from Jim McLay, Permanent Representative.

[26] These points are summarized in a document compiled by the meeting chair. United Nations, General Assembly, Summary by the Chair of discussions at the open-ended meeting of governmental experts on the implementation of the Programme of Action to Prevent, Combat and Eradicate the Illicit Trade in Small Arms and Light Weapons in All Its Aspects, 9–13 May 2011, New York, annex to A/66/157, 19 July 2011. On implementation of the ITI see McDonald, G., 'Fact or fiction? The UN small arms process', *Small Arms Survey 2011: States of Security* (Cambridge University Press: Cambridge, 2011), pp. 49–50.

[27] United Nations (note 26).

[28] McDonald (note 26); and United Nations, Office for Disarmament Affairs, 'ITI National Points of Contact. Updated as of 12 May 2011'.

III. Multilateral arms embargoes

PIETER D. WEZEMAN AND NOEL KELLY

Several substantial developments regarding multilateral arms embargoes occurred during 2011. Early in the year the United Nations Security Council imposed sanctions on Libya, including an arms embargo, but states subsequently disagreed about the scope of the embargo. The Security Council was not able to agree on imposing an arms embargo on Syria despite lengthy discussion.

During 2011, 13 UN arms embargoes, 19 European Union (EU) arms embargoes, 1 Economic Community of West African States (ECOWAS) arms embargo and 1 Arab League arms embargo were in force (see table 10.1).[1] Of the EU's 19 embargoes, 9 implemented UN decisions directly, 3 implemented UN embargoes with modified scope or coverage, and 7 had no UN counterpart.[2] The ECOWAS and Arab League embargoes had no UN counterparts.

The embargo on Libya was the only new embargo imposed by the UN Security Council in 2011.[3] The EU, in addition to its implementation of the new UN embargo on Libya, imposed three new arms embargoes during 2011: on Belarus, on South Sudan and on Syria. The Arab League imposed its first ever arms embargo in 2011: on Syria. ECOWAS's arms embargo on Guinea, imposed in 2009, was lifted in 2011.

Libya

On 26 February 2011, within two weeks of the start of the Libyan uprising, the UN Security Council unanimously voted to impose an embargo on arms supplies to and from Libya in reaction to 'gross and systematic violation of human rights, including the repression of peaceful demonstrators' by the

---

[1] In addition, 1 voluntary multilateral embargo was still in force in 2011: in 1992 the Conference on Security and Co-operation in Europe (CSCE, now renamed the Organization for Security and Co-operation in Europe) requested that all participating states impose an embargo on arms deliveries to Armenian and Azerbaijani forces engaged in combat in the Nagorno-Karabakh area. The request has never been repealed but a number of OSCE participating states have supplied arms to Armenia and Azerbaijan since 1992. Conference on Security and Co-operation in Europe, Committee of Senior Officials, annex 1 to Journal no. 2 of the Seventh Meeting of the Committee, Prague, 27–28 Feb. 1992. On arms transfers to the 2 countries see chapter 6, section IV, in this volume.

[2] The 3 that differed from equivalent UN embargoes were those on Iran and North Korea, which covered more weapon types than the UN embargo, and on Sudan, which covered the whole country whereas the UN embargo applied only to the Darfur region. The 7 with no UN counterpart were those on Belarus, China, Guinea, Myanmar, South Sudan, Syria and Zimbabwe. The 9 that implement UN embargoes are indicated in table 10.1 below.

[3] For administrative reasons, the UN embargo on al-Qaeda, the Taliban and associated individuals and entities was split into an embargo on the Taliban and an embargo on al-Qaeda and associated individuals and entities. UN Security Council resolutions 1988 and 1989, 17 June 2011.

Libyan Government.[4] In contrast to their earlier reluctance to support UN sanctions relating to internal conflicts in Myanmar in 2007 and Zimbabwe in 2008, Russia and China did not delay in voting to support sanctions against Libya.[5] Both countries explained their support for the sanctions as being driven by concern about the violence in Libya and consideration of the views of the Arab League and the African Union.[6] The EU implemented the UN arms embargo by introducing its own arms embargo on 28 February.[7]

On 17 March 2011 the Security Council adopted Resolution 1973, which, while stressing the need to enforce the arms embargo, authorized member states that notified and acted in cooperation with the UN Secretary-General to take all necessary measures to protect civilians under threat of attack in Libya, 'notwithstanding' the paragraph in Resolution 1970 that imposed the arms embargo.[8] Views differed on the extent to which the combined UN Security Council resolutions prohibited arms supplies to forces fighting against the regime of Muammar Gaddafi. The formulation of Resolution 1973, in particular the use of the term 'notwithstanding', caused discussion within and between several countries about whether it allowed the supply of arms to groups in Libya defending themselves against the government as part of efforts to protect civilians.[9] For example, the British Prime Minister, David Cameron, and the US Secretary of State, Hillary Rodham Clinton, argued that it did. In late March the French Foreign Minister, Alain Juppe, and the French Defence Minister, Gerard Longuet, still considered arms supplies to the rebels to be in violation of the UN sanctions.[10] Anders Fogh Rasmussen, Secretary General of the North Atlantic Treaty Organization (NATO), stated that NATO would not support the arming of rebel forces.[11] The UN panel of experts on Libya identified three

---

[4] UN Security Council Resolution 1970, 26 Feb. 2011. On developments in Libya in 2011 see also chapter 2, section I, and chapter 3, section II, in this volume. On arms supplier states' policies on arms exports to Libya see chapter 6, section II, in this volume.

[5] United Nations, Security Council, 6491st meeting, S/PV.6491, 26 Feb. 2011; and Holtom, P. and Kelly, N., 'Multilateral arms embargoes', *SIPRI Yearbook 2009*, p. 484.

[6] United Nations (note 5), p. 4.

[7] Council Decision 2011/137/CFSP of 28 Feb. 2011 concerning restrictive measures in view of the situation in Libya, *Official Journal of the European Union*, L58, 3 Mar. 2011; and Council Regulation (EU) No. 204/2011 of 2 Mar. 2011 concerning restrictive measures in view of the situation in Libya, *Official Journal of the European Union*, L58, 3 Mar. 2011.

[8] UN Security Council Resolution 1973, 17 Mar. 2011, para. 4.

[9] Trevelyan, L., 'Libya: coalition divided on arming rebels', BBC News, 29 Mar. 2011, <http://www.bbc.co.uk/news/world-africa-12900706>; and Lynch, C., 'The United States and its allies explore legal case for arming the Libyan rebels', Turtle Bay blog, *Foreign Policy*, 24 Mar. 2011, <http://turtle bay.foreignpolicy.com/posts/2011/03/24/the_united_states_and_its_allies_explore_legal_case_for_ar ming_the_libyan_rebels>.

[10] 'French defence minister: arming Libyan rebels "not on agenda"', Deutsche Presse-Agentur, 31 Mar. 2011, <http://news.monstersandcritics.com/europe/news/article_1629917.php>.

[11] Bryant, L., 'NATO says arming Libyan rebels not an option', Voice of America, 31 Mar. 2011, <http://www.voanews.com/english/news/africa/north/NATO-Takes-Over-Libya-Air-Operations-11 8977889.html>.

types of transfer: (*a*) transfers that were notified to the UN Secretary-General, which were therefore deemed to be in accordance with Resolution 1973; (*b*) transfers whose notification had been inadequate; and (*c*) non-notified transfers, which violated the arms embargo.[12]

In the end, several countries, acting unilaterally, decided to supply arms to Libyan rebels in the period after 17 March. Transfers by France, Italy, the United Kingdom and the United States fell into the panel's first category. In June France, despite its earlier views, openly admitted to having 'provided self-defensive weapons to the civilian populations', arguing that this was in line with the combined text of the two UN resolutions.[13] Italy, the UK and the USA reported that they had supplied non-lethal equipment such as body armour.[14] Into the second category fell arms transfers from Qatar and, potentially, suspected arms transfers from the United Arab Emirates.[15] It had become an open secret by April that Qatar was supplying arms, with the Qatari Prime Minister, Hamad bin Jasim bin Jabir Al Thani, stating that Resolution 1973 allowed the supply of defensive weapons.[16] Reported arms supplies from Albania and Sudan fell into the third category. The latter declared that it had supplied arms to Libyan rebels in retaliation for Gaddafi's support for Sudanese rebels.[17] There were also unconfirmed reports that Egypt, Italy and Poland supplied arms to the Libyan rebels.[18] Since the EU did not amend its embargo after the adoption of Resolution 1973, it seems that EU member states that supplied arms to the rebels breached the EU embargo. These apparent breaches did not lead to open discussion in the EU.

Russia condemned the supply of arms to groups fighting the Gaddafi regime as a crude violation of the UN arms embargo and, together with South Africa, in July requested a closed meeting of the UN Sanctions Committee on Libya to discuss the French arms supplies.[19] The Russian Foreign Minister, Sergei Lavrov, stated that the arms supplies had damaged the UN Security Council because 'no one had so grossly and openly violated its

---

[12] United Nations, Security Council, Report of the Panel of Experts on Libya established pursuant to Resolution 1973 (2011), 17 Feb. 2012, annex to S/2012/163, 20 Mar. 2012, p. 20.

[13] Charbonneau, L., 'Arming rebels doesn't violate U.N. sanctions: France', Reuters, 29 June 2011, <http://www.reuters.com/article/2011/06/29/us-libya-un-france-idUSTRE75S7XR20110629>.

[14] United Nations (note 12), p. 22.

[15] United Nations (note 12), p. 23.

[16] Black, I., 'Libyan rebels receiving anti-tank weapons from Qatar', *The Guardian*, 14 Apr. 2011; and Dagher, S., Levison, C. and Coker, M., 'Tiny kingdom's huge role in Libya draws concern', *Wall Street Journal*, 17 Oct. 2011.

[17] Copnall, J., 'Sudan armed Libyan rebels, says President Bashir', BBC News, 26 Oct. 2011, <http://www.bbc.co.uk/news/world-africa-15471734>.

[18] Levinson, C. and Rosenberg, M., 'Egypt said to arm Libyan rebels', *Wall Street Journal*, 17 Mar. 2011; Adamowski, J., 'Poland sold arms to Libyan rebels', *Defense News*, 22 Aug. 2011; and Hooper, J., 'Italian government blocks investigation into missing arms cache', *The Guardian*, 19 July 2011.

[19] Reuters, 'Russia says France is violating embargo', *New York Times*, 30 June 2011; and Lee, M. R., 'UN Libya sanctions consensus requirement makes arms embargo a joke', Inner City Press, 7 July 2011, <http://www.innercitypress.com/frun6libya070711.html>

decisions before'.[20] China urged countries to strictly abide by the UN sanctions on Libya but did not explicitly condemn specific countries.[21]

The Gaddafi regime seems to have been successfully cut off from arms supplies after 27 February 2011. Documents found by a journalist in Tripoli indicated that Chinese arms-producing companies had received Libyan officials in July 2011 and had offered to sell them arms.[22] In response the Chinese Ministry of Foreign Affairs announced that the contacts had taken place without the knowledge of the Chinese Government, that no arms had been delivered and that China would strictly implement the UN sanctions on Libya.[23]

On 16 September the UN Security Council amended its arms embargo on Libya to allow arms transfers to the National Transitional Council (NTC), which had been recognized by the UN General Assembly as the new Libyan Government earlier that day.[24]

During 2011 it became clear that there was a major risk that large quantities of arms would leak out of unguarded arsenals in Libya into neighbouring states. Technically, this would be a violation of the embargo on export of arms from Libya, but the real issue was that such arms flows could fuel violent conflict or terrorist activities outside Libya. In October 2011 the UN Security Council adopted a resolution expressing concern about the spread of arms from Libya and calling on the international community to provide assistance in preventing it.[25]

Syria

The swift agreement within the Security Council about a UN arms embargo on Libya was not repeated in the case of Syria, where from March 2011 government forces violently repressed peaceful protests.[26] The EU imposed sanctions on Syria on 9 May 2011, including an embargo on the supply of arms and equipment that could be used for internal repression, and called

---

[20] Russian Ministry of Foreign Affairs, 'Russian Foreign Minister Sergey Lavrov interview to Rossiya 24 TV channel, September 27, 2011', 27 Sep. 2011, <http://www.mid.ru/brp_4.nsf/0/ac216d8 69696b4c4c325791a005c88d6>.

[21] 'China avoids criticising France over Libya arms', Reuters, 30 June 2011, <http://af.reuters.com/article/topNews/idAFJOE75T08J20110630>.

[22] Smith, G., 'China offered Gadhafi huge stockpiles of arms: Libyan memos', *Globe and Mail* (Toronto), 2 Sep. 2011.

[23] Chinese Ministry of Foreign Affairs, 'Foreign Ministry spokesperson Jiang Yu's regular press conference on September 5, 2011', 6 Sep. 2011, <http://www.fmprc.gov.cn/eng/xwfw/s2510/2511/t85 7039.htm>.

[24] UN Security Council Resolution 2009, 16 Sep. 2011.

[25] UN Security Council Resolution 2017, 31 Oct. 2011.

[26] On developments in Syria in 2011 see also chapter 2, section I, and chapter 3, section II, in this volume. On arms supplier states' policies on arms exports to Syria see chapter 6, section II, in this volume.

on the Syrian security forces to exercise restraint.[27] After this first multi-lateral arms embargo had been agreed, in the following months European states and the USA sought support for a Security Council resolution on the situation in Syria. A draft that had been circulated within the UN Security Council before 24 August called for sanctions on Syria, including a full arms embargo and specific financial sanctions.[28] On 26 August Russia circulated an alternative draft resolution that did not include sanctions, which received support from Brazil, China, India and South Africa.[29] Neither draft was put to the vote.

A new draft UN Security Council resolution was introduced by four EU member states in early October. It threatened, but did not impose, sanctions. Instead it called on states to exercise vigilance and restraint over arms transfers to Syria, among other things.[30] China and Russia vetoed the resolution, stressing the principle of non-interference in the internal affairs of states, highlighting the fact that the resolution focused solely on exerting pressure on the Syrian Government and not the opposition, and expressing the concern that threatening sanctions might ultimately result in military intervention as in the case of Libya.[31]

Whereas in the case of Libya calls for UN action from states and multi-lateral organizations in the region had been cited by China and Russia as a reason to vote in favour of UN sanctions, both states continued to oppose sanctions even when the Arab League and Turkey increased pressure on the Syrian Government; by the beginning of December each had imposed economic sanctions and an arms embargo.[32] Statements by Russian Government officials suggested that Russia's strong disagreement with several states' interpretation of the UN arms embargo on Libya contributed to its opposition to an arms embargo on Syria.[33]

[27] Council Decision 2011/273/CFSP of 9 May 2011 concerning restrictive measures against Syria, *Official Journal of the European Union*, L121, 10 May 2011; and Council Regulation no. 442/2011 of 9 May 2011 concerning restrictive measures in view of the situation in Syria, *Official Journal of the European Union*, L121, 10 May 2011.

[28] 'France "three votes short" of putting Syria resolution to UNSC vote', RIA Novosti, 14 June 2011, <http://en.rian.ru/world/20110614/164612668.html.

[29] Lauria, J. and Malas, N., 'Russia introduces competing U.N. draft on Syria', *Wall Street Journal*, 26 Aug. 2011.

[30] United Nations, Security Council, 'France, Germany, Portugal and United Kingdom of Great Britain and Northern Ireland: draft resolution', S/2011/612, 4 Oct. 2011, para. 9.

[31] United Nations, Security Council, 6627th meeting, S/PV.6627, 4 Oct. 2011, pp. 3–5.

[32] League of Arab States, Arab Ministerial Council, Statement on the situation in Syria, 3 Dec. 2011, <http://www.arableagueonline.org/> (in Arabic); 'Turkey announces economic sanctions package against Syria', *Today's Zaman*, 30 Nov. 2011; and Krause-Jackson, F. and Freedman, J., 'Russia shows no sign of buckling to pressure to isolate Syria', *Bloomberg Businessweek*, 2 Dec. 2011.

[33] Yakovenko, A., 'Bending the rules is not the way to resolve conflict', Russia Beyond the Headlines, 26 Oct. 2011, <http://rbth.ru/articles/2011/10/26/bending_the_rules_is_not_the_way_to_resolve_conflict_13646.html>; and Russian Ministry of Foreign Affairs, 'Opening remarks and answers by Russian Foreign Minister Sergey Lavrov at press conference following talks with Icelandic Foreign Minister Ossur Skarphedinsson, Moscow, November 29, 2011', 29 Nov. 2011, <http://www.mid.ru/bdomp/brp_4.nsf/910ea870582bc0f344257959001dace9>.

Other multilateral arms embargoes

Despite the fact that an internationally recognized and UN-supported government took control of Côte d'Ivoire in April 2011, the UN Security Council in the same month voted unanimously to extend the arms embargo on the country for one year.[34]

On 20 June 2011 the EU imposed an arms embargo on Belarus to strengthen its existing sanctions on the leadership of the country in response to the deteriorating human rights, democracy and rule-of-law situation in Belarus.[35] On 18 July 2011, following the independence of South Sudan on 9 July, the EU amended its arms embargo on Sudan so that it continued to cover both Sudan and South Sudan.[36] The EU did not explain the motives or objectives for imposing an arms embargo on South Sudan, but the embargo on Sudan was originally imposed in 1994 in response to the civil war in the south of the country.[37]

Both ECOWAS and the EU imposed an arms embargo on Guinea in October 2009 in response to violence and the deteriorating political situation in the country. During 2010 the political situation improved considerably, and after presidential elections in November Guinea returned to civilian rule. In response, ECOWAS lifted its arms embargo on 25 March 2011.[38] In contrast, in October 2011 the EU extended its embargo until 27 October 2012 without public explanation.[39]

Embargo violations

In 2011, as in previous years, several significant violations of arms embargoes were reported, primarily by the UN panels of experts tasked with monitoring the embargoes.[40] Assessing trends in violations of arms embar-

---

[34] UN Security Council Resolution 1980, 28 Apr. 2011.

[35] Council Decision 2011/357/CFSP of 20 June 2011 amending Decision 2010/639/CFSP concerning restrictive measures against certain officials of Belarus, *Official Journal of the European Union*, L161, 21 June 2011.

[36] Council Decision 2011/423/CFSP of 18 July 2011 concerning restrictive measures against Sudan and South Sudan and repealing Common Position 2005/411/CFSP, *Official Journal of the European Union*, L188, 19 July 2011.

[37] Council Decision of 15 Mar. 1994 on the common position defined on the basis of Article J.2 of the Treaty on European Union concerning the imposition of an embargo on arms, munitions and military equipment on Sudan (94/165/CFSP), *Journal of the European Communities*, L75, 17 Mar. 1994.

[38] ECOWAS, 'Final communiqué of the thirty-ninth ordinary session of the Authority of Heads of State and Government', Press release 040/2011, 25 Mar. 2011, <http://news.ecowas.int/presseshow. php?nb=042&lang=en&annee=2011>.

[39] Council Decision 2011/706/CFSP of 27 Oct. 2011 amending Decision 2010/638/CFSP concerning restrictive measures against the Republic of Guinea, *Official Journal of the European Union*, L281, 28 Oct. 2011.

[40] In 2011 panels existed for all UN arms embargoes except those on non-governmental forces in Iraq and Lebanon. Reports by panels of experts can be found on the website of the UN Security Council sanctions committees, <http://www.un.org/sc/committees/>.

goes has been hindered by efforts of UN Security Council members to prevent or delay the publication of the reports by UN panels.[41] In 2011 two new panel reports—one on Iran and one on the Democratic People's Republic of Korea (DPRK, or North Korea)—were not released to the public. In May 2011 a panel report on the UN embargo on Iran was leaked, but it was not officially released to the public, reportedly because Russia was blocking its publication.[42] During 2011 the committee was not able to reach agreement on when, or whether, the report should be published. Also in May a report by the panel on North Korea was not released, reportedly after China raised objections.[43] It was leaked later that month.[44]

The need for proper investigation and reporting was shown by identified violations of arms embargoes in 2011. Although it did not report new embargo violations by North Korea in 2011, the leaked report by the UN panel of experts provided detailed descriptions of earlier violations and the methods deployed in those violations to stress the need for continued vigilance.[45] Elsewhere it was reported that there were strong suspicions that North Korea tried to export missiles to Myanmar in 2011.[46] During 2011, according to the leaked report on Iran, the panel of experts received information about at least three cases of arms exports from Iran in violation of UN sanctions. These involved a small shipment of small arms to Syria on a plane intercepted in Turkey; a shipment, including six anti-ship missiles, on board a ship en route from Syria to Egypt that was intercepted by the Israeli Navy; and a shipment of 48 122-mm rockets and small arms ammunition originating in Iran that was seized in Afghanistan. The panel also inspected a shipment, intercepted in Singapore, of aluminium powder potentially intended for use in Iranian missiles.[47] The panel concluded that it was likely that other transfers took place undetected.[48]

In Côte d'Ivoire there were strong indications that significant quantities of small arms were supplied from Burkina Faso to the rebel Forces Nouvelles (New Forces) and that the government of President Laurent

---

[41] On efforts to change or block reports in 2010 see Wezeman, P. D. and Kelly, N., 'Multilateral arms embargoes, 2010', *SIPRI Yearbook 2011*, pp. 449–51.

[42] Charbonneau, L., 'Russia blocks UN report on Iran arms sales: envoys', Reuters, 12 May 2011, <http://www.trust.org/alertnet/news/russia-blocks-un-report-on-iran-arms-sales--envoys>.   The leaked report is available at Panel of experts established pursuant to Resolution 1929 (2010), Final report, <http://www.innercitypress.com/1929r051711.pdf>.

[43] Bilefsky, D., 'China delays report suggesting North Korea violated sanctions', *New York Times*, 14 May 2011.

[44] 'N Korea and Iran "sharing ballistic missile technology"', BBC News, 14 May 2011, <http://www.bbc.co.uk/news/world-asia-pacific-13402590>. The leaked report is available at Panel of experts established pursuant to Resolution 1874 (2009), Report, <http://www.scribd.com/doc/558 08872/UN-Panel-of-Experts-NORK-Report-May-2011>.

[45] Panel of experts established pursuant to Resolution 1874 (note 44), pp. 30–32.

[46] Sanger, D. E., 'U.S. said to turn back North Korea missile shipment', *New York Times*, 12 June 2011.

[47] Panel of experts established pursuant to Resolution 1929 (note 42), pp. 15–17.

[48] Panel of experts established pursuant to Resolution 1929 (note 42), p. 2.

Gbagbo tried to import arms before its downfall in April 2011.[49] The acquisitions by the Forces Nouvelles are likely to have played an important role in building its capability to take control of the whole country by force (as part of the larger Republican Forces).[50]

The UN panel on Darfur expressed concern about the Sudanese Government continuing to move military assets into Darfur.[51] The UN monitoring group for Somalia observed that arms continued to be smuggled in by non-state groups. It is believed that Eritrea continued to supply arms to non-state groups in 2011.[52]

---

[49] United Nations, Security Council, Report of the Group of Experts on Côte d'Ivoire pursuant to paragraph 11 of Security Council Resolution 1946 (2010), 17 Mar. 2011, annex to S/2011/272, 27 Apr. 2011, pp. 13–33.

[50] 'Côte d'Ivoire: a changing of the Guard', IRIN, 6 Apr. 2011 <http://www.irinnews.org/report.aspx?reportid=92385>.

[51] United Nations, Security Council, Report of the Panel of Experts on the Sudan established pursuant to Resolution 1591 (2005), 20 Sep. 2010, annex to S/2011/111, 8 Mar. 2011, pp. 30–31. See also Wezeman and Kelly (note 41), pp. 448–49.

[52] United Nations, Security Council, Report of the Monitoring Group on Somalia and Eritrea pursuant to Security Council Resolution 1916 (2010), 20 June 2011, annex to S/2011/433, 18 July 2011, pp. 48–49.

Table 10.1. Multilateral arms embargoes in force during 2011

Target[a]	Date embargo first imposed	Principal instruments establishing or amending the embargo[b]	Developments during 2011
United Nations arms embargoes			
Al-Qaeda and associated individuals and entities	16 Jan. 2002	UNSCR 1390	Amended by UNSCR 1989, 17 June 2011[c]
Congo, Democratic Republic of the (NGF)	28 July 2003	UNSCRs 1493, 1596, 1807	Extended until 30 Nov. 2012 by UNSCR 2021, 29 Nov. 2011
Côte d'Ivoire	15 Nov. 2004	UNSCR 1572, 1946	Amended and extended until 30 Apr. 2012 by UNSCR 1980, 28 Apr. 2011
Eritrea	23 Dec. 2009	UNSCR 1907	
Iran	23 Dec. 2006	UNSCRs 1737, 1747, 1929	
Iraq (NGF)	6 Aug. 1990	UNSCRs 661, 1483, 1546	
Korea, North	15 July 2006	UNSCRs 1695, 1718, 1874	
Lebanon (NGF)	11 Aug. 2006	UNSCR 1701	
Liberia (NGF)	22 Dec. 2003[d]	UNSCRs 1521, 1683, 1903	Extended until 14 Dec. 2012 by UNSCR 2025, 14 Dec. 2011
Libya (NGF)	26 Feb. 2011	UNSCR 1970	New embargo; amended by UNSCR 1973, 17 Mar. 2011, and UNSCR 2009, 16 Sep. 2011[e]
Somalia	23 Jan. 1992	UNSCRs 733, 1725	
Sudan (Darfur)	30 July 2004	UNSCRs 1556, 1591, 1945	
Taliban	16 Jan. 2002	UNSCR 1390	Amended by UNSCR 1988, 17 June 2011[c]
European Union arms embargoes			
Al-Qaeda, the Taliban and associated individuals and entities*	17 Dec. 1996	CPs 96/746/CFSP, 2001/154/CFSP, 2002/402/CFSP	
Belarus	20 June 2011	CD 2011/357/CFSP	New embargo
China	27 June 1989	European Council declaration	
Congo, Democratic Republic of the (NGF)*	7 Apr. 1993	Declaration, CPs 2003/680/CFSP, 2005/440/CFSP, 2008/369/CFSP	

Target[a]	Date embargo first imposed	Principal instruments establishing or amending the embargo[b]	Developments during 2011
Côte d'Ivoire*	13 Dec. 2004	CP 2004/852/CFSP, 2010/656/CFSP	
Eritrea*	1 Mar. 2010	CD 2010/127/CFSP	
Guinea	27 Oct. 2009	CPs 2009/788/CFSP, 2009/1003/CFSP	Amended and extended until 27 Oct. 2012 by CD 2011/706/CFSP, 27 Oct. 2011
Iran	27 Feb. 2007	CPs 2007/140/CFSP, 2007/246/CFSP	
Iraq (NGF)*	4 Aug. 1990	Declaration, CPs 2003/495/CFSP, 2004/553/CFSP	
Korea, North	20 Nov. 2006	CPs 2006/795/CFSP, 2009/573/CFSP	
Lebanon (NGF)*	15 Sep. 2006	CP 2006/625/CFSP	
Liberia (NGF)*	7 May 2001	CPs 2001/357/CFSP, 2004/137/CFSP, 2006/518/CFSP, 2010/129/CFSP	
Libya (NGF)*	28 Feb. 2011	CD 2011/137/CFSP	New embargo; amended by CD 2011/625/CFSP, 22 Sep. 2011[f]
Myanmar	29 July 1991[g]	GAC declaration, CPs 96/635/CFSP, 2003/297/CFSP, 2010/232/CFSP	Extended until 30 Apr. 2012 by CD 2011/239/CFSP, 12 Apr. 2011
Somalia (NGF)*	10 Dec. 2002	CPs 2002/960/CFSP, 2009/138/CFSP, 2010/231/CFSP	
South Sudan[h]	18 July 2011	CD 2011/423/CFSP	New embargo
Sudan	15 Mar. 1994	CPs 94/165/CFSP, 2004/31/CFSP, 2005/411/CFSP	Amended by CD 2011/423/CFSP, 18 July 2011[i]
Syria	9 May 2011	CD 2011/273/CFSP	New embargo
Zimbabwe	18 Feb. 2002	CP 2002/145/CFSP	
Economic Community of West African States (ECOWAS) arms embargo			
Guinea	17 Oct. 2009	ECOWAS statement	Lifted 25 Mar. 2011
Arab League arms embargo			
Syria	3 Dec. 2011	Ministerial Council statement	New embargo

* = EU embargo implementing a UN embargo; CD = Council Decision; CP = Council Common Position; GAC = General Affairs Council; NGF = non-governmental forces; UNSCR = UN Security Council Resolution

[a] The target may have changed since the first imposition of the embargo. The target stated here is as at the end of 2011.

[b] The earlier instruments may have been amended or repealed by subsequent instruments.

[c] In June 2011 the UN Security Council split the embargo on al-Qaeda, the Taliban and associated individuals and entities into separate arms embargoes, one on the Taliban (UNSCR 1988) and one on al-Qaeda and associated individuals and entities (UNSCR 1989).

[d] Liberia has been the target of UN arms embargoes since 1992, with related but different objectives.

[e] To ensure strict implementation of the embargo on Libya, UNSCR 1973 called on UN member states to inspect for compliance ships and aeroplanes in their territory that are bound to or from Libya, including the searching of seaports and airports and allowing for forcible inspections. UNSCR 2009 partly lifted the embargo to allow the transfer of arms to the new Libyan authorities and in support of the United Nations Support Mission in Libya (UNSMIL).

[f] CD 2011/423/CFSP implemented the changes of UNSCR 2009 (see note e).

[g] The EU and its member states first imposed an arms embargo on Myanmar in 1990.

[h] Following the independence of South Sudan in July 2011, CD 2011/423/CFSP amended the EU arms embargo on Sudan so that it continued to cover both Sudan and South Sudan.

Sources: United Nations, Security Council, 'UN Security Council sanctions committees', <http://www.un.org/sc/committees/>; and European Commission, 'Restrictive measures (sanctions) in force', 18 Jan. 2012, <http://eeas.europa.eu/cfsp/sanctions/>.

IV. Limiting conventional arms to promote military security: the case of conventional arms control in Europe

HANS-JOACHIM SCHMIDT AND WOLFGANG ZELLNER

The renewed interest in conventional arms control in Europe that was in evidence in 2010 could not be translated into substantial progress in 2011. On the contrary, after the 2010 Astana Summit of the Organization for Security and Co-operation in Europe (OSCE) failed to adopt a comprehensive Framework for Action because of disagreement over subregional conflicts, particularly in Georgia, the same issue contributed to the suspension of negotiations 'at 36' on conventional arms control in May 2011.[1] By the end of 2011, member states of the North Atlantic Treaty Organization (NATO) had decided to stop sharing information related to the 1990 Treaty on Conventional Armed Forces in Europe (CFE Treaty) with Russia.[2]

The Treaty on Conventional Armed Forces in Europe

Russia was the only CFE state party that did not implement the treaty in 2011.[3] The CFE Treaty is still the framework for pan-European arms control and the only available constraint on military options in unresolved conflicts, particularly the conflict between Armenia and Azerbaijan over Nagorno-Karabakh.[4] Russia has not participated in the obligatory data exchanges since it suspended its participation in the treaty in December 2007 and it has also stopped all active and passive inspection activities, although it still takes part in the treaty committees and thus has not completely left the CFE regime. However, events in 2011 further eroded the regime.

At the fourth, and probably final, CFE review conference on 29 September 2011, there were no strong observable efforts to revive the regime and lift the Russian suspension. Many states parties criticized the Russian suspension and the existence of new 'grey areas' and highlighted the challenge of unaccounted treaty-limited equipment. However, there was no

---

[1] In 2010, at the suggestion of the United States, the 30 parties to the Treaty on Conventional Armed Forces in Europe (CFE Treaty) invited the 6 NATO members that are not treaty parties— Albania, Croatia, Estonia, Latvia, Lithuania and Slovenia—to discuss 'at 36' a framework for strengthening conventional arms control. See Lachowski, Z., 'Conventional arms control and military confidence building', *SIPRI Yearbook 2011*, pp. 411–16.

[2] For a summary and other details of the CFE Treaty see annex A in this volume.

[3] US Department of State, *Compliance with the Treaty on Conventional Armed Forces in Europe*, Unclassified condition (5) (C) report (US Department of State: Washington, DC, Aug. 2011).

[4] However, implementation problems in Armenia and Azerbaijan have contributed to the erosion of the CFE regime. See Lachowski (note 1), p. 414; and chapter 6, section IV, in this volume.

parallel effort 'to find a way forward to reestablish the effectiveness of conventional arms control in Europe'.[5] Russia also behaved in a moderate way but made it clear that the concluding remarks by the chairperson (Andrei Popov of Moldova) have no legally binding effect for Russia because of its suspension of participation in the treaty.[6]

At a meeting of NATO's High-Level Task Force on Conventional Arms Control on 3 November 2011, all NATO member states that are parties to the CFE Treaty decided to stop their data exchange with Russia by the end of the year.[7] Georgia and Moldova followed suit.[8] Russia, which expected this move, did not object because it is in line with the Russian desire to get rid of a regime that it sees as outdated.[9] As a practical consequence, the Netherlands and the United Kingdom decided to significantly reduce their verification personnel, given financial constraints and the uncertain prospects for conventional arms control. Germany plans to reduce the personnel strength of its verification centre by more than 30 posts, to 170, by 2015.[10] Similar steps are being discussed in Russia.

Despite the declared intention to revitalize conventional arms control in Europe in the informal 'at 36' format, it can no longer be taken for granted that the states parties are really willing to negotiate a new agreement. On 8 February 2011 all delegations had agreed on the title for a 'Framework for negotiations to strengthen and to modernize the conventional arms control regime in Europe' that would have opened the way for prospective states parties to participate in negotiating a new agreement with the consent of all parties.[11] This formula would meet the Russian demand to enlarge participation in the regime while still allowing Turkey to block participation by Cyprus.

---

[5] Fourth CFE Treaty Review Conference, Concluding remarks by the Chairperson, RC.DEL/9/11, 29 Sep. 2011.

[6] OSCE, Forum for Security Co-operation, 660th Plenary Meeting of the Forum, FSC.JOUR/666, 19 Oct. 2011, annex 2.

[7] Nuland, V., 'Implementation of the Treaty on Conventional Forces in Europe', Statement, US Department of State, 22 Nov. 2011, <http://www.state.gov/r/pa/prs/ps/2011/11/177630.htm>.

[8] German Federal Foreign Office, *Bericht der Bundesregierung zum Stand der Bemühungen um Rüstungskontrolle, Abrüstung und Nichtverbreitung sowie über die Entwicklung der Streitkräftepotenziale (Jahresabrüstungsbericht 2011)* [Federal government report on the status of arms control, disarmament and non-proliferation efforts and on the development potential of the armed forces (annual disarmament report 2011)] (Federal Foreign Office: Berlin, 2011), p. 60.

[9] Russian Ministry of Foreign Affairs, 'Russian MFA Press and Information Department comment on the decision of a number of NATO countries relating to the CFE Treaty', 23 Nov. 2011, <http://www.mid.ru/brp_4.nsf/0/48f013fdcc0a092444257952005b60a0>.

[10] German Bundestag, 'Deutschlands Rolle im KSE-Prozess' [Germany's role in the CFE process], Response of the federal government to the question by MPs Inge Hoeger, Wolfgang Gehrcke, Sevim Dagdelen, other MPs and the parliamentary group of Die Linke, Bundestagsdrucksache 17/8034, 30 Nov. 2011, p. 8.

[11] On the framework see Rüdiger H. and Schmidt, H.-J., *Konventionelle Ruestungskontrolle in Europa: Wege in die Zukunft* [Conventional arms control in Europe: paths for the future], Hessische Stiftung Friedens– und Konfliktforschung (HSFK) Report 6/2011 (HSFK: Frankfurt am Main, 2011), pp. 16, 40.

In March 2011 the United States, building on an earlier German idea, proposed transparency and verification measures to be implemented outside the CFE Treaty regime by all participants (including all NATO members not party to the CFE Treaty) during an interim period while negotiations on a new agreement take place. However, Russia rejected this proposal.

Russia's stance underlined its long-standing interest in redressing the perceived imbalance created by NATO enlargement. However, Russia has now apparently also linked conventional arms control talks to the issue of missile defence cooperation, although an explicit link has not been made in public. Georgia and Moldova also succeeded in influencing some NATO countries to link unresolved territorial disputes with arms control in addition to the language on host state consent in the Adapted CFE Treaty, which Russia ratified in 2004.[12]

At the final meeting in the 'at 36' format held on 11–12 May 2011 no date was agreed for a future meeting; this can be interpreted as either a pause or an indefinite suspension. Given the complexity of the interlocking issues currently blocking progress, the USA and others have adopted a wait-and-see attitude.[13] Germany has strengthened its efforts to generate some momentum and find a common understanding on the future challenges for European security and the extent to which conventional arms control might help address them. In addition, the German Government has developed a new approach to verified transparency that covers both network-centric warfare capabilities and capabilities for fast transfer and deployment of troops.[14] Where these ideas will lead is uncertain.

Subregional arms control in South Eastern Europe

In stark contrast to the problems with the CFE Treaty, the 1996 Agreement on Sub-Regional Arms Control (Florence Agreement) has not faced any major problems and was implemented in an exemplary manner as in the previous years.[15] The regime currently limits the armed forces of Bosnia and Herzegovina, Croatia, Montenegro and Serbia. Despite the fact that the

---

[12] 'Anatoly Antonov: "The West must not only hear to us, but also listen to us"' *What the Papers Say: Weekly Review*, no. 78 (1 Aug. 2011), p. 3. For a summary and other details of the 1999 Agreement on Adaptation of the CFE Treaty, which has not yet entered into force, see annex A in this volume.

[13] Gottemoeller, R., US Assistant Secretary of State for Verification, Compliance and Implementation, 'Russia and the West: moving the reset forward', Remarks at the Atlantic Council, Washington, DC, 9 Sep. 2011, <http://www.state.gov/t/avc/rls/172055.htm>. However, the fact that the head of the US delegation, Victoria Nuland, took another job on 26 May 2011 suggests that the US Government saw little chance of further progress.

[14] German Bundestag, 'Überwindung des Stillstandes in der konventionellen Rüstungskontrolle in Europa' [Overcoming the standstill in conventional arms control in Europe], Response of the federal government to the question by the MPs Uta Zapf, Dr hc Gernot Erler, Petra Ernstberger, other MPs and the parliamentary group of the SPD, Bundestagsdrucksache 17/8111, 9 Dec. 2011, p. 4.

[15] For a summary and other details of the Florence Agreement see annex A in this volume.

weapon holdings of all states parties are well below the treaty-imposed ceilings, voluntary reductions are still continuing.[16] States parties are also willing to conduct and accept voluntary inspections beyond their treaty obligations.

Because of these positive developments, in 2010 a process to transfer the Florence Agreement to local ownership started in order to reduce the involvement of OSCE participating states (29 of which have supported the regime) and the Personal Representative of the OSCE Chairperson-in-Office. The first phase of the local ownership process progressed successfully in 2011, with international assistance for inspections being reduced by 50 per cent. In a second phase, to be finished by the end of 2014, all other international tasks will be transferred to the four states parties. At its 47th meeting in Belgrade, from 14 to 17 November 2011, the Sub-Regional Consultative Commission was supposed to adopt the common road map for the second phase. However, the Bosnian delegation was not prepared to agree to the common draft for unstated but presumably minor reasons, delaying the anticipated start of the second phase.

Prospects and challenges

Conventional arms control in Europe has reached a dead end even though the need for it is largely undisputed. There is no current consensus on its specific objectives, subjects and instruments and, although some new concepts for and approaches to conventional arms control have been put forward, discussions are in an early phase. Election cycles in Russia and the USA have contributed to a tendency to wait and see how domestic politics of key actors develop and to the assumption that no important initiatives are possible before 2013. Thus, 2012 will be a period of transformation, reorientation and discussion, with the negotiation of new mandates seemingly unlikely.

More broadly, the bilateral Russia–USA 'reset' of relations has not been reflected in European security and arms control policy, where the situation is still characterized by deep mutual mistrust and threat perceptions that lock in place increasingly asymmetric military forces. Russia's current concerns focus less on the military items covered by existing treaties and more on the development of new conventional technologies such as hypersonic cruise and glide vehicles that are not restrained by either conventional or nuclear arms control agreements.[17] Whether these capabilities can ever be

---

[16] Periotto, C. (Brig. Gen.), Personal Representative of the OSCE Chairperson-in-Office, 'Implementation of the Agreement on Sub-Regional Arms Control (Article IV, Annex 1-B, Dayton Peace Accords)', Report to the OSCE Permanent Council, CIO.GAL/158/11, 23 Aug. 2011, p. 1.

[17] See e.g. 'Pentagon successfully tests hypersonic flying bomb', Agence France-Presse, 17 Nov. 2011; and Woolf, A. F., *Conventional Prompt Global Strike and Long-Range Ballistic Missiles:*

covered by purely European approaches is an open question. The unresolved issue of missile defence cooperation represents an additional burden, as does the associated recurring Russian announcements that it could deploy short-range Iskander missiles in the Kaliningrad region.[18]

The unresolved territorial conflicts in the OSCE area, particularly in Georgia, play a key role in blocking progress in security cooperation, including arms control. Both the Astana Framework for Action and the negotiations 'at 36' failed because of disagreement regarding Georgia. Moreover, the territorial conflicts in Georgia and Moldova and between Armenia and Azerbaijan would have an important bearing on European conventional arms control even if new agreements could be reached because they will play a decisive role in the ratification processes of the countries involved and in the US Congress. Therefore, the question is whether status-neutral solutions are still possible or whether politically binding agreements offer a better option.

Background and Issues, Congressional Research Service (CRS) Report for Congress R41464 (US Congress, CRS: Washington, DC, 13 Feb. 2012).

[18] Office of the President of Russia, 'Statement in connection with the situation concerning the NATO countries' missile defence system in Europe', 23 Nov. 2011, <http://eng.kremlin.ru/news/3115>. See also chapter 8, section I, in this volume.

V. Confidence- and security-building measures

HANS-JOACHIM SCHMIDT AND WOLFGANG ZELLNER

In most parts of the world there have, at some point in time, been efforts to elaborate confidence- and security-building measures (CSBMs), not as an aim in themselves, but as part of a broader discussion of a security regime in which the behaviour of states is rendered understandable and predictable. The exact nature of the CSBMs should be tailored to each region's specific conditions.

In Europe, the Vienna Document on CSBMs is the most important element of the CSBM regime, complemented by the 1992 Treaty on Open Skies. In South America, the Union of South American Nations (Unión de Naciones Suramericanas, UNASUR) has become a focal point for the elaboration of CSBMs. Brazil has set an example during the process of elaborating tailor-made CSBMs for South America by providing UNASUR partners with a voluntary report on military activities based on the content of the Vienna Document.

Confidence building in South America[1]

The elaboration of CSBMs by UNASUR culminated in the adoption of a resolution at a meeting of the ministers of foreign affairs and defence on 27 November 2009 creating a 'mechanism to build confidence and security'.[2] This was a tangible outcome of the decision made by UNASUR heads of state in August 2009 at Bariloche, Argentina, to strengthen South America as a zone of peace.[3]

The UNASUR ministers outlined five categories of CSBM: (a) the exchange of information and transparency; (b) advance notification of any defence exercises or manoeuvres along the border of another state; (c) a promise to take action to prevent the presence or operations of illegal armed groups on national territory; (d) a promise never to use force against another UNASUR member state; and (e) provisions for visits and increased military-to-military contact, in particular in border regions, with a mechanism for raising any disputed issues to the level of head of state.[4]

---

[1] This subsection was written by Ian Anthony.

[2] UNASUR, Extraordinary meeting of the ministers of foreign affairs and defence, Resolution, 27 Nov. 2009. For a brief description and list of members of UNASUR see annex B in this volume.

[3] UNASUR, Joint Statement of the Special Meeting of the Council of Heads of State of the Union of South American Nations, San Carlos de Bariloche, 28 Aug. 2009, <http://www.comunidadandina.org/unasur/28-8-09bariloche.htm> (in Spanish).

[4] UNASUR (note 2). See also US Embassy in Quito, 'UNASUR establishes confidence building mechanism', Cable to US Department of State, no. 09QUITO1009, 1 Dec. 2009, <http://wikileaks.org/cable/2009/12/09QUITO1009.html>. On the exchange of information and transparency in Latin

At a meeting of the South American Defence Council (Consejo de Defensa Suramericano, CDS) on 11 November 2011, the UNASUR defence ministers finalized the methodology for one element of the CSBM on exchange of information and transparency: military spending.[5] The development of regional CSBMs has also been facilitated by the creation of a UNASUR Centre for Strategic Defence Studies (Centro de Estudios Estratégicos de la Defensa, CEED), which was inaugurated in May 2011.[6] The CEED is staffed by military personnel from all UNASUR countries and is located in Buenos Aires, Argentina.

Revision of the Vienna Document

At the Ministerial Council meeting in Vilnius, Lithuania, on 6–7 December 2011, the OSCE participating states welcomed a revised version of the Vienna Document—the Vienna Document 2011 on Confidence- and Security-building Measures (VD2011)—which had been adopted by the Forum for Security Co-operation (FSC), the OSCE's negotiation and decision-making body for arms control, a week earlier.[7] The revision had been mandated in 2009 when the Ministerial Council called on the FSC to address 'the role of arms control and CSBMs in the evolving security environment'.[8] By the end of 2010 the FSC had agreed on its approach to updating the previous version, the Vienna Document 1999 of the Negotiations on Confidence- and Security-Building Measures (VD99), and the Astana Commemorative Declaration anticipated the update.[9]

America see Bromley, M. and Solmirano, C., *Transparency in Military Spending and Arms Acquisitions in Latin America and the Caribbean*, SIPRI Policy Paper no 31 (SIPRI: Stockholm, Jan. 2012).

[5] South American Defence Council, Declaration of Lima, 10–11 Nov. 2011, <http://www.unasurcds.org/index.php?option=com_content&id=484> (in Spanish); and Camacho, C., 'South American defense ministers discuss regional security issues in Lima', NTN24 News, 11 Nov. 2011, <http://www.ntn24.com/news/news/south-american-defense-ministers-discuss-regional-security-issues-lima>.

[6] South American Defence Council, Statute of the Center for Strategic Defense Studies of the South American Defense Council, May 2010, <http://www.unasurcds.org/index.php?option=com_content&id=434>; and Santos, L., 'UNASUR founds a Center of Strategic Studies of Defense', Just the Facts, 6 June 2011, <http://justf.org/blog/2011/06/06/unasur-founds-center-strategic-studies-defense>.

[7] Vienna Document 2011 on Confidence- and Security-building Measures, adopted by OSCE, Forum for Security Co-operation, Decision no. 14/11, FSC.DEC/14/11, 30 Nov. 2011, entered into force 1 Dec. 2011, <http://www.osce.org/fsc/86597>. See also OSCE, Ministerial Council, Vilnius 2011, 'Issues relevant to the Forum for Security Co-operation', Decision no. 7/11, MC.DEC/7/11/Corr.1, 7 Dec. 2011.

[8] OSCE, Ministerial Council, Athens 2009, 'Issues relevant to the Forum for Security Co-operation', Decision no. 16/09, MC.DEC/16/09, 2 Dec. 2009. For developments related to the Vienna Document up to 2010 see Lachowski, Z., 'Conventional arms control and military confidence building', *SIPRI Yearbook 2011*, pp. 416–19. For a brief description of the VD2011 and its predecessors see annex A in this volume.

[9] OSCE, Summit Meeting, Astana 2010, 'Astana Commemorative Declaration: towards a security community', SUM.DOC/1/10/Corr.1*, 3 Dec. 2010, <http://www.osce.org/cio/74985>.

Despite this preparation, negotiations did not produce substantial changes. Almost all of the nine decisions that prepared the way for VD2011 were of a purely technical and procedural nature, as assessed by an inter-pretative statement by Germany and supported by 38 other (Western) states, and five of them had already been taken in 2010.[10] The only new decision with any substantive impact concerned a clarification of how briefings for inspectors should be structured and that new measures adopted by all participants should enter into force immediately.[11]

Many substantive proposals that were tabled during the negotiations could not be agreed. Member states of the North Atlantic Treaty Organiza-tion (NATO), supported by some others, concentrated their proposals on lowering the thresholds for prior notification of certain military activities while raising the quota of inspections and evaluation visits. In July 2011 a group of 33 states—the 28 NATO member states joined by Cyprus, Bosnia and Herzegovina, Malta, Sweden and Switzerland—proposed lowering the thresholds for prior notification of military activities to 5000 troops (from 9000 in VD99), 100 battle tanks (from 250 in VD99), 200 armoured combat vehicles (from 500 in VD99) and 80 artillery pieces (from 250 in VD99).[12] This proposal would have led to more notifications as most current military activities are below the VD99 thresholds. The USA proposed raising the number of inspections and evaluations per state and calendar year.[13]

Russia rejected these proposals partly because it is not in favour of add-itional military transparency during the ongoing process of restructuring its armed forces. However, Western and Russian representatives in Vienna agreed that the added military value of the data exchanged under the VD99 is rather limited, and the main impact of the failure to adopt new proposals is political.[14] Western proposals, in particular raising the number of inspec-tions and evaluation visits, were seen by Russia as an attempt to use the Vienna Document to circumvent Russia's suspension of participation in the

---

[10] OSCE, MC.DEC/7/11 (note 7), Attachment, 'Interpretative statement under paragraph IV.1(A)6 of the Rules of Procedure of the Organization for Security and Co-operation'. The list of 9 decisions is contained in OSCE, FSC.DEC/14/11 (note 7), annex.

[11] OSCE, Forum for Security Co-operation, 'Vienna Document Plus: amendments and additions to Chapter IX "Compliance and verification" paragraphs 98 and 127', Decision no. 7/11, FSC.DEC/7/11, 27 July 2011.

[12] OSCE, Forum for Security Co-operation, Delegations of Albania, Germany, the USA, Belgium, Bosnia and Herzegovina, Bulgaria, Cyprus, Croatia, Denmark, Spain, Estonia, Finland, France, the United Kingdom, Greece, Hungary, Ireland, Iceland, Italy, Latvia, Lithuania, Luxembourg, Malta, Montenegro, Norway, Poland, Portugal, Romania, Slovakia, Slovenia, Sweden, Switzerland and the Czech Republic, 'Lowering thresholds for prior notification of certain military activities—Vienna Document 1999', FSC.DEL/107/10/Rev.3/corr.2*, 11 July 2011.

[13] OSCE, Forum for Security Co-operation, US Mission to the OSCE, 'Proposal for a draft decision on inspection quotas', FSC.DEL/92/10, 21 Sep. 2010; and OSCE, Forum for Security Co-operation, US Mission to the OSCE, 'Proposal for a draft decision on quotas for evaluation visits', FSC.DEL/91/10, 21 Sep. 2010.

[14] This paragraph is based on author interviews with members of several OSCE delegations, Vienna, Sep. 2011.

CFE Treaty—not without reason as the effort to upgrade the document was seen by some Western delegations as 'Plan B' should CFE negotiations fail to ensure at least some kind of transparency in the Russian armed forces (see section IV above). Thus, lack of progress in the talks 'at 36' has also blocked progress on the Vienna Document.

Russia also tabled substantive proposals that could not be agreed. A long-standing Russian request to exchange information on naval forces was retabled in October 2010.[15] This proposal has always been rejected by the USA. Two other long-standing Russian proposals—notification of large-scale transits and of the activities of multinational rapid-reaction forces—also failed.[16] The lack of political will to compromise is illustrated by the failure of a joint proposal by Russia, some NATO members and some other states to notify one military exercise per year that is below the current threshold if there is no exercise above the threshold.[17] This proposal failed even though it is already practiced by a number of states on a voluntary basis.

The Vienna Document 2011 represents at best minimal progress over the 1999 document; the objective of adapting to changed military realities has certainly not been achieved. Moreover, the process and its outcome do not provide strategic direction to the FSC, and so it is unclear what its next steps will be. If this trend is not reversed, the Vienna Document regime will continue to lose military and political relevance—a process that is already well under way. Large-scale military manoeuvres have become too costly to conduct and technology has provided other means to evaluate the quality of military training. Even if the remedy proposed by the Western states—lowering the thresholds for the kinds of activities that should be notified—could be agreed, the information gained by inspections would be of less military relevance than one or two decades ago.

---

[15] OSCE, Forum for Security Co-operation, Russian Delegation, 'Proposal for a draft FSC Vienna Document Plus decision on the exchange of information on naval forces', FSC.DEL/134/10, 21 Oct. 2010.

[16] OSCE, Forum for Security Co-operation, Russian Delegation, 'Proposal for a draft FSC Vienna Document Plus decision on notification of military activities of multinational rapid reaction forces', FSC.DEL/98/10/Rev.1, 21 Oct. 2010; and OSCE, Forum for Security Co-operation, Russian Delegation, 'Proposal for a draft FSC Vienna Document Plus decision on prior notification of large-scale military transit', FSC.DEL/133/10/Corr.1, 16 Nov. 2010.

[17] OSCE, Forum for Security Co-operation, Delegations of Russia, the United Kingdom, Greece, Hungary, Austria, Belgium, Kazakhstan, Ireland, Germany, Sweden and Cyprus, 'Proposal for a draft FSC Vienna Document Plus decision on prior notification of major military activities', FSC.DEL/97/10/Corr.4, 21 July 2011.

Blockade of the Open Skies Consultative Commission

In implementing the Open Skies Treaty, only one observation flight was denied in 2011.[18] In the first half of the year Romania proposed an observation flight in Russia close to the border with Georgia—presumably to test again how Russia would interpret the treaty with regard to the territorial conflicts in Georgia.[19] The treaty obliges observation flights to maintain a distance of 10 kilometres from the border of non-state parties. Georgia is party to the Open Skies Treaty, and the mission and flight plan proposed by Romania passed a short distance from the Georgian border. Russian opposition was based on recognition of Abkhazia as an independent state, requiring the 10-km distance to be observed. Romania was unwilling to adapt the flight plan according to the Russian interpretation and the mission was cancelled. While the unresolved territorial conflict limited the observation rights of the parties in this case, other missions over Russia were conducted in accordance with the treaty rules. On 14–18 March 2011 Russia and the USA conducted their first joint observation flight (over Sweden) and Russian observer flights flew over the USA on 26 September–1 October, which underlines the support for the treaty in both states.[20]

The dispute between Greece and Turkey over the unresolved conflict on Cyprus has blocked the membership of Cyprus in the Open Skies Treaty since 2002. Greece has raised the topic at every meeting of the Open Skies Consultative Commission (OSCC) and Turkey has always opposed it. After this issue was mentioned in the Final Document of the Second Review Conference, in 2010, Turkey decided to suspend participation in formal meetings of the OSCC if Greece continued to raise this issue.[21] Because the OSCC can only work by consensus, it was forced to stop its formal activities in February 2011.[22] Informal and extraordinary meetings are still possible and a German proposal for a new informal working group on sharing assets to discuss cooperation and coordination of observation aircraft was accepted in April.[23] Each year, the OSCC must decide the observation flight

---

[18] For a summary and other details of the Treaty on Open Skies see annex A in this volume.

[19] On a similar incident in 2010 see Lachowski (note 8), p. 422.

[20] US Department of State , 'First U.S.–Russian joint Open Skies observation flight', Media note, 14 Mar. 2011, <http://www.state.gov/r/pa/prs/ps/2011/03/158252.htm>; and 'Russian inspectors to make observation flight over US territory', ITAR-TASS, 26 Sep. 2011, <http://www.itar-tass.com/en/c154/233547.html>.

[21] Second Review Conference on the Implementation of the Treaty on Open Skies, Final Document, OSCC.RC/39/10, 9 June 2010.

[22] See e.g. Gottemoeller, R., US Assistant Secretary of State for Verification, Compliance and Implementation, 'Statement at the Annual Security Review Conference', Vienna, 1 July 2011, <http://www.state.gov/t/avc/rls/167477.htm>.

[23] German Bundestag, 'Deutschlands Rolle im KSE-Prozess' [Germany's role in the CFE process], Response of the federal government to the question by MPs Inge Hoeger, Wolfgang Gehrcke, Sevim

quotas for the next year; in an extraordinary meeting on 21 October 2011 at which Greece agreed not to raise the Cyprus issue, all countries were able to agree on the quotas for 2012. This special procedure assured continued implementation of the regime in 2012. However, it is uncertain how issues will be decided beyond that.

Important technical decisions will soon be required on the certification of new inspection aircraft and digital equipment that was authorized in principle at the 2010 review conference. The regime also faces the challenge of a shortage of observation aircraft, which needs further discussions, coordination and cooperation among the states parties. Events in 2011 raised the risk that, like the CFE regime, the Open Skies regime could also become a hostage to unresolved territorial disputes, this time between Greece and Turkey over Cyprus.

Dagdelen, other MPs and the parliamentary group of Die Linke, Bundestagsdrucksache 17/8034, 30 Nov. 2011, p. 2.

Annexes

Annex A. Arms control and disarmament agreements

Annex B. International security cooperation bodies

Annex C. Chronology 2011

Annex A. Arms control and disarmament agreements

NENNE BODELL

This annex lists multi- and bilateral treaties, conventions, protocols and agreements relating to arms control and disarmament. Unless otherwise stated, the status of agreements and of their parties and signatories is as of 1 January 2012.

Notes

1. The agreements are divided into universal treaties (i.e. multilateral treaties open to all states; section I), regional treaties (i.e. multilateral treaties open to states of a particular region; section II) and bilateral treaties (section III). Within each section, the agreements are listed in the order of the date on which they were adopted, signed or opened for signature (multilateral agreements) or signed (bilateral agreements). The date on which they entered into force and the depositary for multilateral treaties are also given.

2. The main source of information is the lists of signatories and parties provided by the depositaries of the treaties. In lists of parties and signatories, states whose name appears in italics ratified, acceded or succeeded to, or signed the agreement during 2011.

3. For some major treaties, the substantive parts of the most important reservations, declarations or interpretive statements made in connection with a state's signature, ratification, accession or succession are given in notes below the entry.

4. States and organizations listed as parties have ratified, acceded to or succeeded to the agreements. Former non-self-governing territories, upon attaining statehood, sometimes make general statements of continuity to all agreements concluded by the former governing power. This annex lists as parties only those new states that have made an uncontested declaration on continuity or have notified the depositary of their succession. The Russian Federation continues the international obligations of the Soviet Union. Serbia continues the international obligations of the State Union of Serbia and Montenegro.

5. Unless stated otherwise, the multilateral agreements listed in this annex are open to all states or to all states in the respective zone (or region) for signature, ratification, accession or succession. Not all the signatories and parties are United Nations members. Taiwan, while not recognized as a sovereign state by many countries, is listed as a party to the agreements that it has ratified.

6. Where possible, the location (in a printed publication or online) of an accurate copy of the treaty text is given. This may be provided by a treaty depositary, an agency or secretariat connected with the treaty, or in the *United Nations Treaty Series* (available online at <http://treaties.un.org/>).

I. Universal treaties

Protocol for the Prohibition of the Use in War of Asphyxiating, Poisonous or Other Gases, and of Bacteriological Methods of Warfare (1925 Geneva Protocol)

Signed at Geneva on 17 June 1925; entered into force on 8 February 1928; depositary French Government

The protocol declares that the parties agree to be bound by the prohibition on the use of these weapons in war.

Parties (138): Afghanistan, Albania, Algeria, Angola, Antigua and Barbuda, Argentina, Australia, Austria, Bahrain, Bangladesh, Barbados, Belgium, Benin, Bhutan, Bolivia, Brazil, Bulgaria, Burkina Faso, Cambodia, Cameroon, Canada, Cape Verde, Central African Republic, Chile, China, Costa Rica, Côte d'Ivoire, Croatia, Cuba, Cyprus, Czech Republic, Denmark, Dominican Republic, Ecuador, Egypt, El Salvador, Equatorial Guinea, Estonia, Ethiopia, Fiji, Finland, France, Gambia, Germany, Ghana, Greece, Grenada, Guatemala, Guinea-Bissau, Holy See, Hungary, Iceland, India, Indonesia, Iran, Iraq, Ireland, Israel, Italy, Jamaica, Japan, Jordan, Kenya, Korea (North), Korea (South), Kuwait, Laos, Latvia, Lebanon, Lesotho, Liberia, Libya, Liechtenstein, Lithuania, Luxembourg, Madagascar, Malawi, Malaysia, Maldives, Malta, Mauritius, Mexico, Monaco, Mongolia, Morocco, Nepal, Netherlands, New Zealand, Nicaragua, Niger, Nigeria, Norway, Pakistan, Panama, Papua New Guinea, Paraguay, Peru, Philippines, Poland, Portugal, Qatar, Romania, Russia, Rwanda, Saint Kitts and Nevis, Saint Lucia, Saint Vincent and the Grenadines, Saudi Arabia, Senegal, Serbia, Sierra Leone, Slovakia, Slovenia, Solomon Islands, South Africa, Spain, Sri Lanka, Sudan, Swaziland, Sweden, Switzerland, Syria, Taiwan, Tanzania, Thailand, Togo, Tonga, Trinidad and Tobago, Tunisia, Turkey, Uganda, UK, Ukraine, Uruguay, USA, Venezuela, Viet Nam, Yemen

Note: On joining the protocol, some states entered reservations which upheld their right to employ chemical or biological weapons against non-parties to the protocol, against coalitions which included non-parties or in response to the use of these weapons by a violating party. Many of these states have withdrawn these reservations, particularly after the conclusion of the 1972 Biological and Toxin Weapons Convention and the 1993 Chemical Weapons Convention since the reservations are incompatible with their obligation under the conventions.

In addition to these, 'explicit', reservations, a number of states that made a declaration of succession to the protocol on gaining independence inherited 'implicit' reservations from their respective predecessor states. For example, these implicit reservations apply to the states that gained independence from France and the UK before the latter states withdrew or amended their reservations. States that acceded (rather than succeeded) to the protocol did not inherit reservations in this way.

Protocol text: International Committee of the Red Cross, International Humanitarian Law, <http://www.icrc.org/ihl.nsf/FULL/280?OpenDocument>

Convention on the Prevention and Punishment of the Crime of Genocide (Genocide Convention)

Adopted at Paris by the UN General Assembly on 9 December 1948; entered into force on 12 January 1951; depositary UN Secretary-General

Under the convention any commission of acts intended to destroy, in whole or in part, a national, ethnic, racial or religious group as such is declared to be a crime punishable under international law.

Parties (142): Afghanistan, Albania*, Algeria*, Andorra, Antigua and Barbuda, Argentina*, Armenia, Australia, Austria, Azerbaijan, Bahamas, Bahrain*, Bangladesh*, Barbados, Belarus*, Belgium, Belize, Bolivia, Bosnia and Herzegovina, Brazil, Bulgaria*, Burkina Faso, Burundi, Cambodia, Canada, *Cape Verde*, Chile, China*, Colombia, Comoros, Congo (Democratic Republic of the), Costa Rica, Côte d'Ivoire, Croatia, Cuba, Cyprus, Czech Republic, Denmark, Ecuador, Egypt, El Salvador, Estonia, Ethiopia, Fiji, Finland, France, Gabon, Gambia, Georgia, Germany, Ghana, Greece, Guatemala, Guinea, Haiti, Honduras, Hungary*, Iceland, India*, Iran, Iraq, Ireland, Israel, Italy, Jamaica, Jordan, Kazakhstan, Korea (North), Korea (South), Kuwait, Kyrgyzstan, Laos, Latvia, Lebanon, Lesotho, Liberia, Libya, Liechtenstein, Lithuania, Luxembourg, Macedonia (Former Yugoslav Republic of), Malaysia*, Maldives, Mali, Mexico, Moldova, Monaco, Mongolia*, Montenegro*, Morocco*, Mozambique, Myanmar*, Namibia, Nepal, Netherlands, New Zealand, Nicaragua, Nigeria, Norway, Pakistan, Panama, Papua New Guinea, Paraguay, Peru, Philippines*, Poland*, Portugal*, Romania*, Russia*, Rwanda*, Saint Vincent and the Grenadines, Saudi Arabia, Senegal, Serbia*, Seychelles, Singapore*, Slovakia, Slovenia, South Africa, Spain*, Sri Lanka, Sudan, Sweden, Switzerland, Syria, Tanzania, Togo, Tonga, Trinidad and Tobago, Tunisia, Turkey, Uganda, UK, Ukraine*, United Arab Emirates, Uruguay, USA*, Uzbekistan, Venezuela*, Viet Nam*, Yemen*, Zimbabwe

* With reservation and/or declaration.

Signed but not ratified (1): Dominican Republic

Convention text: United Nations Treaty Collection, <http://treaties.un.org/Pages/CTCTreaties. aspx?id=4>

Geneva Convention (IV) Relative to the Protection of Civilian Persons in Time of War

Signed at Geneva on 12 August 1949; entered into force on 21 October 1950; depositary Swiss Federal Council

The Geneva Convention (IV) establishes rules for the protection of civilians in areas covered by war and in occupied territories. This convention was formulated at the diplomatic conference held from 21 April to 12 August 1949. Other conventions adopted at the same time were: Convention (I) for the Amelioration of the Condition of the Wounded and Sick in Armed Forces in the Field; Convention (II) for the Amelioration of the Condition of the Wounded, Sick and Shipwrecked Members of Armed Forces at Sea; and Convention (III) Relative to the Treatment of Prisoners of War.

Parties (194): Afghanistan, Albania*, Algeria, Andorra, Angola*, Antigua and Barbuda, Argentina, Armenia, Australia*, Austria, Azerbaijan, Bahamas, Bahrain, Bangladesh*, Barbados*, Belarus, Belgium, Belize, Benin, Bhutan, Bolivia, Bosnia and Herzegovina, Botswana, Brazil, Brunei Darussalam, Bulgaria, Burkina Faso, Burundi, Cambodia, Cameroon, Canada, Cape Verde, Central African Republic, Chad, Chile, China*, Colombia, Comoros, Congo (Democratic Republic of the), Congo (Republic of the), Cook Islands, Costa Rica, Côte d'Ivoire, Croatia, Cuba, Cyprus, Czech Republic*, Denmark, Djibouti, Dominica, Dominican Republic, Ecuador, Egypt, El Salvador, Equatorial Guinea, Estonia, Eritrea, Ethiopia, Fiji, Finland, France, Gabon, Gambia, Georgia, Germany*, Ghana, Greece, Grenada, Guatemala, Guinea, Guinea-Bissau*, Guyana, Haiti, Holy See, Honduras, Hungary, Iceland, India, Indonesia, Iran*, Iraq, Ireland, Israel*, Italy, Jamaica, Japan, Jordan, Kazakhstan, Kenya, Kiribati, Korea (North)*, Korea (South)*, Kuwait*, Kyrgyzstan, Laos, Latvia, Lebanon, Lesotho, Liberia, Libya, Liechtenstein, Lithuania, Luxembourg, Macedonia (Former Yugoslav Republic of)*, Madagascar, Malawi, Malaysia, Maldives, Mali, Malta, Marshall Islands,

Mauritania, Mauritius, Mexico, Micronesia, Moldova, Monaco, Mongolia, Montenegro, Morocco, Mozambique, Myanmar, Namibia, Nauru, Nepal, Netherlands, New Zealand*, Nicaragua, Niger, Nigeria, Norway, Oman, Pakistan*, Palau, Panama, Papua New Guinea, Paraguay, Peru, Philippines, Poland, Portugal*, Qatar, Romania, Russia*, Rwanda, Saint Kitts and Nevis, Saint Lucia, Saint Vincent and the Grenadines, Samoa, San Marino, Sao Tome and Principe, Saudi Arabia, Senegal, Serbia, Seychelles, Sierra Leone, Singapore, Slovakia, Slovenia, Solomon Islands, Somalia, South Africa, Spain, Sri Lanka, Sudan, Suriname*, Swaziland, Sweden, Switzerland, Syria, Tajikistan, Tanzania, Thailand, Timor-Leste, Togo, Tonga, Trinidad and Tobago, Tunisia, Turkey, Turkmenistan, Tuvalu, Uganda, UK*, Ukraine*, United Arab Emirates, Uruguay*, USA*, Uzbekistan, Vanuatu, Venezuela, Viet Nam*, Yemen*, Zambia, Zimbabwe

* With reservation and/or declaration.

Note: In 1989 the Palestine Liberation Organization (PLO) informed the depositary that it had decided to adhere to the four Geneva conventions and the protocols of 1977.

Convention text: Swiss Federal Department of Foreign Affairs, <http://www.eda.admin.ch/eda/fr/home/topics/intla/intrea/chdep/warvic/gvaciv.html>

Protocol I Additional to the 1949 Geneva Conventions, and Relating to the Protection of Victims of International Armed Conflicts

Protocol II Additional to the 1949 Geneva Conventions, and Relating to the Protection of Victims of Non-International Armed Conflicts

Opened for signature at Bern on 12 December 1977; entered into force on 7 December 1978; depositary Swiss Federal Council

The protocols confirm that the right of parties that are engaged in international or non-international armed conflicts to choose methods or means of warfare is not unlimited and that the use of weapons or means of warfare that cause superfluous injury or unnecessary suffering is prohibited.

Parties to Protocol I (171) and Protocol II (166): Afghanistan, Albania, Algeria*, Angola[1]*, Antigua and Barbuda, Argentina*, Armenia, Australia*, Austria*, Bahamas, Bahrain, Bangladesh, Barbados, Belarus*, Belgium*, Belize, Benin, Bolivia*, Bosnia and Herzegovina*, Botswana, Brazil*, Brunei Darussalam, Bulgaria*, Burkina Faso*, Burundi, Cambodia, Cameroon, Canada*, Cape Verde*, Central African Republic, Chad, Chile*, China*, Colombia*, Comoros, Congo (Democratic Republic of the)*, Congo (Republic of the), Cook Islands*, Costa Rica*, Côte d'Ivoire, Croatia, Cuba, Cyprus*, Czech Republic*, Denmark*, Djibouti, Dominica, Dominican Republic, Ecuador, Egypt*, El Salvador*, Equatorial Guinea, Estonia, Ethiopia, Fiji, Finland*, France*, Gabon, Gambia, Georgia, Germany*, Ghana, Greece*, Grenada, Guatemala, Guinea*, Guinea-Bissau, Guyana, Haiti, Holy See, Honduras, Hungary*, Iceland*, Iraq[1], Ireland*, Italy*, Jamaica, Japan*, Jordan, Kazakhstan, Kenya, Korea (North)[1], Korea (South)*, Kuwait, Kyrgyzstan, Laos*, Latvia, Lebanon, Lesotho, Liberia, Libya, Liechtenstein*, Lithuania*, Luxembourg*, Macedonia (Former Yugoslav Republic of)*, Madagascar*, Malawi, Maldives, Mali*, Malta*, Mauritania, Mauritius*, Mexico[1], Micronesia, Moldova, Monaco, Mongolia*, Montenegro, *Morocco*, Mozambique, Namibia*, Nauru, Netherlands*, New Zealand*, Nicaragua, Niger, Nigeria, Norway*, Oman, Palau, Panama*, Paraguay*, Peru, Philippines[2], Poland*,

Portugal*, Qatar*, Romania*, Russia*, Rwanda*, Saint Kitts and Nevis, Saint Lucia, Saint Vincent and the Grenadines, Samoa, San Marino, Sao Tome and Principe, Saudi Arabia*, Senegal, Serbia*, Seychelles*, Sierra Leone, Slovakia*, Slovenia*, Solomon Islands, South Africa, Spain*, Sudan, Suriname, Swaziland, Sweden*, Switzerland*, Syria*[1], Tajikistan*, Tanzania, Timor-Leste, Togo*, Tonga*, Trinidad and Tobago*, Tunisia, Turkmenistan, Uganda, UK*, Ukraine*, United Arab Emirates*, Uruguay*, Uzbekistan, Vanuatu, Venezuela, Viet Nam[1], Yemen, Zambia, Zimbabwe

* With reservation and/or declaration.
[1] Party only to Protocol I.
[2] Party only to Protocol II.

Protocol texts: Swiss Federal Department of Foreign Affairs, <http://www.eda.admin. ch/eda/fr/home/topics/intla/intrea/chdep/warvic.html>

Antarctic Treaty

Signed at Washington, DC, on 1 December 1959; entered into force on 23 June 1961; depositary US Government

The treaty declares the Antarctic an area to be used exclusively for peaceful purposes. It prohibits any measure of a military nature in the Antarctic, such as the establishment of military bases and fortifications, and the carrying out of military manoeuvres or the testing of any type of weapon. The treaty bans any nuclear explosion as well as the disposal of radioactive waste material in Antarctica. The treaty provides a right of on-site inspection of all stations and installations in Antarctica to ensure compliance with its provisions.

In accordance with Article IX, consultative meetings are convened at regular intervals to exchange information and hold consultations on matters pertaining to Antarctica, as well as to recommend to the governments measures in furtherance of the principles and objectives of the treaty.

The treaty is open for accession by UN members or by other states invited to accede with the consent of all the parties entitled to participate in the consultative meetings provided for in Article IX. States demonstrating their interest in Antarctica by conducting substantial scientific research activity there, such as the establishment of a scientific station or the despatch of a scientific expedition, are entitled to become consultative members.

Parties (49): Argentina*, Australia*, Austria, Belarus, Belgium*, Brazil*, Bulgaria*, Canada, Chile*, China*, Colombia, Cuba, Czech Republic, Denmark, Ecuador*, Estonia, Finland*, France*, Germany*, Greece, Guatemala, Hungary, India*, Italy*, Japan*, Korea (North), Korea (South)*, Malaysia, Monaco, Netherlands*, New Zealand*, Norway*, Papua New Guinea, Peru*, Poland*, Portugal, Romania, Russia*, Slovakia, South Africa*, Spain*, Sweden*, Switzerland, Turkey, UK*, Ukraine*, Uruguay*, USA*, Venezuela

* This state is a consultative member under Article IX of the treaty.

Treaty text: Secretariat of the Antarctic Treaty, <http://www.ats.aq/e/ats.htm>

The Protocol on Environmental Protection (**1991 Madrid Protocol**) entered into force on 14 January 1998.

Protocol text: Secretariat of the Antarctic Treaty, <http://www.ats.aq/e/ep.htm>

Treaty Banning Nuclear Weapon Tests in the Atmosphere, in Outer Space and Under Water (Partial Test-Ban Treaty, PTBT)

Signed at Moscow by three original parties on 5 August 1963 and opened for signature by other states at London, Moscow and Washington, DC, on 8 August 1963; entered into force on 10 October 1963; depositaries British, Russian and US governments

The treaty prohibits the carrying out of any nuclear weapon test explosion or any other nuclear explosion: (*a*) in the atmosphere, beyond its limits, including outer space, or under water, including territorial waters or high seas; and (*b*) in any other environment if such explosion causes radioactive debris to be present outside the territorial limits of the state under whose jurisdiction or control the explosion is conducted.

Parties (126): Afghanistan, Antigua and Barbuda, Argentina, Armenia, Australia, Austria, Bahamas, Bangladesh, Belarus, Belgium, Benin, Bhutan, Bolivia, Bosnia and Herzegovina, Botswana, Brazil, Bulgaria, Canada, Cape Verde, Central African Republic, Chad, Chile, Colombia, Congo (Democratic Republic of the), Costa Rica, Côte d'Ivoire, Croatia, Cyprus, Czech Republic, Denmark, Dominican Republic, Ecuador, Egypt, El Salvador, Equatorial Guinea, Fiji, Finland, Gabon, Gambia, Germany, Ghana, Greece, Guatemala, Guinea-Bissau, Honduras, Hungary, Iceland, India, Indonesia, Iran, Iraq, Ireland, Israel, Italy, Jamaica, Japan, Jordan, Kenya, Korea (South), Kuwait, Laos, Lebanon, Liberia, Libya, Luxembourg, Madagascar, Malawi, Malaysia, Malta, Mauritania, Mauritius, Mexico, Mongolia, Montenegro, Morocco, Myanmar, Nepal, Netherlands, New Zealand, Nicaragua, Niger, Nigeria, Norway, Pakistan, Panama, Papua New Guinea, Peru, Philippines, Poland, Romania, Russia, Rwanda, Samoa, San Marino, Senegal, Serbia, Seychelles, Sierra Leone, Singapore, Slovakia, Slovenia, South Africa, Spain, Sri Lanka, Sudan, Suriname, Swaziland, Sweden, Switzerland, Syria, Taiwan, Tanzania, Thailand, Togo, Tonga, Trinidad and Tobago, Tunisia, Turkey, Uganda, UK, Ukraine, Uruguay, USA, Venezuela, Yemen, Zambia

Signed but not ratified (11): Algeria, Burkina Faso, Burundi, Cameroon, Ethiopia, Haiti, Mali, Paraguay, Portugal, Somalia, Viet Nam

Treaty text: United Nations Treaty Series, vol. 480 (1963)

Treaty on Principles Governing the Activities of States in the Exploration and Use of Outer Space, Including the Moon and Other Celestial Bodies (Outer Space Treaty)

Opened for signature at London, Moscow and Washington, DC, on 27 January 1967; entered into force on 10 October 1967; depositaries British, Russian and US governments

The treaty prohibits the placing into orbit around the earth of any object carrying nuclear weapons or any other kind of weapons of mass destruction, the installation of such weapons on celestial bodies, or the stationing of them in outer space in any other manner. The establishment of military bases, installations and fortifications, the testing of any type of weapons and the conducting of military manoeuvres on celestial bodies are also forbidden.

Parties (108): Afghanistan, Algeria, Antigua and Barbuda, Argentina, Australia, Austria, Bahamas, Bangladesh, Barbados, Belarus, Belgium, Benin, Brazil, Brunei Darussalam, Bulgaria,

Burkina Faso, Canada, Chile, China, Cuba, Cyprus, Czech Republic, Denmark, Dominica, Dominican Republic, Ecuador, Egypt, El Salvador, Equatorial Guinea, Fiji, Finland, France, Germany, Greece, Grenada, Guinea-Bissau, Hungary, Iceland, India, Indonesia, Iraq, Ireland, Israel, Italy, Jamaica, Japan, Kazakhstan, Kenya, Korea (South), Kuwait, Laos, Lebanon, Libya, Luxembourg, Madagascar, Mali, Mauritius, Mexico, Mongolia, Montenegro, Morocco, Myanmar, Nepal, Netherlands, New Zealand, Niger, Nigeria, Norway, Pakistan, Papua New Guinea, Peru, Poland, Portugal, Romania, Russia, Saint Kitts and Nevis, Saint Lucia, Saint Vincent and the Grenadines, San Marino, Saudi Arabia, Seychelles, Sierra Leone, Singapore, Slovakia, Solomon Islands, South Africa, Spain, Sri Lanka, Swaziland, Sweden, Switzerland, Syria, Taiwan, Thailand, Togo, Tonga, Tunisia, Turkey, Uganda, UK, Ukraine, United Arab Emirates, Uruguay, USA, Venezuela, Viet Nam, Yemen, Zambia

Signed but not ratified (27): Bolivia, Botswana, Burundi, Cameroon, Central African Republic, Colombia, Congo (Democratic Republic of the), Congo (Republic of the), Ethiopia, Gambia, Ghana, Guyana, Haiti, Holy See, Honduras, Iran, Jordan, Lesotho, Macedonia (Former Yugoslav Republic of), Malaysia, Nicaragua, Panama, Philippines, Rwanda, Serbia, Somalia, Trinidad and Tobago

Treaty text: United Nations Treaty Series, vol. 610 (1967)

Treaty on the Non-Proliferation of Nuclear Weapons (Non-Proliferation Treaty, NPT)

Opened for signature at London, Moscow and Washington, DC, on 1 July 1968; entered into force on 5 March 1970; depositaries British, Russian and US governments

The treaty prohibits the transfer by a nuclear weapon state—defined in the treaty as those which have manufactured and exploded a nuclear weapon or other nuclear explosive device prior to 1 January 1967—to any recipient whatsoever of nuclear weapons or other nuclear explosive devices or of control over them, as well as the assistance, encouragement or inducement of any non-nuclear weapon state to manufacture or otherwise acquire such weapons or devices. It also prohibits the receipt by non-nuclear weapon states from any transferor whatsoever, as well as the manufacture or other acquisition by those states, of nuclear weapons or other nuclear explosive devices.

The parties undertake to facilitate the exchange of equipment, materials and scientific and technological information for the peaceful uses of nuclear energy and to ensure that potential benefits from peaceful applications of nuclear explosions will be made available to non-nuclear weapon parties to the treaty. They also undertake to pursue negotiations in good faith on effective measures relating to cessation of the nuclear arms race at an early date and to nuclear disarmament, and on a treaty on general and complete disarmament.

Non-nuclear weapon states undertake to conclude safeguard agreements with the International Atomic Energy Agency (IAEA) with a view to preventing diversion of nuclear energy from peaceful uses to nuclear weapons or other nuclear explosive devices. A Model Protocol Additional to the Safeguards Agreements, strengthening the measures, was approved in 1997; additional safeguards protocols are signed by states individually with the IAEA.

A Review and Extension Conference, convened in 1995 in accordance with the treaty, decided that the treaty should remain in force indefinitely.

Parties (190): Afghanistan*, Albania*, Algeria*, Andorra, Angola, Antigua and Barbuda*, Argentina*, Armenia*, Australia*, Austria*, Azerbaijan*, Bahamas*, Bahrain, Bangladesh*, Barbados*, Belarus*, Belgium*, Belize*, Benin, Bhutan*, Bolivia*, Bosnia and Herzegovina*, Botswana, Brazil*, Brunei Darussalam*, Bulgaria*, Burkina Faso*, Burundi, Cambodia*, Cameroon*, Canada*, Cape Verde, Central African Republic, Chad, Chile*, China*, Colombia, Comoros, Congo (Democratic Republic of the)*, Congo (Republic of the), Costa Rica*, Côte d'Ivoire*, Croatia*, Cuba*, Cyprus*, Czech Republic*, Denmark*, Djibouti, Dominica*, Dominican Republic*, Ecuador*, Egypt*, El Salvador*, Equatorial Guinea, Eritrea, Estonia*, Ethiopia*, Fiji*, Finland*, France*, Gabon, Gambia*, Georgia, Germany*, Ghana*, Greece*, Grenada*, Guatemala*, Guinea, Guinea-Bissau, Guyana*, Haiti, Holy See*, Honduras*, Hungary*, Iceland*, Indonesia*, Iran*, Iraq*, Ireland*, Italy*, Jamaica*, Japan*, Jordan*, Kazakhstan*, Kenya, Kiribati*, Korea (South)*, Kuwait*, Kyrgyzstan*, Laos*, Latvia*, Lebanon*, Lesotho*, Liberia, Libya*, Liechtenstein*, Lithuania*, Luxembourg*, Macedonia* (Former Yugoslav Republic of), Madagascar*, Malawi*, Malaysia*, Maldives*, Mali*, Malta*, Marshall Islands, Mauritania, Mauritius*, Mexico*, Micronesia, Moldova, Monaco*, Mongolia*, Montenegro, Morocco*, Mozambique, Myanmar*, Namibia*, Nauru*, Nepal*, Netherlands*, New Zealand*, Nicaragua*, Niger, Nigeria*, Norway*, Oman, Palau, Panama, Papua New Guinea*, Paraguay*, Peru*, Philippines*, Poland*, Portugal*, Qatar, Romania*, Russia*, Rwanda, Saint Kitts and Nevis*, Saint Lucia*, Saint Vincent and the Grenadines*, Samoa*, San Marino*, Sao Tome and Principe, Saudi Arabia, Senegal*, Serbia*, Seychelles*, Sierra Leone, Singapore*, Slovakia*, Slovenia*, Solomon Islands*, Somalia, South Africa*, Spain*, Sri Lanka*, Sudan*, Suriname*, Swaziland*, Sweden*, Switzerland*, Syria*, Taiwan, Tajikistan*, Tanzania*, Thailand*, Timor-Leste, Togo, Tonga*, Trinidad and Tobago*, Tunisia*, Turkey*, Turkmenistan, Tuvalu*, Uganda, UK*, Ukraine*, United Arab Emirates*, Uruguay*, USA*, Uzbekistan*, Vanuatu, Venezuela*, Viet Nam*, Yemen*, Zambia*, Zimbabwe*

* Party with safeguards agreements in force with the IAEA, as required by the treaty, or concluded by a nuclear weapon state, as defined in the treaty, on a voluntary basis.

Treaty text: International Atomic Energy Agency, INFCIRC/140, 22 Apr. 1970, <http://www.iaea.org/Publications/Documents/Treaties/npt.html>

Additional Safeguards Protocols in force (115): Afghanistan, Albania, *Andorra*, Angola, Armenia, Australia, Austria, Azerbaijan, *Bahrain*, Bangladesh, Belgium, Botswana, Bulgaria, Burkina Faso, Burundi, Canada, Central African Republic, Chad, Chile, China, Colombia, Comoros, Congo (Democratic Republic of the), *Congo (Republic of)*, Costa Rica, Croatia, Cuba, Cyprus, Czech Republic, Denmark, Dominican Republic, Ecuador, El Salvador, Estonia, Euratom, Fiji, Finland, France, Gabon, *Gambia*, Georgia, Germany, Ghana, Greece, Guatemala, Haiti, Holy See, Hungary, Iceland, Indonesia, Ireland, Italy, Jamaica, Japan, Jordan, Kazakhstan, Kenya, Korea (South), Kuwait, *Kyrgyzstan*, Latvia, Lesotho, Libya, Lithuania, Luxembourg, Macedonia (Former Yugoslav Republic of), Madagascar, Malawi, Mali, Malta, Marshall Islands, Mauritania, Mauritius, *Mexico*, Monaco, Mongolia, *Montenegro*, *Morocco*, *Mozambique*, Netherlands, New Zealand, Nicaragua, Niger, Nigeria, Norway, Palau, Panama, Paraguay, Peru, Philippines, Poland, Portugal, Romania, Russia, Rwanda, Seychelles, Singapore, Slovakia, Slovenia, South Africa, Spain, Swaziland, Sweden, Switzerland, Tajikistan, Tanzania, Turkey, Turkmenistan, Uganda, UK, Ukraine, United Arab Emirates, Uruguay, USA, Uzbekistan

Notes: On 6 Feb. 2007 Iran informed the IAEA that it would no longer act in accordance with the provisions of its unratified Additional Safeguards Protocol. Taiwan, although it has not concluded a safeguards agreement, has agreed to apply the measures contained in the 1997 Model Additional Safeguards Protocol.

Model Additional Safeguards Protocol text: International Atomic Energy Agency, INFCIRC/ 540 (corrected), Sep. 1997, <http://www.iaea.org/Publications/Factsheets/English/sg_over view.html>

Treaty on the Prohibition of the Emplacement of Nuclear Weapons and other Weapons of Mass Destruction on the Seabed and the Ocean Floor and in the Subsoil thereof (Seabed Treaty)

Opened for signature at London, Moscow and Washington, DC, on 11 February 1971; entered into force on 18 May 1972; depositaries British, Russian and US governments

The treaty prohibits implanting or emplacing on the seabed and the ocean floor and in the subsoil thereof beyond the outer limit of a 12-mile (19-kilometre) seabed zone any nuclear weapons or any other types of weapons of mass destruction as well as structures, launching installations or any other facilities specifically designed for storing, testing or using such weapons.

Parties (97): Afghanistan, Algeria, Antigua and Barbuda, Argentina, Australia, Austria, Bahamas, Belarus, Belgium, Benin, Bosnia and Herzegovina, Botswana, Brazil[1], Bulgaria, Canada[2], Cape Verde, Central African Republic, China, Congo (Republic of the), Côte d'Ivoire, Croatia, Cuba, Cyprus, Czech Republic, Denmark, Dominican Republic, Equatorial Guinea, Ethiopia, Finland, Germany, Ghana, Greece, Guatemala, Guinea-Bissau, Hungary, Iceland, India[3], Iran, Iraq, Ireland, Italy[4], Jamaica, Japan, Jordan, Korea (South), Laos, Latvia, Lesotho, Libya, Liechtenstein, Luxembourg, Malaysia, Malta, Mauritius, Mexico[5], Mongolia, Montenegro, Morocco, Nepal, Netherlands, New Zealand, Nicaragua, Niger, Norway, Panama, Philippines, Poland, Portugal, Qatar, Romania, Russia, Rwanda, Saint Kitts and Nevis, Saint Vincent and the Grenadines, Sao Tome and Principe, Saudi Arabia, Serbia[6], Seychelles, Singapore, Slovakia, Slovenia, Solomon Islands, South Africa, Spain, Swaziland, Sweden, Switzerland, Taiwan, Togo, Tunisia, Turkey[7], UK, Ukraine, USA, Viet Nam[8], Yemen, Zambia

[1] It is the understanding of Brazil that the word 'observation', as it appears in para. 1 of Article III of the treaty, refers only to observation that is incidental to the normal course of navigation in accordance with international law.

[2] Canada declared that Article I, para. 1, cannot be interpreted as indicating that any state has a right to implant or emplace any weapons not prohibited under Article I, para. 1, on the seabed and ocean floor, and in the subsoil thereof, beyond the limits of national jurisdiction, or as constituting any limitation on the principle that this area of the seabed and ocean floor and the subsoil thereof shall be reserved for exclusively peaceful purposes. Articles I, II and III cannot be interpreted as indicating that any state but the coastal state has any right to implant or emplace any weapon not prohibited under Article I, para. 1 on the continental shelf, or the subsoil thereof, appertaining to that coastal state, beyond the outer limit of the seabed zone referred to in Article I and defined in Article II. Article III cannot be interpreted as indicating any restrictions or limitation upon the rights of the coastal state, consistent with its exclusive sovereign rights with respect to the continental shelf, to verify, inspect or effect the removal of any weapon, structure, installation, facility or device implanted or emplaced on the continental shelf, or the subsoil thereof, appertaining to that coastal state, beyond the outer limit of the seabed zone referred to in Article I and defined in Article II.

[3] The accession by India is based on its position that it has full and exclusive rights over the continental shelf adjoining its territory and beyond its territorial waters and the subsoil thereof. There cannot, therefore, be any restriction on, or limitation of, the sovereign right of India as a coastal state to verify, inspect, remove or destroy any weapon, device, structure, installation or facility, which might be implanted or emplaced on or beneath its continental shelf by any other country, or to take such other steps as may be considered necessary to safeguard its security.

[4] Italy stated, inter alia, that in the case of agreements on further measures in the field of disarmament to prevent an arms race on the seabed and ocean floor and in their subsoil, the question of

the delimitation of the area within which these measures would find application shall have to be examined and solved in each instance in accordance with the nature of the measures to be adopted.

[5] Mexico declared that the treaty cannot be interpreted to mean that a state has the right to emplace weapons of mass destruction, or arms or military equipment of any type, on the continental shelf of Mexico. It reserves the right to verify, inspect, remove or destroy any weapon, structure, installation, device or equipment placed on its continental shelf, including nuclear weapons or other weapons of mass destruction.

[6] In 1974 the Ambassador of Yugoslavia transmitted to the US Secretary of State a note stating that in the view of the Yugoslav Government, Article III, para. 1, of the treaty should be interpreted in such a way that a state exercising its right under this article shall be obliged to notify in advance the coastal state, in so far as its observations are to be carried out 'within the stretch of the sea extending above the continental shelf of the said state'. The USA objected to the Yugoslav reservation, which it considered incompatible with the object and purpose of the treaty.

[7] Turkey declared that the provisions of Article II cannot be used by a state party in support of claims other than those related to disarmament. Hence, Article II cannot be interpreted as establishing a link with the UN Convention on the Law of the Sea. Furthermore, no provision of the Seabed Treaty confers on parties the right to militarize zones which have been demilitarized by other international instruments. Nor can it be interpreted as conferring on either the coastal states or other states the right to emplace nuclear weapons or other weapons of mass destruction on the continental shelf of a demilitarized territory.

[8] Viet Nam stated that no provision of the treaty should be interpreted in a way that would contradict the rights of the coastal states with regard to their continental shelf, including the right to take measures to ensure their security.

Signed but not ratified (20): Bolivia, Burundi, Cambodia, Cameroon, Colombia, Costa Rica, Gambia, Guinea, Honduras, Lebanon, Liberia, Madagascar, Mali, Myanmar, Paraguay, Senegal, Sierra Leone, Sudan, Tanzania, Uruguay

Treaty text: *United Nations Treaty Series*, vol. 955 (1974)

Convention on the Prohibition of the Development, Production and Stockpiling of Bacteriological (Biological) and Toxin Weapons and on their Destruction (Biological and Toxin Weapons Convention, BTWC)

Opened for signature at London, Moscow and Washington, DC, on 10 April 1972; entered into force on 26 March 1975; depositaries British, Russian and US governments

The convention prohibits the development, production, stockpiling or acquisition by other means or retention of microbial or other biological agents or toxins whatever their origin or method of production of types and in quantities that have no justification of prophylactic, protective or other peaceful purposes, as well as weapons, equipment or means of delivery designed to use such agents or toxins for hostile purposes or in armed conflict. The destruction of the agents, toxins, weapons, equipment and means of delivery in the possession of the parties, or their diversion to peaceful purposes, should be effected not later than nine months after the entry into force of the convention for each country. The parties hold annual political and technical meetings to strengthen implementation of the convention. A three-person Implementation Support Unit (ISU), based in Geneva, supports the parties in implementing the treaty, including facilitating the collection and distribution of annual confidence-building measures and supporting their efforts to achieve universal membership.

Parties (166): Afghanistan, Albania, Algeria, Antigua and Barbuda, Argentina, Armenia, Australia, Austria*, Azerbaijan, Bahamas, Bahrain*, Bangladesh, Barbados, Belarus, Belgium, Belize, Benin, Bhutan, Bolivia, Bosnia and Herzegovina, Botswana, Brazil, Brunei Darussalam, Bulgaria, Burkina Faso, *Burundi*, Cambodia, Canada, Cape Verde, Chile, China*, Colombia, Congo (Democratic Republic of the), Congo (Republic of the), Cook Islands, Costa Rica, Croatia, Cuba, Cyprus, Czech Republic*, Denmark, Dominica, Dominican Republic, Ecuador, El Salvador, Equatorial Guinea, Estonia, Ethiopia, Fiji, Finland, France, Gabon, Gambia, Georgia, Germany, Ghana, Greece, Grenada, Guatemala, Guinea-Bissau, Holy See, Honduras, Hungary, Iceland, India*, Indonesia, Iran, Iraq, Ireland*, Italy, Jamaica, Japan, Jordan, Kazakhstan, Kenya, Korea (North), Korea (South)*, Kuwait*, Kyrgyzstan, Laos, Latvia, Lebanon, Lesotho, Libya, Liechtenstein, Lithuania, Luxembourg, Macedonia (Former Yugoslav Republic of), Madagascar, Malaysia*, Maldives, Mali, Malta, Mauritius, Mexico*, Moldova, Monaco, Mongolia, Montenegro, Morocco, *Mozambique*, Netherlands, New Zealand, Nicaragua, Niger, Nigeria, Norway, Oman, Pakistan, Palau, Panama, Papua New Guinea, Paraguay, Peru, Philippines, Poland, Portugal, Qatar, Romania, Russia, Rwanda, Saint Kitts and Nevis, Saint Lucia, Saint Vincent and the Grenadines, San Marino, Sao Tome and Principe, Saudi Arabia, Senegal, Serbia, Seychelles, Sierra Leone, Singapore, Slovakia*, Slovenia, Solomon Islands, South Africa, Spain, Sri Lanka, Sudan, Suriname, Swaziland, Sweden, Switzerland*, Taiwan, Tajikistan, Thailand, Timor-Leste, Togo, Tonga, Trinidad and Tobago, Tunisia, Turkey, Turkmenistan, Uganda, UK*, Ukraine, United Arab Emirates, Uruguay, USA, Uzbekistan, Vanuatu, Venezuela, Viet Nam, Yemen, Zambia, Zimbabwe

  * With reservation and/or declaration.

Signed but not ratified (12): Central African Republic, Côte d'Ivoire, Egypt, Guyana, Haiti, Liberia, Malawi, Myanmar, Nepal, Somalia, Syria, Tanzania

Treaty text: United Nations Treaty Series, vol. 1015 (1976)

Convention on the Prohibition of Military or Any Other Hostile Use of Environmental Modification Techniques (Enmod Convention)

Opened for signature at Geneva on 18 May 1977; entered into force on 5 October 1978; depositary UN Secretary-General

The convention prohibits military or any other hostile use of environmental modification techniques having widespread, long-lasting or severe effects as the means of destruction, damage or injury to states party to the convention. The term 'environmental modification techniques' refers to any technique for changing—through the deliberate manipulation of natural processes—the dynamics, composition or structure of the earth, including its biota, lithosphere, hydrosphere and atmosphere, or of outer space. The understandings reached during the negotiations, but not written into the convention, define the terms 'widespread', 'long-lasting' and 'severe'.

Parties (76): Afghanistan, Algeria, Antigua and Barbuda, Argentina, Armenia, Australia, Austria, Bangladesh, Belarus, Belgium, Benin, Brazil, Bulgaria, *Cameroon*, Canada, Cape Verde, Chile, China*, Costa Rica, Cuba, Cyprus, Czech Republic, Denmark, Dominica, Egypt, *Estonia*, Finland, Germany, Ghana, Greece, Guatemala, Honduras, Hungary, India, Ireland, Italy, Japan, Kazakhstan, Korea (North), Korea (South)*, Kuwait, Lithuania, Laos, Malawi, Mauritius, Mongolia, Netherlands*, New Zealand, Nicaragua, Niger, Norway, Pakistan, Panama, Papua New Guinea, Poland, Romania, Russia, Saint Lucia, Saint Vincent and the Grenadines, Sao Tome and Principe, Slovakia, Slovenia, Solomon Islands, Spain, Sri Lanka,

Sweden, Switzerland, Tajikistan, Tunisia, UK, Ukraine, Uruguay, USA, Uzbekistan, Viet Nam, Yemen

* With declaration.

Signed but not ratified (16): Bolivia, Congo (Democratic Republic of the), Ethiopia, Holy See, Iceland, Iran, Iraq, Lebanon, Liberia, Luxembourg, Morocco, Portugal, Sierra Leone, Syria, Turkey, Uganda

Convention text: United Nations Treaty Collection, <http://treaties.un.org/Pages/CTCTreaties. aspx?id=26>

Convention on the Physical Protection of Nuclear Material

Original convention opened for signature at New York and Vienna on 3 March 1980; entered into force on 8 February 1987; convention amended in 2005; depositary IAEA Director General

The original convention obligates the parties to protect nuclear material for peaceful purposes while in international transport.

The amended convention—renamed the **Convention on the Physical Protection of Nuclear Material and Nuclear Facilities**—will obligate the parties to protect nuclear facilities and material used for peaceful purposes while in storage as well as transport. The amendments will take effect 30 days after they have been ratified, accepted or approved by two-thirds of the states parties to the convention.

Parties to the original convention (145): Afghanistan, Albania, Algeria*, Andorra*, Antigua and Barbuda, Argentina*, Armenia, Australia, Austria*, Azerbaijan*, Bahamas, Bahrain*, Bangladesh, Belarus, Belgium*, Bolivia, Bosnia and Herzegovina, Botswana, Brazil, Bulgaria, Burkina Faso, Cambodia, Cameroon, Canada, Cape Verde, Central African Republic, Chile, China*, Colombia, Comoros, Congo (Democratic Republic of the), Costa Rica, Croatia, Cuba*, Cyprus*, Czech Republic, Denmark, Djibouti, Dominica, Dominican Republic, Ecuador, El Salvador*, Equatorial Guinea, Estonia, Euratom*, Fiji, Finland*, France*, Gabon, Georgia, Germany, Ghana, Greece*, Grenada, Guatemala*, Guinea, Guinea-Bissau, Guyana, Honduras, Hungary, Iceland, India*, Indonesia*, Ireland*, Israel*, Italy*, Jamaica, Japan, Jordan*, Kazakhstan, Kenya, Korea (South)*, Kuwait*, Laos*, Latvia, Lebanon, Lesotho, Libya, Liechtenstein, Lithuania, Luxembourg*, Macedonia (Former Yugoslav Republic of), Madagascar, Mali, Malta, Marshall Islands, Mauritania, Mexico, Moldova, Monaco, Mongolia, Montenegro, Morocco, Mozambique*, Namibia, Nauru, Netherlands*, New Zealand, Nicaragua, Niger, Nigeria, Niue, Norway*, Oman*, Pakistan*, Palau, Panama, Paraguay, Peru*, Philippines, Poland, Portugal*, Qatar*, Romania*, Russia*, Rwanda, Saint Kitts and Nevis, Saudi Arabia*, Senegal, Serbia, Seychelles, Slovakia, Slovenia, South Africa*, Spain*, Sudan, Swaziland, Sweden*, Switzerland*, Tajikistan, Tanzania, Togo, Tonga, Trinidad and Tobago, Tunisia, Turkey*, Turkmenistan, Uganda, UK*, Ukraine, United Arab Emirates, Uruguay, USA, Uzbekistan, Yemen

* With reservation and/or declaration.

Signed but not ratified (1): Haiti

Convention text: International Atomic Energy Agency, INFCIRC/274/Rev.1, May 1980, <http://www.iaea.org/Publications/Documents/Conventions/cppnm.html>

Ratifications, acceptances or approvals of the amended convention deposited (52): Algeria, Antigua and Barbuda, *Argentina*, Australia, Austria, Bahrain, Bosnia and Herzegovina,

Bulgaria, Chile, China, Croatia, Czech Republic, Denmark*, Estonia, Fiji, *Finland*, Gabon, Germany, *Greece*, Hungary, India, Indonesia, Jordan, *Kazakhstan*, Kenya, Latvia, Libya, Liechtenstein, Lithuania, *Macedonia (Former Yugoslav Republic of)*, Mali, Mauritania, Moldova, Nauru, *Netherlands*, Niger, Nigeria, Norway, Poland, Portugal, Romania, Russia, *Saudi Arabia*, Seychelles, Slovenia, Spain, Switzerland, Tunisia, Turkmenistan, UK, Ukraine, United Arab Emirates

* With reservation and/or declaration.

Amendment convention text: International Atomic Energy Agency, Board of Governors, GOV/INF/2005/10-GC(49)/INF/6, 6 Sep. 2005, <http://www.iaea.org/Publications/Documents/Conventions/cppnm.html>

Convention on Prohibitions or Restrictions on the Use of Certain Conventional Weapons which may be Deemed to be Excessively Injurious or to have Indiscriminate Effects (CCW Convention, or 'Inhumane Weapons' Convention)

The convention, with protocols I, II and III, opened for signature at New York on 10 April 1981; entered into force on 2 December 1983; depositary UN Secretary-General

The convention is an 'umbrella treaty', under which specific agreements can be concluded in the form of protocols. In order to become a party to the convention a state must ratify at least two of the protocols.

The amendment to Article I of the original convention was opened for signature at Geneva on 21 November 2001. It expands the scope of application to non-international armed conflicts. The amended convention entered into force on 18 May 2004.

Protocol I prohibits the use of weapons intended to injure by fragments which are not detectable in the human body by X-rays.

Protocol II prohibits or restricts the use of mines, booby-traps and other devices.

Amended Protocol II, which entered into force on 3 December 1998, reinforces the constraints regarding anti-personnel mines.

Protocol III restricts the use of incendiary weapons.

Protocol IV, which entered into force on 30 July 1998, prohibits the employment of laser weapons specifically designed to cause permanent blindness to unenhanced vision.

Protocol V, which entered into force on 12 November 2006, recognizes the need for measures of a generic nature to minimize the risks and effects of explosive remnants of war.

Parties to the original convention and protocols (114): Albania, Antigua and Barbuda[2], Argentina*, Australia, Austria, Bangladesh, Belarus, Belgium, Benin[1], Bolivia, Bosnia and Herzegovina, Brazil, Bulgaria, Burkina Faso, Cambodia, Cameroon, Canada*, Cape Verde, Chile[1], China*, Colombia, Costa Rica, Croatia, Cuba, Cyprus*, Czech Republic, Denmark, Djibouti, Dominican Republic, Ecuador, El Salvador, Estonia[1], Finland, France*, Gabon[1], Georgia, Germany, Greece, Guatemala, Guinea-Bissau, Holy See*, Honduras, Hungary, Iceland, India, Ireland, Israel*[2], Italy*, Jamaica[1], Japan, Jordan[1], Kazakhstan[1], Korea (South)[3], Laos, Latvia, Lesotho, Liberia, Liechtenstein, Lithuania[1], Luxembourg, Macedonia (Former

Yugoslav Republic of), Madagascar, Maldives[1], Mali, Malta, Mauritius, Mexico, Moldova, Monaco[3], Mongolia, Montenegro, Morocco[4], Nauru, Netherlands*, New Zealand, Nicaragua[1], Niger, Norway, Pakistan, Panama, Paraguay, Peru[1], Philippines, Poland, Portugal, Qatar[1], Romania*, Russia, Saint Vincent and the Grenadines[2], Saudi Arabia[1], Senegal[5], Serbia, Seychelles, Sierra Leone[1], Slovakia, Slovenia, South Africa, Spain, Sri Lanka, Sweden, Switzerland, Tajikistan, Togo, Tunisia, Turkey*[3], Turkmenistan[2], Uganda, UK*, Ukraine, United Arab Emirates[1], Uruguay, USA*, Uzbekistan, Venezuela

* With reservation and/or declaration.
[1] Party only to 1981 protocols I and III.
[2] Party only to 1981 protocols I and II.
[3] Party only to 1981 Protocol I.
[4] Party only to 1981 Protocol II.
[5] Party only to 1981 Protocol III.

Signed but not ratified the original convention and protocols (5): Afghanistan, Egypt, Nigeria, Sudan, Viet Nam

Parties to the amended convention and original protocols (75): Albania, Argentina, Australia, Austria, Belarus, Belgium, Bosnia and Herzegovina, Brazil, Bulgaria, Burkina Faso, Canada, Chile, China, Colombia, Costa Rica, Croatia, Cuba, Czech Republic, Denmark, Dominican Republic, Ecuador, El Salvador, Estonia, Finland, France, Georgia, Germany, Greece, Guatemala, Guinea-Bissau, Holy See*, Hungary, Iceland, India, Ireland, Italy, Jamaica, Japan, Korea (South), Latvia, Liberia, Liechtenstein, Lithuania, Luxembourg, Macedonia (Former Yugoslav Republic of), Malta, Mexico*, Moldova, Montenegro, Netherlands, New Zealand, Nicaragua, Niger, Norway, Panama, Paraguay, Peru, Poland, Portugal, Romania, Russia, Serbia, Sierra Leone, Slovakia, Slovenia, Spain, Sri Lanka, Sweden, Switzerland, Tunisia, Turkey, UK, Ukraine, Uruguay, USA

* With reservation and/or declaration.
Note: In addition to the 75 parties as of 1 Jan. 2012, South Africa deposited its instrument of ratification on 24 Jan. 2012.

Parties to Amended Protocol II (98): Albania, Argentina, Australia, Austria*, Bangladesh, Belarus*, Belgium*, Bolivia, Bosnia and Herzegovina, Brazil, Bulgaria, Burkina Faso, Cambodia, Cameroon, Canada, Cape Verde, Chile, China*, Colombia, Costa Rica, Croatia, Cyprus, Czech Republic, Denmark*, Dominican Republic, Ecuador, El Salvador, Estonia, Finland*, France*, Gabon, Georgia, Germany*, Greece*, Guatemala, Guinea-Bissau, Holy See, Honduras, Hungary*, Iceland, India, Ireland*, Israel*, Italy*, Jamaica, Japan, Jordan, Korea (South)*, Latvia, Liberia, Liechtenstein*, Lithuania, Luxembourg, Macedonia (Former Yugoslav Republic of), Madagascar, Maldives, Mali, Malta, Moldova, Monaco, *Montenegro*, Morocco, Nauru, Netherlands*, New Zealand, Nicaragua, Niger, Norway, Pakistan*, Panama, Paraguay, Peru, Philippines, Poland, Portugal, Romania, Russia*, Saint Vincent and the Grenadines, Senegal, *Serbia*, Seychelles, Sierra Leone, Slovakia, Slovenia, South Africa*, Spain, Sri Lanka, Sweden, Switzerland, Tajikistan, Tunisia, Turkey, Turkmenistan, UK*, Ukraine*, Uruguay, USA*, Venezuela

* With reservation and/or declaration.

Parties to Protocol IV (100): Albania, Antigua and Barbuda, Argentina, Australia*, Austria*, Bangladesh, Belarus, Belgium*, Bolivia, Bosnia and Herzegovina, Brazil, Bulgaria, Burkina Faso, Cambodia, Cameroon, Canada*, Cape Verde, Chile, China, Colombia, Costa Rica, Croatia, Cyprus, Czech Republic, Denmark, Dominican Republic, Ecuador, El Salvador, Estonia, Finland, France, Gabon, Georgia, Germany*, Greece*, Guatemala, Guinea-Bissau, Holy See, Honduras, Hungary, Iceland, India, Ireland*, Israel*, Italy*, Jamaica, Japan, Kazakhstan, Latvia, Liberia, Liechtenstein*, Lithuania, Luxembourg, Macedonia (Former Yugoslav Republic of), Madagascar, Maldives, Mali, Malta, Mauritius, Mexico, Moldova, Mongolia, Montenegro, Morocco, Nauru, Netherlands*, New Zealand, Nicaragua, Niger, Norway,

Pakistan, Panama, Paraguay, Peru, Philippines, Poland*, Portugal, Qatar, Romania, Russia, Saint Vincent and the Grenadines, Saudi Arabia, Serbia, Seychelles, Sierra Leone, Slovakia, Slovenia, South Africa*, Spain, Sri Lanka, Sweden*, Switzerland*, Tajikistan, Tunisia, Turkey, UK*, Ukraine, Uruguay, USA*, Uzbekistan

* With reservation and/or declaration.

Parties to Protocol V (76): Albania, *Argentina**, Australia, Austria, Belarus, Belgium, Bosnia and Herzegovina, Brazil, Bulgaria, Cameroon, Canada, Chile, China*, Costa Rica, Croatia, Cyprus, Czech Republic, Denmark, Dominican Republic, Ecuador, El Salvador, Estonia, Finland, France, Gabon, Georgia, Germany, Guatemala, Guinea-Bissau, Holy See*, Honduras, Hungary, Iceland, India, Ireland, Italy, Jamaica, Korea (South), Latvia, Liberia, Liechtenstein, Lithuania, Luxembourg, Macedonia (Former Yugoslav Republic of), Madagascar, Mali, Malta, Moldova, Netherlands, New Zealand*, Nicaragua, Norway, Pakistan, Panama, Paraguay, Peru, *Poland*, Portugal, Qatar, Romania, Russia, Saint Vincent and the Grenadines, Saudi Arabia, Senegal, Sierra Leone, Slovakia, Slovenia, Spain, Sweden, Switzerland, Tajikistan, Tunisia, Ukraine, United Arab Emirates, Uruguay, USA*

* With reservation and/or declaration.
Note: In addition to the 76 parties as of 1 Jan. 2012, South Africa deposited its instrument of ratification on 24 Jan. 2012 and Laos on 2 Feb. 2012

Convention and protocol texts (original and amendments): United Nations Treaty Collection, <http://treaties.un.org/Pages/CTCTreaties.aspx?id=26>

Convention on the Prohibition of the Development, Production, Stockpiling and Use of Chemical Weapons and on their Destruction (Chemical Weapons Convention, CWC)

Opened for signature at Paris on 13 January 1993; entered into force on 29 April 1997; depositary UN Secretary-General

The convention prohibits the development, production, acquisition, transfer, stockpiling and use of chemical weapons. The CWC regime consists of four 'pillars': disarmament, non-proliferation, assistance and protection against chemical weapons, and international cooperation on the peaceful uses of chemistry.

Each party undertakes to destroy its chemical weapons by 29 April 2012. Old and abandoned chemical weapons will continue to be destroyed as they are uncovered from, for example, former battlefields.

Parties (188): Afghanistan, Albania, Algeria, Andorra, Antigua and Barbuda, Argentina, Armenia, Australia, Austria, Azerbaijan, Bahamas, Bahrain, Bangladesh, Barbados, Belarus, Belgium, Belize, Benin, Bhutan, Bolivia, Bosnia and Herzegovina, Botswana, Brazil, Brunei Darussalam, Bulgaria, Burkina Faso, Burundi, Cambodia, Cameroon, Canada, Cape Verde, Central African Republic, Chad, Chile, China, Colombia, Comoros, Congo (Democratic Republic of the), Congo (Republic of the), Cook Islands, Costa Rica, Côte d'Ivoire, Croatia, Cuba, Cyprus, Czech Republic, Denmark, Djibouti, Dominica, Dominican Republic, Ecuador, El Salvador, Equatorial Guinea, Eritrea, Estonia, Ethiopia, Fiji, Finland, France, Gabon, Gambia, Georgia, Germany, Ghana, Greece, Grenada, Guatemala, Guinea, Guinea-Bissau, Guyana, Haiti, Holy See, Honduras, Hungary, Iceland, India, Indonesia, Iran, Iraq, Ireland, Italy, Jamaica, Japan, Jordan, Kazakhstan, Kenya, Kiribati, Korea (South), Kuwait, Kyrgyzstan, Laos, Latvia, Lebanon, Lesotho, Liberia, Libya, Liechtenstein, Lithuania, Luxembourg, Macedonia (Former Yugoslav Republic of), Madagascar, Malawi, Malaysia, Maldives, Mali, Malta, Marshall Islands, Mauritania, Mauritius, Mexico, Micronesia, Moldova, Monaco,

Mongolia, Montenegro, Morocco, Mozambique, Namibia, Nauru, Nepal, Netherlands, New Zealand, Nicaragua, Niger, Nigeria, Niue, Norway, Oman, Pakistan, Palau, Panama, Papua New Guinea, Paraguay, Peru, Philippines, Poland, Portugal, Qatar, Romania, Russia, Rwanda, Saint Kitts and Nevis, Saint Lucia, Saint Vincent and the Grenadines, Samoa, San Marino, Sao Tome and Principe, Saudi Arabia, Senegal, Serbia, Seychelles, Sierra Leone, Singapore, Slovakia, Slovenia, Solomon Islands, South Africa, Spain, Sri Lanka, Sudan, Suriname, Swaziland, Sweden, Switzerland, Tajikistan, Tanzania, Thailand, Timor-Leste, Togo, Tonga, Trinidad and Tobago, Tunisia, Turkey, Turkmenistan, Tuvalu, Uganda, UK, Ukraine, United Arab Emirates, Uruguay, USA, Uzbekistan, Vanuatu, Venezuela, Viet Nam, Yemen, Zambia, Zimbabwe

Signed but not ratified (2): Israel, Myanmar

Convention text: United Nations Treaty Collection, <http://treaties.un.org/Pages/CTCTreaties. aspx?id=26>

Comprehensive Nuclear-Test-Ban Treaty (CTBT)

Opened for signature at New York on 24 September 1996; not in force; depositary UN Secretary-General

The treaty would prohibit the carrying out of any nuclear weapon test explosion or any other nuclear explosion, and urges each party to prevent any such nuclear explosion at any place under its jurisdiction or control and refrain from causing, encouraging or in any way participating in the carrying out of any nuclear weapon test explosion or any other nuclear explosion.

The treaty will enter into force 180 days after the date of the deposit of the instruments of ratification of the 44 states listed in an annex to the treaty. All the 44 states possess nuclear power reactors and/or nuclear research reactors.

States whose ratification is required for entry into force (44): Algeria, Argentina, Australia, Austria, Bangladesh, Belgium, Brazil, Bulgaria, Canada, Chile, China*, Colombia, Congo (Democratic Republic of the), Egypt*, Finland, France, Germany, Hungary, India*, Indonesia, Iran*, Israel*, Italy, Japan, Korea (North)*, Korea (South), Mexico, Netherlands, Norway, Pakistan*, Peru, Poland, Romania, Russia, Slovakia, South Africa, Spain, Sweden, Switzerland, Turkey, UK, Ukraine, USA*, Viet Nam

* Has not ratified the treaty.

Ratifications deposited (155): Afghanistan, Albania, Algeria, Andorra, Antigua and Barbuda, Argentina, Armenia, Australia, Austria, Azerbaijan, Bahamas, Bahrain, Bangladesh, Barbados, Belarus, Belgium, Belize, Benin, Bolivia, Bosnia and Herzegovina, Botswana, Brazil, Bulgaria, Burkina Faso, Burundi, Cambodia, Cameroon, Canada, Cape Verde, Central African Republic, Chile, Colombia, Congo (Democratic Republic of the), Cook Islands, Costa Rica, Côte d'Ivoire, Croatia, Cyprus, Czech Republic, Denmark, Djibouti, Dominican Republic, Ecuador, El Salvador, Eritrea, Estonia, Ethiopia, Fiji, Finland, France, Gabon, Georgia, Germany, *Ghana*, Greece, Grenada, *Guinea*, Guyana, Haiti, Holy See, Honduras, Hungary, Iceland, Ireland, Italy, Jamaica, Japan, Jordan, Kazakhstan, Kenya, Kiribati, Korea (South), Kuwait, Kyrgyzstan, Laos, Latvia, Lebanon, Lesotho, Liberia, Libya, Liechtenstein, Lithuania, Luxembourg, Macedonia (Former Yugoslav Republic of), Madagascar, Malawi, Malaysia, Maldives, Mali, Malta, Marshall Islands, Mauritania, Mexico, Micronesia, Moldova, Monaco, Mongolia, Montenegro, Morocco, Mozambique, Namibia, Nauru, Netherlands, New Zealand, Nicaragua, Niger, Nigeria, Norway, Oman, Palau, Panama, Paraguay, Peru, Philippines, Poland, Portugal, Qatar, Romania, Russia, Rwanda, Saint Kitts and Nevis, Saint Lucia, Saint Vincent and the Grenadines, Samoa, San Marino, Senegal, Serbia, Seychelles, Sierra Leone, Singapore, Slovakia, Slovenia, South Africa, Spain, Sudan, Suriname, Sweden, Switzerland, Tajikistan, Tanzania,

Togo, Trinidad and Tobago, Tunisia, Turkey, Turkmenistan, Uganda, UK, Ukraine, United Arab Emirates, Uruguay, Uzbekistan, Vanuatu, Venezuela, Viet Nam, Zambia

Note: In addition to the 155 parties as of 1 Jan. 2012, Guatemala deposited its instrument of ratification on 12 Jan. 2012 (with a reservation and/or declaration) and Indonesia on 6 Feb. 2012.

Signed but not ratified (25): Angola, Brunei Darussalam, Chad, China, Comoros, Congo (Republic of the), Egypt, Equatorial Guinea, Gambia, Guinea-Bissau, Iran, Iraq, Israel, Myanmar, Nepal, Papua New Guinea, Sao Tome and Principe, Solomon Islands, Sri Lanka, Swaziland, Thailand, Timor-Leste, USA, Yemen, Zimbabwe

Treaty text: United Nations Treaty Collection, <http://treaties.un.org/Pages/CTCTreaties. aspx?id=26>

Convention on the Prohibition of the Use, Stockpiling, Production and Transfer of Anti-Personnel Mines and on their Destruction (APM Convention)

Opened for signature at Ottawa on 3–4 December 1997 and at New York on 5 December 1997; entered into force on 1 March 1999; depositary UN Secretary-General

The convention prohibits anti-personnel mines (APMs), which are defined as mines designed to be exploded by the presence, proximity or contact of a person and which will incapacitate, injure or kill one or more persons.

Each party undertakes to destroy all its stockpiled APMs as soon as possible but not later that four years after the entry into force of the convention for that state party. Each party also undertakes to destroy all APMs in mined areas under its jurisdiction or control not later than 10 years after the entry into force of the convention for that state party.

Parties (158): Afghanistan, Albania, Algeria, Andorra, Angola, Antigua and Barbuda, Argentina*, Australia*, Austria*, Bahamas, Bangladesh, Barbados, Belarus, Belgium, Belize, Benin, Bhutan, Bolivia, Bosnia and Herzegovina, Botswana, Brazil, Brunei Darussalam, Bulgaria, Burkina Faso, Burundi, Cambodia, Cameroon, Canada*, Cape Verde, Central African Republic, Chad, Chile*, Colombia, Comoros, Congo (Democratic Republic of the), Congo (Republic of the), Cook Islands, Costa Rica, Côte d'Ivoire, Croatia, Cyprus, Czech Republic*, Denmark, Djibouti, Dominica, Dominican Republic, Ecuador, El Salvador, Equatorial Guinea, Eritrea, Estonia, Ethiopia, Fiji, France, Gabon, Gambia, Germany, Ghana, Greece*, Grenada, Guatemala, Guinea, Guinea-Bissau, Guyana, Haiti, Holy See, Honduras, Hungary, Iceland, Indonesia, Iraq, Ireland, Italy, Jamaica, Japan, Jordan, Kenya, Kiribati, Kuwait, Latvia, Lesotho, Liberia, Liechtenstein, Lithuania*, Luxembourg, Macedonia (Former Yugoslav Republic of), Madagascar, Malawi, Malaysia, Maldives, Mali, Malta, Mauritania, Mauritius*, Mexico, Moldova, Monaco, Montenegro*, Mozambique, Namibia, Nauru, Netherlands, New Zealand, Nicaragua, Niger, Nigeria, Niue, Norway, Palau, Panama, Papua New Guinea, Paraguay, Peru, Philippines, Portugal, Qatar, Romania, Rwanda, Saint Kitts and Nevis, Saint Lucia, Saint Vincent and the Grenadines, Samoa, San Marino, Sao Tome and Principe, Senegal, Serbia*, Seychelles, Sierra Leone, Slovakia, Slovenia, Solomon Islands, South Africa*, *South Sudan*, Spain, Sudan, Suriname, Swaziland, Sweden*, Switzerland*, Tajikistan, Tanzania, Thailand, Timor-Leste, Togo, Trinidad and Tobago, Tunisia, Turkey, Turkmenistan, *Tuvalu*, Uganda, UK*, Ukraine, Uruguay, Vanuatu, Venezuela, Yemen, Zambia, Zimbabwe

* With reservation and/or declaration.

Note: In addition to the 158 parties as of 1 Jan. 2012, Finland deposited its instrument of ratification on 9 Jan. 2012.

Signed but not ratified (2): Marshall Islands, Poland

Convention text: United Nations Treaty Collection, <http://treaties.un.org/Pages/CTCTreaties.aspx?id=26>

Convention on Cluster Munitions

Adopted at Dublin on 30 May 2008; opened for signature at Oslo on 3 December 2008; entered into force on 1 August 2010; depositary UN Secretary-General

The convention's objectives are to prohibit the use, production, transfer and stockpiling of cluster munitions that cause unacceptable harm to civilians, and to establish a framework for cooperation and assistance that ensures adequate provision of care and rehabilitation for victims, clearance of contaminated areas, risk reduction education and destruction of stockpiles. The convention does not apply to mines.

Parties (67): Afghanistan, Albania, Antigua and Barbuda, Austria, Belgium*, Bosnia and Herzegovina, *Botswana*, *Bulgaria*, Burkina Faso, Burundi, Cape Verde, Chile, Comoros, *Cook Islands*, *Costa Rica*, Croatia, *Czech Republic*, Denmark, *Dominican Republic*, Ecuador, *El Salvador**, Fiji, France, Germany, *Ghana*, *Grenada*, Guatemala, Guinea-Bissau, Holy See*, Ireland, *Italy*, Japan, Laos, Lebanon, Lesotho, *Lithuania*, Luxembourg, Macedonia (Former Yugoslav Republic of), Malawi, Mali, Malta, Mexico, Moldova, Monaco, Montenegro, *Mozambique*, *Netherlands*, New Zealand, Nicaragua, Niger, Norway, Panama, *Portugal*, Samoa, Saint Vincent and the Grenadines, San Marino, *Senegal*, Seychelles, Sierra Leone, Slovenia, Spain, *Swaziland*, *Trinidad and Tobago*, Tunisia, UK, Uruguay, Zambia

* With reservation and/or declaration.
Note: In addition to the 67 parties as of 1 Jan. 2012, Mauritania deposited its instrument of ratification on 1 Feb. 2012.

Signed but not ratified (43): Angola, Australia, Benin, Bolivia, Cameroon, Canada, Central African Republic, Chad, Colombia, Congo (Democratic Republic of the), Congo (Republic of the), Côte d'Ivoire, Cyprus, Djibouti, Gambia, Guinea, Haiti, Honduras, Hungary, Iceland, Indonesia, Iraq, Jamaica, Kenya, Liberia, Liechtenstein, Madagascar, Namibia, Nauru, Nigeria, Palau, Paraguay, Peru, Philippines, Rwanda, Sao Tome and Principe, Somalia, South Africa, Sweden, Switzerland, Tanzania, Togo, Uganda

Convention text: United Nations Treaty Collection, <http://treaties.un.org/Pages/CTCTreaties.aspx?id=26>

II. Regional treaties

Treaty for the Prohibition of Nuclear Weapons in Latin America and the Caribbean (Treaty of Tlatelolco)

Original treaty opened for signature at Mexico City on 14 February 1967; entered into force on 22 April 1968; treaty amended in 1990, 1991 and 1992; depositary Mexican Government

The treaty prohibits the testing, use, manufacture, production or acquisition by any means, as well as the receipt, storage, installation, deployment and any form of possession of any nuclear weapons by Latin American and Caribbean countries.

The parties should conclude agreements individually with the IAEA for the application of safeguards to their nuclear activities. The IAEA has the exclusive power to carry out special inspections.

The treaty is open for signature by all the independent states of the Latin American and Caribbean zone as defined in the treaty.

Under *Additional Protocol I* states with territories within the zone (France, the Netherlands, the UK and the USA) undertake to apply the statute of military denuclearization to these territories.

Under *Additional Protocol II* the recognized nuclear weapon states—China, France, Russia, the UK and the USA—undertake to respect the statute of military denuclearization of Latin America and the Caribbean and not to contribute to acts involving a violation of the treaty, nor to use or threaten to use nuclear weapons against the parties to the treaty.

Parties to the original treaty (33): Antigua and Barbuda, Argentina[1], Bahamas, Barbados[1], Belize[2], Bolivia, Brazil[1], Chile[1], Colombia[1], Costa Rica[1], Cuba[1], Dominica, Dominican Republic[3], Ecuador[1], El Salvador[1], Grenada[4], Guatemala[1], Guyana[1], Haiti, Honduras, Jamaica[1], Mexico[1], Nicaragua[3], Panama[1], Paraguay[1], Peru[1], Saint Kitts and Nevis, Saint Lucia, Saint Vincent and the Grenadines, Suriname[1], Trinidad and Tobago, Uruguay[1], Venezuela[1]

[1] Has ratified the amendments of 1990, 1991 and 1992.
[2] Has ratified the amendments of 1990 and 1992 only.
[3] Has ratified the amendment of 1992 only.
[4] Has ratified the amendment of 1990 only.

Parties to Additional Protocol I (4): France[1], Netherlands, UK[2], USA[3]

Parties to Additional Protocol II (5): China[4], France[5], Russia[6], UK[2], USA[7]

[1] France declared that Protocol I shall not apply to transit across French territories situated within the zone of the treaty, and destined for other French territories. The protocol shall not limit the participation of the populations of the French territories in the activities mentioned in Article 1 of the treaty, and in efforts connected with the national defence of France. France does not consider the zone defined in the treaty as established in accordance with international law; it cannot, therefore, agree that the treaty should apply to that zone.

[2] When signing and ratifying protocols I and II, the UK made the following declarations of understanding: The signing and ratification by the UK could not be regarded as affecting in any way the legal status of any territory for the international relations of which the UK is responsible, lying within the limits of the geographical zone established by the treaty. Should any party to the treaty carry out any act of aggression with the support of a nuclear weapon state, the UK would be free to reconsider the extent to which it could be regarded as bound by the provisions of Protocol II.

[3] The USA ratified Protocol I with the following understandings: The provisions of the treaty do not affect the exclusive power and legal competence under international law of a state adhering to this Protocol to grant or deny transit and transport privileges to its own or any other vessels or aircraft irrespective of cargo or armaments; the provisions do not affect rights under international law of a state adhering to this protocol regarding the exercise of the freedom of the seas, or regarding passage through or over waters subject to the sovereignty of a state. The declarations attached by the USA to its ratification of Protocol II apply also to Protocol I.

[4] China declared that it will never send its means of transportation and delivery carrying nuclear weapons into the territory, territorial sea or airspace of Latin American countries.

[5] France stated that it interprets the undertaking contained in Article 3 of Protocol II to mean that it presents no obstacle to the full exercise of the right of self-defence enshrined in Article 51 of the UN Charter; it takes note of the interpretation by the Preparatory Commission for the Denuclearization of Latin America according to which the treaty does not apply to transit, the granting or denying of which lies within the exclusive competence of each state party in accordance with international law. In 1974 France made a supplementary statement to the effect that it was prepared to consider its

obligations under Protocol II as applying not only to the signatories of the treaty, but also to the territories for which the statute of denuclearization was in force in conformity with Protocol I.

[6] On signing and ratifying Protocol II, the USSR stated that it assumed that the effect of Article 1 of the treaty extends to any nuclear explosive device and that, accordingly, the carrying out by any party of nuclear explosions for peaceful purposes would be a violation of its obligations under Article 1 and would be incompatible with its non-nuclear weapon status. For states parties to the treaty, a solution to the problem of peaceful nuclear explosions can be found in accordance with the provisions of Article V of the NPT and within the framework of the international procedures of the IAEA. It declared that authorizing the transit of nuclear weapons in any form would be contrary to the objectives of the treaty.

Any actions undertaken by a state or states parties to the treaty which are not compatible with their non-nuclear weapon status, and also the commission by one or more states parties to the treaty of an act of aggression with the support of a state which is in possession of nuclear weapons or together with such a state, will be regarded by the USSR as incompatible with the obligations of those countries under the treaty. In such cases it would reserve the right to reconsider its obligations under Protocol II. It further reserves the right to reconsider its attitude to this protocol in the event of any actions on the part of other states possessing nuclear weapons which are incompatible with their obligations under the said protocol.

[7] The USA signed and ratified Protocol II with the following declarations and understandings: Each of the parties retains exclusive power and legal competence to grant or deny non-parties transit and transport privileges. As regards the undertaking not to use or threaten to use nuclear weapons against the parties, the USA would consider that an armed attack by a party, in which it was assisted by a nuclear weapon state, would be incompatible with the treaty.

Original treaty text: *United Nations Treaty Series*, vol. 634 (1968)

Amended treaty text: Agency for the Prohibition of Nuclear Weapons in Latin America and the Caribbean, <http://www.opanal.org/opanal/Tlatelolco/P-Tlatelolco-i.htm>

South Pacific Nuclear Free Zone Treaty (Treaty of Rarotonga)

Opened for signature at Rarotonga on 6 August 1985; entered into force on 11 December 1986; depositary Secretary General of the Pacific Islands Forum Secretariat

The treaty prohibits the manufacture or acquisition of any nuclear explosive device, as well as possession or control over such device by the parties anywhere inside or outside the zone defined in an annex. The parties also undertake not to supply nuclear material or equipment, unless subject to IAEA safeguards, and to prevent in their territories the stationing as well as the testing of any nuclear explosive device and undertake not to dump, and to prevent the dumping of, radioactive waste and other radioactive matter at sea anywhere within the zone. Each party remains free to allow visits, as well as transit, by foreign ships and aircraft.

The treaty is open for signature by the members of the Pacific Islands Forum.

Under *Protocol 1* France, the UK and the USA undertake to apply the treaty prohibitions relating to the manufacture, stationing and testing of nuclear explosive devices in the territories situated within the zone for which they are internationally responsible.

Under *Protocol 2* China, France, Russia, the UK and the USA undertake not to use or threaten to use a nuclear explosive device against the parties to the treaty or against any territory within the zone for which a party to Protocol 1 is internationally responsible.

Under *Protocol 3* China, France, Russia, the UK and the USA undertake not to test any nuclear explosive device anywhere within the zone.

Parties (13): Australia, Cook Islands, Fiji, Kiribati, Nauru, New Zealand, Niue, Papua New Guinea, Samoa, Solomon Islands, Tonga, Tuvalu, Vanuatu

Parties to Protocol 1 (2): France, UK; *signed but not ratified (1)*: USA

Parties to Protocol 2 (4): China, France[1], Russia, UK[2]; *signed but not ratified (1)*: USA

Parties to Protocol 3 (4): China, France, Russia, UK; *signed but not ratified (1)*: USA

[1] France declared that the negative security guarantees set out in Protocol 2 are the same as the Conference on Disarmament declaration of 6 Apr. 1995 referred to in UN Security Council Resolution 984 of 11 Apr. 1995.

[2] On ratifying Protocol 2 in 1997, the UK declared that nothing in the treaty affects the rights under international law with regard to transit of the zone or visits to ports and airfields within the zone by ships and aircraft. The UK will not be bound by the undertakings in Protocol 2 in case of an invasion or any other attack on the UK, its territories, its armed forces or its allies, carried out or sustained by a party to the treaty in association or alliance with a nuclear weapon state or if a party violates its non-proliferation obligations under the treaty.

Treaty text: United Nations Treaty Series, vol. 1445 (1987)

Treaty on Conventional Armed Forces in Europe (CFE Treaty)

Original treaty signed at Paris on 19 November 1990; entered into force on 9 November 1992; depositary Dutch Government

The treaty sets ceilings on five categories of treaty-limited equipment (TLE)—battle tanks, armoured combat vehicles, artillery of at least 100-mm calibre, combat aircraft and attack helicopters—in an area stretching from the Atlantic Ocean to the Ural Mountains (the Atlantic-to-the-Urals, ATTU).

The treaty was negotiated and signed by the member states of the Warsaw Treaty Organization and NATO within the framework of the Conference on Security and Co-operation in Europe (from 1995 the Organization for Security and Co-operation in Europe, OSCE).

The **1992 Tashkent Agreement**, adopted by the former Soviet republics with territories within the ATTU area of application (with the exception of Estonia, Latvia and Lithuania) and the **1992 Oslo Document** (Final Document of the Extraordinary Conference of the States Parties to the CFE Treaty) introduced modifications to the treaty required because of the emergence of new states after the break-up of the USSR.

Parties (30): Armenia, Azerbaijan, Belarus, Belgium[2], Bulgaria[2], Canada[2], Czech Republic[2], Denmark[2], France, Georgia, Germany[2], Greece, Hungary[2], Iceland[2], Italy[2], Kazakhstan, Luxembourg[2], Moldova[2], Netherlands[2], Norway, Poland, Portugal[2], Romania, Russia[1], Slovakia[2], Spain, Turkey[2], UK[2], Ukraine, USA[2]

[1] On 14 July 2007 Russia declared its intention to suspend its participation in the CFE Treaty and associated documents and agreements, which took effect on 12 Dec. 2007.

[2] In Nov.–Dec. 2011, these countries notified the depositary that they will cease to perform their obligations under the treaty with regard to Russia.

The first review conference of the CFE Treaty adopted the **1996 Flank Document**, which reorganized the flank areas geographically and numerically, allowing Russia and Ukraine to deploy TLE in a less constraining manner.

Original (1990) treaty text: Organization for Security and Co-operation in Europe, <http://www.osce.org/library/14087>

Consolidated (1993) treaty text: Dutch Ministry of Foreign Affairs, <http://www.minbuza.nl/en/treaties/004285>

Flank Document text: Organization for Security and Co-operation in Europe, <http://www.osce.org/library/14099>, annex A

Concluding Act of the Negotiation on Personnel Strength of Conventional Armed Forces in Europe (CFE-1A Agreement)

Signed by the parties to the CFE Treaty at Helsinki on 10 July 1992; entered into force simultaneously with the CFE Treaty; depositary Dutch Government

The politically binding agreement sets ceilings on the number of personnel of the conventional land-based armed forces of the parties within the ATTU area.

Agreement text: Organization for Security and Co-operation in Europe, <http://www.osce.org/library/14093>

Agreement on Adaptation of the Treaty on Conventional Armed Forces in Europe

Signed by the parties to the CFE Treaty at Helsinki on 19 November 1999; not in force; depositary Dutch Government

The agreement would replace the CFE Treaty bloc-to-bloc military balance with regional balance, establish individual state limits on TLE holdings, and provide for a new structure of limitations and new military flexibility mechanisms, flank sub-limits and enhanced transparency. It would open the CFE regime to all the other European states. It will enter into force when it has been ratified by all the signatories. The **1999 Final Act**, with annexes, contains politically binding arrangements with regard to Georgia, Moldova and Central Europe, and withdrawals of armed forces from foreign territories.

Ratifications deposited (3): Belarus, Kazakhstan, Russia*[1]

* With reservation and/or declaration.
[1] On 14 July 2007 Russia declared its intention to suspend its participation in the CFE Treaty and associated documents and agreements, which took effect on 12 Dec. 2007.
  Note: Ukraine has ratified the 1999 Agreement on Adaptation of the CFE Treaty but has not deposited its instrument with the depositary.

Agreement text: Organization for Security and Co-operation in Europe, <http://www.osce.org/library/14108>

Treaty text as amended by 1999 agreement: SIPRI Yearbook 2000, pp. 627–42

Final Act text: Organization for Security and Co-operation in Europe, <http://www.osce.org/library/14114>

Treaty on Open Skies

Opened for signature at Helsinki on 24 March 1992; entered into force on 1 January 2002; depositaries Canadian and Hungarian governments

The treaty obligates the parties to submit their territories to short-notice unarmed surveillance flights. The area of application stretches from Vancouver, Canada, eastward to Vladivostok, Russia.

The treaty was negotiated between the member states of the Warsaw Treaty Organization and NATO. It was opened for signature by the NATO member states, former member states of the Warsaw Treaty Organization and the states of the former Soviet Union (except for Estonia, Latvia and Lithuania). For six months after entry into force of the treaty, any other participating state of the Organization for Security and Co-operation in Europe could apply for accession to the treaty, and from 1 July 2002 any state can apply to accede to the treaty.

Parties (34): Belarus, Belgium, Bosnia and Herzegovina, Bulgaria, Canada, Croatia, Czech Republic, Denmark, Estonia, Finland, France, Georgia, Germany, Greece, Hungary, Iceland, Italy, Latvia, Lithuania, Luxembourg, Netherlands, Norway, Poland, Portugal, Romania, Russia, Slovakia, Slovenia, Spain, Sweden, Turkey, UK, Ukraine, USA

Signed but not ratified (1): Kyrgyzstan

Treaty text: Canada Treaty Information, <http://www.treaty-accord.gc.ca/text-texte.aspx?id=102747>

Treaty on the Southeast Asia Nuclear Weapon-Free Zone (Treaty of Bangkok)

Signed at Bangkok on 15 December 1995; entered into force on 27 March 1997; depository Thai Government

The treaty prohibits the development, manufacture, acquisition or testing of nuclear weapons inside or outside the zone as well as the stationing and transport of nuclear weapons in or through the zone. Each state party may decide for itself whether to allow visits and transit by foreign ships and aircraft. The parties undertake not to dump at sea or discharge into the atmosphere anywhere within the zone any radioactive material or waste or dispose of radioactive material on land. The parties should conclude an agreement with the IAEA for the application of full-scope safeguards to their peaceful nuclear activities.

The zone includes not only the territories but also the continental shelves and exclusive economic zones of the states parties.

The treaty is open for all states of South East Asia.

Under a *Protocol* to the treaty, China, France, Russia, the UK and the USA are to undertake not to use or threaten to use nuclear weapons against any state party to the treaty. They should further undertake not to use nuclear weapons within the South East Asia nuclear weapon-free zone. The protocol will enter into force for each state party on the date of its deposit of the instrument of ratification.

Parties (10): Brunei Darussalam, Cambodia, Indonesia, Laos, Malaysia, Myanmar, Philippines, Singapore, Thailand, Viet Nam

Protocol: no signatures, no parties

Treaty and protocol texts: ASEAN Secretariat, <http://www.aseansec.org/5181.htm>

African Nuclear-Weapon-Free Zone Treaty (Treaty of Pelindaba)

Signed at Cairo on 11 April 1996; entered into force on 15 July 2009; depositary Secretary-General of the African Union

The treaty prohibits the research, development, manufacture and acquisition of nuclear explosive devices and the testing or stationing of any nuclear explosive device. Each party remains free to allow visits and transit by foreign ships and aircraft. The treaty also prohibits any attack against nuclear installations. The parties undertake not to dump or permit the dumping of radioactive waste and other radioactive matter anywhere within the zone. Each party should individually conclude an agreement with the IAEA for the application of comprehensive safeguards to their peaceful nuclear activities.

The zone includes the territory of the continent of Africa, island states members of the African Union (AU) and all islands considered by the AU to be part of Africa.

The treaty is open for signature by all the states of Africa.

Under *Protocol I* China, France, Russia, the UK and the USA are to undertake not to use or threaten to use a nuclear explosive device against the parties to the treaty.

Under *Protocol II* China, France, Russia, the UK and the USA are to undertake not to test nuclear explosive devices within the zone.

Under *Protocol III* states with territories within the zone for which they are internationally responsible are to undertake to observe certain provisions of the treaty with respect to these territories. This protocol is open for signature by France and Spain.

The protocols entered into force simultaneously with the treaty for those protocol signatories that had deposited their instruments of ratification.

Parties (32): Algeria, Benin, Botswana, Burkina Faso, Burundi, Cameroon, Côte d'Ivoire, Equatorial Guinea, Ethiopia, Gabon, Gambia, *Ghana*, Guinea, Kenya, Lesotho, Libya, Madagascar, Malawi, Mali, Mauritania, Mauritius, Mozambique, Nigeria, Rwanda, Senegal, South Africa, Swaziland, Tanzania, Togo, Tunisia, Zambia, Zimbabwe

Note: In addition to the 32 parties as of 1 Jan. 2012, Chad and Guinea-Bissau deposited their instruments of ratification in Jan. 2012.

Signed but not ratified (20): Angola, Cape Verde, Central African Republic, Comoros, Congo (Democratic Republic of the), Congo (Republic of the), Djibouti, Egypt, Eritrea, Liberia, Morocco, Namibia, Niger, Sahrawi Arab Democratic Republic (Western Sahara), Sao Tome and Principe, Seychelles, Sierra Leone, Somalia, Sudan, Uganda

Protocol I, ratifications deposited (4): China, France[1], Russia[2], UK[3]; *signed but not ratified (1):* USA[4]

Protocol II, ratifications deposited (4): China, France, Russia[2], UK[3]; *signed but not ratified (1):* USA[4]

Protocol III, ratifications deposited (1): France

[1] France stated that the protocols did not affect its right to self-defence, as stipulated in Article 51 of the UN Charter. It clarified that its commitment under Article 1 of Protocol I was equivalent to the negative security assurances given by France to non-nuclear weapon states parties to the NPT, as confirmed in its declaration made on 6 Apr. 1995 at the Conference on Disarmament, and as referred to in UN Security Council Resolution 984 of 11 Apr. 1995.

[2] Russia stated that as long as a military base of a nuclear state was located on the islands of the Chagos archipelago these islands could not be regarded as fulfilling the requirements put forward by the treaty for nuclear weapon-free territories. Moreover, since certain states declared that they would consider themselves free from the obligations under the protocols with regard to the mentioned territories, Russia could not consider itself to be bound by the obligations under Protocol I in respect to the same territories. Russia interpreted its obligations under Article 1 of Protocol I as follows: It would not use nuclear weapons against a state party to the treaty, except in the case of invasion or any other armed attack on Russia, its territory, its armed forces or other troops, its allies or a state towards which it had a security commitment, carried out or sustained by a non-nuclear weapon state party to the treaty, in association or alliance with a nuclear weapon state.

[3] The UK stated that it did not accept the inclusion of the British Indian Ocean Territory within the African nuclear weapon-free zone without its consent, and did not accept, by its adherence to Protocols I and II, any legal obligations in respect of that territory. Moreover, it would not be bound by its undertaking under Article 1 of Protocol I in case of an invasion or any other attack on the UK, its dependent territories, its armed forces or other troops, or its allies or a state towards which it had a security commitment, carried out or sustained by a party to the treaty in association or alliance with a nuclear weapon state, or if any party to the treaty was in material breach of its own non-proliferation obligations under the treaty.

[4] The USA stated, with respect to Protocol I, that it would consider an invasion or any other attack on the USA, its territories, its armed forces or other troops, or its allies or on a state towards which it had a security commitment, carried out or sustained by a party to the treaty in association or alliance with a nuclear weapon state, to be incompatible with the treaty party's corresponding obligations. The USA also stated that neither the treaty nor Protocol II would apply to the activities of the UK, the USA or any other state not party to the treaty on the island of Diego Garcia or elsewhere in the British Indian Ocean Territory. Therefore, no change was required in the operations of US armed forces in Diego Garcia and elsewhere in these territories.

Treaty text: African Union, <http://au.int/en/treaties>

Agreement on Sub-Regional Arms Control (Florence Agreement)

Adopted at Florence and entered into force on 14 June 1996

The agreement was negotiated under the auspices of the OSCE in accordance with the mandate in Article IV of Annex 1-B of the 1995 General Framework Agreement for Peace in Bosnia and Herzegovina (Dayton Agreement). It sets numerical ceilings on armaments of the former warring parties. Five categories of heavy conventional weapons are included: battle tanks, armoured combat vehicles, heavy artillery (75 mm and above), combat aircraft and attack helicopters. The limits were reached by 31 October 1997; by that date 6580 weapon items, or 46 per cent of pre-June 1996 holdings, had been destroyed. By 1 January 2010, a further 2650 items had been destroyed voluntarily. The implementation of the agreement is monitored and assisted by the OSCE's Personal Representative of the Chairman-in-Office, the Contact Group (France, Germany, Italy, Russia, the UK and the USA) and supported by other OSCE supporting states.

In 2006 the number of parties fell from five to three with the dissolution of the defence ministries of the sub-national entities of Bosnia and Herzegovina. The remaining parties agreed on six legally binding amendments in March 2006. The number of parties rose to four in 2007, following the independence of Montenegro.

Parties (4): Bosnia and Herzegovina, Croatia, Montenegro, Serbia

Agreement text: OSCE Mission to Bosnia and Herzegovina, <http://www.oscebih.org/documents/11-eng.pdf>

Inter-American Convention Against the Illicit Manufacturing of and Trafficking in Firearms, Ammunition, Explosives, and Other Related Materials (CIFTA)

Adopted at Washington, DC, on 13 November 1997; opened for signature at Washington, DC, on 14 November 1997; entered into force on 1 July 1998; depositary General Secretariat of the Organization of American States

The purpose of the convention is to prevent, combat and eradicate the illicit manufacturing of and trafficking in firearms, ammunition, explosives and other related materials; and to promote and facilitate cooperation and the exchange of information and experience among the parties.

Parties (30): Antigua and Barbuda, Argentina*, Bahamas, Barbados, Belize, Bolivia, Brazil, Chile, Colombia, Costa Rica, Dominica, Dominican Republic, Ecuador, El Salvador, Grenada, Guatemala, Guyana, Haiti, Honduras, Mexico, Nicaragua, Panama, Paraguay, Peru, Saint Kitts and Nevis, Saint Lucia, Suriname, Trinidad and Tobago, Uruguay, Venezuela

   * With reservation.

Signed but not ratified (4): Canada, Jamaica, Saint Vincent and the Grenadines, USA

Convention text: Organization of American States, <http://www.oas.org/juridico/english/treaties/a-63.html>

Inter-American Convention on Transparency in Conventional Weapons Acquisitions

Adopted at Guatemala City on 7 June 1999; entered into force on 21 November 2002; depositary General Secretariat of the Organization of American States

The objective of the convention is to contribute more fully to regional openness and transparency in the acquisition of conventional weapons by exchanging information regarding such acquisitions, for the purpose of promoting confidence among states in the Americas.

Parties (15): Argentina, Brazil, Canada, Chile, *Costa Rica*, Dominican Republic, Ecuador, El Salvador, Guatemala, *Mexico*, Nicaragua, Paraguay, Peru, Uruguay, Venezuela

Signed but not ratified (6): Bolivia, Colombia, Dominica, Haiti, Honduras, USA

Convention text: Organization of American States, <http://www.oas.org/juridico/english/treaties/a-64.html>

ECOWAS Convention on Small Arms and Light Weapons, their Ammunition and Other Related Materials

Adopted by the member states of the Economic Community of West African States (ECOWAS) at Abuja, on 14 June 2006; entered into force on 29 September 2009; depositary President of the ECOWAS Commission

The convention obligates the parties to prevent and combat the excessive and destabilizing accumulation of small arms and light weapons in the 15 ECOWAS member states.

Parties (11): Benin, Burkina Faso, Cape Verde, Ghana, Liberia, Mali, Niger, Nigeria, Senegal, Sierra Leone, Togo

Signed but not ratified (4): Côte d'Ivoire, Gambia, Guinea, Guinea-Bissau

Convention text: ECOWAS Small Arms Control Programme, <http://www.ecosap.ecowas.int/>

Treaty on a Nuclear-Weapon-Free Zone in Central Asia (Treaty of Semipalatinsk)

Signed at Semipalatinsk on 8 September 2006; entered into force on 21 March 2009; depositary Kyrgyz Government

The treaty obligates the parties not to conduct research on, develop, manufacture, stockpile or otherwise acquire, possess or have control over any nuclear weapons or other nuclear explosive device by any means anywhere.

Under a *Protocol* China, France, Russia, the UK and the USA are to undertake not to use or threaten to use a nuclear explosive device against the parties to the treaty. This protocol will enter into force for each party on the date of its deposit of its instrument of ratification.

Parties (5): Kazakhstan, Kyrgyzstan, Tajikistan, Turkmenistan, Uzbekistan

Protocol: no signatures, no parties

Treaty text: United Nations, Office for Disarmament Affairs, Status of Multilateral Arms Regulation and Disarmament Agreements, <http://disarmament.un.org/treatystatus.nsf>

Central African Convention for the Control of Small Arms and Light Weapons, Their Ammunition and All Parts and Components That Can Be Used for Their Manufacture, Repair and Assembly (Kinshasa Convention)

Adopted at Kinshasa on 30 April 2010; opened for signature at Brazzaville on 19 November 2010; not in force; depositary UN Secretary-General

The objectives of the convention are to prevent, combat and eradicate illicit trade and trafficking in small arms and light weapons (SALW) in Central Africa; to strengthen the control in the region of the manufacture, trade, transfer and use of SALW; to combat armed violence and ease the human suffering in the region caused by SALW; and to foster cooperation and confidence among the states parties. The convention will enter into force 30 days after the date of deposit of the sixth instrument of ratification.

Signed but not ratified (11): Angola, *Burundi*, Cameroon, Central African Republic, Chad, Congo (Democratic Republic of the), Congo (Republic of the), *Equatorial Guinea*, Gabon, *Rwanda*, Sao Tome and Principe

Treaty text: United Nations Treaty Collection, <http://treaties.un.org/Pages/CTCTreaties.aspx?id=26>

Vienna Document 2011 on Confidence- and Security-Building Measures

Adopted by the participating states of the Organization for Security and Co-operation in Europe at Vienna on 30 November 2011; entered into force on 1 December 2011

The Vienna Document 2011 builds on the 1986 Stockholm Document on Confidence- and Security-Building Measures (CSBMs) and Disarmament in Europe and previous Vienna Documents (1990, 1992, 1994 and 1999). The Vienna Document 1990 provided for annual exchange of military information, military budget exchange, risk reduction procedures, a communication network and an annual CSBM implementation assessment. The Vienna Document 1992 and the Vienna Document 1994 extended the area of application and introduced new mechanisms and parameters for military activities, defence planning and military contacts. The Vienna Document 1999 introduced regional measures aimed at increasing transparency and confidence in a bilateral, multilateral and regional context and some improvements, in particular regarding the constraining measures.

The Vienna Document 2011 incorporated revisions on such matters as the timing of verification activities and demonstrations of new types of weapon and equipment systems, and established a procedure for updating the Vienna Document every five years.

Document text: Organization for Security and Co-operation in Europe, <http://www.osce.org/fsc/86597>

III. Bilateral treaties

Treaty on the Limitation of Anti-Ballistic Missile Systems (ABM Treaty)

Signed by the USA and the USSR at Moscow on 26 May 1972; entered into force on 3 October 1972; not in force from 13 June 2002

The parties—Russia and the USA—undertook not to build nationwide defences against ballistic missile attack and to limit the development and deployment of permitted strategic missile defences. The treaty prohibited the parties from giving air defence missiles, radars or launchers the technical ability to counter strategic ballistic missiles and from testing them in a strategic ABM mode.

The **1974 Protocol** to the ABM Treaty introduced further numerical restrictions on permitted ballistic missile defences.

In 1997, Belarus, Kazakhstan, Russia, Ukraine and the USA signed a memorandum of understanding designating Belarus, Kazakhstan and Ukraine as parties to the treaty along with Russia as successor states of the USSR and a set of Agreed Statements specifying the demarcation line between strategic missile defences (which are not permitted under the treaty) and non-strategic or theatre missile defences (which are permitted under the treaty). The set of 1997 agreements on anti-missile defence were ratified by Russia in April 2000, but because the USA did not ratify them they did not enter into force. On 13 December 2001 the USA announced its withdrawal from the treaty, which came into effect on 13 June 2002.

Treaty and protocol texts: US Department of State, <http://www.state.gov/t/avc/trty/101888.htm>

Treaty on the Limitation of Underground Nuclear Weapon Tests (Threshold Test-Ban Treaty, TTBT)

Signed by the USA and the USSR at Moscow on 3 July 1974; entered into force on 11 December 1990

The parties—Russia and the USA—undertake not to carry out any underground nuclear weapon test having a yield exceeding 150 kilotons. The 1974 verification protocol was replaced in 1990 with a new protocol.

Treaty and protocol texts: United Nations Treaty Series, vol. 1714 (1993)

Treaty on Underground Nuclear Explosions for Peaceful Purposes (Peaceful Nuclear Explosions Treaty, PNET)

Signed by the USA and the USSR at Moscow and Washington, DC, on 28 May 1976; entered into force on 11 December 1990

The parties—Russia and the USA—undertake not to carry out any individual underground nuclear explosion for peaceful purposes having a yield exceeding 150 kilotons or any group explosion having an aggregate yield exceeding 150 kilotons; and not to carry out any group explosion having an aggregate yield exceeding 1500 kilotons unless the individual explosions in the group could be identified and measured by agreed verification procedures. The 1976 verification protocol was replaced in 1990 with a new protocol.

Treaty text: United Nations Treaty Series, vol. 1714 (1993)

Treaty on the Elimination of Intermediate-Range and Shorter-Range Missiles (INF Treaty)

Signed by the USA and the USSR at Washington, DC, on 8 December 1987; entered into force on 1 June 1988

The treaty obligated the original parties—the USA and the USSR—to destroy all ground-launched ballistic and cruise missiles with a range of 500–5500 kilometre (intermediate-range, 1000–5500 km; and shorter-range, 500–1000 km) and their launchers by 1 June 1991. A total of 2692 missiles were eliminated by May 1991. In 1994 treaty membership was expanded to include Belarus, Kazakhstan and Ukraine. For 10 years after 1 June 1991 on-site inspections were conducted to verify compliance. The use of surveillance satellites for data collection has continued after the end of on-site inspections on 31 May 2001.

Treaty text: US Department of State, <http://www.state.gov/t/avc/trty/102360.htm>

Treaty on the Reduction and Limitation of Strategic Offensive Arms (START I)

Signed by the USA and the USSR at Moscow on 31 July 1991; entered into force on 5 December 1994; expired on 5 December 2009

The treaty obligated the original parties—the USA and the USSR—to make phased reductions in their offensive strategic nuclear forces over a seven-year period. It set numerical limits on deployed strategic nuclear delivery vehicles (SNDVs)—intercontinental ballistic missiles (ICBMs), submarine-launched ballistic missiles (SLBMs) and heavy bombers—and the nuclear warheads they carry. In the Protocol to Facilitate the Implementation of START (**1992 Lisbon Protocol**), which entered into force on 5 December 1994, Belarus, Kazakhstan and Ukraine also assumed the obligations of the former USSR under the treaty.

A follow-on treaty, New START, entered into force on 5 February 2011.

Treaty and protocol texts: US Department of State, <http://www.state.gov/t/avc/trty/146007. htm>

Treaty on Further Reduction and Limitation of Strategic Offensive Arms (START II)

Signed by Russia and the USA at Moscow on 3 January 1993; not in force

The treaty obligated the parties to eliminate their MIRVed ICBMs and reduce the number of their deployed strategic nuclear warheads to no more than 3000–3500 each (of which no more than 1750 may be deployed on SLBMs) by 1 January 2003. On 26 September 1997 the two parties signed a *Protocol* to the treaty providing for the extension until the end of 2007 of the period of implementation of the treaty.

Note: START II was ratified by the US Senate and the Russian Parliament, but the two parties never exchanged the instruments of ratification. The treaty thus never entered into force. On 14 June 2002, as a response to the taking effect on 13 June of the USA's withdrawal from the ABM Treaty, Russia declared that it would no longer be bound by START II.

Treaty and protocol texts: US Department of State, <http://www.state.gov/t/avc/trty/102887. htm>

Treaty on Strategic Offensive Reductions (SORT Treaty, Moscow Treaty)

Signed by Russia and the USA at Moscow on 24 May 2002; entered into force on 1 June 2003; not in force from 5 February 2011

The treaty obligated the parties to reduce the number of their operationally deployed strategic nuclear warheads so that the aggregate numbers did not exceed 1700–2200 for each party by 31 December 2012. The treaty was superseded by New START on 5 February 2011.

Treaty text: US Department of State, <http://www.state.gov/t/avc/trty/127129.htm>

Treaty on Measures for the Further Reduction and Limitation of Strategic Offensive Arms (New START, Prague Treaty)

Signed by Russia and the USA at Prague on 8 April 2010; entered into force on 5 February 2011

The treaty obligates the parties—Russia and the USA—to each reduce their number of (*a*) deployed ICBMs, SLBMs and heavy bombers to 700; (*b*) warheads on deployed ICBMs and SLBMs and warheads counted for deployed heavy bombers to 1550; and (*c*) deployed and non-deployed ICBM launchers, SLBM launchers and heavy bombers to 800. The reductions must be achieved by 5 February 2018; a Bilateral Consultative Commission will resolve questions about compliance and other implementation issues. A protocol to the treaty contains verifications mechanisms.

The treaty follows on from START I and supersedes SORT. It will remain in force for 10 years unless superseded earlier by a subsequent agreement.

Treaty and protocol texts: US Department of State, <http://www.state.gov/t/avc/newstart/c44126.htm>

Annex B. International security cooperation bodies

NENNE BODELL

This annex describes the main international organizations, intergovernmental bodies, treaty-implementing bodies and transfer control regimes whose aims include the promotion of security, stability, peace or arms control and lists their members or participants as of 1 January 2012. The bodies are divided into three categories: those with a global focus or membership (section I), those with a regional focus or membership (section II) and strategic trade control regimes (section III).

The member states of the United Nations and organs within the UN system are listed first, followed by all other bodies in alphabetical order. Not all members or participants of these bodies are UN member states. States that joined or first participated in the body during 2011 are shown in italics. The address of an Internet site with information about each organization is provided where available. On the arms control and disarmament agreements mentioned here, see annex A.

I. Bodies with a global focus or membership

United Nations (UN)

The UN, the world intergovernmental organization, was founded in 1945 through the adoption of its Charter. Its headquarters are in New York, USA. The six principal UN organs are the General Assembly, the Security Council, the Economic and Social Council (ECOSOC), the Trusteeship Council (which suspended operation in 1994), the International Court of Justice (ICJ) and the secretariat.

The General Assembly has six main committees. The First Committee (Disarmament and International Security Committee) deals with disarmament and related international security questions; the Fourth Committee (Special Political and Decolonization Committee) deals with a variety of subjects including decolonization, Palestinian refugees and human rights, peacekeeping, mine action, outer space, public information, atomic radiation and the University for Peace.

The UN Office for Disarmament Affairs (UNODA), a department of the UN Secretariat, promotes disarmament of nuclear, biological, chemical and conventional weapons. The UN also has a large number of specialized agencies and other autonomous bodies.

UN member states (193) and year of membership

Afghanistan, 1946
Albania, 1955
Algeria, 1962
Andorra, 1993
Angola, 1976
Antigua and Barbuda, 1981
Argentina, 1945
Armenia, 1992
Australia, 1945
Austria, 1955
Azerbaijan, 1992
Bahamas, 1973
Bahrain, 1971
Bangladesh, 1974
Barbados, 1966
Belarus, 1945
Belgium, 1945
Belize, 1981
Benin, 1960
Bhutan, 1971
Bolivia, 1945
Bosnia and Herzegovina, 1992
Botswana, 1966
Brazil, 1945
Brunei Darussalam, 1984
Bulgaria, 1955
Burkina Faso, 1960
Burundi, 1962
Cambodia, 1955
Cameroon, 1960
Canada, 1945
Cape Verde, 1975
Central African Republic, 1960
Chad, 1960
Chile, 1945
China, 1945
Colombia, 1945
Comoros, 1975
Congo, Democratic Republic of the, 1960
Congo, Republic of the, 1960
Costa Rica, 1945
Côte d'Ivoire, 1960
Croatia, 1992
Cuba, 1945
Cyprus, 1960
Czech Republic, 1993
Denmark, 1945
Djibouti, 1977
Dominica, 1978
Dominican Republic, 1945

Ecuador, 1945
Egypt, 1945
El Salvador, 1945
Equatorial Guinea, 1968
Eritrea, 1993
Estonia, 1991
Ethiopia, 1945
Fiji, 1970
Finland, 1955
France, 1945
Gabon, 1960
Gambia, 1965
Georgia, 1992
Germany, 1973
Ghana, 1957
Greece, 1945
Grenada, 1974
Guatemala, 1945
Guinea, 1958
Guinea-Bissau, 1974
Guyana, 1966
Haiti, 1945
Honduras, 1945
Hungary, 1955
Iceland, 1946
India, 1945
Indonesia, 1950
Iran, 1945
Iraq, 1945
Ireland, 1955
Israel, 1949
Italy, 1955
Jamaica, 1962
Japan, 1956
Jordan, 1955
Kazakhstan, 1992
Kenya, 1963
Kiribati, 1999
Korea, Democratic People's Republic of (North Korea), 1991
Korea, Republic of (South Korea), 1991
Kuwait, 1963
Kyrgyzstan, 1992
Laos, 1955
Latvia, 1991
Lebanon, 1945
Lesotho, 1966
Liberia, 1945
Libya, 1955
Liechtenstein, 1990

Lithuania, 1991
Luxembourg, 1945
Macedonia, Former Yugoslav Republic of, 1993
Madagascar, 1960
Malawi, 1964
Malaysia, 1957
Maldives, 1965
Mali, 1960
Malta, 1964
Marshall Islands, 1991
Mauritania, 1961
Mauritius, 1968
Mexico, 1945
Micronesia, 1991
Moldova, 1992
Monaco, 1993
Mongolia, 1961
Montenegro, 2006
Morocco, 1956
Mozambique, 1975
Myanmar, 1948
Namibia, 1990
Nauru, 1999
Nepal, 1955
Netherlands, 1945
New Zealand, 1945
Nicaragua, 1945
Niger, 1960
Nigeria, 1960
Norway, 1945
Oman, 1971
Pakistan, 1947
Palau, 1994
Panama, 1945
Papua New Guinea, 1975
Paraguay, 1945
Peru, 1945
Philippines, 1945
Poland, 1945
Portugal, 1955
Qatar, 1971
Romania, 1955
Russia, 1945
Rwanda, 1962
Saint Kitts and Nevis, 1983
Saint Lucia, 1979
Saint Vincent and the Grenadines, 1980
Samoa, 1976
San Marino, 1992
Sao Tome and Principe, 1975

Saudi Arabia, 1945
Senegal, 1960
Serbia, 2000
Seychelles, 1976
Sierra Leone, 1961
Singapore, 1965
Slovakia, 1993
Slovenia, 1992
Solomon Islands, 1978
Somalia, 1960
South Africa, 1945
South Sudan, 2011
Spain, 1955
Sri Lanka, 1955
Sudan, 1956

Suriname, 1975
Swaziland, 1968
Sweden, 1946
Switzerland, 2002
Syria, 1945
Tajikistan, 1992
Tanzania, 1961
Thailand, 1946
Timor-Leste, 2002
Togo, 1960
Tonga, 1999
Trinidad and Tobago, 1962
Tunisia, 1956
Turkey, 1945
Turkmenistan, 1992

Tuvalu, 2000
Uganda, 1962
UK, 1945
Ukraine, 1945
United Arab Emirates, 1971
Uruguay, 1945
USA, 1945
Uzbekistan, 1992
Vanuatu, 1981
Venezuela, 1945
Viet Nam, 1977
Yemen, 1947
Zambia, 1964
Zimbabwe, 1980

Website: <http://www.un.org/>

UN Security Council

Permanent members (the P5): China, France, Russia, UK, USA

Non-permanent members (10): Azerbaijan**, Colombia*, Germany*, *Guatemala**, India*, Morocco**, Pakistan**, Portugal*, South Africa*, *Togo***

Note: Non-permanent members are elected by the UN General Assembly for two-year terms.
    * Member in 2011–12.
    ** Member in 2012–13.

Website: <http://www.un.org/sc/>

Conference on Disarmament (CD)

The CD is a multilateral arms control negotiating body that is intended to be the single multilateral disarmament negotiating forum of the international community. It has been enlarged and renamed several times since 1960. It is not a UN body but reports to the UN General Assembly. It is based in Geneva, Switzerland.

Members (65): Algeria, Argentina, Australia, Austria, Bangladesh, Belarus, Belgium, Brazil, Bulgaria, Cameroon, Canada, Chile, China, Colombia, Congo (Democratic Republic of the), Cuba, Ecuador, Egypt, Ethiopia, Finland, France, Germany, Hungary, India, Indonesia, Iran, Iraq, Ireland, Israel, Italy, Japan, Kazakhstan, Kenya, Korea (North), Korea (South), Malaysia, Mexico, Mongolia, Morocco, Myanmar, Netherlands, New Zealand, Nigeria, Norway, Pakistan, Peru, Poland, Romania, Russia, Senegal, Slovakia, South Africa, Spain, Sri Lanka, Sweden, Switzerland, Syria, Tunisia, Turkey, UK, Ukraine, USA, Venezuela, Viet Nam, Zimbabwe

Website: <http://www.unog.ch/disarmament/>

International Atomic Energy Agency (IAEA)

The IAEA is an intergovernmental organization within the UN system. It is endowed by its Statute, which entered into force in 1957, to promote the peaceful uses of atomic energy and ensure that nuclear activities are not used to further any military purpose. Under the 1968 Non-Proliferation Treaty and the nuclear weapon-free zone treaties, non-nuclear weapon states must accept IAEA nuclear safeguards to demonstrate the fulfilment of their obligation not to manufacture nuclear weapons. Its headquarters are in Vienna, Austria.

Members (152): Afghanistan, Albania, Algeria, Angola, Argentina, Armenia, Australia, Austria, Azerbaijan, Bahrain, Bangladesh, Belarus, Belgium, Belize, Benin, Bolivia, Bosnia and Herzegovina, Botswana, Brazil, Bulgaria, Burkina Faso, Burundi, Cambodia, Cameroon, Canada, Central African Republic, Chad, Chile, China, Colombia, Congo (Democratic Republic of the), Congo (Republic of the), Costa Rica, Côte d'Ivoire, Croatia, Cuba, Cyprus, Czech Republic, Denmark, Dominican Republic, Ecuador, Egypt, El Salvador, Eritrea, Estonia, Ethiopia, Finland, France, Gabon, Georgia, Germany, Ghana, Greece, Guatemala, Haiti, Holy See, Honduras, Hungary, Iceland, India, Indonesia, Iran, Iraq, Ireland, Israel, Italy, Jamaica, Japan, Jordan, Kazakhstan, Kenya, Korea (South), Kuwait, Kyrgyzstan, *Laos*, Latvia, Lebanon, Lesotho, Liberia, Libya, Liechtenstein, Lithuania, Luxembourg, Macedonia (Former Yugoslav Republic of), Madagascar, Malawi, Malaysia, Mali, Malta, Marshall Islands, Mauritania, Mauritius, Mexico, Moldova, Monaco, Mongolia, Montenegro, Morocco, Mozambique, Myanmar, Namibia, Nepal, Netherlands, New Zealand, Nicaragua, Niger, Nigeria, Norway, Oman, Pakistan, Palau, Panama, Paraguay, Peru, Philippines, Poland, Portugal, Qatar, Romania, Russia, Saudi Arabia, Senegal, Serbia, Seychelles, Sierra Leone, Singapore, Slovakia, Slovenia, South Africa, Spain, Sri Lanka, Sudan, Sweden, Switzerland, Syria, Tajikistan, Tanzania, Thailand, Tunisia, Turkey, Uganda, UK, Ukraine, United Arab Emirates, Uruguay, USA, Uzbekistan, Venezuela, Viet Nam, Yemen, Zambia, Zimbabwe

Notes: North Korea was a member of the IAEA until June 1994. In addition to the above-named states, Cape Verde, Dominica, Papua New Guinea, Rwanda, Togo and Tonga have had their membership approved by the IAEA General Conference; it will take effect once the state deposits the necessary legal instruments with the IAEA.

Website: <http://www.iaea.org/>

International Court of Justice (ICJ)

The ICJ was established in 1945 by the UN Charter and is the principal judicial organ of the UN. The court's role is to settle legal disputes submitted to it by states and to give advisory opinions on legal questions referred to it by authorized UN organs and specialized agencies. The Court is composed of 15 judges, who are elected for terms of office of nine years by the UN General Assembly and the Security Council. Its seat is at The Hague, the Netherlands.

Website: <http://www.icj-cij.org/>

Bilateral Consultative Commission (BCC)

The BCC is a forum established under the 2010 Russian–US New START treaty to discuss issues related to the treaty's implementation. It replaced the Joint Compliance and Inspection Commission (JCIC) of the 1991 START treaty. The

BCC is required to meet at least twice each year in Geneva, Switzerland, unless the parties agree otherwise. Its work is confidential.

Commonwealth of Nations

Established in its current form in 1949, the Commonwealth is an organization of developed and developing countries whose aim is to advance democracy, human rights, and sustainable economic and social development within its member states and beyond. Its secretariat is in London, UK.

Members (54): Antigua and Barbuda, Australia, Bahamas, Bangladesh, Barbados, Belize, Botswana, Brunei Darussalam, Cameroon, Canada, Cyprus, Dominica, Fiji*, Gambia, Ghana, Grenada, Guyana, India, Jamaica, Kenya, Kiribati, Lesotho, Malawi, Malaysia, Maldives, Malta, Mauritius, Mozambique, Namibia, Nauru, New Zealand, Nigeria, Pakistan, Papua New Guinea, Rwanda, Saint Kitts and Nevis, Saint Lucia, Saint Vincent and the Grenadines, Samoa, Seychelles, Sierra Leone, Singapore, Solomon Islands, South Africa, Sri Lanka, Swaziland, Tanzania, Tonga, Trinidad and Tobago, Tuvalu, Uganda, UK, Vanuatu, Zambia

* Fiji's membership of the Commonwealth was suspended on 1 Sep. 2009.

Website: <http://www.thecommonwealth.org/>

Comprehensive Nuclear-Test-Ban Treaty Organization (CTBTO)

The CTBTO will become operational when the 1996 Comprehensive Nuclear-Test-Ban Treaty (CTBT) has entered into force. It will resolve questions of compliance with the treaty and act as a forum for consultation and cooperation among the states parties. A Preparatory Commission was established to prepare for the work of the CTBTO, in particular by establishing the International Monitoring System, consisting of seismic, hydro-acoustic, infrasound and radionuclide stations from which data is transmitted to the CTBTO International Data Centre. Its seat is in Vienna, Austria.

Signatories to the CTBT (182): See annex A

Website: <http://www.ctbto.org/>

Group of Eight (G8)

The G8 is a group of (originally seven) leading industrialized countries that have met informally, at the level of head of state or government, since the 1970s. The G8 Global Partnership against the Spread of Weapons and Materials of Mass Destruction was launched in 2002 to address non-proliferation, disarmament, counterterrorism and nuclear safety issues. It was extended for an unspecified period in May 2011.

Members (8): Canada, France, Germany, Italy, Japan, Russia, UK, USA

Website: <http://www.g8.gc.ca/>

International Criminal Court (ICC)

The ICC is an independent, permanent international criminal court dealing with questions of genocide, war crimes and crimes against humanity. The court's statute was adopted in Rome in 1998 and entered into force on 1 July 2002. Its seat is at The Hague, the Netherlands.

Parties (120): Afghanistan, Albania, Andorra, Antigua and Barbuda, Argentina, Australia, Austria, Bangladesh, Barbados, Belgium, Belize, Benin, Bolivia, Bosnia and Herzegovina, Botswana, Brazil, Bulgaria, Burkina Faso, Burundi, Cambodia, Canada, *Cape Verde*, Central African Republic, Chad, Chile, Colombia, Comoros, Congo (Democratic Republic of the), Congo (Republic of the), Cook Islands, Costa Rica, Croatia, Cyprus, Czech Republic, Denmark, Djibouti, Dominica, Dominican Republic, Ecuador, Estonia, Fiji, Finland, France, Gabon, Gambia, Georgia, Germany, Ghana, Greece, *Grenada*, Guinea, Guyana, Honduras, Hungary, Iceland, Ireland, Italy, Japan, Jordan, Kenya, Korea (South), Latvia, Lesotho, Liberia, Liechtenstein, Lithuania, Luxembourg, Macedonia (Former Yugoslav Republic of), Madagascar, Malawi, *Maldives*, Mali, Malta, Marshall Islands, Mauritius, Mexico, Moldova, Mongolia, Montenegro, Namibia, Nauru, Netherlands, New Zealand, Niger, Nigeria, Norway, Panama, Paraguay, Peru, *Philippines*, Poland, Portugal, Romania, Saint Kitts and Nevis, Saint Lucia, Saint Vincent and the Grenadines, Samoa, San Marino, Senegal, Serbia, Seychelles, Sierra Leone, Slovakia, Slovenia, South Africa, Spain, Suriname, Sweden, Switzerland, Tajikistan, Tanzania, Timor-Leste, Trinidad and Tobago, *Tunisia*, Uganda, UK, Uruguay, *Vanuatu*, Venezuela, Zambia

Website: <http://www.icc-cpi.int/>

Non-Aligned Movement (NAM)

NAM was established in 1961 as a forum for consultations and coordination of positions in the United Nations on political, economic and arms control issues among non-aligned states.

Members (120): Afghanistan, Algeria, Angola, Antigua and Barbuda, *Azerbaijan*, Bahamas, Bahrain, Bangladesh, Barbados, Belarus, Belize, Benin, Bhutan, Bolivia, Botswana, Brunei Darussalam, Burkina Faso, Burundi, Cambodia, Cameroon, Cape Verde, Central African Republic, Chad, Chile, Colombia, Comoros, Congo (Democratic Republic of the), Congo (Republic of the), Côte d'Ivoire, Cuba, Djibouti, Dominica, Dominican Republic, Ecuador, Egypt, Equatorial Guinea, Eritrea, Ethiopia, *Fiji*, Gabon, Gambia, Ghana, Grenada, Guatemala, Guinea, Guinea-Bissau, Guyana, Haiti, Honduras, India, Indonesia, Iran, Iraq, Jamaica, Jordan, Kenya, Korea (North), Kuwait, Laos, Lebanon, Lesotho, Liberia, Libya, Madagascar, Malawi, Malaysia, Maldives, Mali, Mauritania, Mauritius, Mongolia, Morocco, Mozambique, Myanmar, Namibia, Nepal, Nicaragua, Niger, Nigeria, Oman, Pakistan, Palestine Liberation Organization, Panama, Papua New Guinea, Peru, Philippines, Qatar, Rwanda, Saint Kitts and Nevis, Saint Lucia, Saint Vincent and the Grenadines, Sao Tome and Principe, Saudi Arabia, Senegal, Seychelles, Sierra Leone, Singapore, Somalia, South Africa, Sri Lanka, Sudan, Suriname, Swaziland, Syria, Tanzania, Thailand, Timor-Leste, Togo, Trinidad and Tobago, Tunisia, Turkmenistan, Uganda, United Arab Emirates, Uzbekistan, Vanuatu, Venezuela, Viet Nam, Yemen, Zambia, Zimbabwe

Website: <http://www.namegypt.org/>

Organisation for Economic Co-operation and Development (OECD)

Established in 1961, the OECD's objectives are to promote economic and social welfare by coordinating policies among the member states. Its headquarters are in Paris, France.

Members (34): Australia, Austria, Belgium, Canada, Chile, Czech Republic, Denmark, Estonia, Finland, France, Germany, Greece, Hungary, Iceland, Ireland, Israel, Italy, Japan, Korea (South), Luxembourg, Mexico, Netherlands, New Zealand, Norway, Poland, Portugal, Slovakia, Slovenia, Spain, Sweden, Switzerland, Turkey, UK, USA

Website: <http://www.oecd.org/>

Organisation for the Prohibition of Chemical Weapons (OPCW)

The OPCW was established by the 1993 Chemical Weapons Convention to oversee implementation of the convention and resolve questions of compliance. Its seat is in The Hague, the Netherlands.

Parties to the Chemical Weapons Convention (188): See annex A

Website: <http://www.opcw.org/>

Organization of the Islamic Conference (OIC)

The OIC was established in 1969 by Islamic states to promote cooperation among the members and to support peace, security and the struggle of the people of Palestine and all Muslim people. Its secretariat is in Jeddah, Saudi Arabia.

Members (57): Afghanistan, Albania, Algeria, Azerbaijan, Bahrain, Bangladesh, Benin, Brunei Darussalam, Burkina Faso, Cameroon, Chad, Comoros, Côte d'Ivoire, Djibouti, Egypt, Gabon, Gambia, Guinea, Guinea-Bissau, Guyana, Indonesia, Iran, Iraq, Jordan, Kazakhstan, Kuwait, Kyrgyzstan, Lebanon, Libya, Malaysia, Maldives, Mali, Mauritania, Morocco, Mozambique, Niger, Nigeria, Oman, Pakistan, Palestine, Qatar, Saudi Arabia, Senegal, Sierra Leone, Somalia, Sudan, Suriname, Syria, Tajikistan, Togo, Tunisia, Turkey, Turkmenistan, Uganda, United Arab Emirates, Uzbekistan, Yemen

Website: <http://www.oic-oci.org/>

Special Verification Commission (SVC)

The Commission was established by the 1987 Treaty on the Elimination of Intermediate-Range and Shorter-Range Missiles (INF Treaty) as a forum to resolve compliance questions and measures necessary to improve the viability and effectiveness of the treaty.

Parties to the INF Treaty (5): See annex A

II. Bodies with a regional focus or membership

African Union (AU)

The AU was formally established in 2001 when the Constitutive Act of the African Union entered into force. In 2002 it replaced the Organization for African Unity. Membership is open to all African states. The AU promotes unity, security and conflict resolution, democracy, human rights, and political, social and economic integration in Africa. The Peace and Security Council (PSC) is a standing decision-making organ for the prevention, management and resolution of conflicts. The AU's headquarters are in Addis Ababa, Ethiopia.

Members (54): Algeria, Angola, Benin, Botswana, Burkina Faso, Burundi, Cameroon, Cape Verde, Central African Republic, Chad, Comoros, Congo (Democratic Republic of the), Congo (Republic of the), Côte d'Ivoire, Djibouti, Egypt, Equatorial Guinea, Eritrea, Ethiopia, Gabon, Gambia, Ghana, Guinea, Guinea-Bissau, Kenya, Lesotho, Liberia, Libya, Madagascar*, Malawi, Mali, Mauritania, Mauritius, Mozambique, Namibia, Niger, Nigeria, Rwanda, Western Sahara (Sahrawi Arab Democratic Republic, SADR), Sao Tome and Principe, Senegal, Seychelles, Sierra Leone, Somalia, South Africa, *South Sudan*, Sudan, Swaziland, Tanzania, Togo, Tunisia, Uganda, Zambia, Zimbabwe

* Madagascar was suspended from the AU in Mar. 2009

Website: <http://www.africa-union.org/>

Asia–Pacific Economic Cooperation (APEC)

APEC was established in 1989 to enhance open trade and economic prosperity in the Asia–Pacific region. Security and political issues, including combating terrorism, non-proliferation of weapons of mass destruction and effective transfer control systems, have been increasingly discussed since the mid-1990s. Its seat is in Singapore.

Member economies (21): Australia, Brunei Darussalam, Canada, Chile, China, Hong Kong, Indonesia, Japan, Korea (South), Malaysia, Mexico, New Zealand, Papua New Guinea, Peru, Philippines, Russia, Singapore, Taiwan, Thailand, USA, Viet Nam

Website: <http://www.apec.org/>

Association of Southeast Asian Nations (ASEAN)

ASEAN was established in 1967 to promote economic, social and cultural development as well as regional peace and security in South East Asia. The seat of the secretariat is in Jakarta, Indonesia.

Members (10): Brunei Darussalam, Cambodia, Indonesia, Laos, Malaysia, Myanmar, Philippines, Singapore, Thailand, Viet Nam

Website: <http://www.aseansec.org/>

ASEAN Regional Forum (ARF)

The ARF was established in 1994 to address security issues.

Participants (27): The ASEAN member states and Australia, Bangladesh, Canada, China, European Union, India, Japan, Korea (North), Korea (South), Mongolia, New Zealand, Pakistan, Papua New Guinea, Russia, Sri Lanka, Timor-Leste, USA

Website: <http://aseanregionalforum.asean.org/>

ASEAN Plus Three (APT)

The APT cooperation began in 1997, in the wake of the Asian financial crisis, and was institutionalized in 1999. It aims to foster economic, political and security cooperation and financial stability among its participants.

Participants (13): The ASEAN member states and China, Japan, Korea (South)

Website: <http://www.aseansec.org/20182.htm>

East Asia Summit (EAS)

The East Asia Summit started in 2005 as a regional forum for dialogue on strategic, political and economic issues with the aim of promoting peace, stability and economic prosperity in East Asia. The annual meetings are held in connection with the ASEAN summits.

Participants (18): The ASEAN member states and Australia, China, India, Japan, Korea (South), New Zealand, *Russia, USA*

Website: <http://www.dfat.gov.au/asean/eas/>

Collective Security Treaty Organization (CSTO)

The CSTO was formally established in 2002–2003 by six signatories of the 1992 Collective Security Treaty. It aims to promote cooperation among its members. An objective is to provide a more efficient response to strategic problems such as terrorism and narcotics trafficking. Its seat is in Moscow, Russia.

Members (7): Armenia, Belarus, Kazakhstan, Kyrgyzstan, Russia, Tajikistan, Uzbekistan

Website: <http://www.dkb.gov.ru/>

Commonwealth of Independent States (CIS)

The CIS was established in 1991 as a framework for multilateral cooperation among former Soviet republics. Its headquarters are in Minsk, Belarus.

Members (11): Armenia, Azerbaijan, Belarus, Kazakhstan, Kyrgyzstan, Moldova, Russia, Tajikistan, Turkmenistan, Ukraine, Uzbekistan

Website: <http://www.cis.minsk.by/>

Communauté Économiques d'États de l'Afrique Centrale (CEEAC, Economic Community of Central African States, ECCAS)

CEEAC was established in 1983 to promote political dialogue, create a customs union and establish common policies in Central Africa. Its secretariat is in Libreville, Gabon. The Council for Peace and Security in Central Africa (COPAX) is a mechanism for promoting joint political and military strategies for conflict prevention, management and resolution in Central Africa.

Members (10): Angola, Burundi, Cameroon, Central African Republic, Chad, Congo (Democratic Republic of the), Congo (Republic of the), Equatorial Guinea, Gabon, Sao Tome and Principe

Website: <http://www.ceeac-eccas.org/>

Conference on Interaction and Confidence-building Measures in Asia (CICA)

Initiated in 1992, CICA was established by the 1999 Declaration on the Principles Guiding Relations among the CICA Member States, as a forum to enhance security cooperation and confidence-building measures among the member states. It also promotes economic, social and cultural cooperation. Its secretariat is in Almaty, Kazahkstan.

Members (24): Afghanistan, Azerbaijan, Bahrain, *Cambodia*, China, Egypt, India, Iran, Iraq, Israel, Jordan, Kazakhstan, Korea (South), Kyrgyzstan, Mongolia, Pakistan, Palestine, Russia, Tajikistan, Thailand, Turkey, United Arab Emirates, Uzbekistan, Viet Nam

Website: <http://www.s-cica.org/>

Council of Europe (COE)

Established in 1949, the Council is open to membership of all European states that accept the principle of the rule of law and guarantee their citizens' human rights and fundamental freedoms. Its seat is in Strasbourg, France. Among its organs are the European Court of Human Rights and the Council of Europe Development Bank.

Members (47): Albania, Andorra, Armenia, Austria, Azerbaijan, Belgium, Bosnia and Herzegovina, Bulgaria, Croatia, Cyprus, Czech Republic, Denmark, Estonia, Finland, France, Georgia, Germany, Greece, Hungary, Iceland, Ireland, Italy, Latvia, Liechtenstein, Lithuania, Luxembourg, Macedonia (Former Yugoslav Republic of), Malta, Moldova, Monaco, Montenegro, Netherlands, Norway, Poland, Portugal, Romania, Russia, San Marino, Serbia, Slovakia, Slovenia, Spain, Sweden, Switzerland, Turkey, UK, Ukraine

Website: <http://www.coe.int/>

Council of the Baltic Sea States (CBSS)

The CBSS was established in 1992 as a regional intergovernmental organization for cooperation among the states of the Baltic Sea region. Its secretariat is in Stockholm, Sweden.

Members (12): Denmark, Estonia, European Commission, Finland, Germany, Iceland, Latvia, Lithuania, Norway, Poland, Russia, Sweden

Website: <http://www.cbss.org/>

Economic Community of West African States (ECOWAS)

ECOWAS was established in 1975 to promote trade and cooperation and contribute to development in West Africa. In 1981 it adopted the Protocol on Mutual Assistance in Defence Matters. Its executive secretariat is in Lagos, Nigeria.

Members (15): Benin, Burkina Faso, Cape Verde, Côte d'Ivoire*, Gambia, Ghana, Guinea, Guinea-Bissau, Liberia, Mali, Niger, Nigeria, Senegal, Sierra Leone, Togo

* Côte d'Ivoire was suspended from participation in the activities of ECOWAS on 7 Dec. 2010.

Website: <http://www.ecowas.int/>

European Union (EU)

The EU is an organization of European states that cooperate in a wide field, including a single market with free movement of people, goods, services and capital, a common currency for some members, and a Common Foreign and Security Policy (CFSP). Its main bodies are the European Council, the Council of the European Union, the European Commission and the European Parliament. The CFSP and the Common Security and Defence Policy (CSDP) are coordinated by the High Representative of the Union for Foreign Affairs and Security Policy. The 2007 Treaty of Lisbon, which modernizes the way in which the EU functions, entered into force on 1 December 2009. The EU's seat is in Brussels, Belgium.

Members (27): Austria, Belgium, Bulgaria, Cyprus, Czech Republic, Denmark, Estonia, Finland, France, Germany, Greece, Hungary, Ireland, Italy, Latvia, Lithuania, Luxembourg, Malta, Netherlands, Poland, Portugal, Romania, Slovakia, Slovenia, Spain, Sweden, UK

Website: <http://europa.eu/>

European Atomic Energy Community (Euratom, or EAEC)

Euratom was created by the 1957 Treaty Establishing the European Atomic Energy Community (Euratom Treaty) to promote the development of nuclear energy for peaceful purposes and to administer the multinational regional safeguards system covering the EU member states. The Euratom Supply Agency, located in Luxembourg, has the task of ensuring a regular and equitable supply of ores, source materials and special fissile materials to EU member states.

Members (27): The EU member states

Website: <http://ec.europa.eu/euratom/>

European Defence Agency (EDA)

The EDA is an agency of the EU, under the direction of the Council. It was established in 2004 to help develop European defence capabilities, to promote European armaments cooperation and to work for a strong European defence technological and industrial base. The EDA's decision-making body is the Steering Board, composed of the defence ministers of the participating member states and the EU's High Representative for Foreign Affairs and Security Policy (as head of the agency). The EDA is located in Brussels, Belgium.

Participating member states (26): Austria, Belgium, Bulgaria, Cyprus, Czech Republic, Estonia, Finland, France, Germany, Greece, Hungary, Ireland, Italy, Latvia, Lithuania, Luxembourg, Malta, Netherlands, Poland, Portugal, Romania, Slovakia, Slovenia, Spain, Sweden, UK

Website: <http://eda.europa.eu/>

Gulf Cooperation Council (GCC)

Formally called the Cooperation Council for the Arab States of the Gulf, the GCC was created in 1981 to promote regional integration in such areas as economy, finance, trade, administration and legislation and to foster scientific and technical progress. The members also cooperate in areas of foreign policy and military and security matters. The Supreme Council is the highest GCC authority. Its headquarters are in Riyadh, Saudi Arabia

Members (6): Bahrain, Kuwait, Oman, Qatar, Saudi Arabia, United Arab Emirates

Website: <http://www.gcc-sg.org/>

Intergovernmental Authority on Development (IGAD)

Initiated in 1986 as the Intergovernmental Authority on Drought and Development, IGAD was formally established in 1996 to promote peace and stability in the Horn of Africa and to create mechanisms for conflict prevention, management and resolution. Its secretariat is in Djibouti.

Members (7): Djibouti, Ethiopia, Kenya, Somalia, *South Sudan*, Sudan, Uganda

Note: Eritrea suspended its membership in 2007 in response to IGAD's support of Ethiopia's intervention in Somalia. Eritrea attempted to reactivate its membership in 2011, but this was not accepted by the other members.

Website: <http://www.igad.int/>

International Conference on the Great Lakes Region (ICGLR)

The ICGLR, which was initiated in 2004, works to promote peace and security, political and social stability, and growth and development in the Great Lakes region. In 2006 the member states adopted the Pact on Peace, Stability and Development in the Great Lakes Region, which entered into force in 2008. The executive secretariat of the ICGLR is in Bujumbura, Burundi.

Members (11): Angola, Burundi, Central African Republic, Congo (Republic of the), Congo (Democratic Republic of the), Kenya, Uganda, Rwanda, Sudan, Tanzania, Zambia

Website: <http://www.icglr.org/>

Joint Consultative Group (JCG)

The JCG was established by the 1990 Treaty on Conventional Armed Forces in Europe (CFE Treaty) to promote the objectives and implementation of the treaty by reconciling ambiguities of interpretation and implementation. Its seat is in Vienna, Austria.

Parties to the CFE Treaty (30): See annex A

Website: <http://www.osce.org/jcg/>

League of Arab States

Also known as the Arab League, it was established in 1945. Its principal objective is to form closer union among Arab states and foster political and economic cooperation. An agreement for collective defence and economic cooperation among the members was signed in 1950. Its permanent headquarters are in Cairo, Egypt.

Members (22): Algeria, Bahrain, Comoros, Djibouti, Egypt, Iraq, Jordan, Kuwait, Lebanon, Libya, Mauritania, Morocco, Oman, Palestine, Qatar, Saudi Arabia, Somalia, Sudan, Syria*, Tunisia, United Arab Emirates, Yemen

* Syria was suspended from the organization as of 16 Nov. 2011.

Website: <http://www.arableagueonline.org/>

North Atlantic Treaty Organization (NATO)

NATO was established in 1949 by the North Atlantic Treaty (Washington Treaty) as a Western defence alliance. Article 5 of the treaty defines the members' commitment to respond to an armed attack against any party to the treaty. Its headquarters are in Brussels, Belgium.

Members (28): Albania, Belgium, Bulgaria, Canada, Croatia, Czech Republic, Denmark, Estonia, France, Germany, Greece, Hungary, Iceland, Italy, Latvia, Lithuania, Luxembourg, Netherlands, Norway, Poland, Portugal, Romania, Slovakia, Slovenia, Spain, Turkey, UK, USA

Website: <http://www.nato.int/>

Euro-Atlantic Partnership Council (EAPC)

The EAPC brings together NATO and its Partnership for Peace (PFP) partners for dialogue and consultation. It is the overall political framework for the bilateral PFP programme.

Members (50): The NATO member states and Armenia, Austria, Azerbaijan, Belarus, Bosnia and Herzegovina, Finland, Georgia, Ireland, Kazakhstan, Kyrgyzstan,

Macedonia (Former Yugoslav Republic of), Malta, Moldova, Montenegro, Russia, Serbia, Sweden, Switzerland, Tajikistan, Turkmenistan, Ukraine, Uzbekistan

Website: <http://www.nato.int/cps/en/natolive/topics_49276.htm>

NATO–Georgia Commission (NGC)

The NGC was established in September 2008 to serve as a forum for political consultations and for practical cooperation to help Georgia achieve its goal of membership in NATO.

Participants (29): The NATO member states and Georgia

Website: <http://www.nato.int/cps/en/natolive/topics_52131.htm>

NATO–Russia Council (NRC)

The NRC was established in 2002 as a mechanism for consultation, consensus building, cooperation, and joint decisions and action on security issues. It focuses on areas of mutual interest identified in the 1997 NATO–Russia Founding Act on Mutual Relations, Cooperation and Security and new areas, such as terrorism, crisis management and non-proliferation.

Participants (29): The NATO member states and Russia

Website: <http://www.nato-russia-council.info/>

NATO–Ukraine Commission (NUC)

The NUC was established in 1997 for consultations on political and security issues, conflict prevention and resolution, non-proliferation, arms transfers and technology transfers, and other subjects of common concern.

Participants (29): The NATO member states and Ukraine

Website: <http://www.nato.int/cps/en/natolive/topics_50319.htm>

Open Skies Consultative Commission (OSCC)

The OSCC was established by the 1992 Treaty on Open Skies to resolve questions of compliance with the treaty.

Parties to the Open Skies Treaty (34): See annex A

Website: <http://www.osce.org/oscc/>

Organisation Conjointe de Coopération en matière d'Armement (OCCAR, Organisation for Joint Armament Cooperation)

OCCAR was established in 1996, with legal status since 2001, by France, Germany, Italy and the UK. Its aim is to provide more effective and efficient arrangements for the management of specific collaborative armament programmes. Its headquarters are in Bonn, Germany.

Members (6): Belgium, France, Germany, Italy, Spain, UK

Website: <http://www.occar-ea.org/>

Organismo para la Proscripción de las Armas Nucleares en la América Latina y el Caribe (OPANAL, Agency for the Prohibition of Nuclear Weapons in Latin America and the Caribbean)

OPANAL was established by the 1967 Treaty of Tlatelolco to resolve, together with the IAEA, questions of compliance with the treaty. Its seat is in Mexico City, Mexico.

Parties to the Treaty of Tlatelolco (33): See annex A

Website: <http://www.opanal.org/>

Organization for Democracy and Economic Development–GUAM

GUAM is a group of four states, established to promote stability and strengthen security, whose history goes back to 1997. The organization was established in 2006. The members cooperate to promote social and economic development and trade in eight working groups. Its secretariat is in Kyiv, Ukraine.

Members (4): Azerbaijan, Georgia, Moldova, Ukraine

Website: <http://guam-organization.org/>

Organization for Security and Co-operation in Europe (OSCE)

The Conference on Security and Co-operation in Europe (CSCE), which had been initiated in 1973, was renamed the OSCE in 1995. It is intended to be the primary instrument of comprehensive and cooperative security for early warning, conflict prevention, crisis management and post-conflict rehabilitation in its area. Its headquarters are in Vienna, Austria. The OSCE Troika consists of the chairperson-in-office and the previous and succeeding chairpersons. The Forum for Security Co-operation (FSC) deals with arms control and confidence- and security-building measures. The OSCE comprises several institutions, all located in Europe.

Participants (56): Albania, Andorra, Armenia, Austria, Azerbaijan, Belarus, Belgium, Bosnia and Herzegovina, Bulgaria, Canada, Croatia, Cyprus, Czech Republic, Denmark, Estonia, Finland, France, Georgia, Germany, Greece, Holy See, Hungary, Iceland, Ireland, Italy, Kazakhstan, Kyrgyzstan, Latvia, Liechtenstein, Lithuania, Luxembourg, Macedonia (Former Yugoslav Republic of), Malta, Moldova, Monaco, Montenegro, Netherlands, Norway, Poland, Portugal, Romania, Russia, San Marino, Serbia, Slovakia, Slovenia, Spain, Sweden, Switzerland, Tajikistan, Turkey, Turkmenistan, UK, Ukraine, USA, Uzbekistan

Website: <http://www.osce.org/>

Minsk Group

The Minsk Group supports the Minsk Process, an ongoing forum for negotiations on a peaceful settlement of the conflict in Nagorno-Karabakh.

Members: Armenia, Azerbaijan, Belarus, Finland, France*, Germany, Italy, Russia*, Sweden, Turkey, USA*, OSCE Troika

* The representatives of these 3 states co-chair the group.

Website: <http://www.osce.org/mg/>

Organization of American States (OAS)

The OAS is a group of states in the Americas that adopted its charter in 1948, with the objective of strengthening peace and security in the western hemisphere. The general secretariat is in Washington, DC, USA.

Members (35): Antigua and Barbuda, Argentina, Bahamas, Barbados, Belize, Bolivia, Brazil, Canada, Chile, Colombia, Costa Rica, Cuba*, Dominica, Dominican Republic, Ecuador, El Salvador, Grenada, Guatemala, Guyana, Haiti, Honduras, Jamaica, Mexico, Nicaragua, Panama, Paraguay, Peru, Saint Kitts and Nevis, Saint Lucia, Saint Vincent and the Grenadines, Suriname, Trinidad and Tobago, Uruguay, USA, Venezuela

* By a resolution of 3 June 2009, the 1962 resolution that excluded Cuba from the OAS ceased to have effect; according to the 2009 resolution, Cuba's participation in the organization 'will be the result of a process of dialogue'. Cuba has declined to participate in OAS activities.

Website: <http://www.oas.org/>

Organization of the Black Sea Economic Cooperation (BSEC)

BSEC was established in 1992. Its aims are to ensure peace, stability and prosperity and to promote and develop economic cooperation and progress in the Black Sea region. Its permanent secretariat is in Istanbul, Turkey.

Members (12): Albania, Armenia, Azerbaijan, Bulgaria, Georgia, Greece, Moldova, Romania, Russia, Serbia, Turkey, Ukraine

Website: <http://www.bsec-organization.org/>

Pacific Islands Forum

The forum was founded in 1971 by a group of South Pacific states that proposed the South Pacific Nuclear-Free Zone, embodied in the 1985 Treaty of Rarotonga. As well as monitoring implementation of the treaty, the forum provides a venue for informal discussions on a wide range of issues. The secretariat is in Suva, Fiji.

Members (16): Australia, Cook Islands, Fiji, Kiribati, Marshall Islands, Micronesia, Nauru, New Zealand, Niue, Palau, Papua New Guinea, Samoa, Solomon Islands, Tonga, Tuvalu, Vanuatu

Website: <http://www.forumsec.org/>

Regional Cooperation Council

The RCC was launched in 2008 as the successor of the Stability Pact for South Eastern Europe that was initiated by the EU at the 1999 Conference on South Eastern Europe. It promotes mutual cooperation and European and Euro-Atlantic integration of South Eastern Europe in order to inspire development in the region for the benefit of its people. It focuses on six priority areas: economic and social development, energy and infrastructure, justice and home affairs, security cooperation, building human capital, and parliamentary cooperation. Its secretariat is based in Sarajevo and its Liaison Office in Brussels.

Members (46): Albania, Austria, Bosnia and Herzegovina, Bulgaria, Canada, Council of Europe, Council of Europe Development Bank, Croatia, Czech Republic, Denmark, European Bank for Reconstruction and Development, European Investment Bank, European Union, Germany, Finland, France, Greece, Hungary, International Organization for Migration, Ireland, Italy, Latvia, Macedonia (Former Yugoslav Republic of), Moldova, Montenegro, North Atlantic Treaty Organization, Norway, Organisation for Economic Co-operation and Development, Organization for Security and Co-operation in Europe, Poland, Romania, Serbia, Slovakia, Slovenia, South East European Cooperative Initiative, Spain, Sweden, Switzerland, Turkey, UK, United Nations, UN Economic Commission for Europe, UN Development Programme, UN Interim Administration Mission in Kosovo, USA, World Bank

Website: <http://www.rcc.int/>

Shanghai Cooperation Organisation (SCO)

The SCO's predecessor group, the Shanghai Five, was founded in 1996; it was renamed the SCO in 2001 and opened for membership of all states that support its aims. The member states cooperate on confidence-building measures and regional security and in the economic sphere. The SCO secretariat is in Beijing, China.

Members (6): China, Kazakhstan, Kyrgyzstan, Russia, Tajikistan, Uzbekistan

Website: <http://www.sectsco.org/>

Six-Party Talks

The talks are a forum for multilateral negotiations on North Korea's nuclear programme. They are held in Beijing and are chaired by China.

Participants (6): China, Japan, Korea (North), Korea (South), Russia, USA

Southeast European Cooperative Initiative (SECI)

SECI was initiated by the USA in coordination with the EU in 1996 to promote cooperation and stability among the countries of South Eastern Europe and facilitate their accession into European structures. The SECI secretariat is located in the OSCE offices in Vienna, Austria.

Members (13): Albania, Bosnia and Herzegovina, Bulgaria, Croatia, Greece, Hungary, Macedonia (Former Yugoslav Republic of), Moldova, Montenegro, Romania, Serbia, Slovenia, Turkey

Website: <http://www.secinet.info/>

Southern African Development Community (SADC)

SADC was established in 1992 to promote regional economic development and the fundamental principles of sovereignty, peace and security, human rights and democracy. The Organ on Politics, Defence and Security Cooperation (OPDS) is intended to promote peace and security in the region. The secretariat is in Gaborone, Botswana.

Members (15): Angola, Botswana, Congo (Democratic Republic of the), Lesotho, Madagascar*, Malawi, Mauritius, Mozambique, Namibia, Seychelles, South Africa, Swaziland, Tanzania, Zambia, Zimbabwe

* Madagascar was suspended from all organs of the SADC in Mar. 2009.

Website: <http://www.sadc.int/>

Sub-Regional Consultative Commission (SRCC)

The SRCC was established by the 1996 Agreement on Sub-Regional Arms Control (Florence Agreement) as the forum in which the parties resolve questions of compliance with the agreement.

Parties to the Florence Agreement (4): See annex A

Website: <http://www.osce.org/item/43725>

Unión de Naciones Suramericanas (UNASUR, Union of South American Nations)

UNASUR is an intergovernmental organization with the aim of strengthening regional integration, political dialogue, economic development and coordination in defence matters among its member states. Its 2008 Constitutive Treaty entered into force on 11 March 2011 and it will gradually replace the Andean Community and the Mercado Común del Sur (MERCOSUR, Southern Common Market). Its headquarters are in Quito, Ecuador.

Members (12): Argentina, Bolivia, Brazil, Chile, Colombia, Ecuador, Guyana, Paraguay, Peru, Suriname, Uruguay, Venezuela

Website: <http://www.unasursg.org/>

Consejo de Defensa Suramericano (CDS, South American Defence Council)

The CDS was approved by the UNASUR member states in December 2008 and had its first meeting in March 2009. The objectives of the CDS are to consolidate South America as a zone of peace and to create a regional identity and strengthen regional cooperation in defence issues.

Members (12): The UNASUR members

Website: <http://www.unasurcds.org/>

Western European Union (WEU)

The WEU was established by the 1954 Modified Brussels Treaty. The WEU's operational activities (the Petersberg Tasks) were transferred to the EU in 2000. The WEU's residual tasks included collective defence commitments, institutional dialogue and support for armaments cooperation. In line with a decision taken in March 2010 by the parties to the treaty, the WEU ceased to exist as a treaty-based international organization on 30 June 2011.

Members as of 30 June 2011 (10): Belgium, France, Germany, Greece, Italy, Luxembourg, Netherlands, Portugal, Spain, UK

Website: <http://www.weu.int/>

III. Strategic trade control regimes

Australia Group (AG)

The AG is a group of states, formed in 1985, that seeks to prevent the intentional or inadvertent supply of materials or equipment to chemical or biological weapon programmes by sharing information on proliferation cases and strategies to manage them, including the harmonization of transfer controls.

Participants (41): Argentina, Australia, Austria, Belgium, Bulgaria, Canada, Croatia, Cyprus, Czech Republic, Denmark, Estonia, European Commission, Finland, France, Germany, Greece, Hungary, Iceland, Ireland, Italy, Japan, Korea (South), Latvia, Lithuania, Luxembourg, Malta, Netherlands, New Zealand, Norway, Poland, Portugal, Romania, Slovakia, Slovenia, Spain, Sweden, Switzerland, Turkey, UK, Ukraine, USA

Website: <http://www.australiagroup.net/>

Financial Action Task Force (FATF)

The FATF is an intergovernmental policymaking body whose purpose is to establish international standards and develop and promote policies, at both national and international levels. It was established in 1989 by the Group of Seven (G7), initially to examine and develop measures to combat money laundering; its mandate was expanded in 2001 to incorporate efforts to combat terrorist financing and again in 2008 to include the financing of WMD proliferation efforts. Its secretariat is in Paris, France.

Members (36): Argentina, Australia, Austria, Belgium, Brazil, Canada, China, Denmark, European Commission, Finland, France, Germany, Greece, Gulf Cooperation Council, Hong Kong (China), Iceland, India, Ireland, Italy, Japan, Korea (South), Luxembourg, Mexico,

Netherlands, New Zealand, Norway, Portugal, Russia, Singapore, South Africa, Spain, Sweden, Switzerland, Turkey, UK, USA

Website: <http://www.fatf-gafi.org/>

Hague Code of Conduct against Ballistic Missile Proliferation (HCOC)

The 2002 HCOC is subscribed to by a group of states that recognize its principles, primarily the need to prevent and curb the proliferation of ballistic missile systems capable of delivering weapons of mass destruction and the importance of strengthening multilateral disarmament and non-proliferation mechanisms. The Austrian Ministry of Foreign Affairs, Vienna, Austria, acts as the HCOC secretariat.

Subscribing states (134): Afghanistan, Albania, Andorra, Argentina, Armenia, Australia, Austria, Azerbaijan, Belarus, Belgium, Benin, Bosnia and Herzegovina, Bulgaria, Burkina Faso, Burundi, Cambodia, Cameroon, Canada, Cape Verde, *Central African Republic*, Chad, Chile, Colombia, Comoros, *Congo (Republic of)*, Cook Islands, Costa Rica, Croatia, Cyprus, Czech Republic, Denmark, Dominican Republic, Ecuador, El Salvador, Eritrea, Estonia, Ethiopia, Fiji, Finland, France, Gabon, Gambia, Georgia, Germany, Ghana, Greece, Guatemala, Guinea, Guinea-Bissau, Guyana, Haiti, Holy See, Honduras, Hungary, Iceland, Iraq, Ireland, Italy, Japan, Jordan, Kazakhstan, Kenya, Kiribati, Korea (South), Latvia, Liberia, Libya, Liechtenstein, Lithuania, Luxembourg, Macedonia (Former Yugoslav Republic of), Madagascar, Malawi, Maldives, Mali, Malta, Marshall Islands, Mauritania, Micronesia, Moldova, Monaco, Mongolia, Montenegro, Morocco, Mozambique, Netherlands, New Zealand, Nicaragua, Niger, Nigeria, Norway, Palau, Panama, Papua New Guinea, Paraguay, Peru, Philippines, Poland, Portugal, Romania, Russia, Rwanda, Samoa, San Marino, Senegal, Serbia, Seychelles, Sierra Leone, *Singapore*, Slovakia, Slovenia, South Africa, Spain, Sudan, Suriname, Sweden, Switzerland, Tajikistan, Tanzania, Timor-Leste, Tonga, Tunisia, Turkey, Turkmenistan, Tuvalu, Uganda, UK, Ukraine, Uruguay, USA, Uzbekistan, Vanuatu, Venezuela, Zambia

Website: <http://www.hcoc.at/>

Missile Technology Control Regime (MTCR)

The MTCR is an informal group of countries that seek to coordinate national export licensing efforts aimed at preventing the proliferation of missile systems capable of delivering weapons of mass destruction. The countries apply the Guidelines for Sensitive Missile-Relevant Transfers.

Partners (34): Argentina, Australia, Austria, Belgium, Brazil, Bulgaria, Canada, Czech Republic, Denmark, Finland, France, Germany, Greece, Hungary, Iceland, Ireland, Italy, Japan, Korea (South), Luxembourg, Netherlands, New Zealand, Norway, Poland, Portugal, Russia, South Africa, Spain, Sweden, Switzerland, Turkey, UK, Ukraine, USA

Website: <http://www.mtcr.info/>

Nuclear Suppliers Group (NSG)

The NSG, formerly also known as the London Club, was established in 1975. It coordinates national transfer controls on nuclear materials according to its Guidelines for Nuclear Transfers (London Guidelines, first agreed in 1978), which contain a 'trigger list' of materials that should trigger IAEA safeguards when they are to be exported for peaceful purposes to any non-nuclear weapon state, and the Guidelines for Transfers of Nuclear-Related Dual-Use Equipment, Materials, Software and Related Technology (Warsaw Guidelines).

Participants (46): Argentina, Australia, Austria, Belarus, Belgium, Brazil, Bulgaria, Canada, China, Croatia, Cyprus, Czech Republic, Denmark, Estonia, Finland, France, Germany, Greece, Hungary, Iceland, Ireland, Italy, Japan, Kazakhstan, Korea (South), Latvia, Lithuania, Luxembourg, Malta, Netherlands, New Zealand, Norway, Poland, Portugal, Romania, Russia, Slovakia, Slovenia, South Africa, Spain, Sweden, Switzerland, Turkey, UK, Ukraine, USA

Website: <http://www.nuclearsuppliersgroup.org/>

Proliferation Security Initiative (PSI)

Based on a US initiative announced in 2003, the PSI is a multilateral forum focusing on law enforcement cooperation for the interdiction and seizure of illegal weapons of mass destruction, missile technologies and related materials when in transit on land, in the air or at sea. The PSI Statement of Interdiction Principles was issued in 2003. The PSI has no secretariat, but its activities are coordinated by an Operational Experts Group.

Participants (98): Afghanistan, Albania, Andorra, Angola, Antigua and Barbuda, Argentina*, Armenia, Australia*[†], Austria, Azerbaijan, Bahamas, Bahrain, Belarus, Belgium, Belize, Bosnia and Herzegovina, Brunei Darussalam, Bulgaria, Cambodia, Canada*, Chile, Colombia, Croatia[†], Cyprus, Czech Republic[†], Denmark*, Djibouti[†], El Salvador, Estonia, Fiji, Finland, France*[†], Georgia, Germany*[†], Greece*, Holy See, Honduras, Hungary, Iceland, Iraq, Ireland, Israel, Italy*[†], Japan*[†], Jordan, Kazakhstan, Korea (South)*[†], Kyrgyzstan, Kuwait, Latvia, Liberia, Libya, Liechtenstein, Lithuania[†], Luxembourg, Macedonia (Former Yugoslav Republic of), Malta, Marshall Islands, Moldova, Mongolia, Montenegro, Morocco, Netherlands*[†], New Zealand*[†], Norway*[†], Oman, Panama, Papua New Guinea, Paraguay, Philippines, Poland*[†], Portugal*[†], Qatar, Romania, Russia*, Saint Vincent and the Grenadines, Samoa, San Marino, Saudi Arabia, Serbia, Singapore*[†], Slovakia, Slovenia[†], Spain*[†], Sri Lanka, Sweden, Switzerland, Tajikistan, Tunisia, Turkey*[†], Turkmenistan, Ukraine[†], United Arab Emirates[†], UK*[†], USA*[†], Uzbekistan, Vanuatu, Yemen

* Member of the Operational Experts Group.
[†] PSI exercise host, 2003–10. No exercises were held during 2011.

Website: US Department of State, <http://www.state.gov/t/isn/c10390.htm>

Wassenaar Arrangement (WA)

The Wassenaar Arrangement on Export Controls for Conventional Arms and Dual-Use Goods and Technologies was formally established in 1996. It aims to prevent the acquisition of armaments and sensitive dual-use goods and technologies for military uses by states whose behaviour is cause for concern to the member states. Its secretariat is in Vienna, Austria.

Participants (40): Argentina, Australia, Austria, Belgium, Bulgaria, Canada, Croatia, Czech Republic, Denmark, Estonia, Finland, France, Germany, Greece, Hungary, Ireland, Italy, Japan, Korea (South), Latvia, Lithuania, Luxembourg, Malta, Netherlands, New Zealand, Norway, Poland, Portugal, Romania, Russia, Slovakia, Slovenia, South Africa, Spain, Sweden, Switzerland, Turkey, UK, Ukraine, USA

Note: In addition, Mexico became a participating state on 25 Jan. 2012.

Website: <http://www.wassenaar.org/>

Zangger Committee

Established in 1971–74, the Nuclear Exporters Committee, called the Zangger Committee, is a group of nuclear supplier countries that meets informally twice a year to coordinate transfer controls on nuclear materials according to its regularly updated trigger list of items which, when exported, must be subject to IAEA safeguards. It complements the work of the Nuclear Suppliers Group.

Members (38): Argentina, Australia, Austria, *Belarus*, Belgium, Bulgaria, Canada, China, Croatia, Czech Republic, Denmark, Finland, France, Germany, Greece, Hungary, Ireland, Italy, Japan, Kazakhstan, Korea (South), Luxembourg, Netherlands, Norway, Poland, Portugal, Romania, Russia, Slovakia, Slovenia, South Africa, Spain, Sweden, Switzerland, Turkey, UK, Ukraine, USA

Website: <http://www.zanggercommittee.org/>

Annex C. Chronology 2011

NENNE BODELL

This chronology lists the significant events in 2011 related to armaments, disarmament and international security. The dates are according to local time. Keywords are indicated in the right-hand column. Definitions of the abbreviations are given on pp. xvii–xx.

9 Jan.	Polling stations open for a referendum on southern Sudan's independence from Sudan. The referendum is a result of the 2005 Comprehensive Peace Agreement, which granted the south the right to self-determination.	Sudan; Southern Sudan
10 Jan.	The Basque separatist group Euzkadi ta Azkatasuna (ETA, Basque Homeland and Liberty) declares 'a permanent and general ceasefire which will be verifiable by the international community'. More than 800 people have been killed in ETA-related violence since the group's founding in 1968.	Spain
11 Jan.	Chinese President Hu Jintao confirms that a first test flight of a stealth jet fighter (the J-20) has been carried out after accounts of the test and pictures of a prototype of the aircraft appear on Chinese websites.	China; Aircraft
14 Jan.	Following weeks of violent anti-government protests throughout Tunisia, President Zine-Al Abidine Ben Ali is forced to leave the country. The Prime Minister, Mohamed Ghannouchi, declares that he will remain in power until elections are held. Ben Ali's overthrow marks the first time an Arab leader has left his post after public demonstrations.	Tunisia
18 Jan.	A suicide bomber kills 50 people and wounds 150 in an attack on police recruits in Tikrit, in the first major attack since the formation of the new Iraqi Government in Dec. 2010. No group claims responsibility, but it is similar to previous bombings by the Islamic State of Iraq, an organization affiliated with al-Qaeda in Mesopotamia.	Iraq; Terrorism
24 Jan.	An explosion in the international terminal at Domodedovo airport, Moscow, kills at least 35 people and injures more than 130. No group claims responsibility, but Russian officials accuse Islamist militants from the North Caucasus.	Russia; Terrorism
25 Jan.	Following violent anti-government protests in Tunisia, tens of thousands of people take to the streets in Cairo and other large cities throughout Egypt, demanding the resignation of President Hosni Mubarak. Violence escalates in subsequent weeks, and protesters loyal to Mubarak clash with anti-government groups.	Egypt

26 Jan.	The Federation Council, the upper house of the Russian Parliament, approves the Treaty on Measures for the Further Reduction and Limitation of Strategic Offensive Arms (New START). The State Duma had ratified the treaty on 25 Jan. and the US Senate on 22 Dec. 2010. The treaty will enter into force on the date of exchange of instruments of ratification.	Russia; USA; Nuclear arms control; New START
4 Feb.	Military clashes on the disputed border between Cambodia and Thailand resume and continue sporadically throughout the spring of 2011. On 4 May a ceasefire is agreed. Indonesia, acting as chair of the Association of Southeast Asian Nations (ASEAN), attempts to mediate, and on 6 May both parties agree terms of reference for an Indonesian observer team.	ASEAN; Cambodia; Thailand
5 Feb.	The Treaty on Measures for the Further Reduction and Limitation of Strategic Offensive Arms (New START) enters into force after Russia and the USA exchange instruments of ratification.	Russia; USA; Nuclear arms control; New START
7 Feb.	Sudanese President Omar al-Bashir announces the Sudanese Government's acceptance of the results of the 9 Jan. referendum on independence for southern Sudan, in which nearly 99 per cent of the registered voters participated. Southern Sudan will become independent in July 2011.	Sudan; Southern Sudan
9–10 Feb.	The Sudan People's Liberation Army clashes in the state of Jonglei with rebel forces loyal to General George Athor, leaving almost 200 dead. The fighting breaks a one-month armistice signed days before the 9 Jan. referendum on independence for southern Sudan.	Southern Sudan
11 Feb.	After weeks of protests, Egyptian President Hosni Mubarak is forced to leave power.	Egypt
16–22 Feb.	The violent anti-government protests that have taken place throughout the Middle East and North Africa reach Libya; demonstrations against the regime of Muammar Gaddafi occur in several cities. On 21 Feb. hundreds are killed and injured when government forces respond in Tripoli and Benghazi. The UN Security Council condemns the 'violence and use of force against civilians', deplores the 'repression against peaceful demonstrators' and expresses 'deep regret at the deaths of hundreds of civilians'. On 22 Feb. Gaddafi states that anyone using 'force against the authority of the state will be sentenced to death'.	Libya
26 Feb.	The UN Security Council unanimously adopts Resolution 1970, which demands an end to violence against civilian demonstrators in Libya, refers the situation to the International Criminal Court (ICC), imposes an arms embargo and a travel ban on the country, and freezes the assets of Muammar Gaddafi's family and those of government officials.	UN; ICC; Libya; Arms embargoes
28 Feb.	The Council of the European Union adopts restrictive measures on trade with Libya, including an arms embargo, imposes a travel ban and freezes the assets of Muammar Gaddafi's family and those of government officials.	EU; Libya; Arms embargoes

1 Mar.	The UN General Assembly suspends Libya from the UN Human Rights Council for 'gross and systematic' human rights violations.	UN; Libya
8 Mar.	Violent fighting between protesters and forces loyal to Muammar Gaddafi in the town of Az Zawiyah leaves dozens of people dead and many wounded. Fighting, which began on 16 Feb., persists throughout Libya as Gaddafi tries to regain control of cities held by rebel forces, using air strikes, armour and artillery.	Libya
12 Mar.	Following a devastating earthquake and tsunami that kill over 18 400 people in northern Japan on 11 Mar., the Fukushima Daiichi nuclear reactors are partly destroyed and an explosion occurs. Radioactive steam is released and people are evacuated from the area. Following the disaster, many countries re-evaluate their nuclear energy programmes, and anti-nuclear demonstrations take place globally.	Japan; Nuclear energy
12 Mar.	The Arab League asks the UN Security Council to impose a no-fly zone over Libya to protect civilians. It suspends Libya from the organization and opens contact with rebel forces via the Libyan National Transitional Council (NTC).	Libya; Arab League
14 Mar.	Following weeks of anti-government protest in Manama, the Bahraini Government requests assistance from the Gulf Cooperation Council (GCC) to quell the unrest. Troops are provided by Saudi Arabia and the United Arab Emirates. Several protesters are killed or wounded.	GCC; Bahrain
17 Mar.	The UN Security Council adopts Resolution 1973 by a vote of 10–0, with Brazil, China, Germany, India and Russia abstaining. The resolution approves a no-fly zone over Libya and authorizes UN member states to act individually or through regional organizations and to use all necessary measures to protect civilians under threat of attack in Libya, including in Benghazi. It excludes the sending of any foreign occupation force to any part of Libya.	UN; Libya
18 Mar.	Following the adoption of UN Security Council Resolution 1973 on 17 Mar., the Libyan Foreign Minister, Moussa Koussa, announces an 'immediate ceasefire and the stoppage of all military operations'. In eastern Libya, government armed forces reportedly continue to attack cities held by rebel forces.	Libya
18 Mar.	Security forces and government supporters open fire on demonstrators in Sana'a, killing at least 40 people and injuring more than 100. The anti-government demonstration is the largest to occur in Yemen and follows weeks of escalating protests and violence.	Yemen

19 Mar.	A coalition including Canada, France, Italy, the UK and the USA launches an operation to enforce the no-fly zone in Libya that was authorized by UN Security Council Resolution 1973. French fighter aircraft attack Libyan tanks south of Benghazi, in eastern Libya, and British and US cruise missiles are fired at Libyan military installations along the coastline.	UN; Libya
23 Mar.	As part of Operation Unified Protector, NATO warships and aircraft patrol Libyan territorial waters to reduce the flow of arms, related material and mercenaries to Libya, in accordance with UN Security Council Resolution 1970.	NATO; Libya
29 Mar.	The Republican Forces of presidential claimant Alassane Ouattara take control of a number of towns in Côte d'Ivoire and proceed towards the capital, Abidjan, which is held by troops loyal to the incumbent president, Laurent Gbagbo. Ouattara had been declared the winner of presidential elections on 28 Nov. 2010, but Gbagbo had refused to accept defeat. Fighting between their supporters had escalated. On 7 Dec. 2010 the Economic Community of West African States (ECOWAS) had recognized Ouattara as the winner, but attempts by the African Union and ECOWAS to solve the crisis by peaceful means failed.	Côte d'Ivoire
29 Mar.	Following presidential elections on 4 Feb., the new civilian president of Myanmar, Thein Sein, together with two vice-presidents, takes power after almost 50 years of military rule. The former ruling body, the State Peace and Development Council (SPDC), is 'officially dissolved'.	Myanmar
30 Mar.	The UN Security Council unanimously adopts Resolution 1975, imposing targeted sanctions against Ivorian President Laurent Gbagbo and his associates. On 31 Mar. heavy fighting erupts in Abidjan. The UN estimates that about 500 people have been killed and more than 1 million displaced in the fighting since Nov. 2010.	UN; Côte d'Ivoire
31 Mar.	NATO and its allies take the lead in Operation Unified Protector, a military operation in Libya conducted under UN Security Council Resolution 1973, with the goal of protecting civilians and civilian-populated areas that are under threat of attack by the regime of Muammar Gaddafi.	NATO; Libya
1 Apr.	Following the burning of the Koran by US Christian extremists at the Dove World Outreach Center, Florida, on 20 Mar., thousands of protesters storm the compound of the UN Assistance Mission in Afghanistan (UNAMA) in Mazar i Sharif. At least 20 people are killed. Massive protests occur throughout Afghanistan for several days.	UN; Afghanistan
1 Apr.	Richard Goldstone, head of the 2009 UN Human Rights Council Fact-Finding Mission on the Gaza Conflict, retracts some of the conclusions made in its report on Israel's intentional targeting of civilians during the conflict. On 14 Apr. the three other members of the mission criticize Goldstone and state that they stand by the report's conclusions.	UN; Israel; Palestinians; War crimes

2 Apr.	International humanitarian organizations report that a massacre, killing at least 800, was committed in Duékoué by the Republican Forces loyal to Alassane Ouattara. The killings are alleged to have taken place between 27 and 29 Mar. during inter-ethnic fighting.	Côte d'Ivoire
4 Apr.	An aircraft in use by the UN Organization Stabilization Mission in the Democratic Republic of the Congo (MONUSCO) crashes while landing in poor weather conditions in Kinshasa, killing 32 people, in one of the worst accidents involving a UN aircraft.	UN; DRC
4 Apr.	Forces from the UN Operation in Côte d'Ivoire (UNOCI), supported by French forces, carry out a military operation and attack weapon stores at President Laurent Gbagbo's military camp in Abidjan. The UN forces have been instructed by the UN Secretary-General, Ban Ki-moon, to take 'all necessary measures' to prevent the use of heavy weapons against civilians.	UN; Côte d'Ivoire
10 Apr.	The African Union sends representatives from the Democratic Republic of the Congo, Mali, Mauritania, South Africa and Uganda to Libya to negotiate a 'roadmap to peace', including an immediate ceasefire, suspension of NATO air strikes and talks to reach a political solution to the conflict in Libya. Muammar Gaddafi accepts the road map, but the rebel forces' National Transitional Council (NTC) rejects it because it does not require the regime to leave power immediately.	AU; Libya
11 Apr.	Following attacks by UN helicopters on Ivorian President Laurent Gbagbo's residence on 10 Apr., the Republican Forces loyal to Alassane Ouattara, and supported by French and UN forces, capture and arrest Gbagbo.	Côte d'Ivoire
13–15 Apr.	At a plenary meeting in Buenos Aires, Argentina, the Missile Technology Control Regime (MTCR) partners agree to strengthen cooperation with non-partners in missile non-proliferation and underline the importance of transit and trans-shipment controls.	MTCR
19 Apr.	After a month of violent anti-government protests, with nearly 200 people killed, the Syrian Government announces that the 48-year-old emergency powers law will be lifted. Demonstrations continue.	Syria
19 Apr.	The UN Security Council unanimously adopts Resolution 1977, which extends the mandate of the 1540 Committee for 10 years. The committee is urged to intensify its efforts to promote full implementation by all states of Resolution 1540 (2004) on the non-proliferation of weapons of mass destruction, and is requested to carry out a comprehensive review of implementation.	UN; WMD

20 Apr.	The UN Office of the High Commissioner for Human Rights (OHCHR) condemns the alleged repeated use of cluster munitions and heavy weapons in Misratah by Libyan Government forces, claiming that their use could be considered a war crime and a serious violation of international humanitarian law.	Libya; War crimes
24 Apr.	Two NATO missiles hit Muammar Gaddafi's compound, Bab al-Azizia, in Tripoli. The Libyan Government accuses NATO of trying to assassinate Gaddafi. On 30 Apr., in the second air strike in a week, NATO again attacks one of Gaddafi's residences, killing members of his family.	NATO; Libya
25 Apr.	Violence escalates throughout Syria and at least 3000 troops, backed by tanks and heavy weapons, open fire in the town of Dará, the centre of the anti-government protests. The Office of the UN High Commissioner for Human Rights (OHCHR) condemns the violence.	Syria
28 Apr.	The UN Security Council unanimously adopts Resolution 1980 extending the arms embargo and the diamond trade ban on Côte d'Ivoire until 30 Apr. 2012, stating that it can be lifted or modified earlier depending on progress in the peace process.	UN; Côte d'Ivoire; Arms embargoes
30 Apr.	At the second meeting of the Non-Proliferation and Disarmament Initiative (NPDI), which was formed in Sep. 2010, its 10 members—Australia, Canada, Chile, Germany, Japan, Mexico, the Netherlands, Poland, Turkey and the United Arab Emirates—adopt the Berlin Statement on Nuclear Disarmament and Non-proliferation, containing four proposals for nuclear disarmament and non-proliferation.	Disarmament; Nuclear weapons
1 May	US President Barack Obama announces that US special forces have located and killed al-Qaeda's leader, Osama bin Laden, in Abbottadad, Pakistan.	USA; al-Qaeda
4 May	In Cairo, in a deal brokered by the Egyptian Government, the leaders of the main Palestinian factions, President Mahmoud Abbas (Fatah) and Khaled Meshaal (Hamas), sign a reconciliation agreement committing them to form an interim unity government and hold elections in the Gaza Strip and the West Bank within a year.	Palestinian territories; Egypt
9 May	In response to the violent repression by Syrian Government forces of peaceful protests, the Council of the European Union adopts an embargo against Syria on arms and equipment that could be used for internal repression and imposes a visa ban and freezes the assets of officials and individuals with ties to the Syrian regime.	EU; Arms embargoes; Syria
13 May	Two suicide bomb attacks at a paramilitary training centre in the Charsadda district, north-western Pakistan, kill at least 70 people and injure 100. Pakistani Taliban groups claim responsibility and state that the attacks are revenge for the death of Osama bin Laden on 1 May.	Pakistan; Terrorism

15 May	Thousands of Palestinians in East Jerusalem, the Gaza Strip and the West Bank demonstrate to commemorate Nakba Day, marking the Palestinian displacement and the creation of Israel in 1948. The protesters clash with the Israeli Army and police on Israeli's borders with Jordan, Lebanon and Syria. At least 13 people are killed. Israel accuses Syria of provoking the confrontations.	Israel; Palestinian territories
16 May	The prosecutor at the International Criminal Court (ICC), The Hague, Netherlands, formally requests arrest warrants for Libyan leader Muammar Gaddafi, his son Saif al-Islam Gaddafi and the head of the Libyan intelligence service, Abdullah al-Senussi, on charges of war crimes. The ICC prosecutor states that the three are operating as an 'inner circle', orchestrating the killing of peaceful protesters.	ICC; Libya
17 May	The International Criminal Tribunal for Rwanda (ICTR) in Arusha, Tanzania, finds the former head of the Rwandan Army, Augustin Bizimungu, guilty of genocide and crimes against humanity that were committed in the 1994 civil war and sentences him to 30 years in prison. Bizimungu has been on trial since his arrest in 2002.	ICTR; Rwanda
26 May	The Bosnian Serb military leader Ratko Mladić is arrested by Serbian police and indicted by the International Criminal Tribunal for the former Yugoslavia (ICTY), The Hague, Netherlands, for war crimes and genocide during the 1990s Bosnian War.	ICTY; Bosnia and Herzegovina
27 May	The leaders of the Group of Eight (G8) industrialized states, meeting in Deauville, France, agree to extend its 2002 Global Partnership against the Spread of Weapons and Materials of Mass Destruction for an unspecified period beyond its 2012 expiration.	G8; WMD
31 May	At the All Darfur Stakeholders Conference in Doha, Qatar, the Doha Peace Document is adopted as the basis for a comprehensive and final peace agreement to end the conflict in Darfur, Sudan.	Sudan
2–3 June	Meeting in Vienna, Austria, the participants in the Hague Code of Conduct against Ballistic Missile Proliferation (HCOC) welcome the accession of Iraq and the Central African Republic to the regime, bringing the number of subscribing states to 132.	HCOC; Ballistic missiles
3 June	In an attack on the presidential compound in Sana'a, Yemeni President Ali Abdullah Saleh is seriously wounded and some senior officials are killed or wounded. Saleh is taken to Saudi Arabia for treatment. Violence has escalated in Yemen since the end of May.	Yemen
10 June	Meeting in Paris, France, the Australia Group approves a new manual containing guidance on how to manage intangible transfers of technology .	Australia Group

14 June	The Arab League publicly criticizes the ongoing violence in Syria, stating that it is 'angry and actively monitoring' the crisis.	Arab League; Syria
20 June	Protests erupt throughout Syria following the first public speech in two months by President Bashar al-Assad, who promises national dialogue and reforms. The opposition forces claim that at least 1400 people have been killed and 10 000 arrested since violent protests against the regime started in Mar. The European Union strengthens its financial sanctions against the Syrian regime.	Syria
20 June	Meeting in Addis Ababa, Ethiopia, the Sudan People's Liberation Movement (SPLM) and the Sudanese Government sign a demilitarization agreement for the contested region of Abyei on the border of southern Sudan. The deal, negotiated under the auspices of the African Union High-Level Implementation Panel (AUHIP), permits Ethiopian peacekeeping troops to be deployed in the area. On 27 June the UN Security Council adopts Resolution 1990, establishing the UN Interim Security Force for Abyei (UNISFA).	AU; UN; Sudan; Southern Sudan
20 June	NATO officials confirm that an air strike on 19 June in Tripoli that was intended to hit a military missile site instead struck a residential area, killing and injuring several civilians.	NATO; Libya
20 June	The Council of the European Union adopts Council Decision 2011/357/CFSP, imposing an arms embargo on Belarus, to strengthen its existing sanctions on the leadership of the country in response to the deteriorating human rights, democracy and rule-of-law situation in Belarus.	EU; Belarus; Arms embargoes
22 June	US President Barack Obama announces that the USA has largely achieved its goals in Afghanistan and plans to withdraw 10 000 troops from the country by the end of 2011, and an additional 20 000 troops by the summer of 2012. The drawdown will then continue 'at a steady pace' until 2014. The troop reductions are larger and the pace more rapid than suggested by military commanders.	USA; Afghanistan
23–24 June	Meeting in Noordwijk, the Netherlands, the Nuclear Suppliers Group (NSG) agrees to strengthen the NSG guidelines on the transfer of sensitive enrichment and reprocessing technologies.	Nuclear Suppliers Group
27 June	Pre-Trial Chamber I of the International Criminal Court (ICC), The Hague, Netherlands, issues warrants for the arrest of Muammar Gaddafi, Saif al-Islam Gaddafi and Abdullah al-Senussi on charges of crimes against humanity (murder and persecution) in Libya. The crimes were allegedly committed throughout Libya during Feb. 2011 using the state apparatus and security forces.	ICC; Libya; War crimes

29 June	Meeting in Addis Ababa, Ethiopia, the Government of Sudan and the Sudan People's Liberation Movement–North (SPLM-N) sign a framework agreement for the states of South Kordufan and Blue Nile, under which a Joint Security Committee and a Joint Political Committee are formed to address remaining issues regarding border security.	Sudan
30 June	The Western European Union (WEU) ceases to exist as a treaty-based international organization. Residual administrative tasks are transferred to the European Union Satellite Centre.	WEU
30 June–1 July	The five permanent members of the UN Security Council—China, France, Russia, the UK and the USA—meet in Paris, France, to consider how to follow through with the commitments they made at the 2010 Review Conference of the 1968 Non-Proliferation Treaty. They establish a regular multilateral dialogue among themselves on nuclear transparency, verification and confidence-building measures.	P5; Nuclear arms control
8 July	The UN Security Council unanimously adopts Resolution 1996, establishing the UN Mission in the Republic of South Sudan (UNMISS) as of 9 July to consolidate peace and security. The mandate of the UN Mission in the Sudan (UNMIS) ends on the same date.	UN; South Sudan; Peacekeeping operations
9 July	The Republic of South Sudan is officially declared an independent state at a ceremony in the new capital, Juba. On 14 July the UN General Assembly admits it as its 193rd member.	South Sudan
18 July	The International Court of Justice (ICJ), The Hague, Netherlands, decides that the disputed temple area Preah Vihear belongs to Cambodia, under a 1962 ICJ decision, and that both Cambodia and Thailand should immediately withdraw military personnel from the demilitarized zone around the temple. The two countries should also continue their cooperation initiated within the framework of the Association of Southeast Asian Nations (ASEAN). The conflict has been ongoing since 2008.	ICJ; Thailand; Cambodia
18 July	The Council of the European Union adopts Council Decision 2011/423/CFSP, amending its 2005 decision imposing an arms embargo on Sudan so that it covers arms supplies to both Sudan and newly independent South Sudan.	EU; South Sudan; Arms embargoes
22 July	A bomb kills 8 people and damages government buildings in Oslo; a few hours later a shooting attack occurs at a Labour Party youth camp on an island outside Oslo, killing a further 69 people and injuring many. A Norwegian right-wing extremist is arrested and charged with carrying out both attacks.	Norway; Terrorism

31 July	At least 140 civilians are killed in clashes between Syrian Government forces and anti-government protesters. The largest number of deaths occurs in the city of Hamah when government security forces attack using tanks. On 3 Aug. the UN Security Council issues a statement condemning the Syrian authorities' 'widespread violations of human rights and use of force against civilians'.	Syria
6 Aug.	Following an offensive by government troops and forces of the African Union Mission in Somalia (AMISOM), the Islamist rebel group al-Shabab announces a 'tactical' withdrawal from Mogadishu. The group still controls several towns in southern Somalia.	AU; Somalia
15 Aug.	In a series of suicide attacks and car bombings targeted at civilians and security forces throughout Iraq, at least 90 people are killed and 300 are injured. No group claims responsibility.	Iraq; Terrorism
17 Aug.	Following an appeal by the UN Secretary-General, Ban Ki-moon, to halt the violence, Syrian President Bashar al-Assad states that all military and police operations against anti-government protesters have ceased. Syria is criticized for its violence against civilians by several states in the Middle East. On 18 Aug. the European Union and the USA demand al-Assad's resignation.	Syria
17–22 Aug.	Following an attack by rebel forces of the Partiya Karkerên Kurdistan (PKK, Kurdistan Workers' Party), the Turkish Army conducts a series of air strikes over six days, targeting 132 PKK strongholds in northern Iraq. Up to 100 rebels are killed and more than 80 wounded.	Turkey; Iraq; Kurds
18 Aug.	In coordinated attacks on civilian and military vehicles by gunmen in southern Israel, several people are killed or injured. Hamas denies responsibility for the attacks. Israel immediately retaliates, launching air attacks on Rafah in the Gaza Strip.	Israel; Palestinian territories
23 Aug.	Rebel forces, backed by NATO air strikes, capture Muammar Gaddafi's compound, Bab al-Azizia, in Tripoli, but are unable to gain control of the whole capital and fighting continues. Government forces still control the cities of Sirte and Sabha. Gaddafi himself is not located.	NATO; Libya
26 Aug.	An explosion at UN headquarters in Abuja kills at least 18 people and injures many. An Islamist group linked to al-Qaeda, Boko Haram ('Western education is forbidden'), claims responsibility for the attack, the first on UN representatives in Nigeria.	UN; Nigeria; Terrorism
26 Aug.	Violent ethnic clashes in Jonglei state, South Sudan, that began on 18 Aug. and leave at least 600 people dead and 1000 injured, prompt the deployment of peacekeepers from the UN Mission in the Republic of South Sudan (UNMISS) together with members of the Sudan People's Liberation Army (SPLA) in an attempt restore peace and stability.	UN; South Sudan

1 Sep.	At a conference in Paris, France, hosted by French President Nicolas Sarkozy and the British Prime Minister, David Cameron, leaders of the Libyan National Transitional Council (NTC) and over 60 states and international organizations discuss a road map for Libya's humanitarian, political and economic future. The participants agree to continue NATO operations, to bring those guilty of war crimes to justice and to help the NTC achieve political transition.	Libya
2 Sep.	The organization WikiLeaks releases the complete, unredacted archive of 250 000 confidential US diplomatic cables (Cablegate) on the Internet.	USA; Foreign policy
6 Sep.	Meeting in Mogadishu under the auspices of the UN Special Representative for Somalia, at the Consultative Meeting on Ending the Transition, delegates from the Transitional Federal Institutions (TFIs) and regional representatives agree on a road map of measures and principles for their implementation leading to the end of transition on 20 Aug. 2012.	UN; Somalia
13–14 Sep.	Taliban militants launch an attack on government buildings, the US Embassy and the headquarters of the NATO-led International Security Assistance Force (ISAF) in Kabul, killing several people. NATO blames the attack on the Haqqani Network, an al-Qaeda ally, based in Pakistan.	Afghanistan; Terrorism
16 Sep.	The UN General Assembly recognizes the National Transitional Council (NTC) as Libya's representative in the UN, and the Security Council unanimously adopts Resolution 2009, establishing the UN Support Mission in Libya (UNSMIL) to support the NTC. The resolution lifts parts of the arms embargo, the assets freeze and the no-fly zone imposed earlier in 2011.	UN; Libya
22 Sep.	Meeting in Vienna, Austria, the International Atomic Energy Agency (IAEA) General Conference unanimously endorses an action plan on nuclear safety to enhance transparency in the ongoing efforts to set effective global safety standards.	IAEA; Nuclear safety
23 Sep.	Palestinian President Mahmoud Abbas submits an application for full UN membership for Palestine to the UN Secretary-General, Ban Ki-moon. The application is transmitted to the UN Security Council.	UN; Palestine
29 Sep.	China launches an experimental space laboratory module, Tiangong-1, from Jiuquan Satellite Launch Centre, to lay the groundwork for a future space station. This is China's most ambitious space project since its first manned space flight, in 2003.	China; Space programmes
29 Sep.	The fourth Review Conference of the 1990 Treaty on Conventional Armed Forces in Europe (CFE Treaty) is held in Vienna, Austria.	CFE Treaty

30 Sep.	In northern Yemen, Anwar al-Awlaki, a US citizen and lead-ing figure in al-Qaeda in the Arabian Peninsula, is killed by a missile fired from an unmanned aircraft by the US Central Intelligence Agency (CIA). This is the first CIA strike in Yemen since 2002.	USA; Yemen; CIA; al-Qaeda
30 Sep.	The UN Security Council unanimously adopts Resolution 2010, requesting the African Union (AU) to 'urgently increase' the strength of the AU Mission in Somalia (AMISOM) to the mandated level of 12 000 uniformed personnel and to extend the mission's authorization until 31 Oct. 2012. The resolution calls on member states and international and regional organ-izations to provide additional equipment, technical aid and funding to the enlarged force.	AU; UN; Somalia
4 Oct.	A truck loaded with bombs explodes in a government district in Mogadishu, killing more than 80 people and injuring many. The Islamist group al-Shabab claims responsibility for the attack, the largest since the group withdrew from Mogadishu on 6 Aug. and one of the most devastating attacks to date.	Somalia; Terrorism
11 Oct.	Israel and Hamas announce that they have reached an agree-ment to exchange more than 1000 Palestinian prisoners for an Israeli soldier, Gilad Shalit, who has been held prisoner in the Gaza Strip since June 2006. The deal is negotiated under the auspices of Egypt. The exchange of prisoners starts on 18 Oct.	Israel; Palestinian territories
11 Oct.	The US Attorney General accuses Iranian officials of con-spiring to assassinate the Saudi Arabian ambassador to the USA and of planning to bomb the Israeli Embassy in the USA and the Israeli and Saudi embassies in Argentina. Iran 'strongly and categorically rejects' the accusations.	USA; Iran; Saudi Arabia; Israel
19 Oct.	In fighting with armed rebels of the Partiya Karkerên Kurdi-stan (PKK, Kurdistan Workers' Party), 26 Turkish soldiers are killed.	Turkey; Kurds
20 Oct.	The Libyan National Transitional Council (NTC) announces the capture and subsequent killing of the former Libyan leader Muammar Gaddafi, when NTC forces, supported by NATO air strikes, liberate the city of Sirte, the last stronghold of the forces loyal to Gaddafi.	Libya
20 Oct.	The Basque separatist group Euzkadi ta Azkatasuna (ETA, Basque Homeland and Liberty) announces 'the definite ces-sation of its military activities' and declares its desire for 'direct dialogue' with the governments of France and Spain. ETA has sought Basque independence since 1968.	Spain
23 Oct.	In Benghazi, Libya, leaders of the Libyan National Trans-itional Council (NTC) declare an end to the uprising in the country. The NTC is to select a new interim government within three months, elections to a national council are to be held within eight months and a full government is to be elected a year after that.	Libya

31 Oct.	By 107 votes in favour, 14 against and 52 abstentions, the UN Educational, Scientific and Cultural Organization (UNESCO) General Conference admits Palestine as its 195th member.	UNESCO; Palestine
31 Oct.	NATO ends its Operation Unified Protector in Libya.	NATO; Libya
2 Nov.	With the agreement of the Syrian Government, the Arab League adopts an Arab Plan of Action on the conflict in Syria. The plan calls on the Syrian Government to immediately halt the violence directed at civilians, withdraw all its security forces from civilian areas and release tens of thousands of political prisoners.	Arab League; Syria
5 Nov.	At least 63 people are killed in a series of coordinated gun and bomb attacks in Yobe, a north-eastern state in Nigeria. Boko Haram ('Western education is forbidden'), an Islamist group linked to al-Qaeda, claims responsibility for the attacks. The violence is among the worst seen since the group launched its insurgency against the government, demanding wider application of sharia law in Nigeria in 2009.	Nigeria; Terrorism
8 Nov.	The Director General of the International Atomic Energy Agency (IAEA), Yukiya Amano, releases his report on implementation by Iran of its 1968 Non-Proliferation Treaty (NPT) safeguards agreement and relevant provisions of UN Security Council resolutions, covering developments since 2 Sep. 2011. The report states that 'Iran has carried out activities relevant to the development of a nuclear device' that might still be ongoing. Iran rejects the report, claiming it is 'unbalanced, unprofessional and politically motivated'.	UN; IAEA; Iran
12 Nov.	Meeting in Cairo, Egypt, the Arab League decides to suspend Syria from its activities as of 16 Nov. because of the violent repression of anti-government protesters and its failure to implement the Arab Plan of Action. On 13 Nov. the European Union decides to strengthen its sanctions against Syria.	Arab League; EU; Syria
14–25 Nov.	The Fourth Review Conference of the 1981 Certain Conventional Weapons Convention (CCW Convention) is held in Geneva, Switzerland.	CCW Convention
16 Nov.	The Free Syrian Army, composed of defectors from the Syrian Army, claims to have launched several attacks on government military bases near Damascus, including on an air force intelligence compound. The attacks are not independently confirmed. Violence in Syria has escalated and several attacks on foreign diplomatic missions have occurred in recent weeks. The UN estimates that more than 3500 people have been killed since Mar. 2011.	Syria
16 Nov.	Meeting in Rabat, Morocco, the foreign ministers of the Arab League offer Syria a new deadline to accept the League's peace plan, calling on the Syrian Government to stop its violent repression of anti-government protesters. The Arab League also offers to send civilian and military monitors to Syria.	Arab League; Syria

21 Nov.	Following the 8 Nov. release of an International Atomic Energy Agency (IAEA) report on the Iranian nuclear programme, Canada, the UK and the USA impose new sanctions on Iran's banks and oil industry. In protest against the sanctions, on 28 Nov. students storm the British Embassy in Tehran.	Canada; UK; USA; Iran; Sanctions
22 Nov.	Sixteen states parties—Belgium, Bulgaria, Canada, the Czech Republic, Denmark, Germany, Hungary, Iceland, Italy, Luxembourg, the Netherlands, Portugal, Slovakia, Turkey, the UK and the USA—announce, in Vienna, Austria, that they will cease carrying out certain obligations under the 1990 Treaty on Conventional Armed Forces in Europe (CFE Treaty) with regard to Russia. They will continue to implement the treaty and carry out all obligations with all other states parties and will resume full treaty implementation if Russia resumes implementation of its treaty obligations. Russia suspended its participation in the CFE Treaty in 2007.	CFE Treaty
23 Nov.	Yemeni President Ali Abdullah Saleh signs an agreement brokered by the Gulf Cooperation Council (GCC) in Riyadh, Saudi Arabia, under which power is transferred to the vice-president in an attempt to restore calm to Yemen after 10 months of political instability and violence.	GCC; Yemen
26 Nov.	NATO helicopters from the International Security Assistance Force (ISAF) in Afghanistan launch an air attack on a border checkpoint in Mohmand agency in Pakistan's Federally Administered Tribal Areas, killing 24 Pakistani soldiers. Pakistan calls the attack 'unprovoked' and 'deliberate' and closes ISAF's cross-border supply routes through Torkham in Khyber Pakhtunkhwa and Chaman in Balochistan. US officials claim that the ISAF troops came under fire and acted in self-defence. NATO initiates an investigation.	NATO; ISAF; Pakistan; Afghanistan
27 Nov.	Meeting in Cairo, Egypt, the Arab League agrees to impose immediate broad economic sanctions on Syria. The Syrian Foreign Minister, Walid Muallem, states that the Arab League has declared 'economic war' on Syria by imposing sanctions and that Syria will use 'its strategic location to retaliate'. On 3 Dec. the sanctions are expanded to include an arms embargo. This is the first time that the Arab League has imposed an arms embargo.	Arab League; Syria; Arms embargoes
30 Nov.	Following the storming of its embassy in Tehran, the British Foreign Secretary, William Hague, announces that the UK is closing the embassy and ordering the expulsion of Iranian diplomats from the UK.	UK; Iran
30 Nov.	Meeting in Vienna, Austria, the Forum for Security Co-operation (FSC) of the Organization for Security and Co-operation in Europe (OSCE) adopts the Vienna Document 2011 on Confidence- and Security-Building Measures, a revised version of the Vienna Document 1999.	OSCE; CSBMs

5–22 Dec.	The Seventh Review Conference of the States Parties to the 1972 Biological and Toxin Weapons Convention (BTWC) is held in Geneva, Switzerland.	BTWC
5 Dec.	The UN Security Council adopts, by a vote of 13–0, with China and Russia abstaining, Resolution 2023, which expands the sanctions imposed by Resolution 1907 (2009) and demands that Eritrea cease providing support to all direct or indirect efforts to destabilize Somalia and other parts of the Horn of Africa.	UN; Eritrea; Sanctions
5 Dec.	Former Ivorian President Laurent Gbagbo appears before the International Criminal Court (ICC), having been detained by the ICC on 30 Nov. Gbagbo is brought to account for his individual responsibility in the violence during the civil war in Côte d'Ivoire following the elections in 2010. He is the first former head of state to appear before the court.	ICC; Côte d'Ivoire
6 Dec.	A series of coordinated suicide bomb attacks at Shia shrines in Kabul, Kandahar and Mazar i Sharif, Afghanistan, kills at least 63 people and injures many more.	Afghanistan; Terrorism
12 Dec.	The Council of the European Union approves the establishment of the Regional Maritime Capacity Building (RMCB) mission under the EU's Common Security and Defence Policy (CSDP) in order to strengthen the maritime capacities of eight countries in the Horn of Africa and the western Indian Ocean—Djibouti, Kenya, Mauritius, Mozambique, the Seychelles, Somalia (the regions of Puntland, Somaliland and Galmudug), Tanzania and Yemen. The RMCB will be a civilian mission that will complement the EU Naval Force Somalia (EU NAVFOR Somalia, Operation Atalanta) and the EU Training Mission Somalia (EUTM). The mission's launch date is to be decided by the Council.	EU; Horn of Africa; Indian Ocean
15 Dec.	A ceremony at Baghdad airport marks the end of the nine-year US military presence in Iraq, which started with the US- and British-led invasion in Mar. 2003. The last US soldiers leave Iraq on 18 Dec. and the 2008 Iraqi–US status of forces agreement expires on 31 Dec.	USA; Iraq
19 Dec.	North Korea announces the death of its leader, Kim Jong-il, on 17 Dec. Following the news of Kim's death, South Korea puts its military on alert along the border with North Korea. Over the following weeks his youngest son, Kim Jong-un, assumes power as the country's leader.	North Korea
19 Dec.	Meeting in Cairo, Egypt, the Arab League and Syria sign a deal allowing Arab League observers into Syria. Under the agreement Syria is also to withdraw its troops from insurgent towns, release thousands of political prisoners and open dialogue with the opposition. The observer mission, comprising 150 observers, will be fully deployed by 25 Dec.	Arab League; Syria

22 Dec.	A series of coordinated bomb attacks across Baghdad, Iraq, kills at least 72 people and injures more than 200. The sectarian violence has been provoked by the issuing of an arrest warrant for Vice-President Tariq al-Hashemi (a Sunni) by the Prime Minister, Nouri al-Maliki (a Shia).	Iraq; Terrorism
29 Dec.	The Turkish military carries out air strikes in Iraq, killing 35 civilian smugglers mistaken for rebels of the Partiya Karkerên Kurdistan (PKK, Kurdistan Workers' Party).	Turkey; Iraq; Kurds

About the authors

Marie Allansson (Sweden) is a Research Assistant with the Uppsala Conflict Data Program (UCDP) at the Uppsala University Department of Peace and Conflict Research. Prior to joining the UCDP, she conducted an internship at the United Nation Development Programme (UNDP) Iraq Country Office, based in Jordan, focusing on small arms and light weapons.

Dr Ian Anthony (United Kingdom) is SIPRI Research Coordinator and Director of the SIPRI Arms Control and Non-proliferation Programme. His publications include *Reforming Nuclear Export Controls: The Future of the Nuclear Suppliers Group*, SIPRI Research Report no. 22 (2007, co-author), and *The Future of Nuclear Weapons in NATO* (Friedrich-Ebert-Stiftung, 2010, co-author). He has contributed to the SIPRI Yearbook since 1988

Dr Sibylle Bauer (Germany) is Director of the SIPRI Dual-use and Arms Trade Control Programme. Before joining SIPRI, she was a Researcher with the Institute for European Studies in Brussels. Since 2005 she has designed and implemented capacity-building activities in Europe and, more recently also South East Asia, with a focus on legal and enforcement issues related to the enhancement of transit, brokering and export controls. Her publications include *The European Union Code of Conduct on Arms Exports: Improving the Annual Report*, SIPRI Policy Paper no. 8 (2004, co-author), and chapters in *From Early Warning To Early Action? The Debate on the Enhancement of the EU's Crisis Response Capability Continues* (European Commission, 2008, co-author) and *The Arms Trade* (Routledge, 2010). She has contributed to the SIPRI Yearbook since 2004.

Jonas Baumann (Switzerland) is a Research Assistant with the Uppsala University Department of Peace and Conflict Research. He previously worked as a research fellow for the Parliamentary Assembly of the Organization for Security and Co-operation in Europe (OSCE).

Nenne Bodell (Sweden) is Director of the SIPRI Library and Documentation Department and of the SIPRI Arms Control and Disarmament Documentary Survey Programme. She has contributed to the SIPRI Yearbook since 2003.

Mark Bromley (United Kingdom) is a Senior Researcher with the SIPRI Arms Transfers Programme, where his work focuses on European arms exports and arms export controls and South American arms acquisitions. Previously, he was a policy analyst for the British American Security Information Council (BASIC). His recent publications include *Implementing an Arms Trade Treaty: Lessons on Reporting and Monitoring from Existing Mechanisms*, SIPRI Policy Paper no. 28 (July 2011, co-author), *Transparency in Military Spending and Arms Acquisitions in Latin America and the Caribbean*, SIPRI Policy Paper no. 31 (Jan. 2012, co-author), and 'The review of the EU Common Position on arms exports: prospects for strengthened controls', Non-proliferation Papers no. 7 (Jan. 2012). He has contributed to the SIPRI Yearbook since 2004.

Gareth Evans (Australia) is Chancellor of Australian National University, Professorial Fellow at the University of Melbourne and President Emeritus of the International Crisis Group, which he led from 2000 to 2009. He was a member of the Australian Parliament for 21 years, and a cabinet minister for 13, including as foreign minister between 1988 and 1996. He co-chaired the International Commission on Intervention and State Sovereignty (2000–2001), which initiated the 'responsibility to protect' concept, and the International Commission on Nuclear Non-Proliferation and Disarmament (2008–10). He has written or edited nine books, including *The Responsibility to Protect: Ending Mass Atrocity Crimes Once and for All* (Brookings Institution Press, 2008).

Claire Fanchini (France) is a Research Assistant with the SIPRI Armed Conflict and Conflict Management Programme, where her research focuses on peace operations and the triggers of armed conflict. She also contributes to the SIPRI Project on Security, Democratization and Good Governance in Africa. Prior to joining SIPRI, she worked for Amnesty International France as a creative writer. Her recent publications include 'Ressources et conflits: de nouveaux défis à la sécurité internationale du XXIe siècle' [Resources and conflicts: emerging challenges to international security in the 21st century], *Diplomatie*, Grands Dossiers no. 7 (Feb.–Mar. 2012).

Vitaly Fedchenko (Russia) is a Senior Researcher with the SIPRI Arms Control and Non-proliferation Programme, with responsibility for nuclear security issues and the political, technological and educational dimensions of nuclear arms control and non-proliferation. Previously, he was a visiting researcher at SIPRI and worked at the Center for Policy Studies in Russia and the Institute for Applied International Research in Moscow. He is the author or co-author of several publications on nuclear forensics, nuclear security and verification, and the international nuclear fuel cycle, including *Reforming Nuclear Export Controls: The Future of the Nuclear Suppliers Group*, SIPRI Research Report no. 22 (2007, co-author). He has contributed to the SIPRI Yearbook since 2005.

Dr Bates Gill (United States) is Director of SIPRI. Before joining SIPRI in 2007, he held the Freeman Chair in China Studies at the Center for Strategic and International Studies (CSIS) in Washington, DC. He previously served as a Senior Fellow in Foreign Policy Studies and inaugural Director of the Center for Northeast Asian Policy Studies at the Brookings Institution. At the end of 2012 he will take up a new appointment as the Chief Executive Officer of the United States Studies Centre in Sydney, Australia. He has a long record of research and publication on international and regional security issues, particularly regarding arms control, non-proliferation, strategic nuclear relations, peacekeeping and military–technical development, especially with regard to

China and Asia. His most recent publications include *Governing the Bomb: Civilian Control and Democratic Accountability of Nuclear Weapons* (2010, Oxford University Press, co-editor), *Asia's New Multilateralism: Cooperation, Competition, and the Search for Community* (Columbia University Press, 2009, co-editor) and *Rising Star: China's New Security Diplomacy* (Brookings, 2007, revised edn 2010). He contributed to the SIPRI Yearbook in 1994, 1996, 2004 and since 2008.

Dr Alexander Glaser (Germany) is Assistant Professor at the Woodrow Wilson School of Public and International Affairs and in the Department of Mechanical and Aerospace Engineering at Princeton University. He is a participant in the university's Program on Science and Global Security and works with the International Panel on Fissile Materials, which publishes the annual Global Fissile Material Report. He holds a PhD in physics from Darmstadt University of Technology and works on nuclear energy and security policy with a focus on nuclear non-proliferation and arms control. He is co-editor of *Science & Global Security*. He has contributed to the SIPRI Yearbook since 2007.

Mikael Grinbaum (Sweden) is studying for a master's degree in global studies at Gothenburg University. He holds a bachelor's degree in peace and conflict studies from Uppsala University. He was an intern at SIPRI in 2011–12.

Lina Grip (Sweden) is a Researcher with the SIPRI Arms Control and Non-proliferation Programme and is SIPRI's coordinator for the EU Non-proliferation Consortium. She is also a doctoral candidate in political science at Helsinki University. Her research interests include regional and multilateral non-proliferation and arms control policies and processes, with a focus on the European Union. Her recent publications include 'Mapping the European Union institutional actors related to WMD non-proliferation', Non-proliferation Papers no. 1 (May 2011), and 'Assessing selected European Union external assistance and cooperation projects on WMD non-proliferation', Non-proliferation Papers no. 6 (Dec. 2011).

John Hart (United States) is a Senior Researcher and Head of the Chemical and Biological Security Project of the SIPRI Arms Control and Non-proliferation Programme. He is also a doctoral candidate in military sciences at the Finnish National Defence University. In 2011 he headed an expert group to facilitate EU support for public health in Central Asia and the South Caucasus under the Instrument for Stability. His publications include *Chemical Weapon Destruction in Russia: Political, Legal and Technical Aspects*, SIPRI Chemical & Biological Warfare Studies No. 17 (1998, co-editor), and *Historical Dictionary of Nuclear, Biological and Chemical Warfare* (Scarecrow Press, 2007, co-author). He has contributed to the SIPRI Yearbook since 1997.

Dr Paul Holtom (United Kingdom) is Director of the SIPRI Arms Transfers Programme. Previously, he was a Research Fellow with the University of Glamorgan Centre for Border Studies. His research interests include the monitoring of international conventional arms transfers, with a particular focus on Russia, Eastern Europe and Central Asia, promoting greater transparency in international arms transfers, and strengthening conventional arms transfer controls to prevent trafficking. His most recent publications include *Implementing an Arms Trade Treaty: Lessons on Reporting and Monitoring from Existing Mechanisms*, SIPRI Policy Paper no. 28 (July 2011, co-author), *China's Energy and Security Relations with Russia: Hopes, Frustrations and Uncertainties*, SIPRI Policy Paper no. 29 (Oct. 2011, co-author), and 'European Union arms export control outreach activities in Eastern and South Eastern Europe', Non-proliferation Papers no. 14 (Apr. 2012, co-author). He has contributed to the SIPRI Yearbook since 2007.

Dr Olawale Ismail (Nigeria) is a Researcher with the SIPRI Military Expenditure and Arms Production Programme and coordinator of the SIPRI Project on Security, Democratization and Good Governance in Africa. He holds a PhD in peace studies from the University of Bradford. He previously worked with the Conflict, Security and Development Group (CSDG), King's College London, and for the SIPRI Project on Budgeting for the Military Sector in Africa. His recent publications include *Dynamics of Post-conflict Reconstruction and Peace Building in West Africa: Between Change and Security* (Nordic Africa Institute, 2009) and 'The dialectics of "junctions" and "bases": youth, "securo-commerce" and the crises of order in downtown Lagos', *Security Dialogue* (2009). He contributed to the SIPRI Yearbook in 2003 and since 2010.

Dr Susan T. Jackson (United States) is Head of the Arms Production Project of the SIPRI Military Expenditure and Arms Production Programme. Her work focuses on the links between militarization and globalization. She has published on the national security exception and the marketing of militarism. She has contributed to the SIPRI Yearbook since 2010.

Noel Kelly (Ireland) is a Research Assistant with the SIPRI Military Expenditure and Arms Production and Arms Transfers programmes. He is responsible for the electronic archive common to these three research areas and maintains the SIPRI reporting system for military expenditure. He has contributed to the SIPRI Yearbook since 2009.

Shannon N. Kile (United States) is a Senior Researcher and Head of the Nuclear Weapons Project of the SIPRI Arms Control and Non-proliferation Programme. His principal areas of research are nuclear arms control and non-proliferation, with a special interest in Iran and regional security issues. His publications include *Europe and Iran: Perspectives on Non-proliferation*, SIPRI Research Report no. 21 (2005, editor), and *Verifying a Fissile Materials Cut-off Treaty: Technical and Organizational Considerations*, SIPRI Policy Paper no. 33 (2012). He has contributed to the SIPRI Yearbook since 1993.

Hans M. Kristensen (Denmark) is Director of the Nuclear Information Project at the Federation of American Scientists (FAS). He is a frequent consultant to the news media and institutes on nuclear weapon matters and is co-author of the 'Nuclear notebook' column in the *Bulletin of the Atomic Scientists*. His recent publications include *Obama and the Nuclear War Plan* (FAS, 2010) and *Non-Strategic Nuclear Weapons* (FAS, 2012). He has contributed to the SIPRI Yearbook since 2001.

Glenn McDonald (Canada) is a Senior Researcher and Yearbook Coordinator at the Small Arms Survey, where he specializes in small arms control measures. He has played an advisory role in successive United Nations small arms processes and in 2012 is an adviser to the president-designate of the Second Review Conference for the UN Programme of Action. He has also worked in UN peacekeeping (Somalia, 1994–95) and post-conflict peacebuilding (Rwanda, 1995). His recent publications include 'Weapons tracing and peace support operations: theory or practice?', Small Arms Survey Issue Brief no. 4 (Mar. 2012, co-author), and 'Precedent in the making: the UN meeting of governmental experts', Small Arms Survey Issue Brief no. 5 (Mar. 2012).

Dr Neil Melvin (United Kingdom) is Director of the SIPRI Armed Conflict and Conflict Management Programme. Prior to joining SIPRI he held senior adviser positions in the Energy Charter Secretariat and the Organization for Security and Co-operation in Europe (OSCE). He has also worked at a variety of leading policy institutes in Europe and has published widely on issues of conflict, with a particular focus on ethno-religious issues. In recent years he has broadened his research interests to consider the impact of resources on conflict, notably the issue of energy and conflict. His recent publications include 'New social media and conflict in Kyrgyzstan', SIPRI Insights on Peace and Security 2011/1 (Aug. 2011, co-author). He contributed to the SIPRI Yearbook in 2006, 2007 and 2011.

Zia Mian (Pakistan/United Kingdom) is a physicist with Princeton University's Program on Science and Global Security, where he directs the Project on Peace and Security in South Asia. He is co-deputy chair of the International Panel on Fissile Materials and co-editor of *Science & Global Security*. His work focuses on nuclear weapons, arms control and disarmament, and nuclear energy issues in India and Pakistan. He contributed to the SIPRI Yearbook in 2003 and since 2007.

Thomas Morgan (Australia) is a Research Fellow at the Institute for Economics and Peace (IEP). He leads the development of IEP's United States Peace Index, the first index to rank all the states of the USA by their peacefulness and has worked extensively on data analysis to investigate what leads to peaceful societies. He has worked on the Global Peace Index since 2010.

Marcus Nilsson (Sweden) is a Research Assistant with the Uppsala Conflict Data Program (UCDP) at the Uppsala University Department of Peace and Conflict Research. His publications include 'Reaping what was sown: conflict outcome and post-civil war democratization', *Cooperation and Conflict* (forthcoming 2012).

Dr Sam Perlo-Freeman (United Kingdom) is a Senior Researcher with the SIPRI Military Expenditure and Arms Production Programme, responsible for monitoring data on military expenditure worldwide. Previously, he was a Senior Lecturer at the University of the West of England, working in the field of defence and peace economics. His recent publications include 'The demand for military expenditure in developing countries: hostility vs capability', *Defence and Peace Economics* (August 2008, co-author), a chapter on the UK's arms industry in *The Global Arms Trade: A Handbook* (Routledge, 2009) and 'Budgetary priorities in Latin America: military, health and education spending', SIPRI Insights on Peace and Security 2011/2 (Dec. 2011). He has contributed to the SIPRI Yearbook since 2003.

Phillip Schell (Germany) is a Researcher with the SIPRI Arms Control and Non-Proliferation Programme. Before joining SIPRI in September 2011, he worked at NATO's Emerging Security Challenges Division and the James Martin Center for Nonproliferation Studies.

Camilla Schippa (Italy/Sweden) is Director of the Institute for Economics and Peace (IEP), where she manages the development of the Global Peace Index as well as the research carried out internationally on and around the index. Until 2008 she was chief of office of the United Nations Office for Partnerships, where she guided the creation of strategic alliances between the UN and corporations, foundations and philanthropists. She has contributed to the SIPRI Yearbook since 2010.

Dr Hans-Joachim Schmidt (Germany) is a Senior Research Fellow at the Peace Research Institute Frankfurt (PRIF/HSFK). His work focuses on military confidence building and conventional arms control in Europe and on the Korean Peninsula. He also studies the Six Party Talks on the nuclear issue with North Korea. His publications include *The Future of Conventional Arms Control in Europe* (Nomos 2009, co-editor), *Konventionelle Rüstungskontrolle in Europa: Wege in die Zukunft* [Conventional arms control in Europe: paths towards the future], HSFK Report no. 6/2011 (co-author), 'Caps and bans: limiting, reducing, and prohibiting missiles and missile defence' in *Arms Control and Missile Proliferation in the Middle East* (Routledge, 2011, co-author), and Nordkorea als Nuklearmacht: Chancen der Kontrolle [North Korea as a nuclear power: chances of its control], HSFK Report no. 1/2012.

Dr Elisabeth Sköns (Sweden) is Director of the SIPRI Military Expenditure and Arms Production Programme. Her current research focus is on the security-related activities of external actors in Africa and she leads the SIPRI Project on Security, Democratization and Good Governance in Africa. Her recent publications include 'The private military services industry', SIPRI Insights on Peace and Security no. 2008/1 (Sep. 2008, co-author), 'The economics of arms production' in *Encyclopedia of Violence, Peace and Conflict* (Elsevier, 2008, co-author), 'The military-industrial complex' in *The Global Arms Trade* (Routledge, 2010, co-author) and 'The US defence industry after the cold war' in *The Global Arms Trade* (Routledge 2010). She has contributed to the SIPRI Yearbook since 1983.

Carina Solmirano (Argentina) is a Researcher with the SIPRI Military Expenditure and Arms Production Programme responsible for monitoring military expenditure in Latin America, the Middle East and South Asia. Prior to joining SIPRI, she worked at the Josef Korbel School of International Studies at the University of Denver, Colorado, where she is a doctoral candidate. She has also worked on arms control issues at the Argentine NGO Asociacion para Politicas Publicas and as an adviser at the Argentine Senate. Her recent publications include *Transparency in Military Spending and Arms Acquisitions in Latin America and the Caribbean*, SIPRI Policy Paper no. 31 (Jan. 2012, co-author). She has contributed to the SIPRI Yearbook since 2010.

Samuel Taub (Sweden) is a Research Assistant with the Uppsala Conflict Data Program (UCDP) at the Uppsala University Department of Peace and Conflict Research. He is the UCDP's regional expert covering the Middle East and North Africa during the Arab Spring.

Lotta Themnér (Sweden) is a Research Coordinator with the Uppsala Conflict Data Program (UCDP) at the Uppsala University Department of Peace and Conflict Research. She has edited eight editions of the UCDP's *States in Armed Conflict* and has co-authored a number of articles and book chapters on armed conflicts. She has contributed to the SIPRI Yearbook since 2005.

Professor Peter Wallensteen (Sweden) has held the Dag Hammarskjöld Chair in Peace and Conflict Research at Uppsala University since 1985 and has been the Richard G. Starmann Sr Research Professor of Peace Studies at the University of Notre Dame since 2006. He directs the Uppsala Conflict Data Program (UCDP) and the Special Program on International Targeted Sanctions (SPITS). His publications include *Understanding Conflict Resolution: War, Peace and the Global System* (Sage, 3rd edn, 2011), *Peace Research: Theory and Practice* (Routledge 2011) and *The Go-Between: Jan Eliasson and the Styles of Mediation* (US Institute of Peace Press, 2010, co-author). He has contributed to the SIPRI Yearbook since 1988.

Pieter D. Wezeman (Netherlands) is a Senior Researcher with the SIPRI Arms Transfers Programme. Prior to rejoining SIPRI in 2006 he was a Senior Analyst for the Dutch Ministry of Defence in the field of proliferation of conventional and nuclear weapon technology. His recent publications include *Arms Flows to Sub-Saharan Africa*, SIPRI Policy Paper no. 30 (Dec. 2011, co-author). He has contributed to the SIPRI Yearbook since 1995.

Siemon T. Wezeman (Netherlands) is a Senior Fellow with the SIPRI Arms Transfers Programme, where he has worked since 1992. Among his publications are several relating to international transparency in arms transfers, *The Future of the United Nations Register of Conventional Arms*, SIPRI Policy Paper no. 4 (Aug. 2003), *Cluster Weapons: Necessity or Convenience?* (Pax Christi Netherlands, 2005, co-author) and *Arms Flows to Sub-Saharan Africa*, SIPRI Policy Paper no. 30 (Dec. 2011, co-author). He has contributed to the SIPRI Yearbook since 1993.

Sharon Wiharta (Indonesia) is a Senior Researcher with the SIPRI Armed Conflict and Conflict Management Programme, where she leads research on peacekeeping and peacebuilding issues. She currently directs the SIPRI Project on the New Geopolitics of Peace Operations, which seeks to better understand the perspectives and motives of emerging powers on the future of peace operations. Her publications include *Peace Operations: Trends, Progress and Prospects* (Georgetown University Press, 2008, co-editor) and *The Civilian Contribution to Peace Operations*, SIPRI Research Report (forthcoming 2012). She has contributed to the SIPRI Yearbook since 2002.

Helen Wilandh (Sweden) is a Research Assistant with the SIPRI Military Expenditure and Arms Production Programme. Her main research interest is African security issues and she has worked on the SIPRI Project on Security, Democratization and Good Governance in Africa. She holds a master's degree from Uppsala University and studied political science, international relations and international law at the Paris Institute of Political Studies (Sciences Po).

Dr Wolfgang Zellner (Germany) is Deputy Director of the Institute for Peace Research and Security Policy at the University of Hamburg (IFSH) and Head of the IFSH's Centre for OSCE Research (CORE). He received his PhD in Political Science from the Free University of Berlin in 1994. From 1984 to 1991, he advised a member of the German Bundestag on military and security policy and arms control. He has (co-)authored and edited around 100 publications, mainly on European security, conventional arms control, national minorities, OSCE-related subjects, and transnational threats and challenges.

Errata

SIPRI Yearbook 2011: Armaments, Disarmament and International Security

Page 308, table 6B.1   *In the line for Denmark, for '2 607' (2009) read '336'*
In the line for South Korea, for '1 625' (2009) read '1 170'

SIPRI Yearbook 2012: Armaments, Disarmament and International Security

Errata for this printed edition of *SIPRI Yearbook 2012* will appear at <http://www.sipri.org/yearbook/> and in *SIPRI Yearbook 2013*. The online edition of *SIPRI Yearbook 2012* at <http://www.sipriyearbook.org/> will be updated as errors are discovered.

Index

AAR Corp. 232, 255
ABACC (Brazilian–Argentine Agency for
  Accounting and Control of Nuclear
  Materials) 379, 381
Abbas, President Mahmoud 514, 519
Abkhazia 451
ABM Treaty (Treaty on the Limitation of
  Anti-Ballistic Missile Systems, 1972)
  482–83
Abyei 91, 95, 96, 97–99, 121, 516
  see also UNISFA
Academi 236
Adams, Gordon 163–64
Aeronautics 292
Aerospace Corp. 247
Afghanistan:
  armed conflict 3, 44, 71
  arms imports 271, 437
  arms industry and 247–49
  civilian casualties 15
  economic cost of war 3, 147, 148, 156–61
  EUPOL Afghanistan 132
  GPI ranking 85
  ISAF see ISAF
  Italian troops 177
  length of war 7, 67
  lessons from conflict 30, 36
  logistics support 235–36
  non-state actors 44
  peace operations in 89
  terrorism 519, 523
  UNAMA 123, 158, 512
  US troop withdrawal 4, 163, 219, 516
Africa:
  arms transfers, reports 294–95
  military expenditure 167–72
    GDP percentages 202–203
    increases 147, 148
    reporting 183
    tables 150, 153, 188–89, 195–96,
      202–203
  organized violence 80
    non-state conflicts 72, 74–75
    one-sided violence 76, 77, 78
    state-based armed conflicts 68
  peace operations 106–108
  peacefulness 84
Africa Contingency Operations Training
  and Assistance (ACOTA) 237

African Union (AU) 494
  Côte d'Ivoire policy 512
  higher profile 8
  Libya and 32, 54, 100, 432, 513
  military expenditure, table 150
  peace operations
    AMISOM 59, 60, 61, 106–107, 126,
      518, 520
    training 237
    UNAMID 92, 125, 237
  responsibility to protect and 37
  Sudan and 98, 516
Agility 232, 253
AgustaWestland 250, 252
Ahlu Sunna Waljamaca 59
Al Jazeera 16
al-Qaeda 67, 78, 263, 392, 509, 514, 518
al-Qaeda in the Arabian Peninsula (AQAP)
  51, 54–55, 520
al-Qaeda in the Islamic Maghreb (AQIM)
  148, 167, 168
al-Shabab 57, 59–61, 106–107, 167, 518, 520
Albania:
  arms supply to Libya 433
  chemical weapons 399
  OSCE Presence in 138
Albright, Madeleine 30
Alenia Aeronautica 253
Algeria:
  Arab Spring 45
  arms imports 265, 268, 271
  de-escalation of conflict 71
  military expenditure 8, 148, 167–69
  rivalry with Morocco 169
Alion Science and Technology 232, 254
Aliyev, President Ilham 290
Alliant Techsystems 252
Almaz-Antei 251
AM General 253
Amano, Yukiya 363, 365, 366, 375, 521
Americas:
  arms export control 427–28
  CSBMs in South America 447–48
  military expenditure 154–55
    GDP percentages 204
    reporting 184
    South American transparency 5
    tables 150, 153, 190, 197, 204
    trend 149

organized violence
  non-state conflicts 72, 74, 75–76
  one-sided violence 76, 77, 78–79
  state-based armed conflicts 68, 71
peace operations 108–109
AMISOM (AU Mission to Somalia) 59, 60,
  61, 106–107, 126, 518, 520
Angola:
  end of conflict 71
  military expenditure 171
  UNITA conflict 67
Annan, Kofi 18, 20, 21, 34
Antarctic Treaty (1959) 459
  Madrid Protocol (1991) 459
Anteon 231–32
anthrax 409
anti-personnel mines:
  APM Convention (1997) 415, 422,
    471–72
  destruction 422
APEC (Asia–Pacific Economic
  Cooperation) 494
APM Convention (Anti-Personnel Mines
  Convention, 1997) 415, 422, 471–72
Arab League 499
  Arab Spring and 55
  arms embargoes 11, 275, 416, 431, 440
  higher profile 8
  Libya and 26, 27, 31, 53, 55, 100, 432, 511
  military expenditure 150
  responsibility to protect and 37
  Syria and 3, 31
    arms embargo 11, 275, 416
    attempted mediation 55
    evolution of position 54, 435, 516
    Observer Mission 89, 91, 104–105, 110,
      127, 523
    Plan of Action 521
    public criticism 516
    sanctions 522
Arab Spring 3
  arms transfers and 259, 275–79
  assessment 55–56
  effect on peacefulness 84
  external support 52–54
  first year 45–56
  level of violence 45, 46
  media and 16
  patterns 43
  table 46
  third-party involvement 54–55
  see also individual countries

Argentina:
  NSG transfer guidelines and 378–79, 381
  uranium-enrichment facilities 349
ARINC 247
armed conflicts:
  Arab Spring see Arab Spring
  Horn of Africa 57–64
  intensity 71
  non-state conflicts 71–77
    casualties 73, 74–75
    comparisons 79–80
    definition 71–73, 81–82
    ethnic or religious conflicts 73–74
    meaning 43, 65
    tables 72, 74
    trend 73
  numbers 4
  one-sided violence 77–79
    casualties 77–78
    comparisons 79–80
    definition 82
    meaning 43, 65
    non-state actors 78
    tables 76, 77
  overview 43–44
  protection of civilians see protection of
    civilians
  protracted conflicts 43
  reduction 15, 43
  state-based armed conflicts 66–71
    comparisons 79
    definition 66, 81
    meaning 43, 65
    tables 68–70, 71
    types 67
  types 43, 57, 65–80
    comparisons 79–80
  see also individual countries
Armenia:
  arms imports 260, 287, 288–90
  map 287
  military expenditure 286–87, 288
  Nagorno-Karabakh conflict 137–38, 260,
    286, 288, 292, 442, 446
  OSCE arms embargo 260, 287–88
arms control:
  2011 overview 10–11
  chemical and biological weapons
    391–414
  conventional arms 415–52
  exports control regimes 425–30,
    505–508

nuclear arms control 353–89
strategic trade control regimes 505–508
treaties 455–86
see also specific treaties
arms embargoes:
Arab League 11, 275, 416, 431
Arab Spring and 275–79
ECOWAS 431, 436, 440
EU 431
Arab Spring and 278–79
arms transfers and 278–79
Belarus 431, 436, 516
Libya 11, 275, 278, 433, 510
Sudan and South Sudan 431, 436, 517
Syria 11, 53, 275, 278, 416, 431, 434–35, 514
table 439–40
OSCE 260, 287–88
purpose 416
survey 431–41
United Nations
Côte d'Ivoire 436, 437–38, 514
Darfur 438
Iran 437
Libya 11, 27, 100, 275, 416, 431–34
protection of civilians and 19
Syria 265–67, 276, 431, 437
table 439
violations 11, 27, 437–38
arms industry:
definitions 257
European cooperation 180, 224–27
financial crisis and 217, 219
international sales *see* arms transfers
key developments 219–29
mergers and acquisitions
cybersecurity 228, 231–32
USA 222–24
methodology 257–58
overview 217–18
sales reports 219–20
sources 257
technology transfer 218
Top 100 producers 247–58
regional and national shares 248
tables 248, 251–56
see also individual countries and companies; military services
arms trade treaty 425
arms transfers:
2011 developments 4
exporters 261–69
importers 269–73

Arab Spring and 259, 275–79
definition 274
exporters
10 largest 264
50 largest 266–67
developments 261–69
largest exporters 259, 261
tables 264, 266–67
financial value, table 303–305
importers
10 largest 270
50 largest 272–73
developments 269–73
largest importers 259, 269–71
licensed production 268, 271
tables 270, 272–73
methodology 274
overview 259–60
sources 273
South East Asia
maritime security 280–83
naval equipment 280–85
transfers of technology 259–60
transparency 293–98
EU reports 297–98
national reports 296–97
UNROCA 260, 293–96, 299–301
see also arms embargoes
Asaad, Riyad al- 50, 54
ASEAN (Association of Southeast Asian Nations) 12, 282, 494, 510, 517
ASEAN Plus Three (APT) 495
ASEAN Regional Forum (ARF) 495
Aselsan 219, 254
Asia and Oceania:
military expenditure
GDP percentages 205–206
increases 147, 149, 153–54
reporting 184
tables 150, 153, 191–92, 198–99, 205–206
organized violence
non-state conflicts 72, 74
one-sided violence 76, 77
state-based armed conflicts 69, 71
peace operations 109–10
South East Asia
map 282
maritime security 280–83
naval equipment imports 280–85
Assad, President Bashar al- 31, 49–50, 53, 54, 516, 518
Assad, President Hafez al- 49

Athor, George 510
Australia:
    arms imports from US 262
    military expenditure 7
    NPDI member 514
    South East Asia and 282
Australia Group 411, 505, 515
Austria: arms transfer reports 295
avian influenza 9, 392, 410–11
Avio 247
Avnet 228
Aweys, Hassan Dahir 59
Awlaki, Anwar al- 520
Azad Systems 292
Azerbaijan:
    arms imports 260, 287, 290–92
    map 287
    military expenditure 149, 174, 286–87
    Nagorno-Karabakh conflict 137–38, 260,
        286, 288, 292, 442, 446
    OSCE arms embargo 260, 287–88

Babcock 232, 250, 252
BAE Systems 219, 226, 228, 229, 236–37,
    249, 251, 253
Bahrain:
    Arab Spring 3, 45–47, 52, 268, 275, 511
    arms imports 276, 277, 278
    governance 55
Ban Ki-moon 19, 24, 102, 103, 518
Bangkok Treaty (1995) 477–78
Bangladesh: peace operations contribution
    93
Bashir, President Omar al- 510
Belarus:
    arms exports 287, 290, 292
    EU arms embargo 431, 436, 516
Belgium:
    CFE Treaty and 522
    deployment of US nuclear weapons 314
    old chemical weapons 403
Ben Ali, President Zine-Al Abidine 51, 509
Berdennikov, Grigory 370
Berlusconi, Silvio 175
Bharat Electronics Ltd (BEL) 241, 244,
    254
Bilmes, Linda 159, 161
bin Laden, Osama 4, 514
biological weapons:
    allegations 406–408
    biosecurity 9, 288, 294, 410–12
    control 393–96
    DNA recovery 411–12

flu viruses 392, 410–11
    overview 391–92
    prevention 409–14
    research 392, 410–14
    terrorism 409–10, 414
    see also BTWC
BioWeapons Prevention Project (BWPP)
    393–94
Bizimungu, Augustin 515
Black Death 411–12
Blackwater 236
Boeing 228, 229, 235, 251
Boko Haram 148, 167, 169, 170, 518, 521
Bosnia and Herzegovina:
    armed forces limits 444–45
    EUFOR Althea 130
    EUPM 129
    OSCE Mission to 138
    Srebrenica massacre 21
    Vienna Document and 449
Bouazizi, Mohamed 50–51
Brahimi Report (2000) 20
Brazil:
    arms industry 218, 247
    cluster munitions and CCW Convention
        420
    criminal gangs 76
    CSBMs 447
    Libyan policy 27, 33, 511
    military expenditure 154
    military services to 234
    NSG transfer guidelines and 378–79, 381
    one-sided violence 79
    peace operations contribution 89
    responsibility to protect and 17, 32–33
    responsibility while protecting 35
    Syria and 435
    uranium-enrichment facilities 349
BRICS (Brazil, Russia, India, China and
    South Africa): Libya and 27, 30–33, 34, 35
Brunei Darussalam: arms imports 259,
    280, 281, 285
BTWC (Biological and Toxin Weapons
    Convention, 1972) 464–65
    7th Review Conference (2011) 391,
        393–96, 523
    8th Review Conference (2016) 395
    drafting 407
    Implementation Support Unit 393, 395,
        464
    new parties 393
    scientific research and 412–13
    VEREX 396

Bulgaria: CFE Treaty and 522
Burkina Faso:
    arms supplies to Côte d'Ivoire 437
    UNROCA and 295
Burundi:
    BTWC membership 393
    end of conflict 71
Bush, President George W. 312, 378

CACI International 228, 229, 232, 252
CAE 254
Camber Corp. 228
Cambodia:
    1970s atrocities 20, 25
    cluster munitions 423
    military expenditure 154
    Thai border dispute 5, 510, 517
Cameron, David 432, 519
Cameroon: counterterrorism 170
Canada:
    arms transfer reports 296
    CFE Treaty and 522
    Indian nuclear cooperation agreement
        383
    Iran and sanctions 522
    Libyan operation 512
    military expenditure in Afghanistan
        158–59
    NPDI member 514
    NSG transfer guidelines and 379
Carter, Ashton 223
Cassidian 226–27
CCM (Convention on Cluster Munitions,
    2008) 11, 415, 420, 421, 422–23, 472
CCW Convention (Certain Conventional
    Weapons Convention, 1981) 467–69
    3rd Review Conference (2006) 417–18
    4th Review Conference (2011) 417,
        419–22, 521
    cluster munitions and 11, 417–22
    international divisions 415
    protocols 467
CEA 252
CEEAC (Economic Community of Central
    African States) 127–28, 496
Central African Republic:
    HCOC participant 515
    MICOPAX 127–28
CFE Treaty (Treaty on Conventional
    Armed Forces in Europe, 1990) 475–77
    2011 Review Conference 11, 519
    CFE-1A Agreement (1992) 476

Flank Document (1996) 475–76
Joint Consultative Group (JCG) 499
Nagorno-Karabakh and 286
Russia and 442–44, 450, 522
Tashkent Agreement (1992) 475
violations 11
Chad: armed conflict 71, 170
Chechnya 44
chemical weapons:
    allegations 406–408
    control 397–405
    destruction 399–403
        abandoned weapons 403
        Iraq 399–400
        Libya 400–402
        old weapons 403
        Russia 402
        United States 402–403
    overview 391–92
    political tension 404–405
    prevention 409–14
    research 412–14
    terrorism 409–10, 414
    victim support 398
    see also CWC
Chemring Group 254
Chile: NPDI member 514
China:
    abandoned chemical weapons 403
    arms exports 259, 269, 284
    arms imports 8, 259, 265, 269, 271
    arms industry 250, 271
    arms trade treaty and 425
    biological weapons in 406
    BTWC and 395
    Central Military Commission 327
    Defence White Paper (2010) 327, 330
    humanitarian intervention and 30
    Indian relations 239
    Libyan policy 26, 27, 30, 53, 101, 432,
        434, 511
    maritime rights disputes 281
    military expenditure 4, 8, 149, 153–54,
        282
    nuclear disarmament and 389
    nuclear forces 327–31
        aircraft and cruise missiles 331, 509
        ballistic missile submarines 330
        expansion 307, 327
        fissile material 327, 345
        lack of transparency 5, 307, 327
        land-based ballistic missiles 329

numbers 328
recognized nuclear weapon state 307, 389
reprocessing facilities 350
uranium-enrichment facilities 349
nuclear non-proliferation and
Iran 370
North Korea 375
NPT commitments 389, 517
Pakistan 384–85
Syria 364, 365
Pakistan relations 337, 384–85
peace operations contribution 89
Philippines and 154
responsibility to protect and 17, 30
rising power 178
space programme 519
Syrian policy 30–31, 55, 105, 364, 365, 435
terrorism 3
USA and 165, 263, 283, 331
CICA (Conference on Interaction and Confidence-building Measures in Asia) 496
CIFTA (Inter-American Convention against the Illicit Manufacturing and Trafficking in Firearms, Ammunition, Explosives, and Other Related Materials) 427–28, 480
civilian protection see protection of civilians
Clapper, James 369–70
Clinton, Hillary Rodham 355, 383, 432
cluster munitions:
CCM (2008) 415, 420, 421, 422–23, 472
CCW Convention and 417–22
control 417–24
definition 417
destructions 422
international divisions 11
Libya 514
NGO role 421–22
Oslo Process 418
prospects 423–24
trade 423–24
Vientiane Action Plan 415–16, 423
Cluster Munitions Coalition 418
Cobham 252
Cohen, Roberta 21
Colombia:
United Self-defence Forces of Colombia (AUC) 73
MAPP/OEA 136

non-state conflict 73, 76
Revolutionary Armed Forces of Colombia (FARC) 73, 76
Commonwealth of Independent States (CIS) 495
Joint Control Commission Peacekeeping Force (JCC) 128
military expenditure 150
Computer Sciences Corp. 232, 251
Conference on Disarmament (CD) 489
confidence- and security-building measures:
2011 developments 416, 447–52
South America 447–48
Vienna Document 447, 448–50, 482, 522
Congo, Democratic Republic of (DRC):
Bundu-dia-Kongo 66
civilian casualties 15
EUPOL RD Congo 132
EUSEC RD Congo 130
Libya and 513
MONUSCO 92–93, 116–17, 513
peace operations in, reinforcement 91
Congo, Republic of: arms transfers and 294–95
Convention on the Physical Protection of Nuclear Material (1980) 466–67
conventional arms control 415–52
embargoes see arms embargoes
European control 442–46
exports control regimes 416, 425–30
informal regimes 416
overview 415–16
trend 11
Côte d'Ivoire:
armed conflict 3, 44, 512, 513
arms embargo 436
ICC arrest 523
Indian policy 32
international actors 8
Operation Licorne 108, 141
peace operations 36
French operation 36, 44, 108
UNOCI 107–108, 118, 513
protection of civilians 10, 32, 89
UN arms embargo 11, 437–38, 514
UN Security Council
policy 36, 44
Resolution 1967 107
Resolution 1975 108, 512
Resolution 1980 108, 436, 514
Resolution 2000 108

Council of Europe (COE) 496
Council of the Baltic Sea States (CBSS)
    496–97
counterterrorism:
    Africa 167
    Algeria 167–69
    chemical and biological weapons
        409–10, 414
    global war on terrorism 67, 110–11,
        147–48, 167, 168
    Nigeria 169–71
    nuclear terrorism 354, 377, 388
    oil and 167–71
    UN Global Counter-Terrorism Strategy
        409–10
Croatia:
    arms export reports 297
    limits on armed forces 444–45
CSTO (Collective Security Treaty
    Organization) 151, 495
CTBT (Comprehensive Nuclear-Test-Ban
    Treaty, 1996) 311, 354, 470–71
CTBTO (Comprehensive Nuclear-Test-
    Ban Treaty Organization) 491
Cuba: responsibility to protect and 23
Cubic Corp. 232, 254
Curtiss-Wright Corp. 254
CWC (Chemical Weapons Convention,
    1993) 469–70
    3rd Review Conference (2013) 391
    16th CSP 391, 397–99
    budget (2012) 397
    detecting violations 392
    ratifications 397
    scientific research and 412–13
    verification regime 392
cybersecurity 9, 218, 228–29, 233
Cyprus:
    CFE Treaty and 443
    Greece–Turkey relations and 177,
        451–52
    Open Skies Treaty 451–52
    UNFICYP 114
    Vienna Document and 449
Czech Republic:
    arms exports to Azerbaijan 291, 292
    CFE Treaty and 522

Dagestan 44
Darfur:
    civilian casualties 15–16
    Doha Peace Agreement 515
    Janjaweed 77

    one-sided violence 78
    UN arms embargo violations 11, 438
    UNAMID 92, 125, 237
    UN Security Council Resolution 1706
        100
Dassault 226, 245–46, 253, 268
Davies, Glyn 374
DCNS 252
Deng, Francis 21
Denmark:
    CFE Treaty and 522
    NORDEFCO 226
Diehl 253
Djibouti:
    armed conflict with Eritrea 67
    maritime capacity 523
Dominican Republic: arms transfer
    reporting 293
drones see unmanned aerial systems
dual-use items 227, 381, 382, 386, 393, 411,
    425
Duelfer, Charles 400
DynCorp International 232, 252

EADS 226, 249, 251, 252
East African Community 151
East Asia Summit (EAS) 495
Economist Intelligence Unit (EIU) 84
ECOWAS (Economic Community of West
    African States) 497
    arms embargo 431, 436, 440
    Côte d'Ivoire policy 512
    military expenditure 151
    responsibility to protect and 37
    SALW Convention (2006) 481
Ecuador: arms transfer reporting 293
Edwards, Ryan 161
Egeland, Jan 24
Egypt:
    Arab Spring 3, 47–48, 52, 55, 275, 509,
        510
    arms imports 275, 276, 277–78, 278
    arms supply to Libya 433
    MFO 140
    monocracy 55
    National Democratic Party 47
    Palestine territories and 514
    Supreme Council of the Armed Forces
        (SCAF) 47–48
Eisenhower Research Project 159
Elbit Systems 252
Embraer 218, 247, 255
Enmod Convention 465–66

Eritrea:
  arms supplies to Darfur 438
  external conflict 57
  UN Security Council Resolution 1907 523
  UN Security Council Resolution 2023 523
  armed conflict with Djibouti 67
Esterline Technologies 254
ETA 5, 509, 520
Ethiopia:
  Kenyan border disputes 62–64
  military expenditure 167
  one-sided violence 57–58
  Somali conflict 57, 59
  Operation Linda Nchi
  violence in Somali region 61–62
EU BAM Rafah (EU Border Assistance Mission for the Rafah Crossing Point) 131
EUFOR Althea (EU Military Operation in Bosnia and Herzegovina) 130
EUJUST LEX (EU Integrated Rule of Law Mission for Iraq) 130–31
EULEX Kosovo (EU Rule of Law Mission in Kosovo) 133
EUMM (EU Monitoring Mission) 133
EUPM (EU Police Mission in Bosnia and Herzegovina) 129
EUPOL Afghanistan (EU Police Mission in Afghanistan) 132
EUPOL COPPS (EU Coordinating Office for Palestinian Police Support) 131
EUPOL RD Congo (EU Police Mission in the DRC) 132
Euratom (European Atomic Energy Community) 497
Eurocopter Group 252
Europe:
  arms industry
    cooperation debate 224–27
    defence cooperation treaties 180, 225–26
    top producers 247
    UASs 226–27
  military expenditure 147, 149, 173–80
    financial crisis and 173–80, 217
    implications of reduction 178–80
    reporting 183, 184
    tables 150, 153, 192–93, 199–200
  organized violence
    one-sided violence 76, 77
    state-based armed conflicts 69, 71

peace operations 110
  see also European Union; OSCE
European Defence Agency (EDA) 498
European Scientific Working Group on Influenza 410
European Union (EU) 497–98
  arms embargoes see arms embargoes
  arms exports
    control 426–27
    dual-use goods 425
    reports 297–98
  arms industry 218
    cooperation debate 224–27
  BTWC and 394
  Côte d'Ivoire policy 36
  euro crisis 147, 175
  Horn of Africa and 523
  Iran and 372
  Libyan policy 53, 99, 510
  members 497
  military expenditure
    debate 180
    table 151
    UASs 217
  Nagorno-Karabakh and 292
  peace operations
    table 129–35
    see also specific operations
  responsibility to protect and 37
  Satellite Centre 517
  Syrian policy 3, 53, 516, 518, 521
EUSEC RD Congo (EU Advisory and Assistance Mission for Security Reform in the DRC) 130
EUTM (EU Training Mission Somalia) 107, 134, 523

F-35 (Joint Strike Fighter) 217, 221–22, 249, 263, 314
Facebook 50
Fakhrizadeh, Mohsen 366
FARC (Revolutionary Armed Forces of Colombia) 73, 76
Fiat 247
Financial Action Task Force (FATF) 505–506
financial crisis:
  arms industry and 217, 219
  instability 3
  military expenditure and 147
    Europe 173–80
Fincantieri 254

Finland:
  arms imports 249
  NORDEFCO 226
Finmeccanica 250, 251, 253, 254
fissile material:
  categories 308, 345
  China 327, 345
  global stocks 345–50
  India 308, 332, 345
  Iran 371–73
  Israel 308, 345
  legitimate use 379
  North Korea 343–44, 345
  Pakistan 308, 337–38, 339, 345
  reprocessing facilities 350
  Russia 345
  treaty negotiations 354
  UK 345
  uranium-enrichment facilities 349
  USA 345
Flank Document (1996) 475–76
Florence Agreement (1996) 444–45,
  479–80, 504
Fluor 232, 249, 253
Force Protection 255
Fouchier, Ron 410
France:
  Arab Spring and 55, 279
  arms exports 268
    Arab Spring and 278, 279
    to Greece 176–77
    major supplier 259, 261
    naval equipment to South East Asia
      283, 284
    reports 298
  arms industry 225, 226–27
  arms trade treaty and 425
  German defence cooperation 226
  humanitarian intervention and 29–30,
    34, 35
  Indian relations 383, 384
  Iranian policy 370, 372
  Libyan operation 27, 52–53, 55, 512
  military expenditure 7, 149, 158–59, 175
  NPT commitments 389, 517
  nuclear disarmament and 389
  nuclear forces 325–26
    disclosure 307
    fissile material 345
    recognized nuclear weapon state 307,
      389
    reprocessing facilities 350
    transparency 5, 307

  UK cooperation 324
  uranium-enrichment facilities 349
  old chemical weapons 403
  peace operations contribution 93
    Côte d'Ivoire 36, 44, 108
    DRC 30
  responsibility to protect and 17–18
  UK Defence and Security Cooperation
    Treaty (2010) 180, 225, 324
  UN arms embargo on Libya and 27, 433

G8 354, 388, 491, 515
G20 12
Gaddafi, Muammar:
  African Union and 100
  Arab Spring 48–49, 510–12
  attacks on civilians 16, 25–26, 28, 100
  chemical weapons 392, 400, 407
  death 4, 27, 49, 102, 520
  ICC arrest warrant 515, 516
  NATO and 514, 518
  Russian contacts 54
  South Africa and 32
  Sudanese policy 433
  superior forces 102
Gaddafi, Saif al-Islam 515, 516
Gates, Robert 179
Gbagbo, President Laurent 44, 108,
  437–38, 512, 513, 523
GenCorp 255
General Atomics 235
General Dynamics 228, 231, 251
General Electric 251
Geneva Conventions (1949) 18, 457–58
  Additional Protocols (1977) 18, 458–59
Geneva Protocol (1925) 456
genocide 15, 16, 17, 21, 22, 25, 77, 79, 515
Genocide Convention (1948) 456–57
Georgia:
  arms control and 11, 443, 444, 446
  EUMM 133
  NATO–Georgia Commission (NGC) 500
  Open Skies Treaty 451
  Russian invasion 31
  territorial conflict 446, 451
German Institute for Economic Research
  (DIW Berlin) 156, 159
Germany:
  anti-personnel mines, destruction 422
  arms exports 267–68
    Arab Spring and 278–79
    to Greece 176
    to Israel 268, 341

major supplier 259, 261
naval equipment to South East Asia
284
reports 298
arms industry 225, 226–27
CFE Treaty and 443, 522
cluster munitions and CCW Convention
420
deployment of US nuclear weapons 314
Iran and 370, 372
Iraqi chemical weapons and 399–400
Italian arms industry cooperation
225–26
Libya and 7, 401, 511
military expenditure 7, 149, 158–59, 175
reporting proposal 181
NPDI member 514
nuclear energy 385
old chemical weapons 403
Open Skies Treaty 451
peace operations contribution 93
uranium-enrichment facilities 349
Vienna Document and 449
Ghannouchi, Mohamed 51, 509
Gilbert, Martin 22
GKN 253
Global Partnership against the Spread of
Weapons and Materials of Mass
Destruction 354, 388, 515
Global Peace Index (GPI) 84–88
methodology 87–88
table 86–87
Global Peace Operations Initiative 237
Goa Shipyard 244
Goldstone, Richard 512
Goodrich 223, 252
Gottemoeller, Rose 362
Greece:
arms imports 176–77
austerity programme 173
financial crisis 175, 176–77
KFOR contribution 176
military expenditure 147, 176–77
Open Skies Treaty 451–52
Turkish relations 177, 451–52
Grenada: arms transfer reports 295
GUAM (Organization for Democracy and
Economic Development) 501
Guinea: arms embargos 436
Gulf Cooperation Council 498
Bahrain and 511
higher profile 8
Libya and 100

US policy 263
Yemen and 51, 54–55, 55, 522
Guyana:
arms transfer reports 293, 295
organized violence 79

Hadi, President Abdo Rabu Mansour al-
52
Hague, William 372, 522
Hague Code of Conduct against Ballistic
Missile Proliferation (HCOC) 506, 515
Haiti: MINUSTAH 91, 108–109, 119
Halliburton 232
Haqqani network 44, 519
Harris 252
Hashemi, Tariq al- 524
Hawker Beechcraft 247, 249, 254
HEU see fissile material
Hewlett-Packard 232, 250, 252
Hindustan Aeronautics Ltd (HAL) 240,
241, 244, 245–46, 252
Hindustan Shipyard 244
Hizbul-Islam 59
Honeywell 251
Horn of Africa:
border conflicts 62–64
map 58
organized violence 57–64
non-state conflicts 44, 57
one-sided violence 57–58
state-based armed conflicts 57
see also individual countries
Howaldtswerke-Deutsche Werft AG 341
Hu Jintao, President 509
Human Rights Watch 16
humanitarian interventions:
criteria 33–35
debate 20–21
Libya 25–33
Hungary: CFE Treaty and 522

IAEA (International Atomic Energy
Agency) 489–90
additional safeguards protocol 372,
378–81, 382
Iran and 353, 366–73, 521
members 490
North Korea and 375
NSG and 376–77
Syria and 4, 353, 363–65
transparency and global safety
standards 519
IBM 229

Iceland:
    CFE Treaty and 522
    GPI ranking 84
    NORDEFCO 226
ICISS (International Commission on
    Intervention and State Sovereignty) 21,
    27–28, 34
IGAD (Intergovernmental Authority on
    Development) 498
IHI Group 253, 254
IJssel, Paul van den 395
Ilyumzhínov, Kirsan 54
India:
    arms exports 241
    arms imports 8, 242, 259, 262, 265, 268,
        269
    arms industry 218, 239–46
        FDI 240, 242–43
        joint ventures 240–41, 245–46
        military services 244–46
        R&D 239, 242, 243–44
    BTWC and 395
    chemical weapons 399
    Chinese relations 239
    cluster munitions and 420, 422
    conflicts 67
    Côte d'Ivoire and 32
    Kargil conflict with Pakistan 239
    Libyan policy 27, 511
    military expenditure 4, 8, 154, 220
    Myanmar and 67
    Non-Aligned Movement 32
    nuclear forces 332–36
        Cold Start doctrine 340
        fissile material 308, 332, 345
        lack of transparency 307, 333
        land-based missiles 333–35
        missile tests 333
        numbers 332, 334
        reprocessing facilities 350
        sea-based missiles 334, 336
        strategy 332–33
        strike aircraft 333
        transfer of nuclear technology to 377
        uranium-enrichment facilities 332,
            349
    US Civil Nuclear Cooperation
        Agreement 383
    nuclear non-proliferation and
        bilateral agreements 383
        IAEA safeguards 383
        NPT 383
        NSG 382–84

    Pakistan relations 67, 239, 333, 340
    responsibility to protect and 17, 31–32
    Russian nuclear fuel 377
    South East Asia and 282
    Syrian policy 32, 435
    UNMOGIP 114
    US relations 165, 262, 377, 383–84
Indian Ordnance Factories 240, 241, 243,
    249, 253
Indonesia:
    arms imports 259, 280, 281, 283, 284–85
    maritime rights disputes 281
    military expenditure 8, 154
    military services to 234
    peace operations contribution 89
    Thai–Cambodian dispute and 5, 510
Indra 254
INF Treaty (Treaty on the Elimination of
    Intermediate-Range and Shorter-Range
    Missiles, 1987) 483–84
Ingushetia 44
Inhumane Weapons Convention see CCW
    Convention
Institute for Economics and Peace 84
Inter-American Convention on
    Transparency in Conventional Weapons
    Acquisitions (1999) 480–81
International Committee of the Red Cross
    (ICRC) 18, 62, 418, 421–22
International Conference on the Great
    Lakes (ICGLR) 498–99
International Court of Justice (ICJ) 5,
    490, 517
International Criminal Court (ICC):
    deterrence 23
    function and parties 492
    Gbagbo arrest 523
    Libya and 49, 510, 515, 516
    protection of civilians and 19
International Criminal Tribunal for
    Rwanda (ICTR) 19, 515
International Criminal Tribunal for the
    former Yugoslavia (ICTY) 19, 515
international criminal tribunals:
    deterrence 23
International Crisis Group 16
International Monetary Fund (IMF) 147,
    175
International Organization for Migration
    102
International Security Forces (ISF) 142
International Stability Operations
    Association 236–37

Iran:
  BTWC and 394, 395
  European Union and 372
  Libyan policy 53, 407
  military expenditure 155
  MTCR and 426
  nuclear activities 4, 10
    2003 halt order 367
    alleged weaponization 367–68
    AMAD Plan 366–67
    concerns 353, 366–73
    Fordow enrichment plant 371–73
    IAEA assessment 366–69, 521
    IAEA resolution 370
    international sanctions 522
    NSG and 382
    uranium-enrichment facilities 349
    US intelligence 369–70
  UK embassy attacks 522
  UN arms embargo violations 11, 437
  USA and 165, 263, 371
    assassination attempt 520
    chemical weapons 391, 404, 407
    nuclear intelligence 369–70
    nuclear non-proliferation 370
    sanctions 522
Iraq:
  anti-personnel mines 422
  arms imports 271
  arms industry and 247–49
  chemical weapons 391, 399–400
  conflict 67
    civilian casualties 15
    economic costs 3, 147, 148, 156–61
    lessons from 30, 36
    logistics support 233, 235–36
    US troop withdrawal 4, 163, 523
  GPI ranking 85
  HCOC participant 515
  military expenditure 155
  one-sided violence 78
  peace operations 89
    EUJUST LEX 130–31
    MNF-I 110–11
    NTM-I 135
    UNAMI 123, 400
  popular uprisings 55
  terrorism 3, 509, 518, 524
  UNSCOM 399, 400
  USA and 4, 237
    armed conflict 67
    chemical weapons 400
    global war on terrorism 110–11
    military expenditure 156–61, 163, 164
    troop withdrawal 4, 163, 523
Iraq Family Health Survey 157–58
Ireland:
  arms transfer reports 296–97
  cluster munitions and CCW Convention 420
  financial crisis 175
Irkut Corp. 253
ISAF (International Security Assistance Force):
  largest peace operation 91–92
  Pakistan, attack in 522
  perceptions of peacekeeping and 111
  table 135
  Taliban violence on 519
  withdrawal 89, 109
Isaikin, Anatoly 275
ISF (International Security Forces) 142
Islamic State of Iraq (ISI) 78–79, 509
Israel:
  arms exports to Azerbaijan 260, 291, 292
  destruction of Syrian nuclear facility 4, 353, 363
  EU BAM Rafah 131
  exchange of prisoners 520
  Gaza Strip violence 512
  MFO 140
  nuclear forces 341–42
    fissile material 308, 345
    lack of transparency 307–308, 341
    reprocessing facilities 350
  Palestinian violence 515, 518
  UNDOF 114–15
  UNTSO 113
Israel Aerospace Industries 252
Italy:
  arms industry 247
  austerity programme 173
  CFE Treaty and 522
  deployment of US nuclear weapons 314
  financial crisis 175, 177–78
  German arms industry cooperation 225–26
  Libya and 53, 177, 512
    violation of arms embargo 433
  military expenditure 147, 149, 177–78
  old chemical weapons 403
  overseas operations 177
  peace operations contribution 93
ITT 224, 249, 251
Ivins, Bruce E. 409

Jacobs Engineering 228, 232, 253
Jamaica: organized violence 79–80
Jamalov, Yavar 292
Japan:
  arms industry 220
  biological weapons 406
  chemical weapons 403
  earthquake and tsunami 385, 511
  Fukushima Daiichi nuclear power plant
    385, 511
  military expenditure 7, 149, 155
  NPDI member 514
  nuclear energy 385, 511
  nuclear reprocessing facilities 350
  South East Asia and 282
  uranium-enrichment facilities 349
Jonathan, President Goodluck 170
Jordan
  Libyan policy and 7
  monarchy 55
Juppe, Alain 432
just war 29

Kabardino-Balkaria 44
Kawaoka, Yoshihiro 410
Kawasaki Heavy Industries 254
KBR 232, 235, 249, 252
Kellenberger, Jakob 421
Kelley, Robert 368
Kenya:
  2008 massacres 25
  al-Shabab attacks 167
  military expenditure 167
  non-state conflicts 62–64
  one-sided violence 57–58
  Somali conflict 57, 59, 60, 107
KFOR (NATO Kosovo Force) 110, 134, 176
Khan network 343, 368, 375, 378
Kidwai, Khalid Ahmed 340
Kim Jong-il 4, 374, 523
Kim Jong-un 523
Kinshasa Convention (2010) 481–82
Kongsberg 249, 253
Korea: Neutral Nations Supervisory
  Commission 139
Korea, Democratic People's Republic of
  (DPRK, North Korea):
  chemical weapons, allegations 406–407
  MTCR and 426
  Myanmar and 437
  nuclear forces
    capabilities 343–44
    fissile material 343–44, 345

lack of transparency 308
  reprocessing facilities 350
  tests 343
  uranium-enrichment facilities 349
  nuclear programme 4, 10, 354, 374–75,
    382
  Six-Party Talks 354, 374, 503
  succession 523
  Syrian nuclear programme and 363
  UN arms embargo violations 11, 437
  UN sanctions 375
Korea, Republic of (ROK, South Korea):
  arms exports 284, 424
  arms imports 8, 259, 262, 269
  chemical weapons 399
  Indian nuclear cooperation agreement
    383
  military expenditure 4, 7, 149
  North Korean nuclear programme and
    374
  South East Asia and 282, 284
Kosovo:
  EULEX Kosovo 133
  humanitarian intervention 21, 29
  KFOR 110, 134
    Italian contribution to 177
  OMIK 138–39
  UNMIK 116
Kouchner, Bernard 20
Koussa, Moussa 511
Kratos 228
Krauss-Maffei Wegmann 253
Kirloskar Group 240–41
Kyrgyzstan: Uzbek conflict 80

L-3 Communications 224, 232, 251
Larsen 240–41
Lavrov, Sergei 355, 362, 433–34
Lebanon:
  UNIFIL 115, 177
  uprisings 55
Le Guelte, Georges 179
Liberia:
  end of conflict 71
  UNMIL 117
Libya:
  African Union and 32, 54
  Arab Spring 48–49, 275
    chronology 510–16
    civilian casualties 10, 16
    cluster munitions 514
    end of conflict 520
    external support 52–53, 55

international responses 8, 99–100
level of violence 45
militias 103
regional responses 37
revolution 43
third-party involvement 54
arms control 103
arms embargoes 11, 100
EU 11, 275, 278, 433, 510
Russia and 275, 432, 433–34
United Nations 11, 27, 100, 275, 416,
431–34
US policy 276
violations 27, 433
arms imports 275, 278, 424
chemical weapons
allegations 407
declaration 399
destruction 10, 392, 397–98, 400–402
Chinese policy 26, 27, 30, 53, 101, 432,
434, 511
ICC arrest warrants 515, 516
Indian policy 31–32
Iran and 407
NATO operation 55, 100–102
Arab League and 53
arms embargo 432–33
civilian casualties 3, 516
debate 101, 105
difficulties 7
end 521
Italian contribution 177
military importance 48–49, 518
not a peace operation 90
objectives 512, 514
overreach 26–28, 33
patrol of territorial waters 512
perceptions of peacekeeping and 111
UASs 226
UN mandate 3
NTC (National Transitional Council)
48, 49, 54, 103, 511, 513, 520
arms transfers 434
recognition 102, 519
Paris conference 519
peace operations 99–103
UNSMIL 91, 102–103, 124, 519
responsibility to protect and 23–24, 89
Russian policy
arms embargoes 275, 432, 433–34
mediation 54
NATO operation 101
UN Security Council 26, 27, 30, 31, 511

South African policy 17, 32
UN Security Council and
chemical weapons 401, 402
condemnation of violence 510
UN Security Council Resolution 1970
25, 100, 510, 512
UN Security Council Resolution 1973
aftermath 18, 29–33
Arab League and 53
arms embargo 432–33
China and Russia 26, 27, 30, 31, 511
implementation 25–29, 512
NATO operation and 3, 101
objectives 48, 100, 511
overreach debate 25–29
protection of civilians 24, 25, 100
responsibility to protect 17, 24, 25,
100
vote 511
UN Security Council Resolution 2009
519
US policy 26, 27, 53, 433, 512
war crimes 49
Licorne, Operation 108, 141
LIG Nex1 254
Lockheed Martin 219, 221, 249, 251
Longuet, Gérard 432
Lord's Resistance Army (LRA) 77, 79
LTTE (Liberation Tigers of Tamil Eelam)
67
Luck, Edward 22
Luxembourg: CFE Treaty and 522

Macedonia, Former Yugoslav Repubic of:
OSCE Spillover Monitor Mission to
Skopje 136–37
McLay, Jim 430
Mahindra Group 240–41
Mahley, Donald A. 407
maintenance, repair and overhaul (MRO)
217–18, 231, 233–34, 238
Malaysia:
arms imports 259, 280, 281, 284
maritime rights disputes 281
Mali:
AQIM operations 167, 168
Libya and 513
Maliki, Nouri al- 524
Malta: Vienna Document and 449
ManTech 228, 229, 232, 250, 252
MAPP/OEA (Mission to Support the
Peace Process in Colombia) 136
Martin, Ian 101–103

Marzouki, Moncef 51
Mauritania:
    AQIM operations 167, 168
    Libya and 513
Mauritius: maritime capacity 523
MBDA 251, 252, 255
Médecins sans Frontières (MSF) 62
media: Arab Spring and 16, 50
Medvedev, President Dmitry 361, 374
Meggitt 254
Méndez, Constantino 178
Meshaal, Khaled 514
Mexico:
    CWC and 398–99
    drug cartels 73, 76
    military expenditure, increase 154–55
    NPDI member 514
MFO (Multinational Force and Observers)
    140
MICOPAX (Mission for the Consolidation
    of Peace in the Central African Republic)
    127–28
Middle East:
    military expenditure
        GDP percentages 207–208
        increases 149, 155
        reporting 183, 184
        tables 150, 153, 193–94, 200–201,
            207–208
    organized violence
        non-state conflicts 72, 74
        one-sided violence 76, 77, 79, 80
        state-based armed conflicts 69–70, 71
    peace operations 110–11
    peacefulness change 84
military expenditure:
    Afghanistan and Iraq wars 156–61
    definition 214
    financial crisis and 147
        Europe 173–80
    global developments 149–55
    global war on terrorism and 147–48
    income groups 151
    organizations 150–51
    overview 147–48
    tables 187–213
        GDP percentages 202–208
        highest spenders 152
        local currency listing 188–94
        methodology 187, 214–16
        regional breakdown 150, 153, 188–213
        sources 216
        US dollar listings 195–201

    trend 4, 7
    UN reporting system 11, 148, 181–86
    see also specific regions and countries
military services 217–18, 230–38
    categories 233
    logistics support 235–37
    MRO 217–18, 231, 233–34, 238
    operational support 235–38
    SIPRI Top 100 230, 231–33
    systems support 234–35
    training 236, 237–38
Minsk Conference (1995) 137–38
Minsk Group 288, 502
MINURSO (UN Mission for the
    Referendum in Western Sahara) 115
MINUSTAH (UN Stabilization Mission in
    Haiti) 91, 108–109, 119
Missile Technology Control Regime
    (MTCR) 416, 425–26, 506, 513
Mitre 232, 254
Mitsubishi 252, 253
Mladić, Ratko 515
MMPP Salut 254
Moldova:
    arms exports to Armenia 289–90
    CFE Treaty and 11, 443, 444
    Joint Control Commission
        Peacekeeping Force 128
    OSCE Mission to 137
    territorial conflict 446
monocracies 55
Montenegro:
    arms exports to Armenia 288
    limits on armed forces 444–45
MONUSCO (UN Organization
    Stabilization Mission to the DRC) 92–93,
    116–17, 513
Moog 254
Moreno-Ocampo, Luis 49
Morocco:
    Algerian rivalry 169
    Arab Spring 45
    MINURSO 115
    monarchy 55
Moscow Treaty see SORT
Mozambique:
    BTWC membership 393
    maritime capacity 523
MTU Aero Engines 255
Mubarak, President Hosni 47, 51, 509, 510
Mukherjee, Pranab 31
Mungiki 57
Muslim Brotherhood 49

Myanmar:
  arms embargo violations 437
  elections 512
  India and 67
  UN policy 432

Nagorno-Karabakh 137–38, 260, 286, 288, 292, 442, 446
Namibia:
  Angolan conflict and 67
  Indian nuclear energy 383
national interest: rethinking 38–39
National Security Partners 228
National Socialist Council of Nagaland–Khaplang faction (NSCN-K) 67
NATO (North Atlantic Treaty Organization):
  Central European membership 175
  CFE Treaty, Russia and 442–44
  conventional arms control 416
  Euro-Atlantic Partnership Council (EAPC) 499–500
  function and members 499–500
  ISAF see ISAF
  Kosovo intervention 21, 29
  Libya see Libya
  military expenditure 7, 151, 179–80
  missile defence 360–61
  NATO–Georgia Commission (NGC) 500
  NATO–Russia Council (NRC) 500
  NATO–Ukraine Commission (NUC) 500
  nuclear disarmament and 362
  peace operations 91
    KFOR 110, 134, 176
    personnel numbers 93
    table 134–35
  Vienna Document and 449, 450
Navantia 253
Navistar 249, 252
NEC 254
Nepal: peace operation in 91
Netherlands:
  arms exports 284
  avian flu research 9, 410
  CFE Treaty and 443, 522
  deployment of US nuclear weapons 314
  naval weapons 283, 284
  NPDI member 514
  nuclear non-proliferation and 382
  UNROCA and 295
  uranium-enrichment facilities 349

Neutral Nations Supervisory Commission (NNSC) 139
New START (Treaty on Measures for the Further Reduction and Limitation of Strategic Offensive Arms, 2010) 485
  Bilateral Consultative Commission 359, 490–91
  commencement 307, 353, 510
  disclosures 309, 315, 353, 357–58
  inspections made 358–59
  missile defence and 359–61
  next step 354, 361–62
  notification process 359
  ratification 5, 355, 510
  reduction numbers 356, 357
  Russian reductions 315
  verification regime 355–57, 485
  withdrawal right 361
Nexter 253
Nicaragua: responsibility to protect and 23
Niger: counterterrorism 167, 168, 170
Nigeria:
  anti-personnel mines, destruction 422
  Boko Haram 148, 167, 169, 170, 518, 521
  military expenditure, counterterrorism 169–71
  terrorism 3
Non-Aligned Movement (NAM) 32, 365, 370, 492
Non-Proliferation and Disarmament Initiative (NPDI) 514
non-state actors:
  Afghanistan 44
  cluster munitions 419–20
  engaging with 12–13, 19
  garage science 414
  Horn of Africa 44, 57, 61–64
  organized violence 65, 77, 78, 80
  terrorist threats 414, 393, 414
  trend 8–9
NORDEFCO (Nordic Defence Cooperation) 226
North Korea see Korea, Democratic People's Republic of
Northrop Grumman 237, 250, 251
Norway:
  arms imports 249
  assistance with cluster munition clearance 423
  CCM and 418
  military expenditure 174
  NORDEFCO 226
  terrorism 3, 84, 517

NPT (Non-Proliferation Treaty, 1968)
  461–63
    2010 Review Conference 389, 517
    civil nuclear programmes and 365, 372
    India and 383
    Iran and 372
    NSG and 385
    recognized nuclear states 307, 389
    violations 353
NTM-I (NATO Training Mission in Iraq)
  135
nuclear arms control and disarmament:
  multilateral discussions 389
  overview 353–54
  see also specific treaties
nuclear forces:
  China 327–31
  fissile material see fissile material
  France 325–26
  India 332–36
  Israel 341–42
  North Korea 343–44
  overview 307–308
  Pakistan 337–40
  recognized nuclear weapon states 307,
    389
  Russia 315–21
  sources of information 307
  total number of weapons 307, 308
  trend 4
  UK 322–24
  USA 309–14
nuclear non-proliferation:
  dual-use items 227, 381, 382, 386, 393,
    411, 425
  future of export control 385–86
  G8 Global Partnership 354, 388, 515
  international cooperation 387–89
  Iran 353, 366–73
  North Korea 374–75
  overview 353–54
  Syria 353, 363–65
  terrorism 354, 377, 388
  transfer of technology 354, 376–81
  UN Security Council Resolution 1540
    354, 380, 382, 387, 388, 513
  UN Security Council Resolution 1977
    354, 387
  see also Nuclear Suppliers Group
Nuclear Suppliers Group (NSG) 506–507
  2011 developments 376–86
  brokering and transit issues 381–82
  Chinese supplies to Pakistan 384–85

  future of nuclear export control 385–86
  India and 382–84
  plenary meeting 376, 516
  transfer guidelines 354, 376–81, 382,
    383, 516
nuclear tests:
  CTBT 311, 354, 470–71
  India 333
  North Korea 343
  Pakistan 340
  PTBT 460
  TTBT 483

Obama, President Barack:
  Afghan policy 4
  bin Laden and 514
  Egyptian policy 277–78
  Indian membership of NSG 383
  military expenditure and budget crisis
    162–63, 165
  nuclear arms control 361
  nuclear strategy 312
  withdrawal from Afghanistan 516
OCCAR (Organisation for Joint Armament
  Cooperation) 500–501
Oceania see Asia and Oceania
OECD (Organisation for Economic
  Co-operation and Development) 493
Ogaden National Liberation Front (ONLF)
  57, 61–62
Ohanyan, Seyran 289
oil: counterterrorism and 167–71
OMIK (OSCE Mission in Kosovo) 138–39
OPANAL (Agency for the Prohibition of
  Nuclear Weapons in Latin America and
  the Caribbean) 501
OPCW (Organisation for the Prohibition
  of Chemical Weapons) 391–92, 397–402,
  404–405, 407–408, 493
Open Skies Consultative Commission
  (OSCC) 451–52, 500
Open Skies Treaty (1992) 477, 451–52, 500
Organization of American States (OAS)
  136, 425, 427–28, 502
Organization of the Black Sea Economic
  Cooperation (BSEC) 502
Organization of the Islamic Conference
  (OIC) 493
OSCE (Organization for Security and
  Co-operation in Europe) 501
  Albania, Presence in 138
  Armenia and Azerbaijan arms embargo
    260, 287–88, 431fn

arms export control 425, 428–29
Astana Summit (2010) 442, 446, 448
Bosnia and Herzegovina Mission 138
conventional arms control 442–46
Forum for Security Co-operation (FSC)
    448, 450, 501, 522
military expenditure 151
Moldova Mission 137
OMIK 138–39
peace operations 8, 136–39
Personal Representative of the
    Chairman-in-Office on the Conflict
    Dealt with by the OSCE Minsk
    Conference 137–38
Serbia Mission 139
Skopje, Spillover Monitor Mission to
    136–37
Vienna Document 447, 448–50, 482,
    522
Oshkosh 249, 251
Oslo Process 418
Ottoman Empire 29
Ouattara, President Alassane 44, 107, 108,
    512, 513
Outer Space Treaty (1967) 460–61

Pacific Islands Forum 502
Pakistan:
    Afghanistan and 44
    armed conflicts 44, 67, 71, 239
    arms exports to Azerbaijan 292
    arms imports 8, 259, 262, 269, 424
    BTWC and 395
    CWC and 398
    Indian relations 67, 239, 333, 340
    ISAF attack in 522
    National Defence Complex 339
    National Engineering and Scientific
        Commission (NESCOM) 340
    nuclear forces 337–40
        China and 337, 384–85
        cruise missiles 338, 340
        fissile material 308, 337–38, 339, 345
        lack of transparency 307
        land-based missiles 338, 339–40
        numbers 337, 338
        reprocessing facilities 350
        strike aircraft 338, 339
        tests 340
        uranium-enrichment facilities 349
    peace operations contribution 93
    terrorism 3, 514
    UNMOGIP 114

Palestinian territories:
    EU BAM Rafah 131
    EUPOL COPPS 131
    exchange of prisoners with Israel 520
    Goldstone Report 512
    Hamas–Fatah agreement 514
    Nakba Day 515
    TIPH 2 140
    UN membership application 519
    UNESCO membership 521
    UNTSO 113
    uprisings 55
Panetta, Leon 222
Partial Test-Ban Treaty (PTBT, 1963) 460
Patria 255
peace operations:
    2011 new operations 95–105
        Libya 99–103
        Sudan and South Sudan 95–99
        Syria 104–105
    ad hoc coalitions 139–42
    Africa 106–108
    African Union see African Union
    Americas 108–109
    Arab League see Arab League
    Asia and Oceania 109–10
    AU see African Union
    CEEAC 127
    CIS 128
    civilian capacities 13, 90, 93
    contributors 89, 93
    costs 94
    definition 112
    Europe 110
    European Union see European Union
    global trends 91–94
    Middle East 110–11
    NATO see NATO
    numbers 92
    OAS 136
    OSCE 136–39
    overview 89–90
    personnel numbers 92
    regional developments 106–11
    resources 111
    table 112–42
        methods 143
        sources 144
    trend 8, 10
    United Nations
        Africa 106
        alternatives 90
        costs 94

funding 10, 94
logistics support 233, 236
overstretch 89
personnel numbers 93
protection of civilians and 19–20
table 113–25
trends 91–94
see also specific operations
see also specific countries and operations
Peaceful Nuclear Explosions Treaty
(PNET, 1976) 483
Pelindaba Treaty (1996) 478–79
Philippines:
arms imports 259, 280, 281, 285
Chinese relations 154
military expenditure 154
PKK (Kurdistan Workers' Party) 44, 518,
520, 524
plutonium *see* fissile material
Poinar, Hendrick 412
Poland:
arms exports
to Libya 433
reports 260, 296
arms imports 249
arms industry 225
cluster munitions and CCW Convention
420
Libya and 433
military expenditure 174
missile defence base 360
NPDI member 514
Popov, Andrei 443
Portugal:
CFE Treaty and 522
financial crisis 175
Prague Treaty *see* New START
Pratt & Whitney 251
Precision Castparts Corp. 254
Proliferation Security Initiative (PSI) 507
protection of civilians (POC) 5–6, 15, 16,
18–20, 89, 105
2011 developments 89
boundaries 90
casualties 15–16
challenge 15–39
consciousness of problem 16
Côte d'Ivoire 32, 89
future 33–39
Geneva Convention (1949) 457–59
legal history 18–20
Libya 25–33, 89, 100, 101
responsibility to protect and 24–25

South Sudan 97
Syria 89
trend 10
PTBT (Partial Test-Ban Treaty, 1963) 460
PZL-Świdnik 250

Qatar:
Libyan policy 7, 53
UN arms embargo on Libya and 27, 433
QinetiQ 232, 245, 253

Rafael 253
RAMSI (Regional Assistance Mission to
Solomon Islands) 141
Rarotonga Treaty (1985) 474–75
Ras Kamboni 59
Rasmussen, Anders Fogh 179, 432
Raytheon 228, 251, 255
Red Cross *see* ICRC
Regional Cooperation Council 503
regional organizations:
responsibility to protect and 37–38
survey 494–505
treaties 472–82
United Nations and 12
responsibility to protect (R2P):
2011 developments 89
criteria 33–35
debate 105
elements 21
emergence of concept 16–17
future 33–39
ICISS report (2001) 21
institutional response capacities 37–38
legal history 20–24
Libya 25–33, 100
long-term strategies 36–37
national interest and 38–39
non-military measures 36
non-war situations 25
protection of civilians and 24–25
responsibility while protecting 33, 35
UN Office 16
Rheinmetall 226–27, 252
Rideau Institute 159
Rieff, David 29
Rockwell Collins 252
Rolls-Royce 251
Romania:
arms exports to Azerbaijan 291
military expenditure, reporting
proposal 181
missile defence base 360

Open Skies Treaty and 451
Russian relations 451
Rosoboronexport 275, 289
Rowat, Colin 157
RUAG 254
Russia:
arms exports 263–67
Arab Spring and 265–67, 275–76
to Armenia and Azerbaijan 260, 287–91
to India 242, 265
major supplier 259, 261
naval equipment to South East Asia 284, 285
to Syria 53, 265–67, 275, 276
arms imports from France 268
arms industry, top producers 247
arms trade treaty and 425
biological weapons 394–95
BTWC and 394, 395
CFE Treaty and 11, 442–44, 445–46, 450, 522
chemical weapons 391, 397–98, 399, 402, 404–405
conventional arms control 416
Côte d'Ivoire policy 36
Georgian dispute 446, 451
humanitarian intervention and 30, 31
India and 383, 384
Joint Control Commission Peacekeeping Force (JCC) 128
Libyan policy
arms embargo 275, 432, 433–34
mediation 54
NATO operation and 101
UN Security Council 26, 27, 30, 31, 511
military expenditure 4, 8, 147, 149, 173
NATO–Russia Council (NRC) 500
North Caucasus conflict 44, 509
nuclear disarmament and
ABM Treaty 482–83
INF Treaty 483–84
multilateralism 389
New START see New START
PNET 483
SORT 355, 356, 485
START 355–57, 484
TTBT 483
nuclear forces 315–21
fissile material 345
lack of transparency 5, 307, 321
land-based ballistic missiles 318–19
non-strategic weapons 316, 321
numbers 315, 316
recognized nuclear weapon state 307, 389
reduction 307, 315
reprocessing facilities 350
sea forces 319–20
strategic weapons 316, 317–20
uranium-enrichment facilities 349
nuclear non-proliferation and
Iran 370
North Korea 374
NPT commitments 389, 517
Syria 364, 465
transfer of technology 377
Open Skies Treaty 451
responsibility to protect and 17, 30, 31
Syria and
arms supplies 53, 265–67, 275, 276
nuclear non-proliferation 364, 365
responsibility to protect and 55, 105
UN Security Council resolutions 265–67, 435
terrorism 3, 509
Tupolev Design Bureau 318
US relations
on biological weapons 394
nuclear disarmament 355–62
Vienna Document and 449–50
Rwanda:
Democratic Liberation Forces (FDLR) 77
genocide 16, 20, 21, 25, 77, 515
ICTR 19, 515
one-sided violence 77

Saab 252
Sabaot Land Defence Force (SLDF) 57
SADC (Southern African Development Community) 151, 504
Saddam Hussein, President 157, 404
Safran 219, 251
SAIC 232, 251
Saleh, President Ali Abdullah 51, 55, 515, 522
Salehi, Ali Akbar 373
Samsung 253
Saraswat, Vijay Kumar 335
Sargsyan, Serzh 289
Sarkozy, President Nicolas 519
Saudi Arabia:
arms imports 263, 268, 279, 424
Bahrain intervention 52, 268, 511
cluster munitions 424

military expenditure 4, 8, 149
monarchy 55
SCO (Shanghai Cooperation Organisation) 151, 503
Seabed Treaty (1971) 463–64
Selex Communications 254
Selex Galileo 254
Semipalatinsk Treaty (2006) 481
Senegal: Movement of the Democratic Forces of Casamance 77
Sensor Technologies Incorporated (STI) 250
Senussi, Abdullah al- 515, 516
Serbia:
  armed forces limits 444–45
  cluster munitions 423
  Mladić arrest 515
  OSCE Mission to 139
Serco 232, 253
Sevmash 253
Seychelles: maritime capacity 523
Shanghai Cooperation Organisation (SCO) 151, 503
Shaw Group 232, 254
Sierra Leone:
  UK intervention 29
  UNIPSIL 124
Signal Corp. 231
Sikorsky 233, 251
Singapore:
  arms imports 8, 259, 262, 269, 280, 281, 283
  military services 234
Singh, Manmohan 333
Six-Party Talks 354, 374, 503
Slovakia: CFE Treaty and 522
smart defence 180
Solomon Islands: RAMSI 141
Soltanieh, Ali Asgahr 369
Somalia:
  AMISOM 59, 60, 61, 106–107, 126, 518, 520
  armed conflicts 57, 59–61, 167
  conflict with al-Shabab 57
  EU NAVFOR Somalia 523
  EUTM 107, 134, 523
  GPI ranking 85
  maritime capacity 523
  terrorism 3, 518, 520
  transition road map 519
  Transitional Federal Government (TFG) 57, 59–60, 107, 519

SORT (Treaty on Strategic Offensive Reductions, 2002) 355, 356, 485
Sotera Defence Solutions 228
South Africa:
  arms exports to Azerbaijan 260, 291, 292
  arms transfer reports 294
  cluster munitions and CCW Convention 421
  Côte d'Ivoire policy 36
  Libya and 27, 32, 433, 513
  military expenditure 171–72
  NSG transfer guidelines and 378–79
  responsibility to protect and 17, 32
  Syria and 435
South American Defence Council (CDS) 5, 504–505
South Korea see Korea, Republic of
South Sudan:
  border violence 5, 97–99, 516, 517
  civilian casualties 16
  EU arms embargo 431, 517
  independence 4–5, 95, 98, 509, 510, 517
  Jonglei violence 510, 518
  map 96
  UNISFA 91, 97–99, 106, 121
  UNMISS 91, 95–97, 106, 122, 517, 518
Southeast European Cooperative Initiative (SECI) 503–504
Spain:
  arms exports 259, 269, 284, 424
  arms industry, cooperation 226
  austerity programme 173
  ETA ceasefire 5, 509, 520
  financial crisis 175, 176, 178
  military expenditure 147, 178
Special Verification Commission (SVC) 493
SRA International 254
Sri Lanka:
  Indian relations 31
  LTTE conflict 67
ST Engineering 234, 253
START I (Treaty on the Reduction and Limitation of Strategic Offensive Arms, 1991) 355–57, 484
START II (Treaty on Further Reduction and Limitation of Strategic Offensive Arms, 1993) 484
state sovereignty:
  defence cooperation and 180
  Latin America 33

meaning 16
national interest and 38–39
responsibility to protect and 20–22
Russia and 30
Stiglitz, Joseph 161
Sub-Regional Consultative Commission
(SRCC) 504
Sudan:
border violence 5, 97–99, 516, 517
civilian casualties 15–16
Darfur *see* Darfur
de-escalation of conflict 71
EU arms embargo 436, 517
Libya and 53, 433
map 96
one-sided violence 78
Peace Agreement (2005) 95
responsibility to protect and 23
South Sudan *see* South Sudan
UNISFA 91, 97–99, 106, 121
UNMIS 91, 95, 97, 99, 106, 120, 517
Sukhoi 253
Swaziland: military expenditure 172
Sweden:
arms exports 268
Libyan policy and 7
military expenditure 174
NORDEFCO 226
Vienna Document and 449
Switzerland:
arms imports 268
military expenditure 174
old chemical weapons 403
Vienna Document and 449
Syria:
Arab Spring 43, 49–50
Arab League and *see* Arab League
BRICS countries and 32, 33
emergency powers lifted 513
escalating violence 3, 518, 521
EU policy 3, 516, 518, 521
external support 53–54, 55
Free Syrian Army (FSA) 50, 54, 521
intense conflict 275, 516
international actors 8
Iran and 53
level of violence 45
OHCHR protest 514
plight of civilians 10
regional responses 37
responsibility to protect and 23, 89
third-party involvement 54

arms embargoes 275, 431
Arab League 11, 275, 416
EU 11, 53, 275, 278, 416, 431, 434–35,
514
Russia and 265–67, 275, 276
Turkey and 279
United Nations 265–67, 276, 431, 437
chemical and biological weapons 10,
392, 408
Chinese policy 30–31, 55, 105, 364, 365,
435
GPI ranking 85
Iran and 53
media and 50
monocracy 55
nuclear non-proliferation and 4, 10, 353,
363–65, 382
Russia and *see* Russia
Turkey and 3, 53, 105, 279, 435
UNDOF 114–15
UN Security Council and
Ban Ki-moon 518
Chinese position 30–31
Indian position 32
international disagreement 27
nuclear non-proliferation 364–65
paralysis 11, 17, 35
Resolution 2042 105
Russian position 265–67, 435
slippery side argument 35
USA and 3, 105, 408, 435, 518

Taiwan:
arms imports 262–63, 424
cluster munitions 424
international status 455
maritime rights disputes 281
Taliban 44, 67, 157, 514, 519
Tantawi, Mohamed Hussein 47
Tanzania: maritime capacity 523
Tashkent Agreement (1992) 475
Tata Group 240–41, 245
Teledyne Technologies 255
Temasek 253
Terbil, Fathi 48
Textron 252
Thailand:
Cambodian border dispute 5, 510, 517
military coup (2006) 154
military expenditure 154
Patani conflict 44
Thales 251, 253, 255

Thani, Hamad bin Jasim bin Jahir Al 433
Thein Sein, President 512
Threshold Test-Ban Treaty (TTBT, 1974)
   483
Thyssen-Krupp 253
Timor-Leste:
   ISF 142
   UNMIT 91, 109–10, 121
TIPH 2 (Temporary International
   Presence in Hebron) 140
Tlatelolco Treaty (1967) 472–74
Toubro 240–41
training services 236, 237–38
Trans-Dniester: peace operation 128
Trans-Sahara Counterterrorism
   Partnership (TSCTP) 168
transfer of technology:
   to Asia 259, 260, 283
   BTWC and CWC 413
   India 218, 243, 246
   intangible transfers 9, 386, 515
   NSG guidelines 354, 376–81, 382, 383,
      516
   nuclear material 354, 376–81
   peace operations and 90
Trinidad and Tobago: arms transfer
   reporting 293
Triumph Group 247, 253
TRV Corp. 254
TTP (Taliban Movement of Pakistan) 67
Tunisia:
   AQIM operations 167
   Arab Spring 50–51, 509
      casualties 3
      external support 52, 55
      revolt 43
   arms imports 276, 278
   monocracy 55
Turkey:
   arms exports
      Arab Spring and 279
      to Armenia and Azerbaijan 260, 287,
         291, 292
   arms imports 263
   CFE Treaty and 522
   deployment of US nuclear weapons 314
   Greek relations 177, 451–52
   Libyan policy 53–54
   military expenditure 4, 7, 149, 174
   NPDI member 514
   NSG transfer guidelines and 379
   Open Skies Treaty 451–52
   PKK 44, 518, 520

   responsibility to protect and 33
   Syria and 3, 105, 279, 435
Twitter 47

Uganda:
   al-Shabab attacks 60, 167
   arms imports from Russia 265
   de-escalation of conflict 71
   Libya and 513
   LRA 77, 79
   military expenditure 167
   Somali policy 61
Ukraine:
   arms exports to Armenia and
      Azerbaijan 287, 290, 292
   NATO–Ukraine Commission (NUC)
      500
Ultra Electronics 228, 229, 254
UNAMA (UN Administration in
   Afghanistan) 123, 158, 512
UNAMI (UN Assistance Mission in Iraq)
   123, 400
UNAMID (AU/UN Hybrid Operation in
   Darfur) 92, 125, 237
UNASUR (Union of South American
   Nations) 447–48, 504–505
UNDOF (UN Disengagement Observer
   Force) 114–15
UNESCO (UN Educational, Scientific and
   Cultural Organization) 521
UNFICYP (UN Peacekeeping Force in
   Cyprus) 114
UNHCR (UN High Commissioner for
   Refugees) 18, 158
UNICEF (United Nations Children's
   Fund) 18
UNIFIL (UN Interim Force in Lebanon)
   115, 177
UNIPSIL (UN Integrated Peacebuilding
   Office in Sierra Leone) 124
UNISFA (UN Interim Security Force for
   Abyei) 91, 97–99, 106, 121
UNITA 67
United Aircraft Corp. 252, 253
United Arab Emirates:
   arms imports 262, 263, 268
   Bahrain and 52, 511
   Libyan policy 7
   military expenditure 155
   NPDI member 514
   UN arms embargo on Libya and 433
United Engine Corp. 253

United Kingdom:
anti-personnel mines 422
arms exports 268–69
Arab Spring and 278, 279
major supplier 259, 261
reports 298
arms trade treaty and 425
austerity programme 173
CFE Treaty and 443, 522
cluster munition clearance 423
French Defence and Security
Cooperation Treaty (2010) 180, 225,
324
humanitarian intervention and 29–30,
34, 35
Indian nuclear cooperation agreement
383
Iran and
embassy attack 522
nuclear non-proliferation 370, 372
sanctions 372, 522
Iraqi chemical weapons and 399–400
Libyan operation 27, 52–53, 175, 512
military expenditure 7, 175
Afghanistan war 158–59
Nigeria and counterterrorism 170
NPT commitments 389, 517
nuclear forces 322–24
Atomic Weapons Establishment
323–24
Continuous at Sea Deterence 322
disarmament issue 389
disclosure 307
fissile material 345
French cooperation 324
recognized nuclear weapon state 307,
389
replacement submarines 323
reprocessing facilities 350
Strategic Defence and Security
Review 322–23
transparency 5, 307
uranium-enrichment facilities 349
old chemical weapons 403
peace operations contribution 93
responsibility to protect and 17–18
Sierra Leone intervention 29
UAS training 235
UN arms embargo on Libya and 433
United Nations 487–89
Arab Human Development Reports 45
arms embargoes see arms embargoes
arms export control 425, 429–30

arms trade treaty 425
Charter 487
Chapter VII 17, 19, 364
Chapter VIII 37
state sovereignty 20
genocide and responsibility to protect
16
Global Counter-Terrorism Strategy
409–10
Human Rights Council
Goldstone Report 512
Libyan suspension 511
members 488–89
military expenditure reporting system
11, 148, 181–86
Myanmar and 432
Office of Disarmament Affairs
(UNODA) 181–82, 295
OHCHR
Libyan cluster munitions and 514
protection of civilians 16, 18
Syria 514
Palestinian membership application 519
peace operations see peace operations
regional organizations and 12
Register of Conventional Arms see
UNROCA
Security Council see United Nations
Security Council
WMD Working Group 10–11
World Summit (2005) 22, 30–32,
Zimbabwe and 432
see also specific UN agencies
United Nations Security Council:
arms embargoes see arms embargoes
Côte d'Ivoire 36, 44
Kosovo 21
Libya see Libya
members 489
North Korea and 375, 407
nuclear non-proliferation, efficacy
353–54
protection of civilians and 18–19
reform 12, 17
Resolution 1540 (WMDs) 354, 380, 382,
387, 388, 513
Resolution 1674 (R2P) 22
Resolution 1706 (Darfur) 100
Resolution 1907 (Eritrea) 523
Resolution 1967 (Côte d'Ivoire) 107
Resolution 1970 (Libya) 25, 100, 510, 512
Resolution 1973 see Libya
Resolution 1975 (Côte d'Ivoire) 108, 512

Resolution 1977 (WMDs) 354, 387, 513
Resolution 1980 (Côte d'Ivoire) 108,
    436, 514
Resolution 1996 (UNMISS) 517
Resolution 2000 (Côte d'Ivoire) 108
Resolution 2009 (Libya) 519
Resolution 2010 (Somalia) 520
Resolution 2023 (Eritrea) 523
Resolution 2042 (Syria) 105
responsibility to protect and
    criteria 33–35
    development 22, 23
    long-term strategies 36–37
    non-military measures 36
    Resolution 1973 17, 24–25, 100
    Western powers 17–18
Somali policy 60, 519, 520
Syria see Syria
United Shipbuilding Corp. 247, 253
United States:
    11 September 2001 attacks 78–79, 156
    2011 budget crisis, military expenditure
        and 162–66, 219
    Aerospace Industries Association 222
    Afghanistan see Afghanistan
    alliance system 7–8
    anthrax 409
    Arab Spring and 55
        arms transfers 276–78
    arms exports 261–63
        to Armenia and Azerbaijan 287
        cluster munitions 424
        major supplier 259, 261
        naval weapons to South East Asia
            283, 285
        reporting 297
    arms imports 249, 269
    arms industry
        mergers and acquisitions 222–24
        NDAA and 217, 220–22
        top producer 218, 247
        UASs 226
    arms trade treaty and 425
    Atrocities Prevention Board 23
    biosecurity 9, 410
    BTWC and 394
    chemical weapons
        declaration 399
        destruction 391, 397–98, 402–403,
            404–405
        Iran and 391, 404, 407
    China and 165, 263, 283
        on Chinese nuclear forces 331

    cluster munitions 420, 424
    European arms control and 444, 445,
        446, 522
    financial constraints 6–7, 162–66, 219
    global war on terrorism 67
        Africa 167, 168
        Iraq 110–11
        military expenditure and 147–48
    GPOI and 237
    humanitarian intervention and 30, 34,
        35
    Indian relations 165, 262
        Civil Nuclear Cooperation
            Agreement 383
        nuclear issues 383–84
    Iran and 165, 263
        assassination attempt 520
        chemical weapons 391, 404, 407
        nuclear fuel exchange 371
        nuclear intelligence 369–70
        nuclear non-proliferation 370
        sanctions 522
    Iraq and 4, 237
        armed conflict 67
        chemical weapons 400
        Multinational Force 110–11
        withdrawal of troops 4, 110, 163, 523
    Libya and 26, 27, 53, 55, 433, 512
    military expenditure 7, 147, 149
        2011 budget crisis 162–66, 219
        Afghanistan and Iraq wars 156–61,
            163, 164
        European free riding 178–80
        global war on terrorism 147–48
        NDAA 217, 220–22
    military power 415
    military services 230–31
        logistics support 235–36
        MRO 234
    National Science Advisory Board for
        Biosecurity 410
    nuclear disarmament and
        ABM Treaty 482–83
        INF Treaty 483–84
        multilateralism 389
        New START see New START
        PNET 483
        SORT 485
        START 355–57, 484
        TTBT 483
    nuclear forces 309–14
        ballistic missile submarines 313
        disclosure 307, 309

European Phased Adaptive Approach 360

fissile material 345

Global Thunder exercise 312

land-based ballistic missiles 312–13

modernization 309–11, 312

non-strategic weapons 310, 313–14

NPR 311, 312–13, 314

numbers 309, 310

recognized nuclear weapon state 307, 389

reduction 307

reprocessing facilities 350

Russia–USA arms control 355–62

strategic weapons 310, 312–13

strategy 312

transparency 5, 307

uranium-enrichment facilities 349

nuclear non-proliferation and

  Chinese supplies to Pakistan 384–85

  Iran 369–70, 371

  North Korea 374–75

  NPT commitments 389, 517

  transfer of technology 377–78, 379

Open Skies Treaty 451

peace operations contribution 93

responsibility to protect and 23

Russian relations

  on biological weapons 394

  nuclear disarmament 355–62

South East Asia and 282

Syrian policy 3, 105, 435

  allegation of chemical weapons 408

  demand for Assad resignation 518

UAS training 235

Vienna Document and 449, 450

Viet Nam War defoliants 410

WikiLeaks releases 519

Yemen and 54–55, 520

United Technologies (UTC) 223, 233, 251

unmanned aerial systems (UASs) 90, 217, 225, 226–27, 234–35

UNMIK (UN Interim Administration Mission in Kosovo) 116

UNMIL (UN Mission in Liberia) 117

UNMIN (UN Mission in Nepal) 91

UNMIS (UN Mission in the Sudan) 91, 95, 97, 99, 106, 120, 517

UNMISS (UN Mission in the Republic of South Sudan) 91, 95–97, 106, 122, 517, 518

UNMIT (UN Integrated Mission in Timor-Leste) 91, 109–10, 121

UNMOGIP (UN Military Observer Group in India and Pakistan) 114

UNMOVIC (UN Monitoring, Verification and Inspection Commission) 399

UNOCI (UN Operation in Côte d'Ivoire) 107–108, 118, 513

UNODA (UN Office for Disarmament Affairs) 181–82, 295

UNROCA (UN Register of Conventional Arms) 260, 293–96

  reporting level 293–95

  review 295–96

  SALW reporting 295

  table 299–301

UNSCOM (UN Special Commission on Iraq) 399, 400

UNSMIL (UN Support Mission in Libya) 91, 102–103, 124, 519

UNTSO (UN Truce Supervision Organization) 113

Uppsala Conflict Data Program (UCDP) 6, 43, 65, 79

Uralvagonzavod 254

URS Corp. 252

Uruguay: arms transfer reporting 293

Üzümcü, Ahmet 397

Valasek, Tomas 180

Vectra Group India 245

Venezuela:

  arms imports from Russia 265

  responsibility to protect and 23

Veridian 231

Vertex Corp. 232

Vertolety Rossii 245, 247, 253

Vienna Document on CSBMs (2011) 447, 448–50, 482, 522

Vientiane Action Plan 415–16

Viet Nam:

  arms imports 259, 265, 280, 281, 285

  cluster munitions 423

  military expenditure 8

  US use of defoliants in 410

Vought Aircraft Industries 247

VSE Corp. 232, 255

VT Group 250

Wassenaar Agreement 416, 425, 426, 507–508

weapons of mass destruction:

  chemical and biological weapons 391–414

  G8 and 354, 388, 515

international control cooperation 376
nuclear *see* nuclear
trend 10–11
UN Working Group, 2011 report 10–11
UN Security Council Resolution 1540
354, 380, 382, 387, 388, 513
UN Security Council Resolution 1977
354, 387, 513
Western European Union (WEU) 505, 517
Wi Sung-lac 374
Wifaq 47
WikiLeaks 519
World Bank: Libya and 102
World Health Organization (WHO) 409, 411
World Organization for Animal Health (OIE) 409

Xe Services 236

Yemen:
Arab Spring 51–52
casualties 3
external support 52, 515
government violence 275, 511
maritime capacity 523
Saleh's departure for Saudi Arabia 515
third-party involvement 54–55
transfer of power 51–52, 54–55, 522
arms imports from Russia 275
monocracy 55
USA and 54–55, 520
Yersinia pestis 411–12
YouTube 50
Yugoslavia: special tribunal 19, 515

Zangger Committee 376, 508
Zimbabwe: UN policy 432